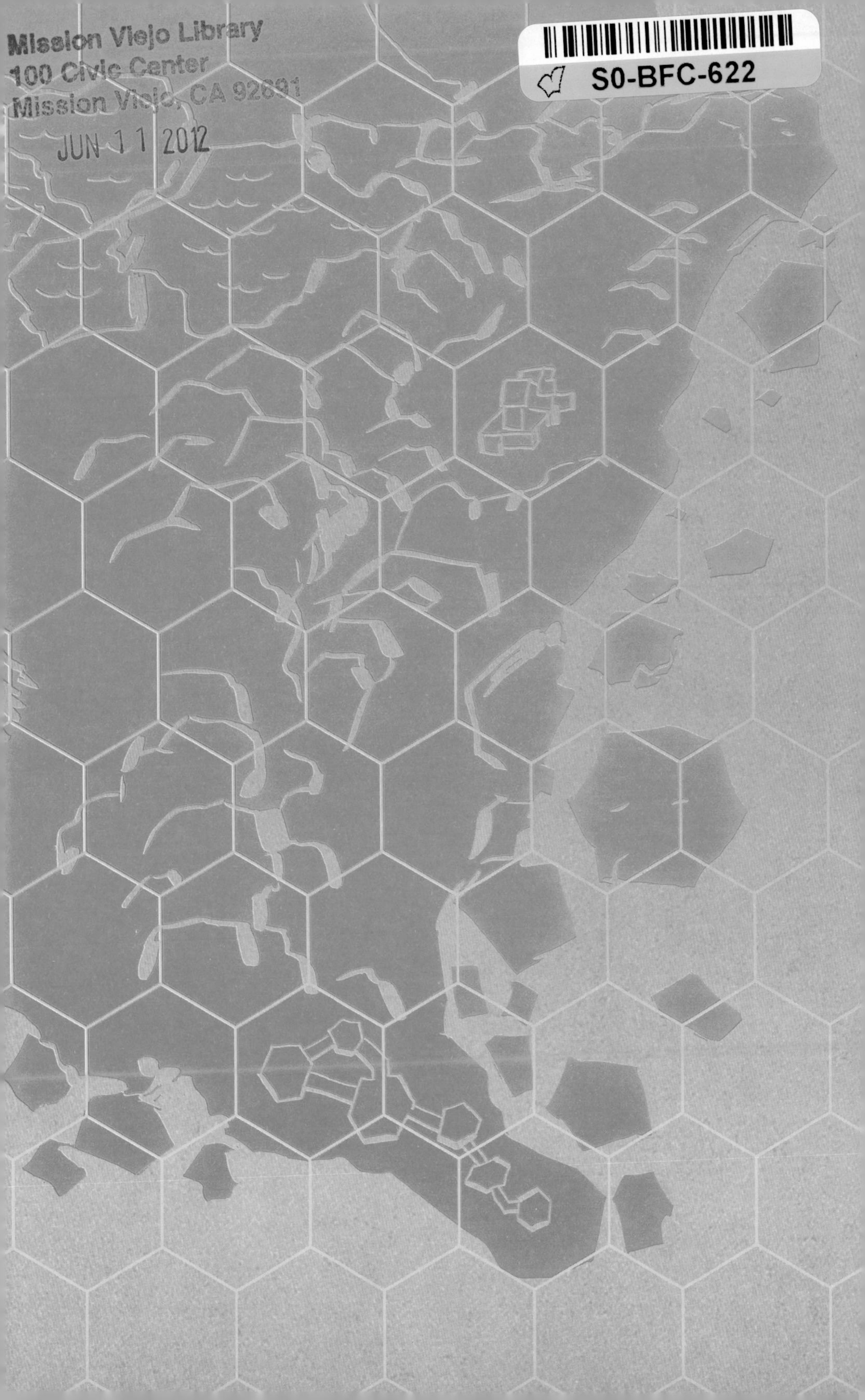

TOM SCIOLI

AMERICAN BARBARIAN

ADHOUSE BOOKS ✚ RICHMOND, VA

American Barbarian
Published by AdHouse Books.

Content is © copyright 2012 Tom Scioli.
AdHouse logo is © copyright 2012 AdHouse Books.

ISBN 1-9352331-7-3
ISBN 978-1-9352331-7-6
10 9 8 7 6 5 4 3 2 1

Design: Pitzer + Scioli

AdHouse Books
1224 Greycourt Ave.
Richmond, VA 23227-4042
www.adhousebooks.com

First Printing, March 2012

Printed in Malaysia

BOOK ONE: SEVEN BROTHERS
MY SEVEN SONS.
THE TWINS
HANIBULL AND TRISTON
BOBERT
SHEM
JIMOTHY
GUNTHOR, THE ELDEST
AND MERIC, THE YOUNGEST
MY NAME IS YOOSAMON, BUT THEY CALL ME "PA."
SEVEN FUTURES,
ALL ABOUT TO CHANGE.
THIS IS THE RITUAL THAT DEFINES OUR FAMILY.
THEY REACH INTO THE ABYSS...
AND PULL FORTH...
THE TANGLE OF SWORDS.

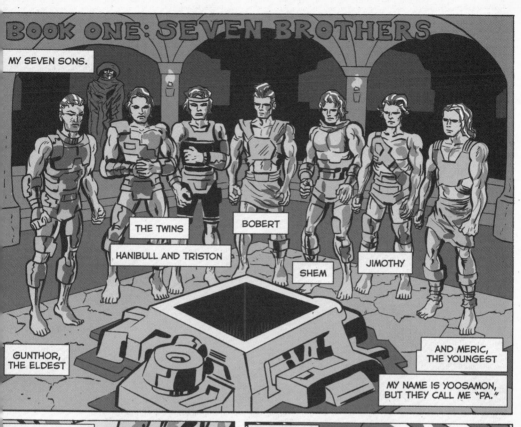

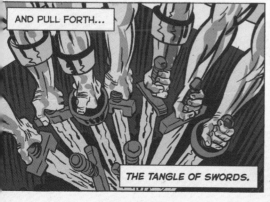

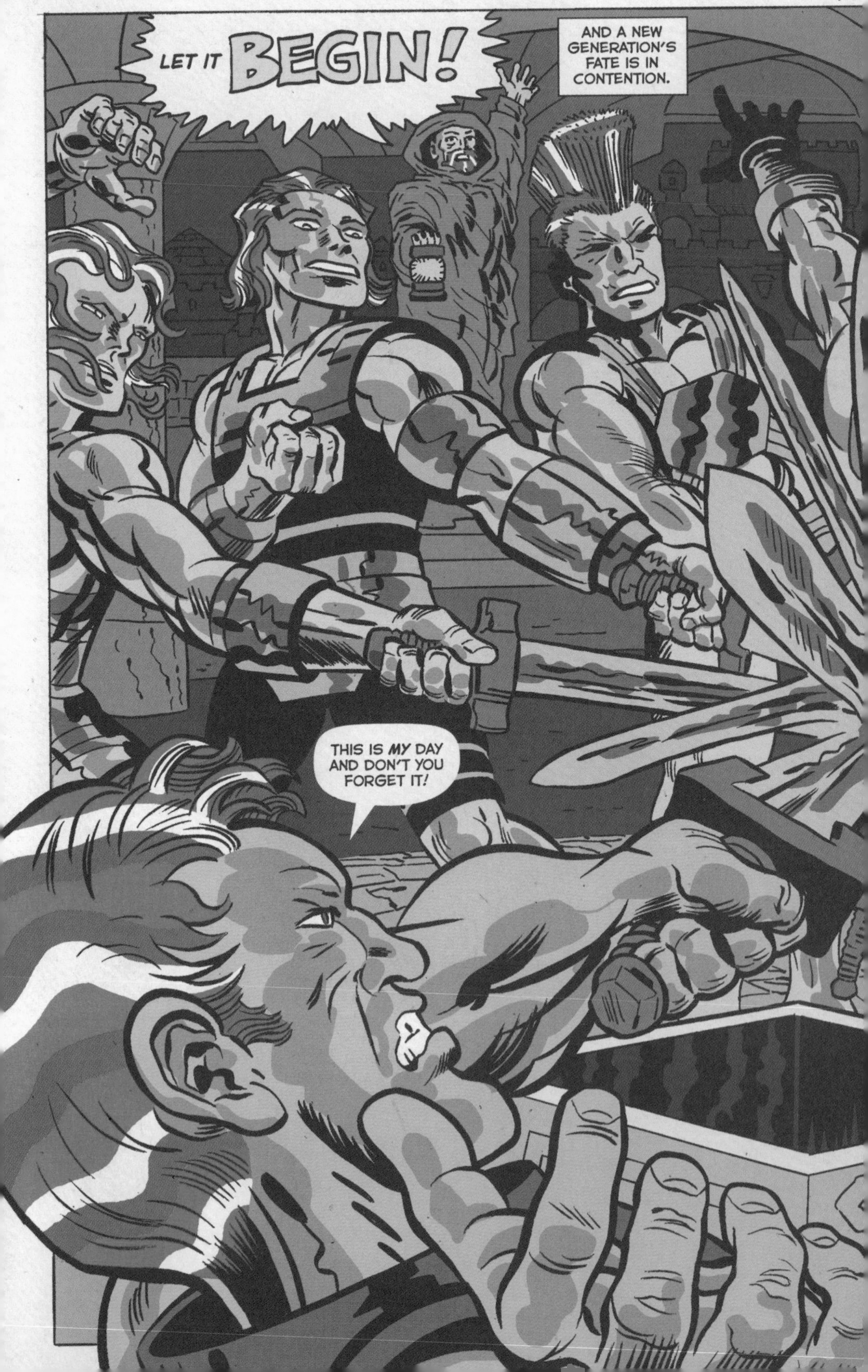
LET IT BEGIN!
AND A NEW GENERATION'S FATE IS IN CONTENTION.
THIS IS MY DAY AND DON'T YOU FORGET IT!

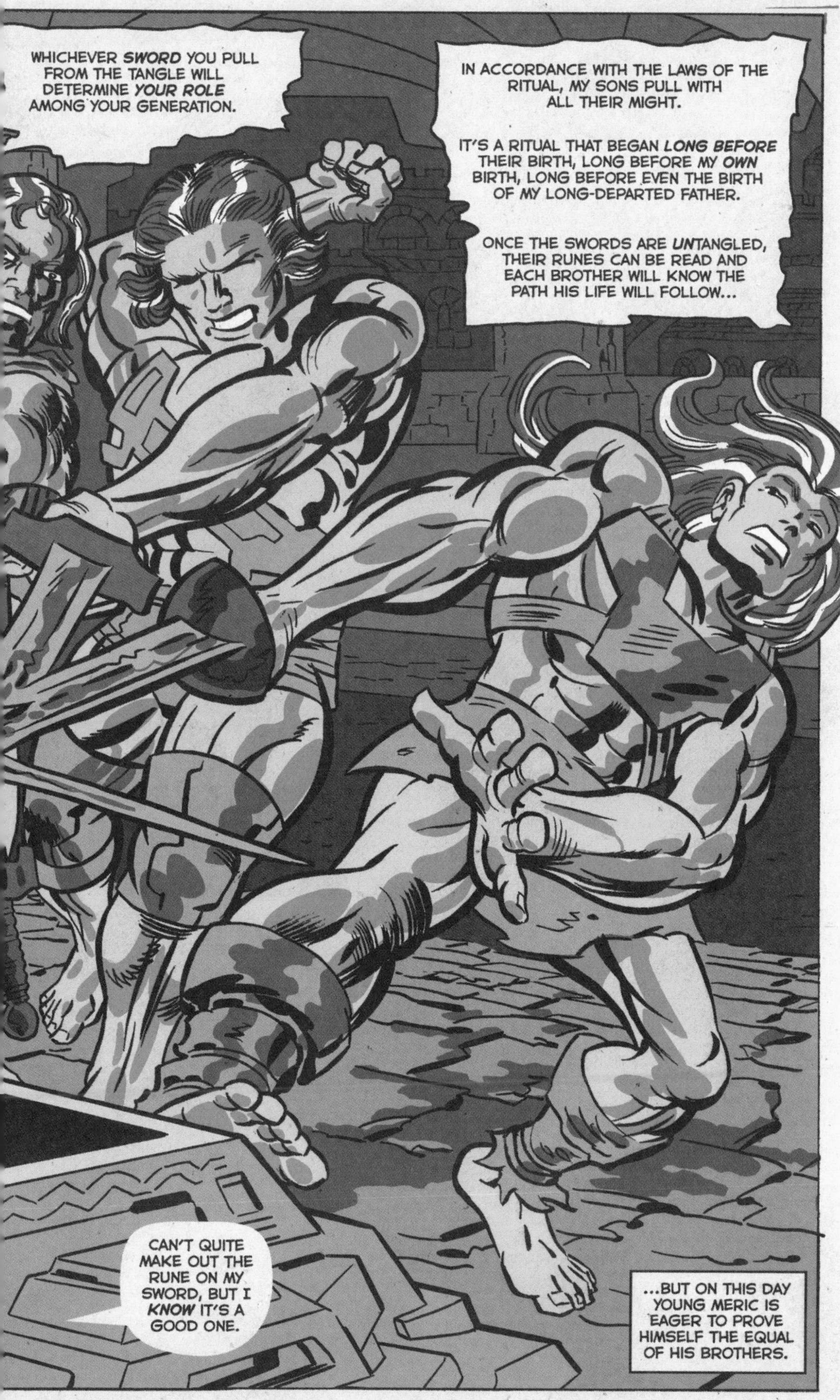
WHICHEVER SWORD YOU PULL FROM THE TANGLE WILL DETERMINE YOUR ROLE AMONG YOUR GENERATION.
IN ACCORDANCE WITH THE LAWS OF THE RITUAL, MY SONS PULL WITH ALL THEIR MIGHT.
IT'S A RITUAL THAT BEGAN LONG BEFORE THEIR BIRTH, LONG BEFORE MY OWN BIRTH, LONG BEFORE EVEN THE BIRTH OF MY LONG-DEPARTED FATHER.
ONCE THE SWORDS ARE UNTANGLED, THEIR RUNES CAN BE READ AND EACH BROTHER WILL KNOW THE PATH HIS LIFE WILL FOLLOW...
CAN'T QUITE MAKE OUT THE RUNE ON MY SWORD, BUT I KNOW IT'S A GOOD ONE.
...BUT ON THIS DAY YOUNG MERIC IS EAGER TO PROVE HIMSELF THE EQUAL OF HIS BROTHERS.

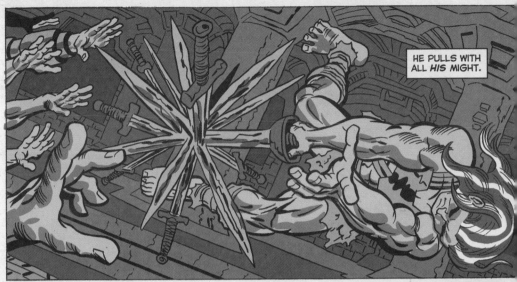

HE PULLS WITH ALL *HIS* MIGHT.

HE PULLED THE *WHOLE* TANGLE!

NO FAIR! WHAT A *FREAK!*

NOW HE HOLDS *ALL* THE SWORDS? *DO OVER!!*

THAT'S NOT SUPPOSED TO *HAPPEN,* IS IT?

THIS IS A *SPECIAL* CASE.

THOUGH IT IS MOST *UNUSUAL,* THIS *ONE-IN-A-MILLION* CIRCUMSTANCE IS *NOT* WITHOUT *PRECEDENT.*

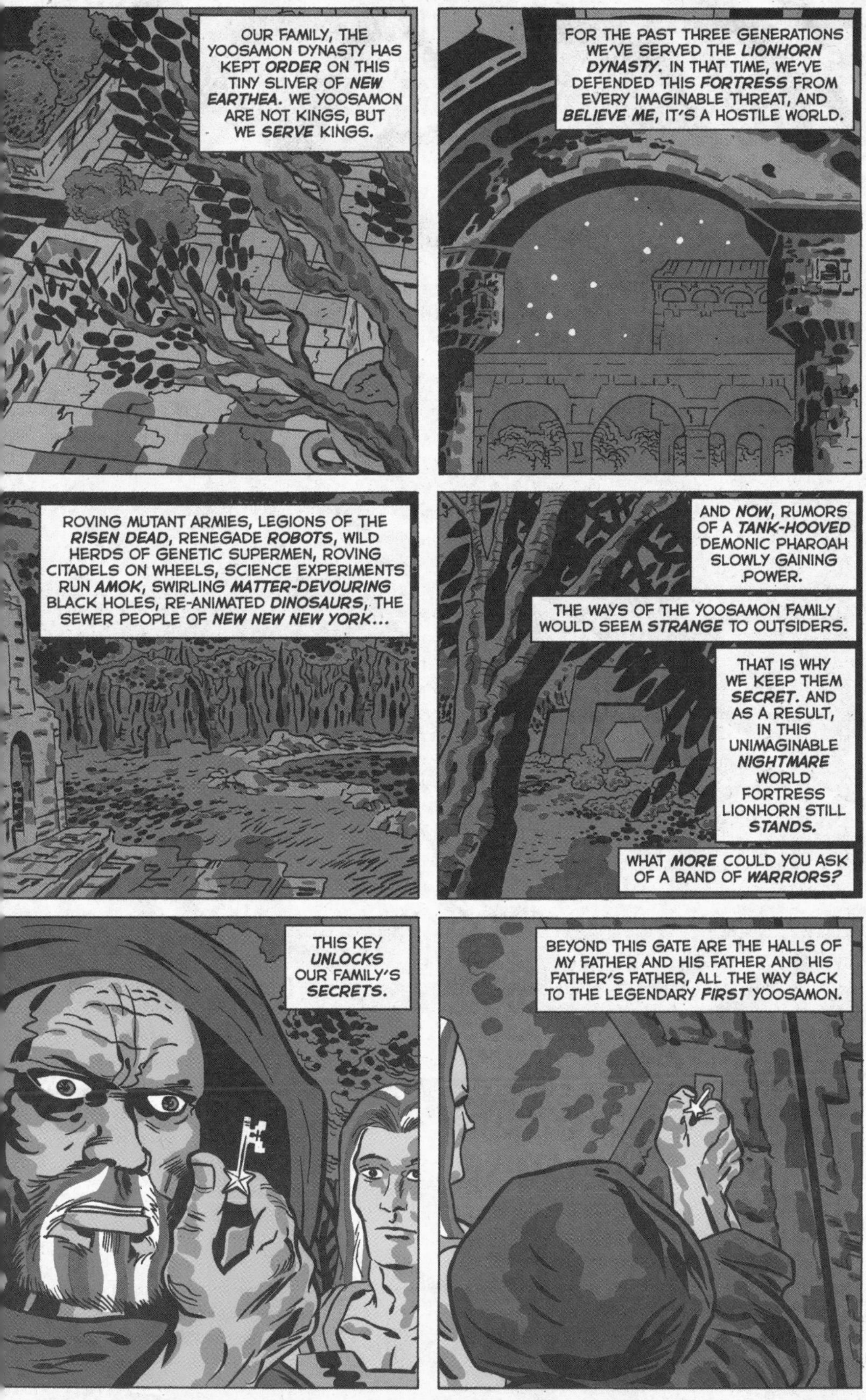
OUR FAMILY, THE YOOSAMON DYNASTY HAS KEPT ORDER ON THIS TINY SLIVER OF NEW EARTHEA. WE YOOSAMON ARE NOT KINGS, BUT WE SERVE KINGS.
FOR THE PAST THREE GENERATIONS WE'VE SERVED THE LIONHORN DYNASTY. IN THAT TIME, WE'VE DEFENDED THIS FORTRESS FROM EVERY IMAGINABLE THREAT, AND BELIEVE ME, IT'S A HOSTILE WORLD.
ROVING MUTANT ARMIES, LEGIONS OF THE RISEN DEAD, RENEGADE ROBOTS, WILD HERDS OF GENETIC SUPERMEN, ROVING CITADELS ON WHEELS, SCIENCE EXPERIMENTS RUN AMOK, SWIRLING MATTER-DEVOURING BLACK HOLES, RE-ANIMATED DINOSAURS, THE SEWER PEOPLE OF NEW NEW NEW YORK...
AND NOW, RUMORS OF A TANK-HOOVED DEMONIC PHAROAH SLOWLY GAINING POWER.
THE WAYS OF THE YOOSAMON FAMILY WOULD SEEM STRANGE TO OUTSIDERS.
THAT IS WHY WE KEEP THEM SECRET. AND AS A RESULT, IN THIS UNIMAGINABLE NIGHTMARE WORLD FORTRESS LIONHORN STILL STANDS.
WHAT MORE COULD YOU ASK OF A BAND OF WARRIORS?
THIS KEY UNLOCKS OUR FAMILY'S SECRETS.
BEYOND THIS GATE ARE THE HALLS OF MY FATHER AND HIS FATHER AND HIS FATHER'S FATHER, ALL THE WAY BACK TO THE LEGENDARY FIRST YOOSAMON.

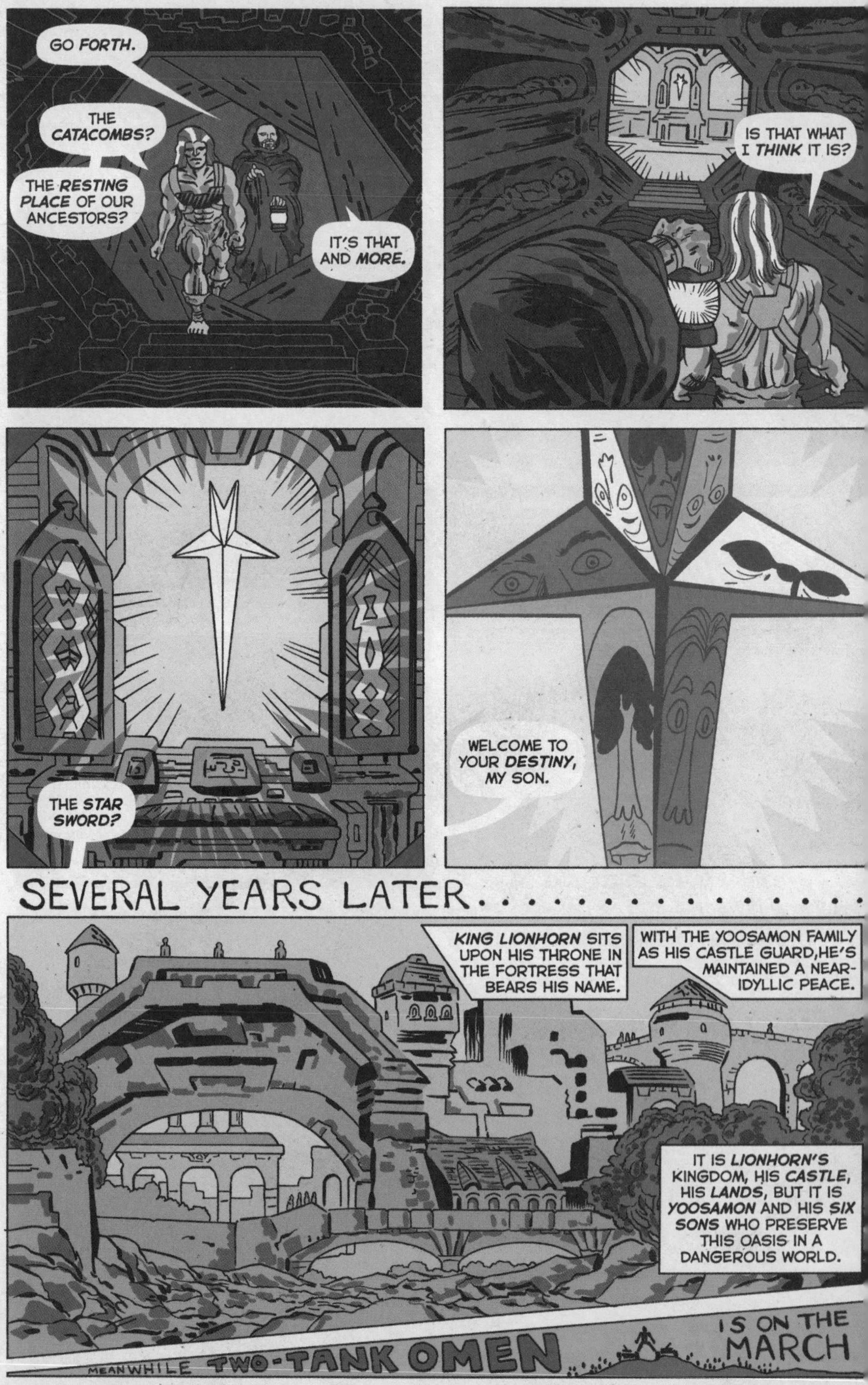
GO FORTH.
THE CATACOMBS?
THE RESTING PLACE OF OUR ANCESTORS?
IT'S THAT AND MORE.
IS THAT WHAT I THINK IT IS?
THE STAR SWORD?
WELCOME TO YOUR DESTINY, MY SON.
SEVERAL YEARS LATER.........
KING LIONHORN SITS UPON HIS THRONE IN THE FORTRESS THAT BEARS HIS NAME.
WITH THE YOOSAMON FAMILY AS HIS CASTLE GUARD, HE'S MAINTAINED A NEAR-IDYLLIC PEACE.
IT IS LIONHORN'S KINGDOM, HIS CASTLE, HIS LANDS, BUT IT IS YOOSAMON AND HIS SIX SONS WHO PRESERVE THIS OASIS IN A DANGEROUS WORLD.
MEANWHILE TWO-TANK OMEN IS ON THE MARCH

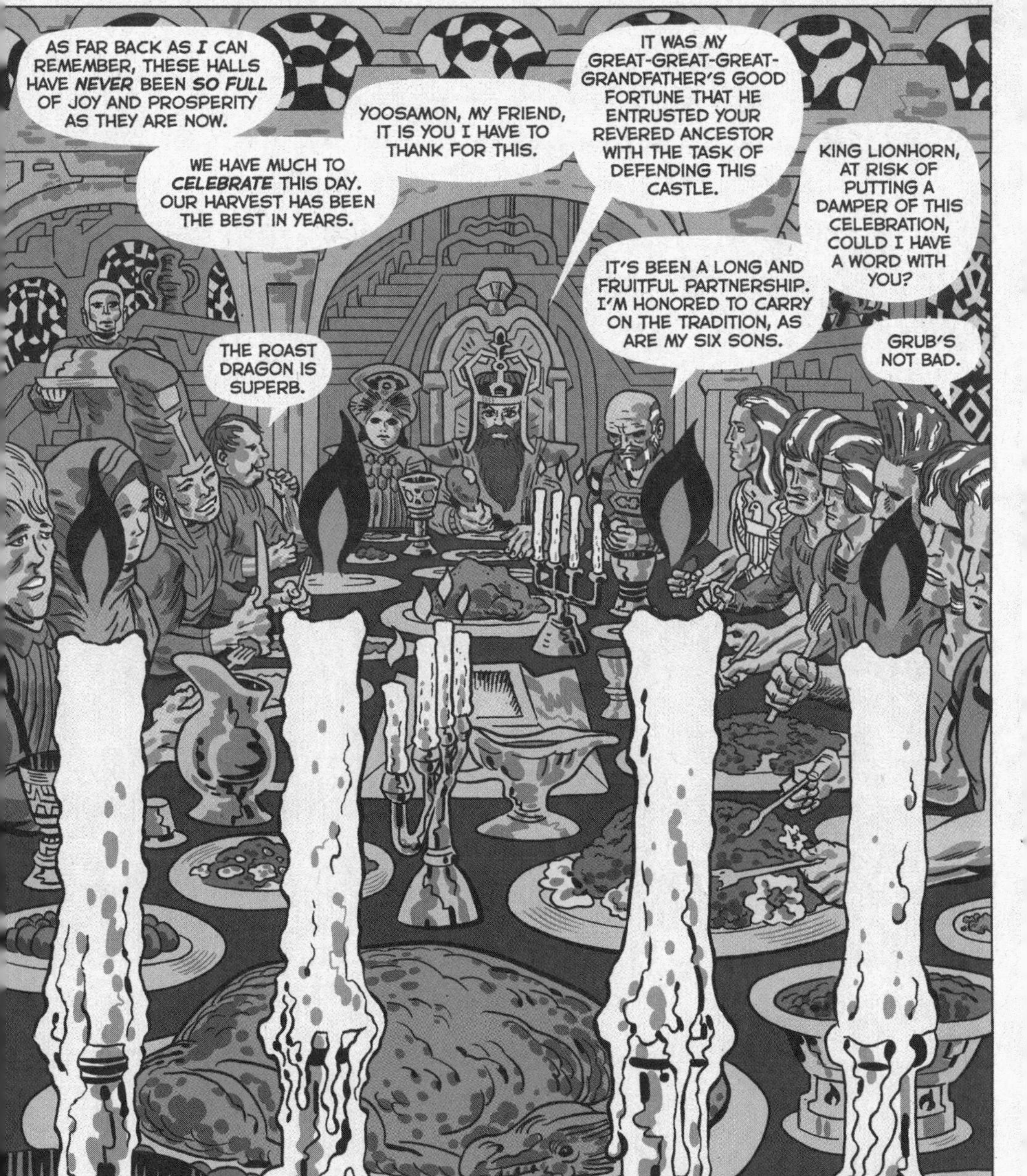
AS FAR BACK AS *I* CAN REMEMBER, THESE HALLS HAVE ***NEVER*** BEEN ***SO FULL*** OF JOY AND PROSPERITY AS THEY ARE NOW.
WE HAVE MUCH TO ***CELEBRATE*** THIS DAY. OUR HARVEST HAS BEEN THE BEST IN YEARS.
YOOSAMON, MY FRIEND, IT IS YOU I HAVE TO THANK FOR THIS.
IT WAS MY GREAT-GREAT-GREAT-GRANDFATHER'S GOOD FORTUNE THAT HE ENTRUSTED YOUR REVERED ANCESTOR WITH THE TASK OF DEFENDING THIS CASTLE.
IT'S BEEN A LONG AND FRUITFUL PARTNERSHIP. I'M HONORED TO CARRY ON THE TRADITION, AS ARE MY SIX SONS.
KING LIONHORN, AT RISK OF PUTTING A DAMPER OF THIS CELEBRATION, COULD I HAVE A WORD WITH YOU?
THE ROAST DRAGON IS SUPERB.
GRUB'S NOT BAD.
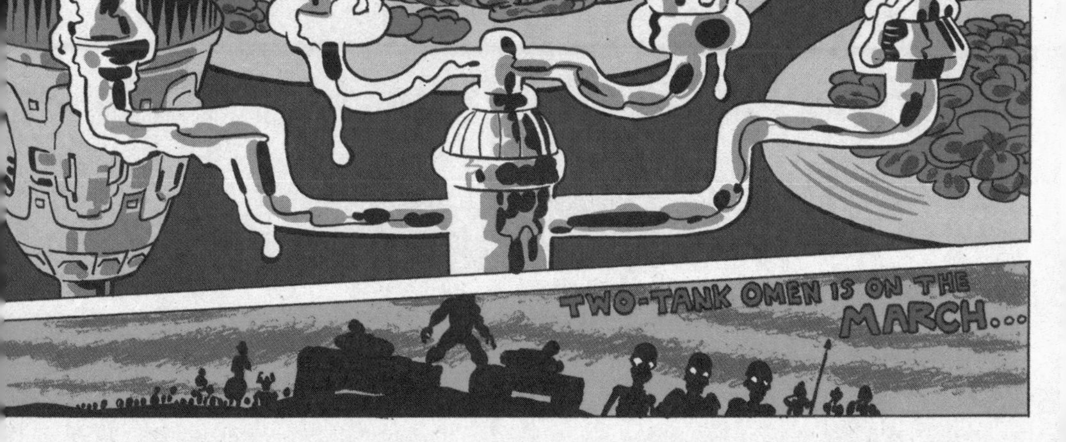
TWO-TANK OMEN IS ON THE MARCH...

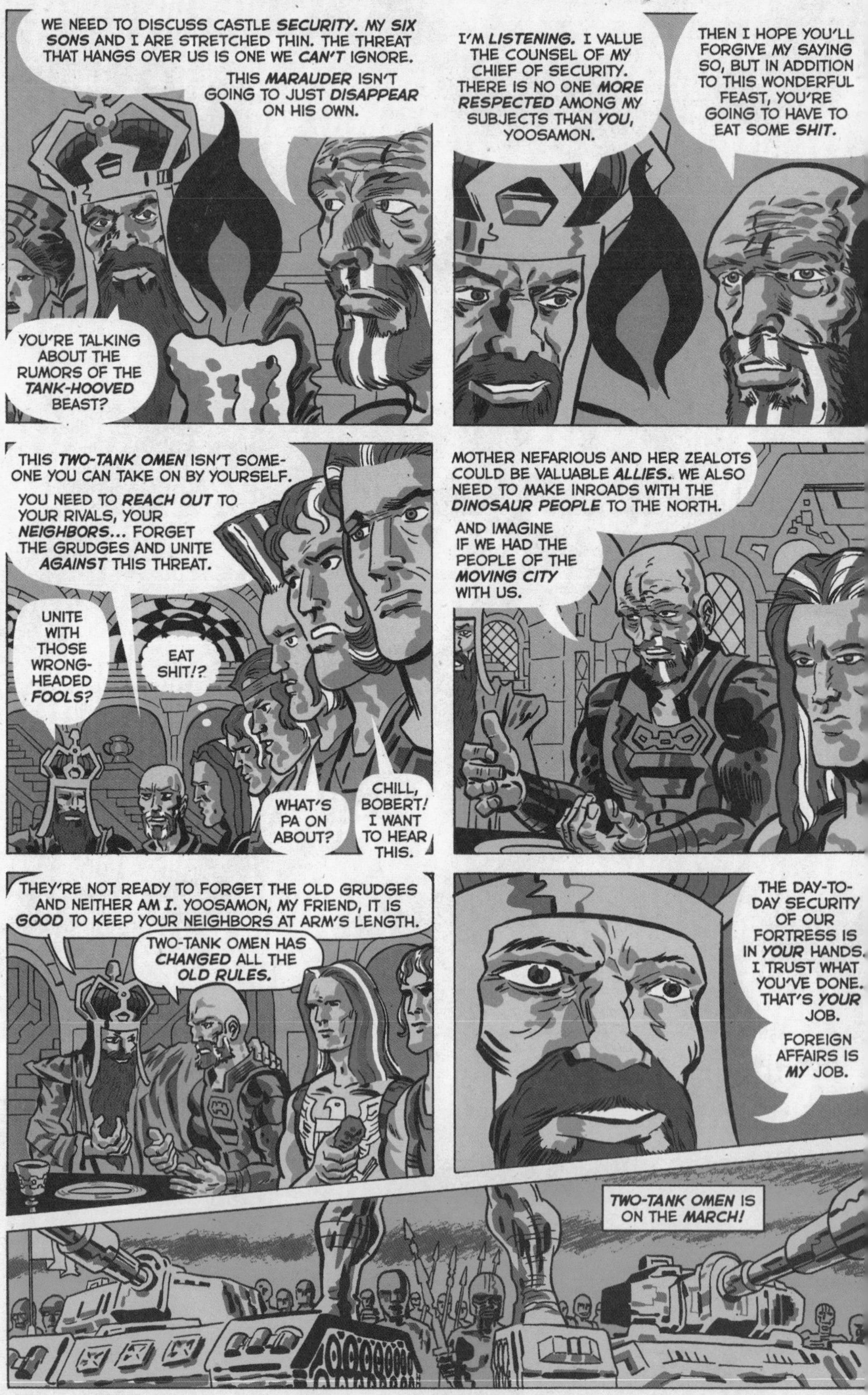
WE NEED TO DISCUSS CASTLE SECURITY. MY SIX SONS AND I ARE STRETCHED THIN. THE THREAT THAT HANGS OVER US IS ONE WE CAN'T IGNORE.
THIS MARAUDER ISN'T GOING TO JUST DISAPPEAR ON HIS OWN.
YOU'RE TALKING ABOUT THE RUMORS OF THE TANK-HOOVED BEAST?
I'M LISTENING. I VALUE THE COUNSEL OF MY CHIEF OF SECURITY. THERE IS NO ONE MORE RESPECTED AMONG MY SUBJECTS THAN YOU, YOOSAMON.
THEN I HOPE YOU'LL FORGIVE MY SAYING SO, BUT IN ADDITION TO THIS WONDERFUL FEAST, YOU'RE GOING TO HAVE TO EAT SOME SHIT.
THIS TWO-TANK OMEN ISN'T SOMEONE YOU CAN TAKE ON BY YOURSELF.
YOU NEED TO REACH OUT TO YOUR RIVALS, YOUR NEIGHBORS... FORGET THE GRUDGES AND UNITE AGAINST THIS THREAT.
UNITE WITH THOSE WRONG-HEADED FOOLS?
EAT SHIT!?
WHAT'S PA ON ABOUT?
CHILL, BOBERT! I WANT TO HEAR THIS.
MOTHER NEFARIOUS AND HER ZEALOTS COULD BE VALUABLE ALLIES. WE ALSO NEED TO MAKE INROADS WITH THE DINOSAUR PEOPLE TO THE NORTH.
AND IMAGINE IF WE HAD THE PEOPLE OF THE MOVING CITY WITH US.
THEY'RE NOT READY TO FORGET THE OLD GRUDGES AND NEITHER AM I. YOOSAMON, MY FRIEND, IT IS GOOD TO KEEP YOUR NEIGHBORS AT ARM'S LENGTH.
TWO-TANK OMEN HAS CHANGED ALL THE OLD RULES.
THE DAY-TO-DAY SECURITY OF OUR FORTRESS IS IN YOUR HANDS. I TRUST WHAT YOU'VE DONE. THAT'S YOUR JOB.
FOREIGN AFFAIRS IS MY JOB.
TWO-TANK OMEN IS ON THE MARCH!

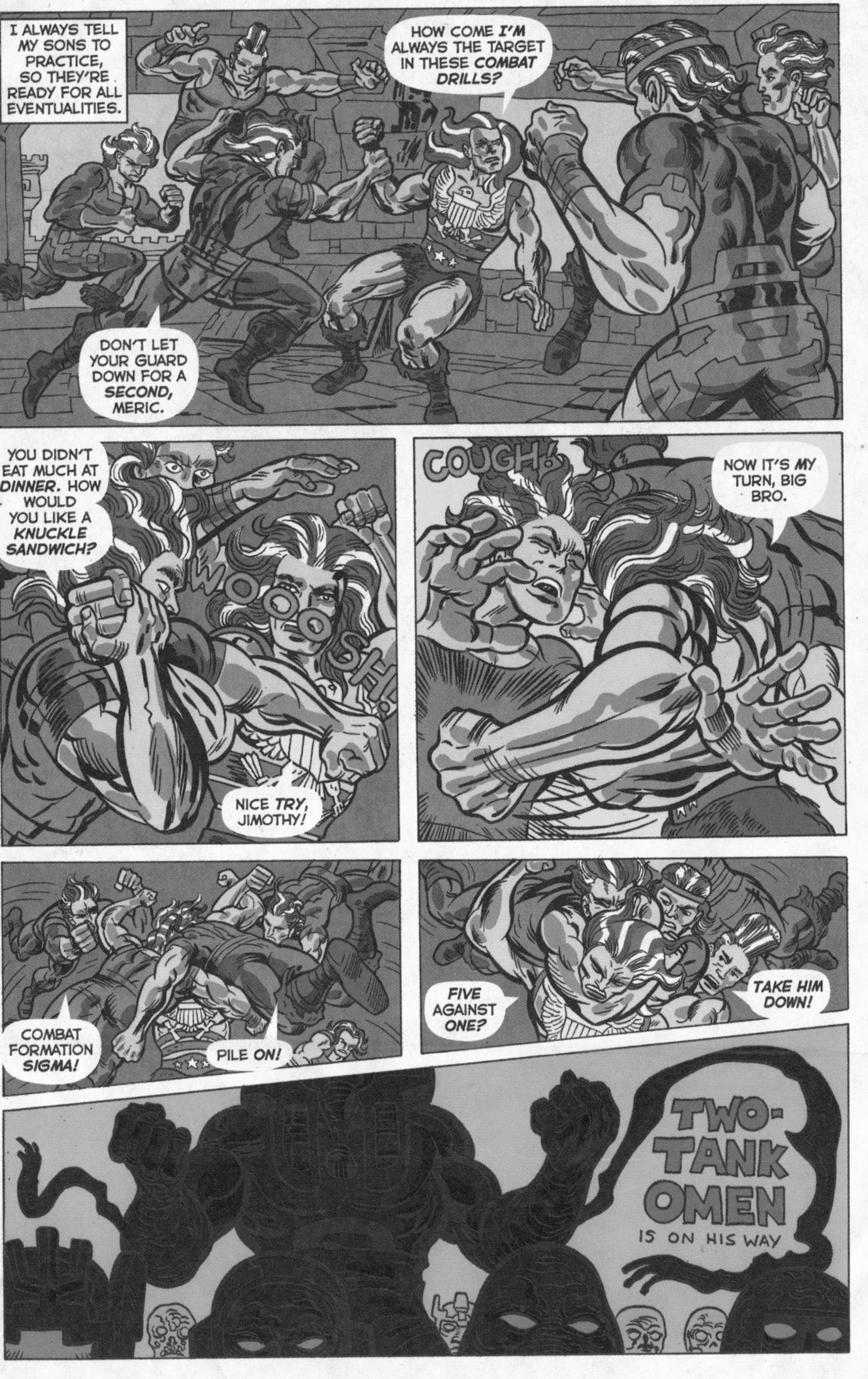
I ALWAYS TELL MY SONS TO PRACTICE, SO THEY'RE READY FOR ALL EVENTUALITIES.
HOW COME I'M ALWAYS THE TARGET IN THESE COMBAT DRILLS?
DON'T LET YOUR GUARD DOWN FOR A SECOND, MERIC.
YOU DIDN'T EAT MUCH AT DINNER. HOW WOULD YOU LIKE A KNUCKLE SANDWICH?
WOOOOSH!
NICE TRY, JIMOTHY!
COUGH!
NOW IT'S MY TURN, BIG BRO.
COMBAT FORMATION SIGMA!
PILE ON!
FIVE AGAINST ONE?
TAKE HIM DOWN!
TWO-TANK OMEN
IS ON HIS WAY

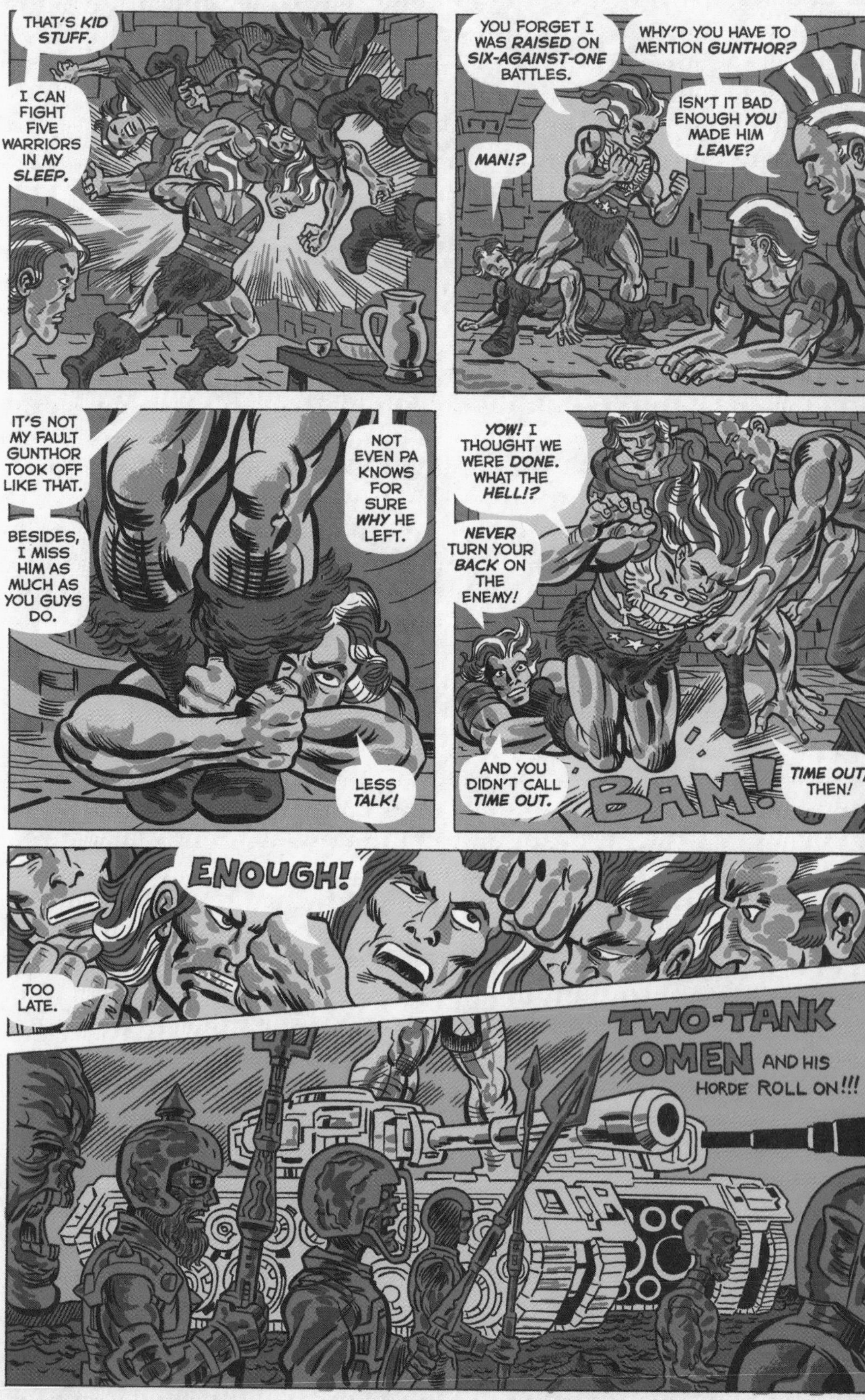

THAT'S KID STUFF.
I CAN FIGHT FIVE WARRIORS IN MY SLEEP.
YOU FORGET I WAS RAISED ON SIX-AGAINST-ONE BATTLES.
MAN!?
WHY'D YOU HAVE TO MENTION GUNTHOR?
ISN'T IT BAD ENOUGH YOU MADE HIM LEAVE?
IT'S NOT MY FAULT GUNTHOR TOOK OFF LIKE THAT.
BESIDES, I MISS HIM AS MUCH AS YOU GUYS DO.
NOT EVEN PA KNOWS FOR SURE WHY HE LEFT.
LESS TALK!
YOW! I THOUGHT WE WERE DONE. WHAT THE HELL!?
NEVER TURN YOUR BACK ON THE ENEMY!
AND YOU DIDN'T CALL TIME OUT.
BAM!
TIME OUT, THEN!
ENOUGH!
TOO LATE.
TWO-TANK OMEN AND HIS HORDE ROLL ON!!!

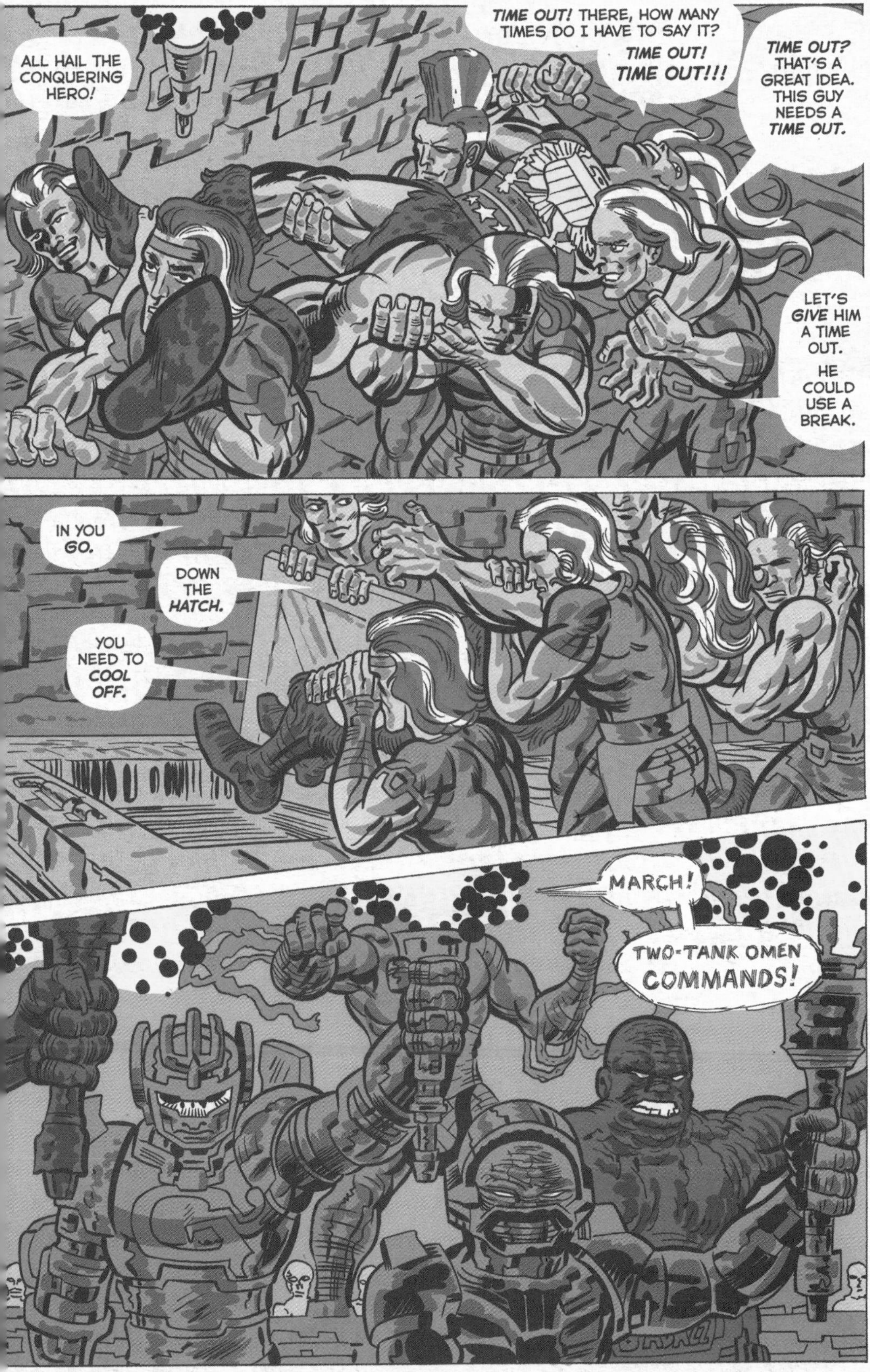

ALL HAIL THE CONQUERING HERO!
TIME OUT! THERE, HOW MANY TIMES DO I HAVE TO SAY IT? TIME OUT! TIME OUT!!!
TIME OUT? THAT'S A GREAT IDEA. THIS GUY NEEDS A TIME OUT.
LET'S GIVE HIM A TIME OUT.
HE COULD USE A BREAK.
IN YOU GO.
DOWN THE HATCH.
YOU NEED TO COOL OFF.
MARCH!
TWO-TANK OMEN COMMANDS!

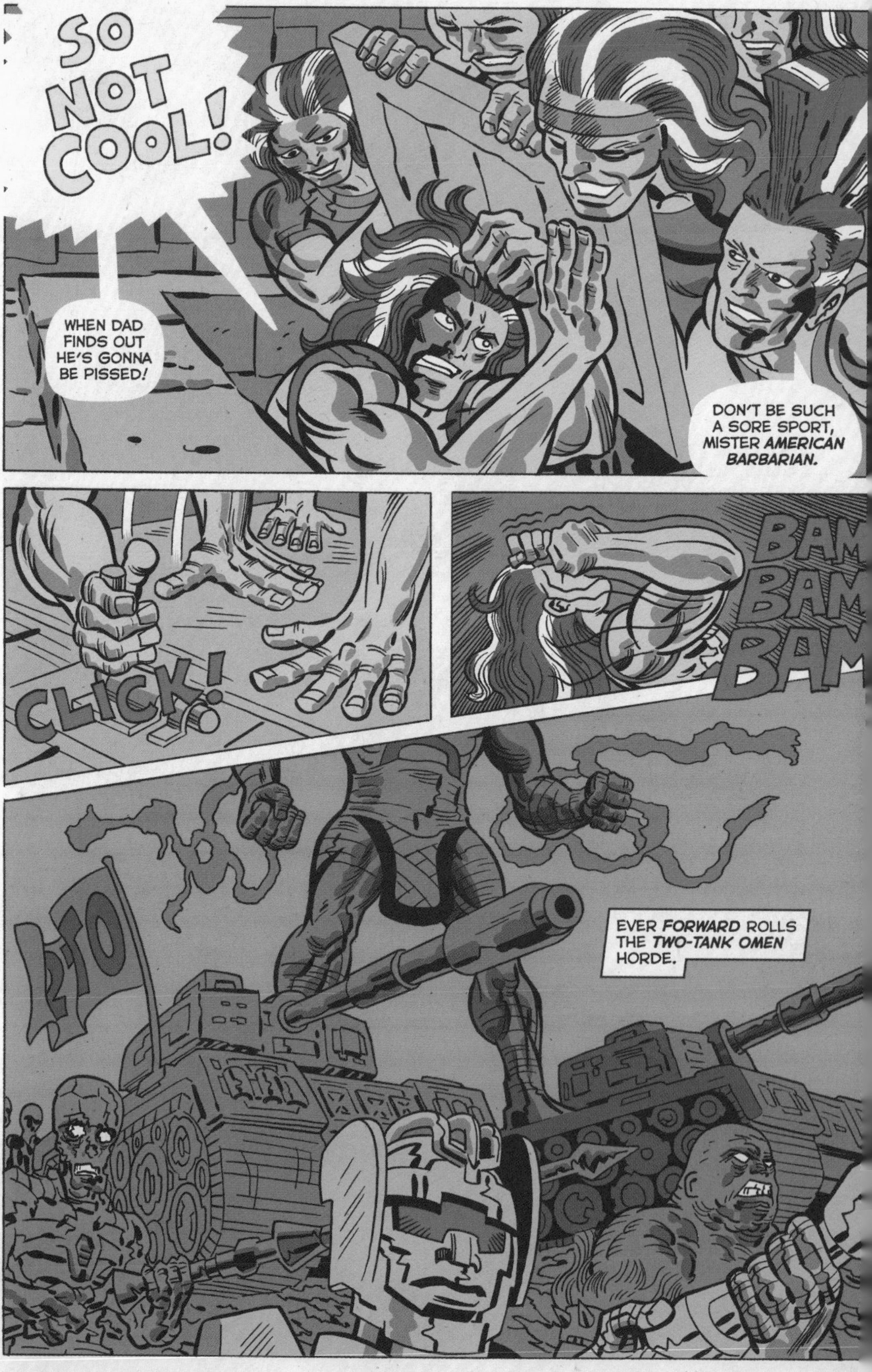
SO NOT COOL!
WHEN DAD FINDS OUT HE'S GONNA BE PISSED!
DON'T BE SUCH A SORE SPORT, MISTER *AMERICAN BARBARIAN.*
CLICK!
BAM BAM BAM
2TO
EVER *FORWARD* ROLLS THE *TWO-TANK OMEN* HORDE.

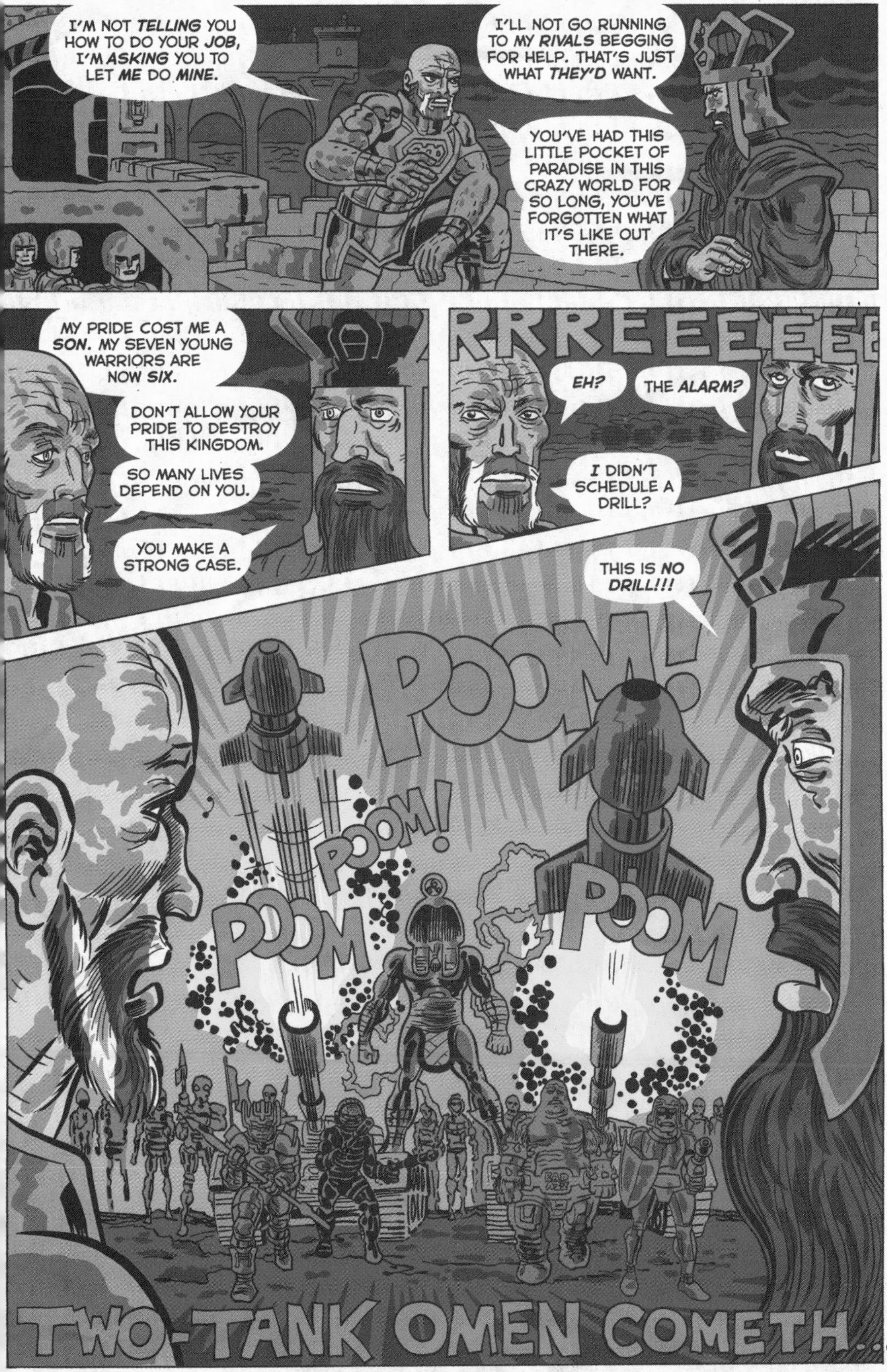
I'M NOT TELLING YOU HOW TO DO YOUR JOB, I'M ASKING YOU TO LET ME DO MINE.
I'LL NOT GO RUNNING TO MY RIVALS BEGGING FOR HELP. THAT'S JUST WHAT THEY'D WANT.
YOU'VE HAD THIS LITTLE POCKET OF PARADISE IN THIS CRAZY WORLD FOR SO LONG, YOU'VE FORGOTTEN WHAT IT'S LIKE OUT THERE.
MY PRIDE COST ME A SON. MY SEVEN YOUNG WARRIORS ARE NOW SIX.
DON'T ALLOW YOUR PRIDE TO DESTROY THIS KINGDOM.
SO MANY LIVES DEPEND ON YOU.
YOU MAKE A STRONG CASE.
RRREEEEEE
EH?
THE ALARM?
I DIDN'T SCHEDULE A DRILL?
THIS IS NO DRILL!!!
POOM!
POOM!
POOM
POOM
TWO-TANK OMEN COMETH...

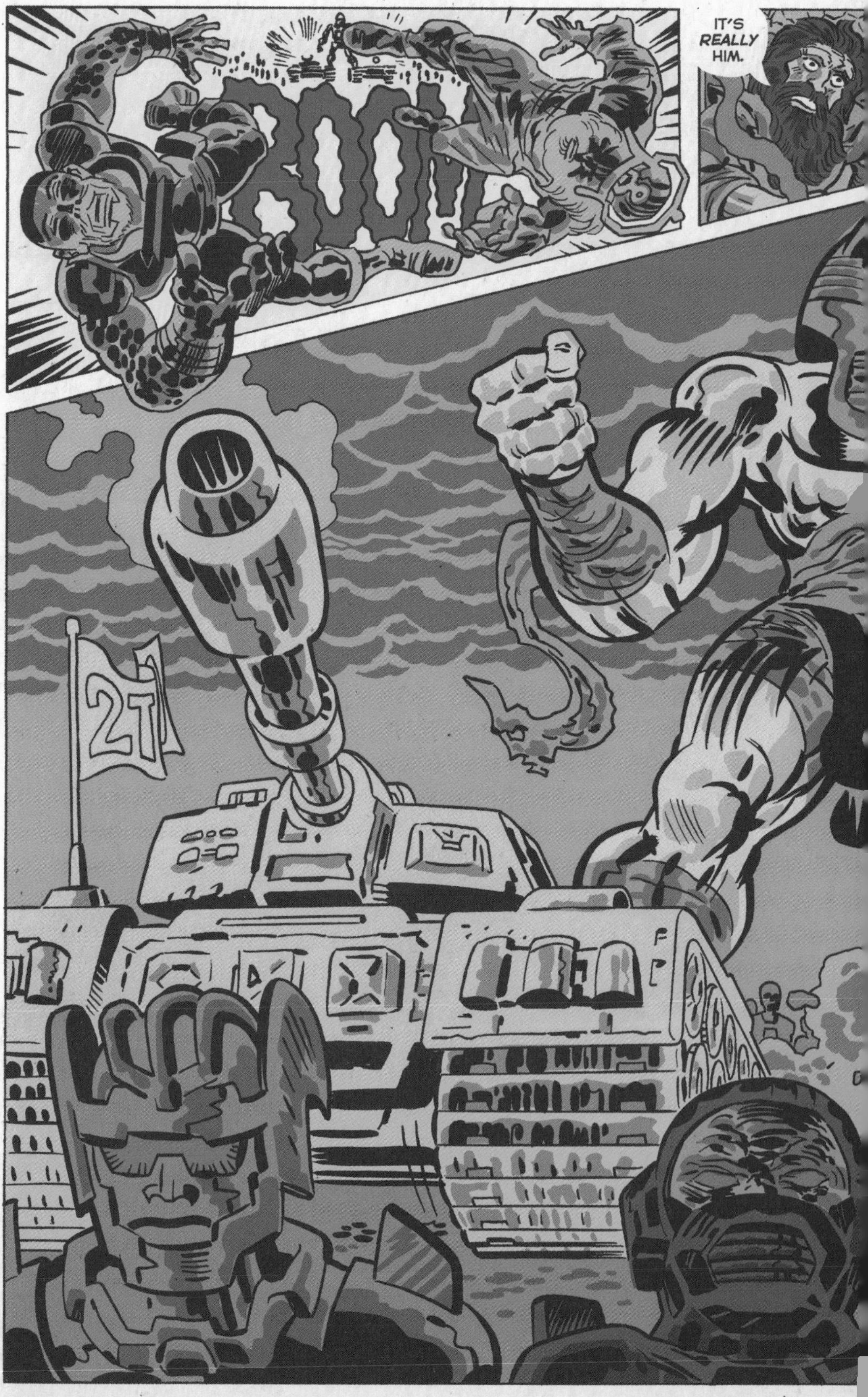
BOOM
IT'S REALLY HIM.
2T

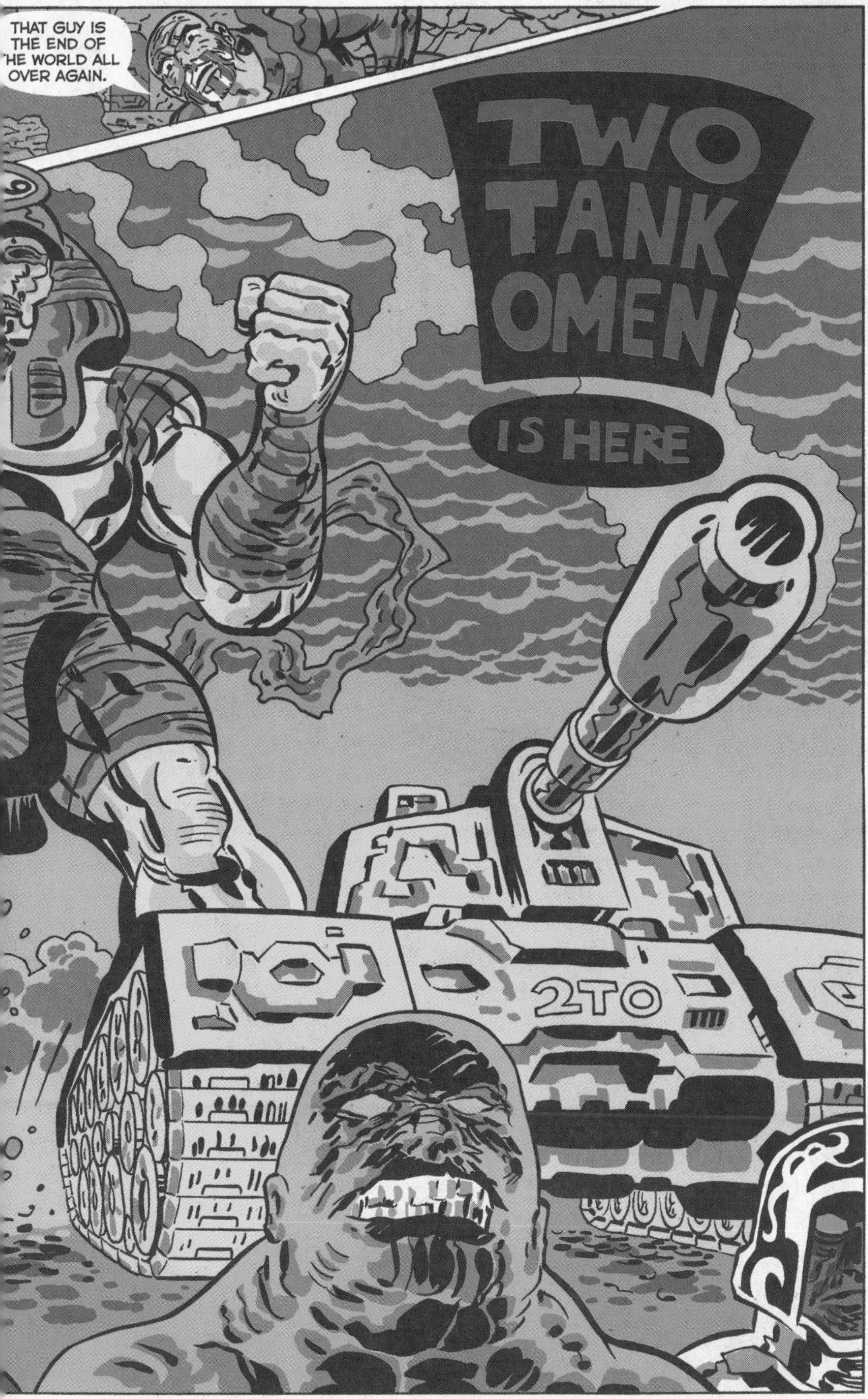

THAT GUY IS THE END OF HE WORLD ALL OVER AGAIN.
TWO TANK OMEN
IS HERE
2TO

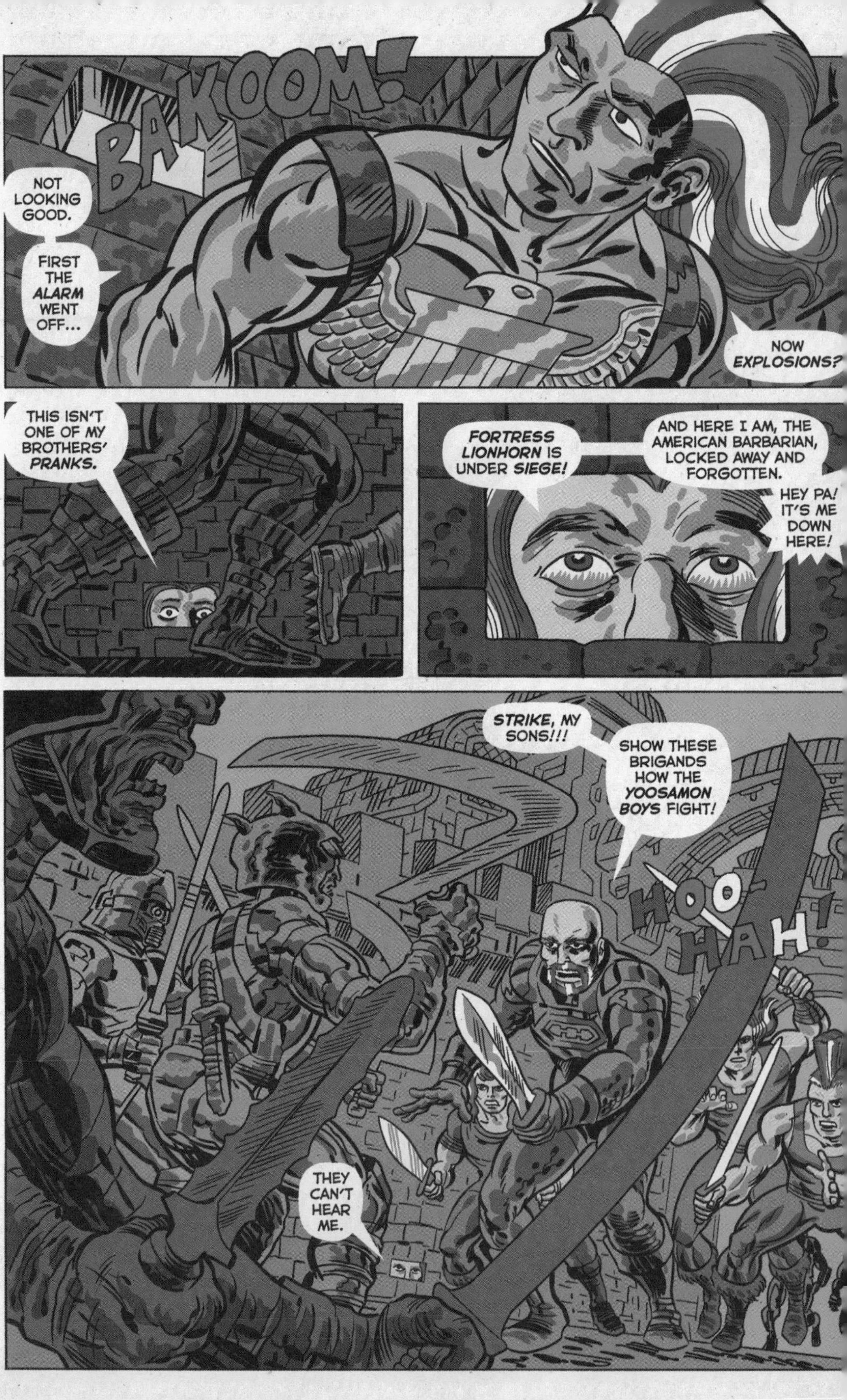
BAKOOM!
NOT LOOKING GOOD.
FIRST THE ALARM WENT OFF...
NOW EXPLOSIONS?
THIS ISN'T ONE OF MY BROTHERS' PRANKS.
FORTRESS LIONHORN IS UNDER SIEGE!
AND HERE I AM, THE AMERICAN BARBARIAN, LOCKED AWAY AND FORGOTTEN.
HEY PA! IT'S ME DOWN HERE!
STRIKE, MY SONS!!!
SHOW THESE BRIGANDS HOW THE YOOSAMON BOYS FIGHT!
HOO-HAH!
THEY CAN'T HEAR ME.

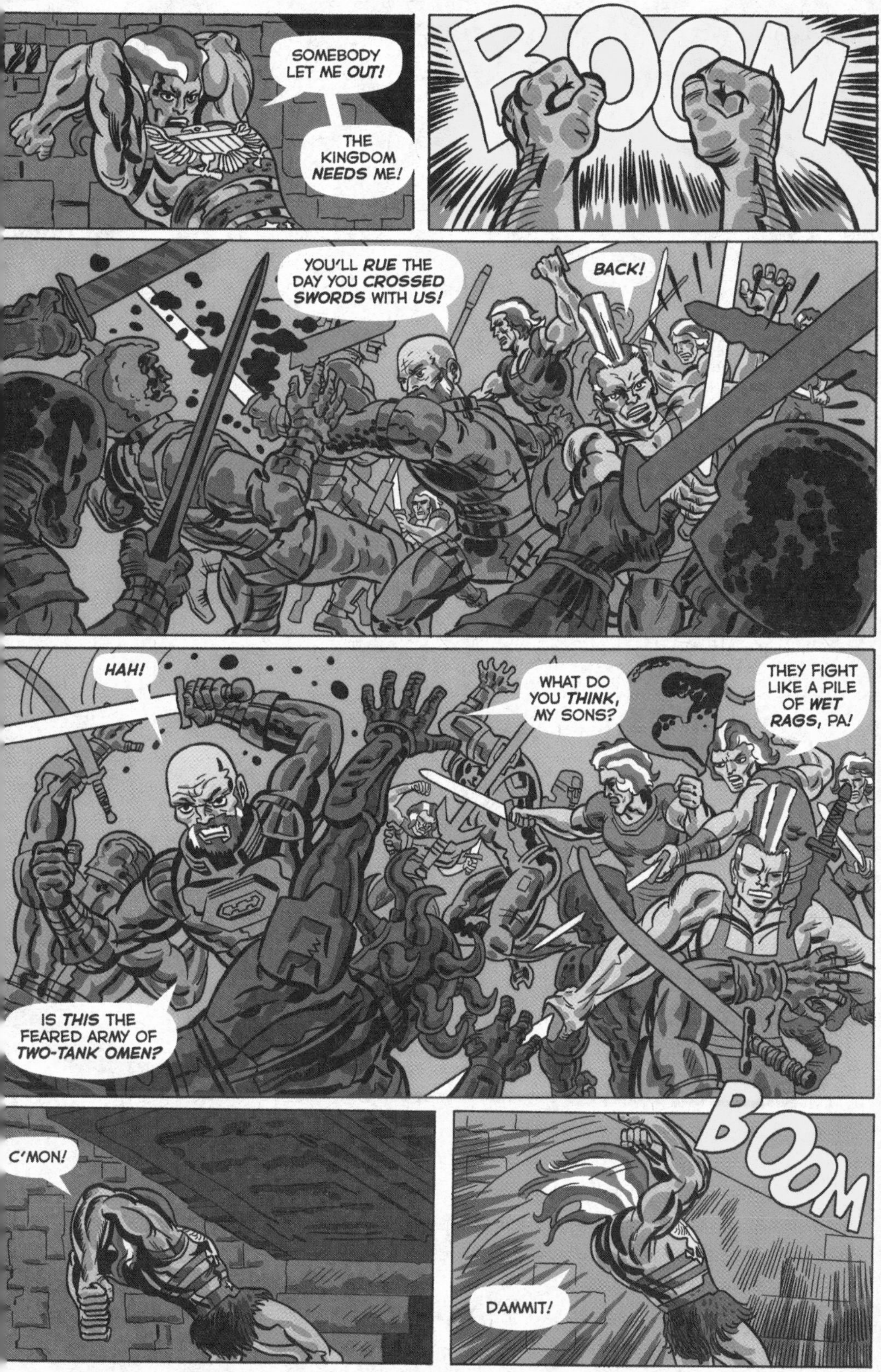
SOMEBODY LET ME OUT!
THE KINGDOM NEEDS ME!
BOOM
YOU'LL RUE THE DAY YOU CROSSED SWORDS WITH US!
BACK!
HAH!
WHAT DO YOU THINK, MY SONS?
THEY FIGHT LIKE A PILE OF WET RAGS, PA!
IS THIS THE FEARED ARMY OF TWO-TANK OMEN?
C'MON!
BOOM
DAMMIT!

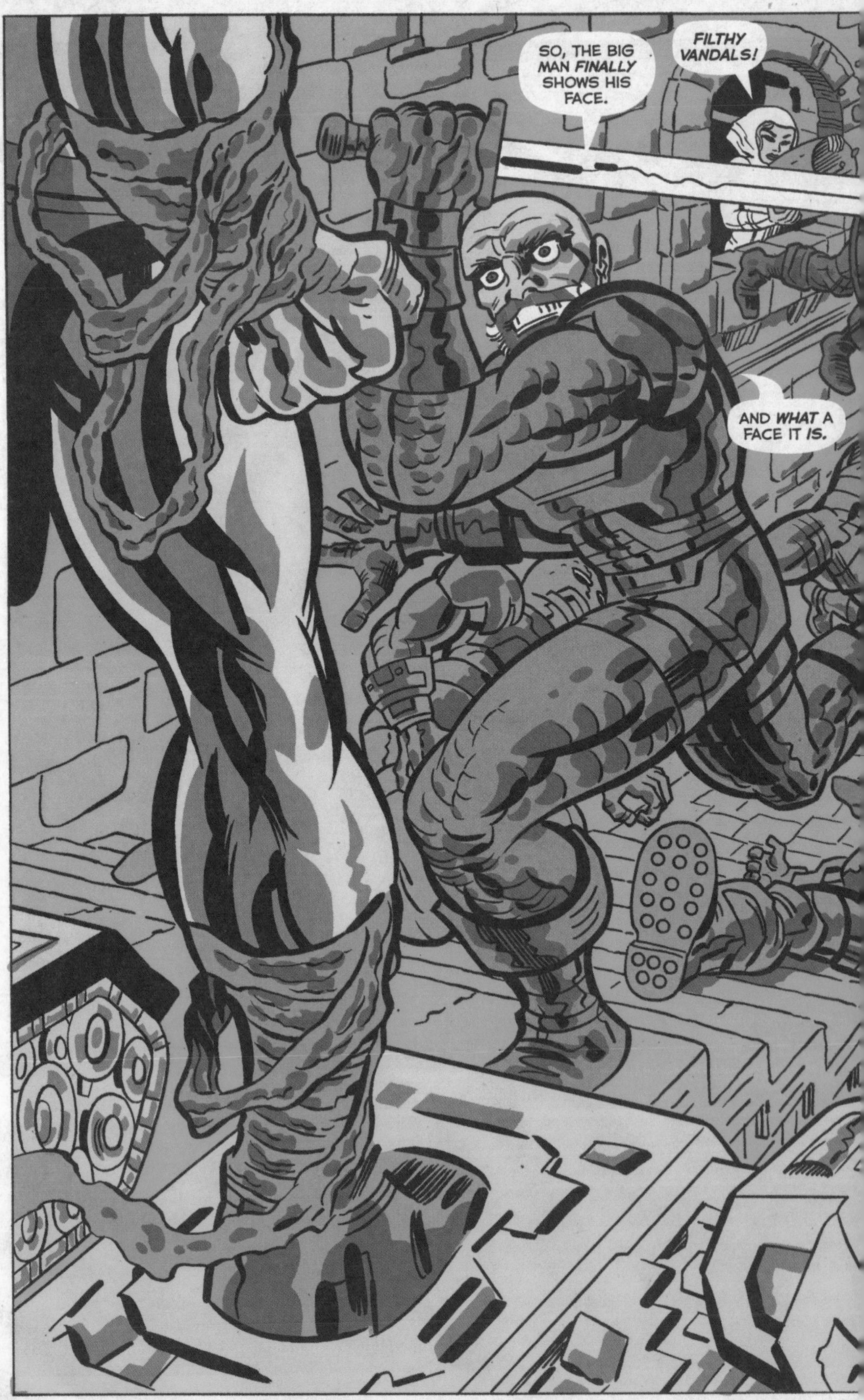
SO, THE BIG MAN FINALLY SHOWS HIS FACE.
FILTHY VANDALS!
AND WHAT A FACE IT IS.

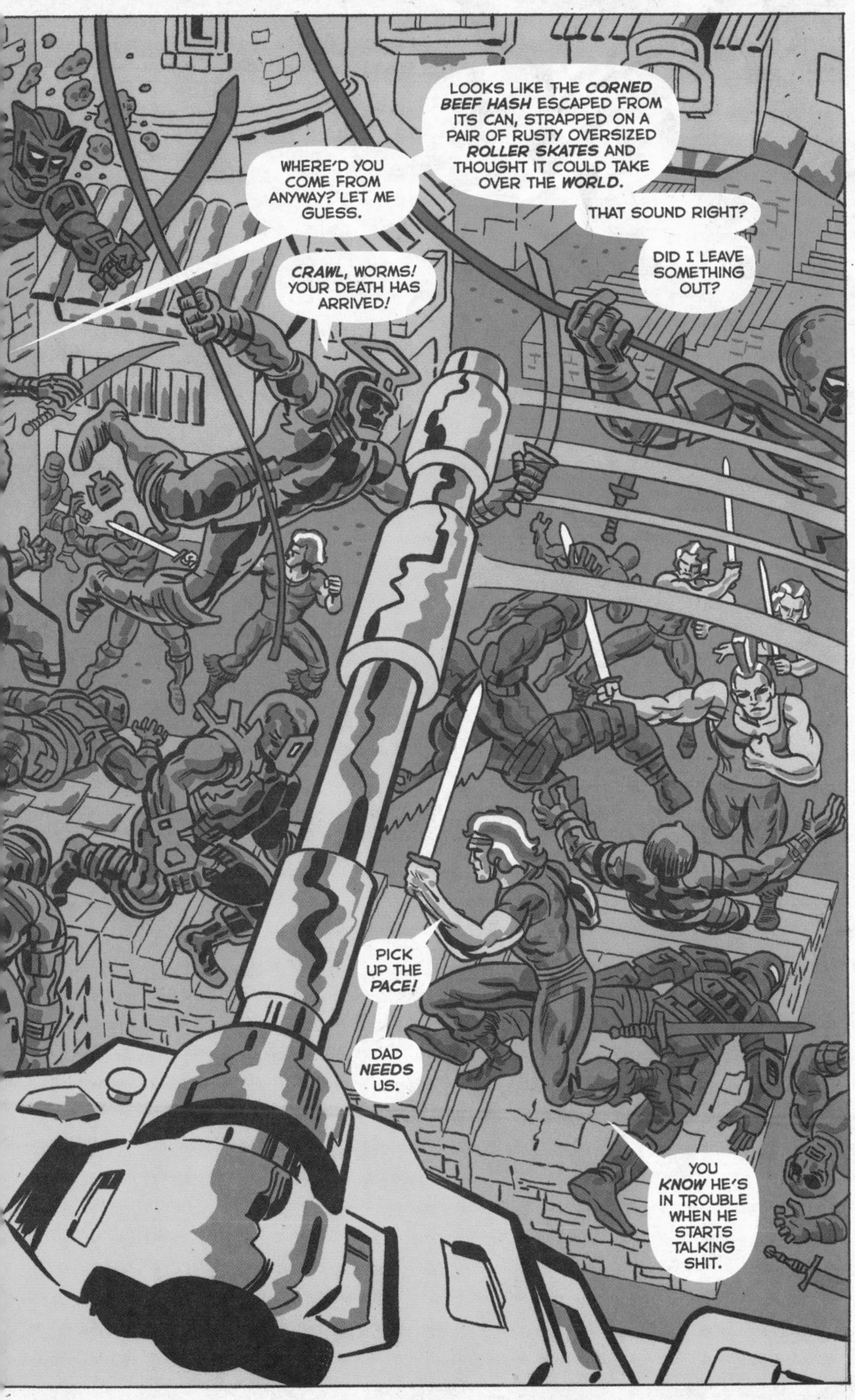
WHERE'D YOU COME FROM ANYWAY? LET ME GUESS.
LOOKS LIKE THE CORNED BEEF HASH ESCAPED FROM ITS CAN, STRAPPED ON A PAIR OF RUSTY OVERSIZED ROLLER SKATES AND THOUGHT IT COULD TAKE OVER THE WORLD.
THAT SOUND RIGHT?
DID I LEAVE SOMETHING OUT?
CRAWL, WORMS! YOUR DEATH HAS ARRIVED!
PICK UP THE PACE!
DAD NEEDS US.
YOU KNOW HE'S IN TROUBLE WHEN HE STARTS TALKING SHIT.

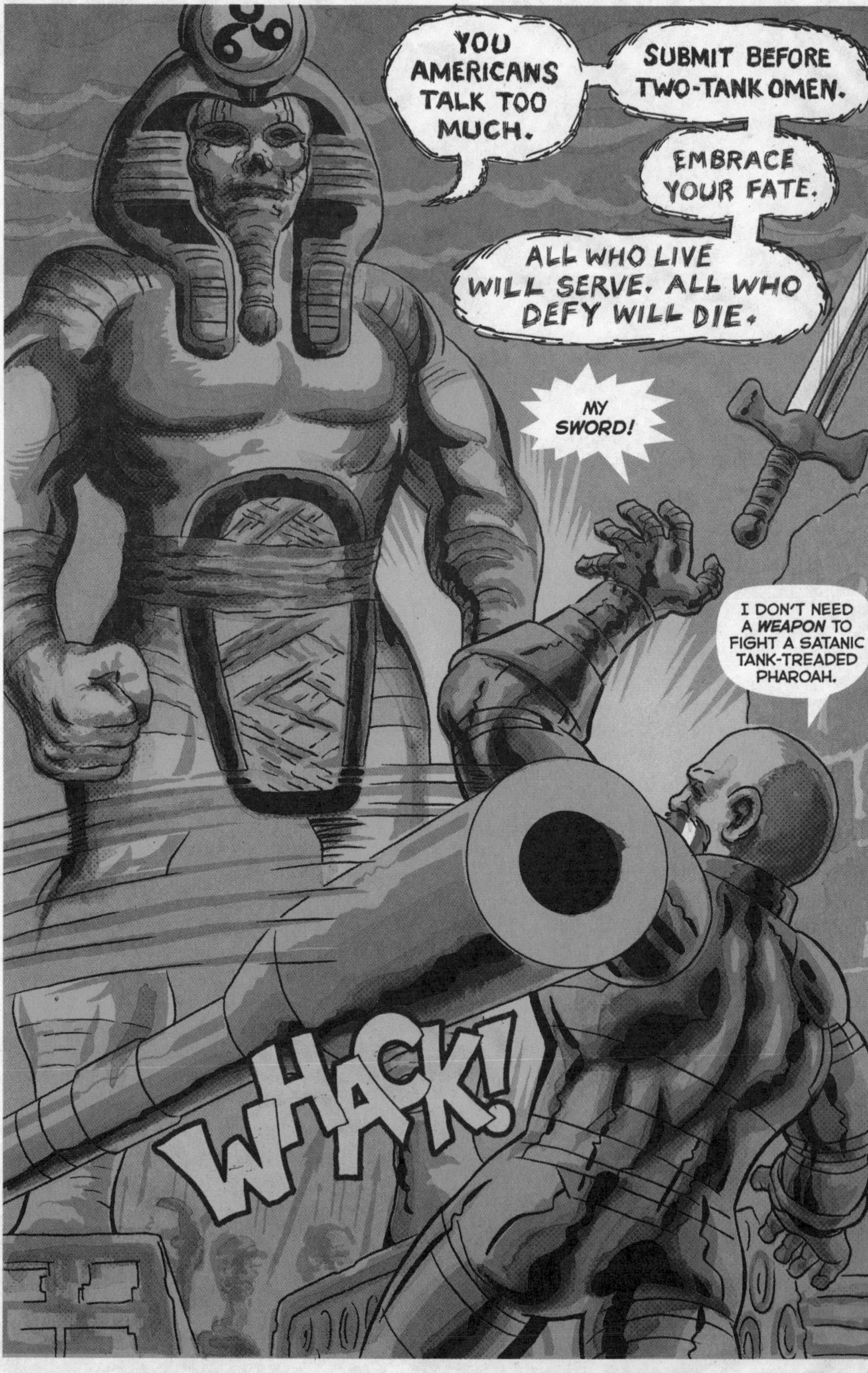
YOU AMERICANS TALK TOO MUCH.
SUBMIT BEFORE TWO-TANK OMEN.
EMBRACE YOUR FATE.
ALL WHO LIVE WILL SERVE. ALL WHO DEFY WILL DIE.
MY SWORD!
I DON'T NEED A *WEAPON* TO FIGHT A SATANIC TANK-TREADED PHAROAH.
WHACK!

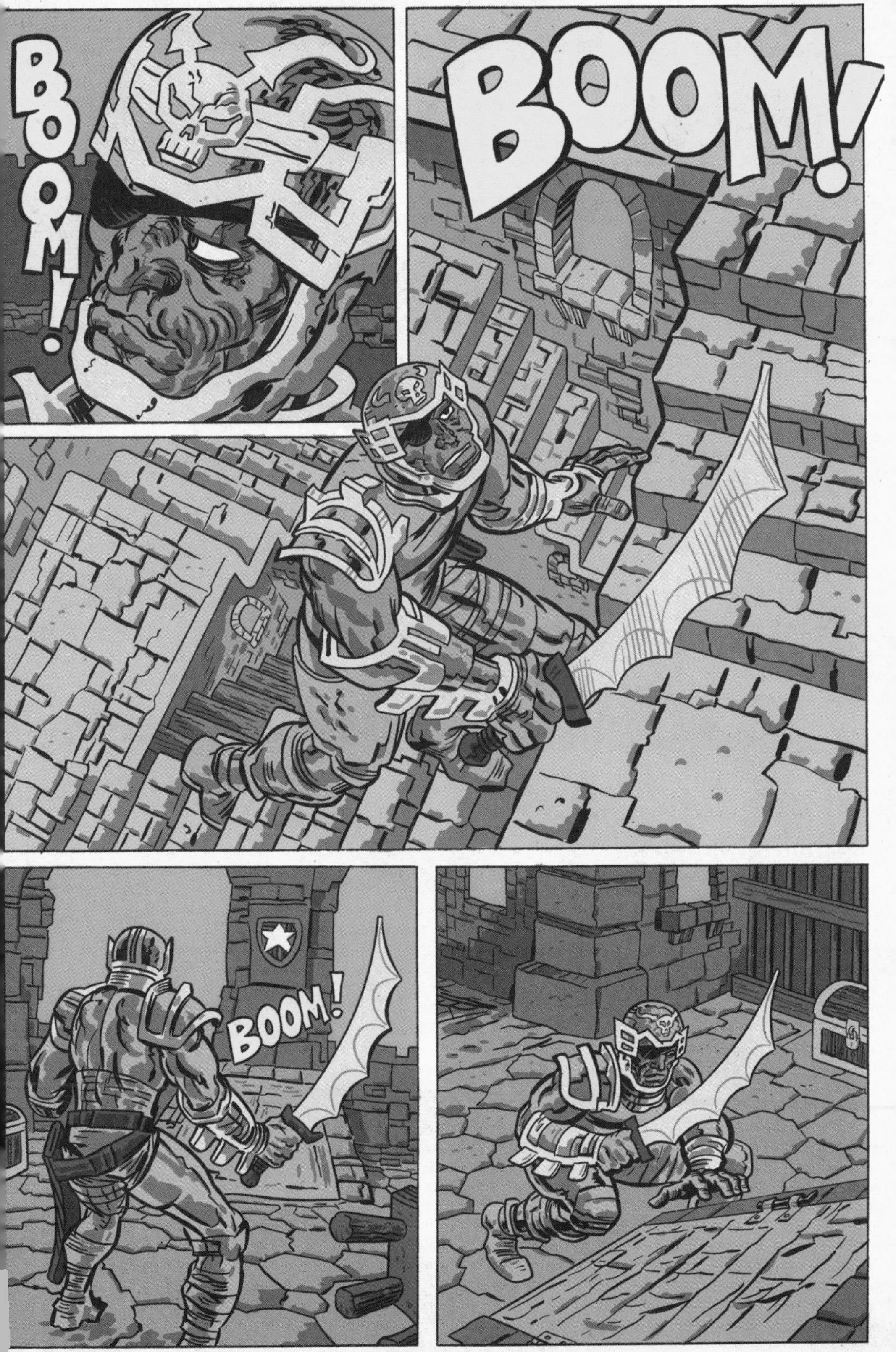
BOOM!
BOOM!
BOOM!

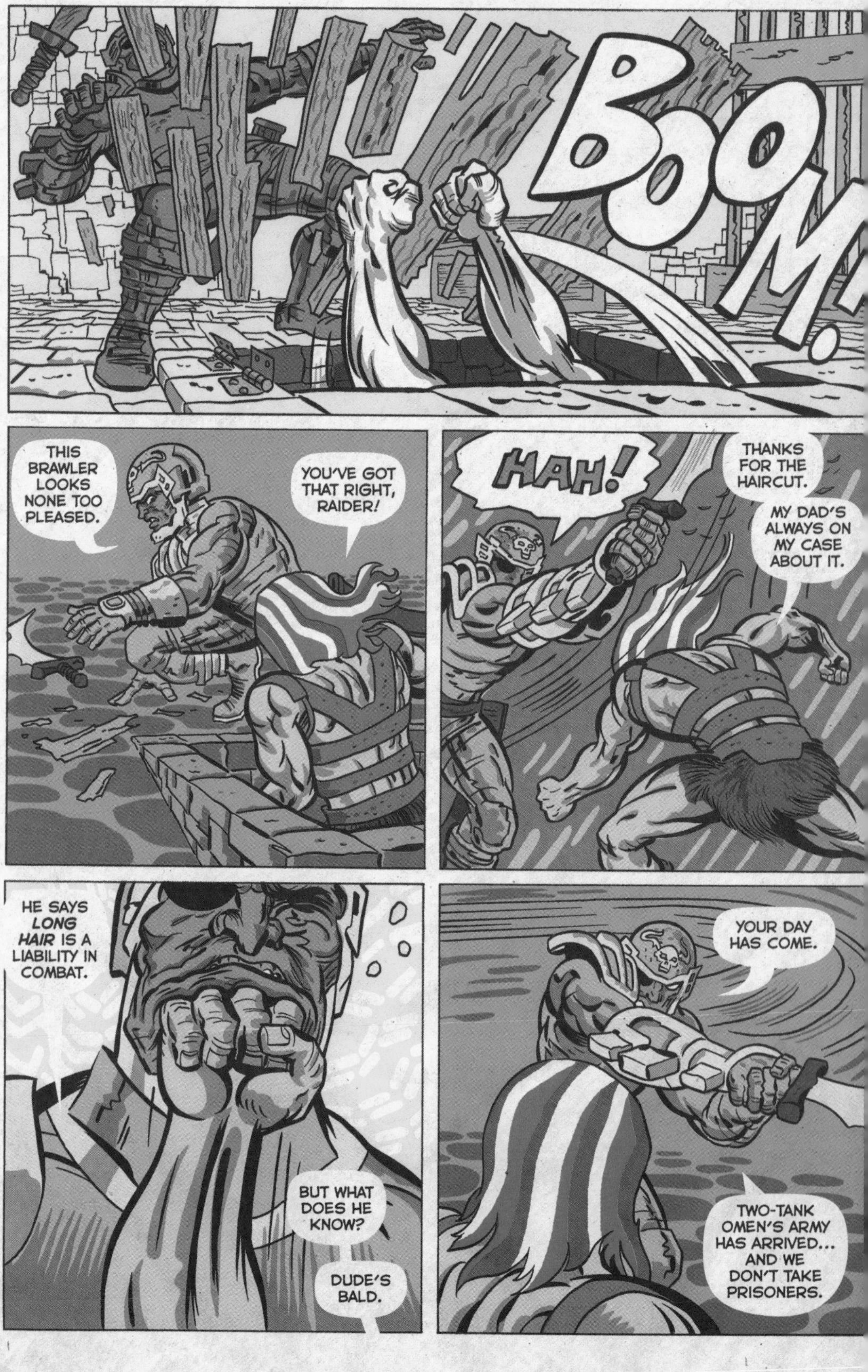
BOOM!
THIS BRAWLER LOOKS NONE TOO PLEASED.
YOU'VE GOT THAT RIGHT, RAIDER!
HAH!
THANKS FOR THE HAIRCUT.
MY DAD'S ALWAYS ON MY CASE ABOUT IT.
HE SAYS LONG HAIR IS A LIABILITY IN COMBAT.
BUT WHAT DOES HE KNOW?
DUDE'S BALD.
YOUR DAY HAS COME.
TWO-TANK OMEN'S ARMY HAS ARRIVED... AND WE DON'T TAKE PRISONERS.

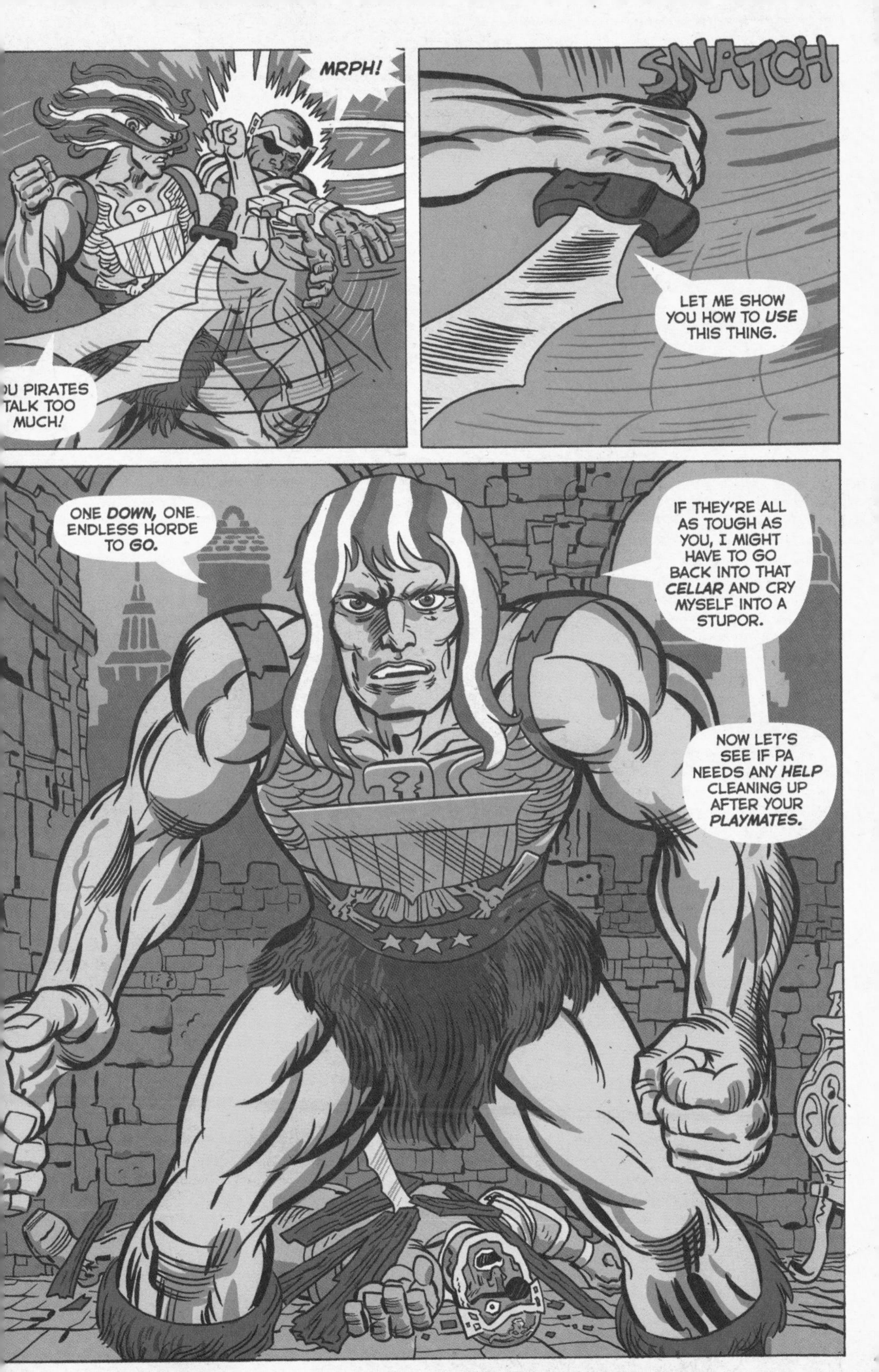
MRPH!
OU PIRATES TALK TOO MUCH!
SNATCH
LET ME SHOW YOU HOW TO USE THIS THING.
ONE DOWN, ONE ENDLESS HORDE TO GO.
IF THEY'RE ALL AS TOUGH AS YOU, I MIGHT HAVE TO GO BACK INTO THAT CELLAR AND CRY MYSELF INTO A STUPOR.
NOW LET'S SEE IF PA NEEDS ANY HELP CLEANING UP AFTER YOUR PLAYMATES.

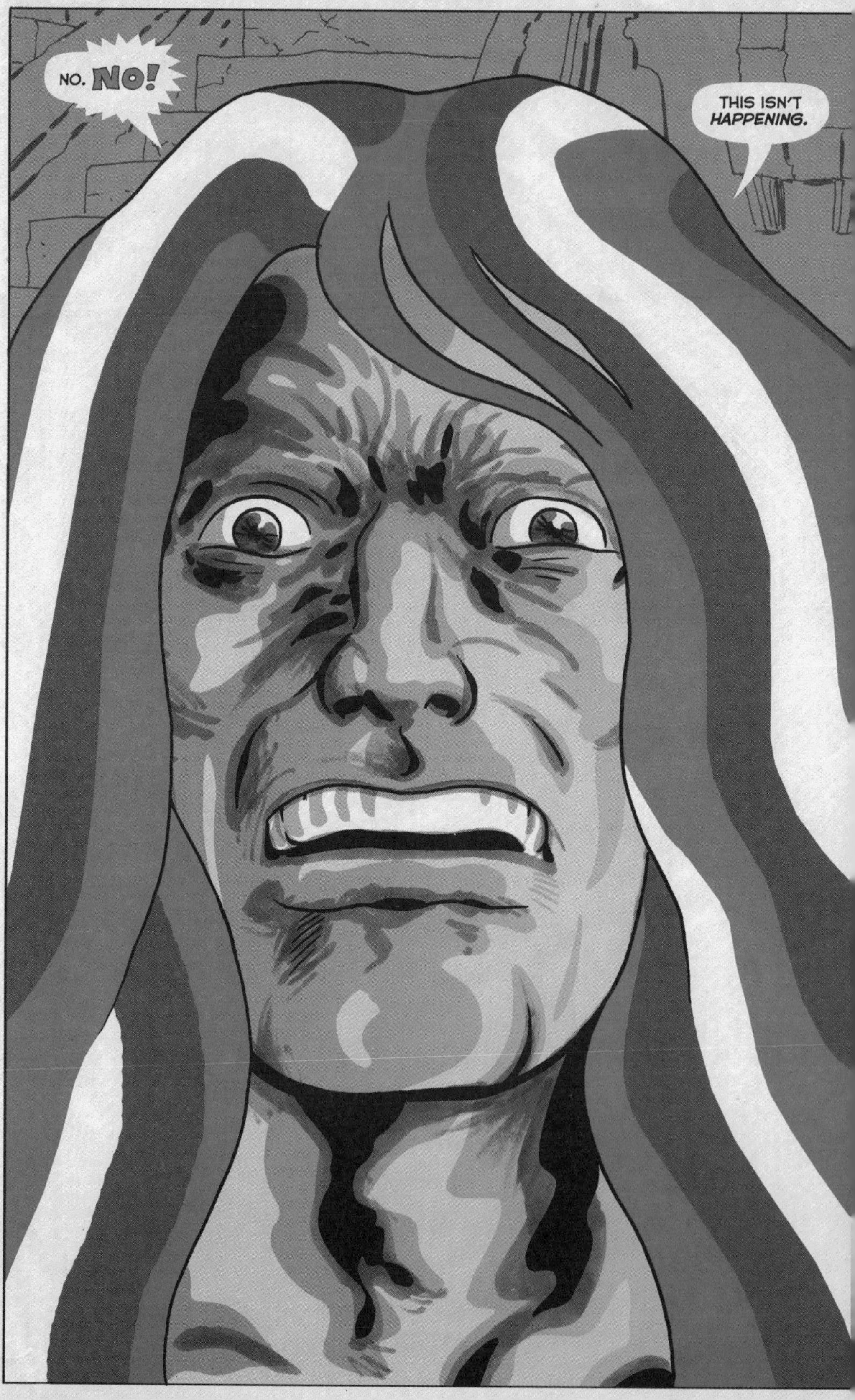
NO. NO!
THIS ISN'T HAPPENING.

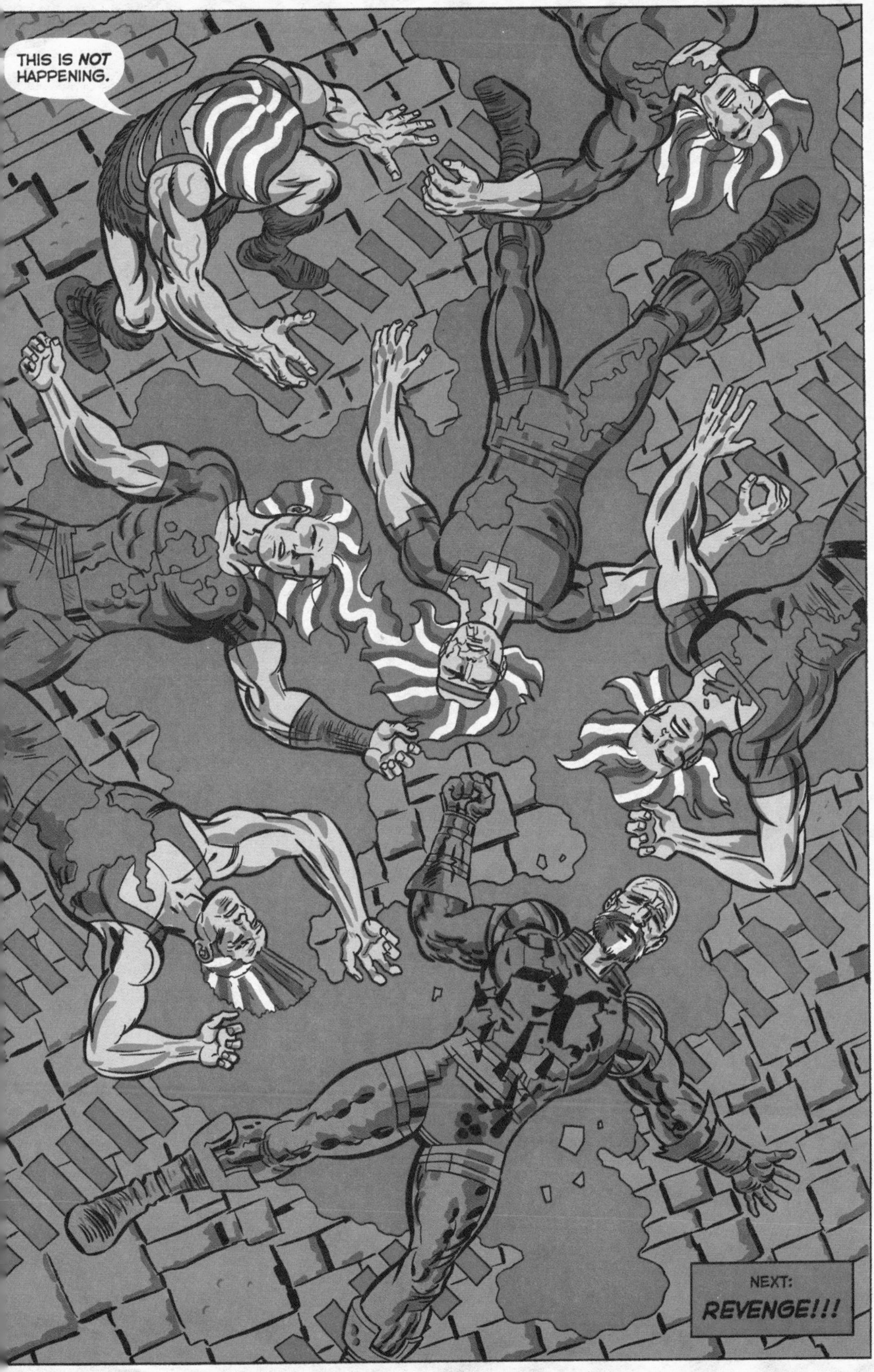
THIS IS *NOT* HAPPENING.
NEXT: REVENGE!!!

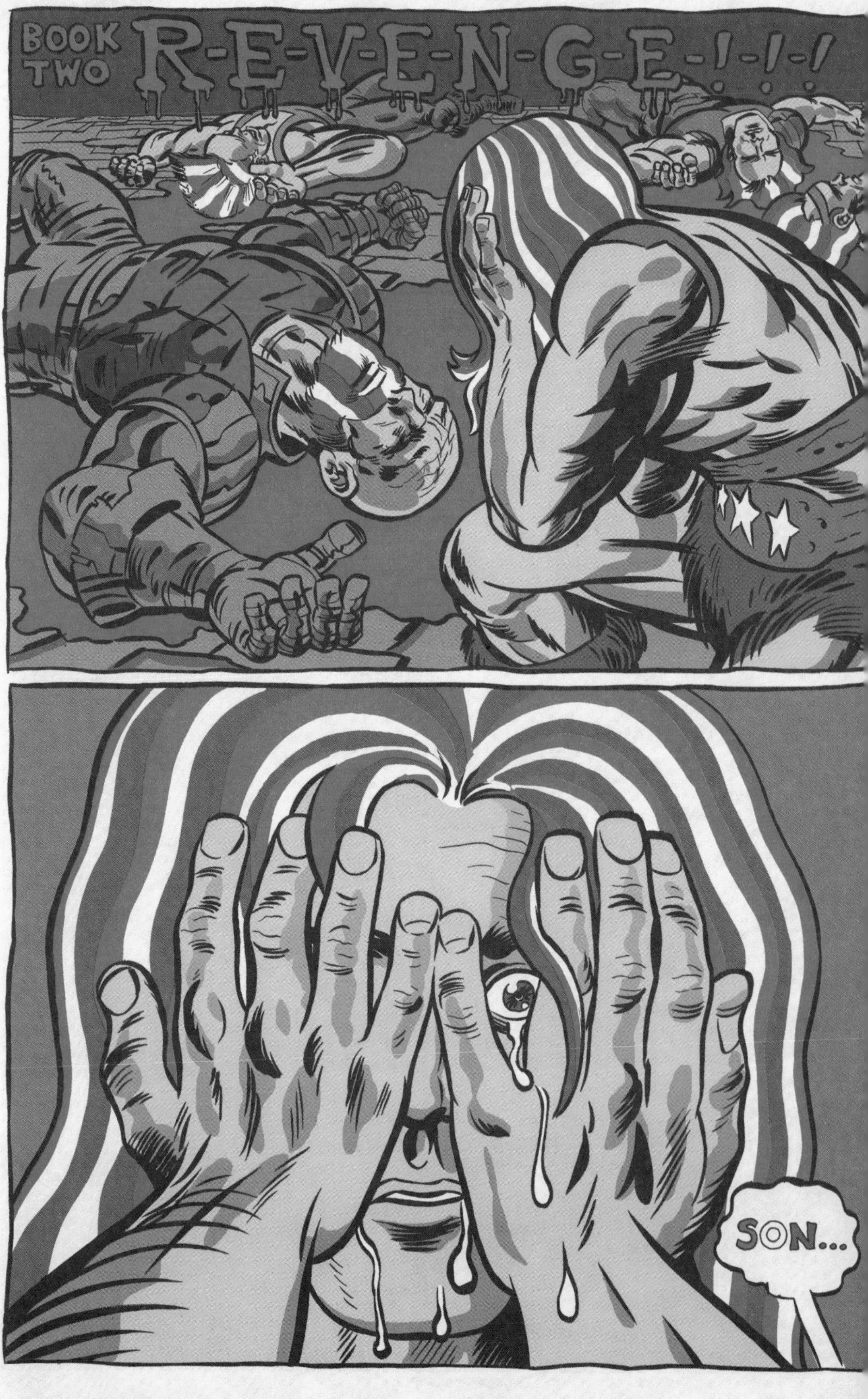
BOOK TWO R-E-V-E-N-G-E-!-!-!
SON...

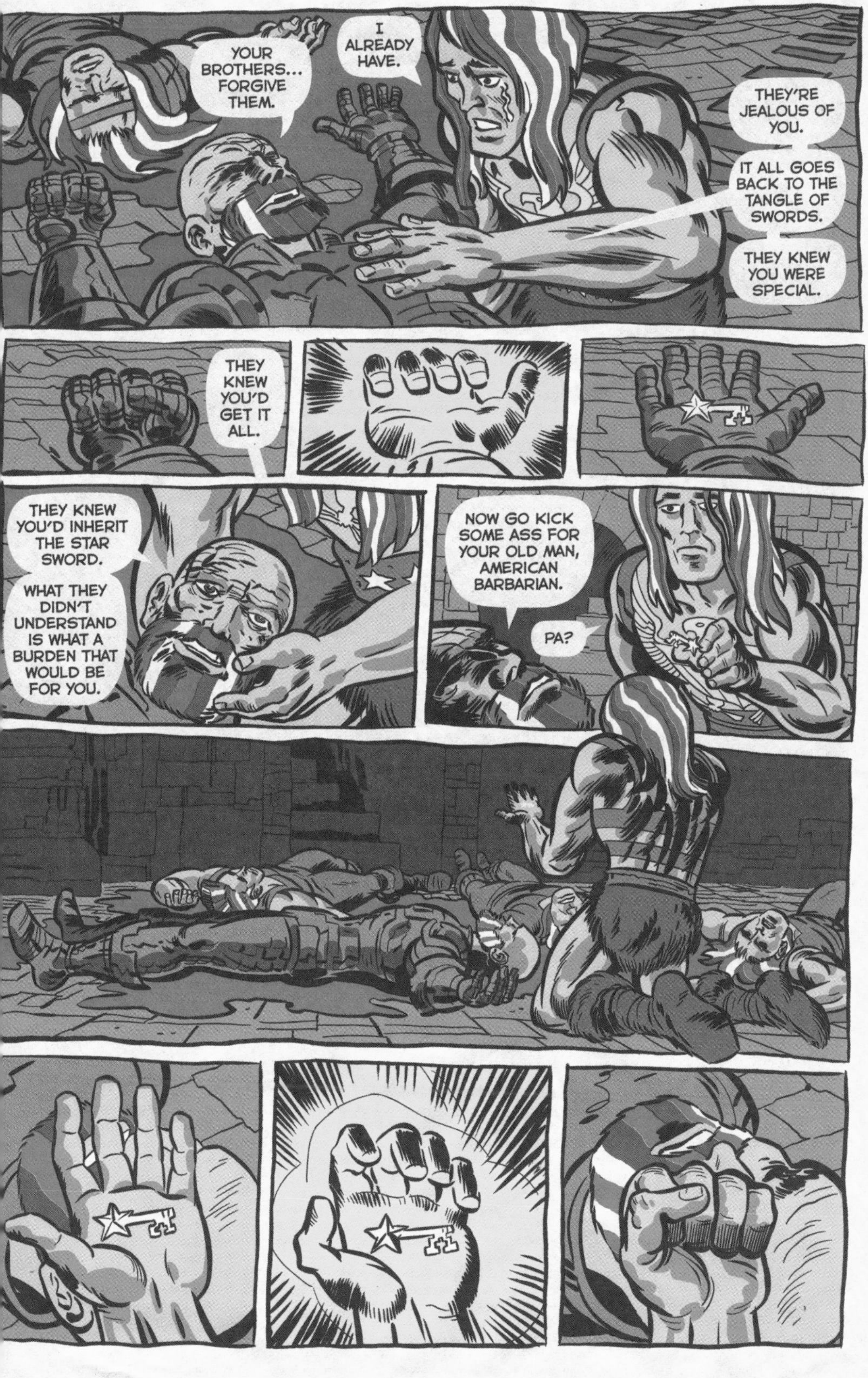
YOUR BROTHERS... FORGIVE THEM.
I ALREADY HAVE.
THEY'RE JEALOUS OF YOU.
IT ALL GOES BACK TO THE TANGLE OF SWORDS.
THEY KNEW YOU WERE SPECIAL.
THEY KNEW YOU'D GET IT ALL.
THEY KNEW YOU'D INHERIT THE STAR SWORD.
WHAT THEY DIDN'T UNDERSTAND IS WHAT A BURDEN THAT WOULD BE FOR YOU.
NOW GO KICK SOME ASS FOR YOUR OLD MAN, AMERICAN BARBARIAN.
PA?

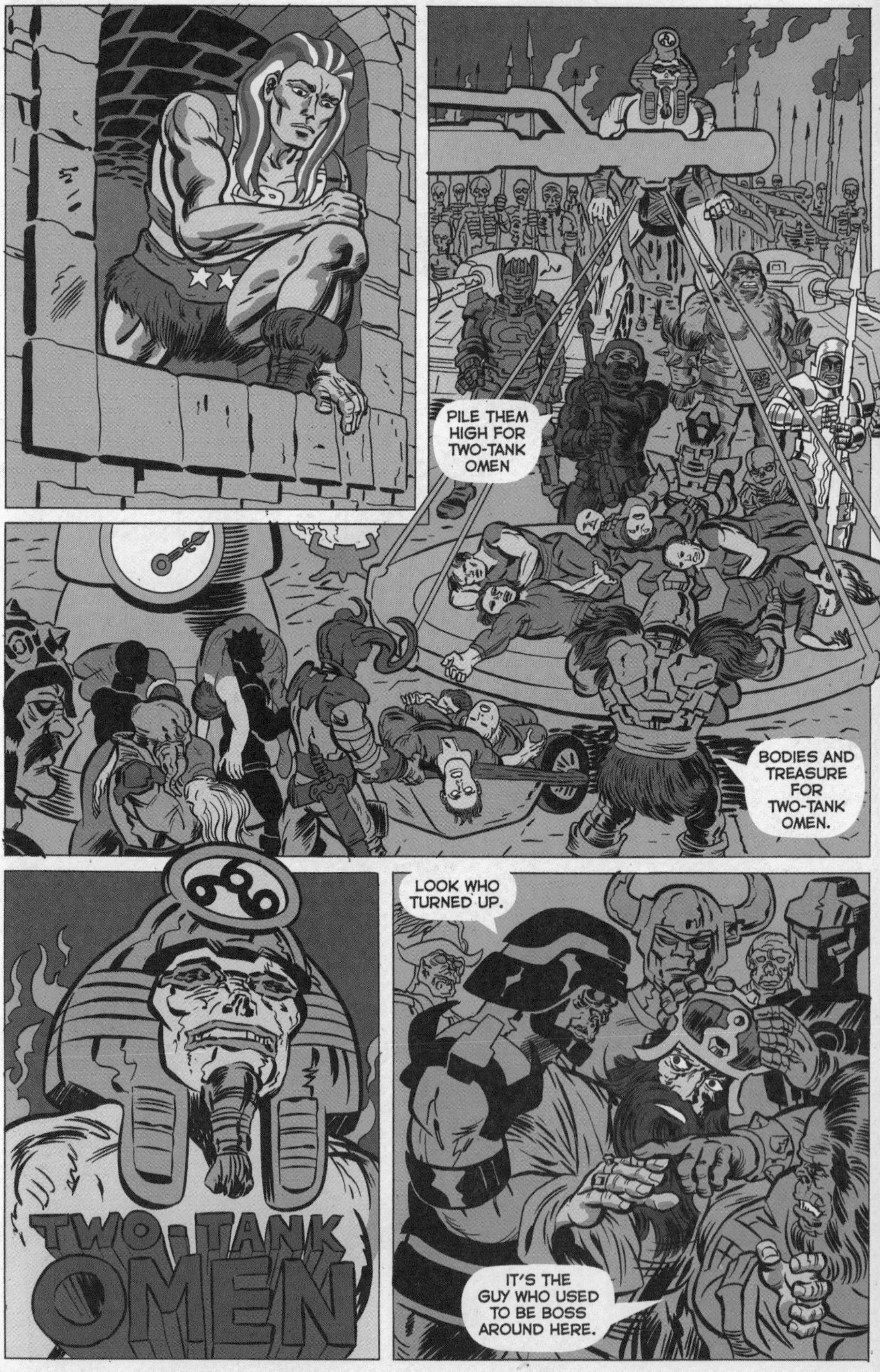
PILE THEM HIGH FOR TWO-TANK OMEN
BODIES AND TREASURE FOR TWO-TANK OMEN.
TWO-TANK OMEN
LOOK WHO TURNED UP.
IT'S THE GUY WHO USED TO BE BOSS AROUND HERE.

THE CROWN OF LIONHORN IS YOURS, OH GREAT ONE.

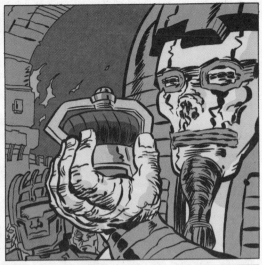

TWO-TANK OMEN IS A MERCIFUL GOD.

THOUGH YOU ARE UNWORTHY, HE OFFERS YOU A CHOICE.

JOIN THE INEVITABLE SWELL OF HIS ARMY...OR DIE.

TWO-TANK OMEN IS A BUTCHER.

HE'S A MOLDY BLOT ON THIS SHATTERED SPHERE.

TWO-TANK OMEN CAN RETURN TO THE HELL PIT THAT SPAWNED HIM...

PTOOooo

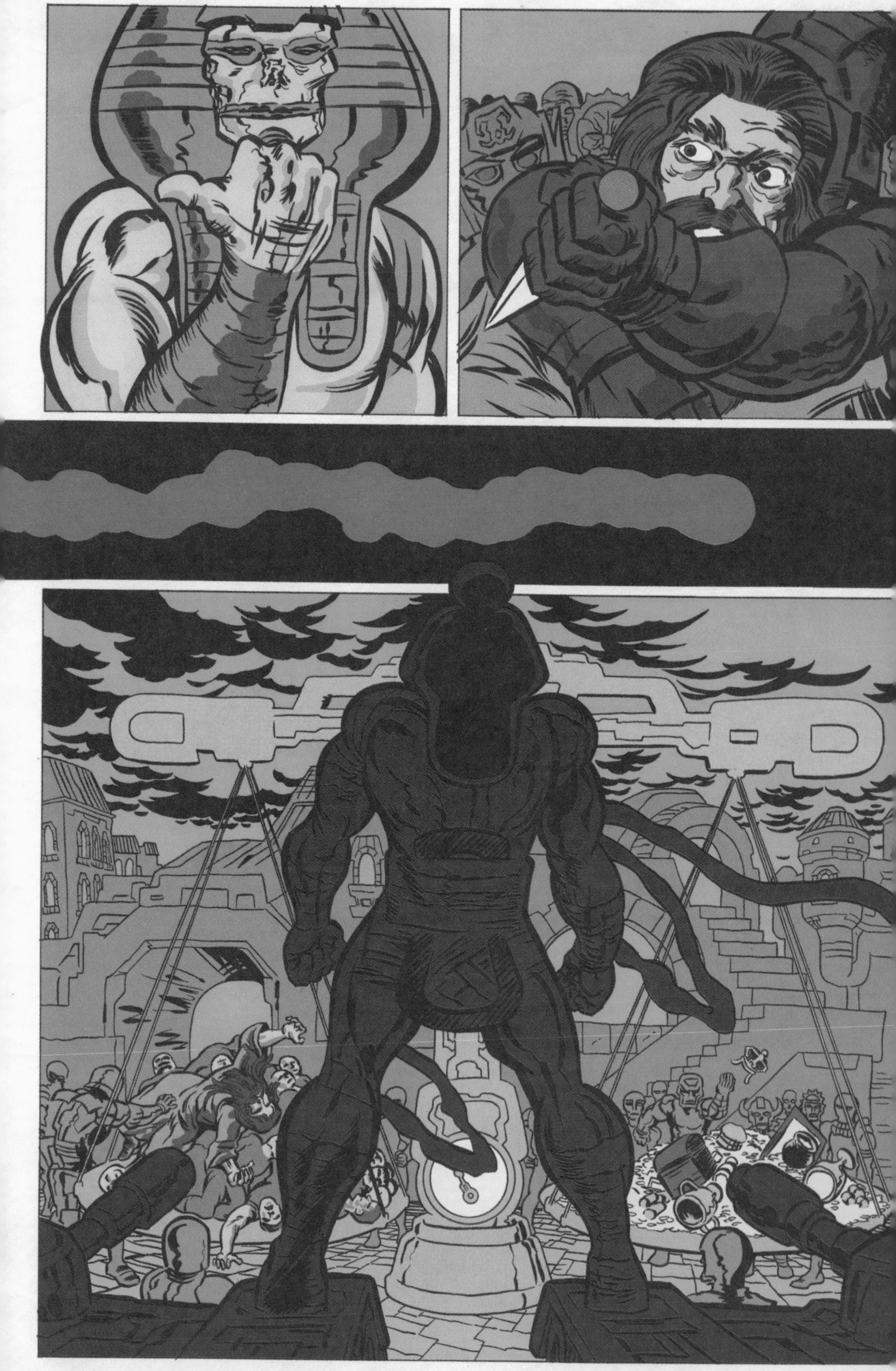

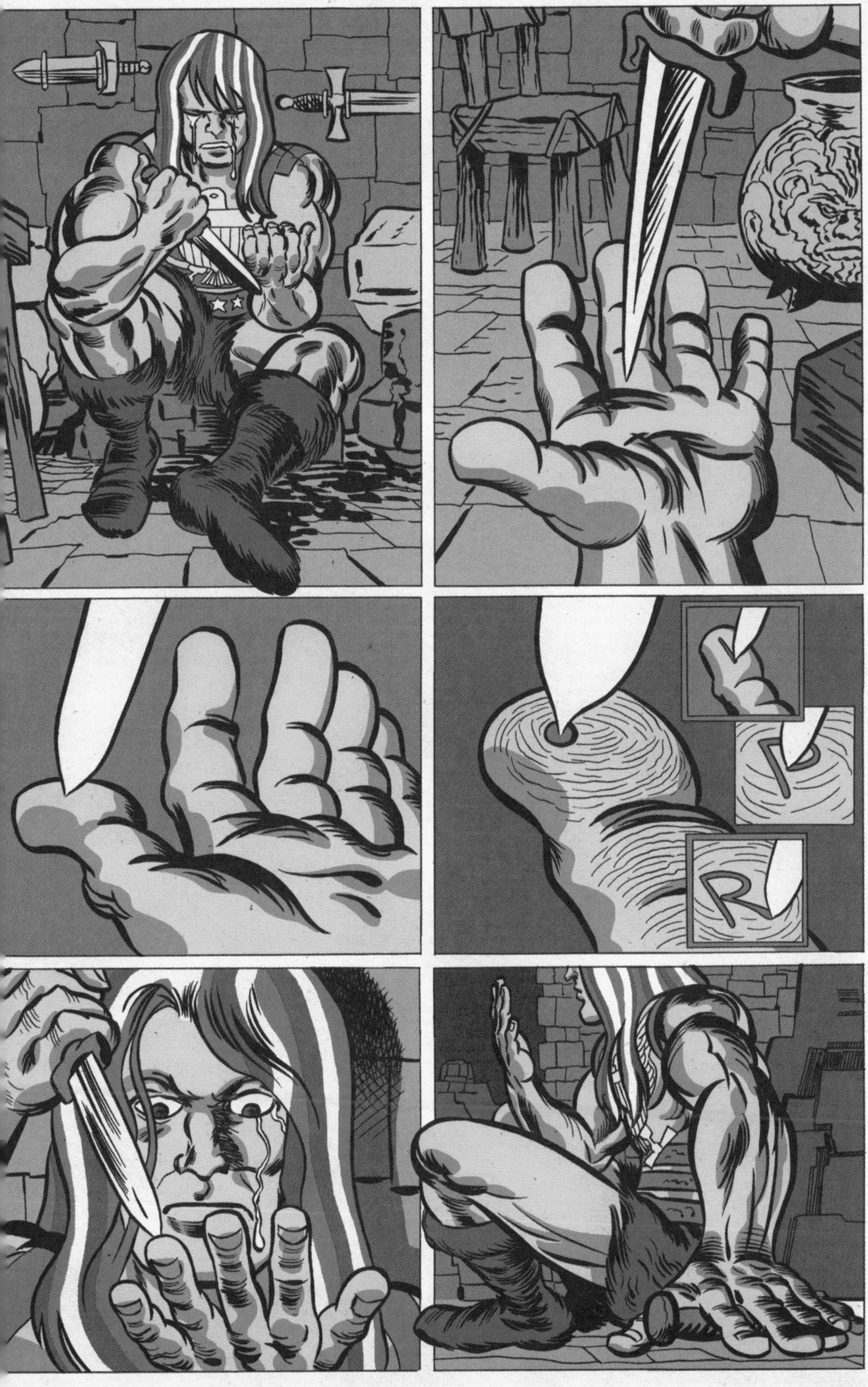
R

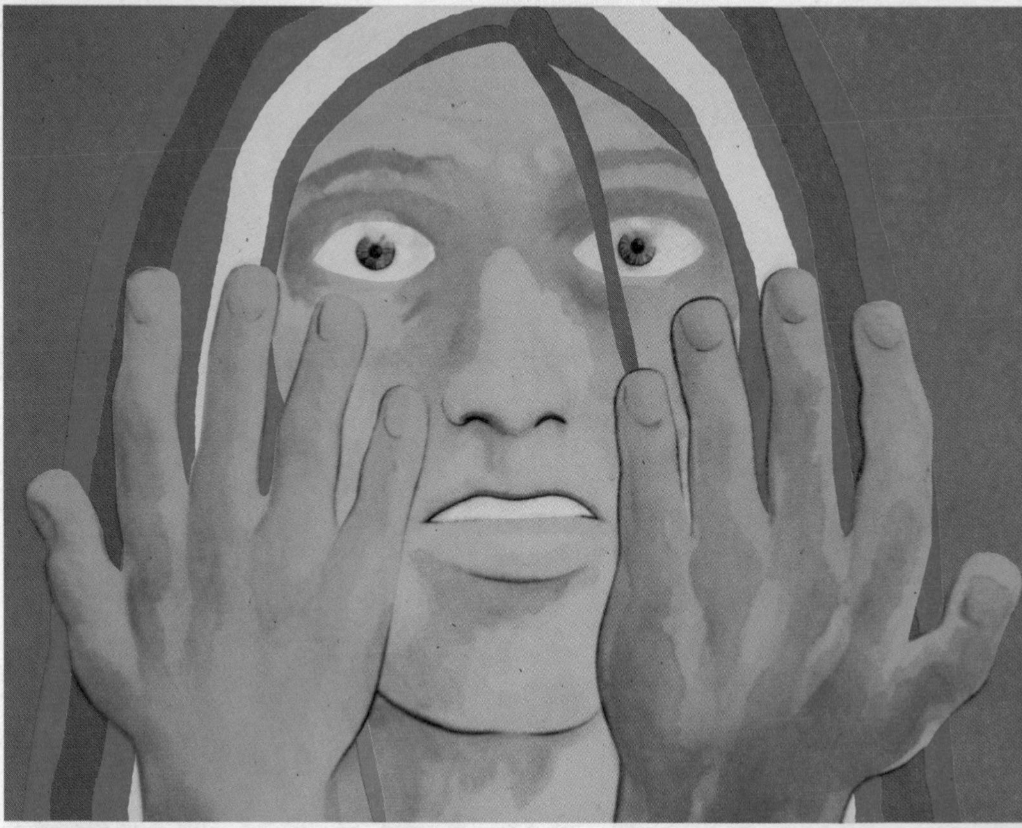

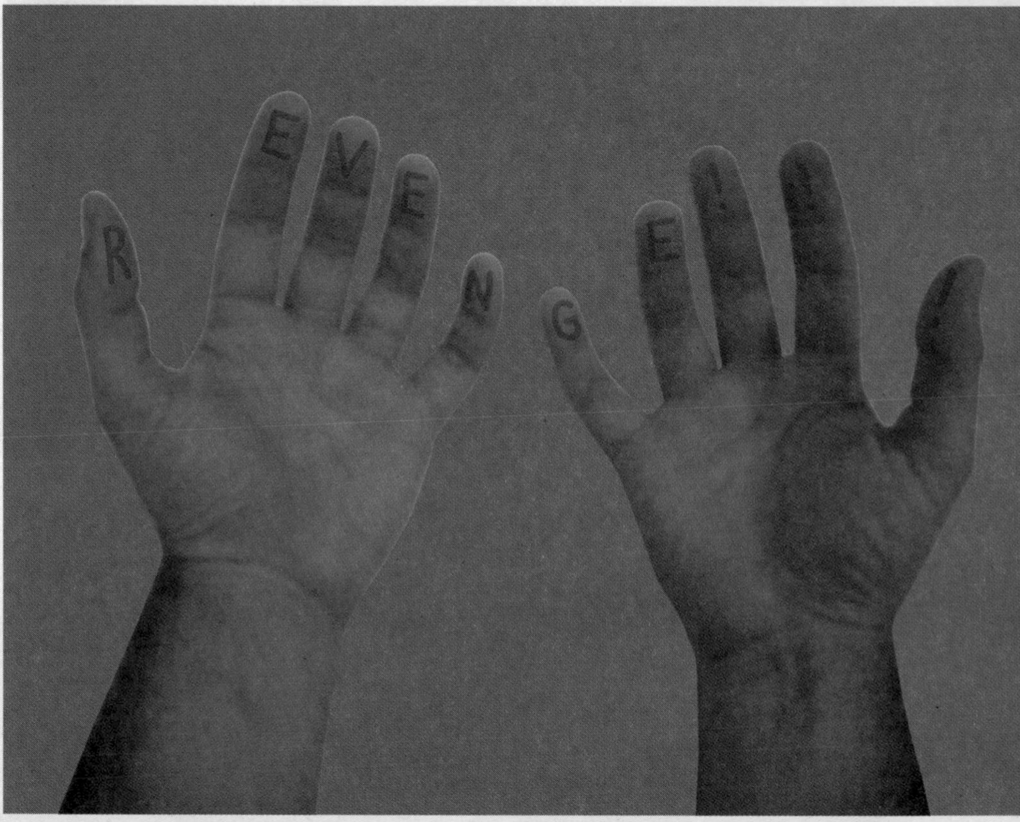
REVENGE

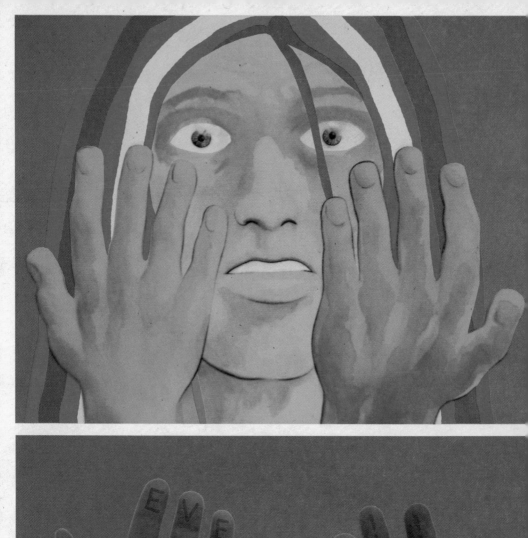

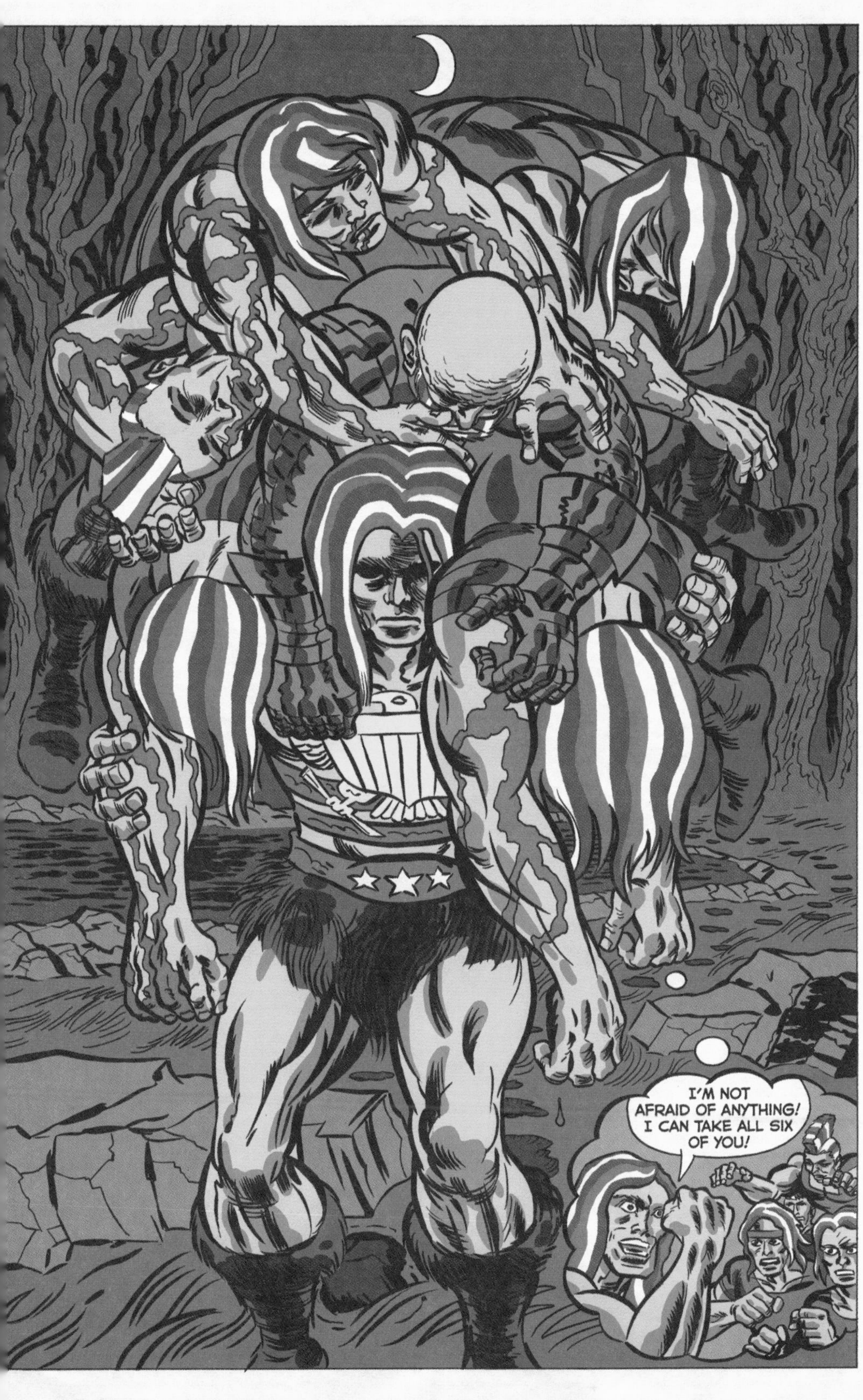
I'M NOT AFRAID OF ANYTHING! I CAN TAKE ALL SIX OF YOU!

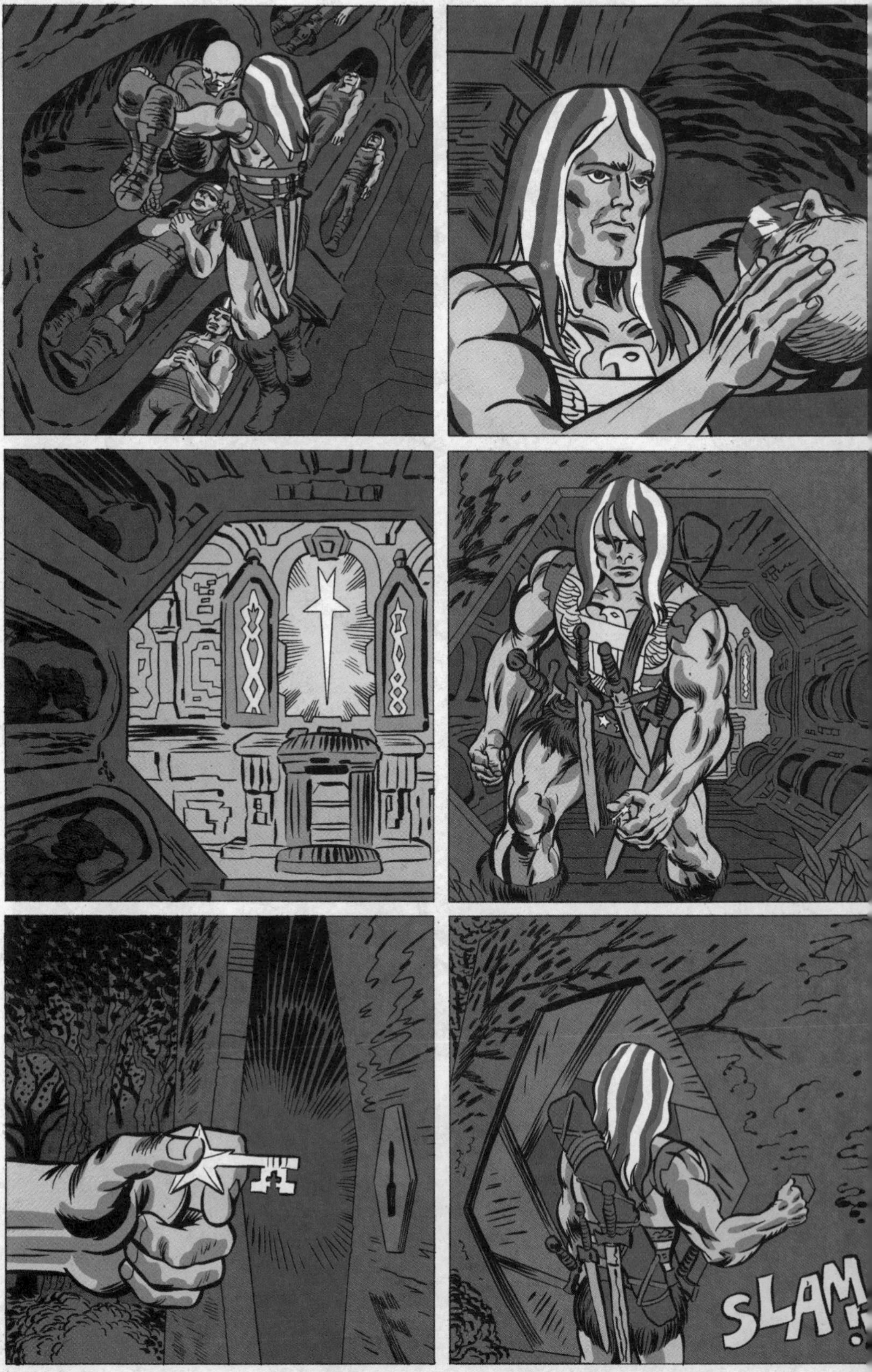
SLAM!

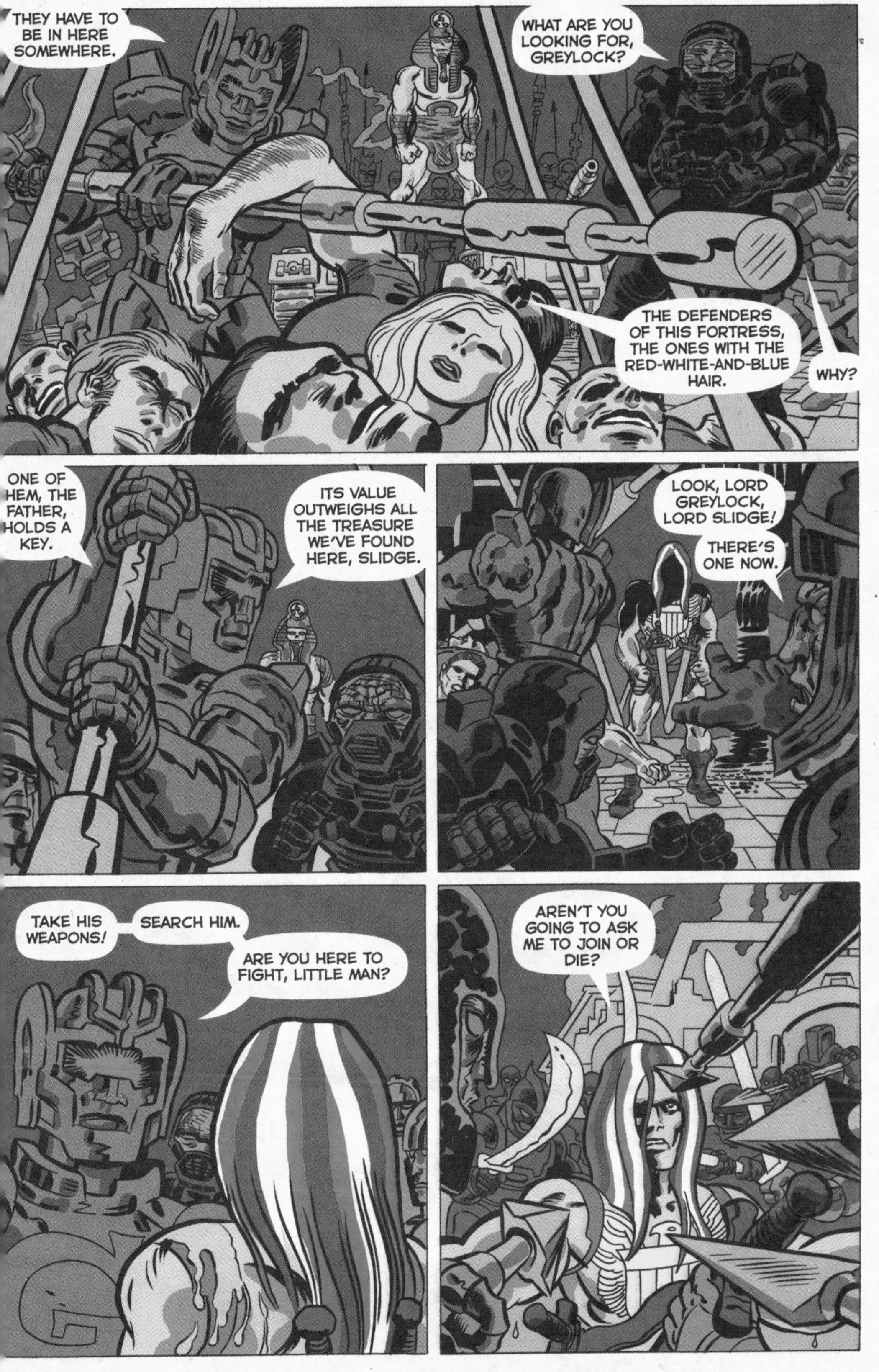
THEY HAVE TO BE IN HERE SOMEWHERE.
WHAT ARE YOU LOOKING FOR, GREYLOCK?
THE DEFENDERS OF THIS FORTRESS, THE ONES WITH THE RED-WHITE-AND-BLUE HAIR.
WHY?
ONE OF HEM, THE FATHER, HOLDS A KEY.
ITS VALUE OUTWEIGHS ALL THE TREASURE WE'VE FOUND HERE, SLIDGE.
LOOK, LORD GREYLOCK, LORD SLIDGE!
THERE'S ONE NOW.
TAKE HIS WEAPONS!
SEARCH HIM.
ARE YOU HERE TO FIGHT, LITTLE MAN?
AREN'T YOU GOING TO ASK ME TO JOIN OR DIE?

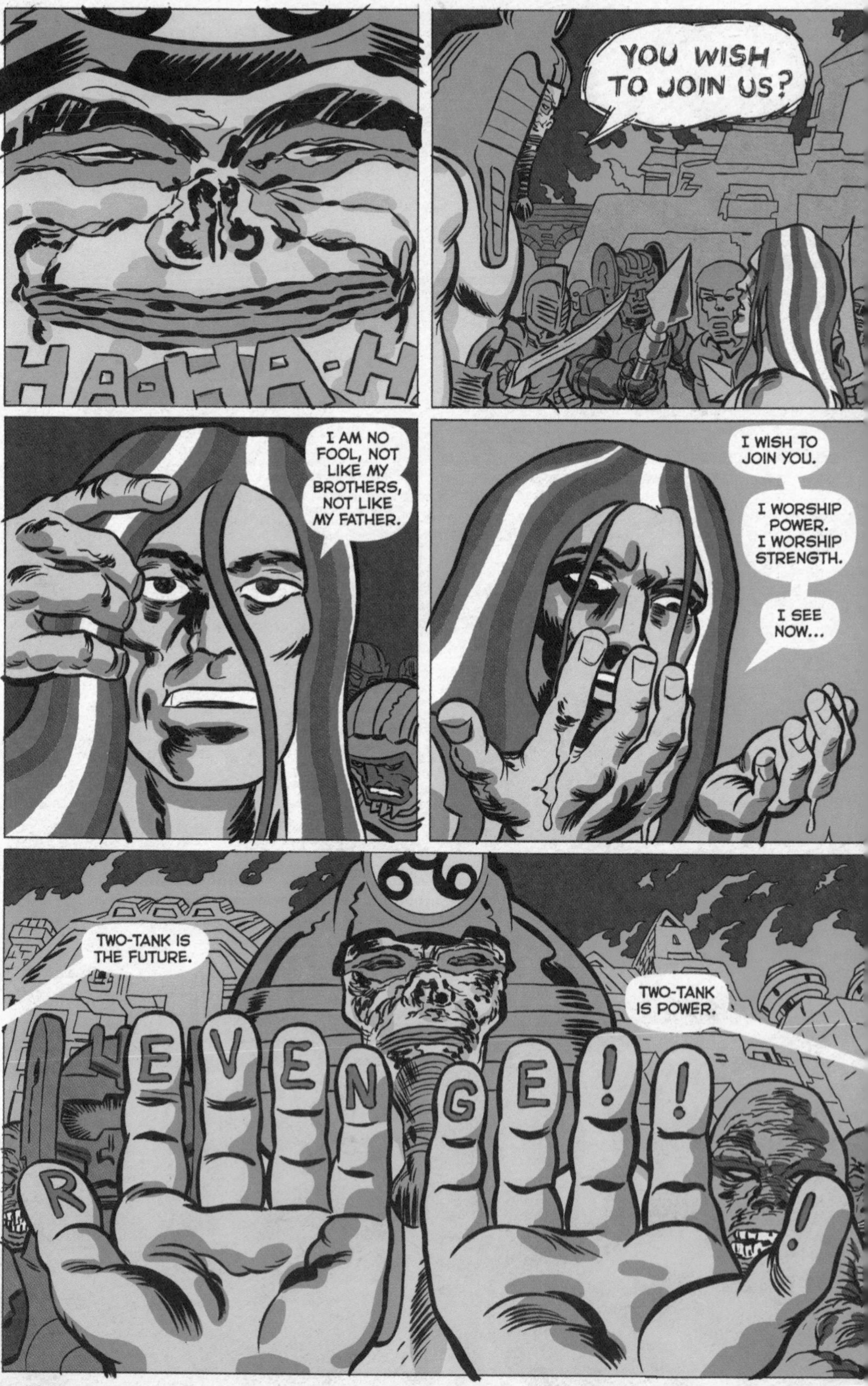

HA-HA-HA-H
YOU WISH TO JOIN US?
I AM NO FOOL, NOT LIKE MY BROTHERS, NOT LIKE MY FATHER.
I WISH TO JOIN YOU.
I WORSHIP POWER. I WORSHIP STRENGTH.
I SEE NOW...
TWO-TANK IS THE FUTURE.
TWO-TANK IS POWER.
REVENGE!!

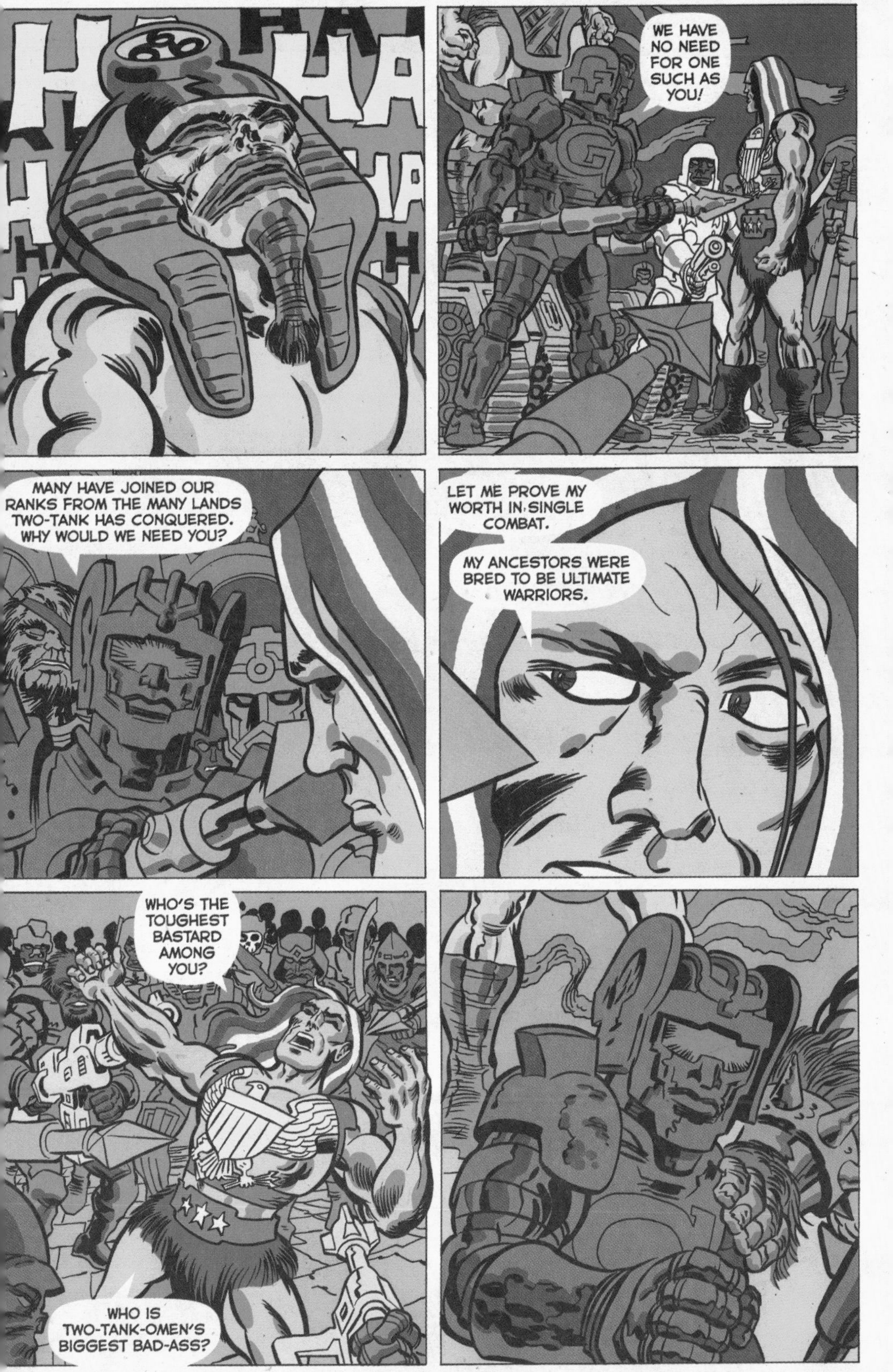
HA HA HA HA HA HA HA
WE HAVE NO NEED FOR ONE SUCH AS YOU!
MANY HAVE JOINED OUR RANKS FROM THE MANY LANDS TWO-TANK HAS CONQUERED. WHY WOULD WE NEED YOU?
LET ME PROVE MY WORTH IN SINGLE COMBAT.
MY ANCESTORS WERE BRED TO BE ULTIMATE WARRIORS.
WHO'S THE TOUGHEST BASTARD AMONG YOU?
WHO IS TWO-TANK-OMEN'S BIGGEST BAD-ASS?

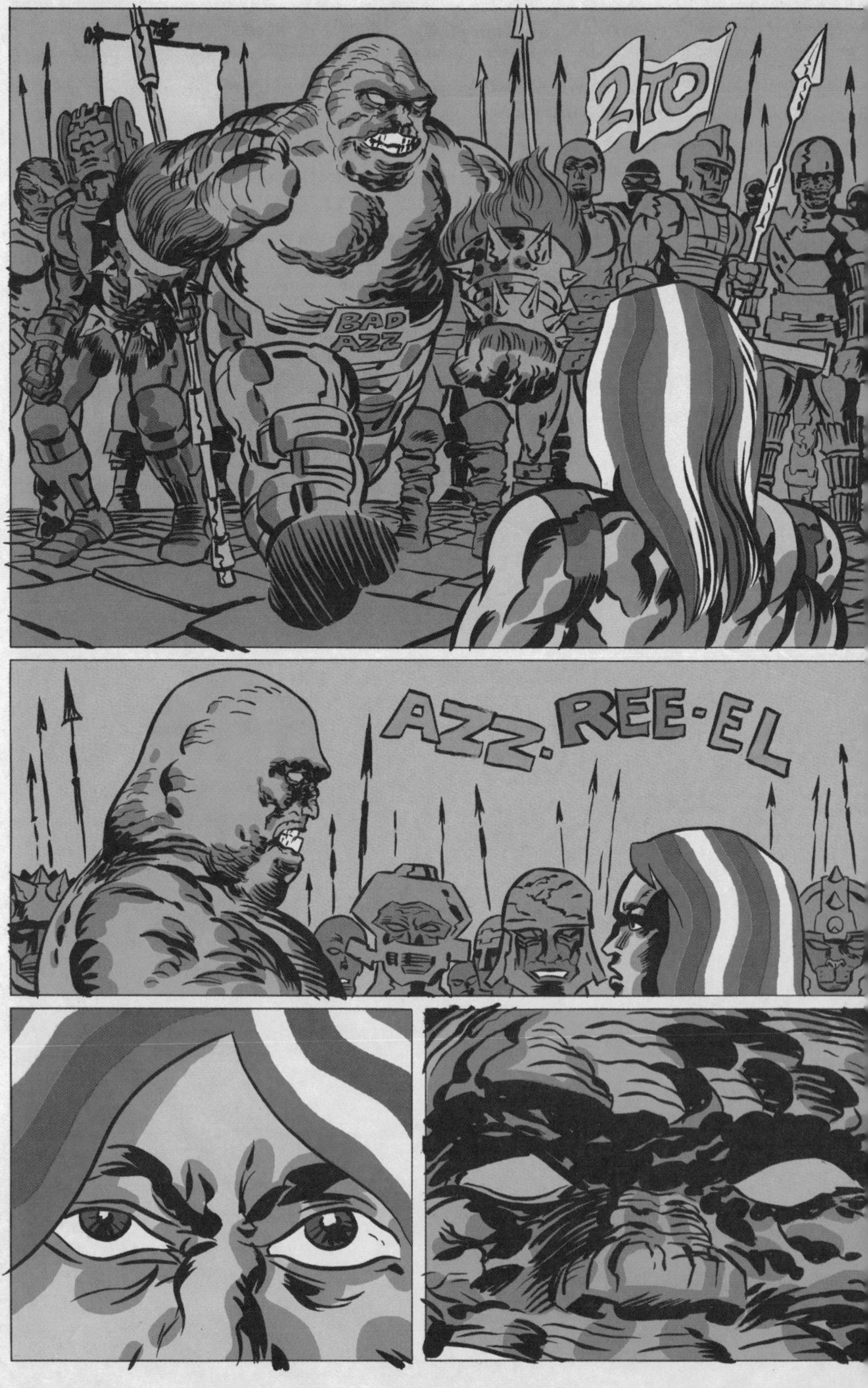
2TO
BAD AZZ
AZZ-REE-EL

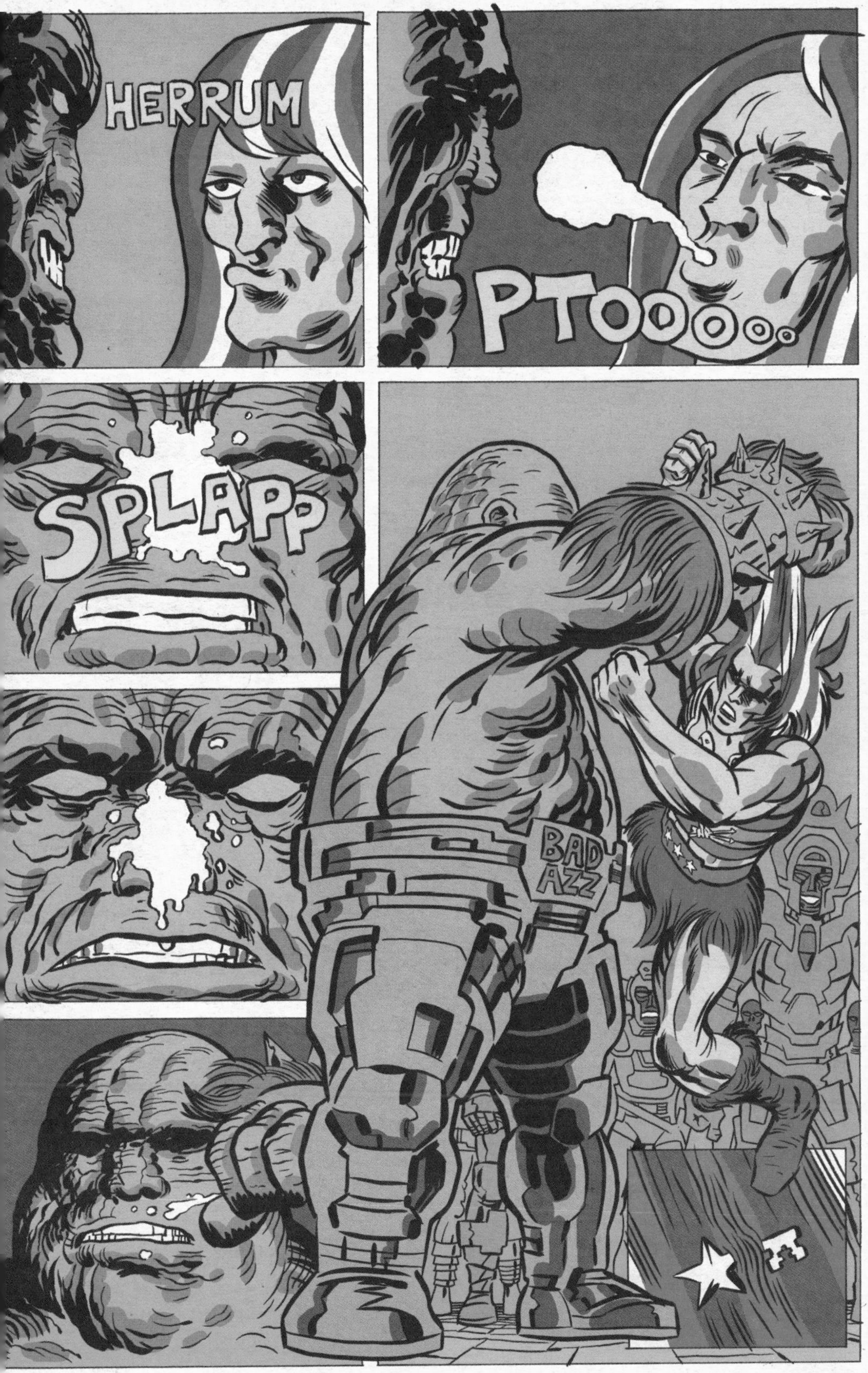
HERRUM
PTOOOOO..
SPLAPP
BAD AZZ

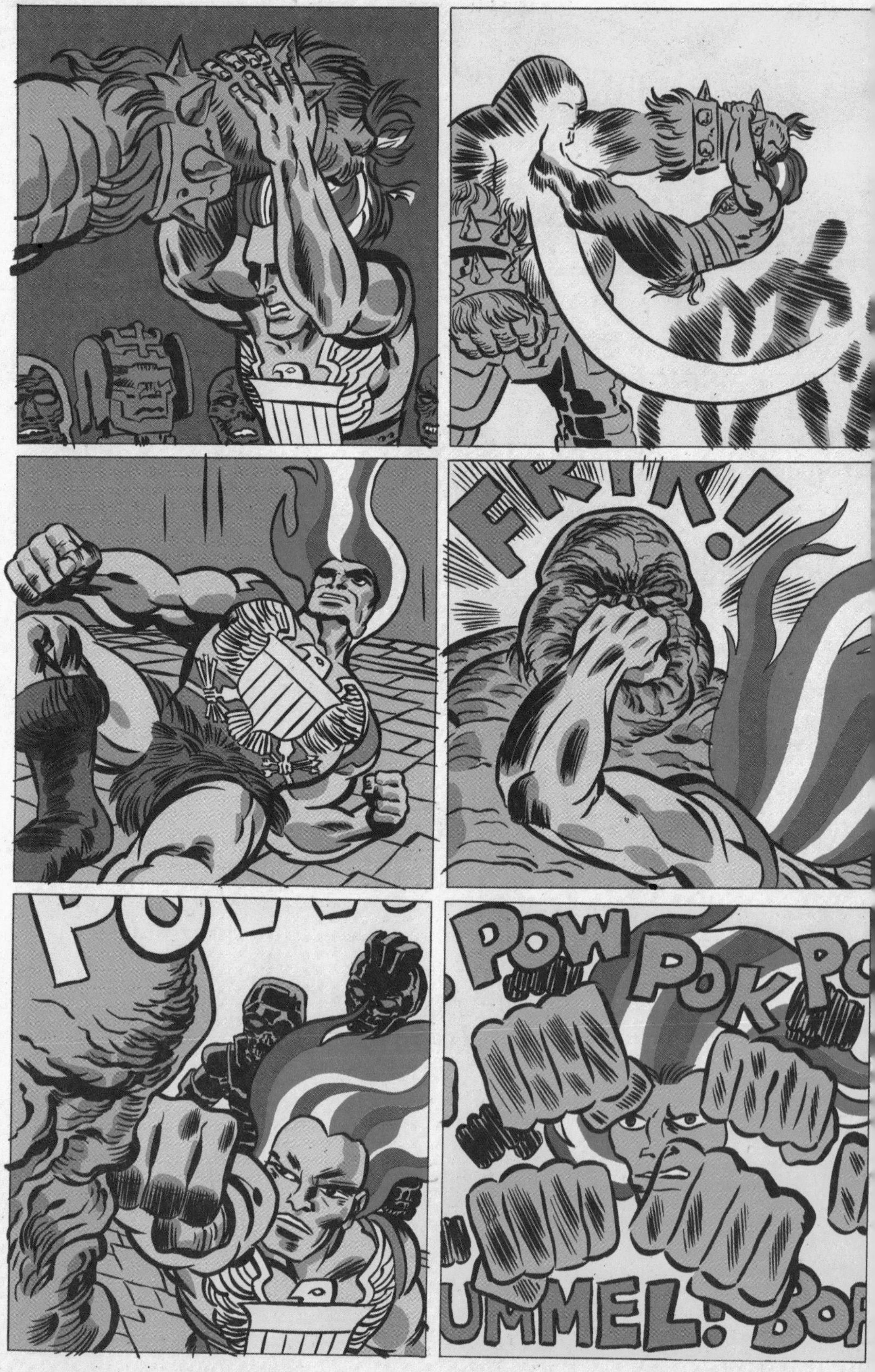
FRIK!
POW
POK
UMMEL!

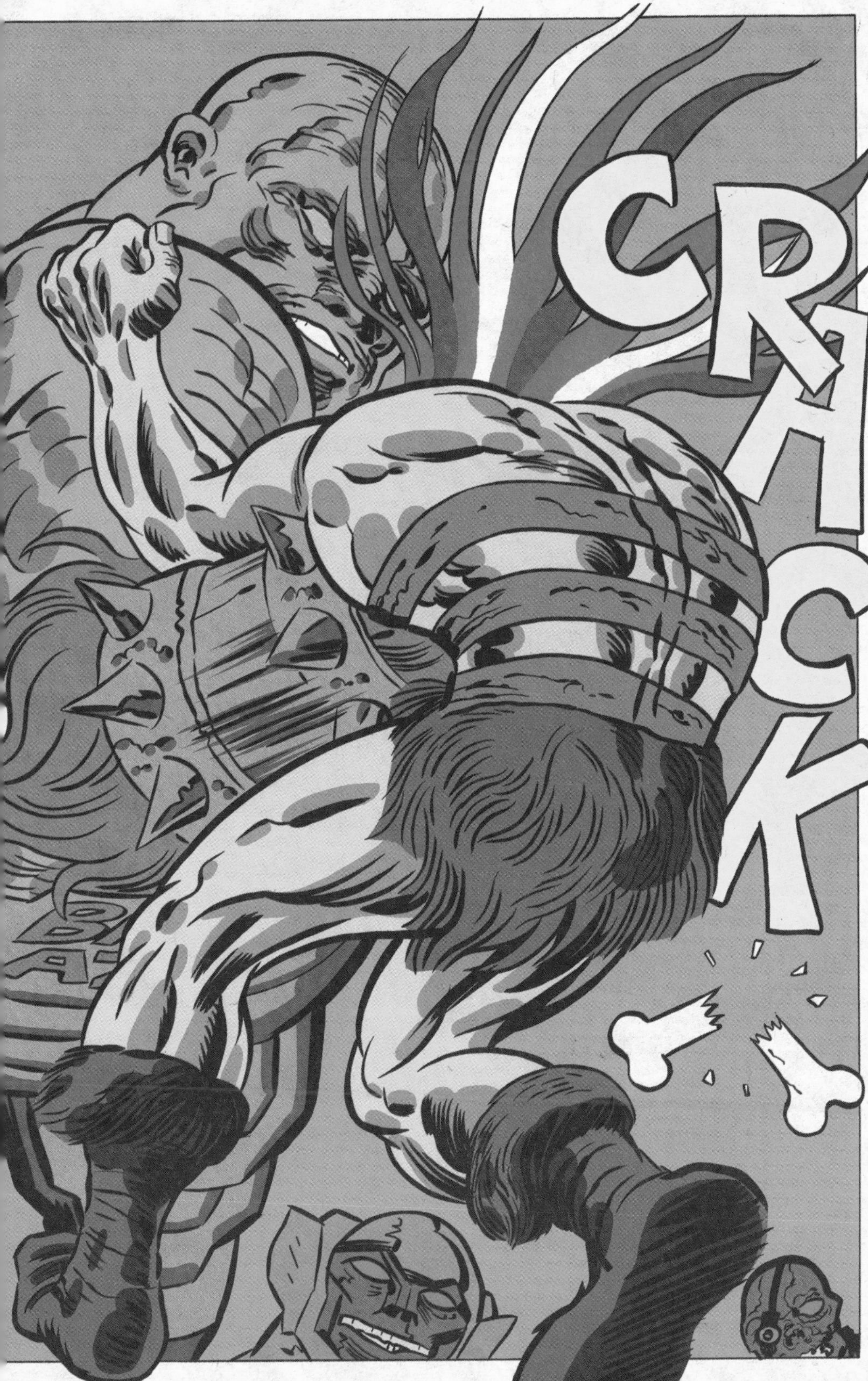
CRACK

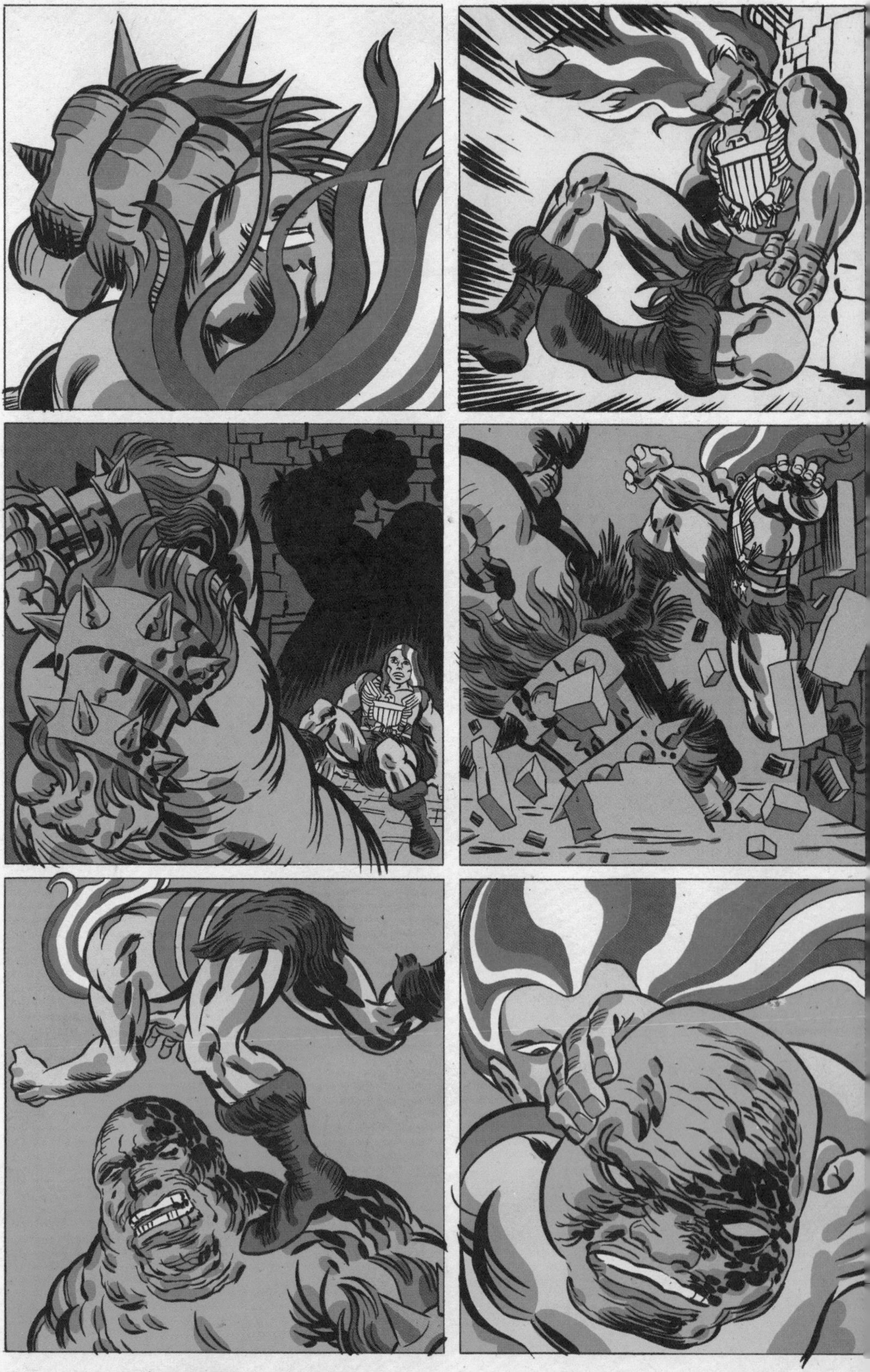

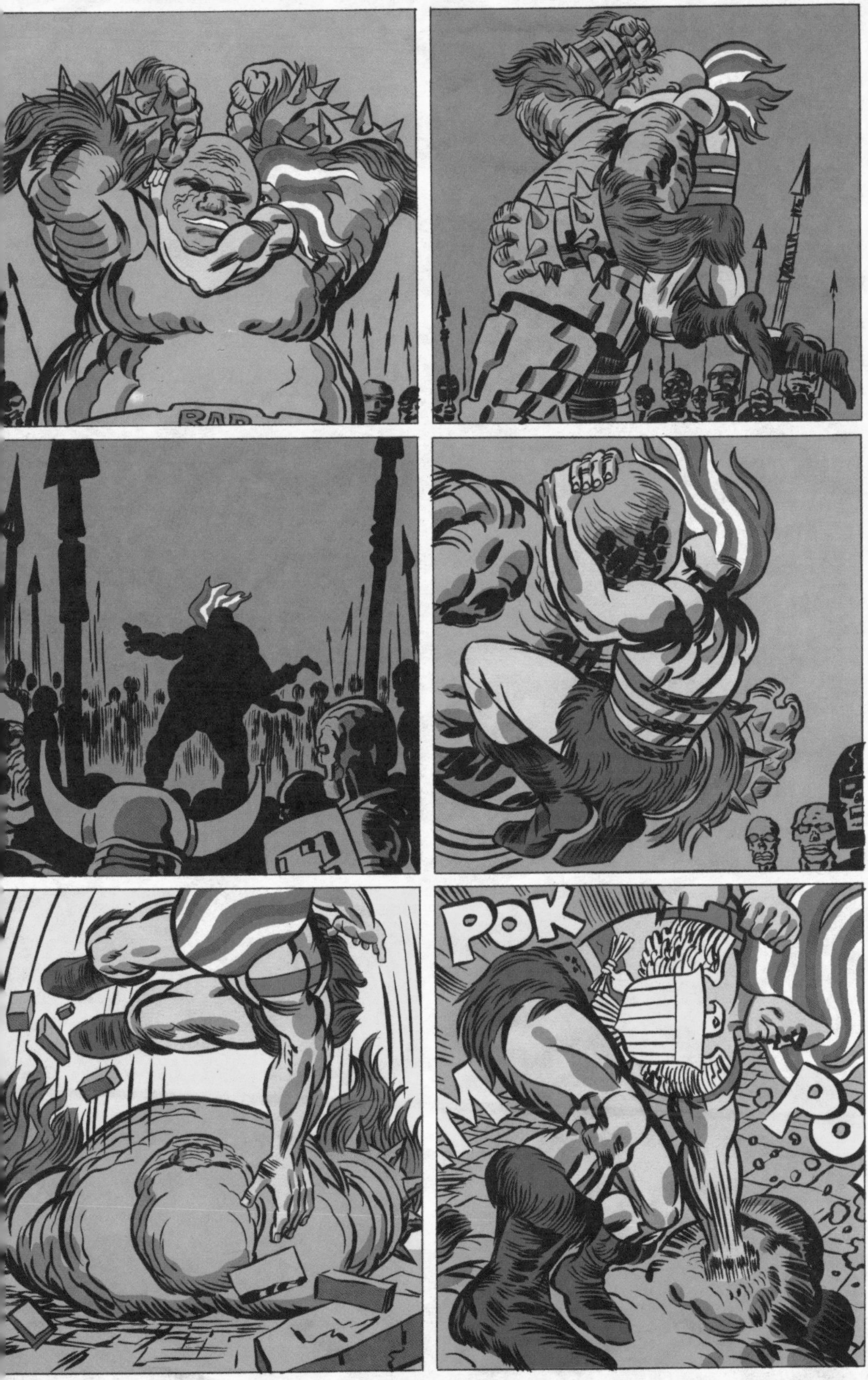
POK

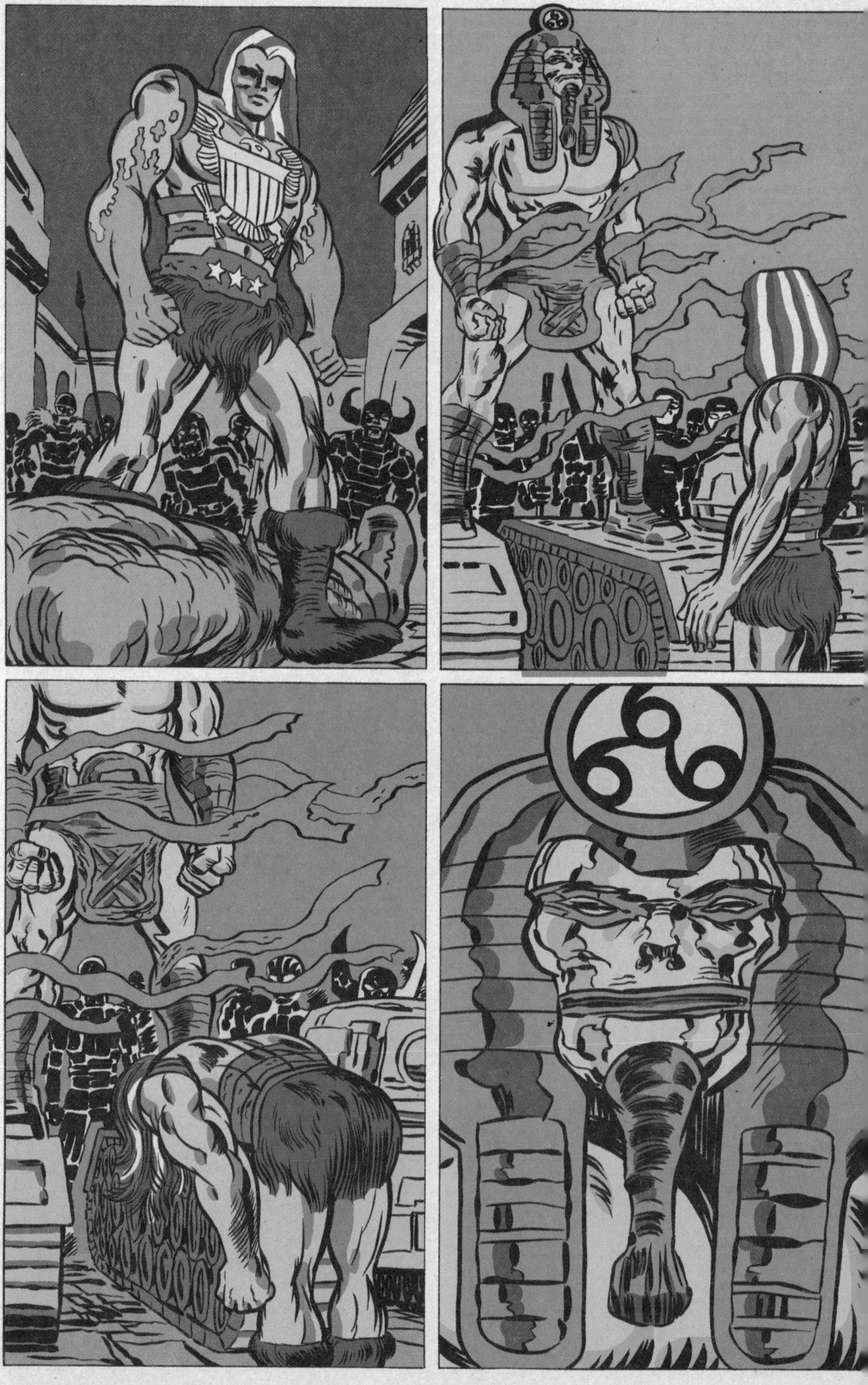

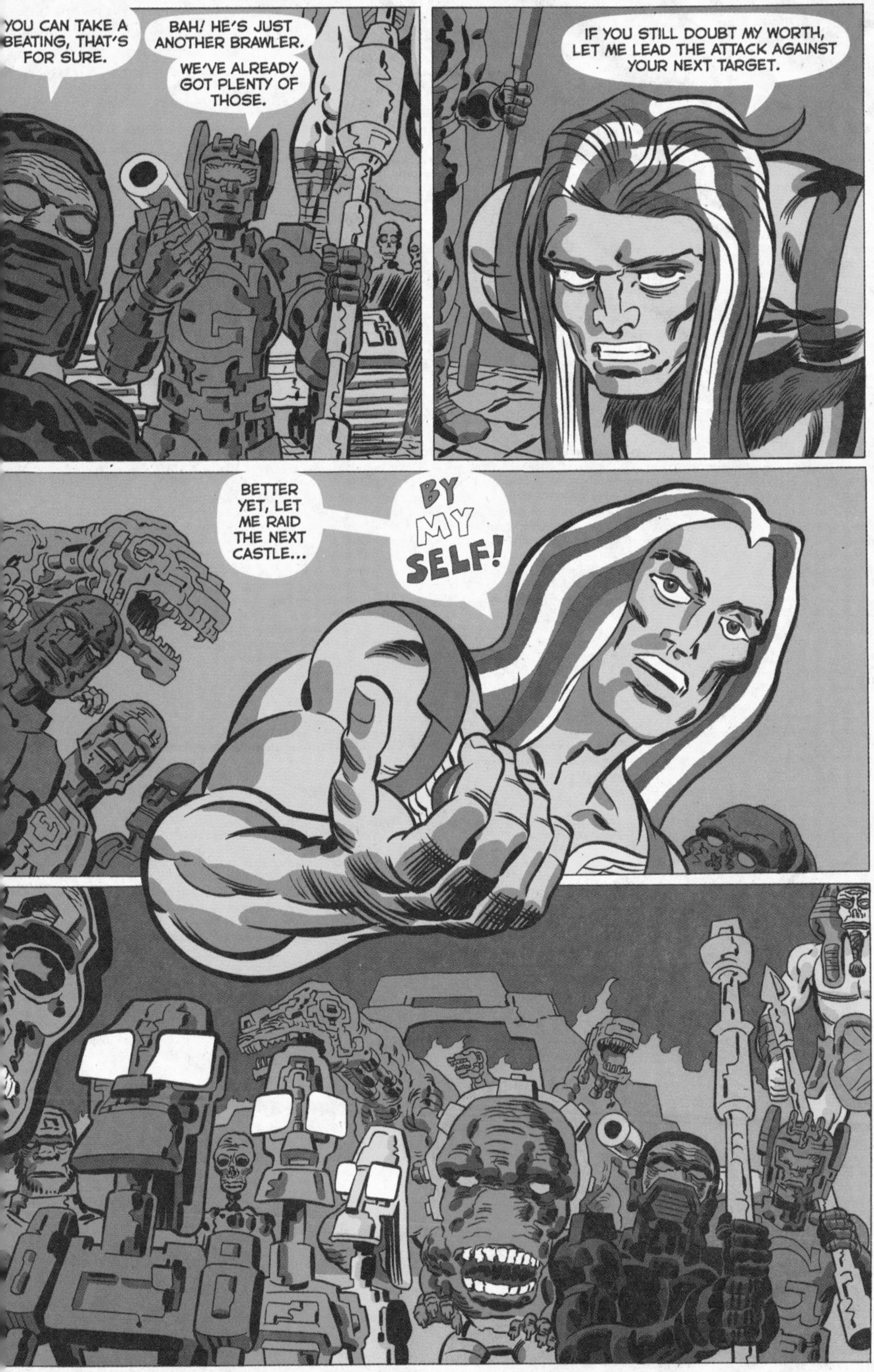
YOU CAN TAKE A BEATING, THAT'S FOR SURE.
BAH! HE'S JUST ANOTHER BRAWLER.
WE'VE ALREADY GOT PLENTY OF THOSE.
IF YOU STILL DOUBT MY WORTH, LET ME LEAD THE ATTACK AGAINST YOUR NEXT TARGET.
BETTER YET, LET ME RAID THE NEXT CASTLE...
BY MY SELF!

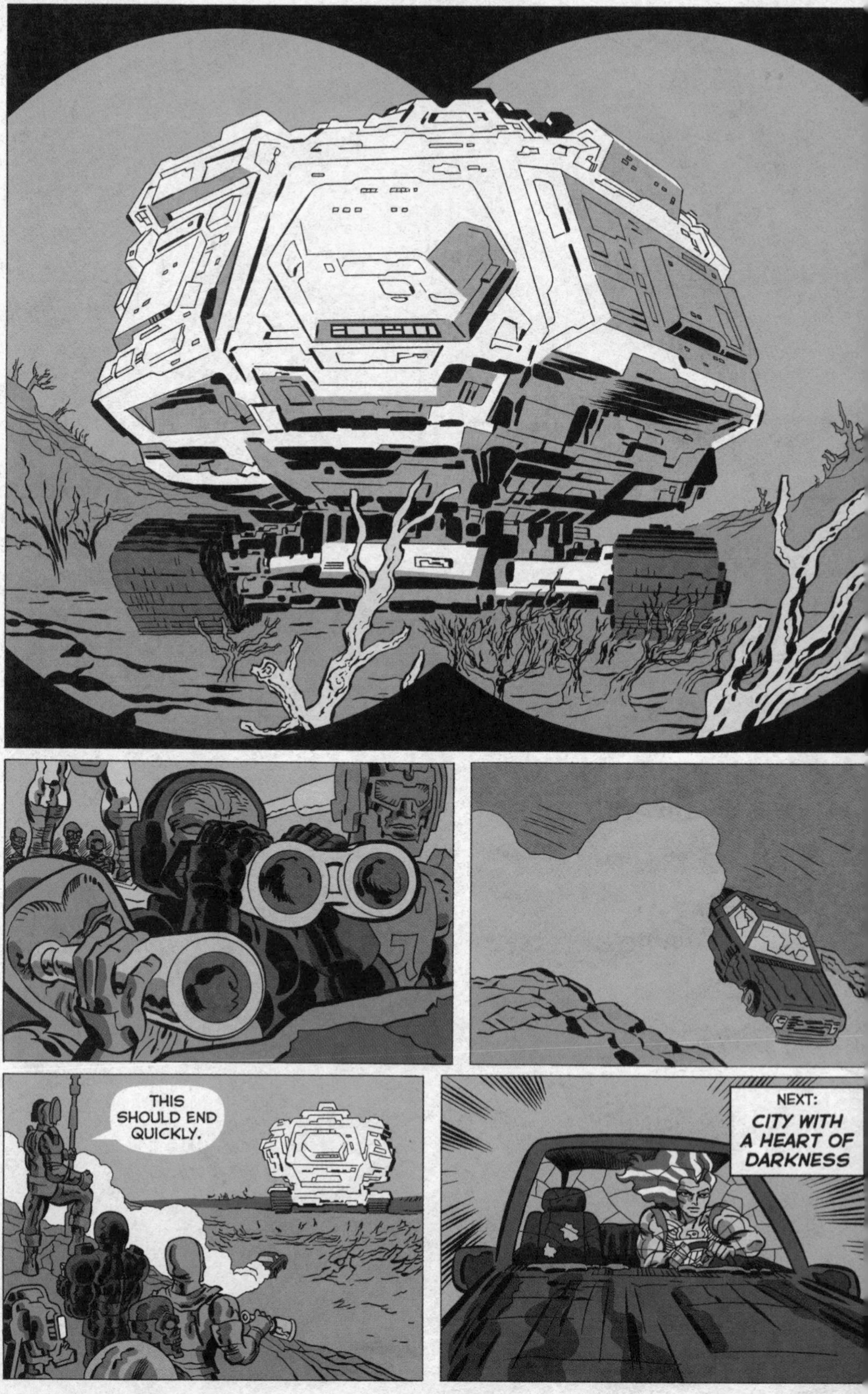
THIS SHOULD END QUICKLY.
NEXT:
CITY WITH A HEART OF DARKNESS

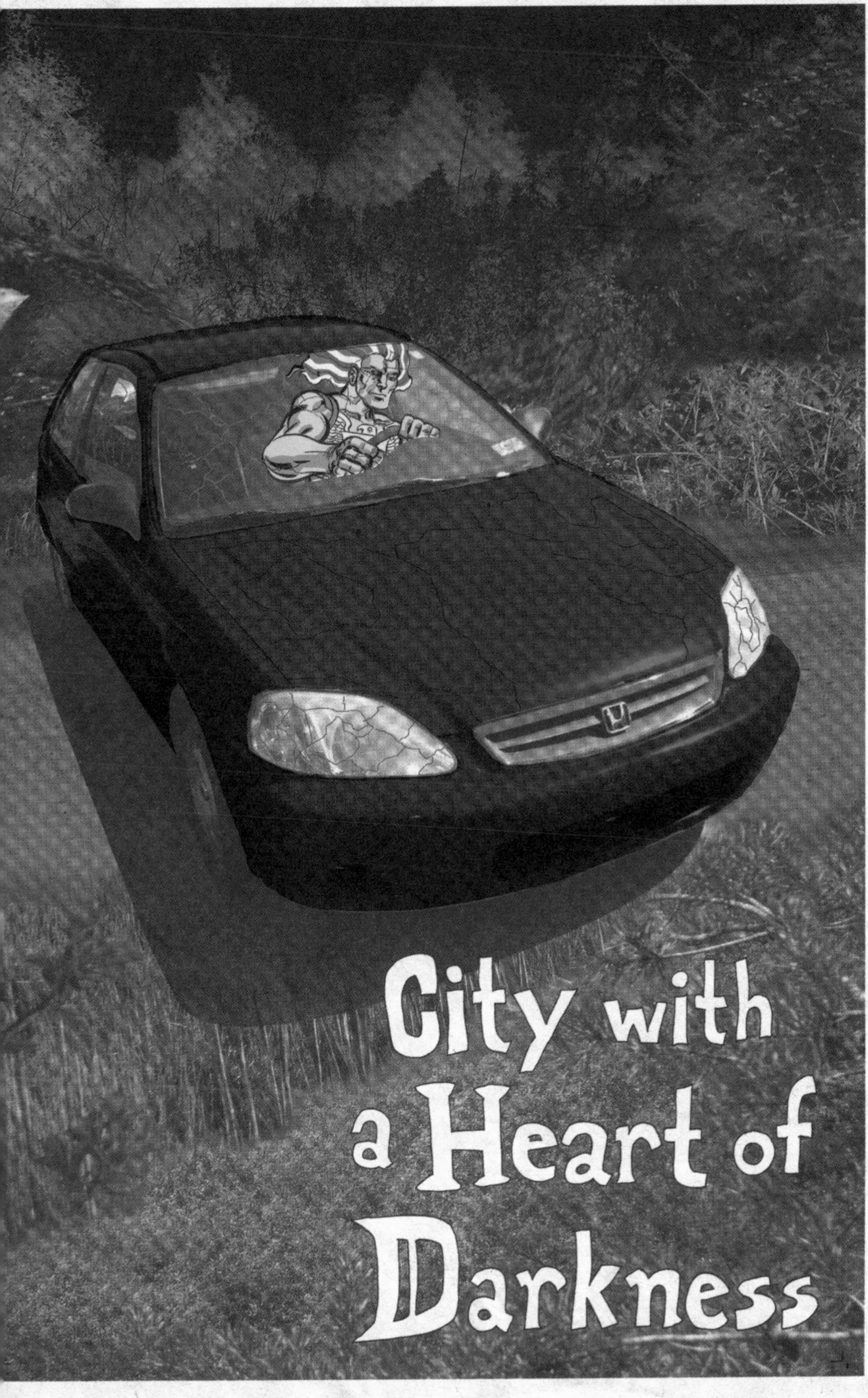
City with a Heart of Darkness

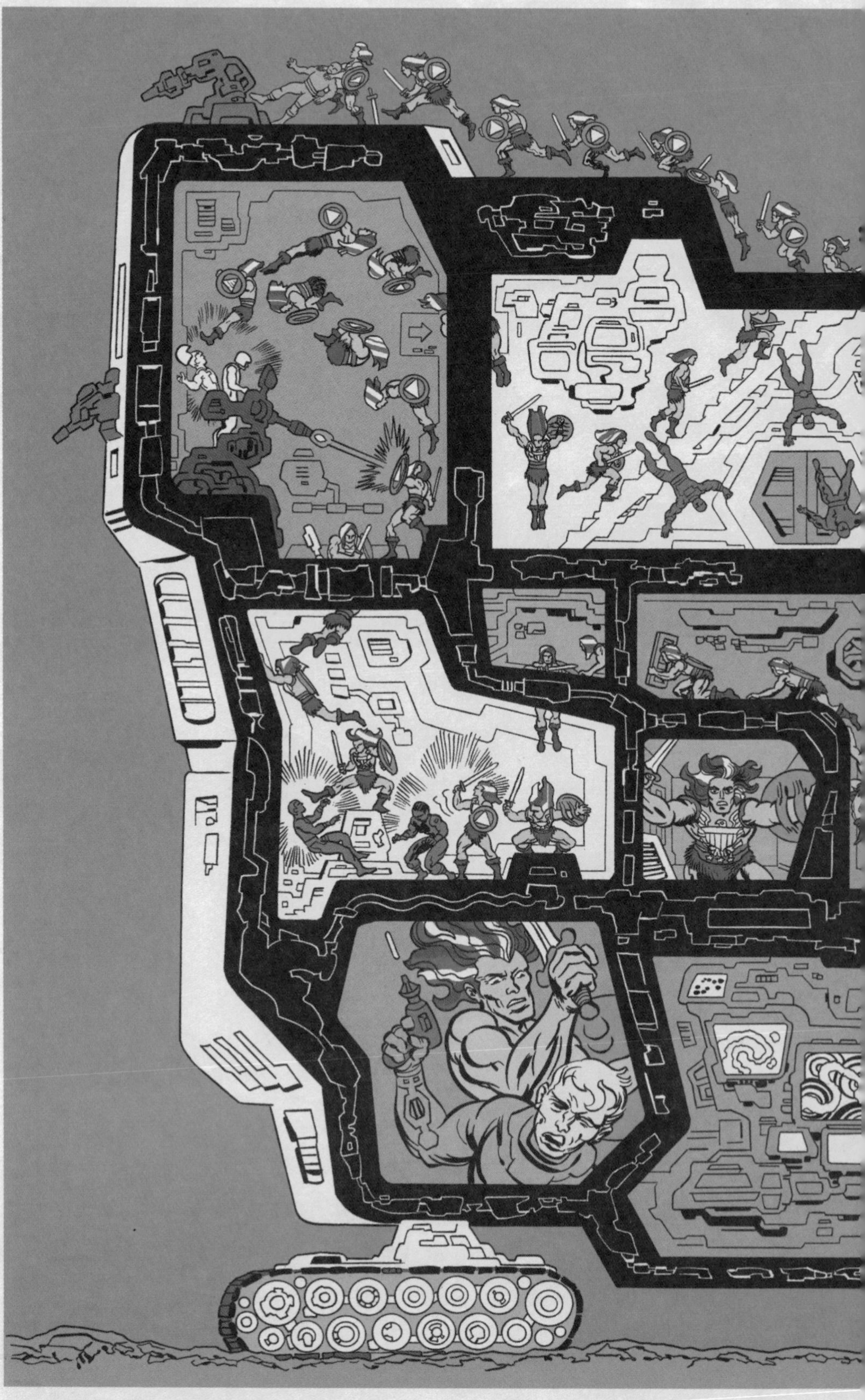

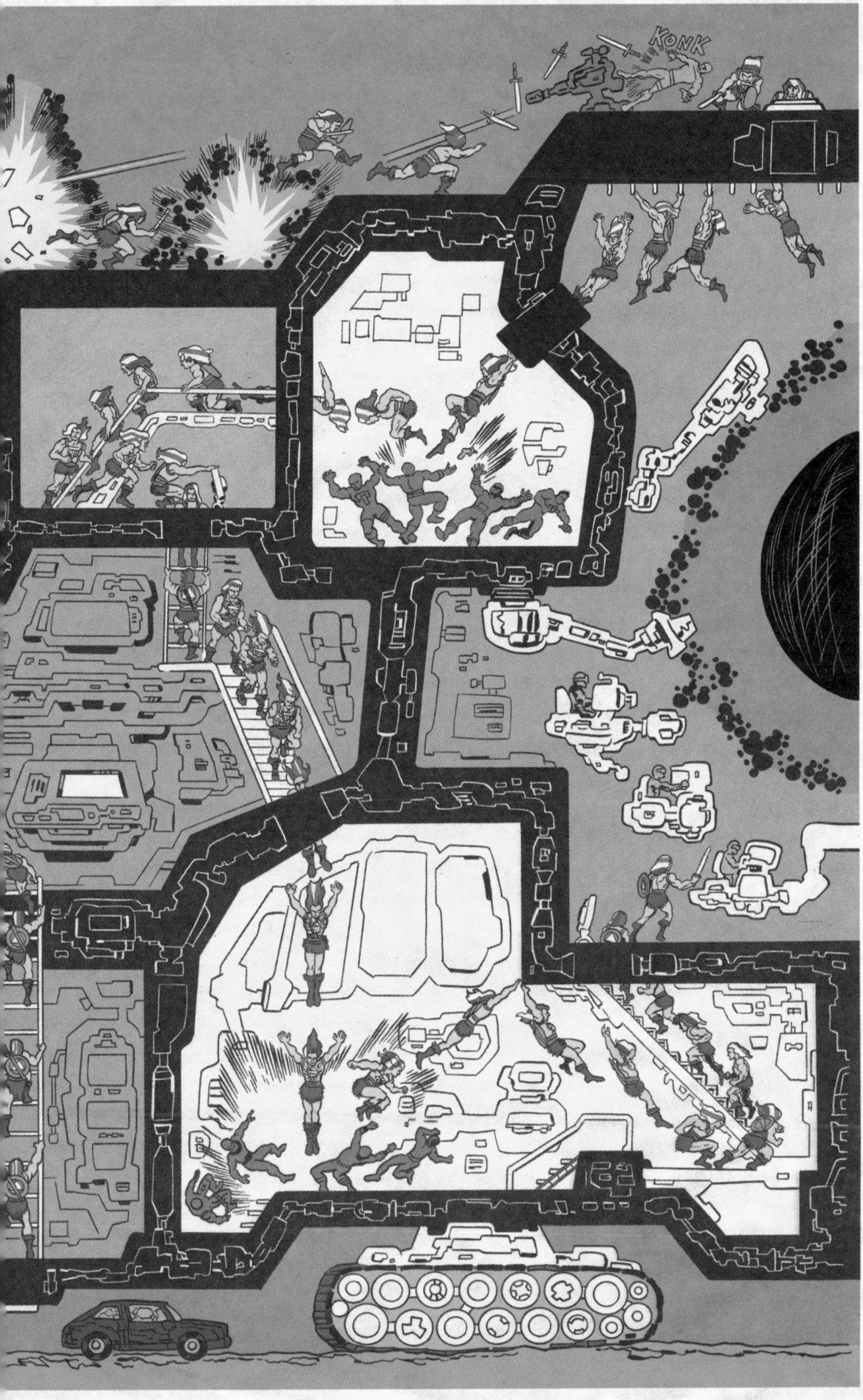
KONK

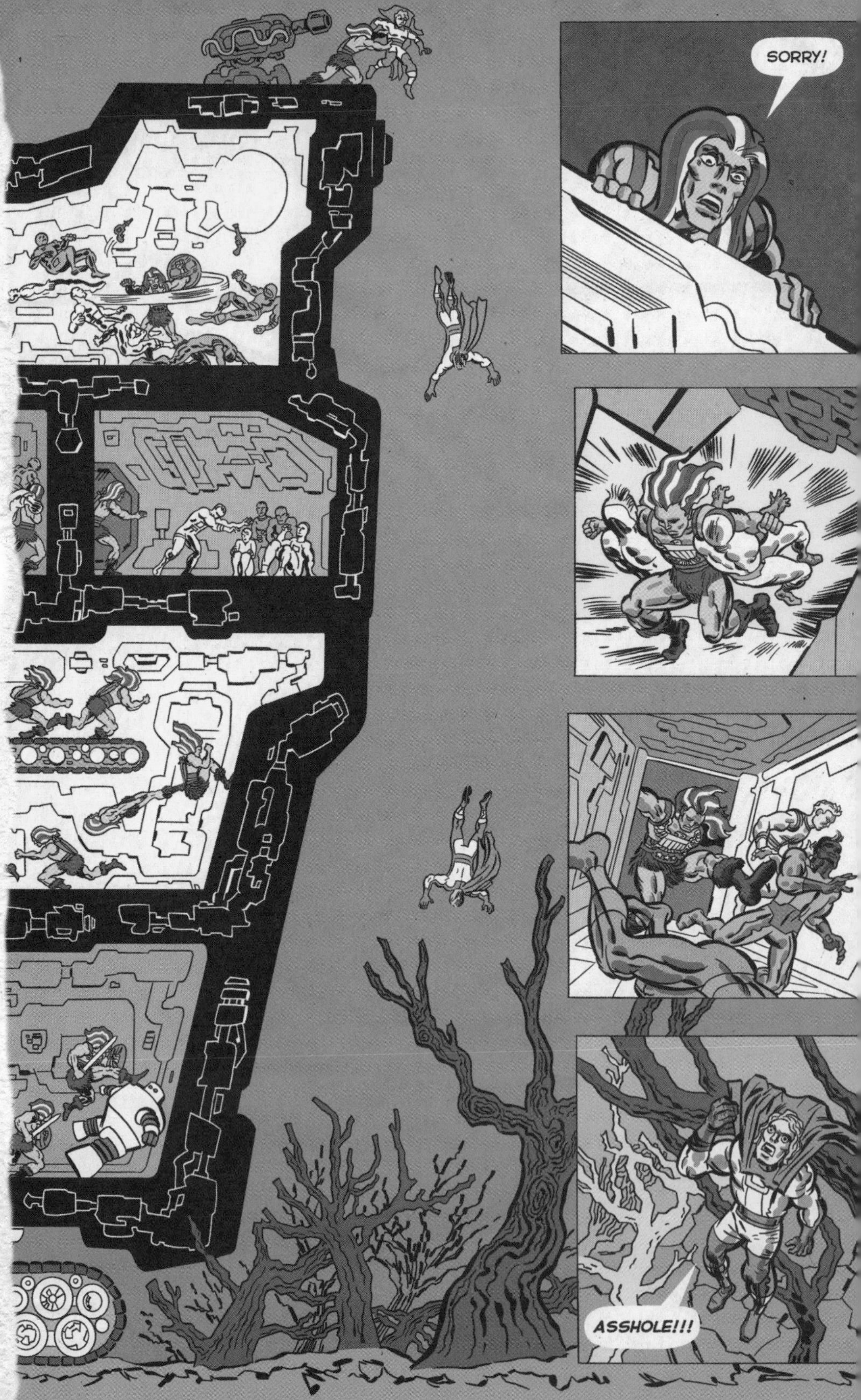
SORRY!
ASSHOLE!!!

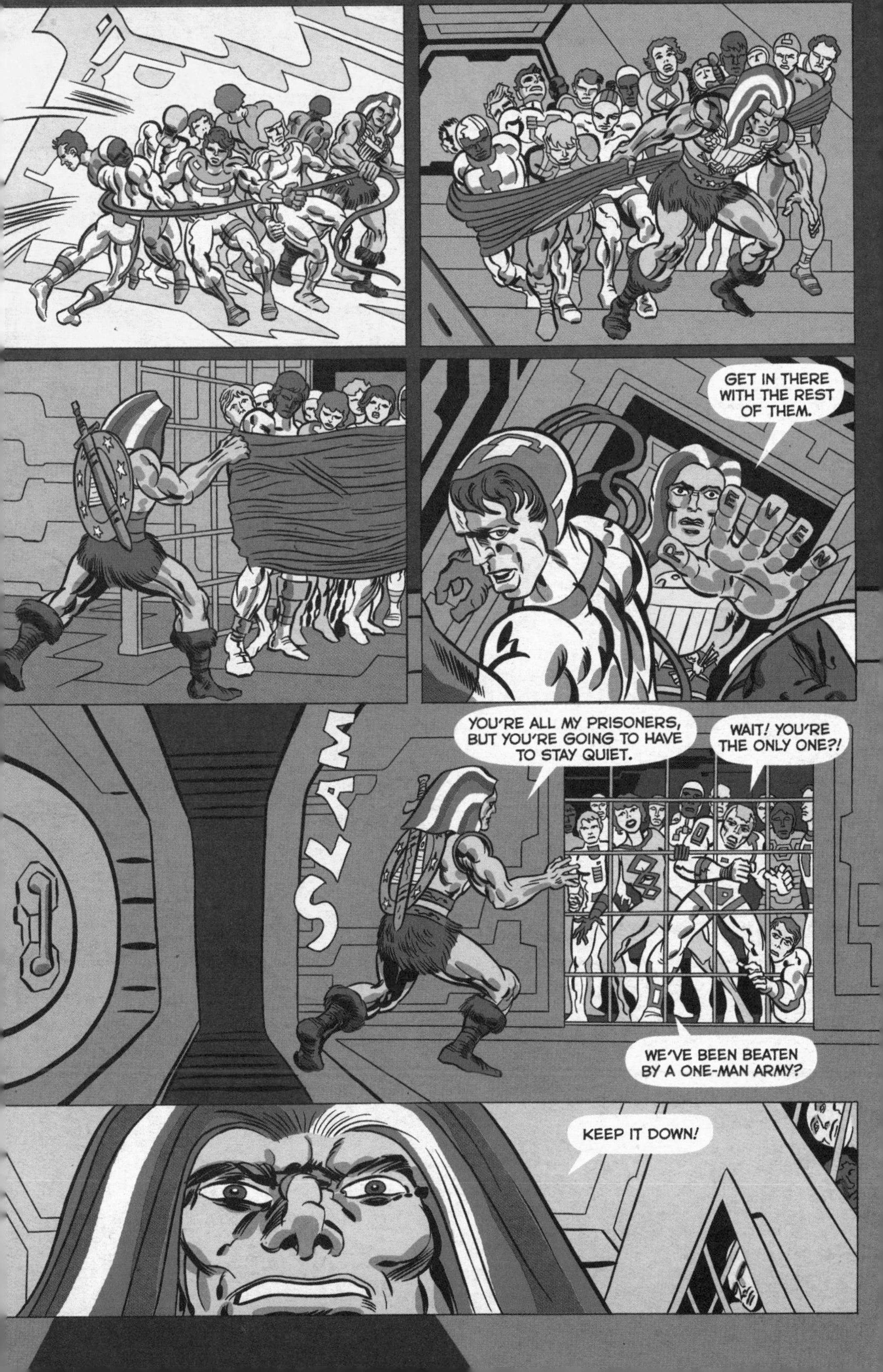
GET IN THERE WITH THE REST OF THEM.
EVEN
SLAM
YOU'RE ALL MY PRISONERS, BUT YOU'RE GOING TO HAVE TO STAY QUIET.
WAIT! YOU'RE THE ONLY ONE?!
WE'VE BEEN BEATEN BY A ONE-MAN ARMY?
KEEP IT DOWN!

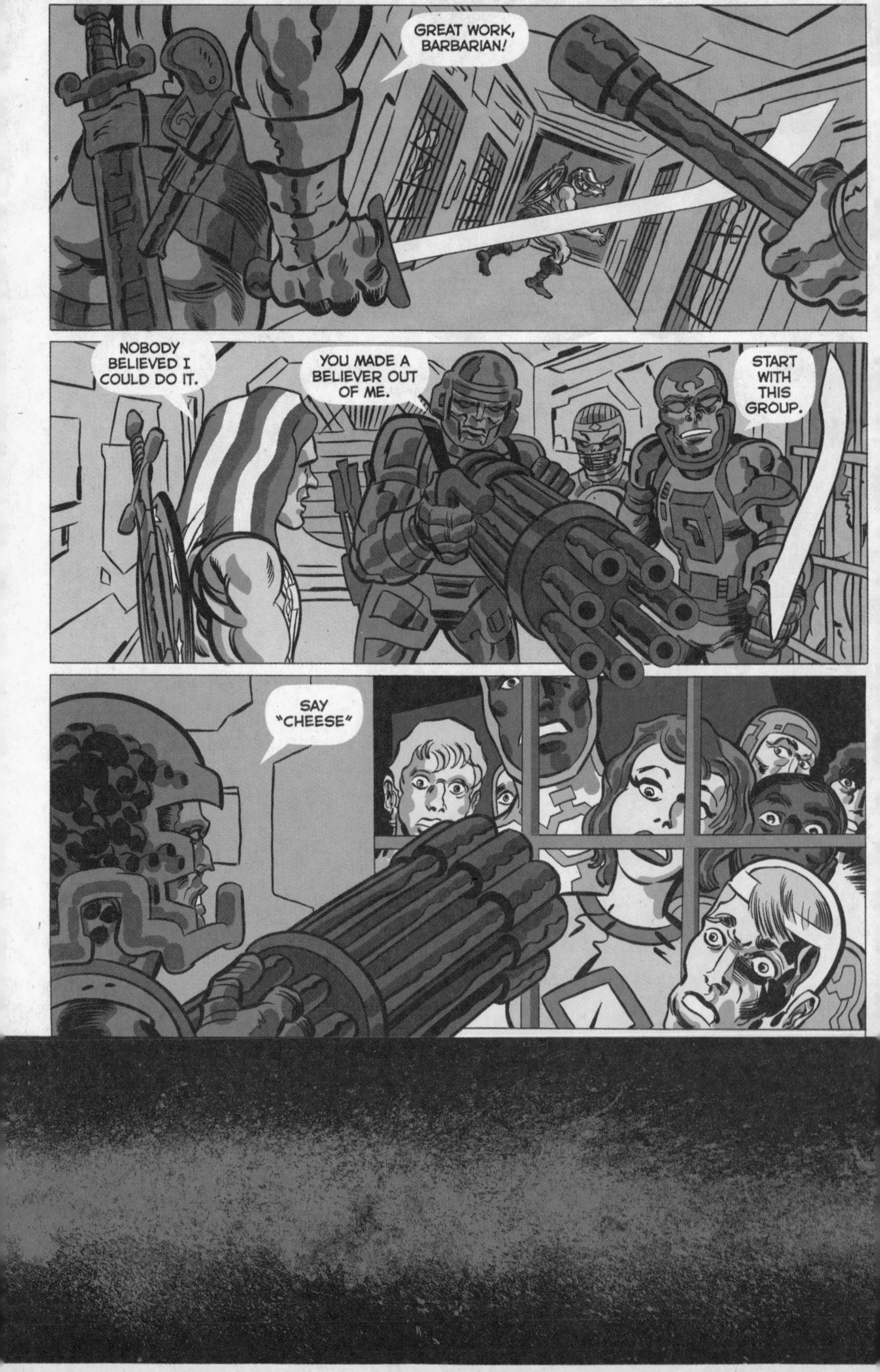
GREAT WORK, BARBARIAN!
NOBODY BELIEVED I COULD DO IT.
YOU MADE A BELIEVER OUT OF ME.
START WITH THIS GROUP.
SAY "CHEESE"

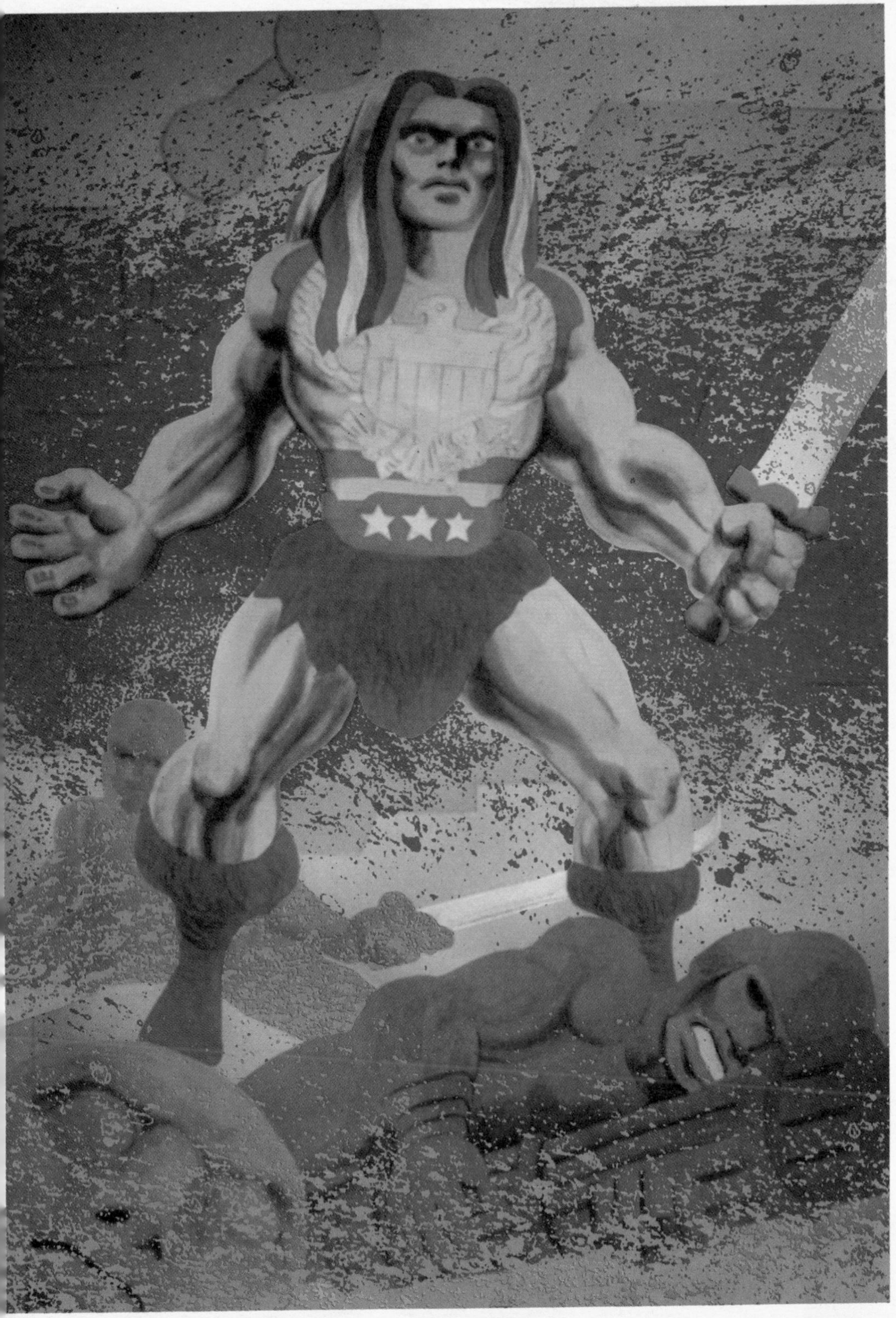

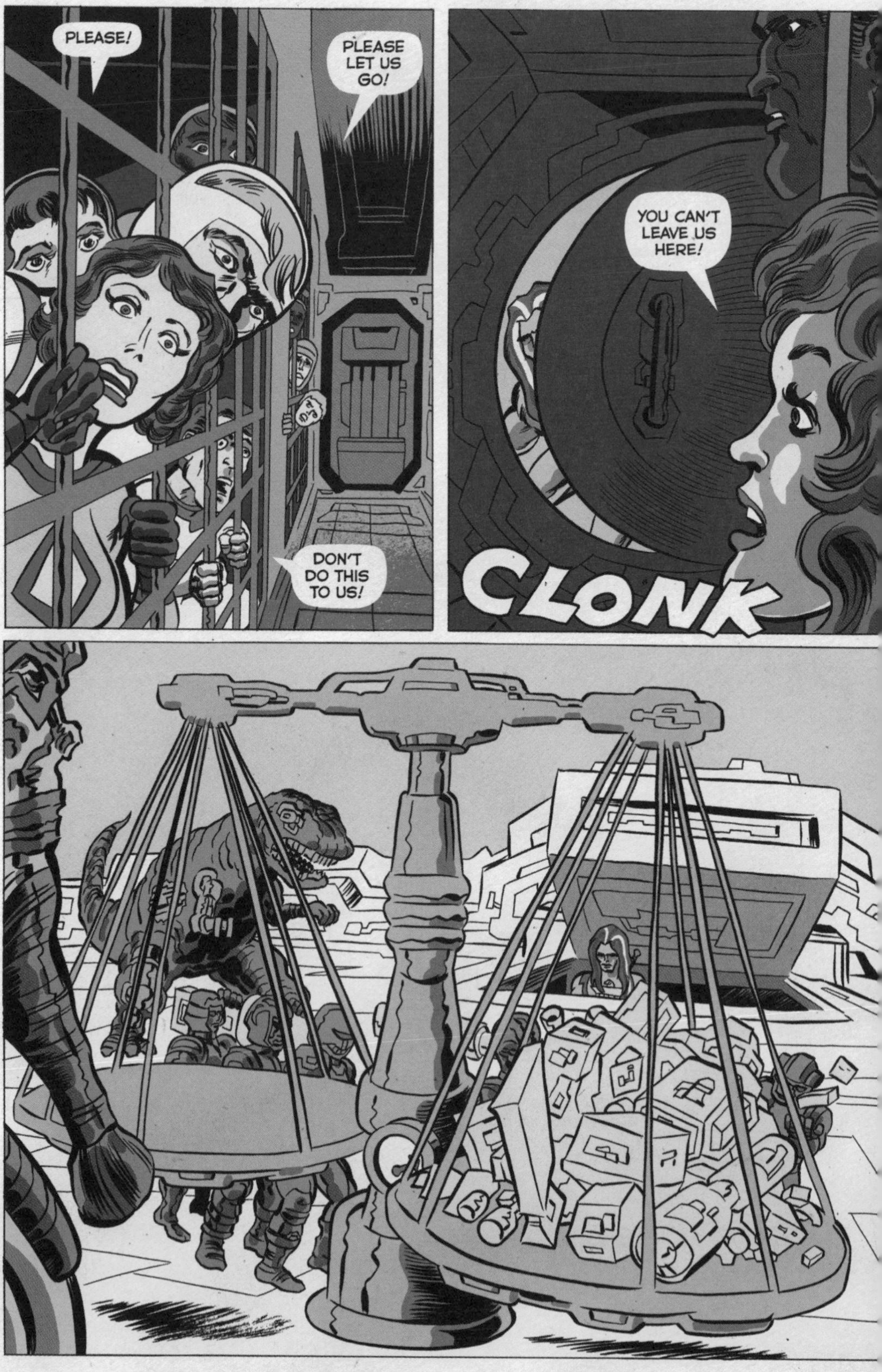
PLEASE!
PLEASE LET US GO!
DON'T DO THIS TO US!
YOU CAN'T LEAVE US HERE!
CLONK

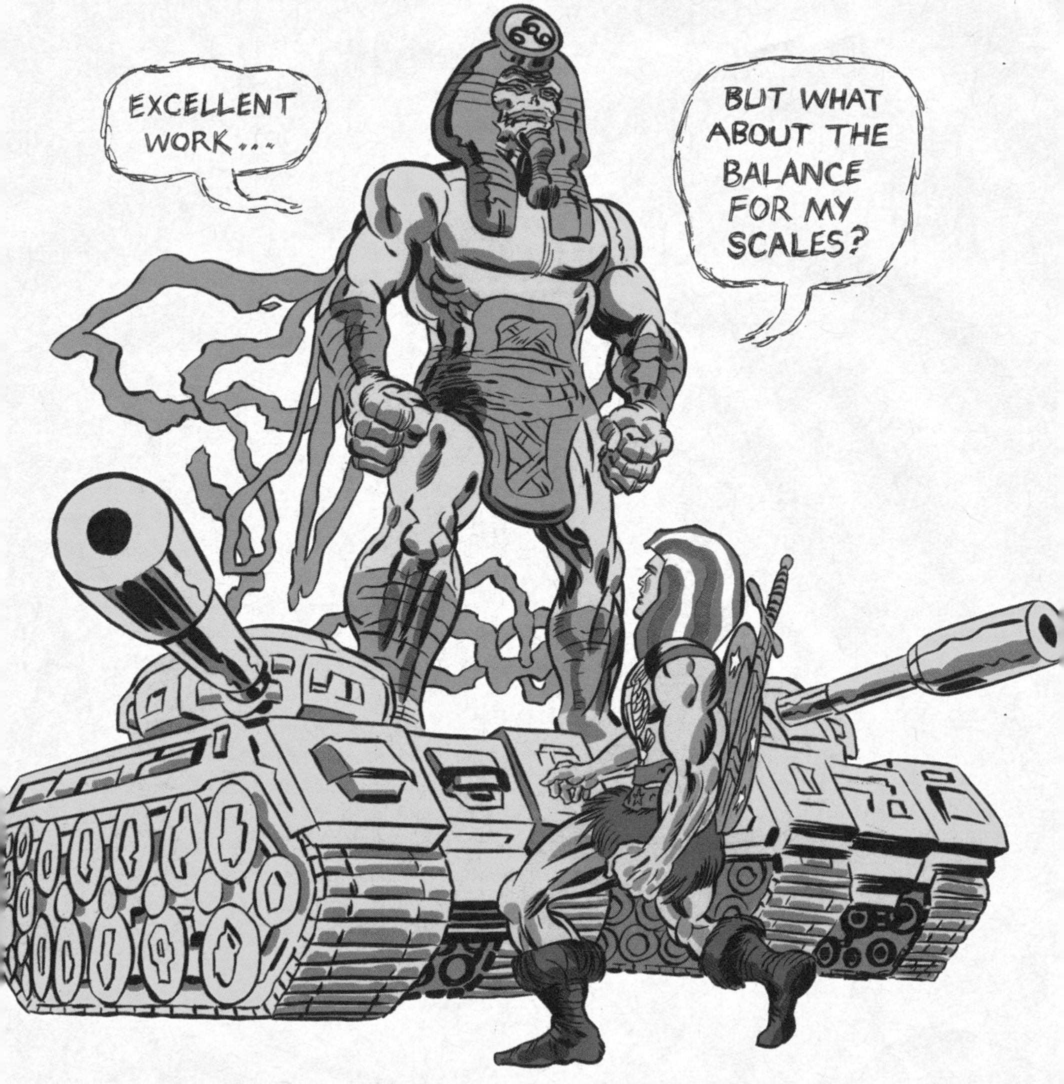
EXCELLENT WORK...
BUT WHAT ABOUT THE BALANCE FOR MY SCALES?

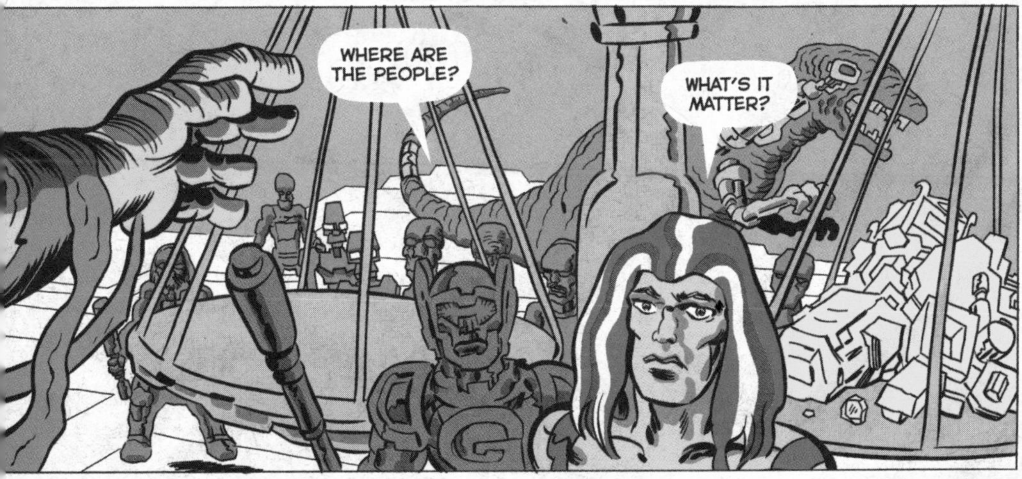
WHERE ARE THE PEOPLE?
WHAT'S IT MATTER?

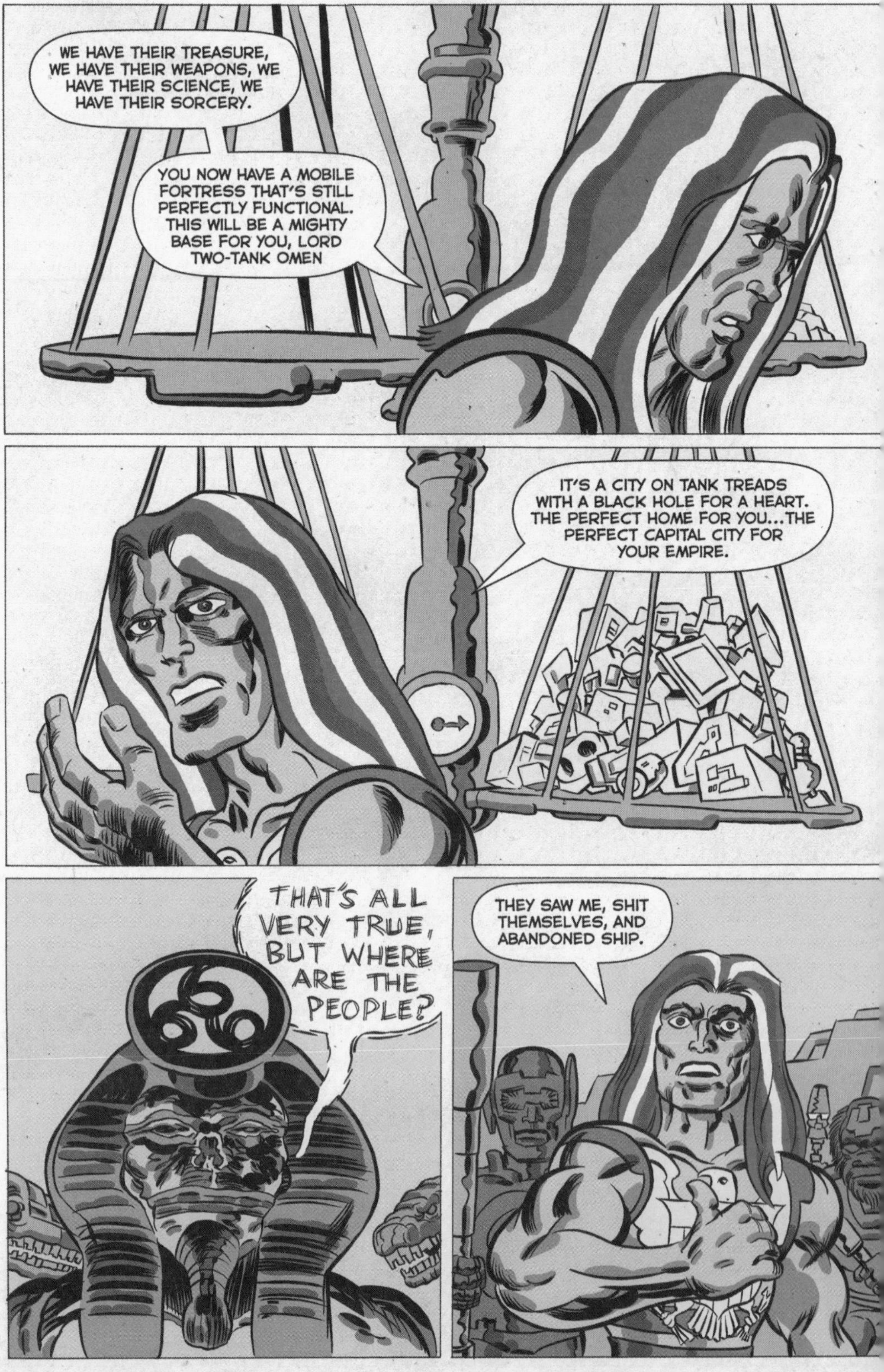
WE HAVE THEIR TREASURE, WE HAVE THEIR WEAPONS, WE HAVE THEIR SCIENCE, WE HAVE THEIR SORCERY.
YOU NOW HAVE A MOBILE FORTRESS THAT'S STILL PERFECTLY FUNCTIONAL. THIS WILL BE A MIGHTY BASE FOR YOU, LORD TWO-TANK OMEN
IT'S A CITY ON TANK TREADS WITH A BLACK HOLE FOR A HEART. THE PERFECT HOME FOR YOU...THE PERFECT CAPITAL CITY FOR YOUR EMPIRE.
THAT'S ALL VERY TRUE, BUT WHERE ARE THE PEOPLE?
THEY SAW ME, SHIT THEMSELVES, AND ABANDONED SHIP.

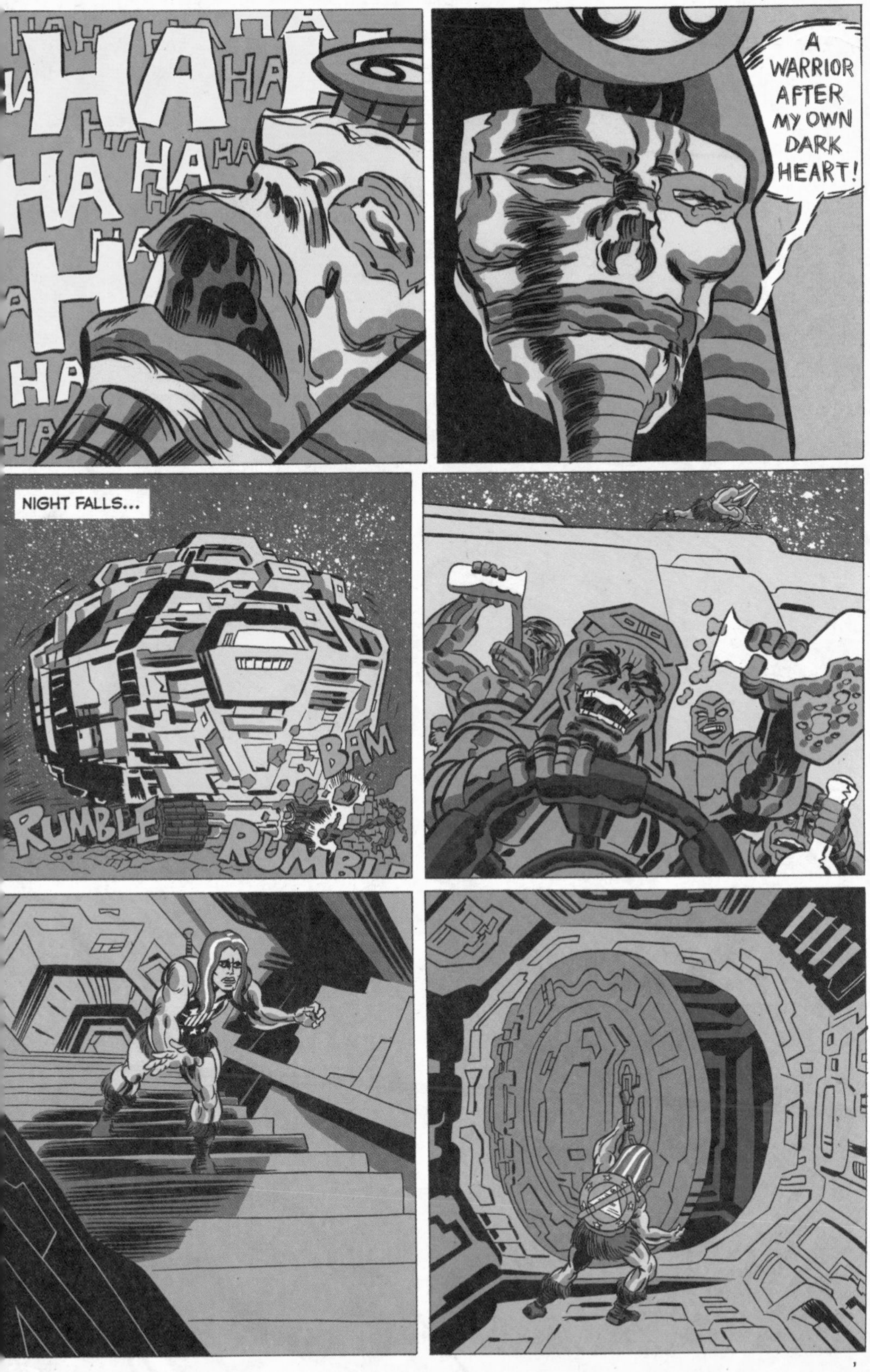

HA HA HA HA HA HA HA HA HA HA
A WARRIOR AFTER MY OWN DARK HEART!
NIGHT FALLS...
BAM
RUMBLE

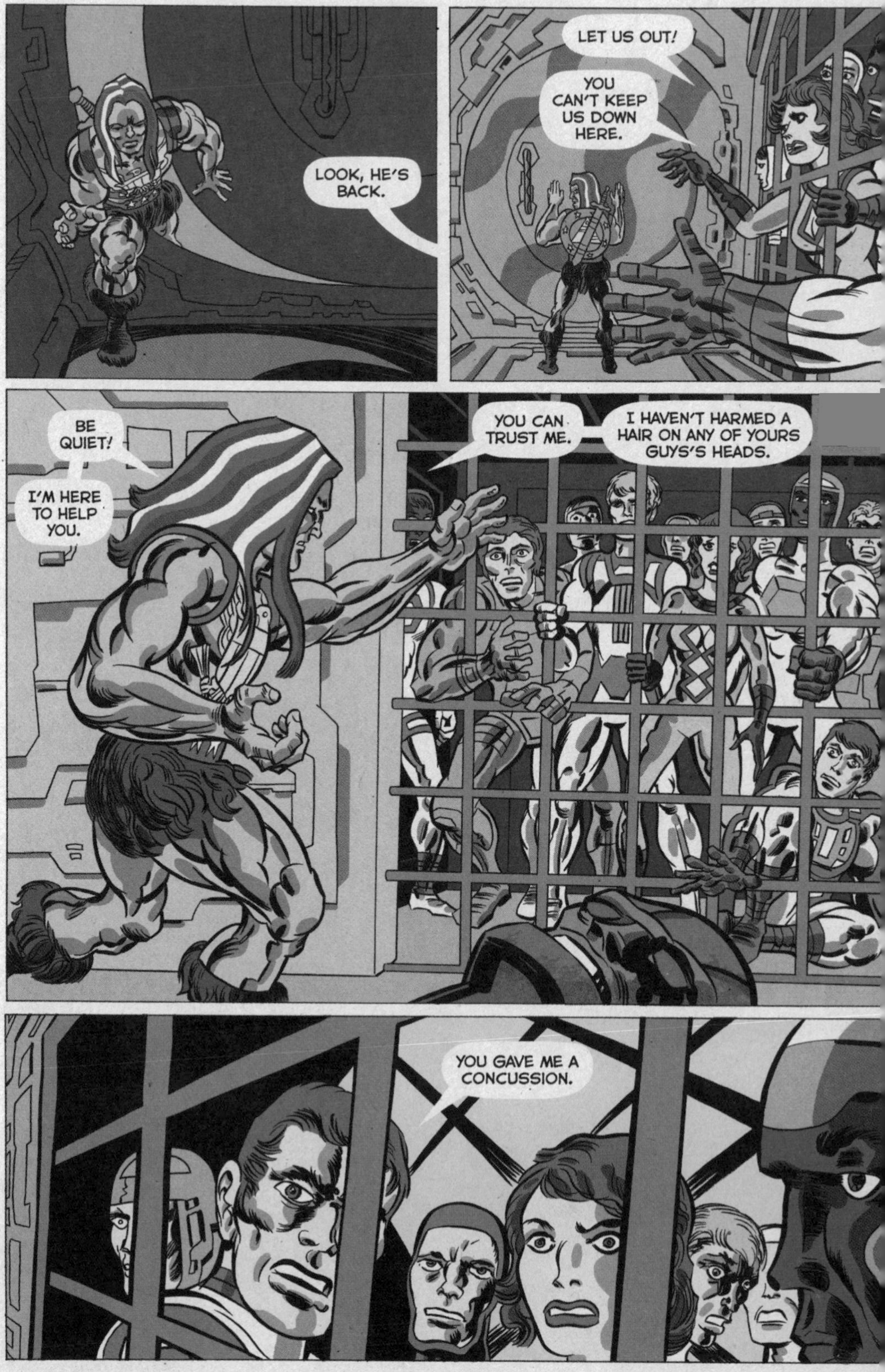
LOOK, HE'S BACK.
LET US OUT!
YOU CAN'T KEEP US DOWN HERE.
BE QUIET!
I'M HERE TO HELP YOU.
YOU CAN TRUST ME.
I HAVEN'T HARMED A HAIR ON ANY OF YOURS GUYS'S HEADS.
YOU GAVE ME A CONCUSSION.

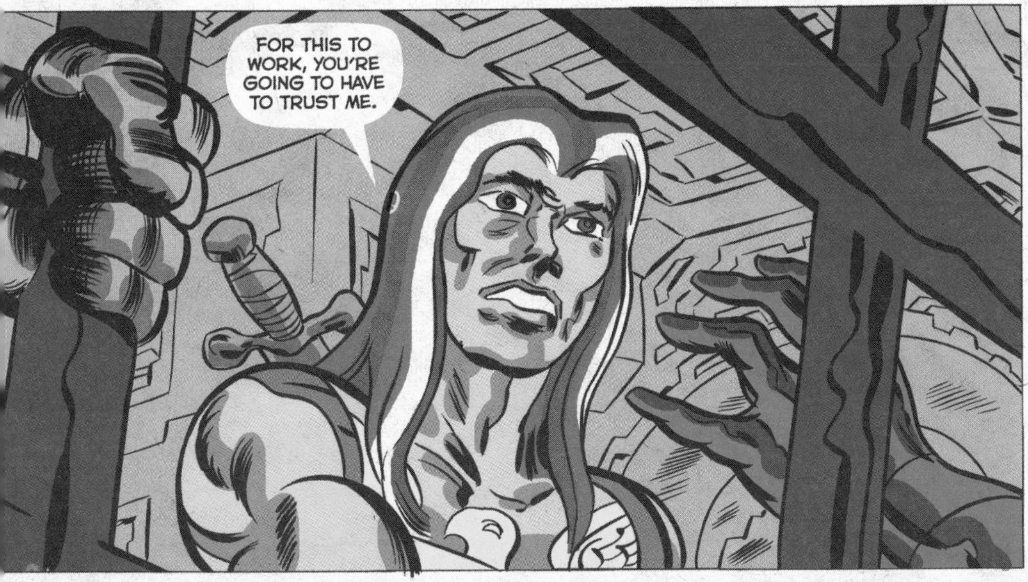
FOR THIS TO WORK, YOU'RE GOING TO HAVE TO TRUST ME.

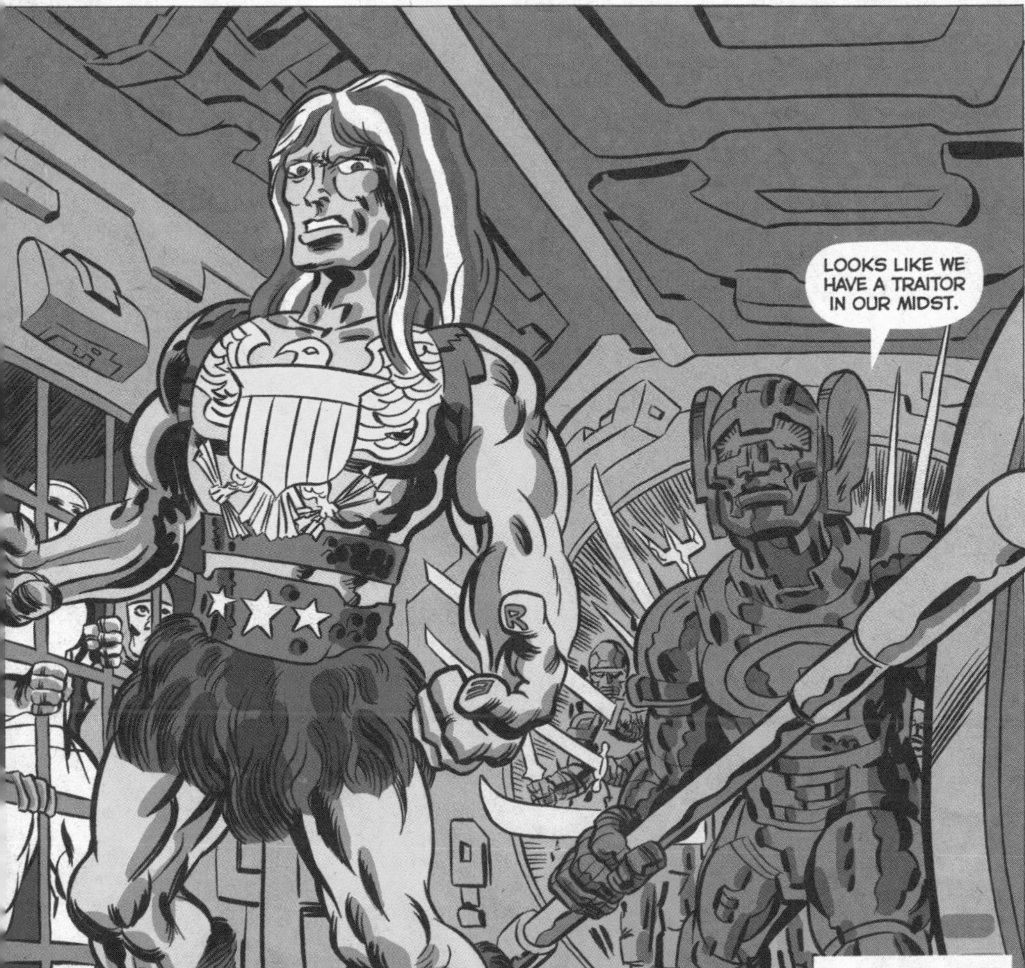
LOOKS LIKE WE HAVE A TRAITOR IN OUR MIDST.
NEXT: EXECUTION

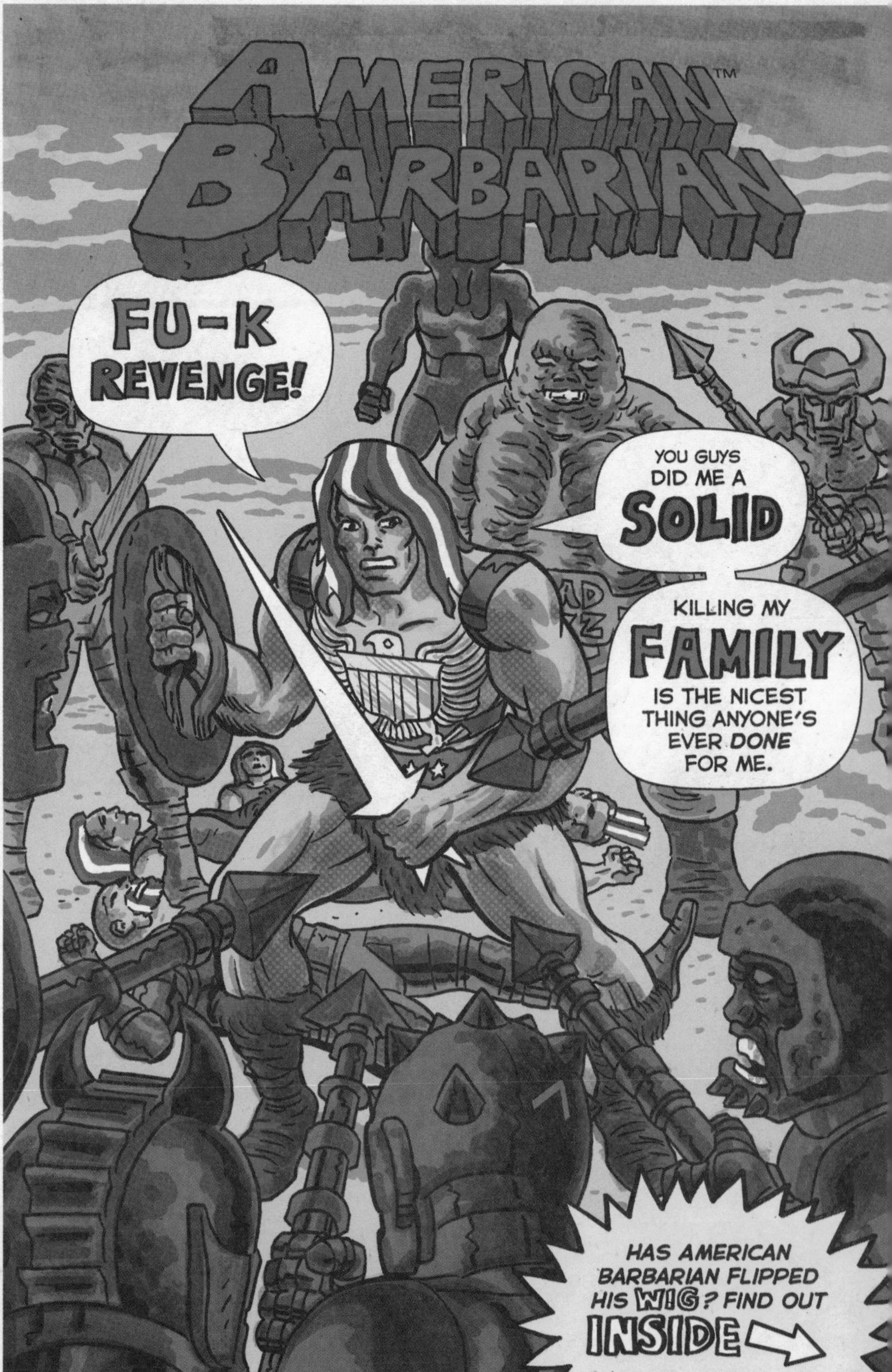
AMERICAN™ BARBARIAN
FU-K REVENGE!
YOU GUYS DID ME A SOLID
KILLING MY FAMILY IS THE NICEST THING ANYONE'S EVER DONE FOR ME.
HAS AMERICAN BARBARIAN FLIPPED HIS WIG? FIND OUT INSIDE

EXECUTION

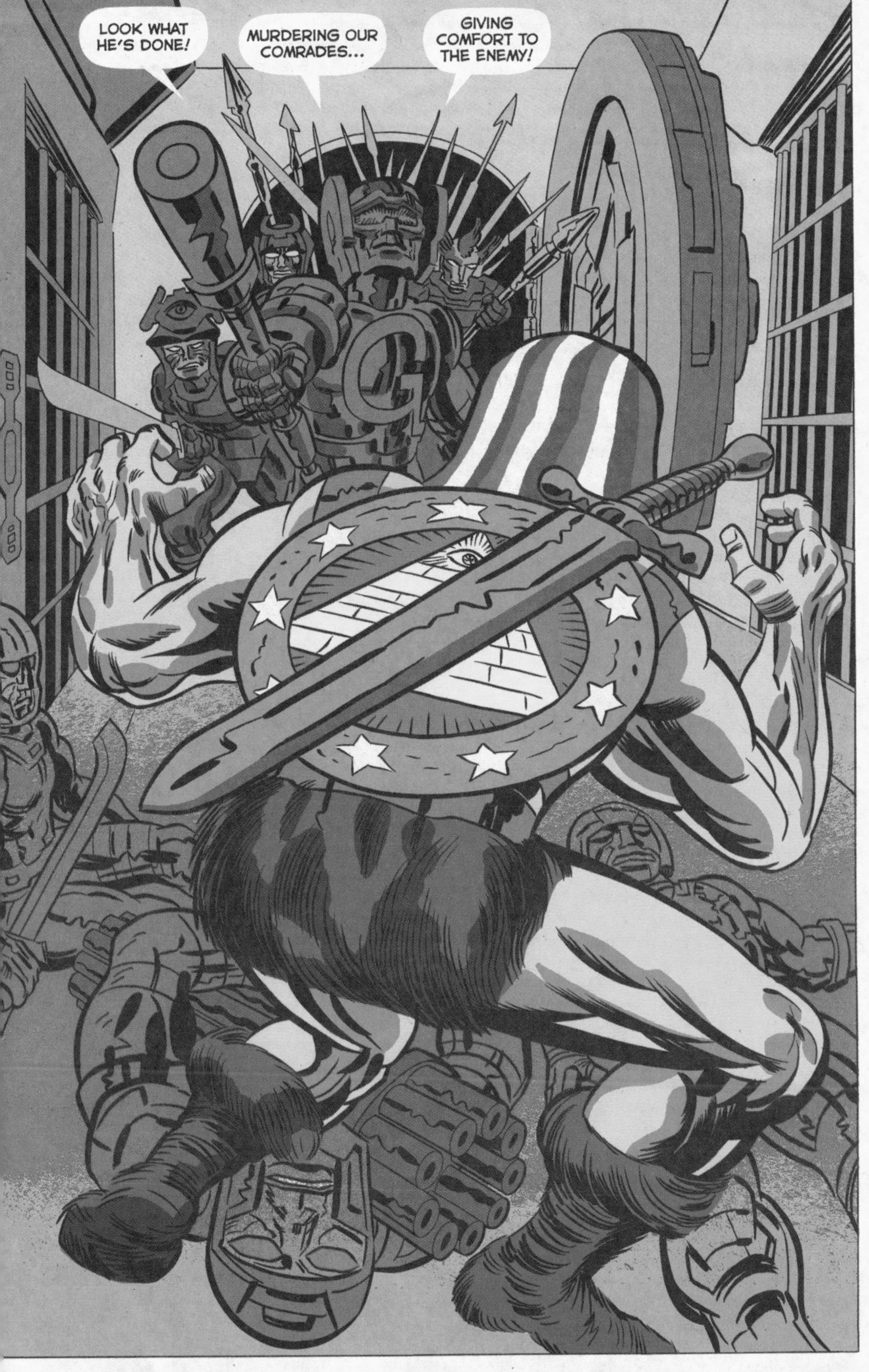
LOOK WHAT HE'S DONE!
MURDERING OUR COMRADES...
GIVING COMFORT TO THE ENEMY!

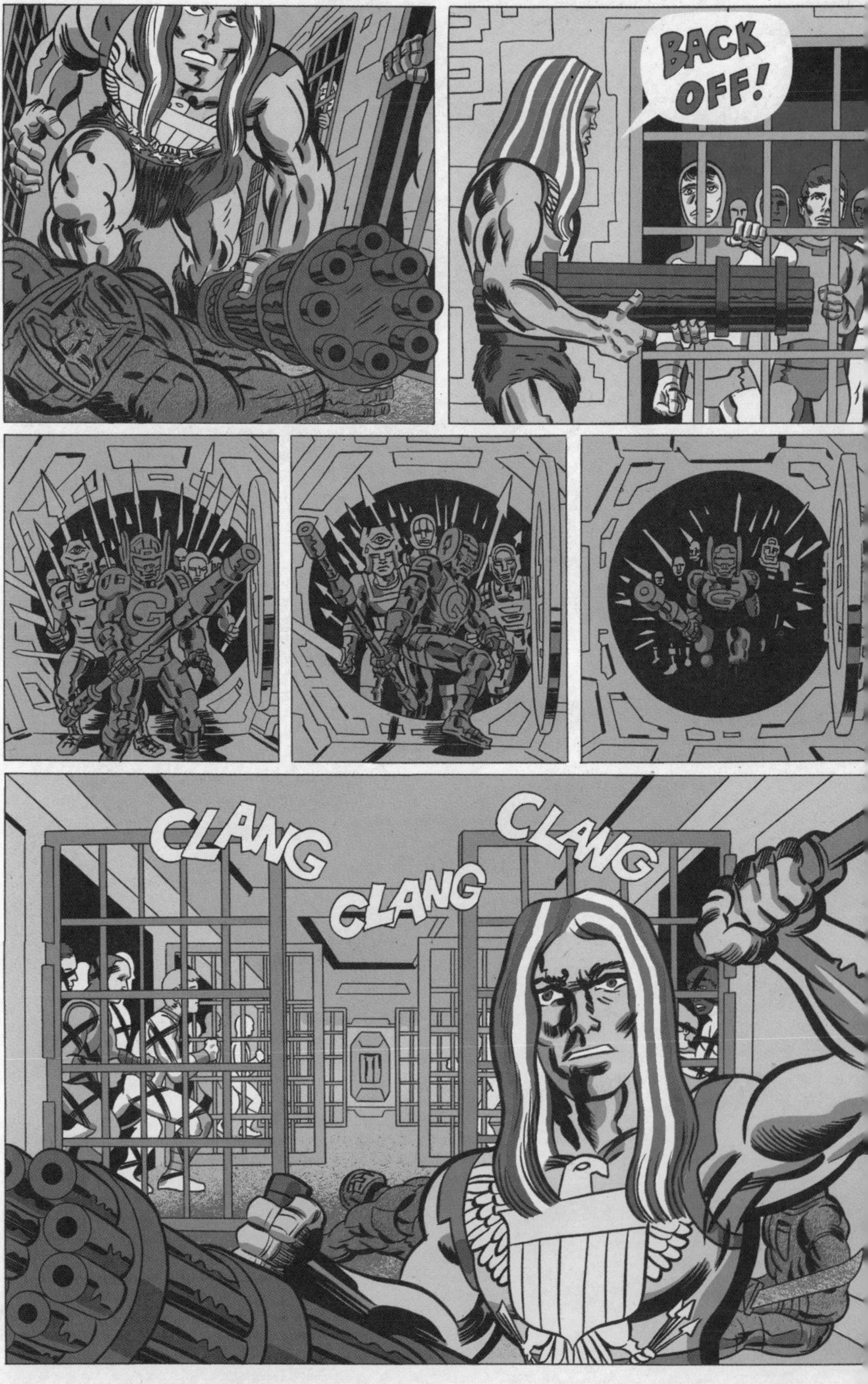
BACK OFF!
CLANG
CLANG
CLANG

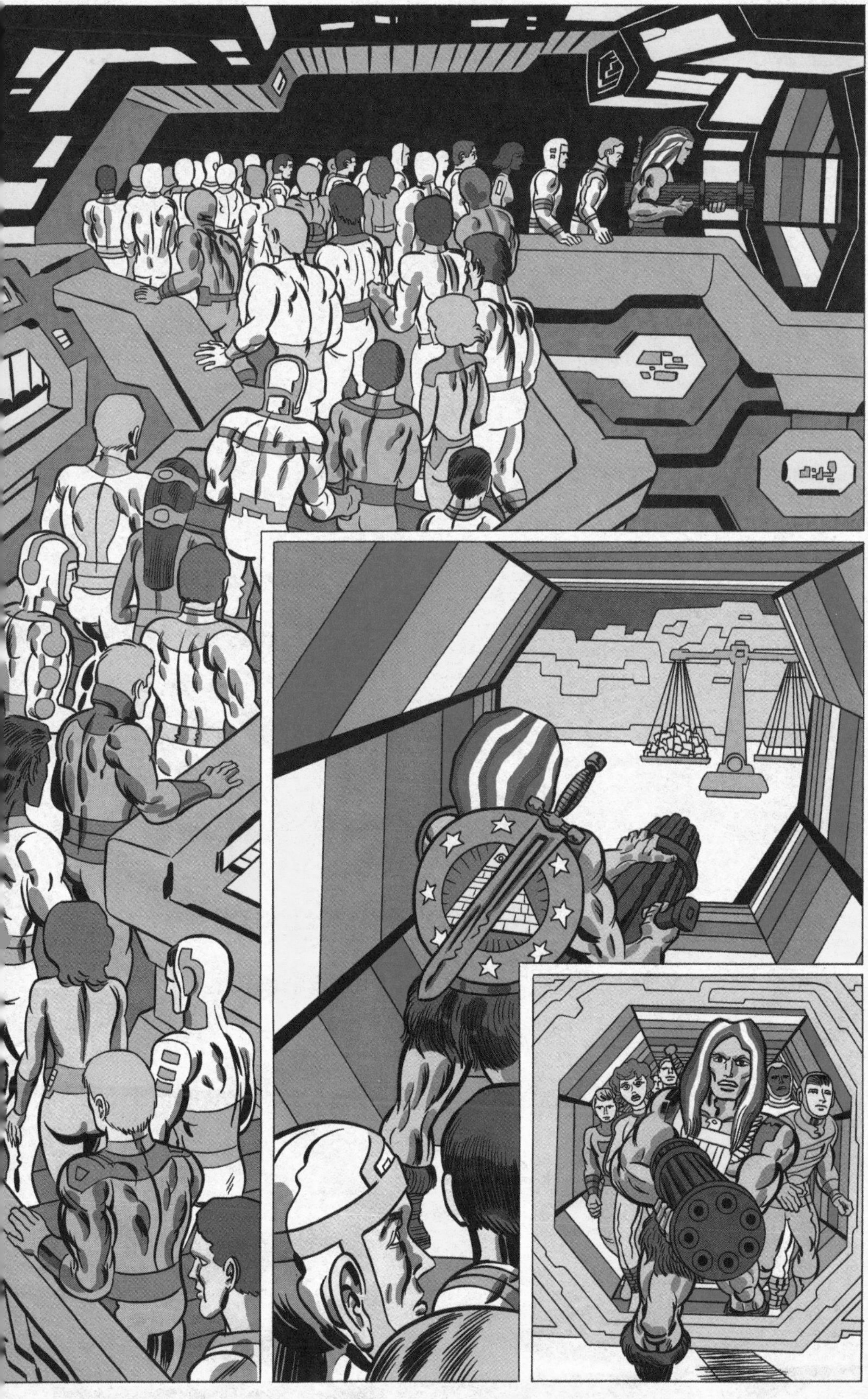

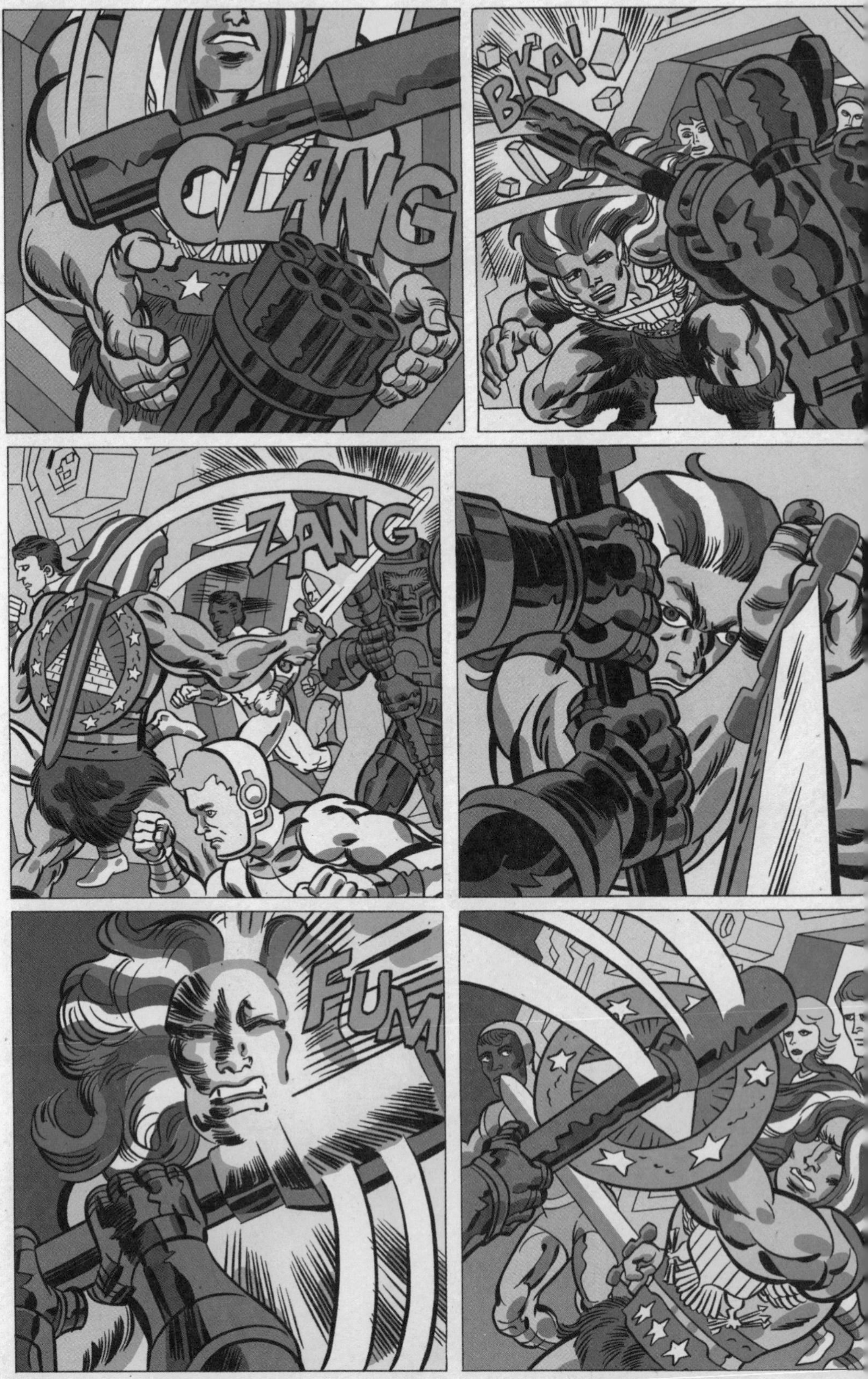
CLANG
BKA!
ZANG
FUM

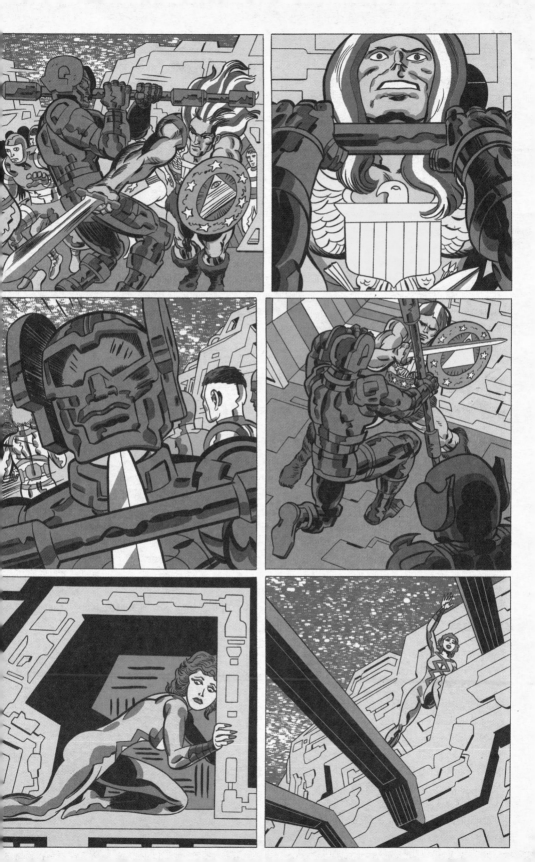

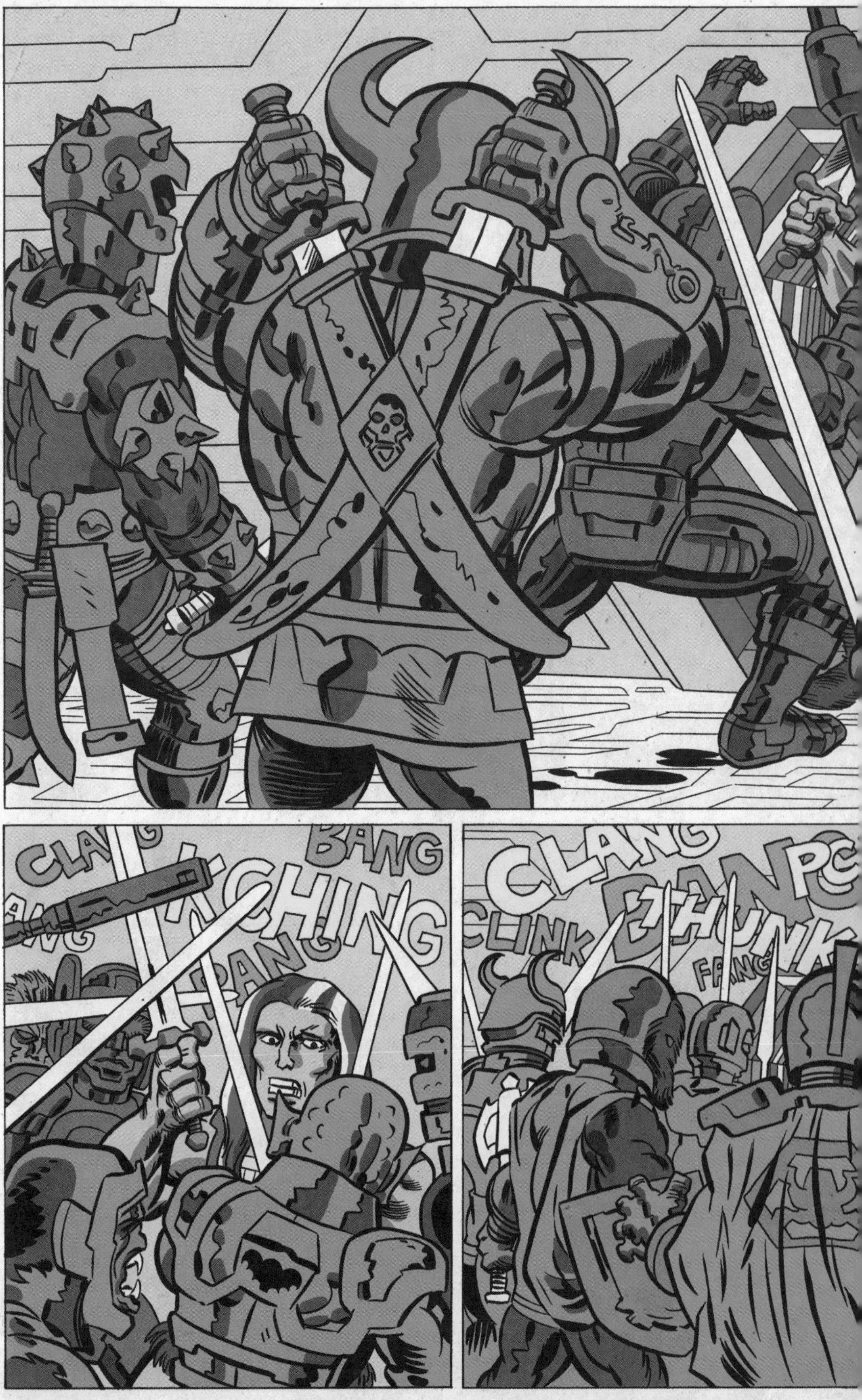
BANG
CHING
CLANG
CLINK
THUNK

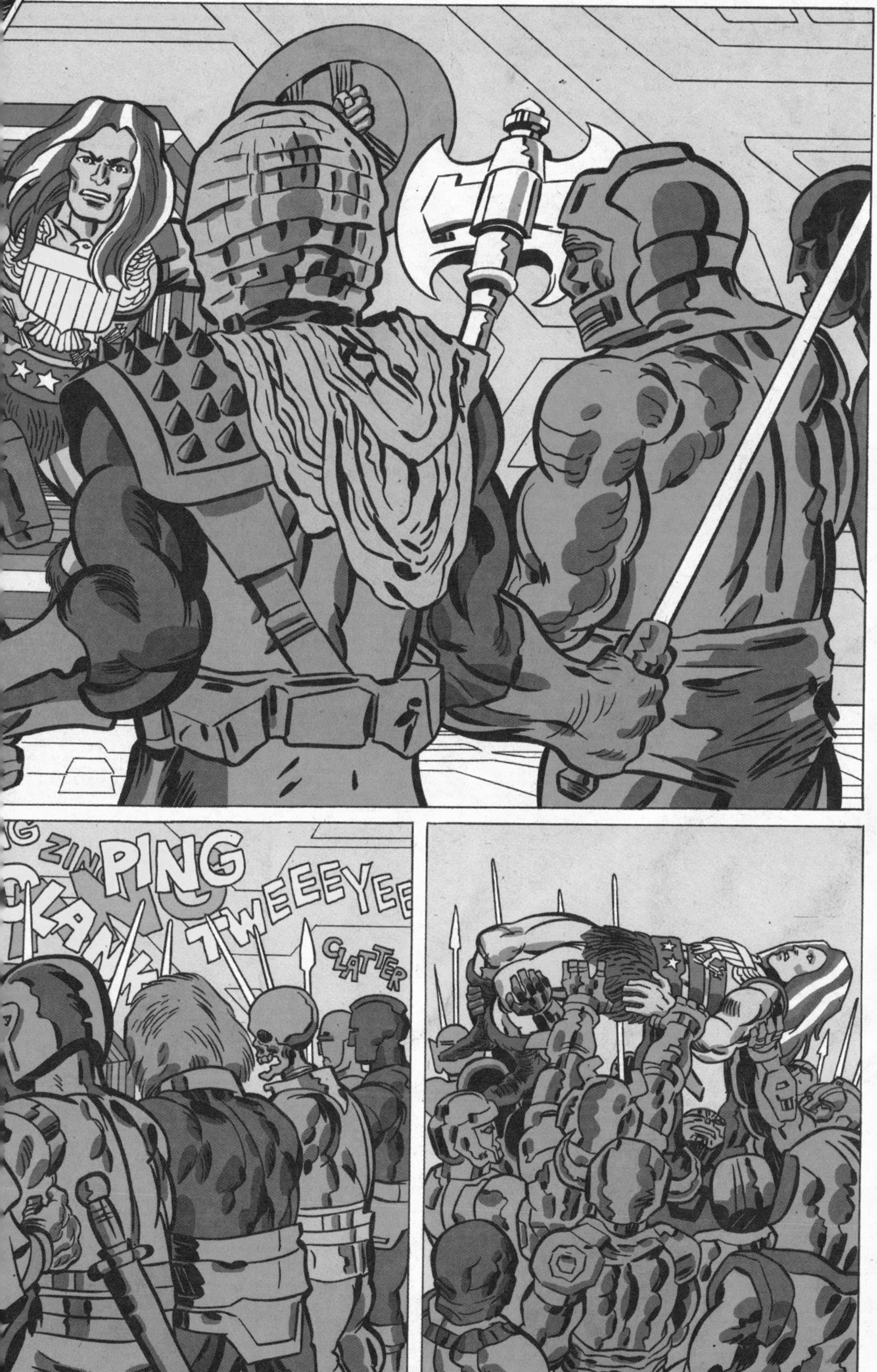
ZIN PING
CLANK
TWEEEEYEE
CLATTER

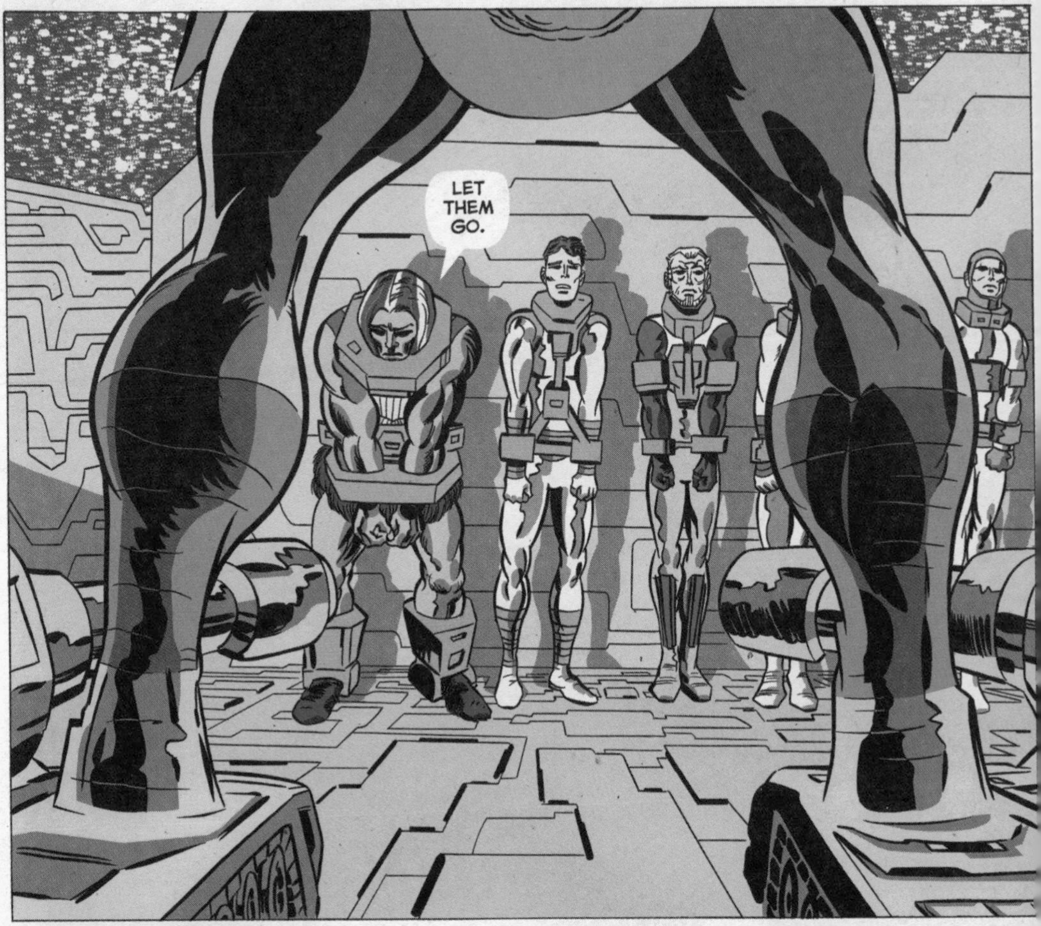
LET THEM GO.

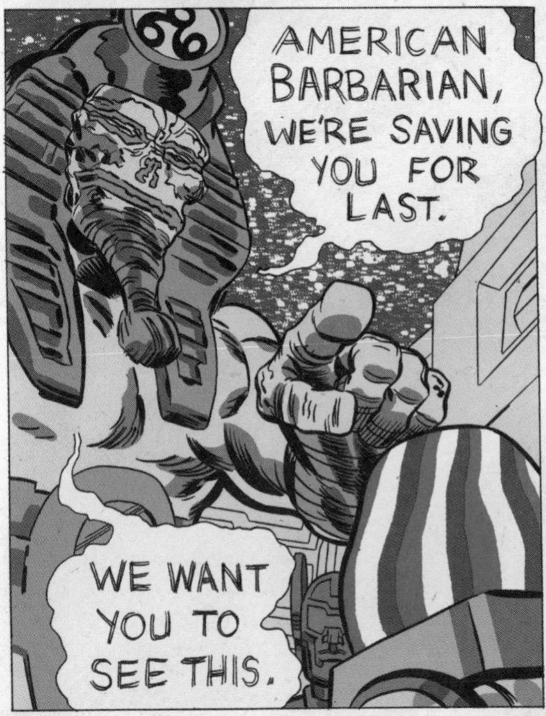
AMERICAN BARBARIAN, WE'RE SAVING YOU FOR LAST.
WE WANT YOU TO SEE THIS.

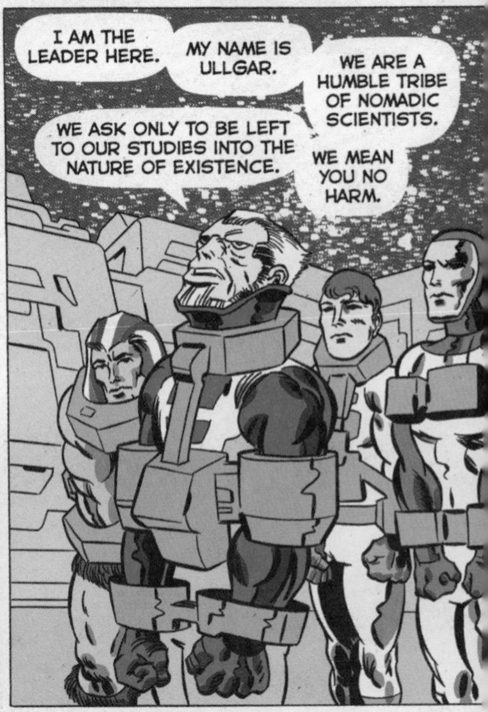
I AM THE LEADER HERE.
MY NAME IS ULLGAR.
WE ARE A HUMBLE TRIBE OF NOMADIC SCIENTISTS.
WE ASK ONLY TO BE LEFT TO OUR STUDIES INTO THE NATURE OF EXISTENCE.
WE MEAN YOU NO HARM.

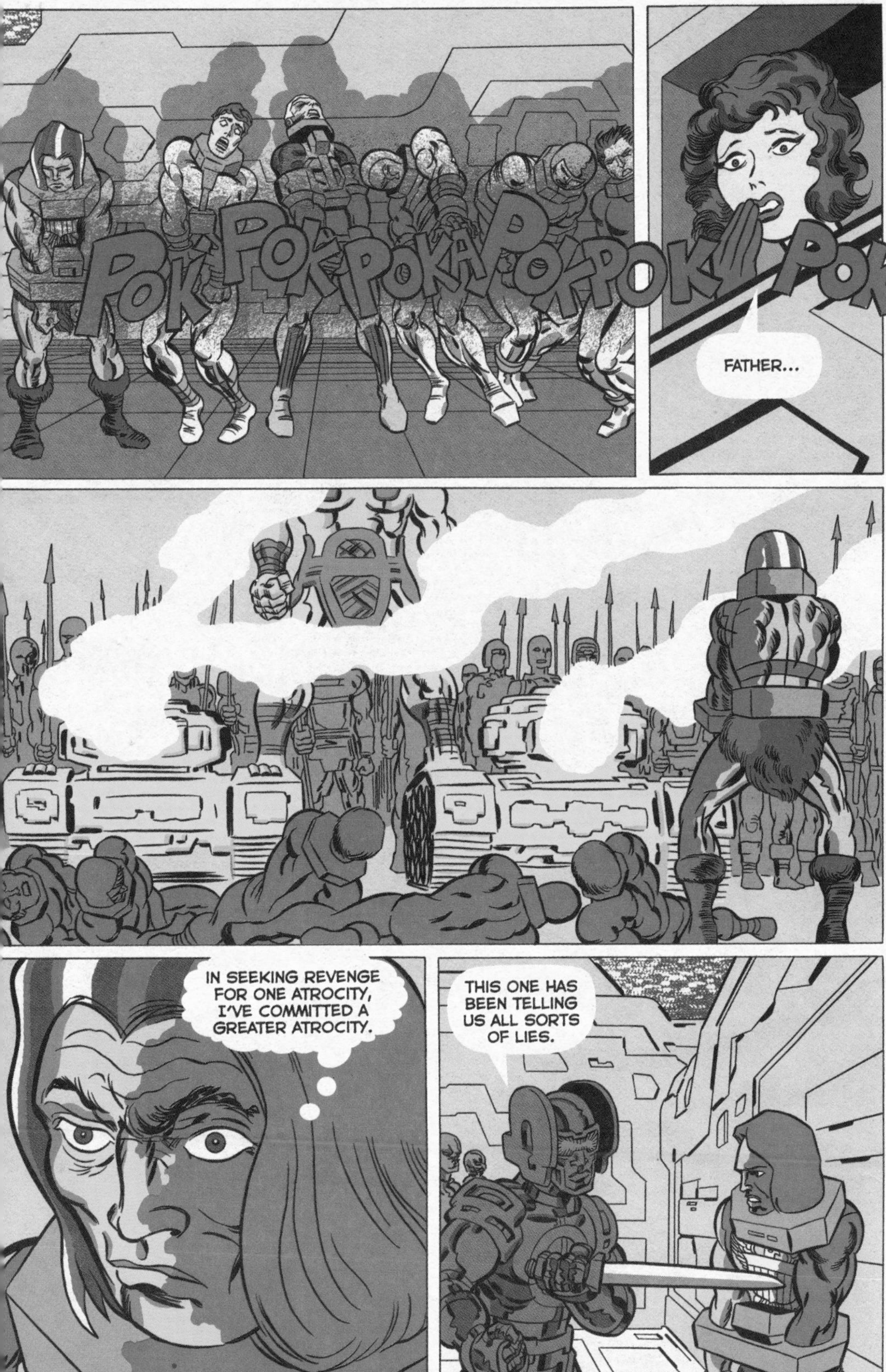
POK POK POKA POK POK POK POK
FATHER...
IN SEEKING REVENGE FOR ONE ATROCITY, I'VE COMMITTED A GREATER ATROCITY.
THIS ONE HAS BEEN TELLING US ALL SORTS OF LIES.

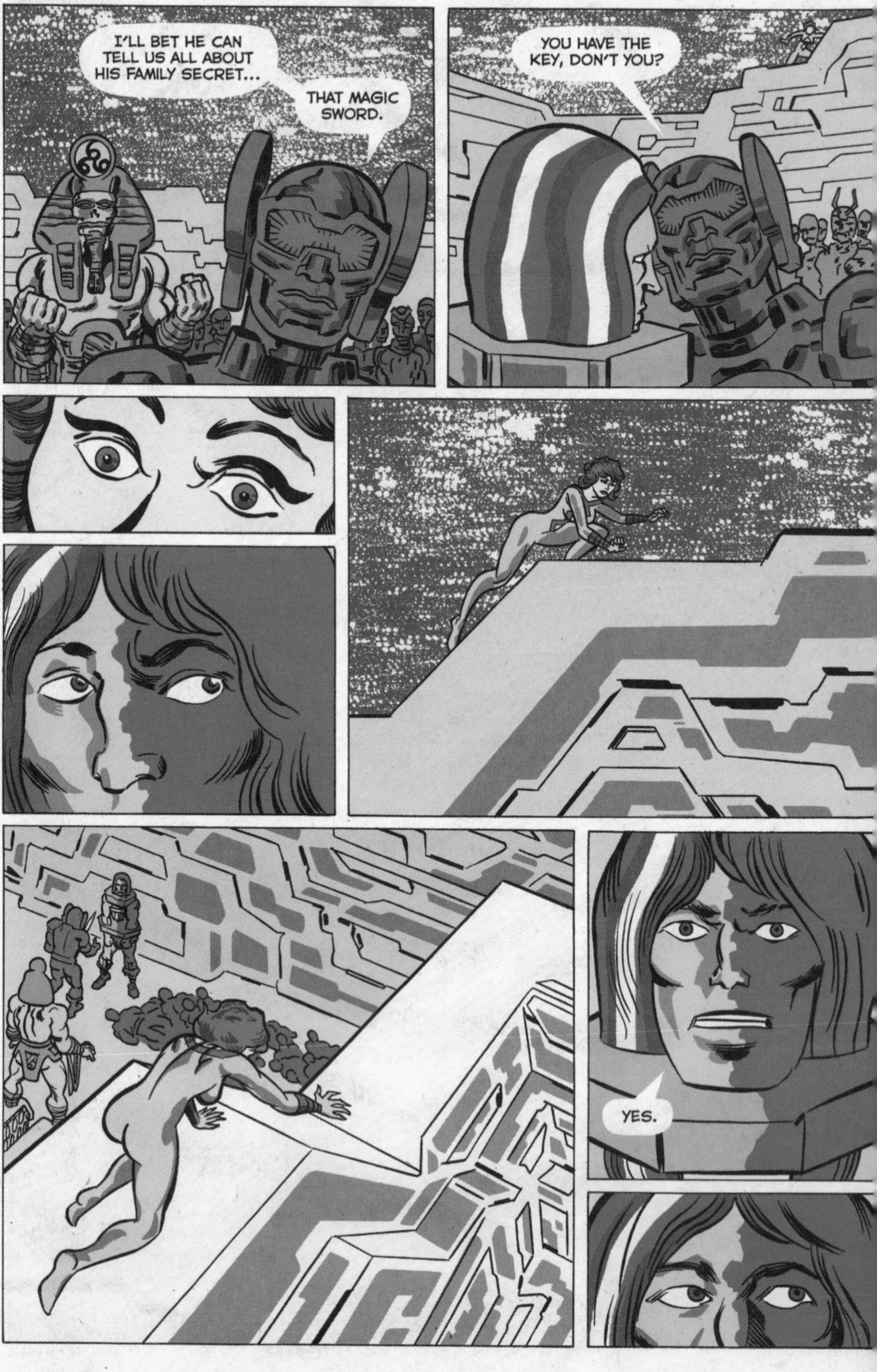
I'LL BET HE CAN TELL US ALL ABOUT HIS FAMILY SECRET...
THAT MAGIC SWORD.
YOU HAVE THE KEY, DON'T YOU?
YES.

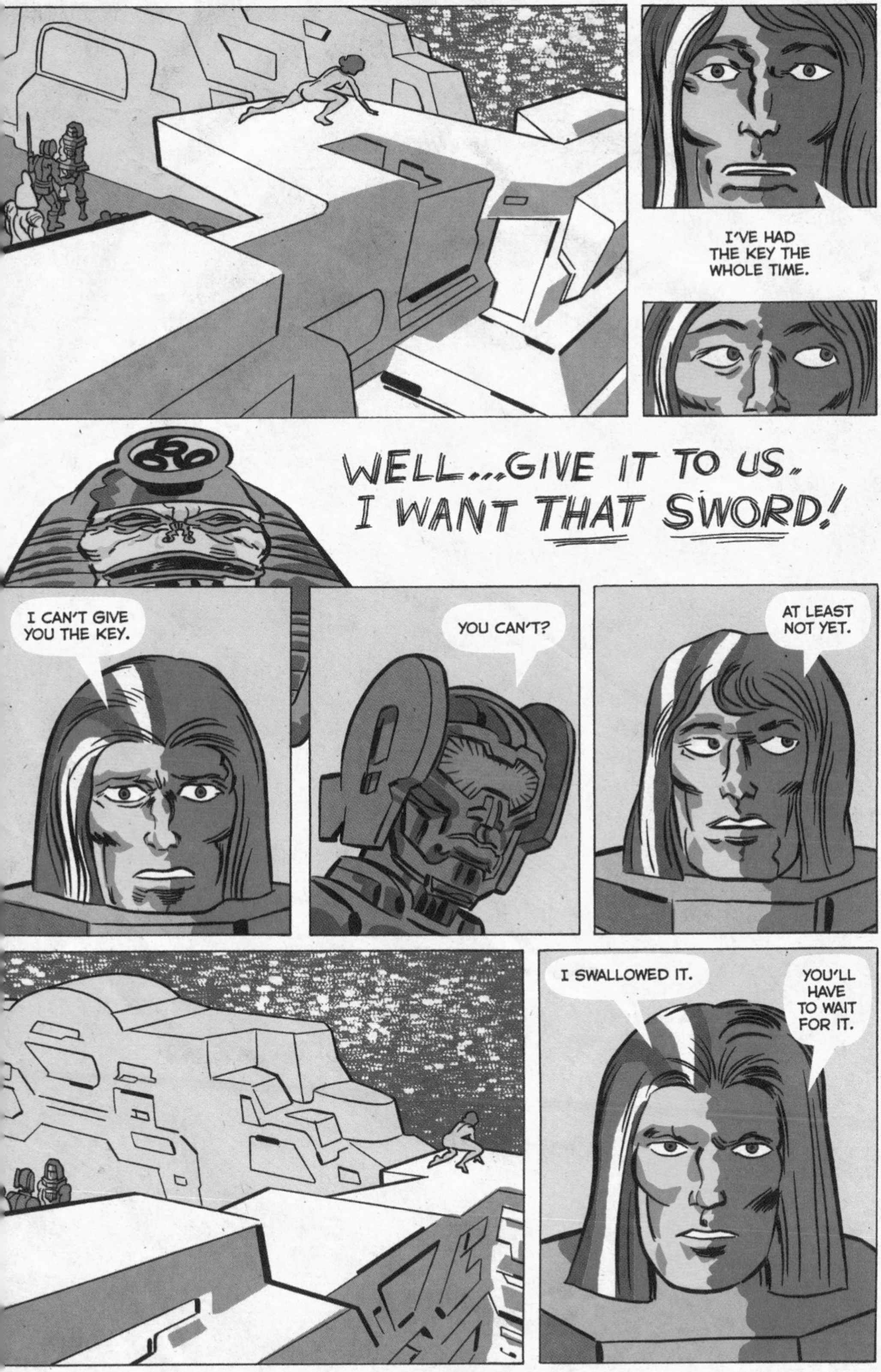
I'VE HAD THE KEY THE WHOLE TIME.
WELL...GIVE IT TO US. I WANT THAT SWORD!
I CAN'T GIVE YOU THE KEY.
YOU CAN'T?
AT LEAST NOT YET.
I SWALLOWED IT.
YOU'LL HAVE TO WAIT FOR IT.

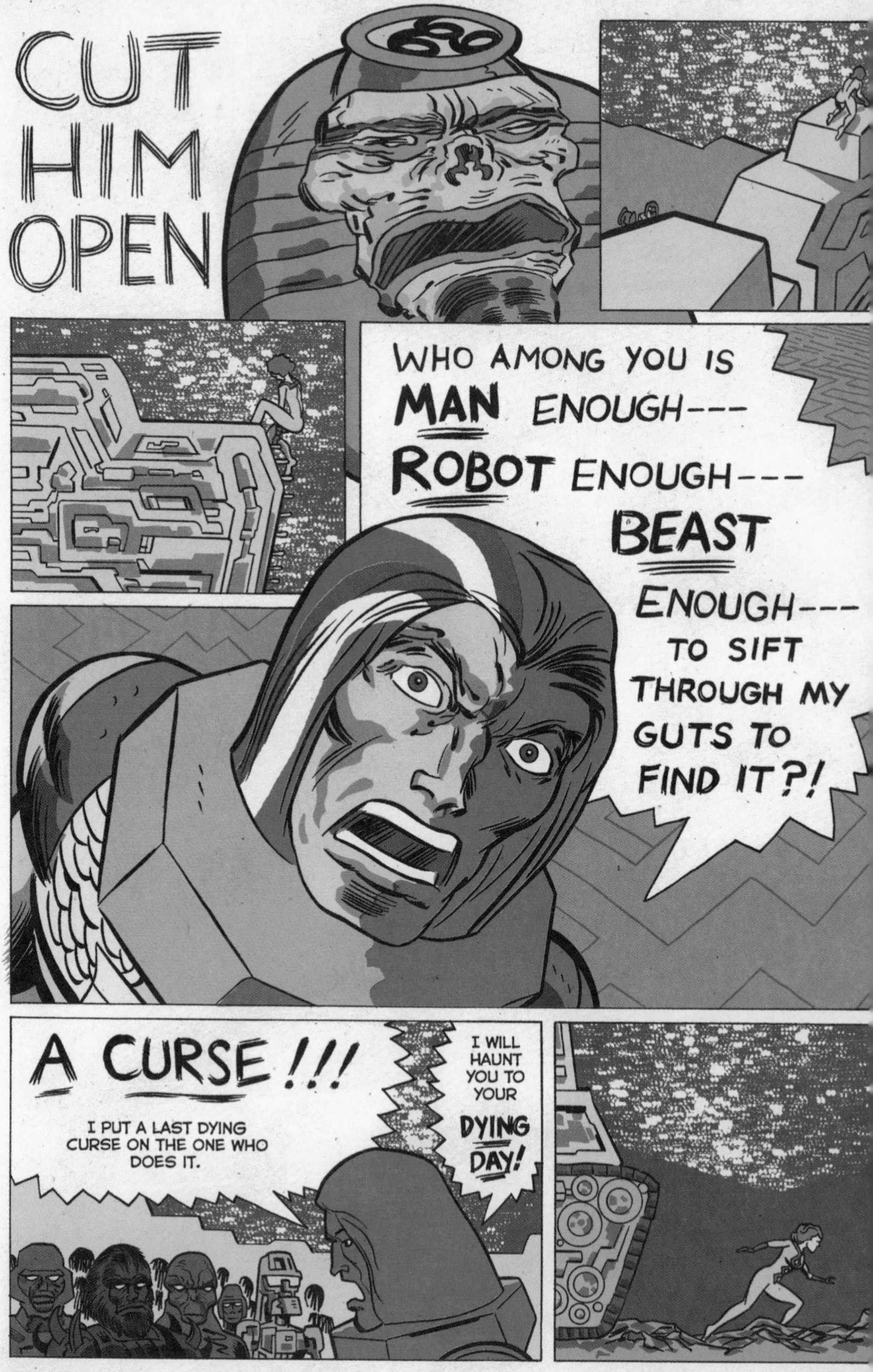
CUT HIM OPEN
WHO AMONG YOU IS MAN ENOUGH--- ROBOT ENOUGH--- BEAST ENOUGH--- TO SIFT THROUGH MY GUTS TO FIND IT?!
A CURSE!!!
I PUT A LAST DYING CURSE ON THE ONE WHO DOES IT.
I WILL HAUNT YOU TO YOUR DYING DAY!

ENOUGH HISTRIONICS!

THE KEY WAS TIED TO HIS GOOFY HAIR THE WHOLE TIME.

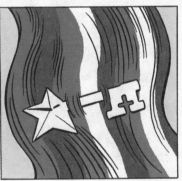

I KNEW I SAW SOMETHING WHEN HE FOUGHT BAD AZZ.

I HAVE WHAT I WANT... NOW HOW SHOULD WE KILL HIM?

DEATH BY DINOSAUR!

LEMME POP HIS EYES OUT!

GROO GRAA GROGGLE!

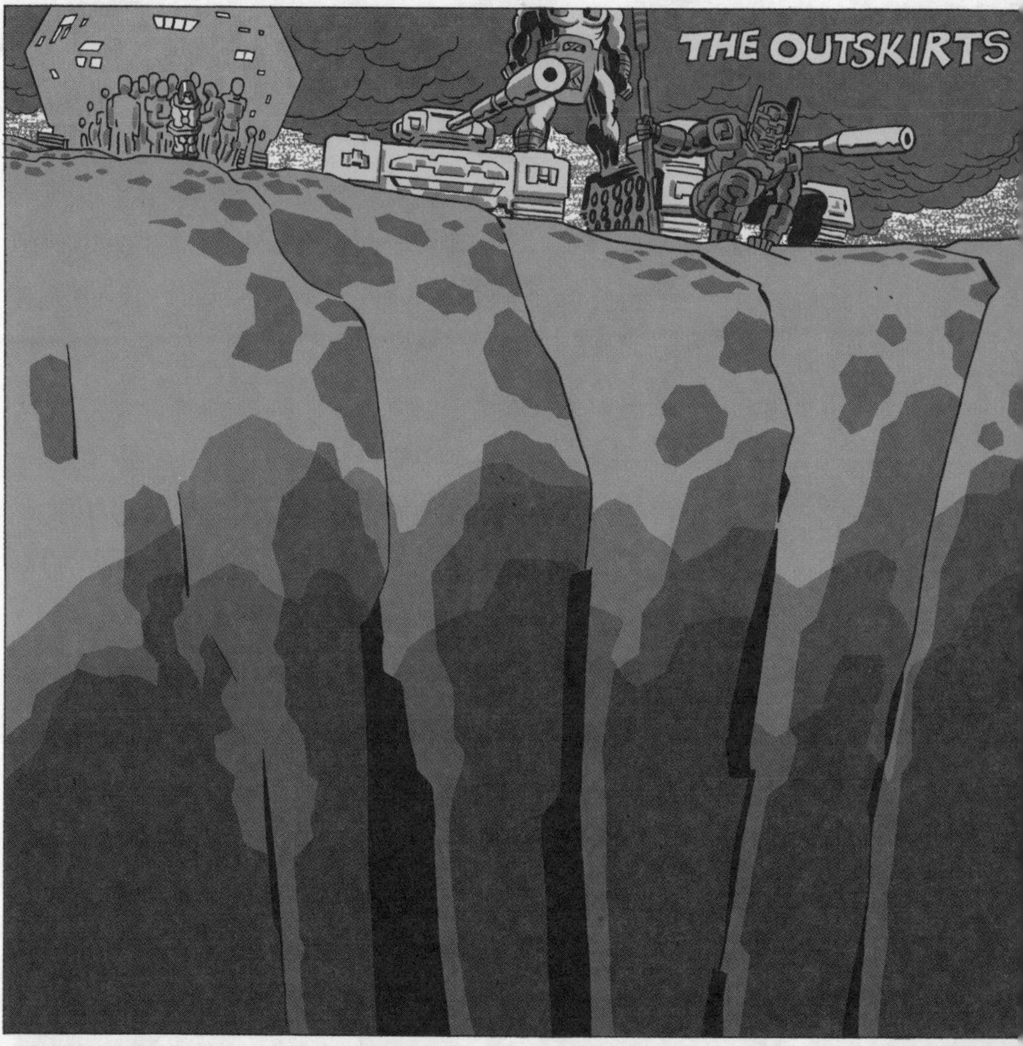
THE OUTSKIRTS
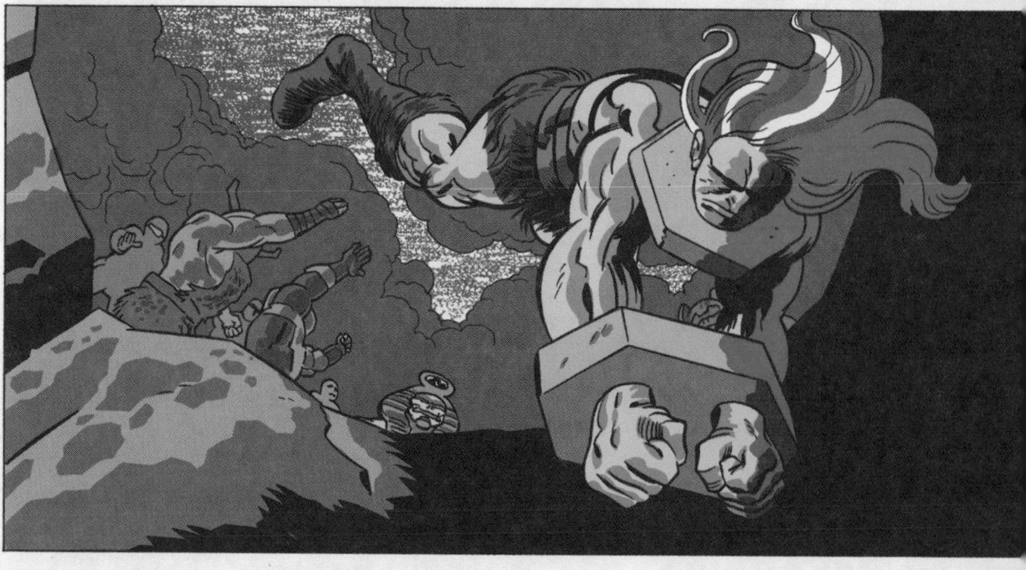

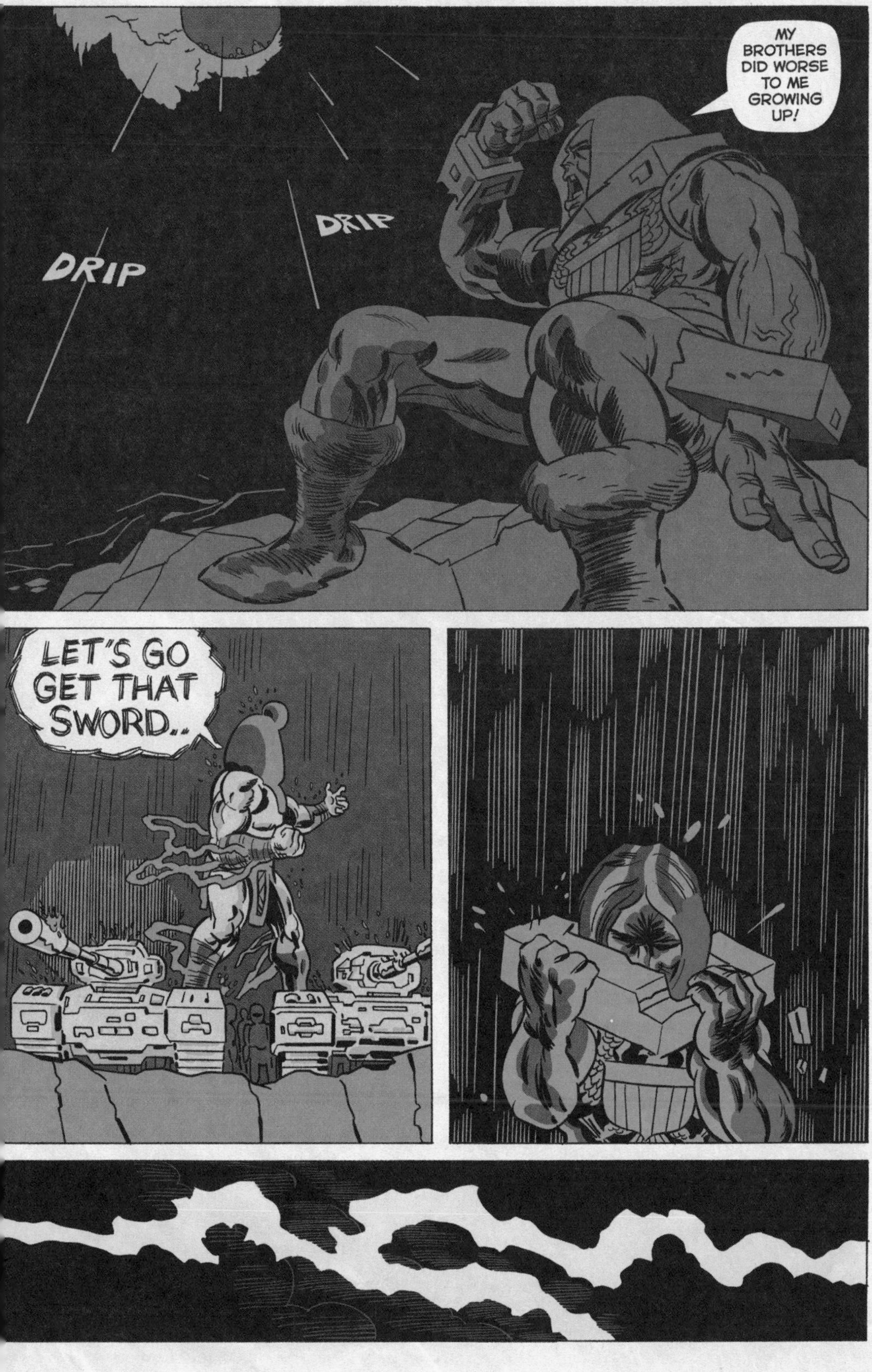

MY BROTHERS DID WORSE TO ME GROWING UP!
DRIP
DRIP
LET'S GO GET THAT SWORD..

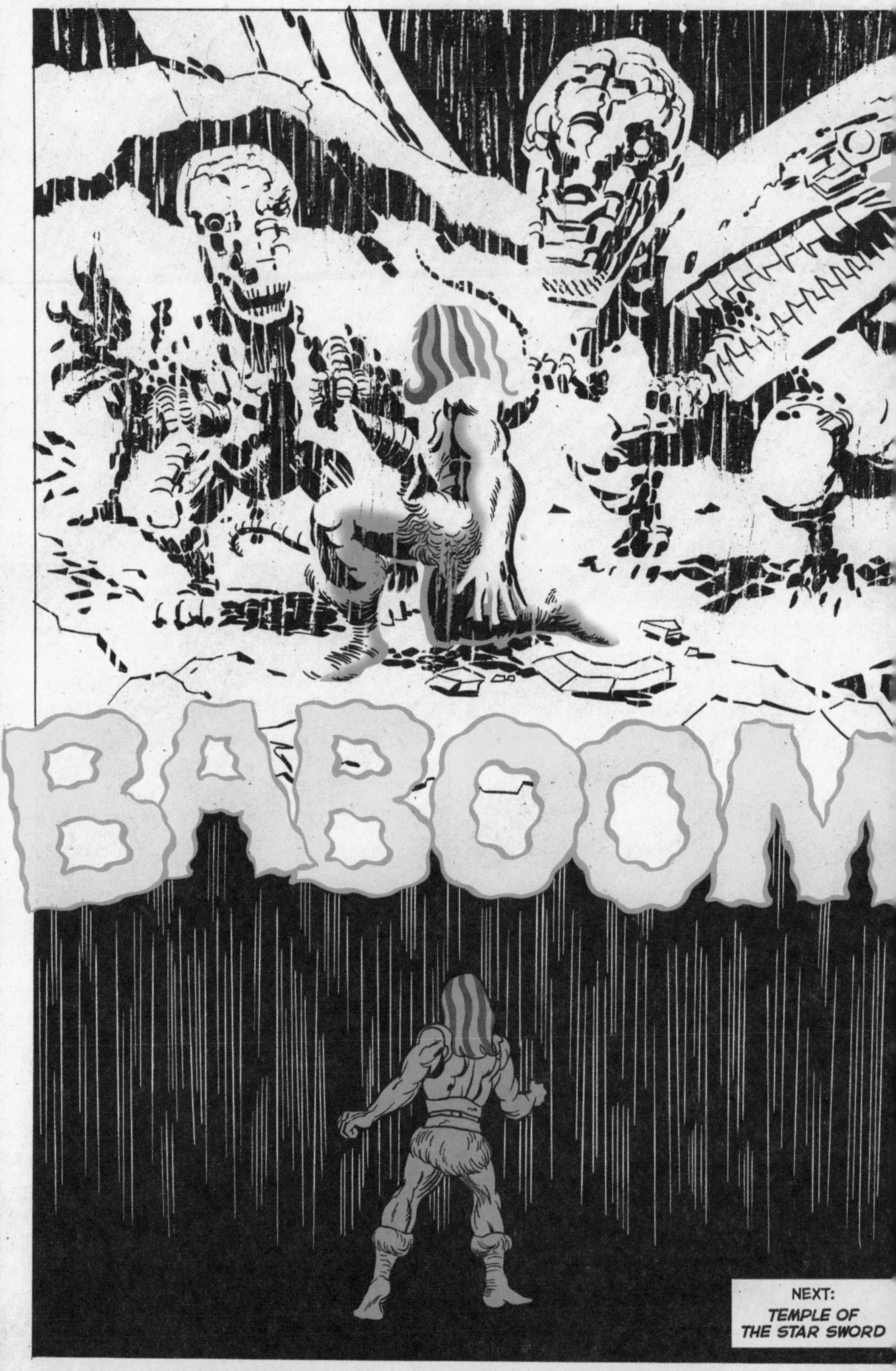

BABOOM
NEXT: TEMPLE OF THE STAR SWORD

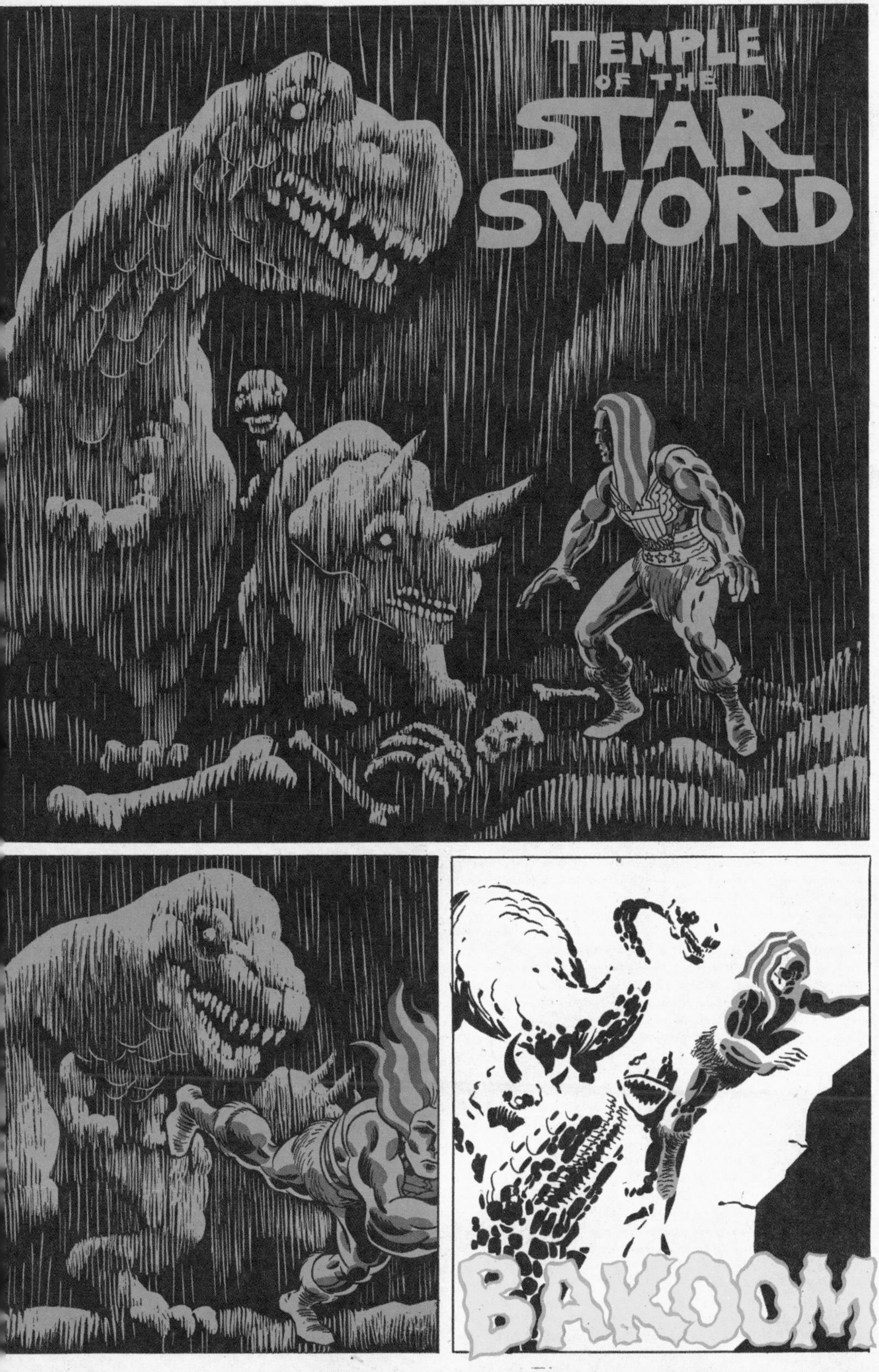
TEMPLE OF THE STAR SWORD
BAKOOM

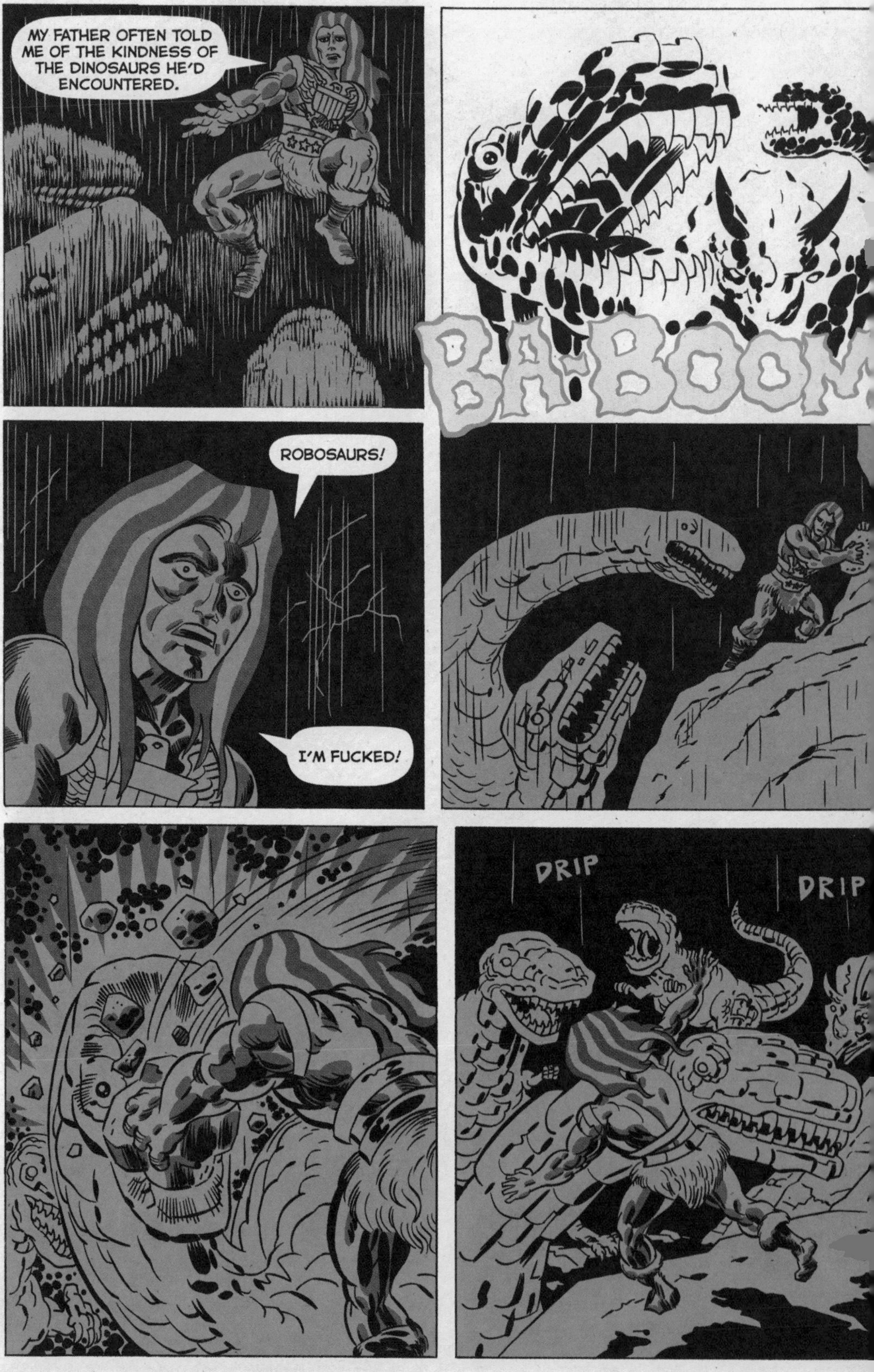
MY FATHER OFTEN TOLD ME OF THE KINDNESS OF THE DINOSAURS HE'D ENCOUNTERED.
BA-BOOM
ROBOSAURS!
I'M FUCKED!
DRIP
DRIP

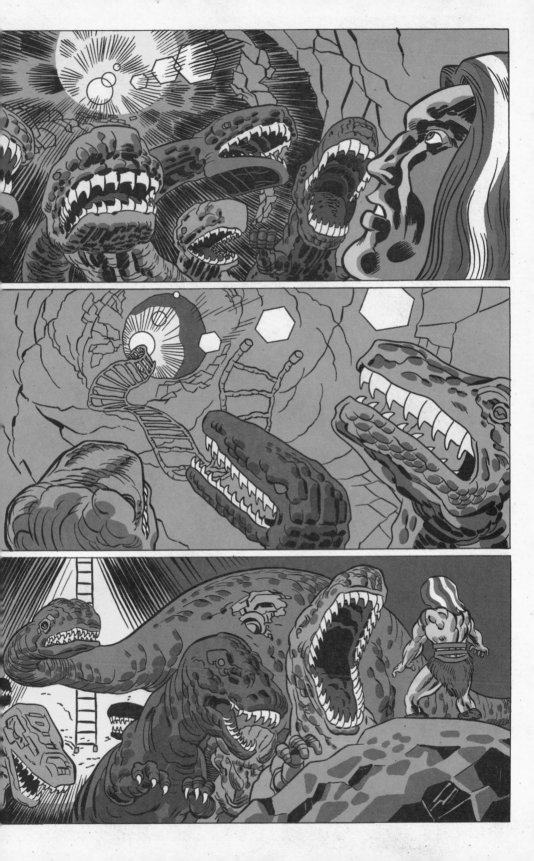

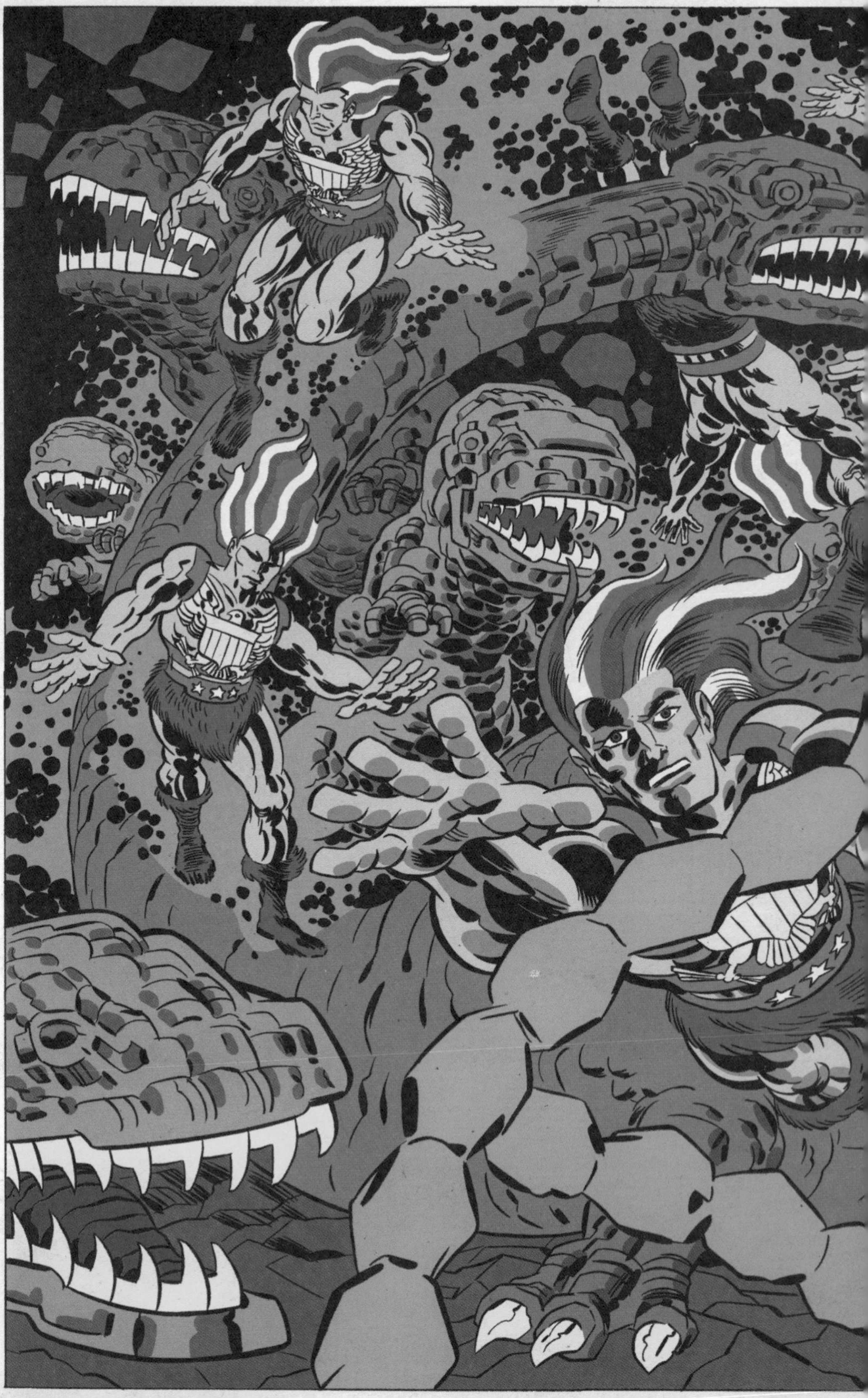

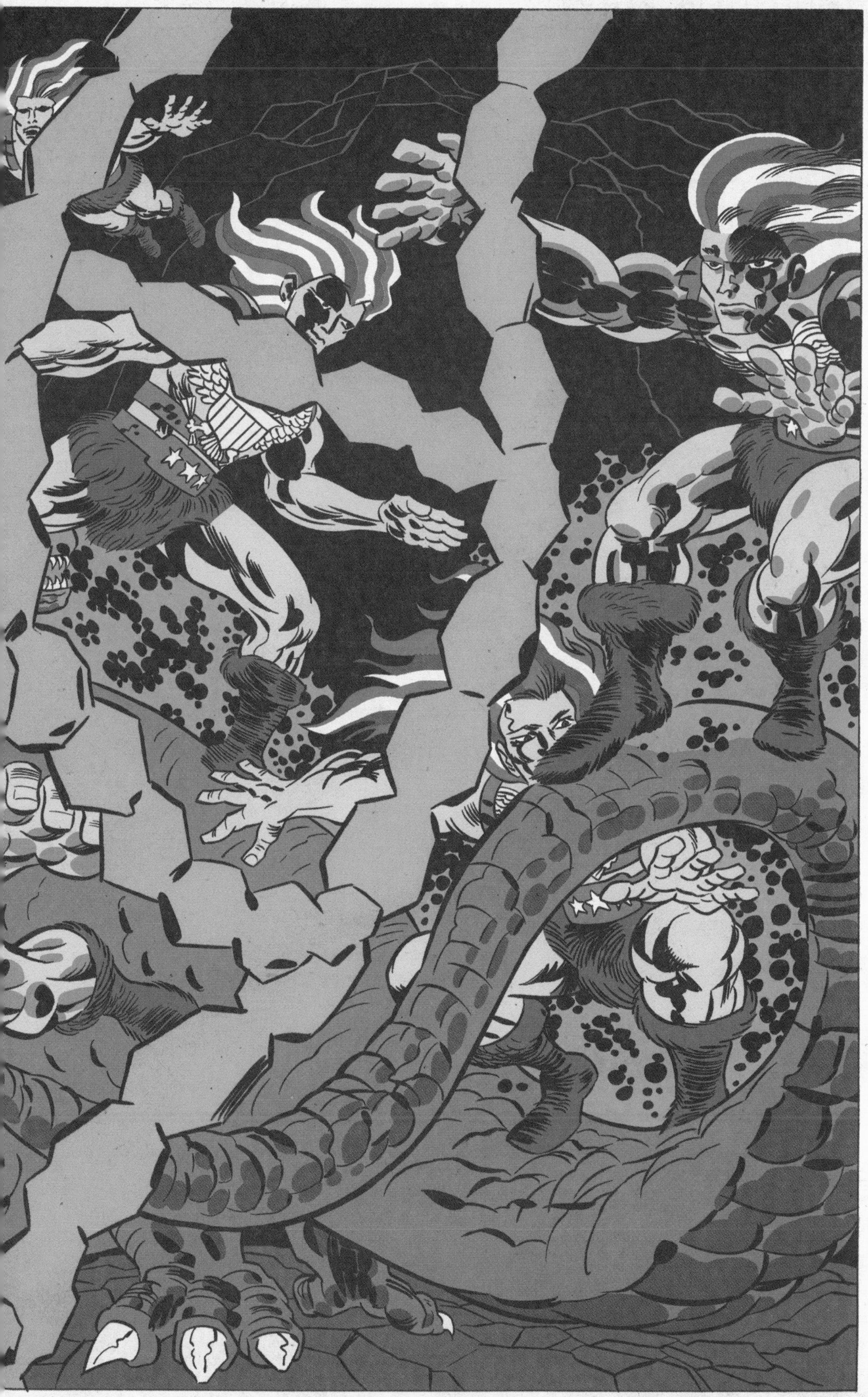

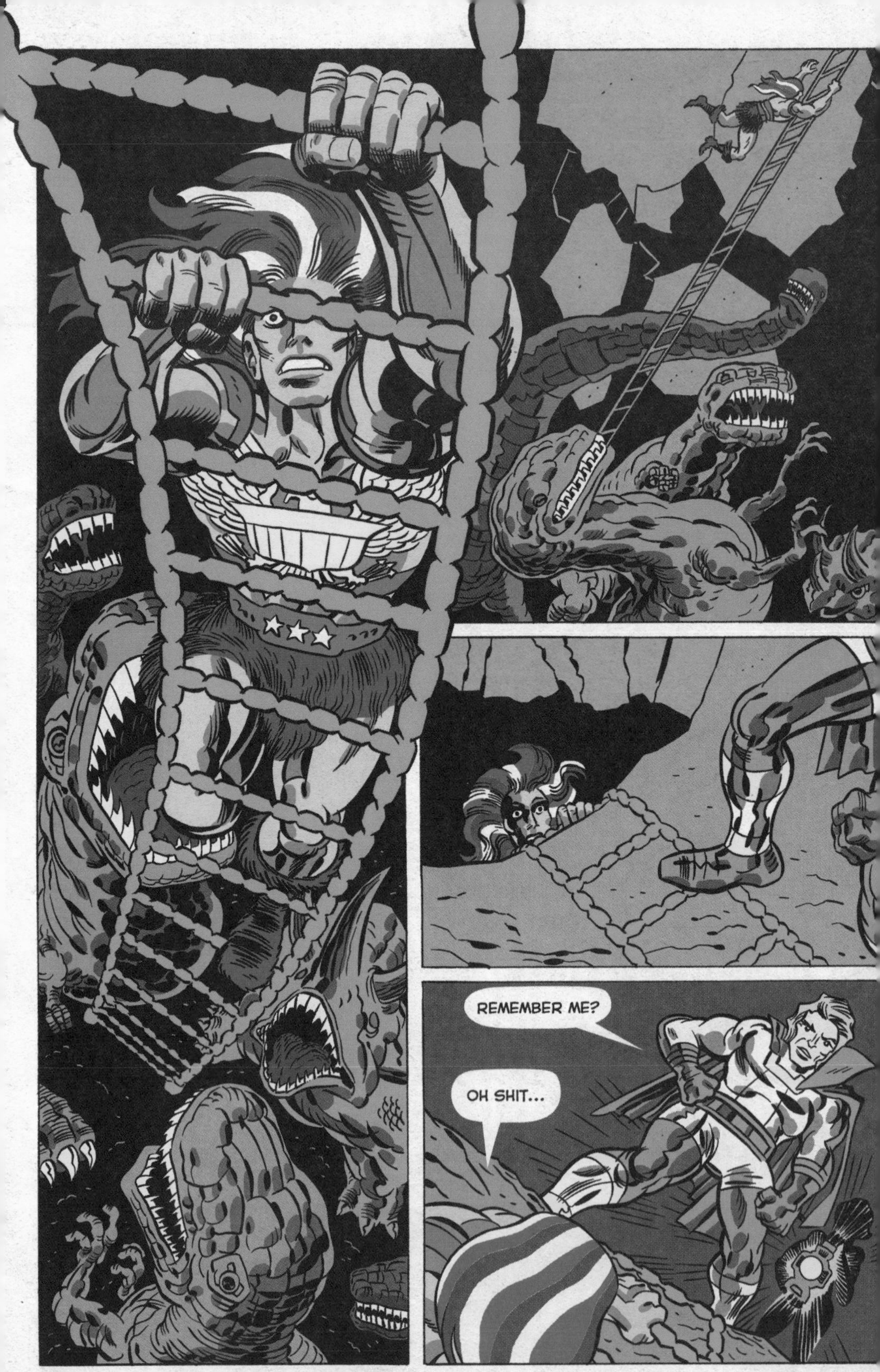
REMEMBER ME?
OH SHIT...

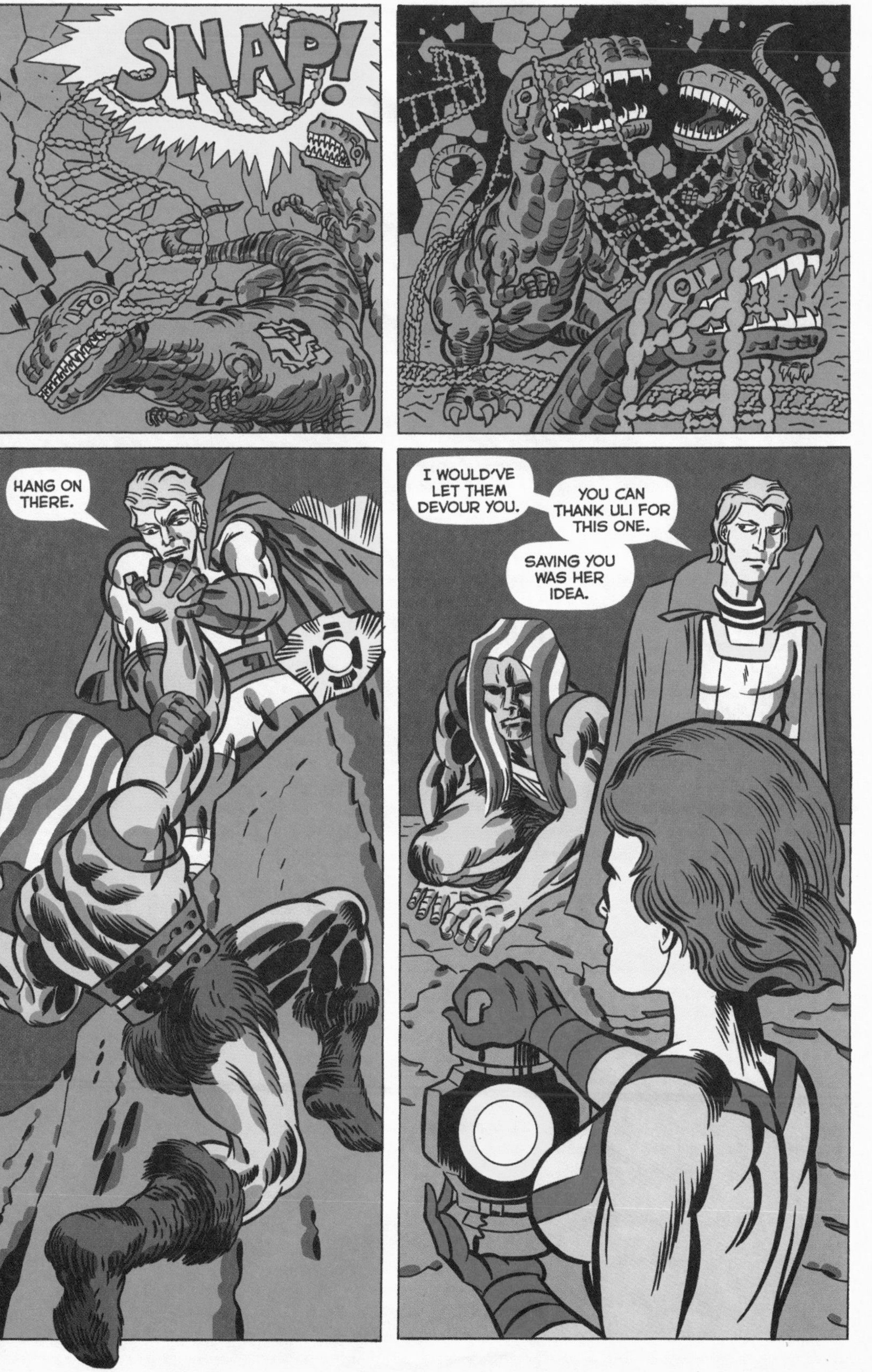
SNAP!
HANG ON THERE.
I WOULD'VE LET THEM DEVOUR YOU.
YOU CAN THANK ULI FOR THIS ONE.
SAVING YOU WAS HER IDEA.

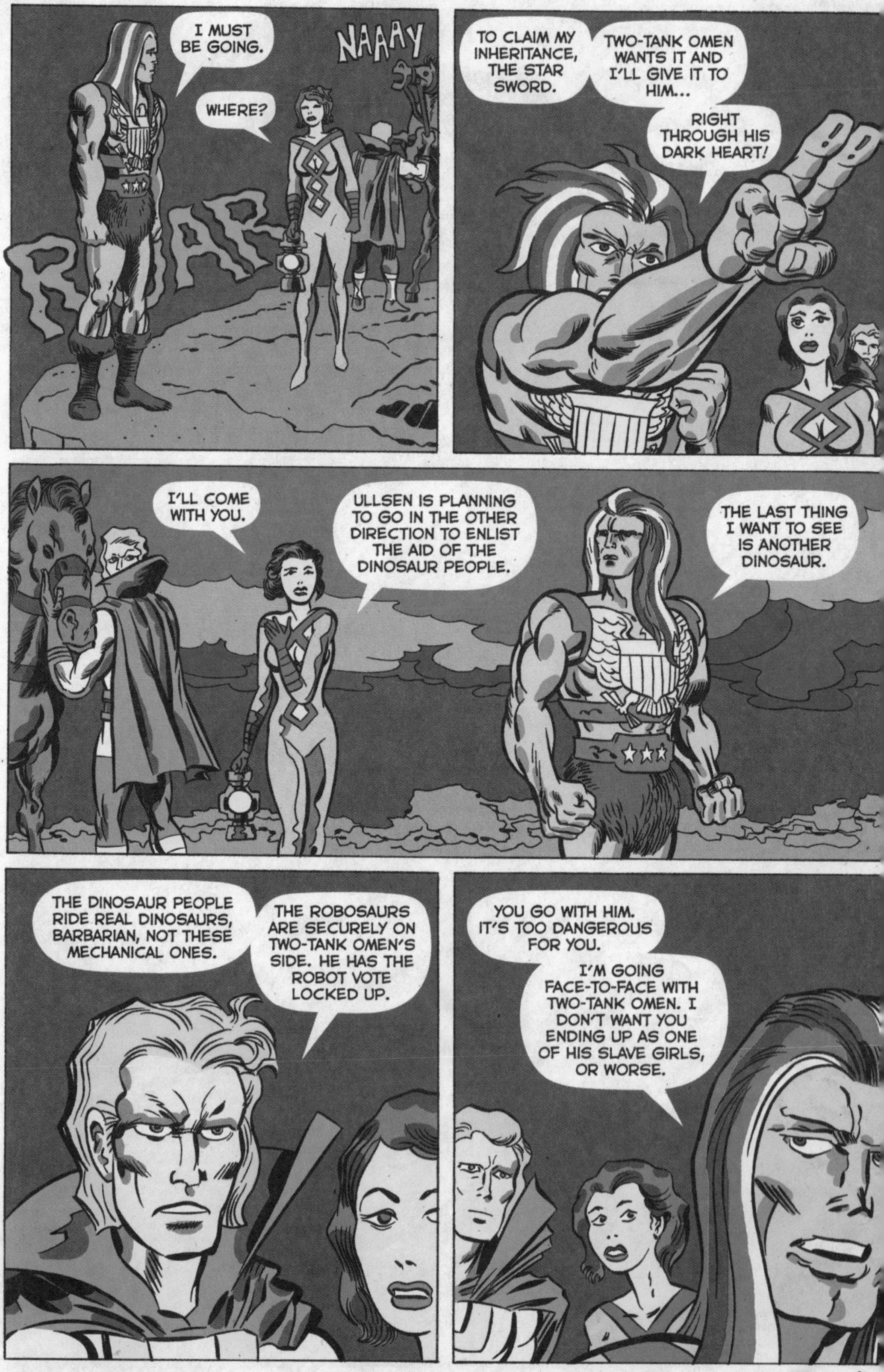
I MUST BE GOING.
NAAAY
WHERE?
ROAR
TO CLAIM MY INHERITANCE, THE STAR SWORD.
TWO-TANK OMEN WANTS IT AND I'LL GIVE IT TO HIM...
RIGHT THROUGH HIS DARK HEART!
I'LL COME WITH YOU.
ULLSEN IS PLANNING TO GO IN THE OTHER DIRECTION TO ENLIST THE AID OF THE DINOSAUR PEOPLE.
THE LAST THING I WANT TO SEE IS ANOTHER DINOSAUR.
THE DINOSAUR PEOPLE RIDE REAL DINOSAURS, BARBARIAN, NOT THESE MECHANICAL ONES.
THE ROBOSAURS ARE SECURELY ON TWO-TANK OMEN'S SIDE. HE HAS THE ROBOT VOTE LOCKED UP.
YOU GO WITH HIM. IT'S TOO DANGEROUS FOR YOU.
I'M GOING FACE-TO-FACE WITH TWO-TANK OMEN. I DON'T WANT YOU ENDING UP AS ONE OF HIS SLAVE GIRLS, OR WORSE.

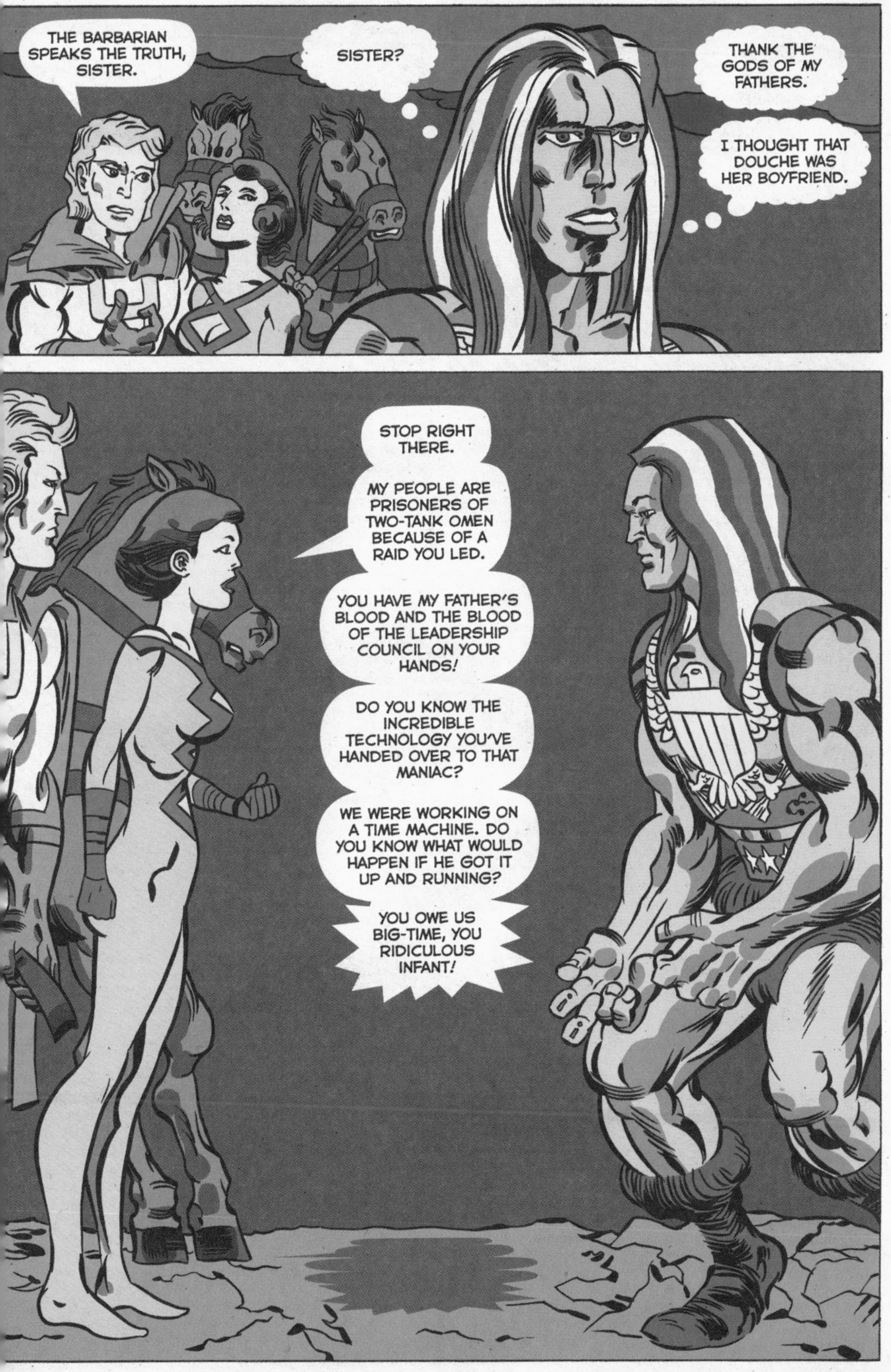
THE BARBARIAN SPEAKS THE TRUTH, SISTER.
SISTER?
THANK THE GODS OF MY FATHERS.
I THOUGHT THAT DOUCHE WAS HER BOYFRIEND.
STOP RIGHT THERE.
MY PEOPLE ARE PRISONERS OF TWO-TANK OMEN BECAUSE OF A RAID YOU LED.
YOU HAVE MY FATHER'S BLOOD AND THE BLOOD OF THE LEADERSHIP COUNCIL ON YOUR HANDS!
DO YOU KNOW THE INCREDIBLE TECHNOLOGY YOU'VE HANDED OVER TO THAT MANIAC?
WE WERE WORKING ON A TIME MACHINE. DO YOU KNOW WHAT WOULD HAPPEN IF HE GOT IT UP AND RUNNING?
YOU OWE US BIG-TIME, YOU RIDICULOUS INFANT!

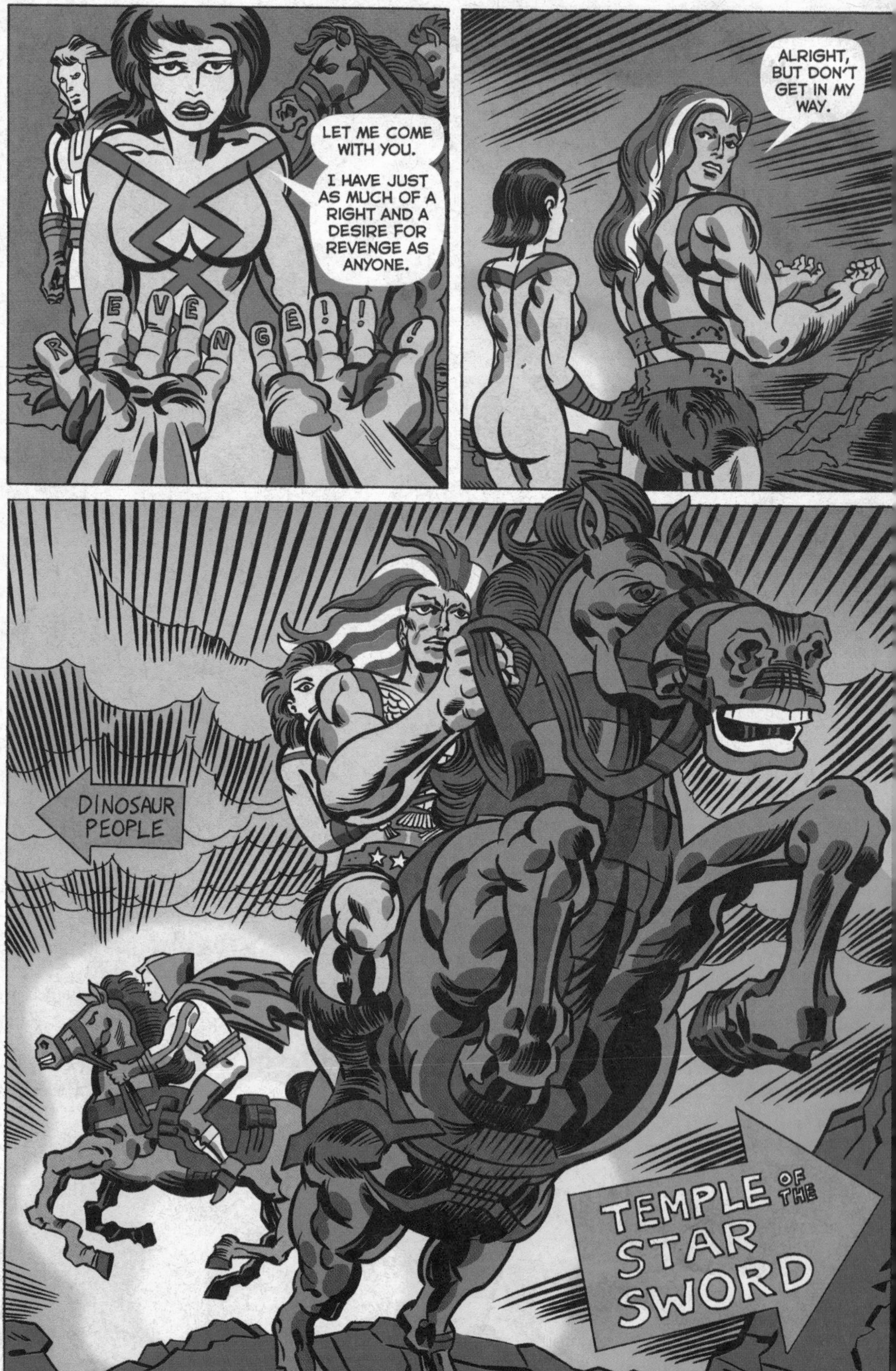
LET ME COME WITH YOU.
I HAVE JUST AS MUCH OF A RIGHT AND A DESIRE FOR REVENGE AS ANYONE.
REVENGE!!!
ALRIGHT, BUT DON'T GET IN MY WAY.
DINOSAUR PEOPLE
TEMPLE OF THE STAR SWORD

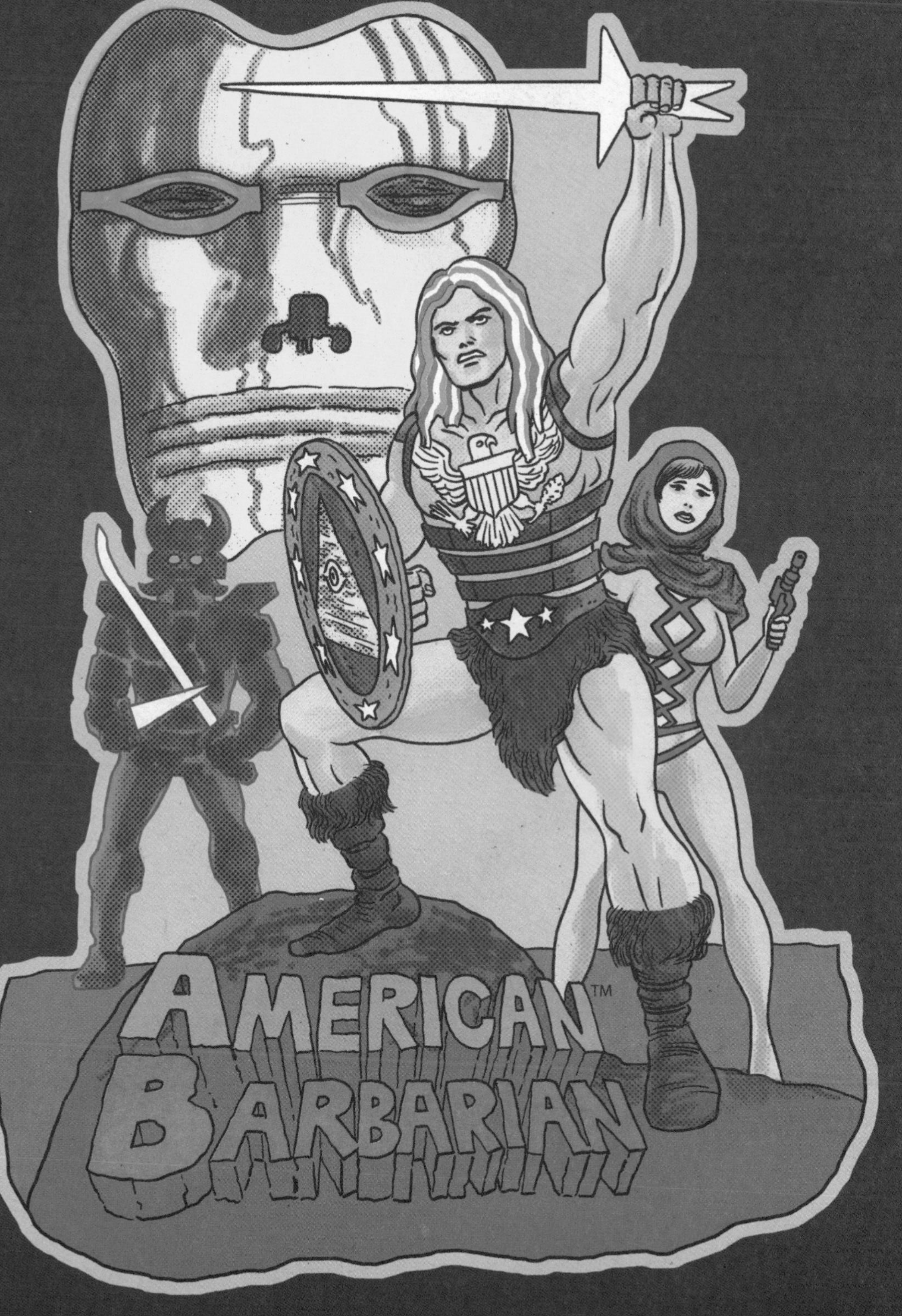
AMERICAN BARBARIAN™

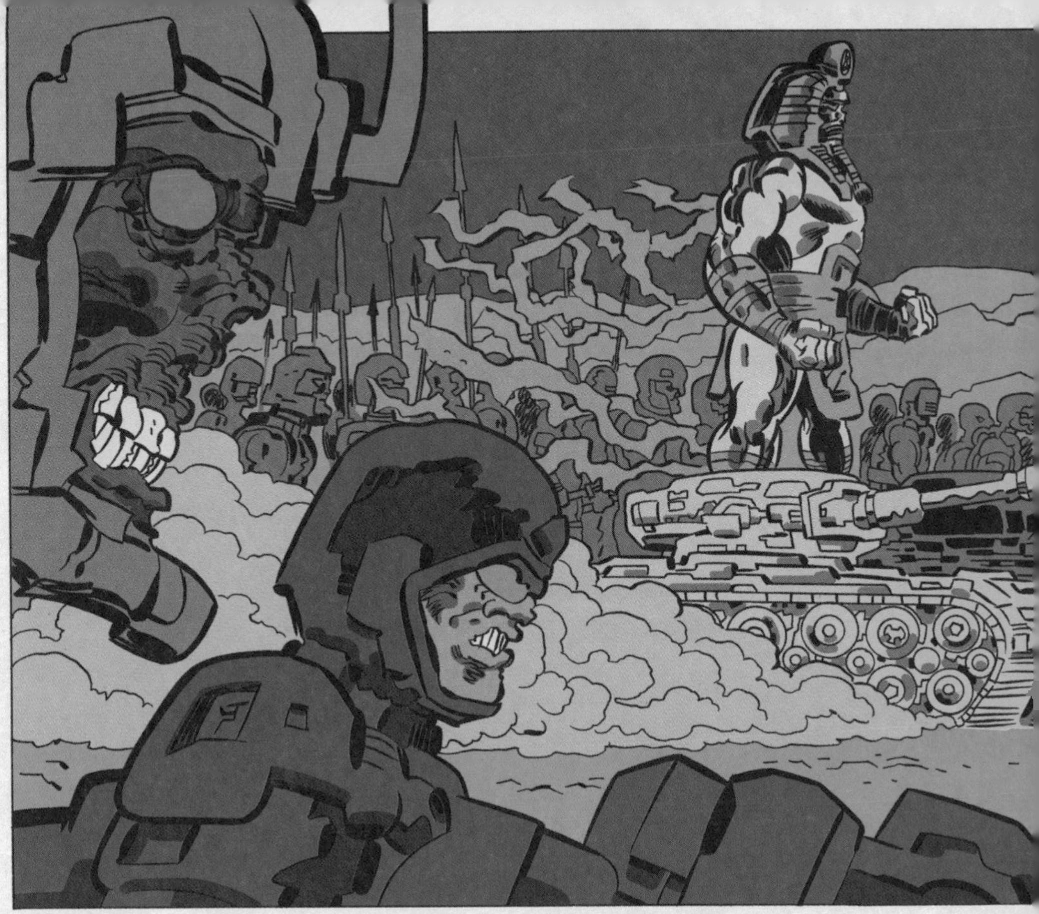

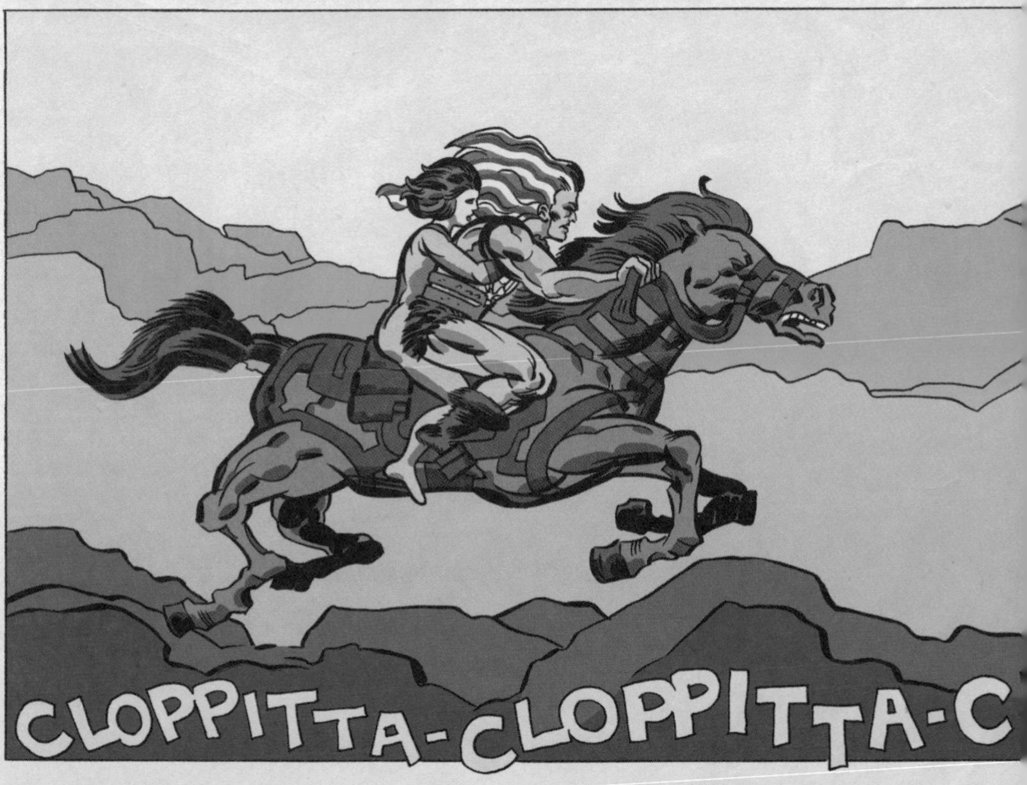
CLOPPITTA-CLOPPITTA-C

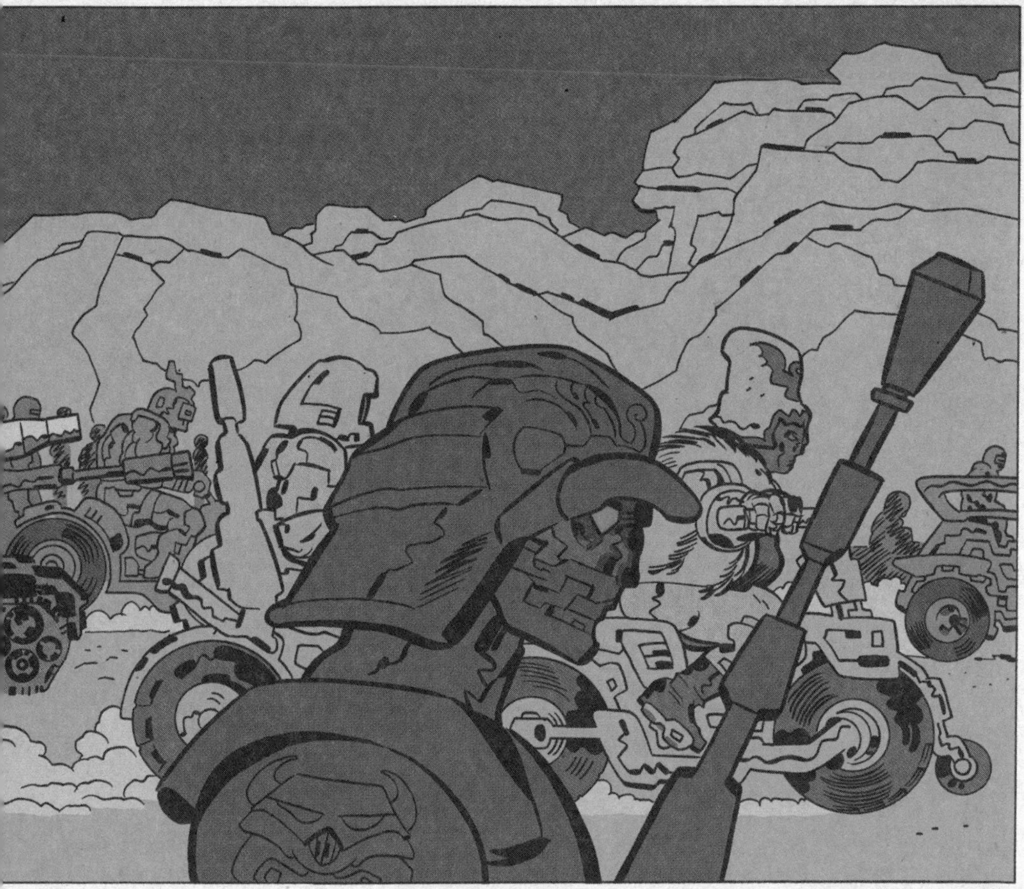

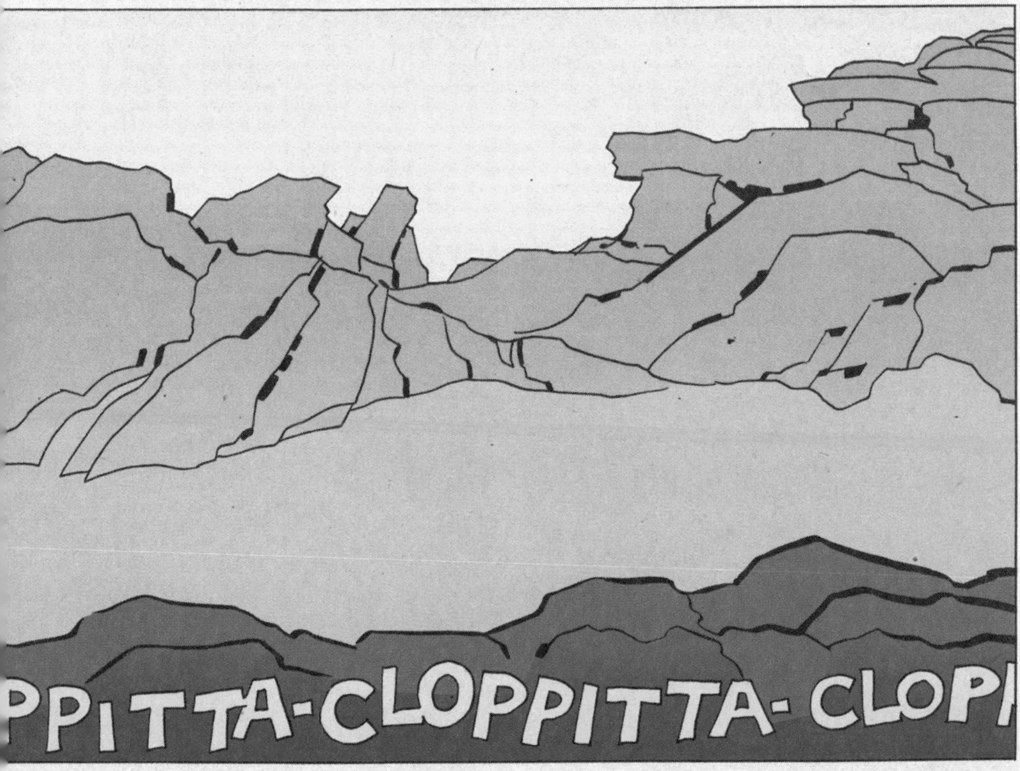
PPITTA-CLOPPITTA-CLOP

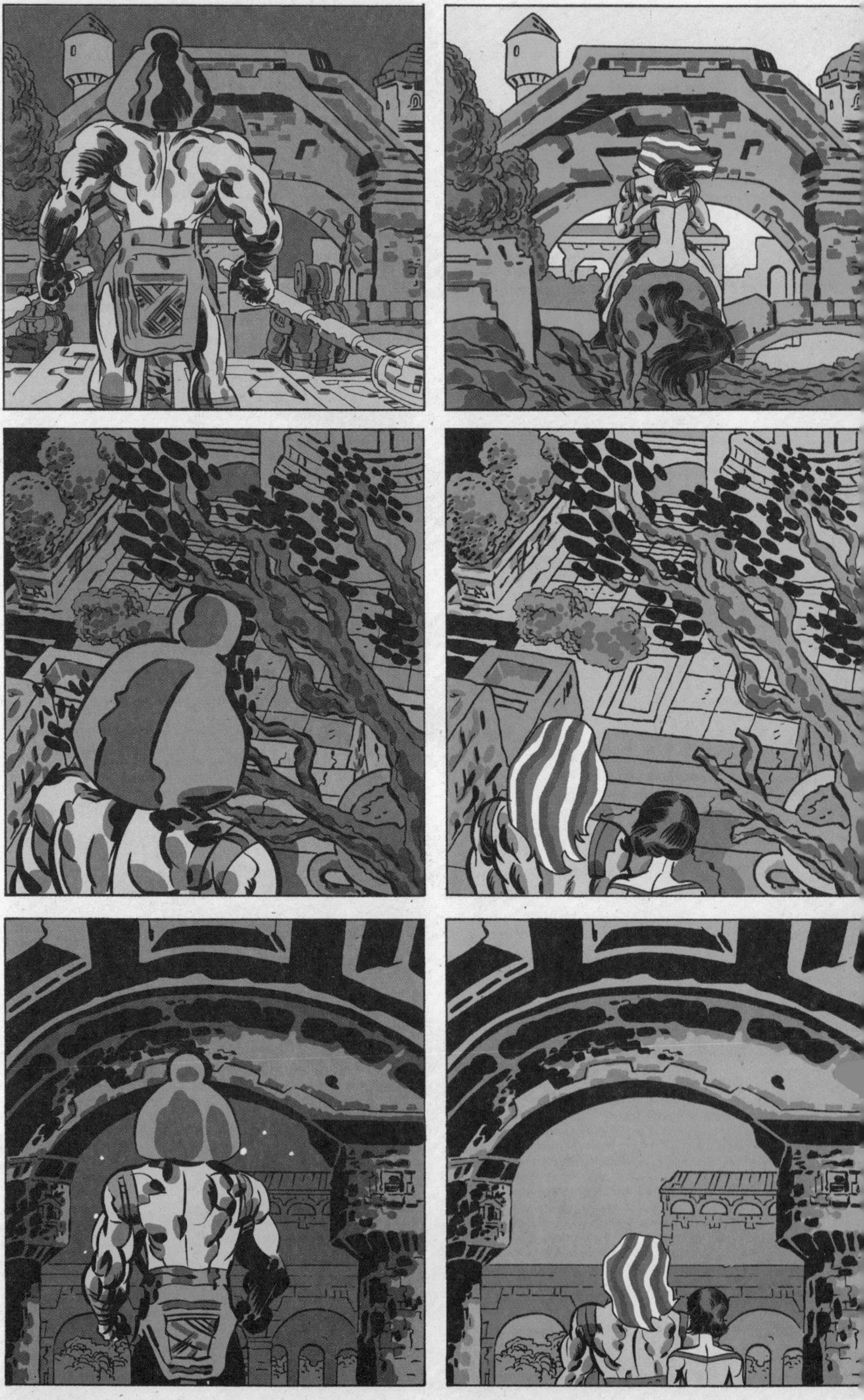

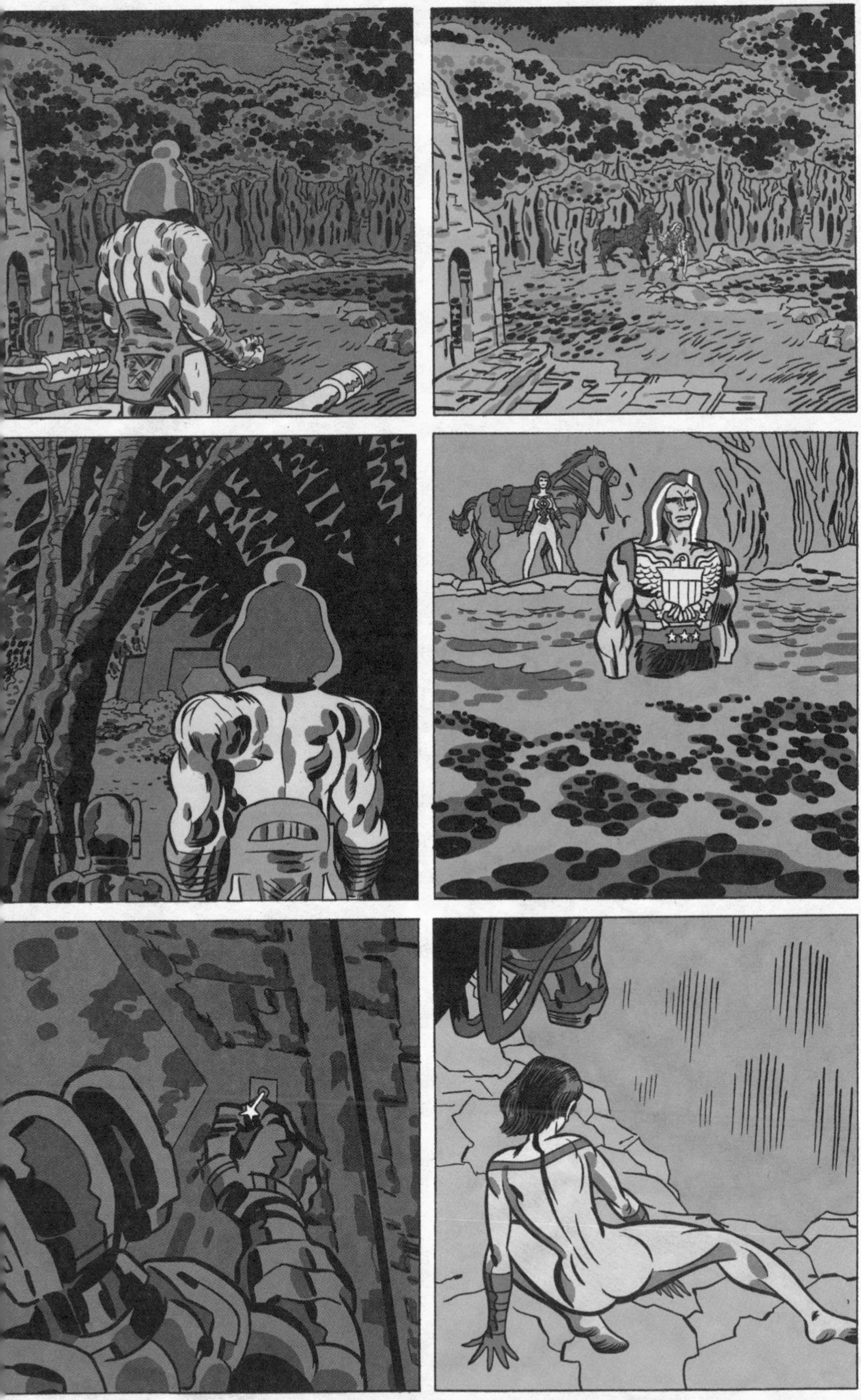

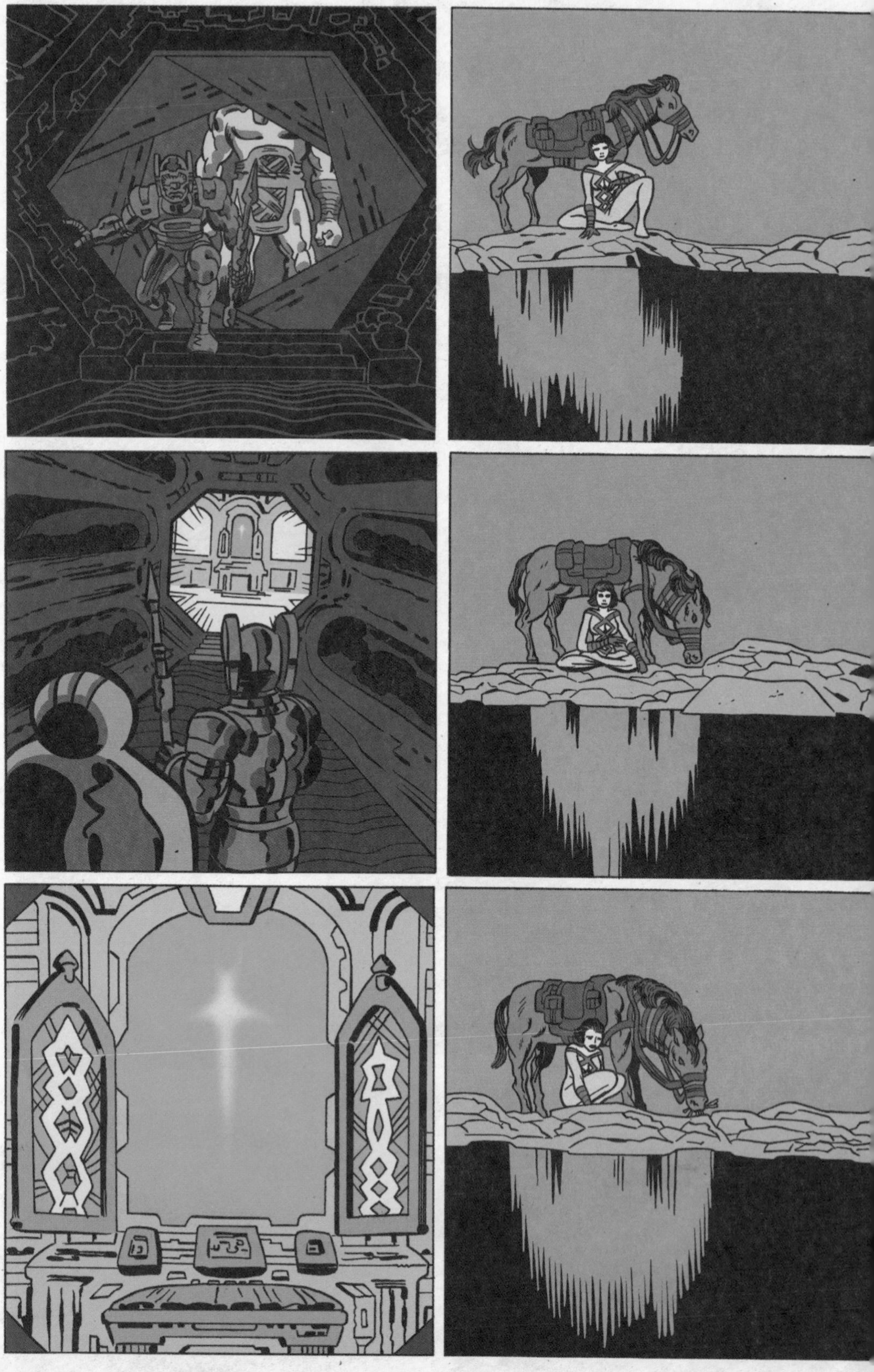

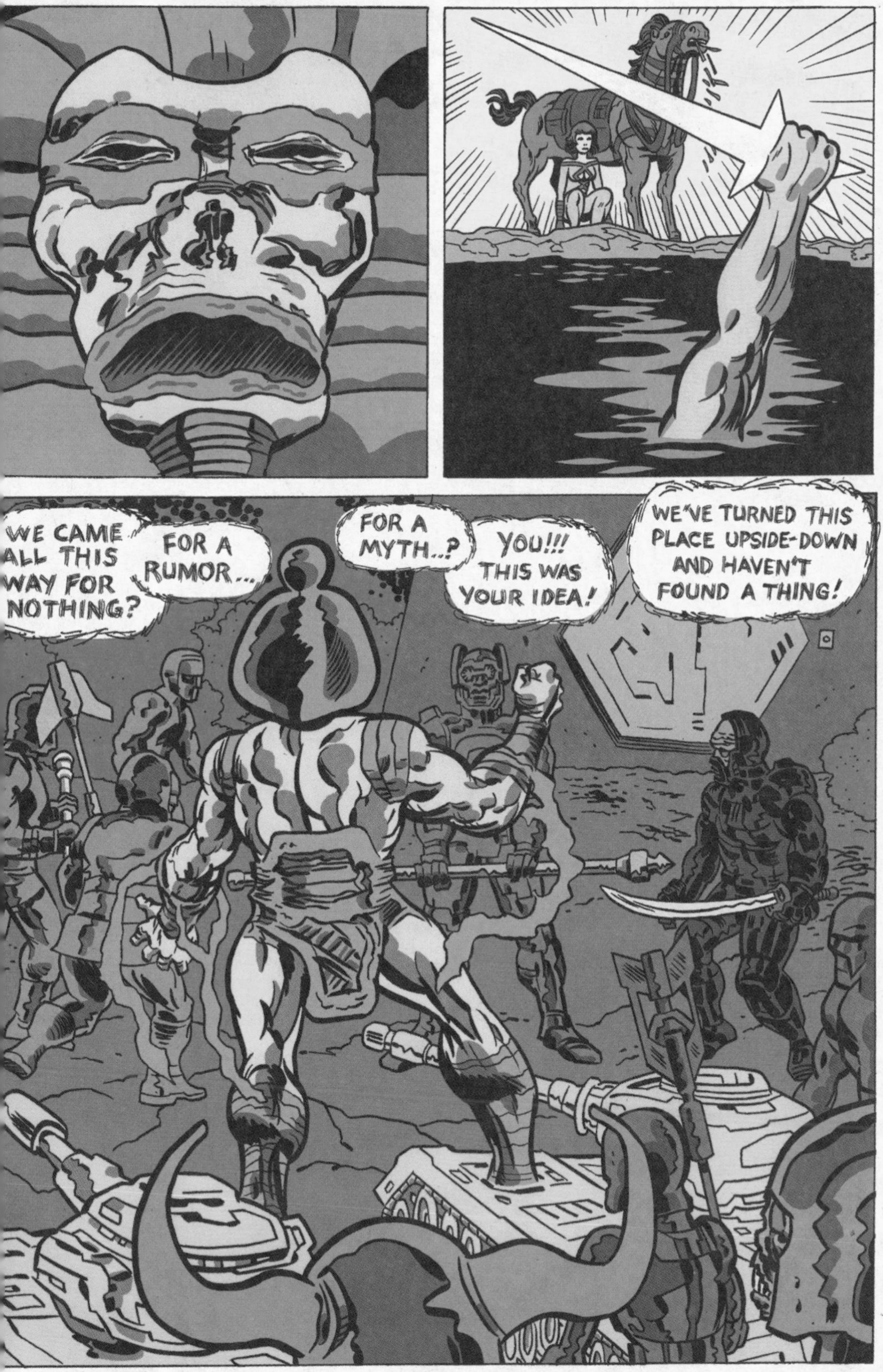
WE CAME ALL THIS WAY FOR NOTHING?
FOR A RUMOR...
FOR A MYTH..?
YOU!!! THIS WAS YOUR IDEA!
WE'VE TURNED THIS PLACE UPSIDE-DOWN AND HAVEN'T FOUND A THING!

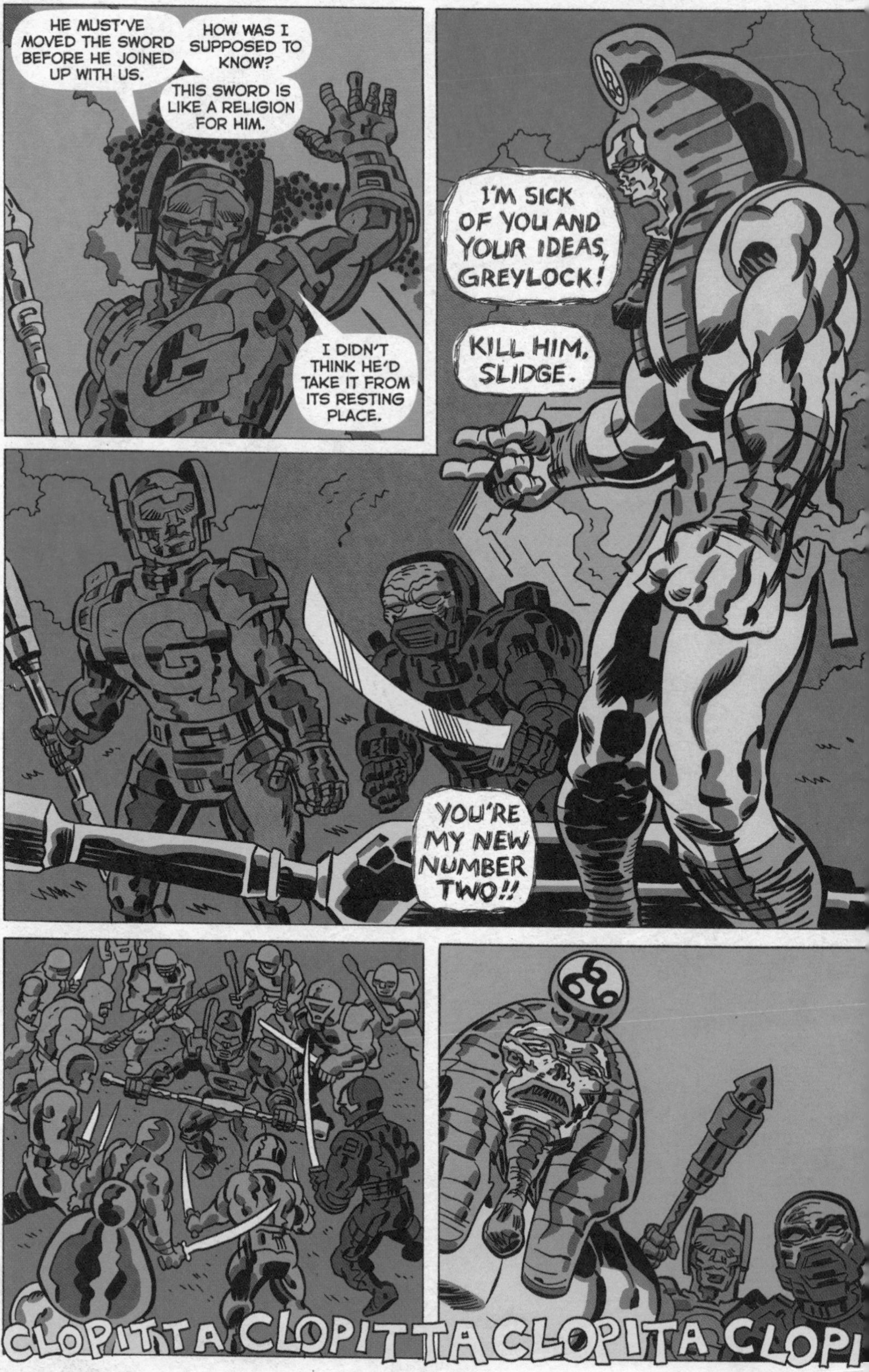
HE MUST'VE MOVED THE SWORD BEFORE HE JOINED UP WITH US.
HOW WAS I SUPPOSED TO KNOW?
THIS SWORD IS LIKE A RELIGION FOR HIM.
I DIDN'T THINK HE'D TAKE IT FROM ITS RESTING PLACE.
I'M SICK OF YOU AND YOUR IDEAS, GREYLOCK!
KILL HIM, SLIDGE.
YOU'RE MY NEW NUMBER TWO!!
CLOPITTA CLOPITTA CLOPITA CLOPI

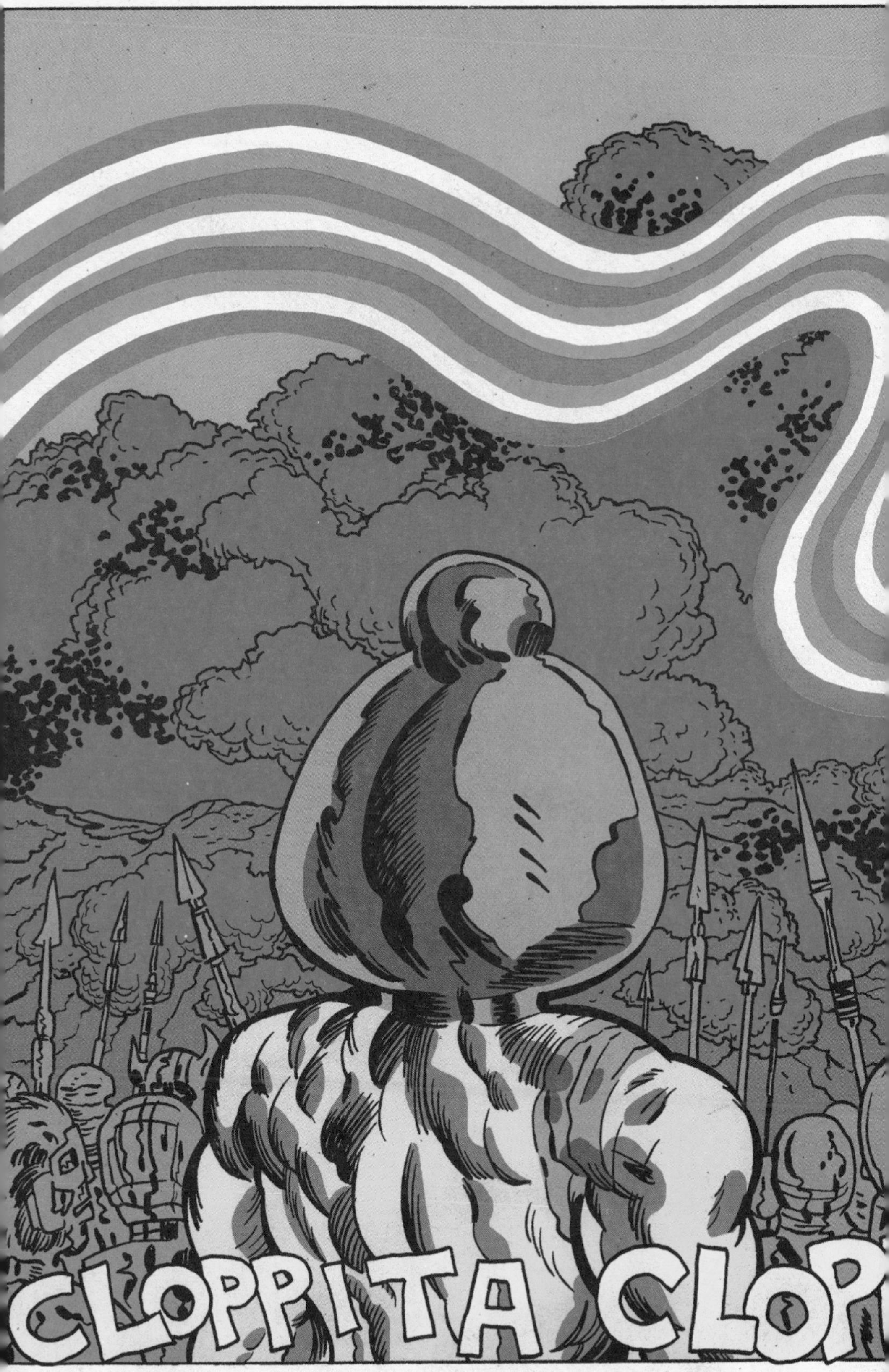
CLOPPITA CLOP

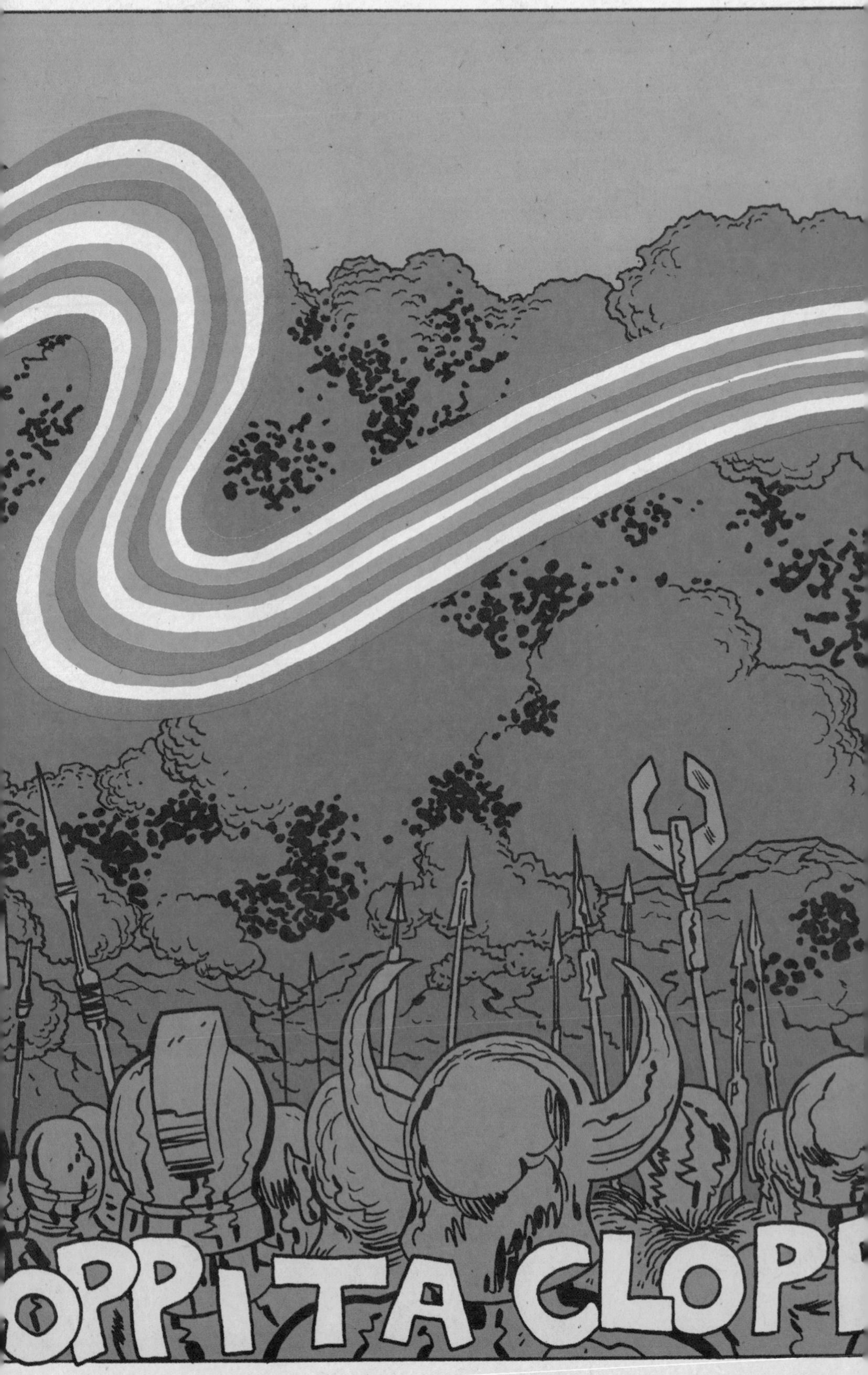
OPPITA CLOP

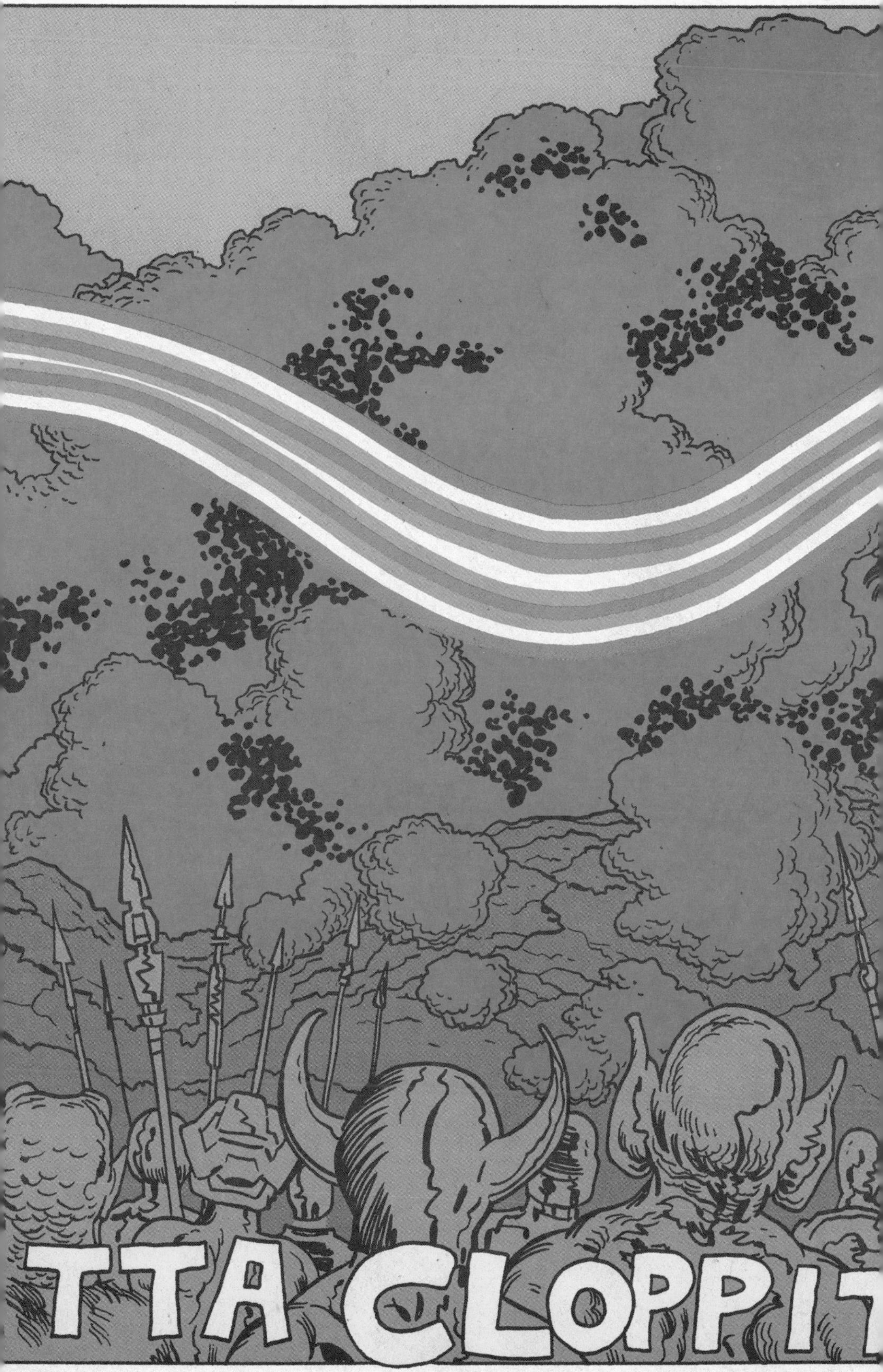
TTA CLOPPIT

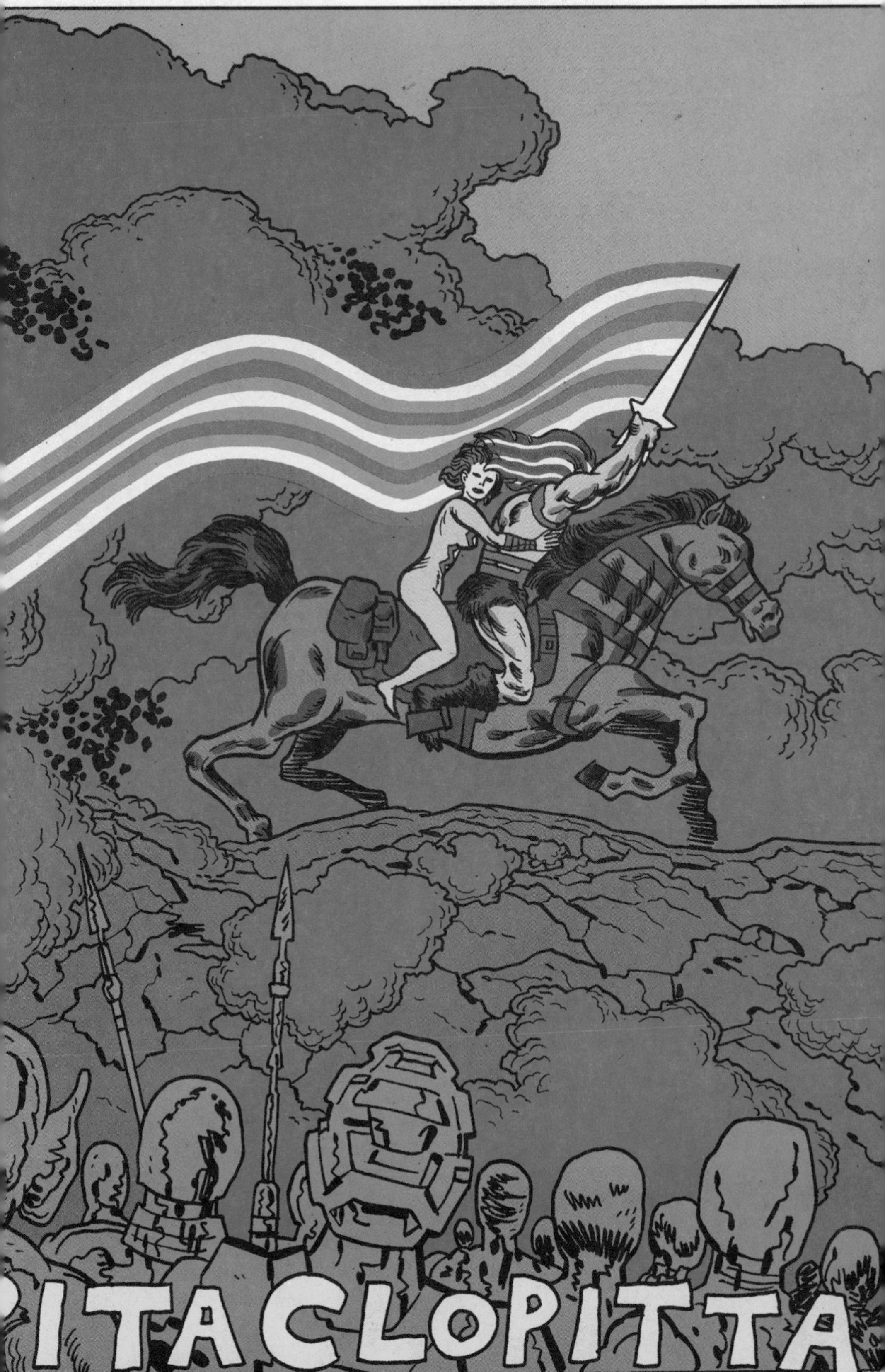
ITACLOPITTA

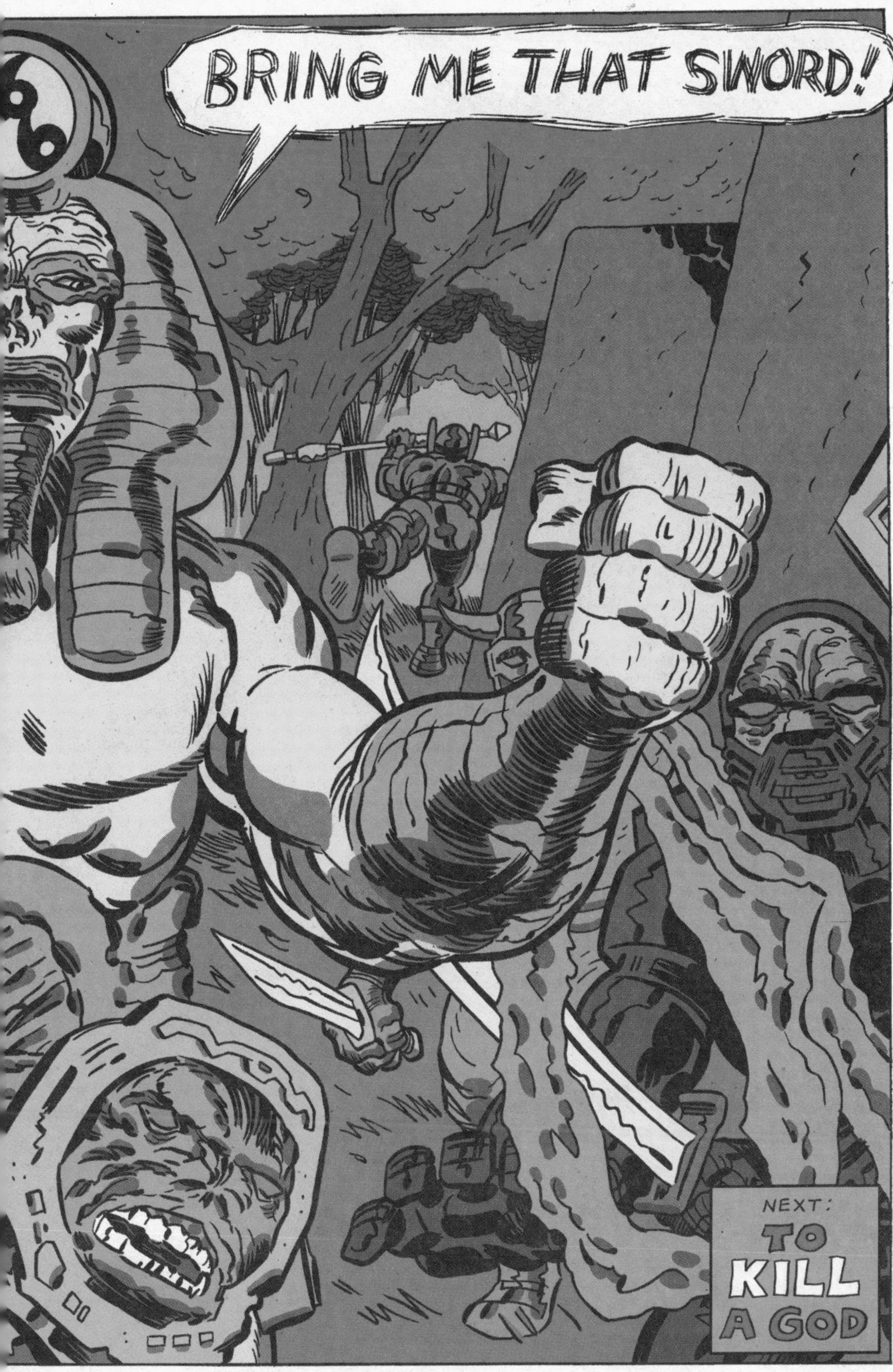
BRING ME THAT SWORD!
NEXT:
TO
KILL
A GOD

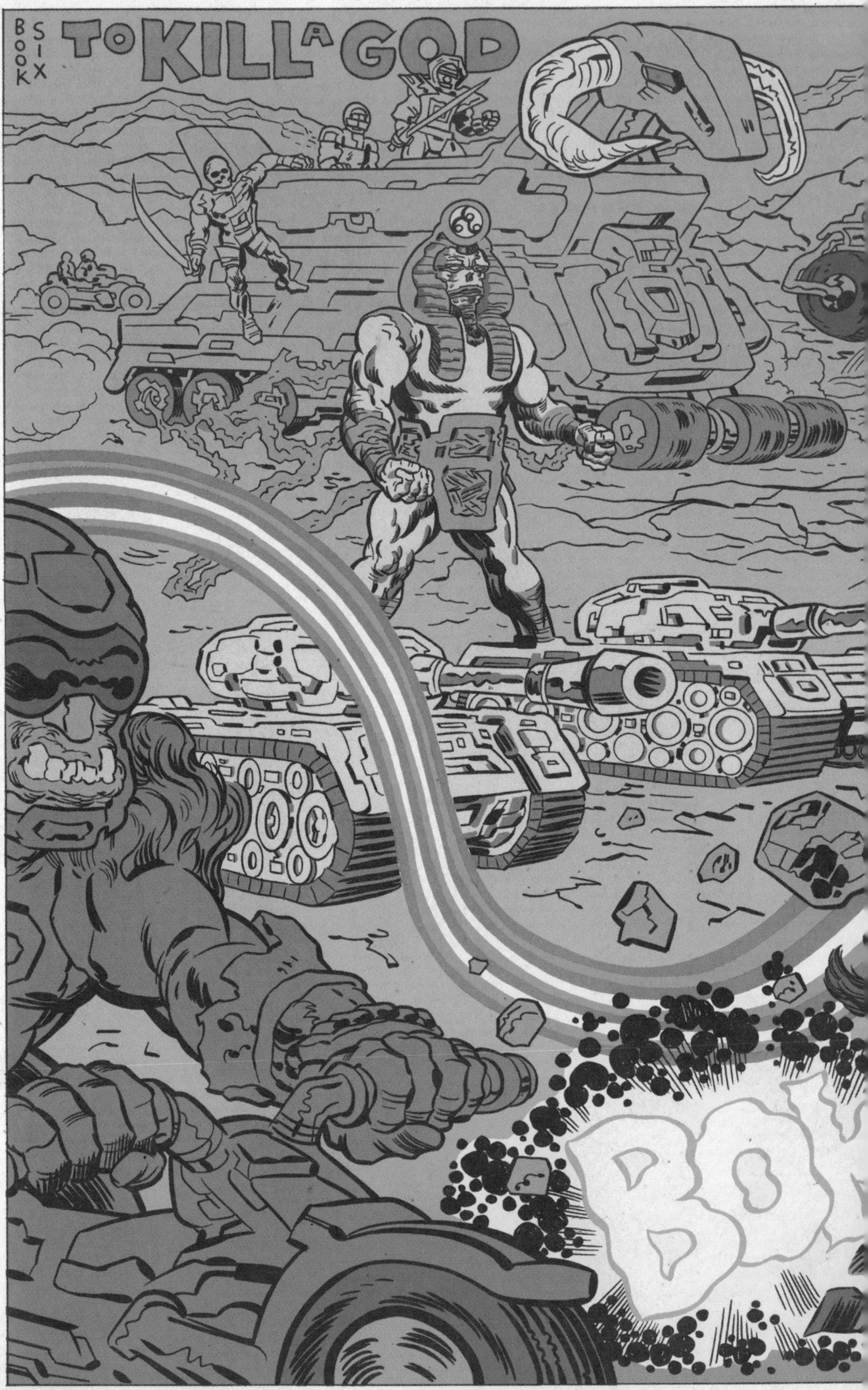
BOOK SIX
TO KILL A GOD

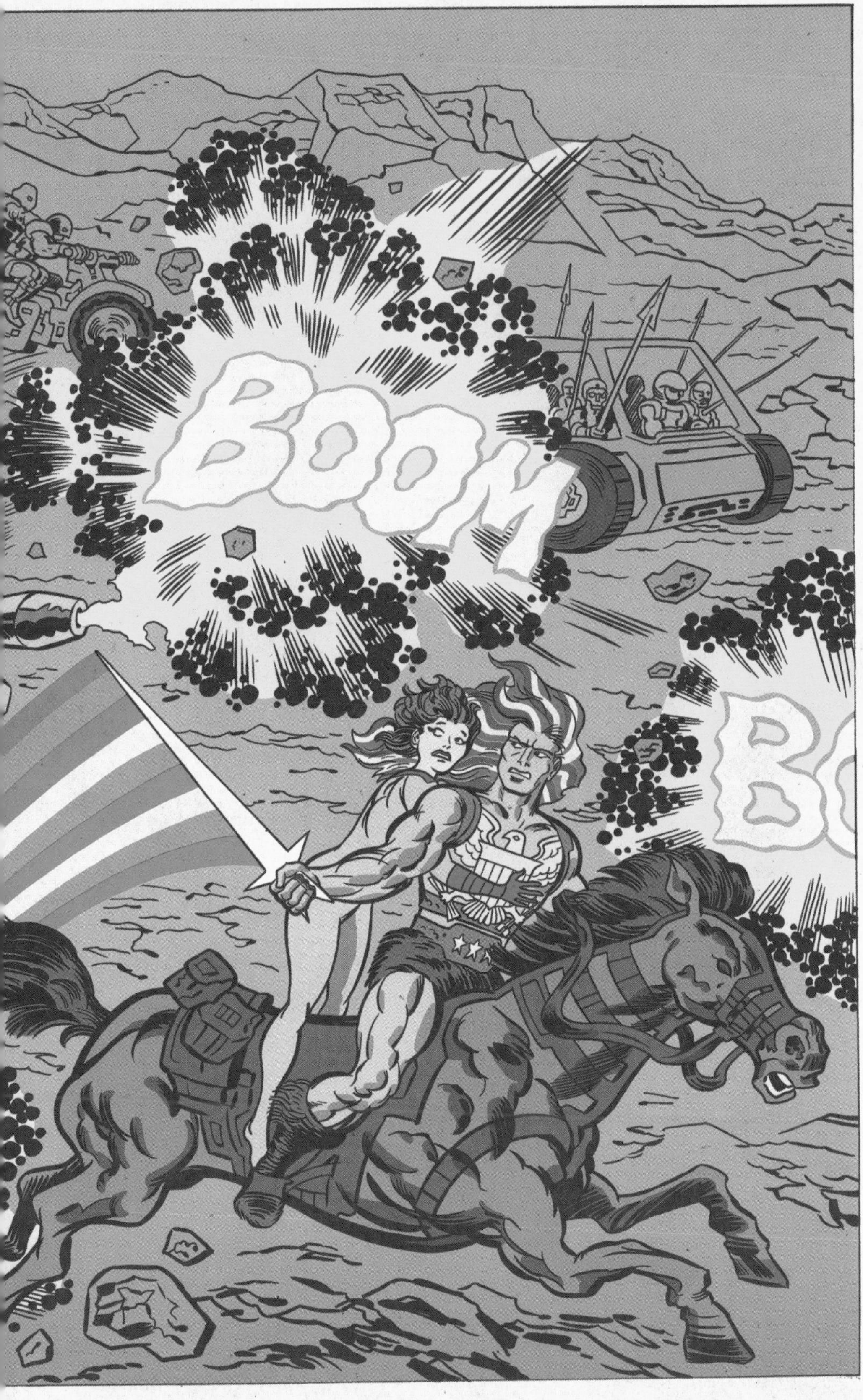
BOOM

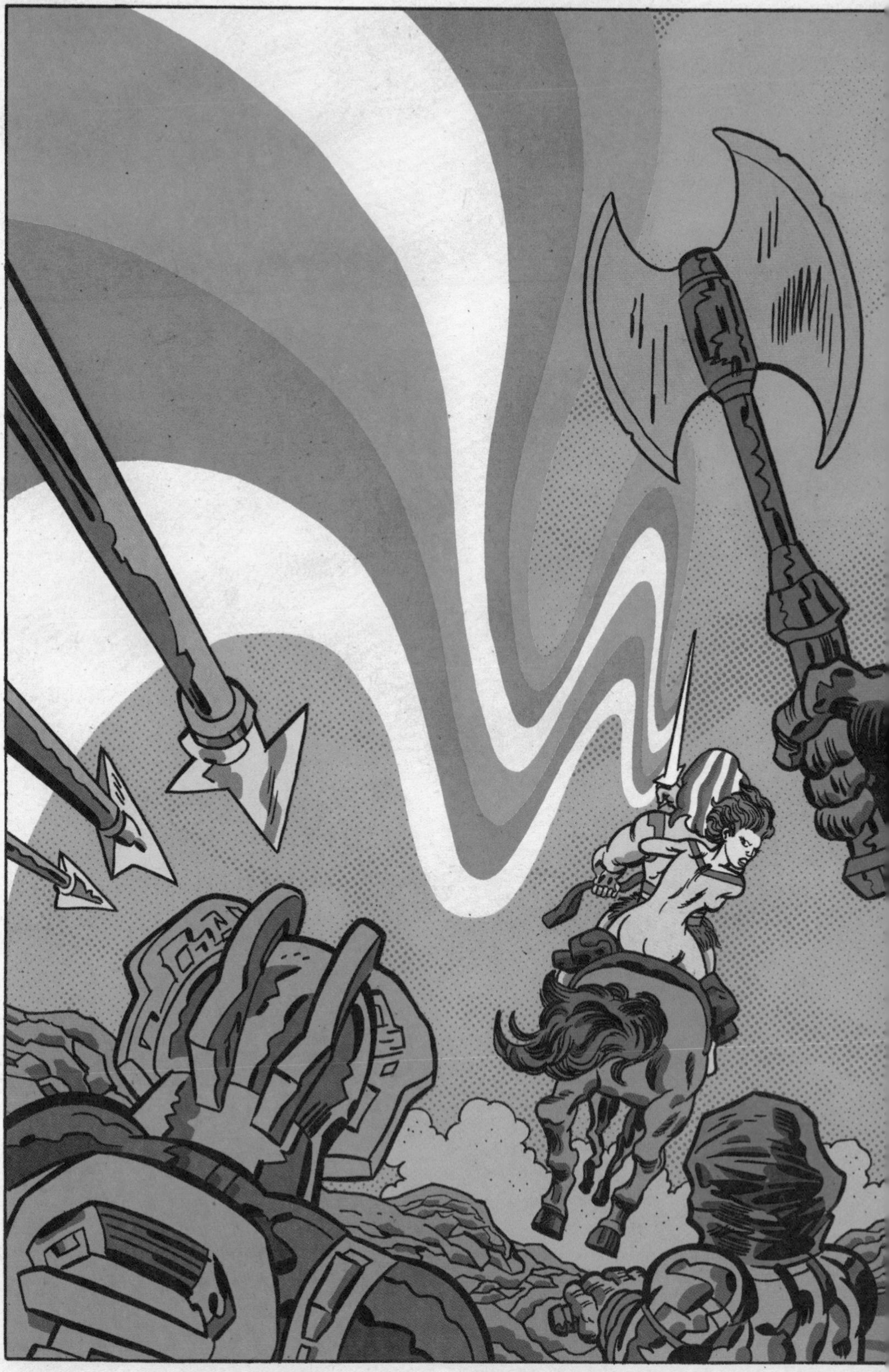

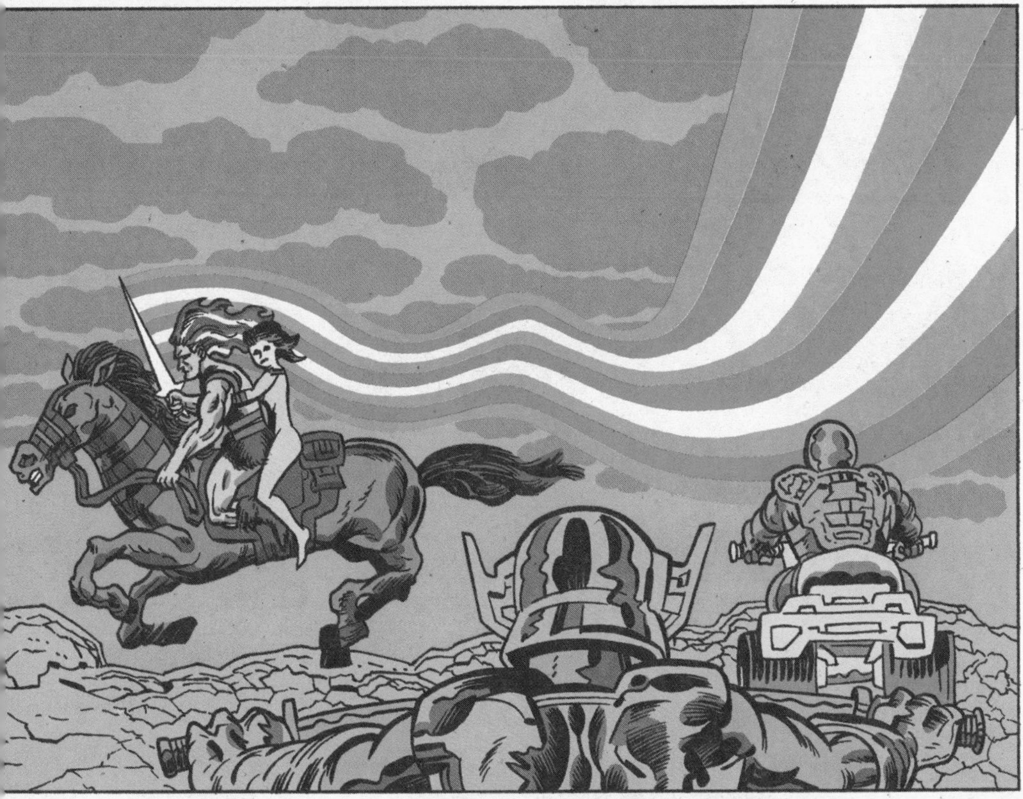
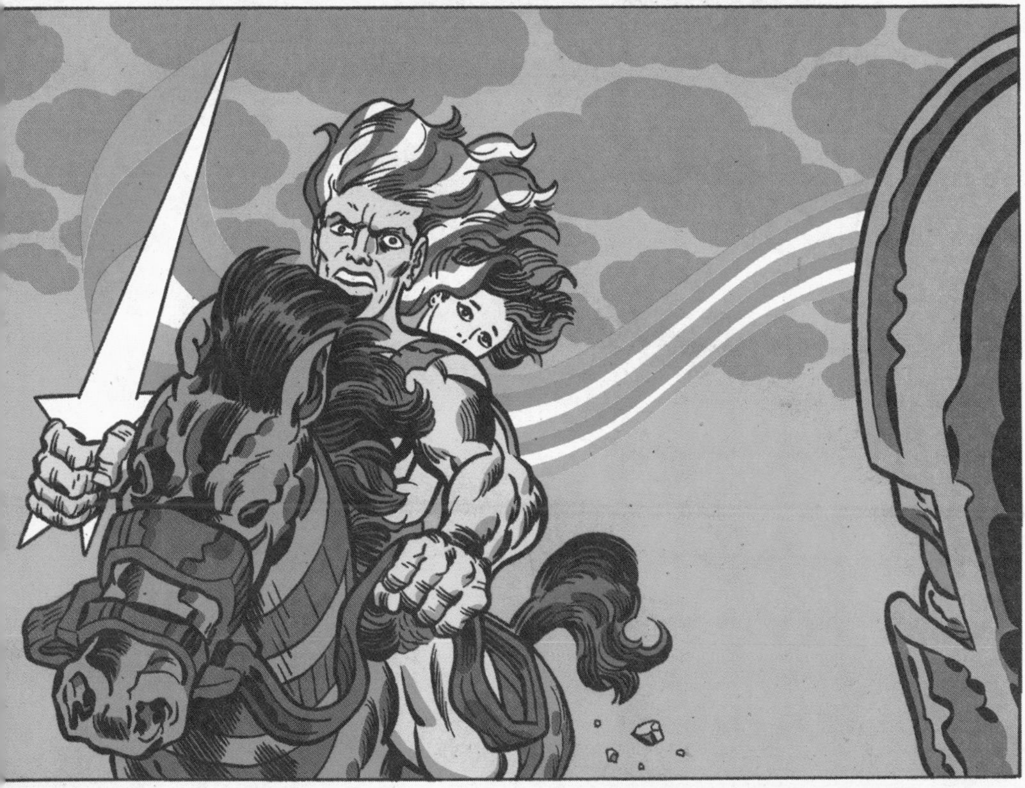

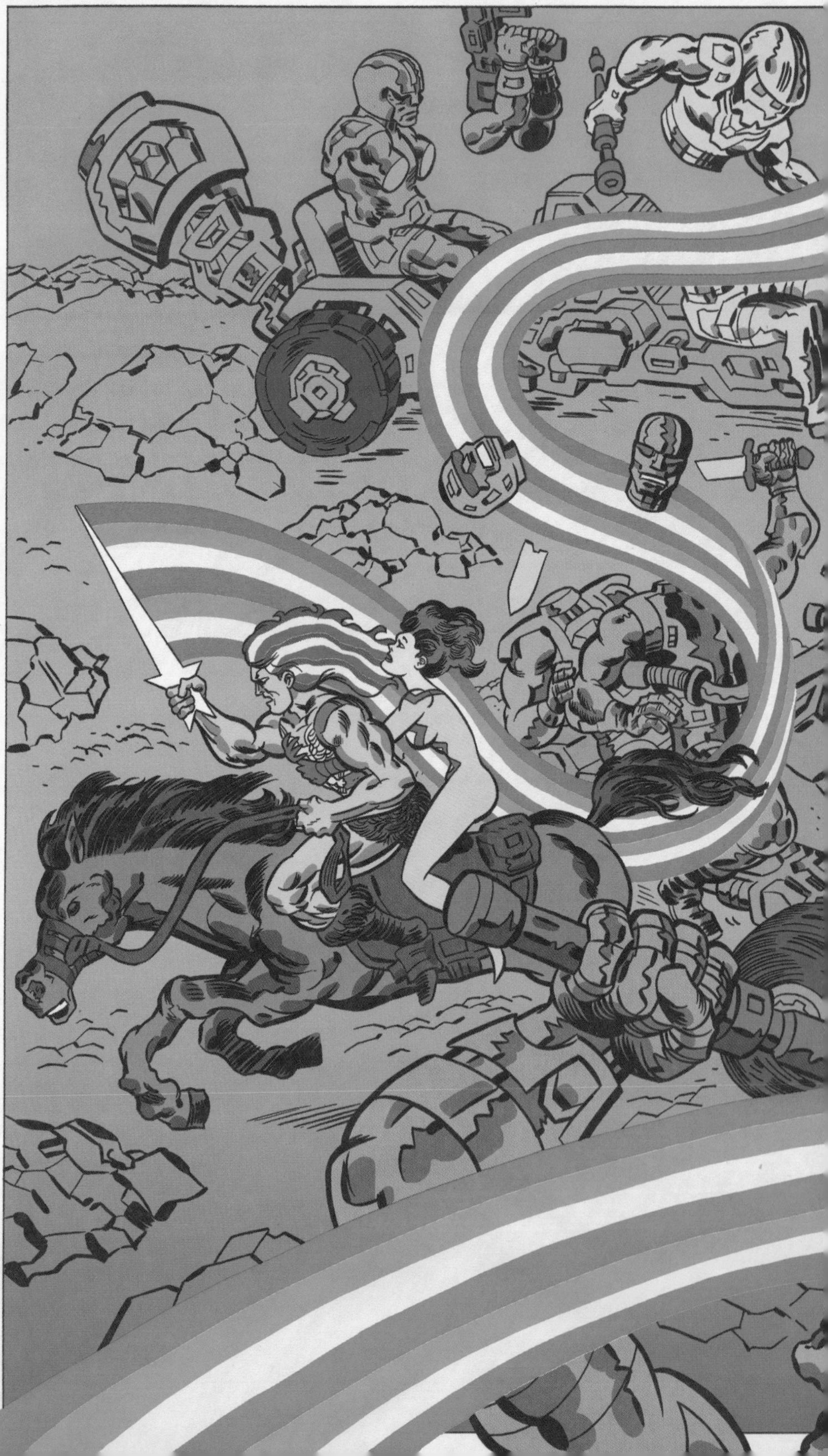

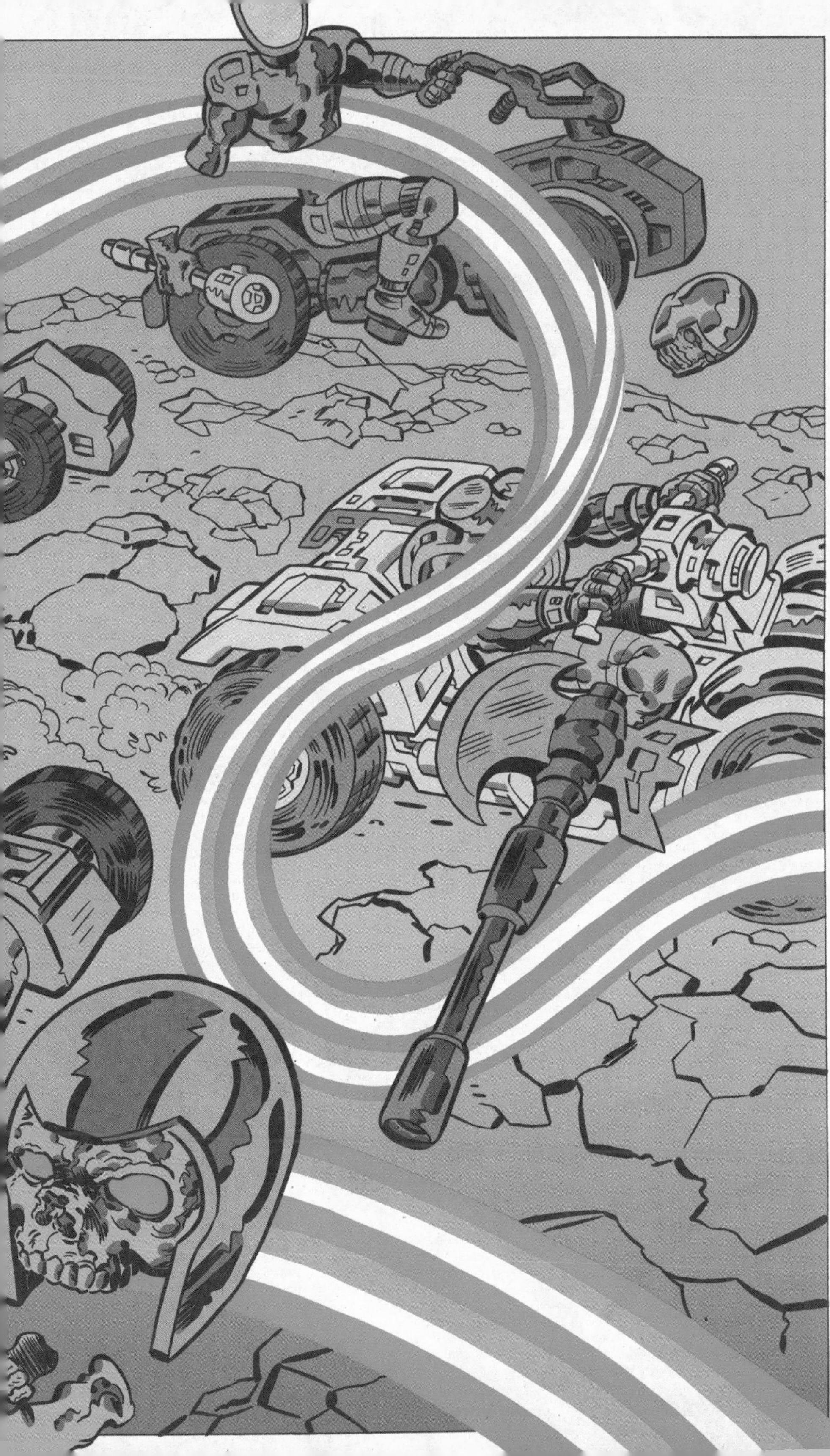

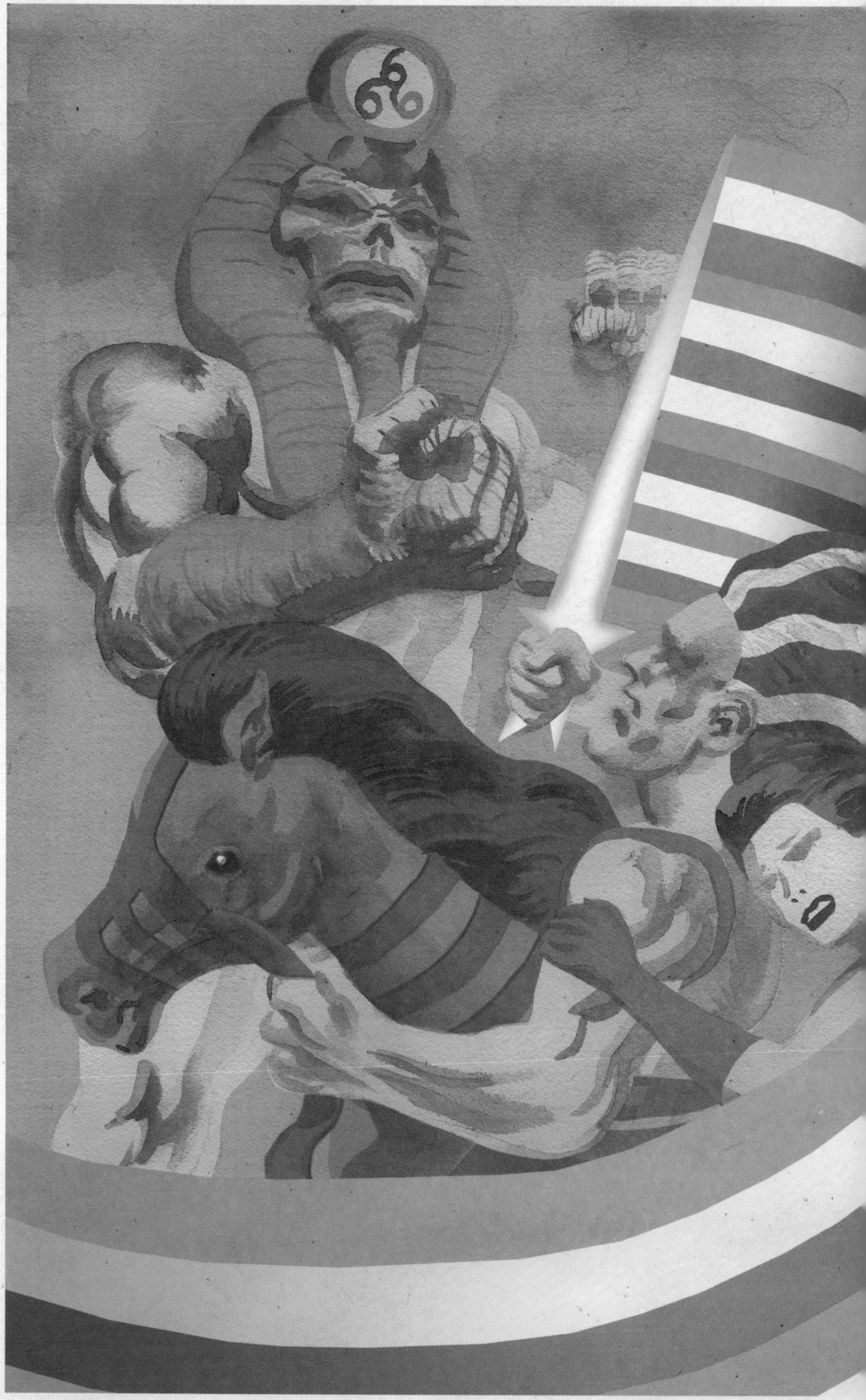

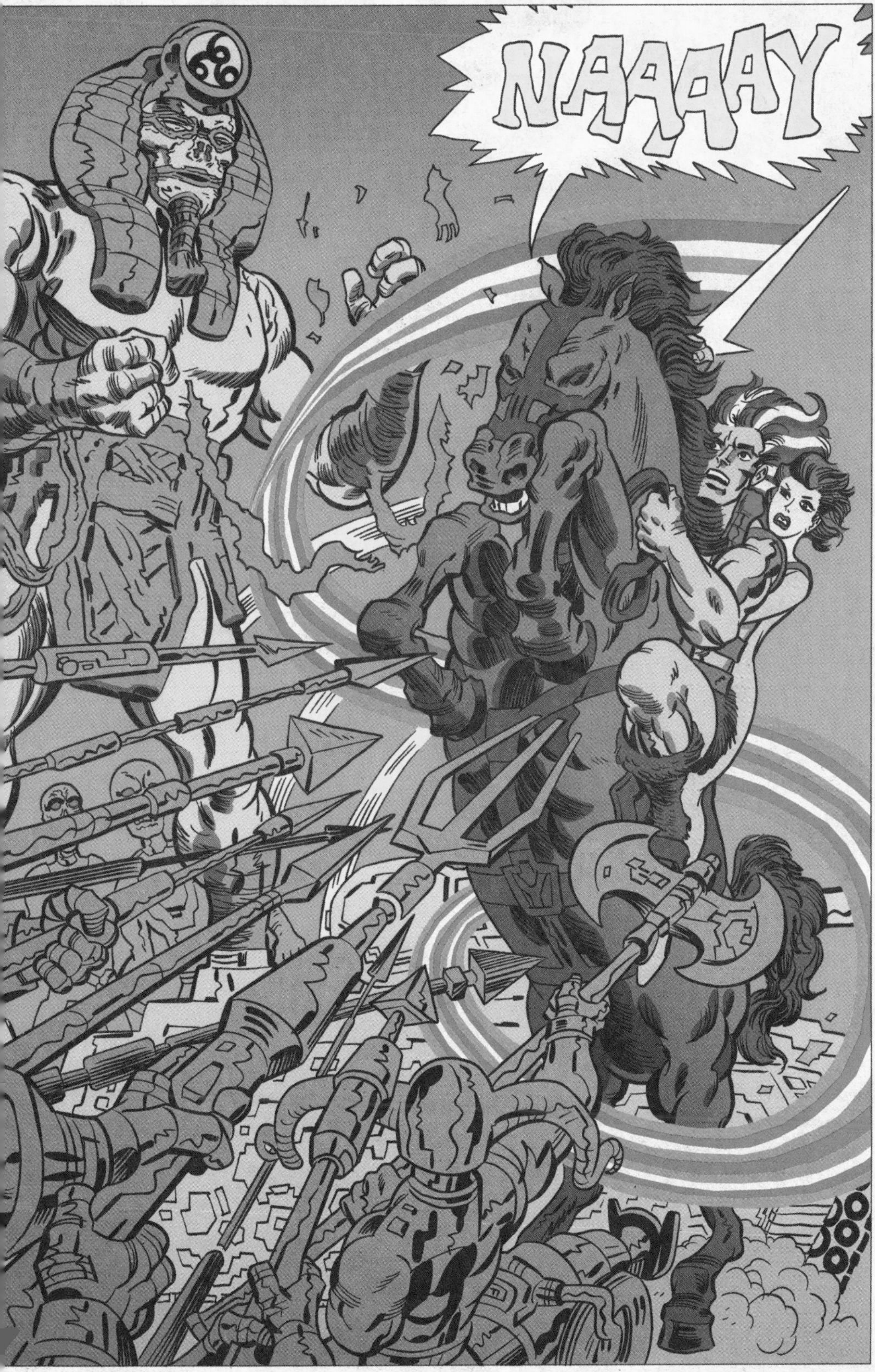
NAAAAY

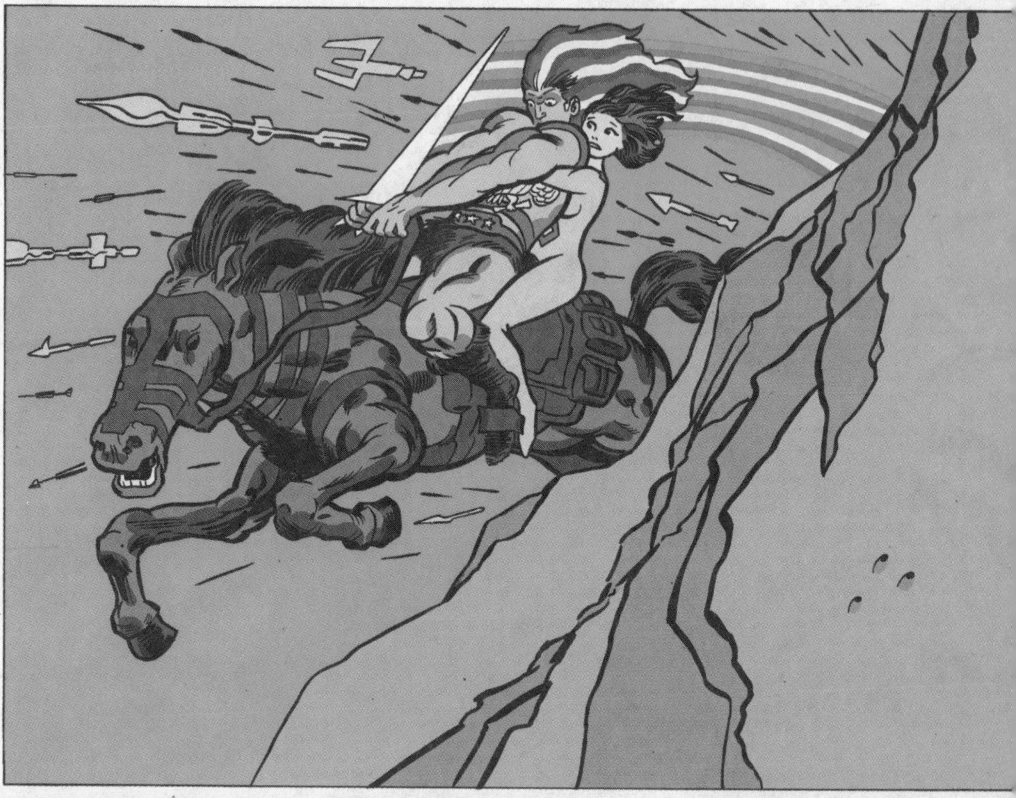
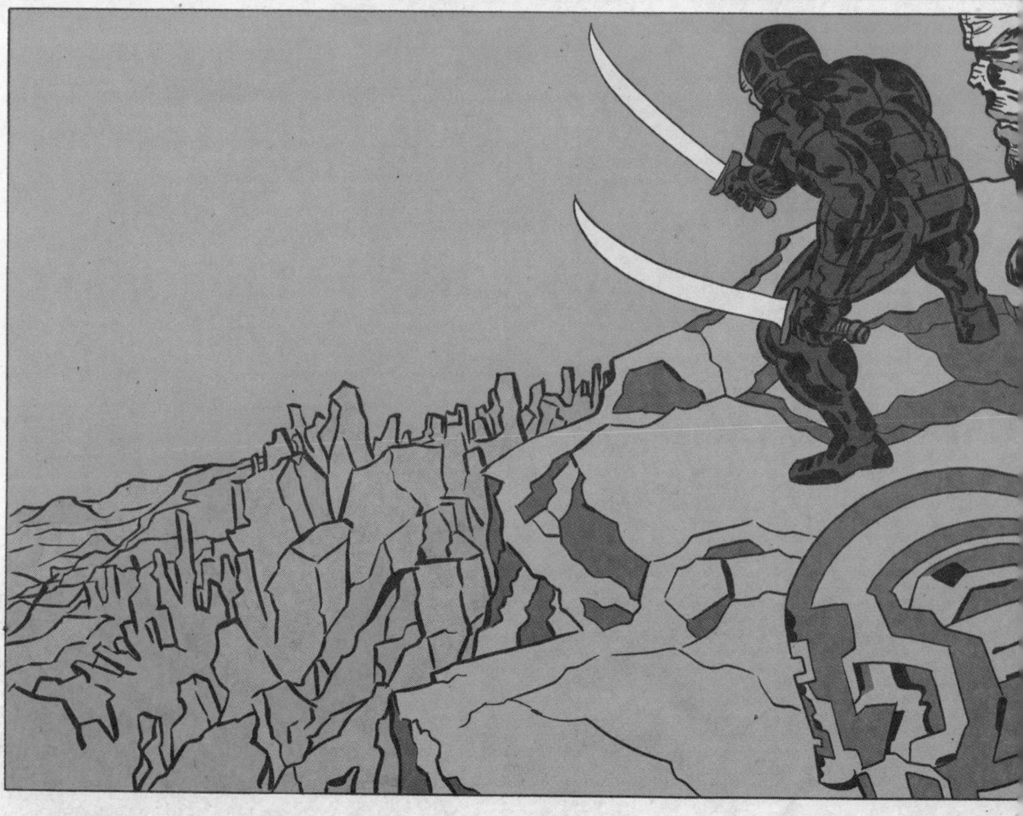

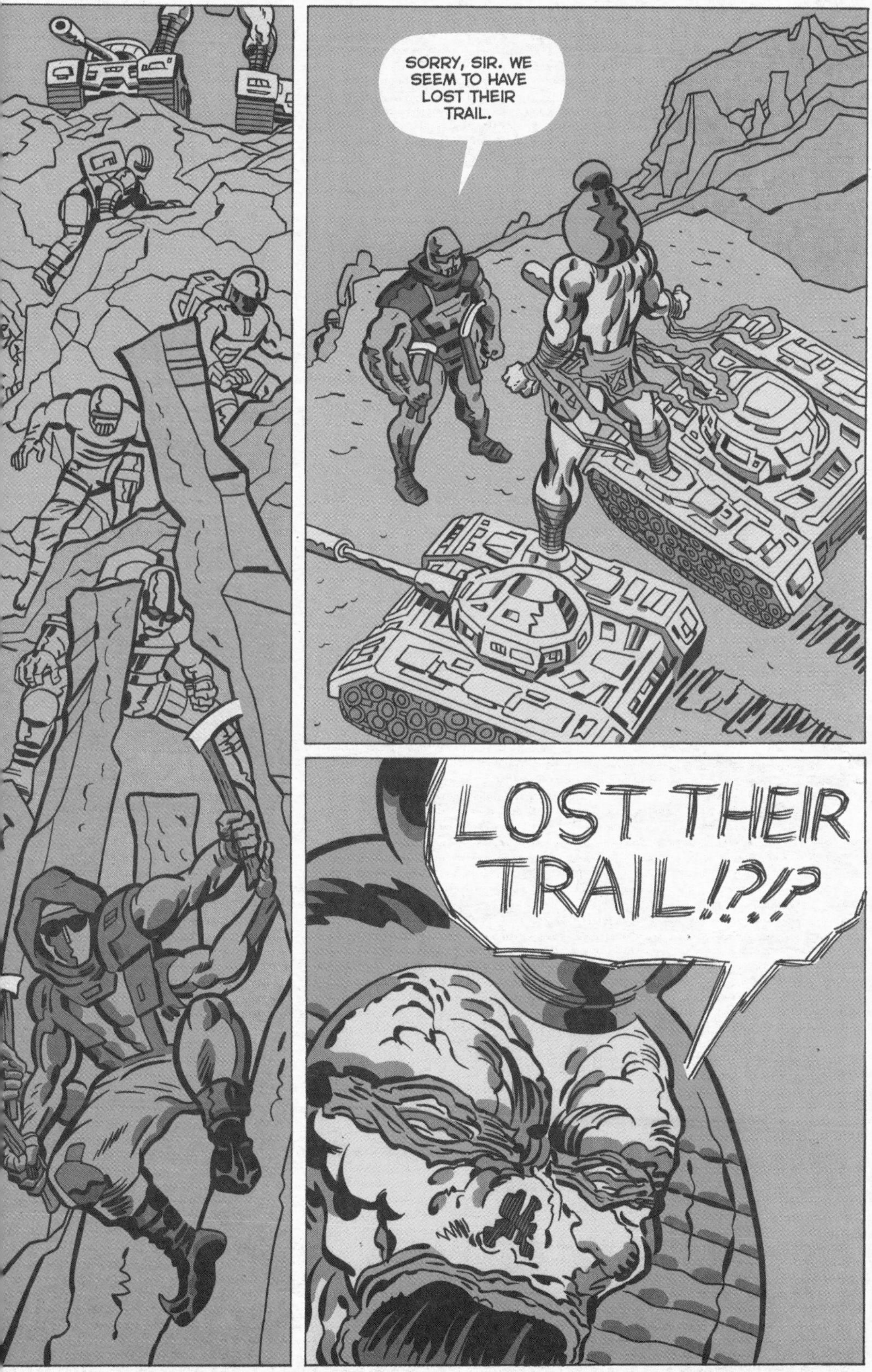
SORRY, SIR. WE SEEM TO HAVE LOST THEIR TRAIL.
LOST THEIR TRAIL!?!?

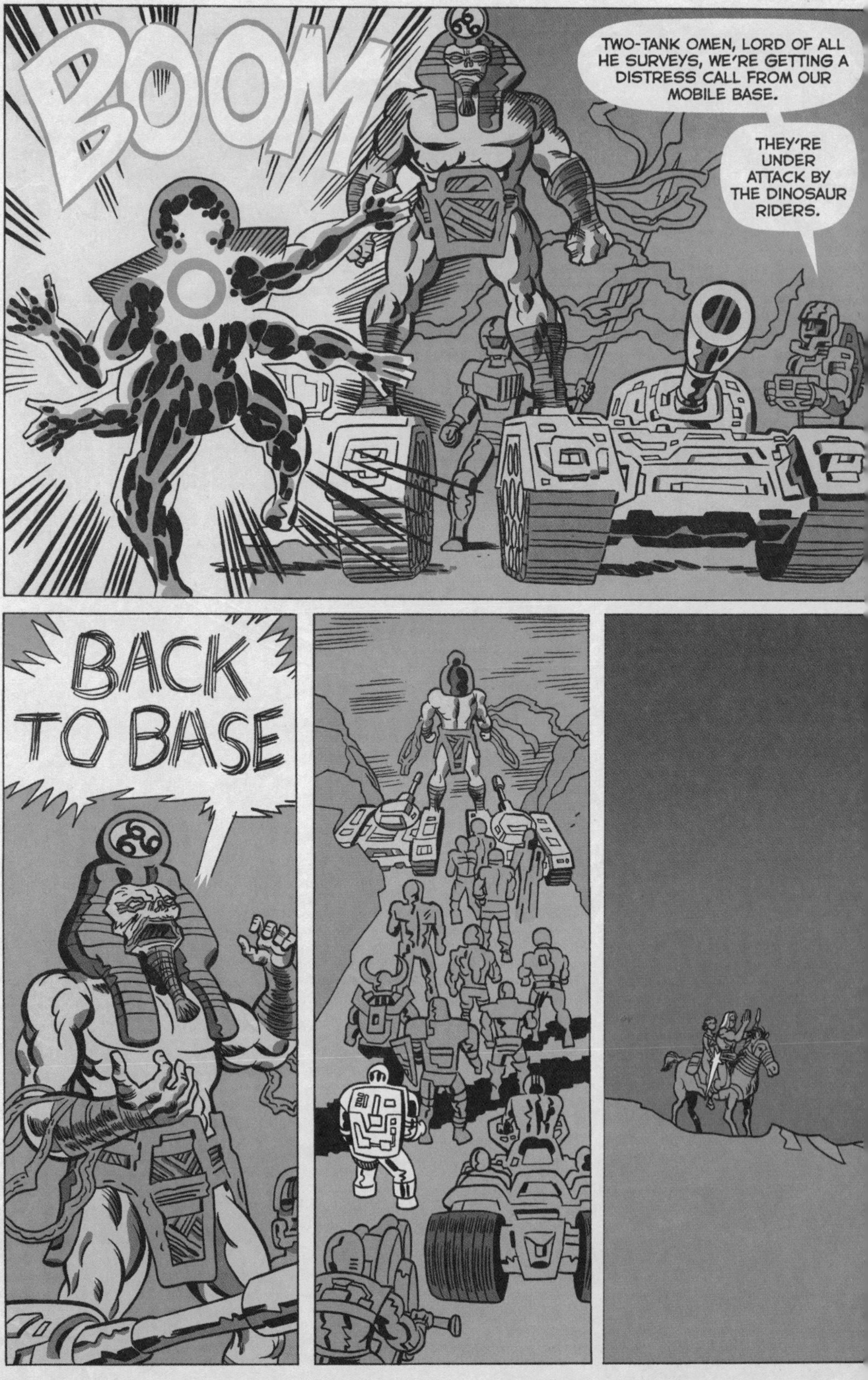
BOOM
TWO-TANK OMEN, LORD OF ALL HE SURVEYS, WE'RE GETTING A DISTRESS CALL FROM OUR MOBILE BASE.
THEY'RE UNDER ATTACK BY THE DINOSAUR RIDERS.
BACK TO BASE

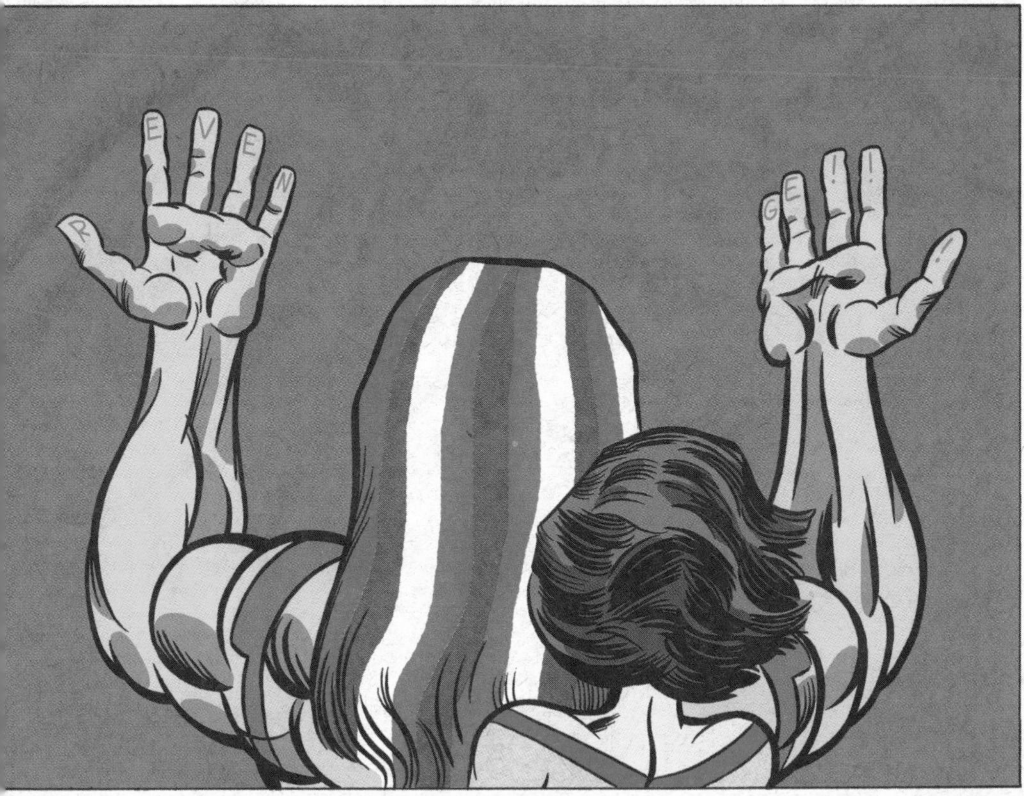
REVEN
GE!!!

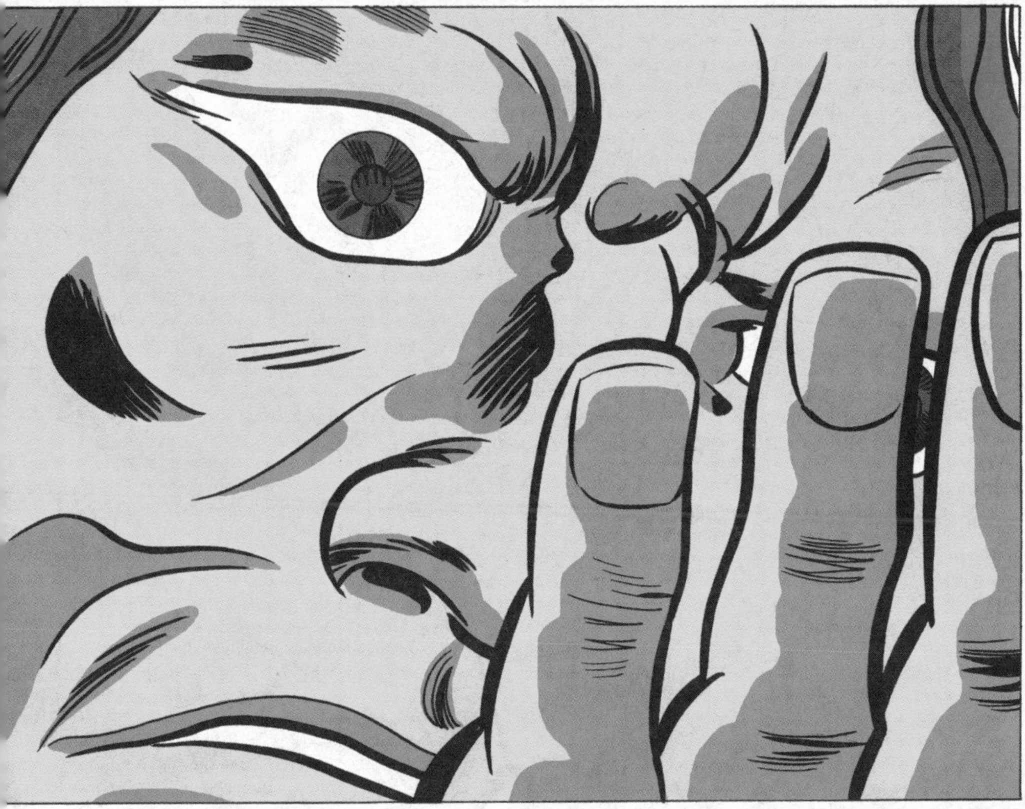

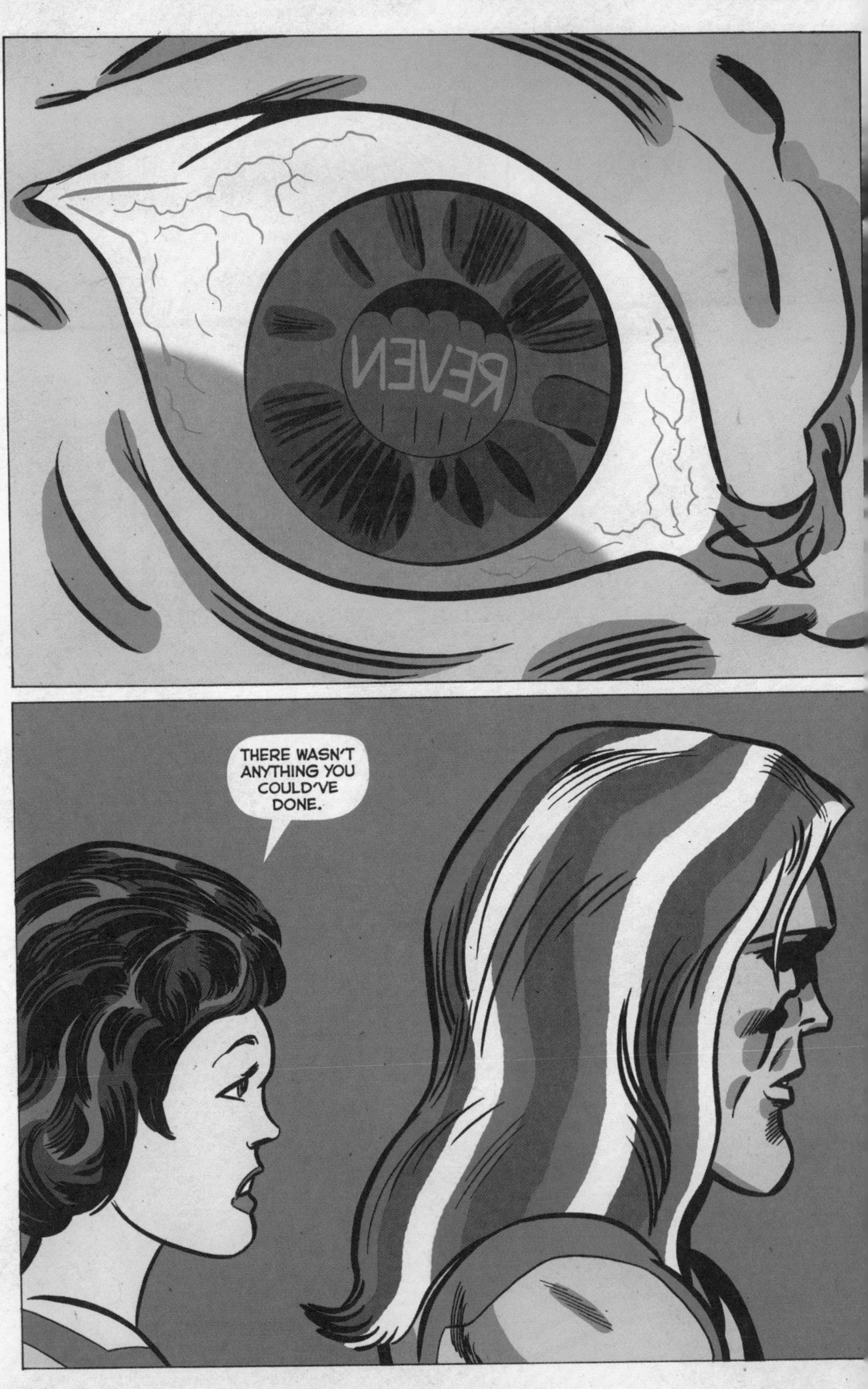
THERE WASN'T ANYTHING YOU COULD'VE DONE.

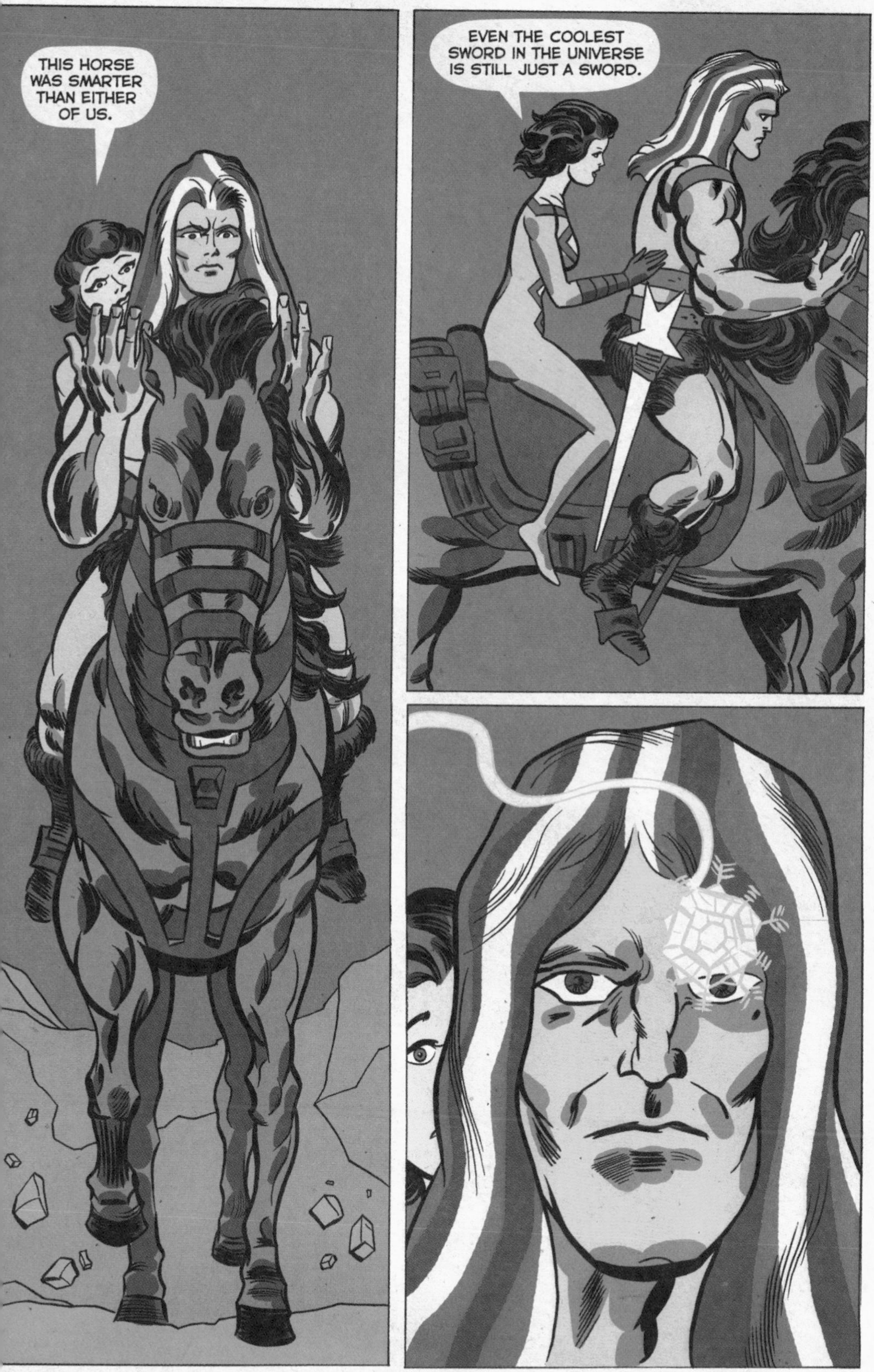
THIS HORSE WAS SMARTER THAN EITHER OF US.
EVEN THE COOLEST SWORD IN THE UNIVERSE IS STILL JUST A SWORD.

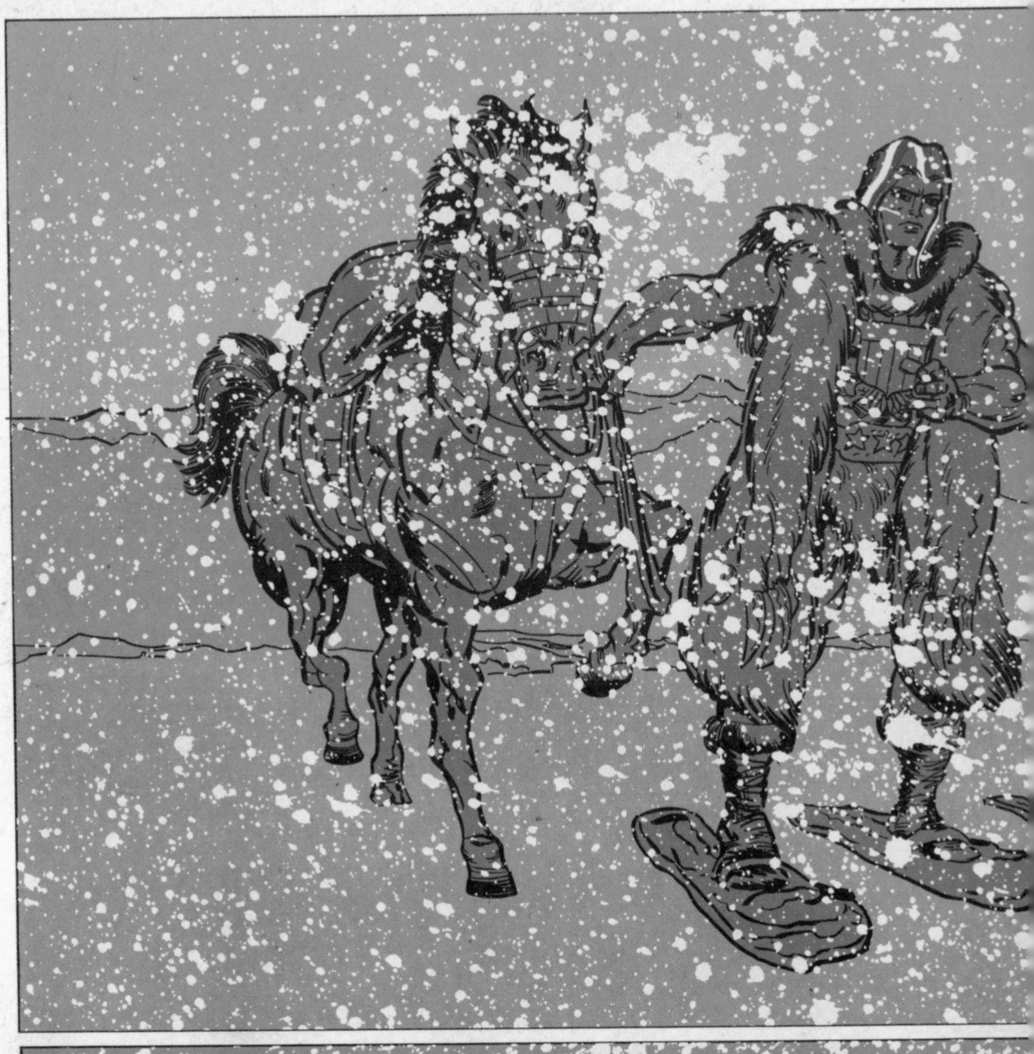
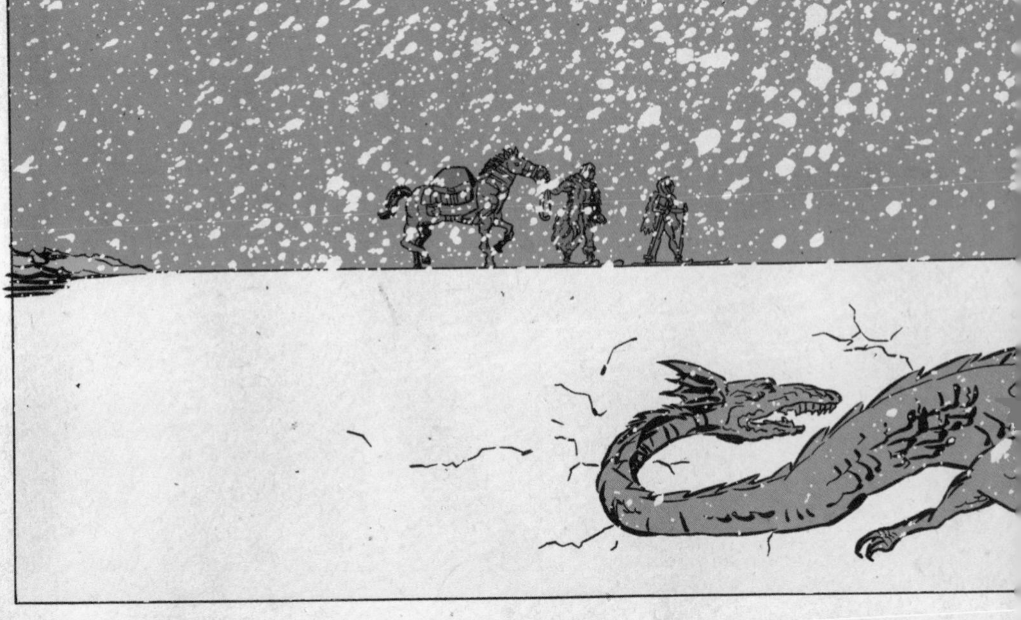

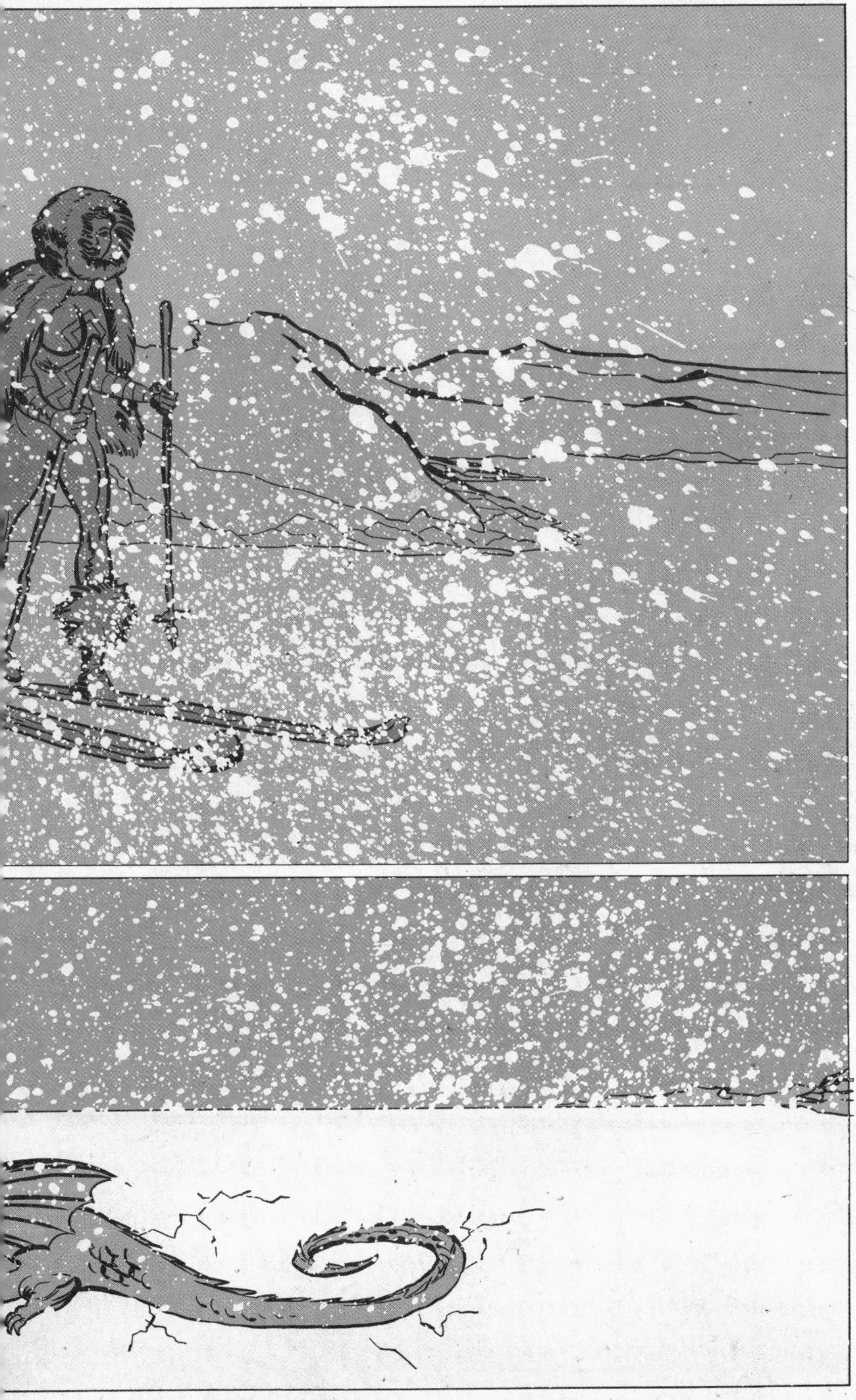

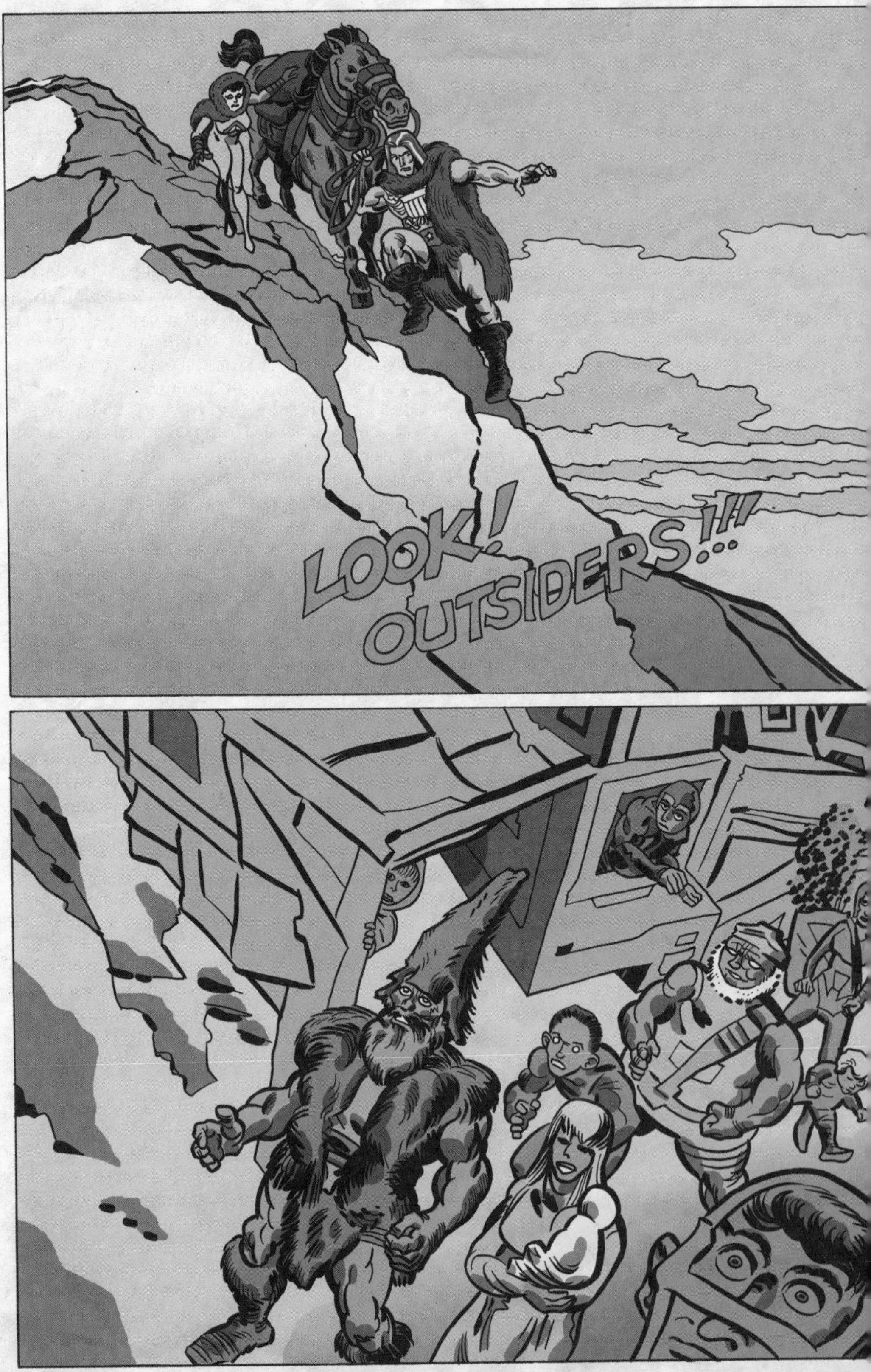
LOOK! OUTSIDERS!!!...

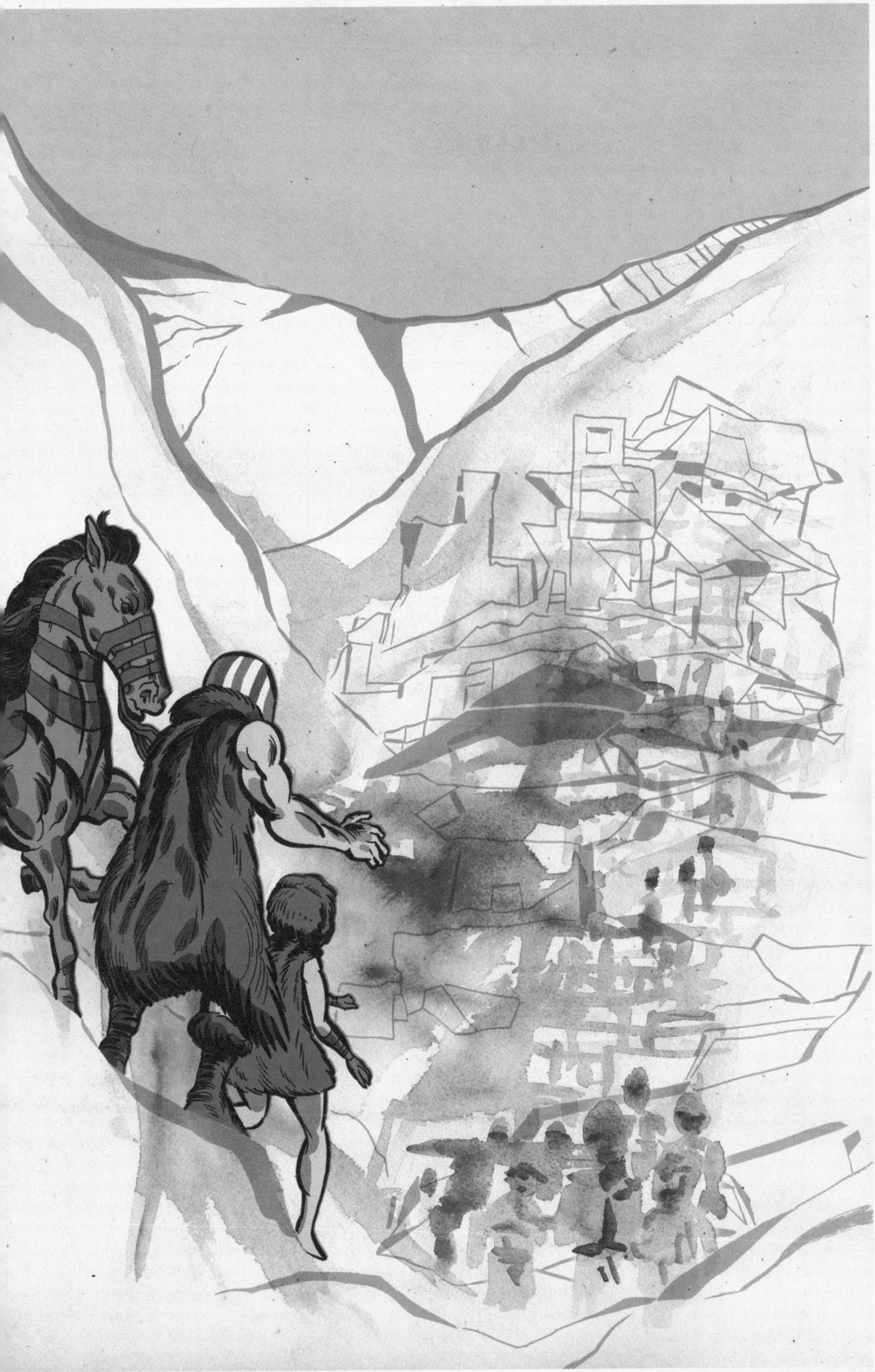

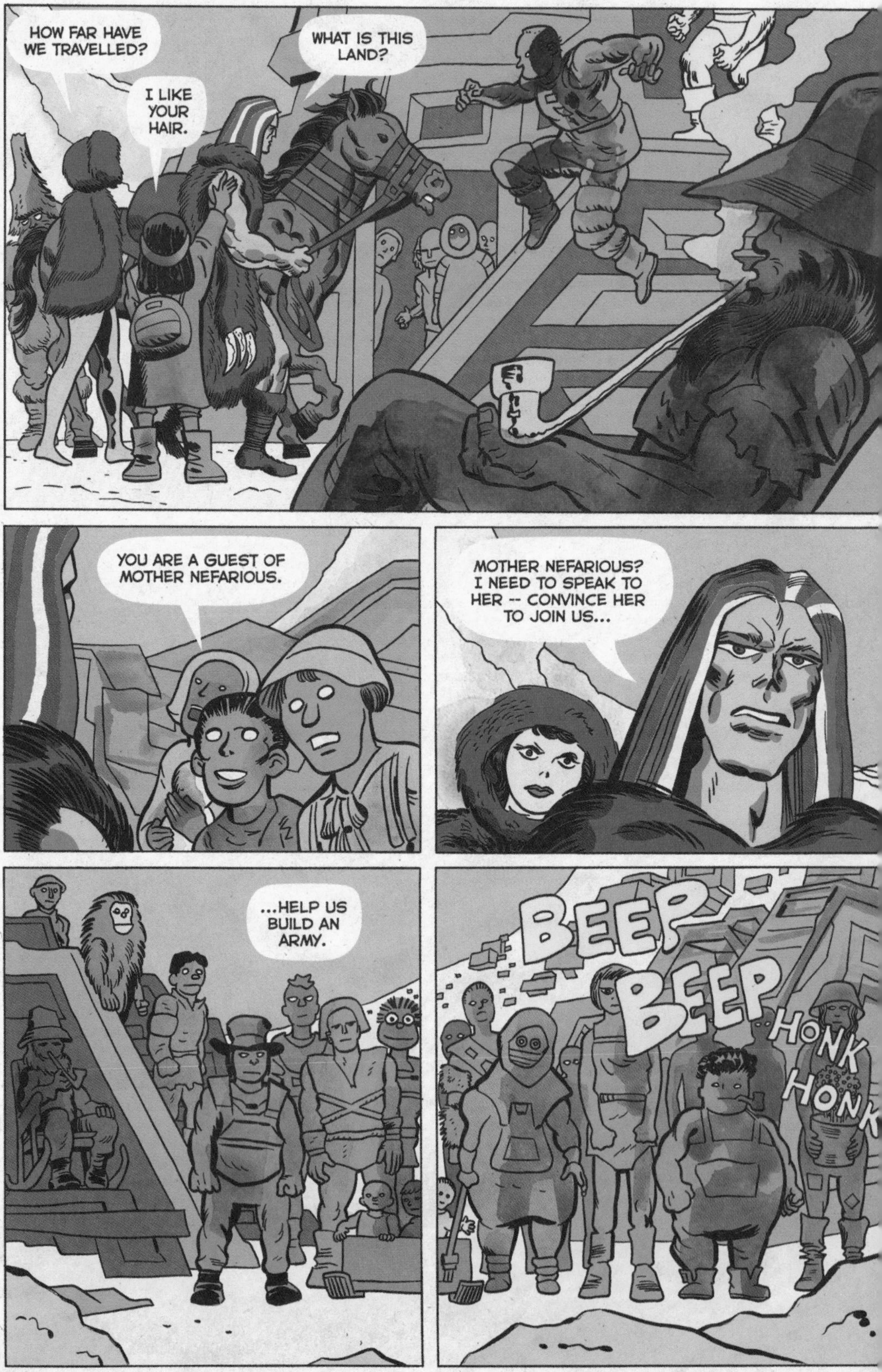
HOW FAR HAVE WE TRAVELLED?
I LIKE YOUR HAIR.
WHAT IS THIS LAND?
YOU ARE A GUEST OF MOTHER NEFARIOUS.
MOTHER NEFARIOUS? I NEED TO SPEAK TO HER -- CONVINCE HER TO JOIN US...
...HELP US BUILD AN ARMY.
BEEP
BEEP
HONK
HONK

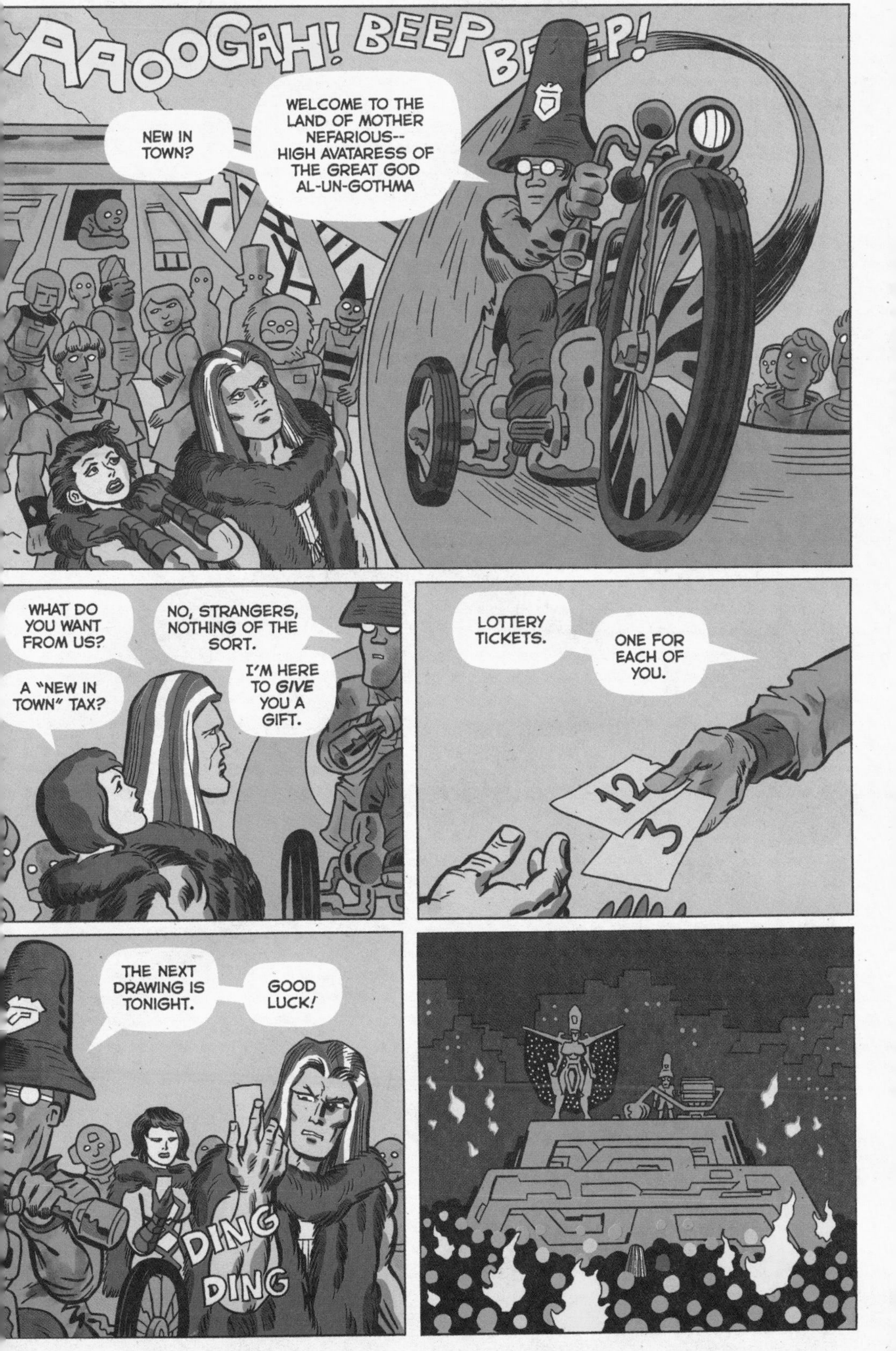
AAOOGAH! BEEP BEEP!
NEW IN TOWN?
WELCOME TO THE LAND OF MOTHER NEFARIOUS-- HIGH AVATARESS OF THE GREAT GOD AL-UN-GOTHMA
WHAT DO YOU WANT FROM US?
A "NEW IN TOWN" TAX?
NO, STRANGERS, NOTHING OF THE SORT.
I'M HERE TO GIVE YOU A GIFT.
LOTTERY TICKETS.
ONE FOR EACH OF YOU.
12
3
THE NEXT DRAWING IS TONIGHT.
GOOD LUCK!
DING
DING

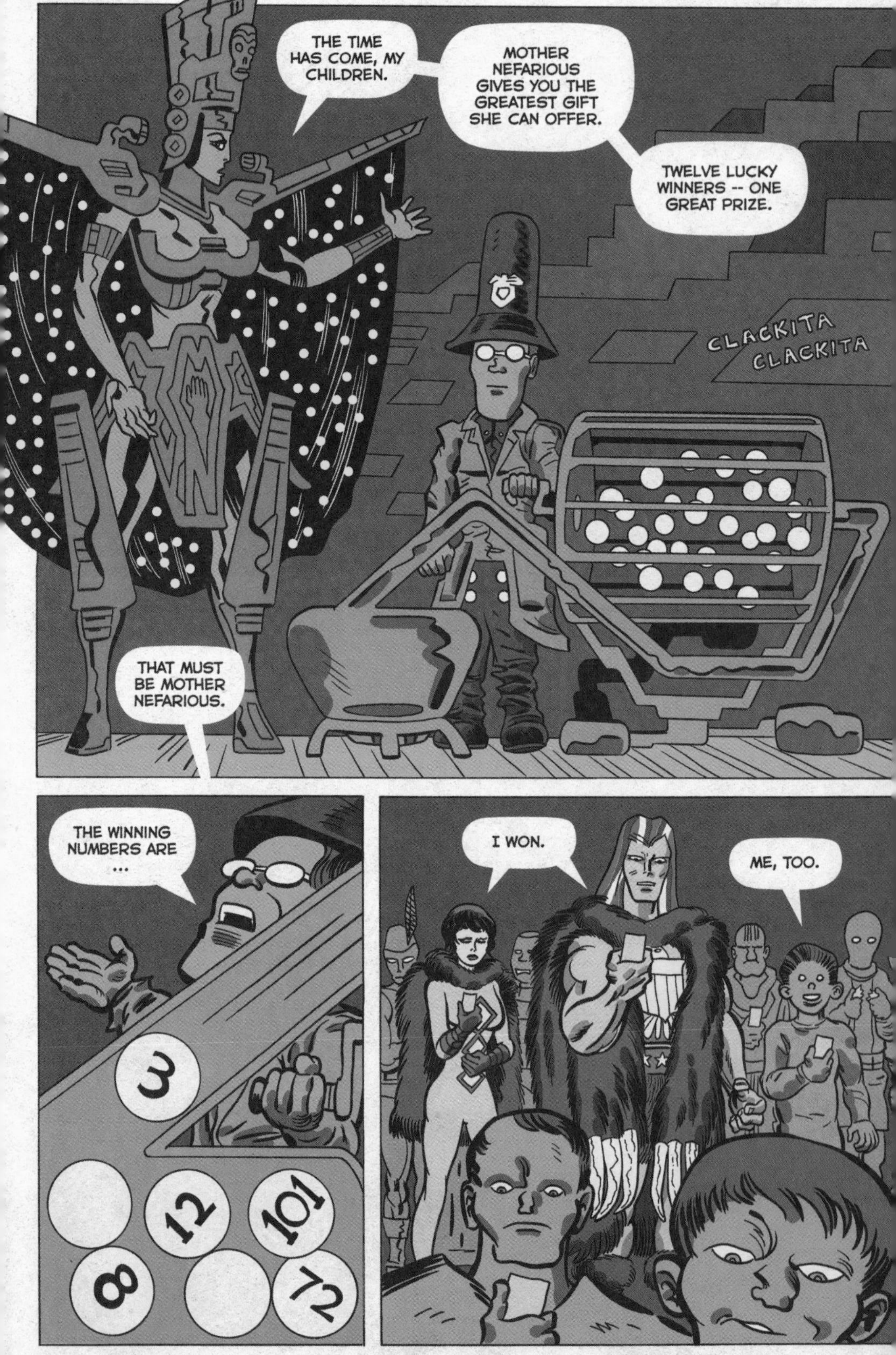
THE TIME HAS COME, MY CHILDREN.
MOTHER NEFARIOUS GIVES YOU THE GREATEST GIFT SHE CAN OFFER.
TWELVE LUCKY WINNERS -- ONE GREAT PRIZE.
CLACKITA CLACKITA
THAT MUST BE MOTHER NEFARIOUS.
THE WINNING NUMBERS ARE ...
3
12
101
8
72
I WON.
ME, TOO.

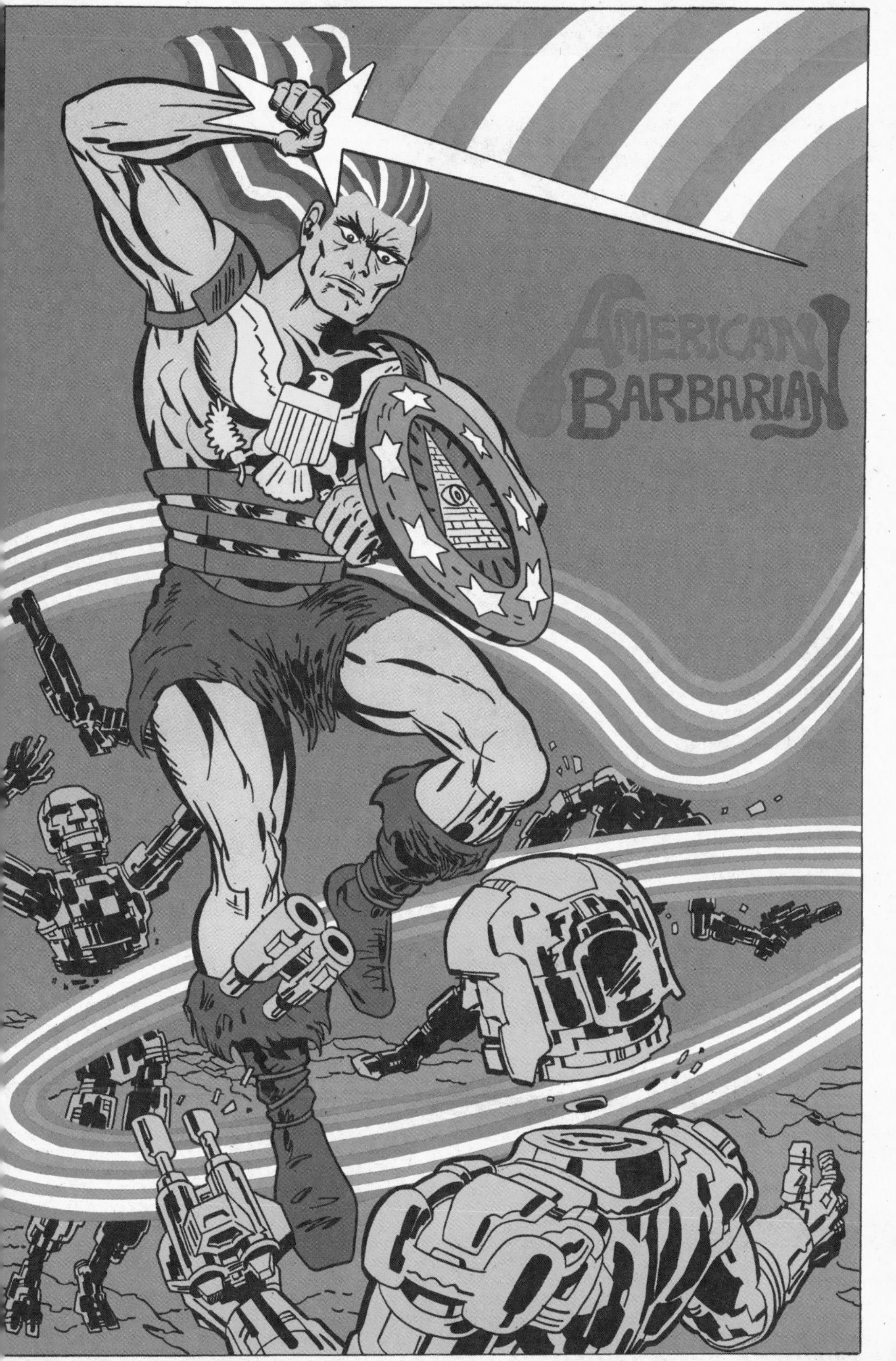
AMERICAN
BARBARIAN

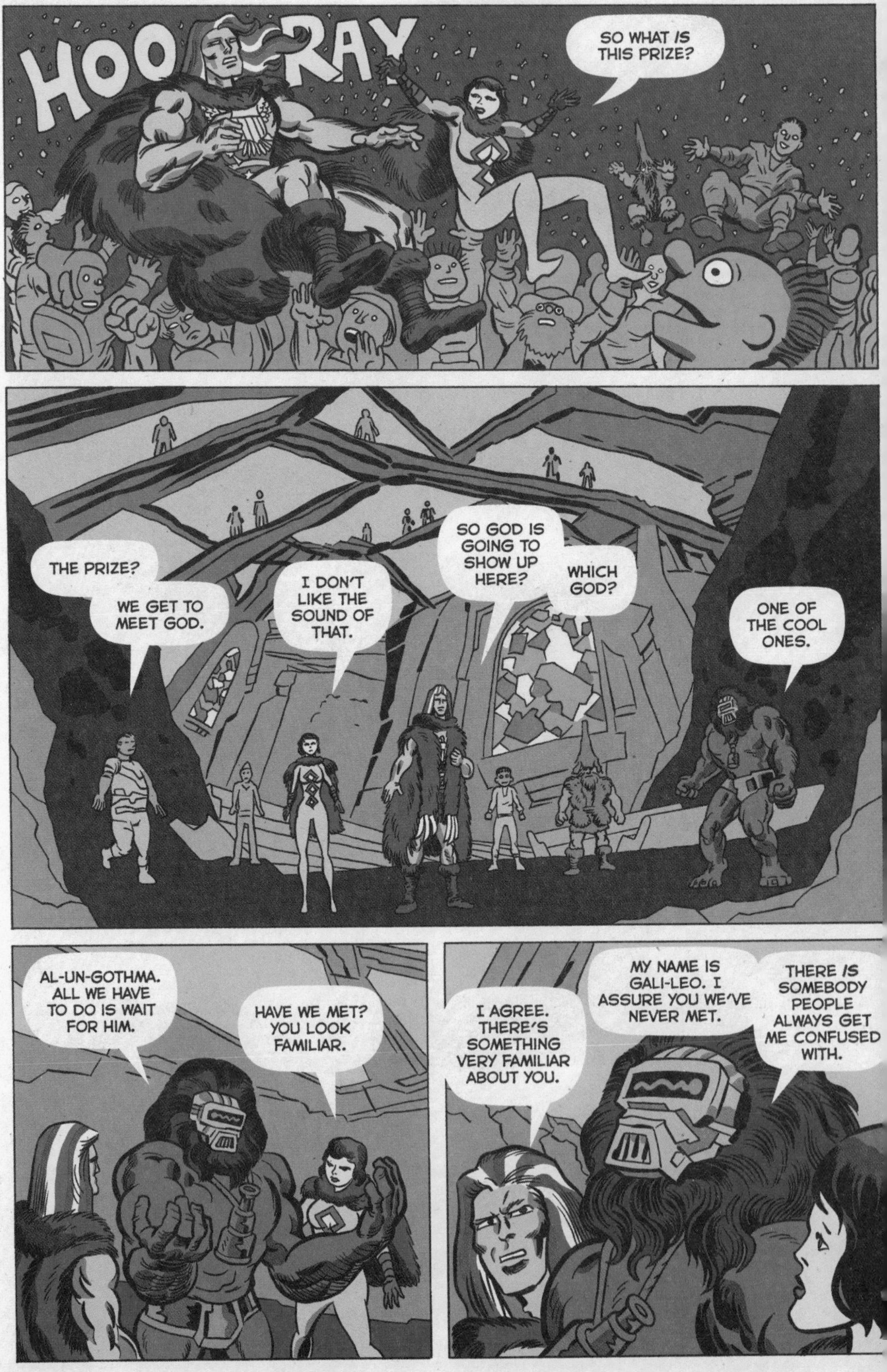
HOORAY
SO WHAT IS THIS PRIZE?
THE PRIZE?
WE GET TO MEET GOD.
I DON'T LIKE THE SOUND OF THAT.
SO GOD IS GOING TO SHOW UP HERE?
WHICH GOD?
ONE OF THE COOL ONES.
AL-UN-GOTHMA. ALL WE HAVE TO DO IS WAIT FOR HIM.
HAVE WE MET? YOU LOOK FAMILIAR.
I AGREE. THERE'S SOMETHING VERY FAMILIAR ABOUT YOU.
MY NAME IS GALI-LEO. I ASSURE YOU WE'VE NEVER MET.
THERE IS SOMEBODY PEOPLE ALWAYS GET ME CONFUSED WITH.

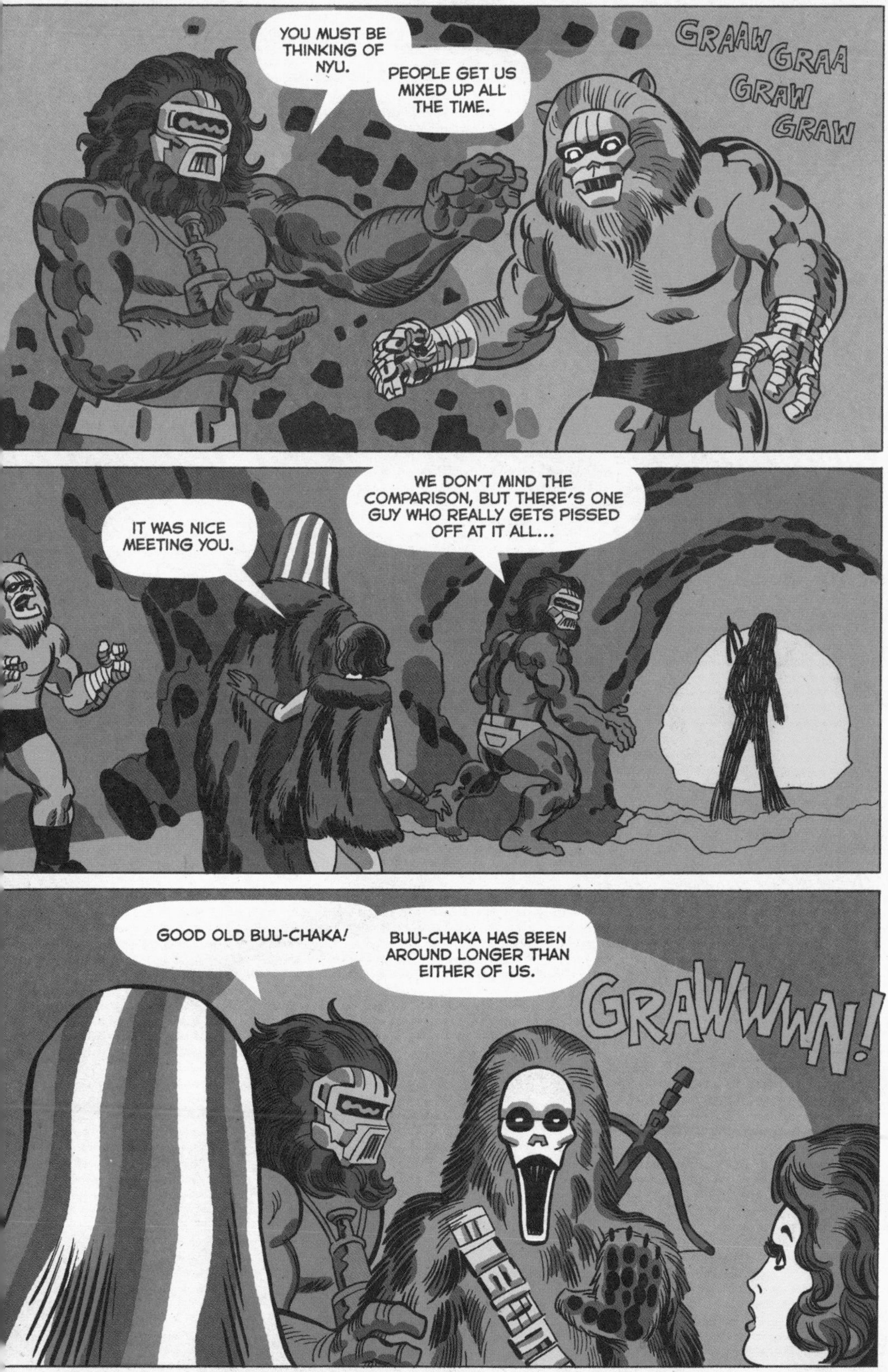

YOU MUST BE THINKING OF NYU.
PEOPLE GET US MIXED UP ALL THE TIME.
GRAAW GRAA GRAW GRAW
IT WAS NICE MEETING YOU.
WE DON'T MIND THE COMPARISON, BUT THERE'S ONE GUY WHO REALLY GETS PISSED OFF AT IT ALL...
GOOD OLD BUU-CHAKA!
BUU-CHAKA HAS BEEN AROUND LONGER THAN EITHER OF US.
GRAWWWN!

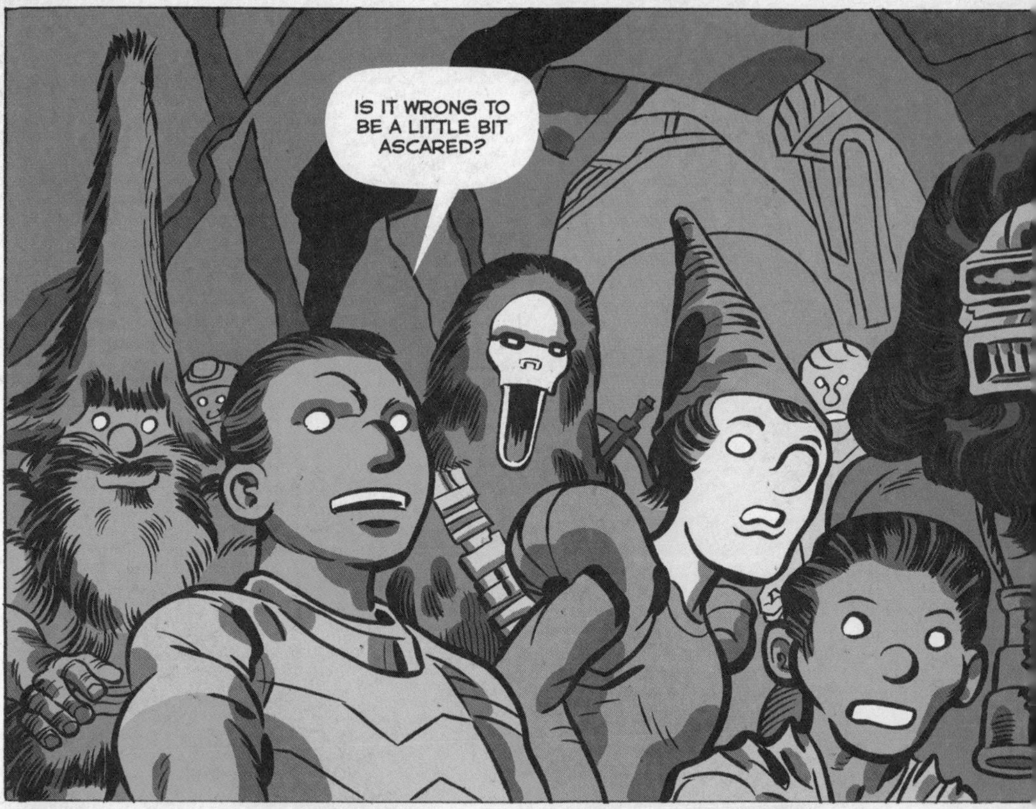
IS IT WRONG TO BE A LITTLE BIT ASCARED?

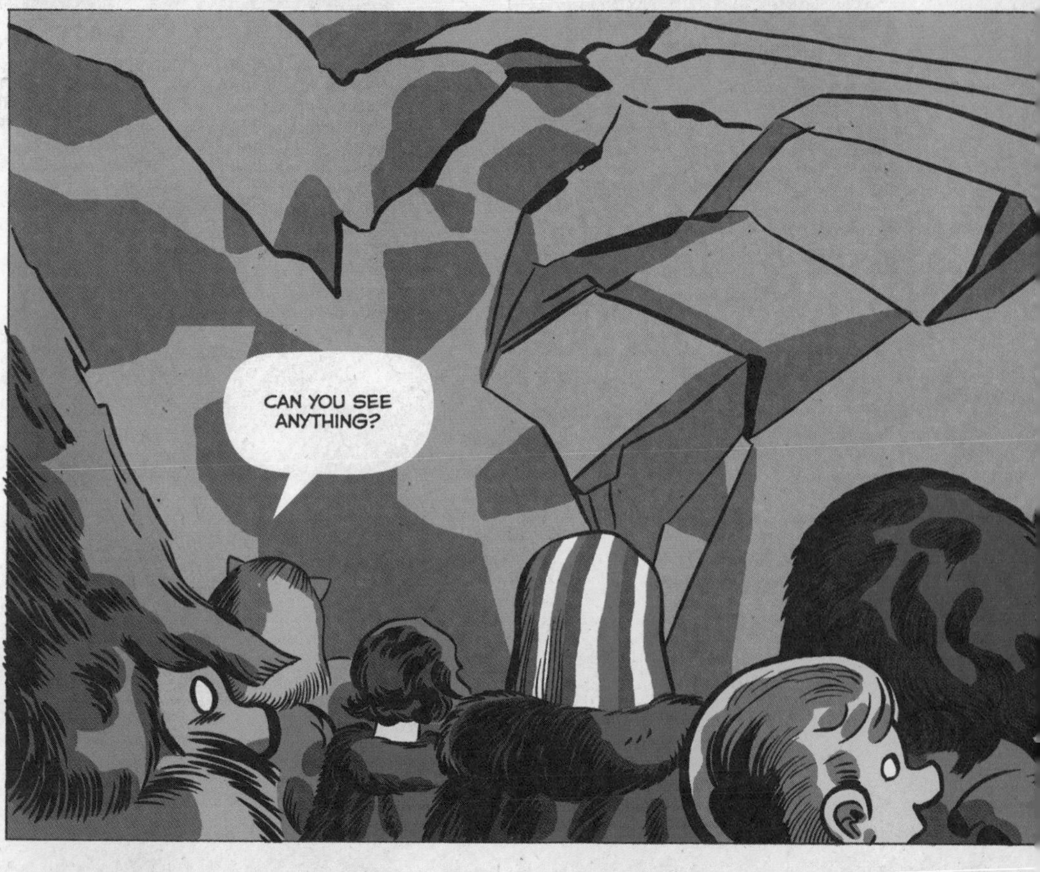
CAN YOU SEE ANYTHING?

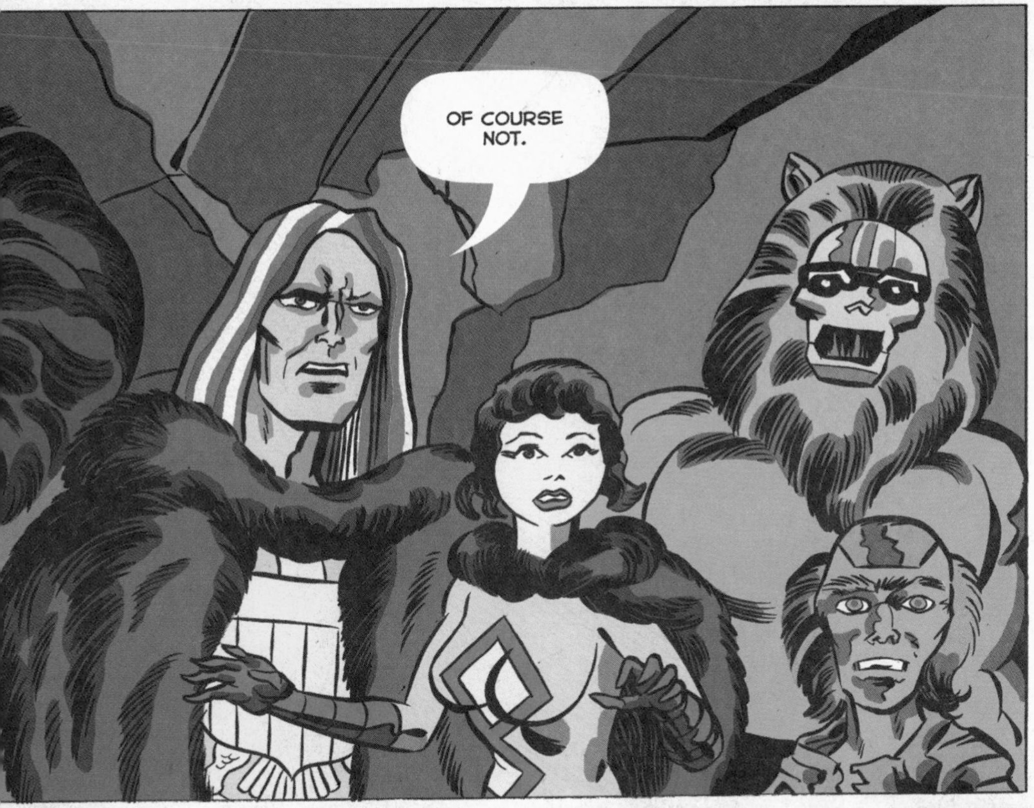
OF COURSE NOT.
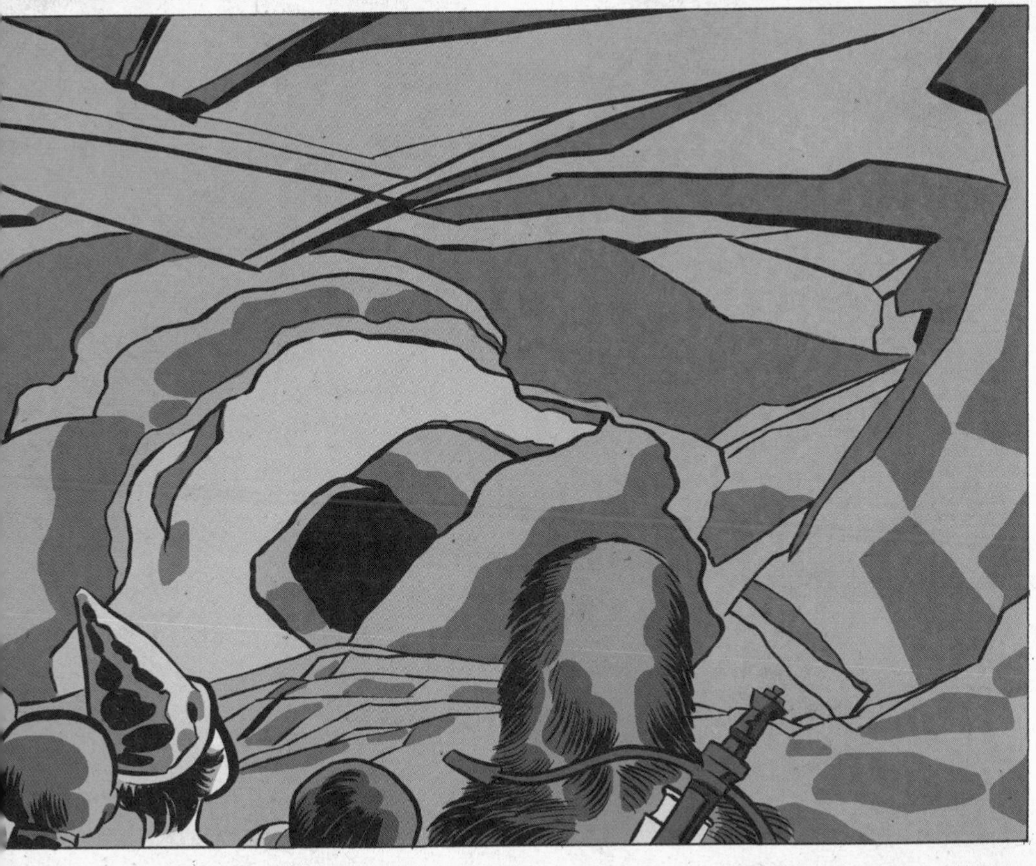

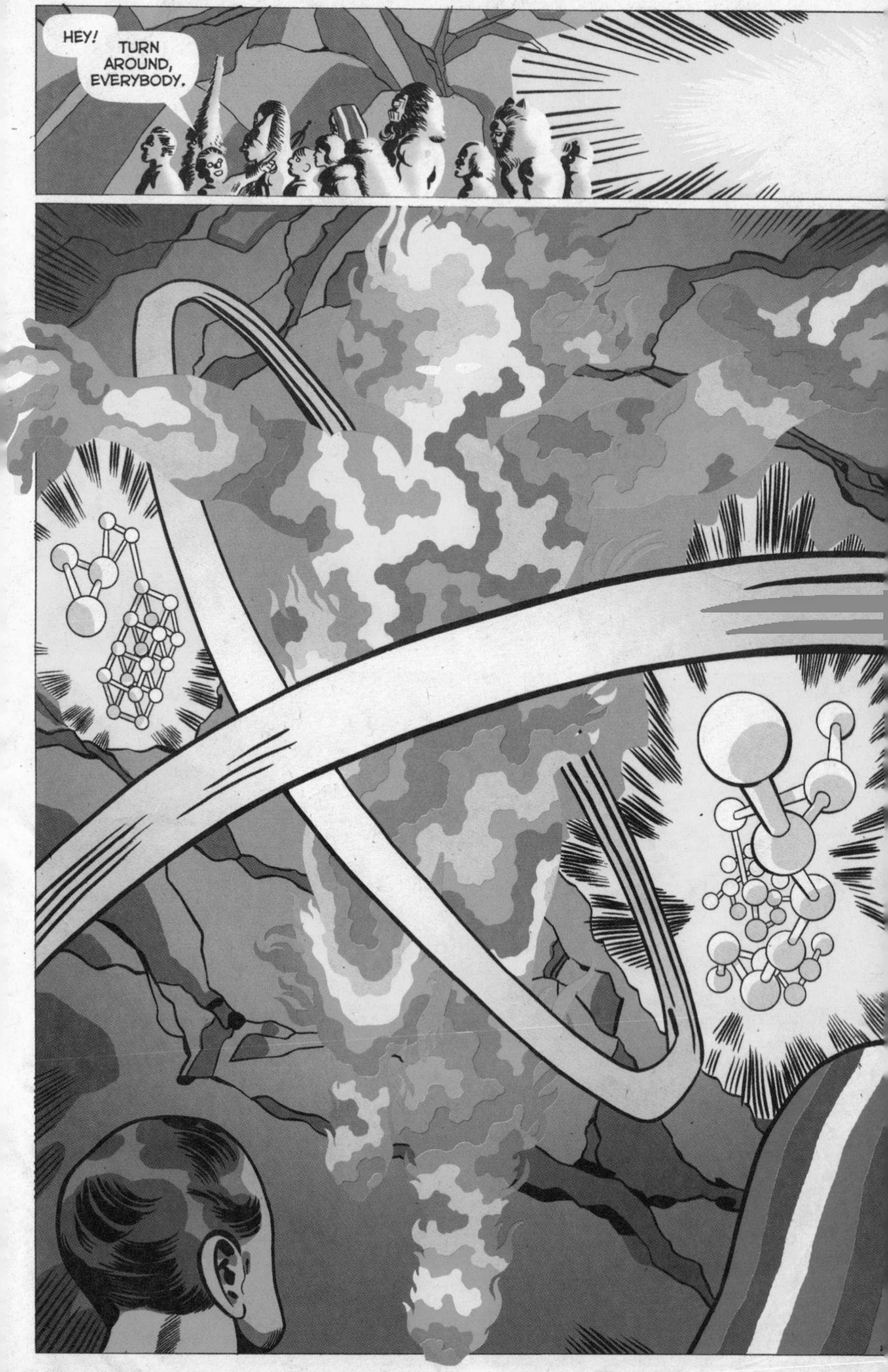
HEY!
TURN AROUND, EVERYBODY.

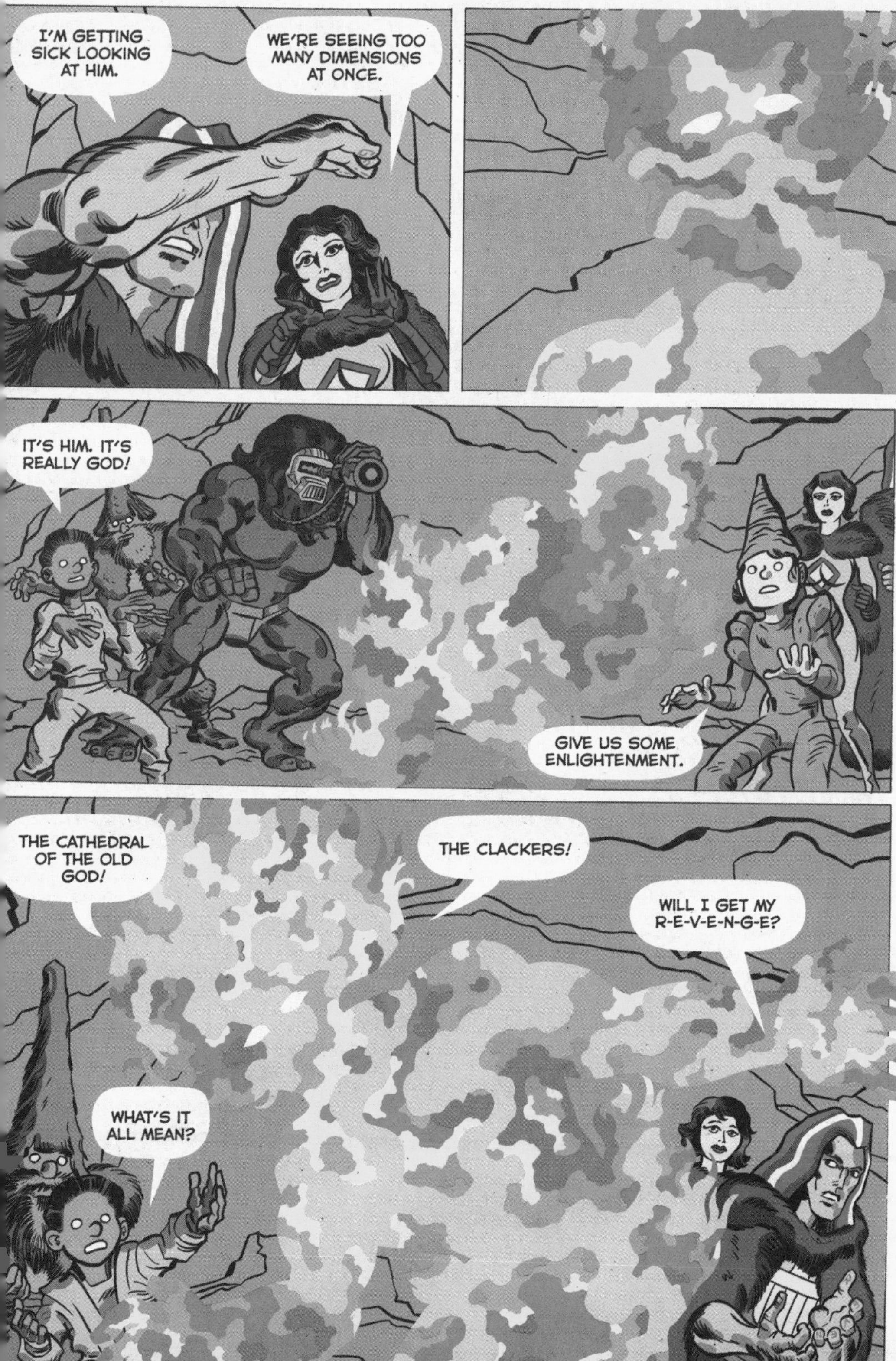
I'M GETTING SICK LOOKING AT HIM.
WE'RE SEEING TOO MANY DIMENSIONS AT ONCE.
IT'S HIM. IT'S REALLY GOD!
GIVE US SOME ENLIGHTENMENT.
THE CATHEDRAL OF THE OLD GOD!
THE CLACKERS!
WILL I GET MY R-E-V-E-N-G-E?
WHAT'S IT ALL MEAN?

THE CLACKERS!

DON'T LET GO OF THEM LAZER-ZAPPING CLACKERS!

OH, AND BEWARE OF MY BROTHER!

GOD HAS A BROTHER?

SO SICK! SO DISORIENTED!

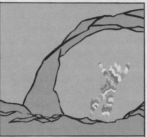

THAT WAS A DISAPPOINTMENT AS PRIZES GO.

AND AS GODS GO.

HAVE YOU NOTICED HOW THINGS KEEP CHANGING IN THIS CATHEDRAL?

I SWEAR THAT WALL WAS OVER THERE A SECOND AGO.

IF YOU SAY SO.

MAYBE IT'S SOME KIND OF TEMPORAL DISTORTION CAUSED BY THE GOD PASSING THROUGH OUR PLANE OF EXISTENCE.

RUMBLE!

WHAT WAS THAT SOUND!?

I DON'T LIKE THIS.

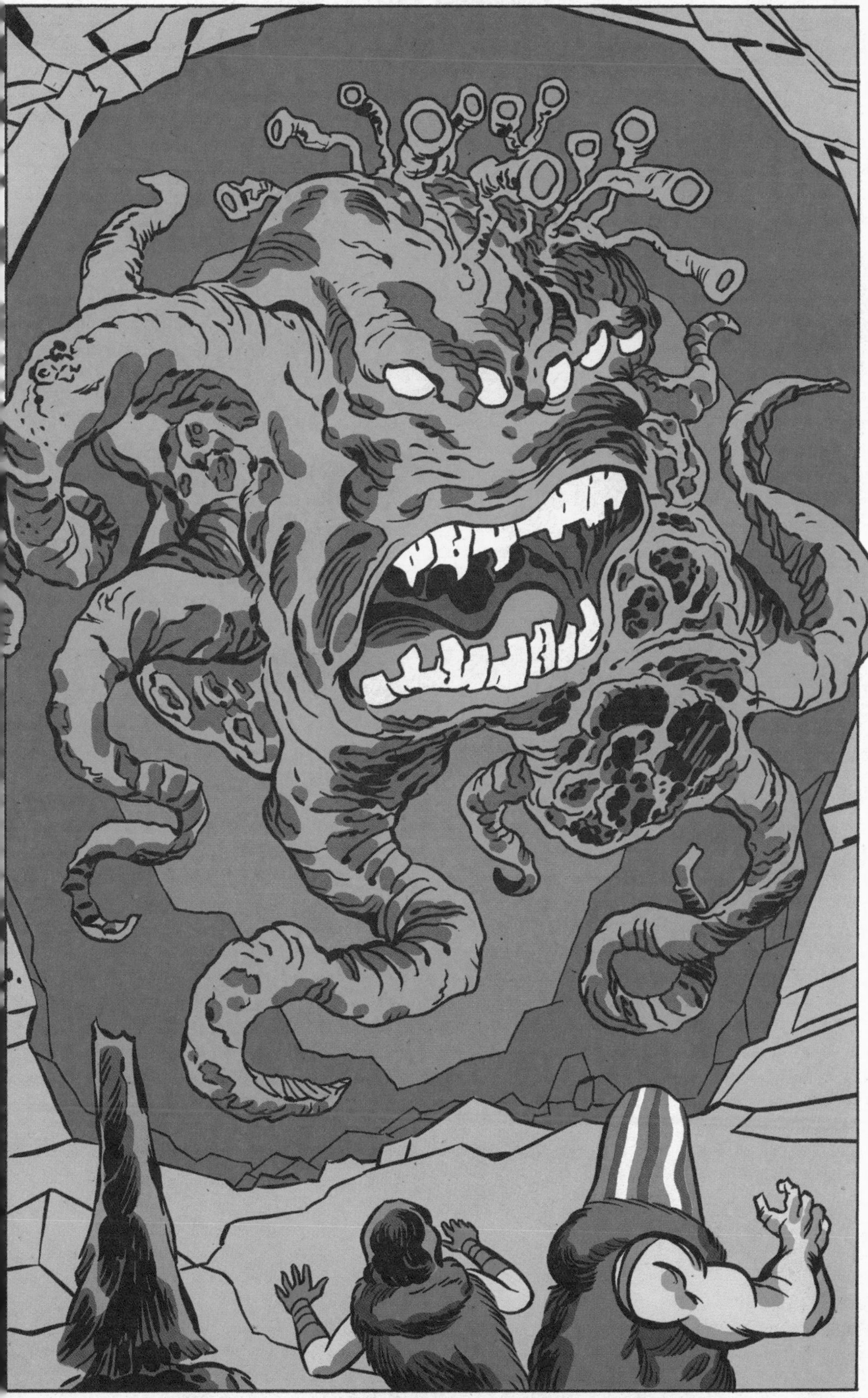

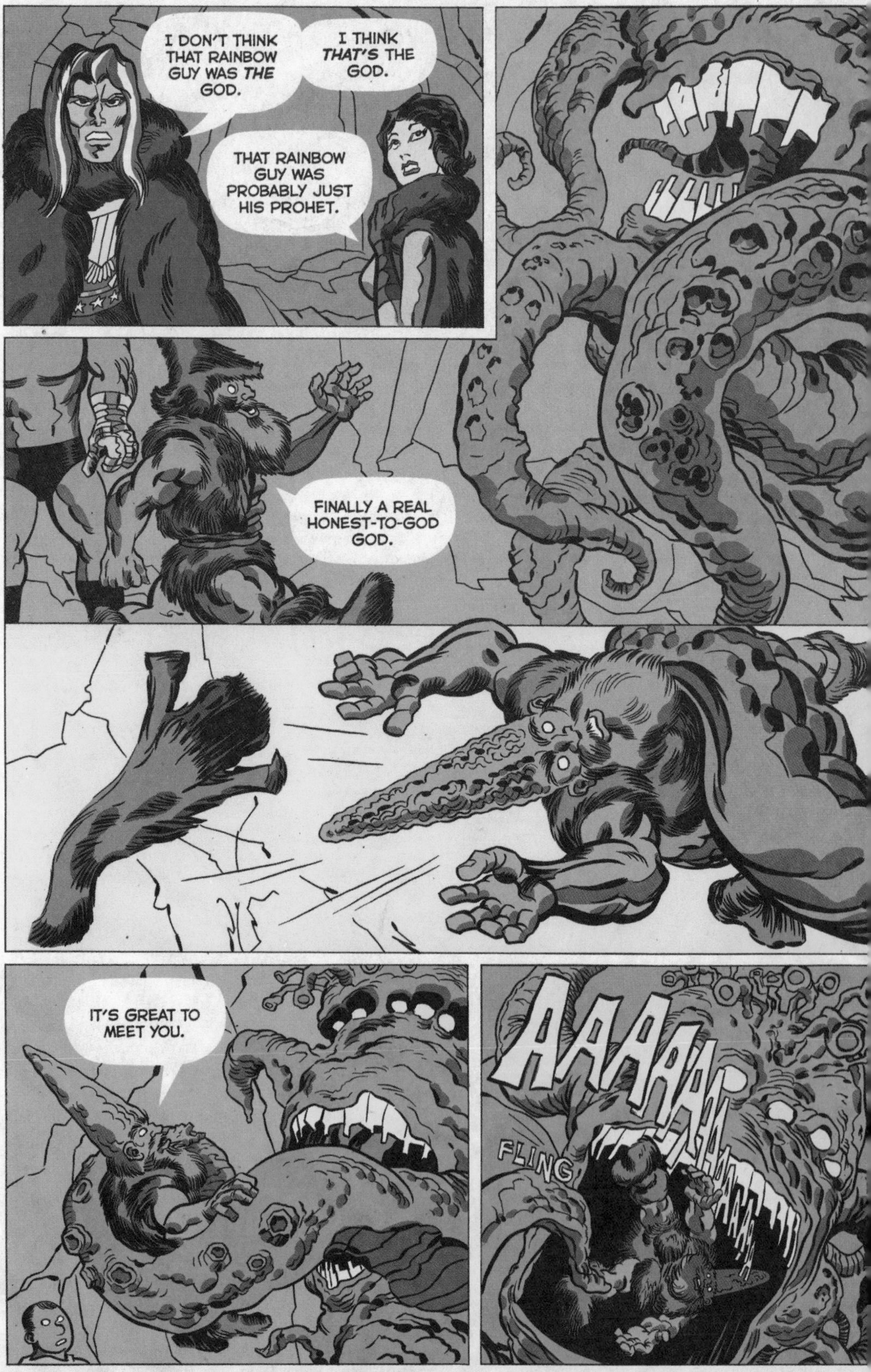
I DON'T THINK THAT RAINBOW GUY WAS *THE* GOD.
I THINK *THAT'S* THE GOD.
THAT RAINBOW GUY WAS PROBABLY JUST HIS PROHET.
FINALLY A REAL HONEST-TO-GOD GOD.
IT'S GREAT TO MEET YOU.
FLING
AAAAAAAAAAAAAAA

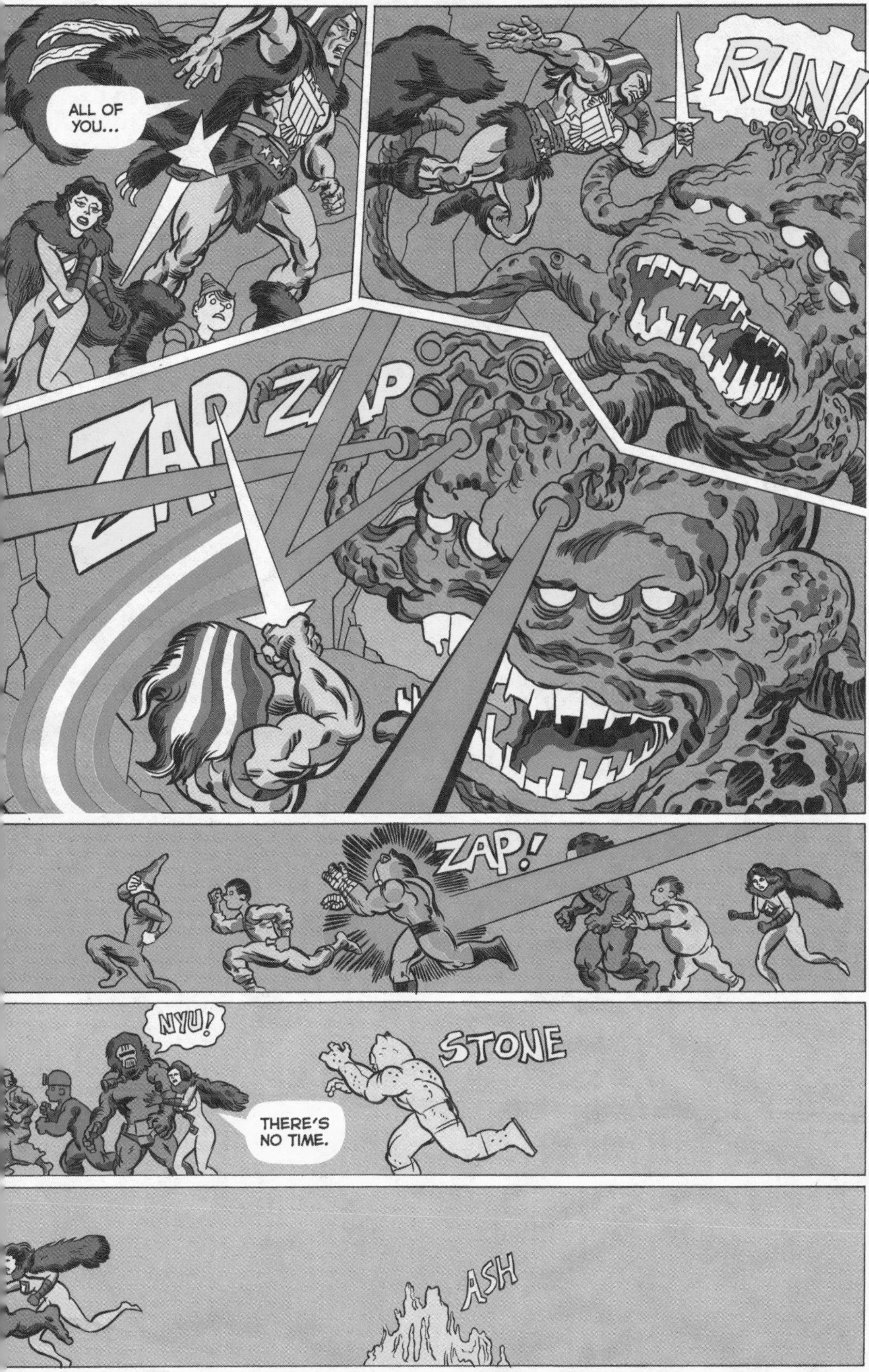
ALL OF YOU...
RUN!
ZAP
ZAP
ZAP!
NYU!
THERE'S NO TIME.
STONE
ASH

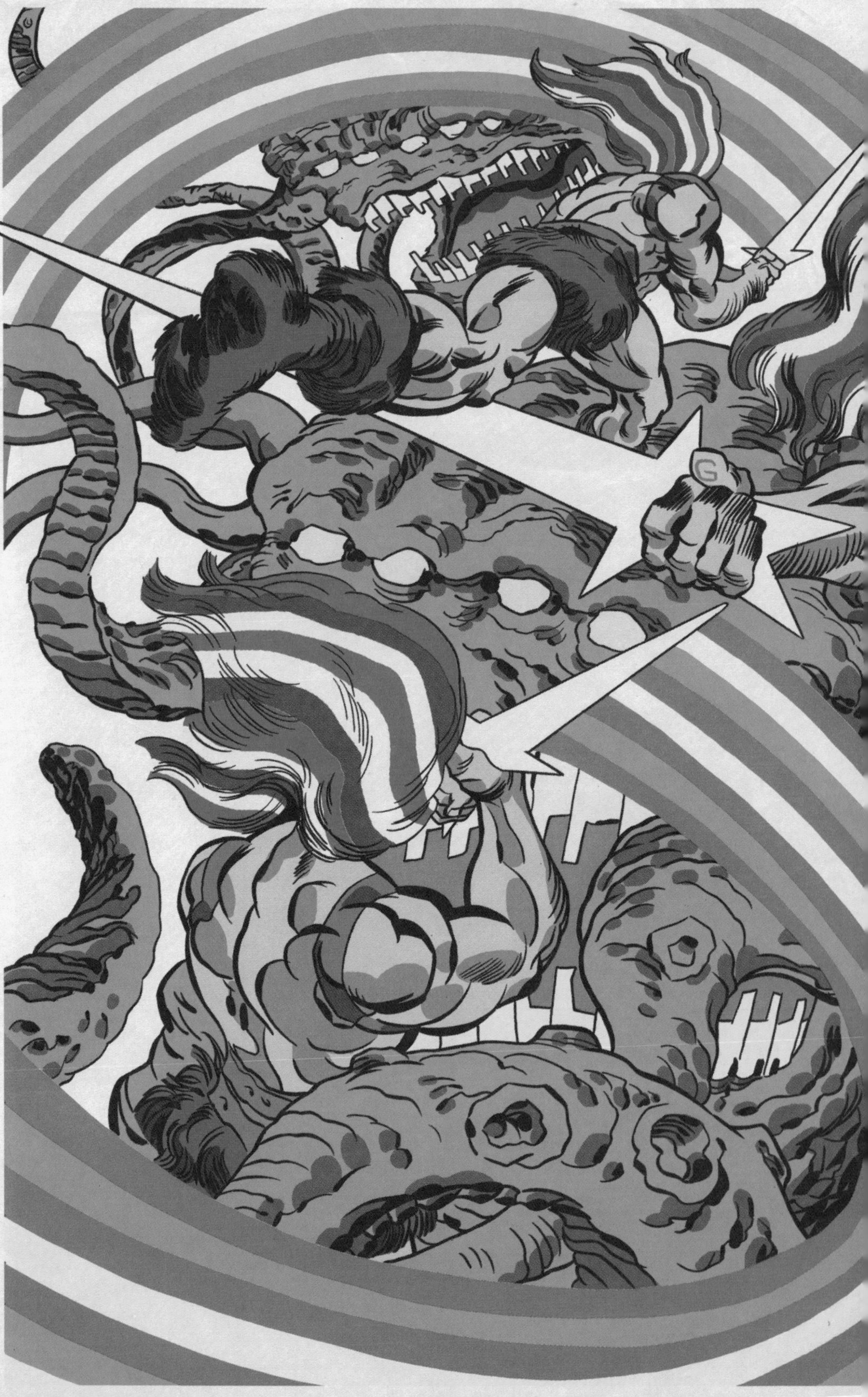

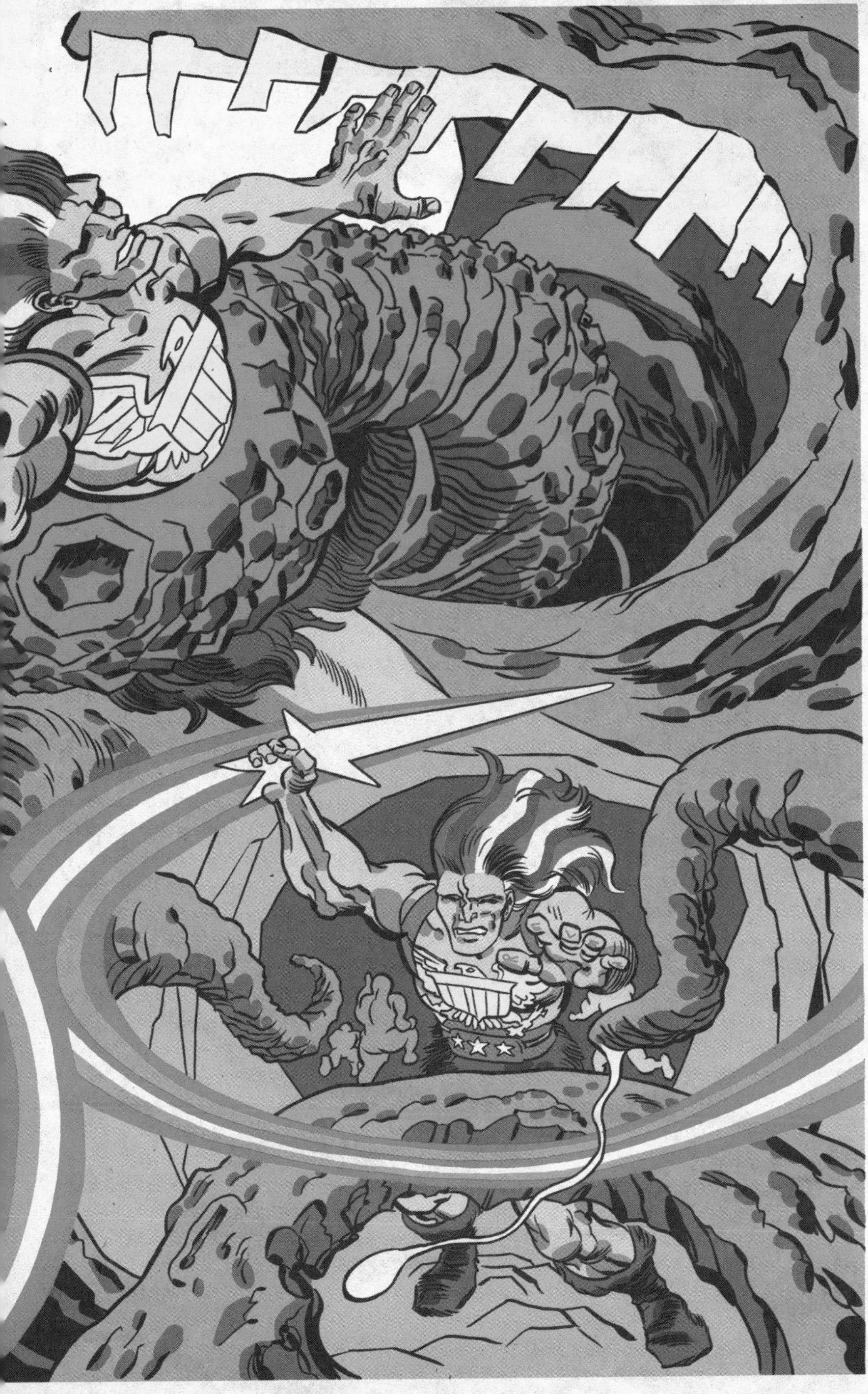

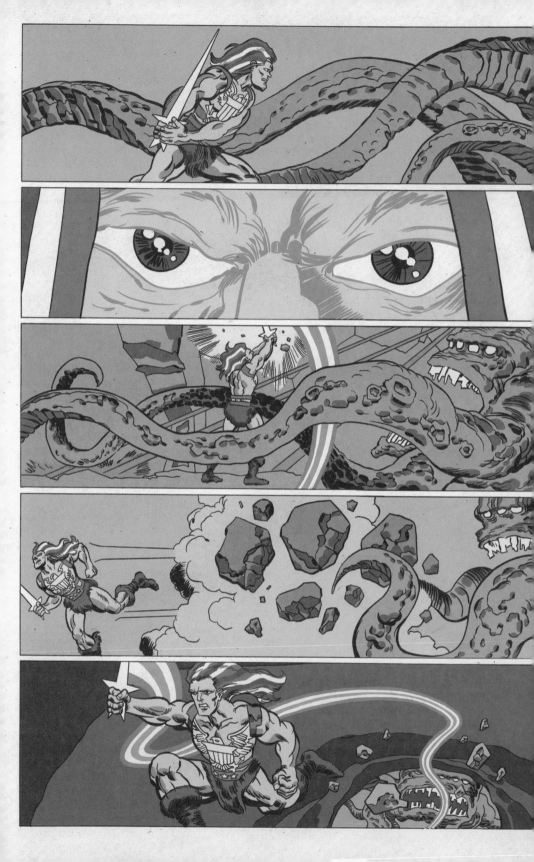

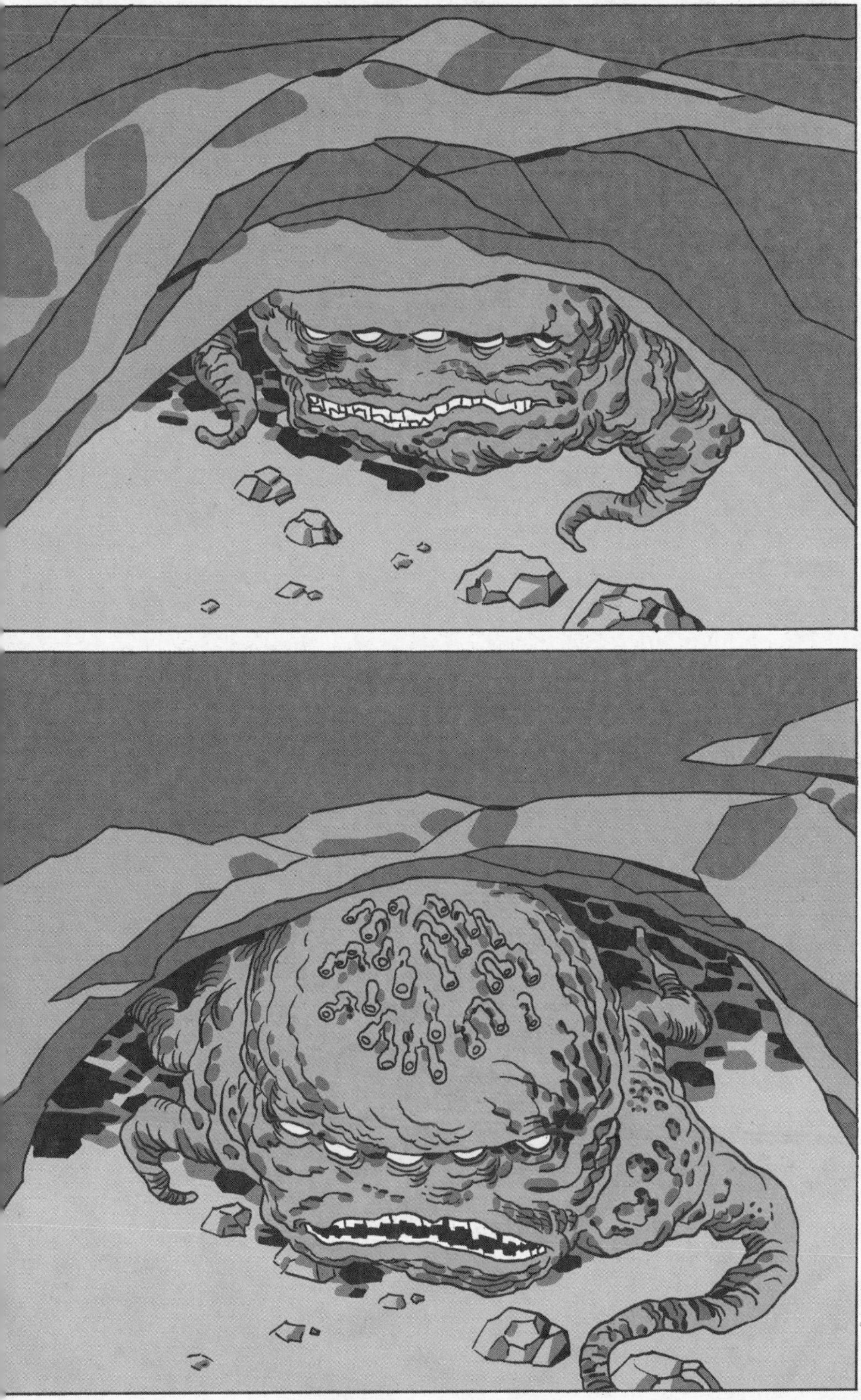

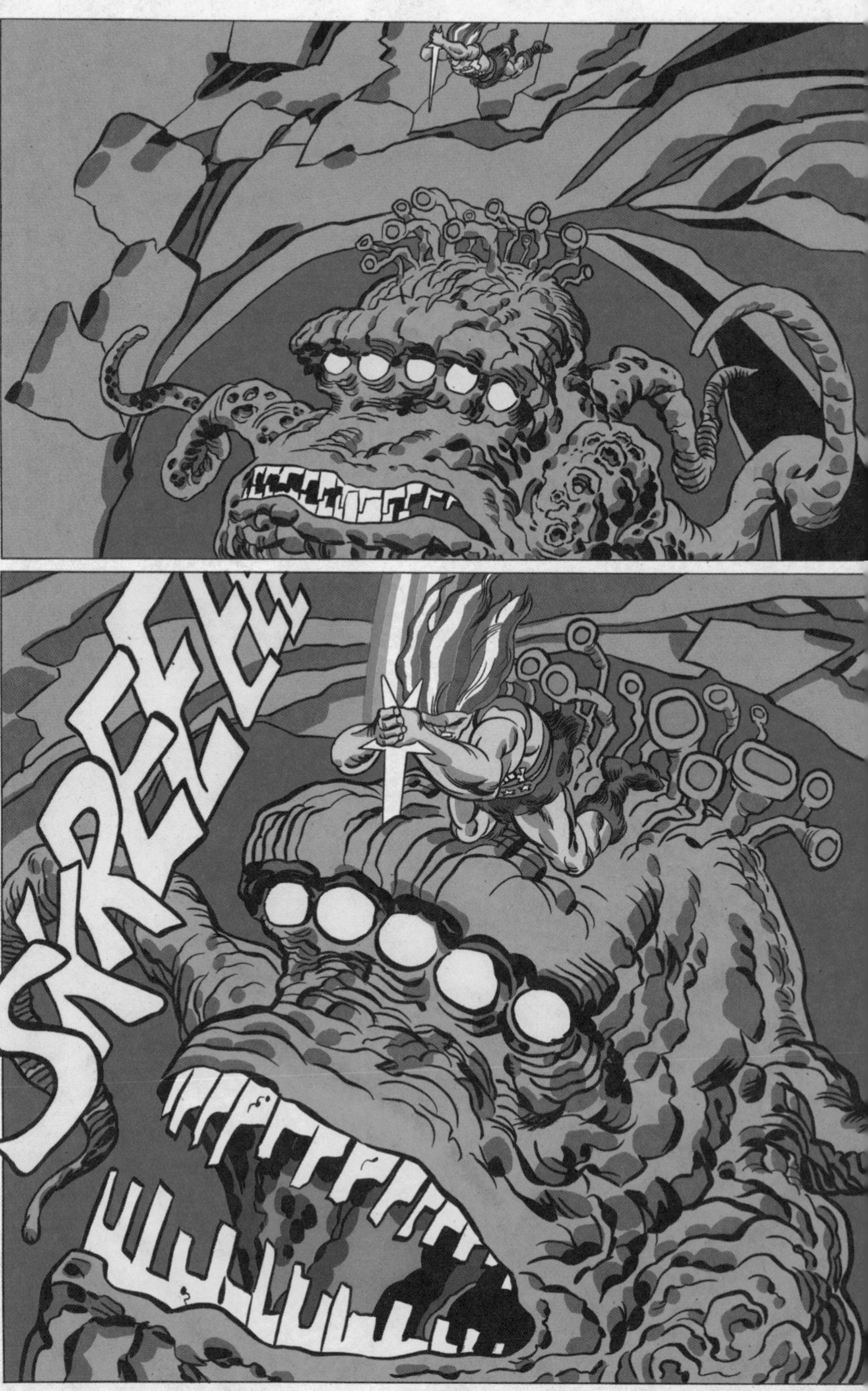

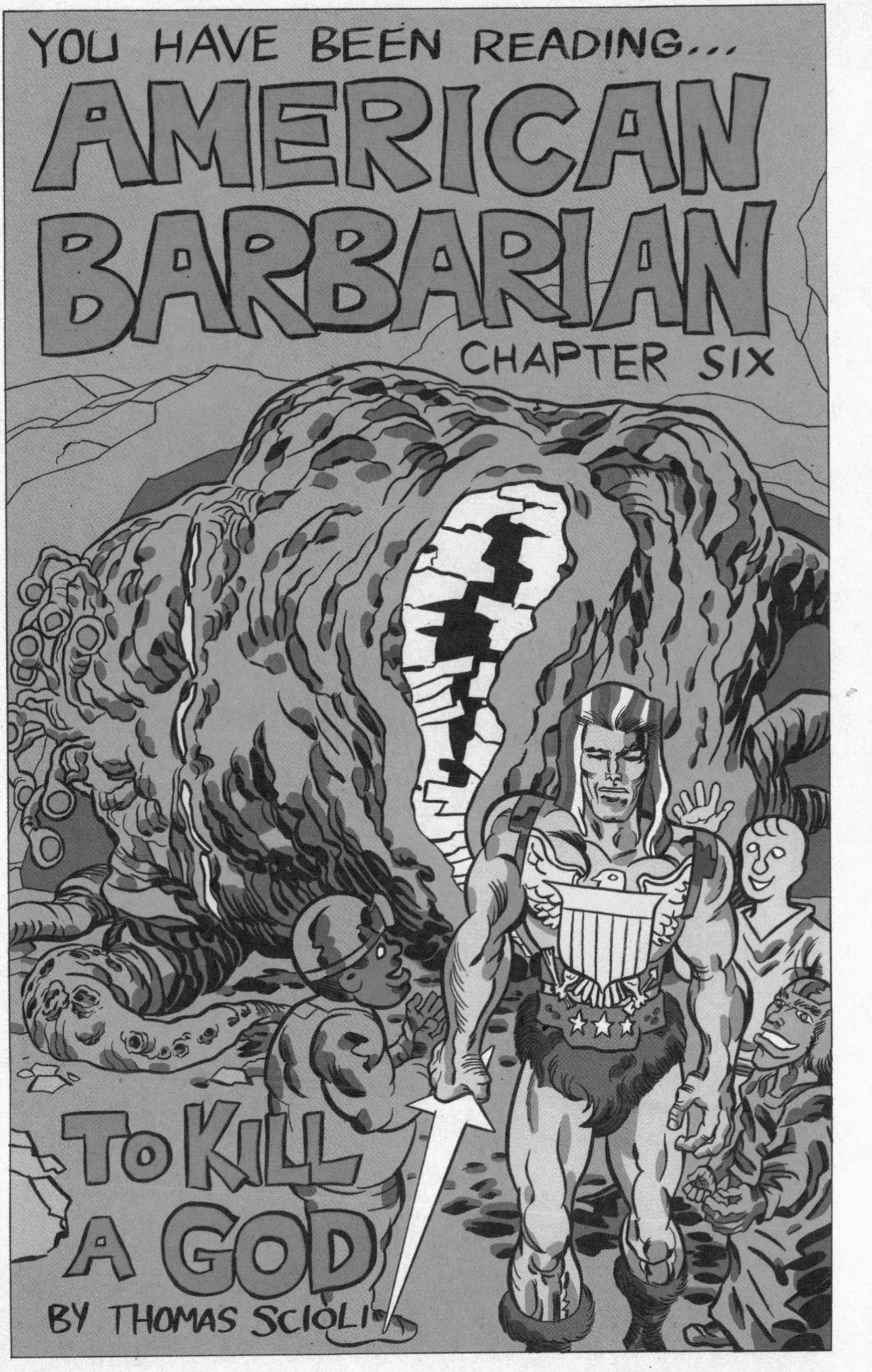
YOU HAVE BEEN READING...
AMERICAN BARBARIAN
CHAPTER SIX
TO KILL A GOD
BY THOMAS SCIOLI

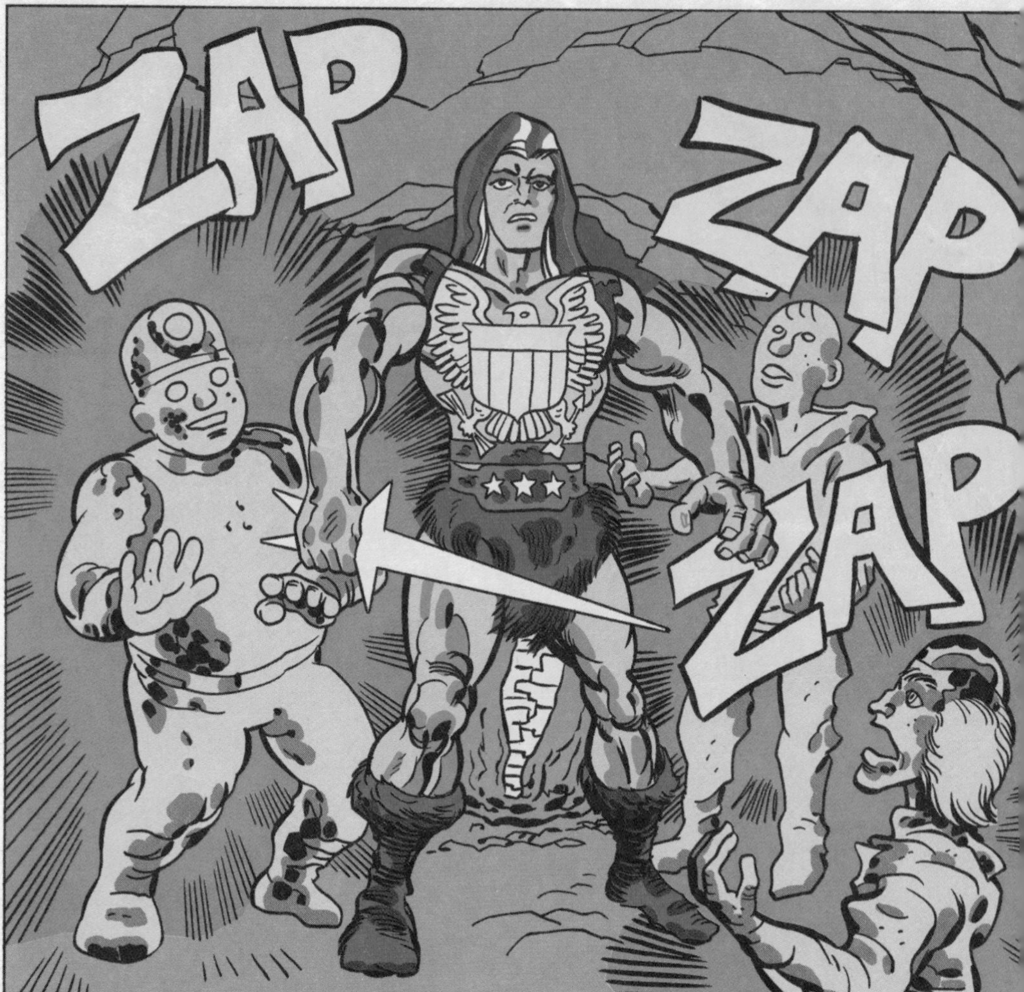
ZAP
ZAP
ZAP

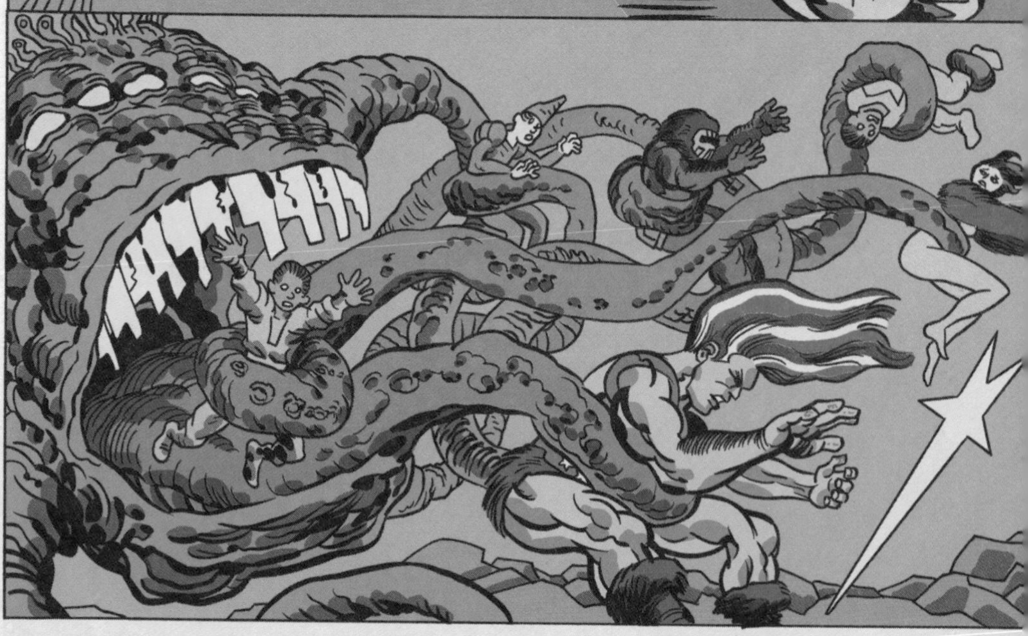

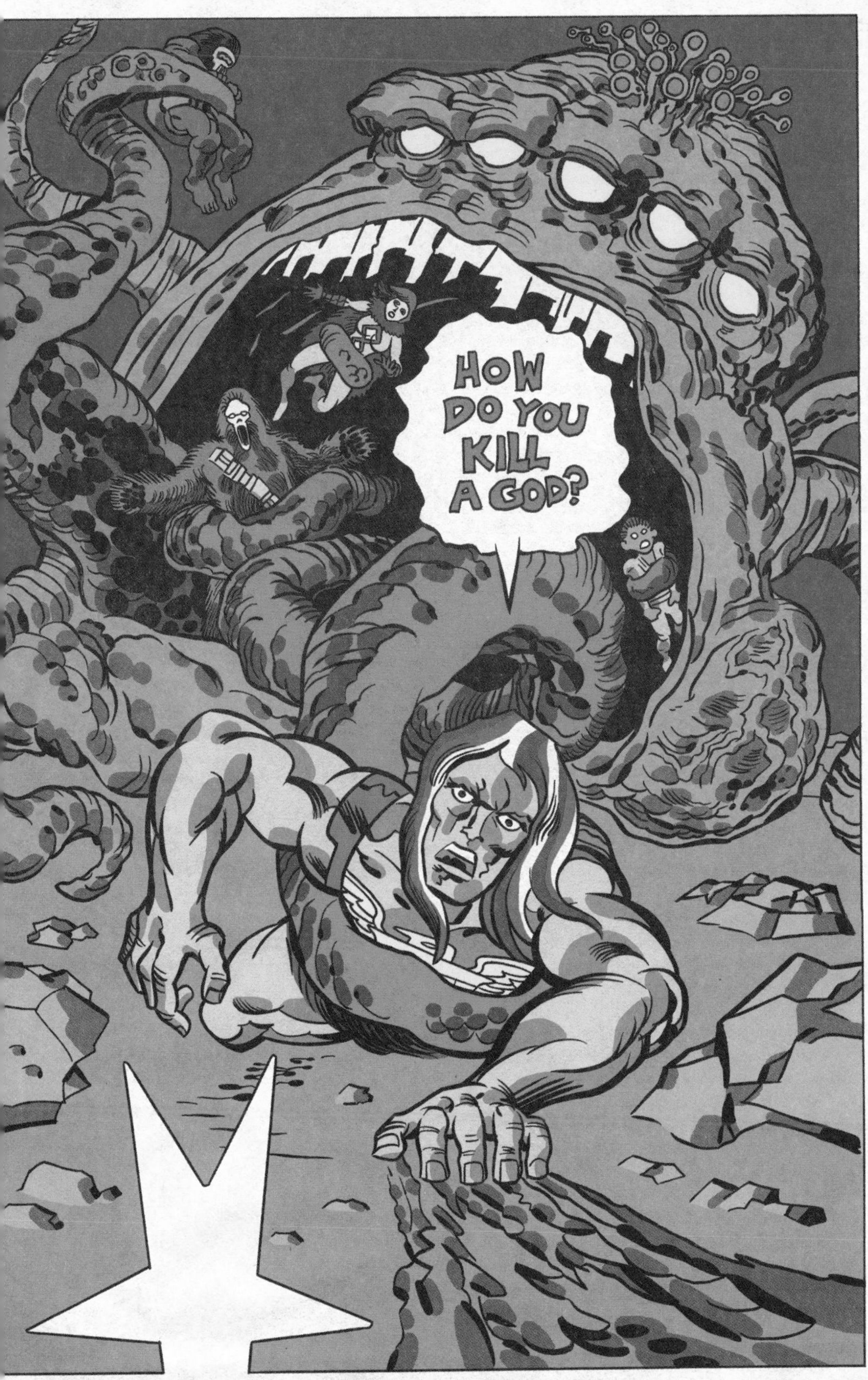
HOW DO YOU KILL A GOD?

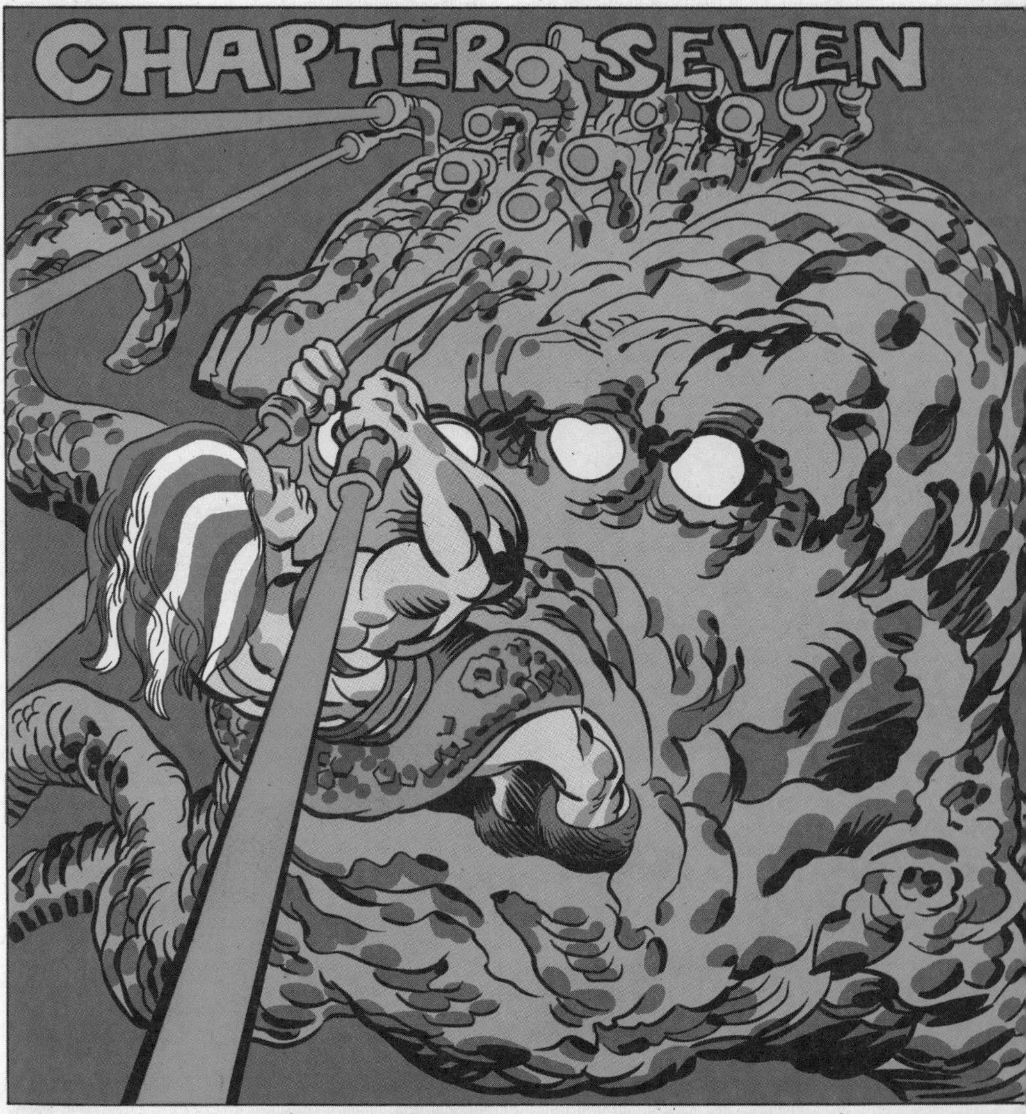
CHAPTER SEVEN

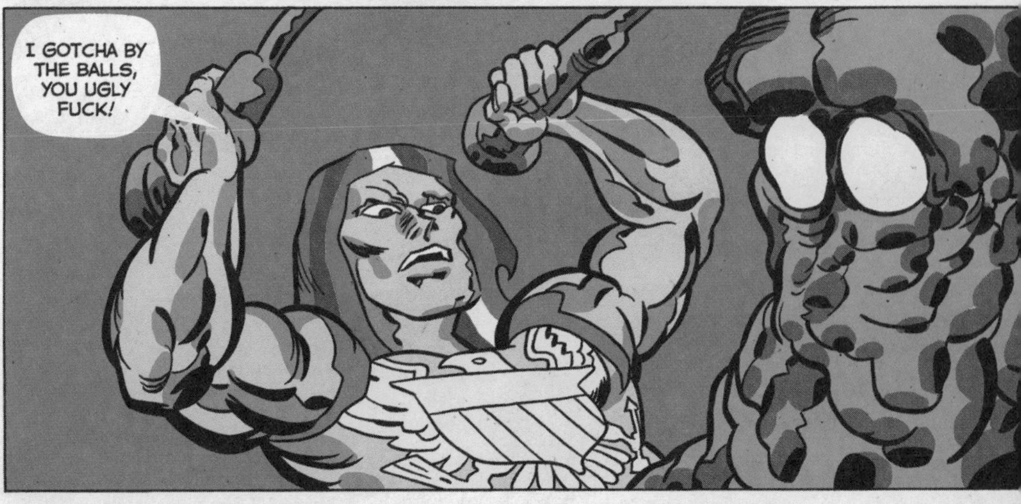
I GOTCHA BY THE BALLS, YOU UGLY FUCK!

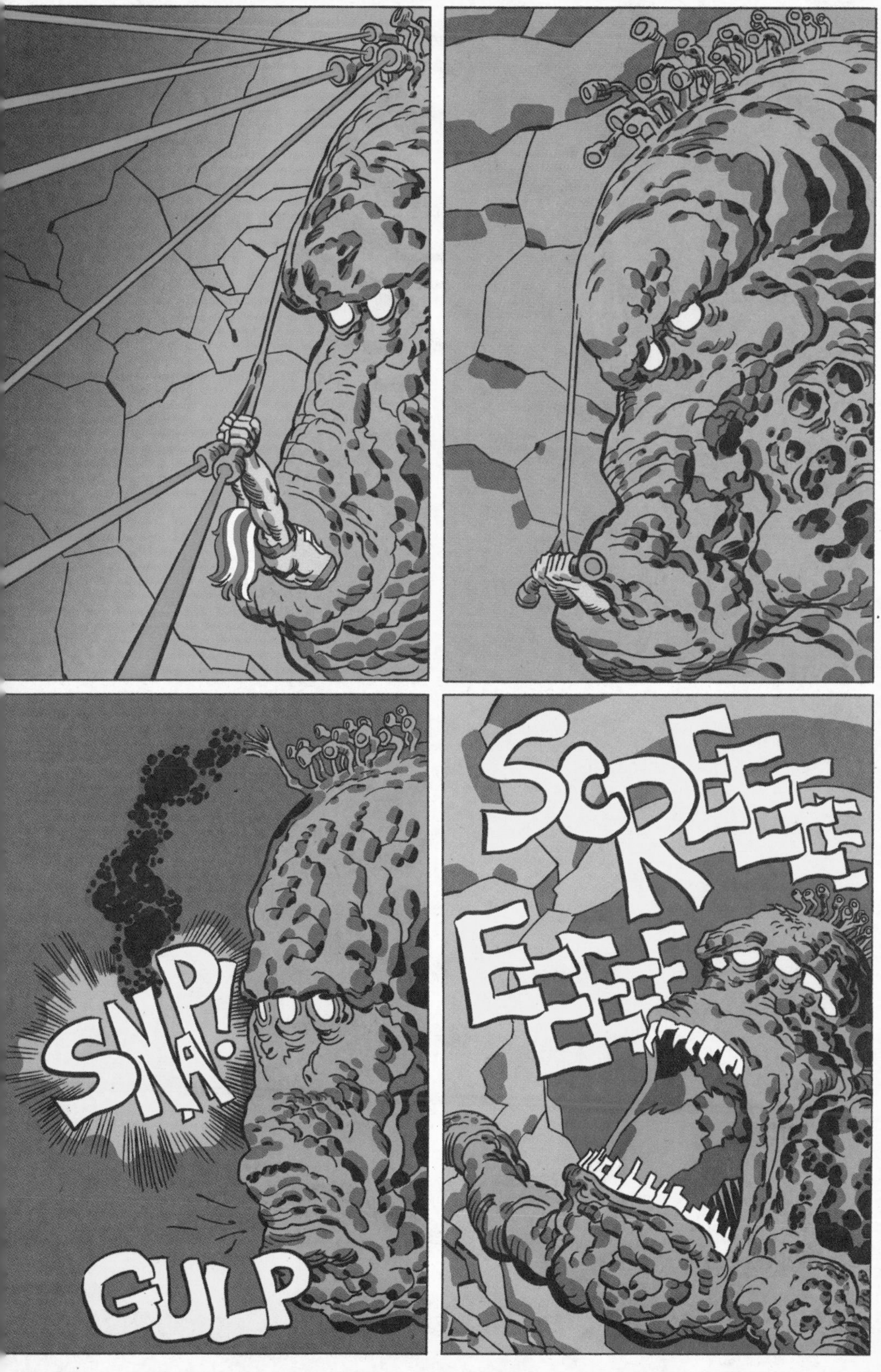
SNAP!
GULP
SCREEEEE
EEEEE

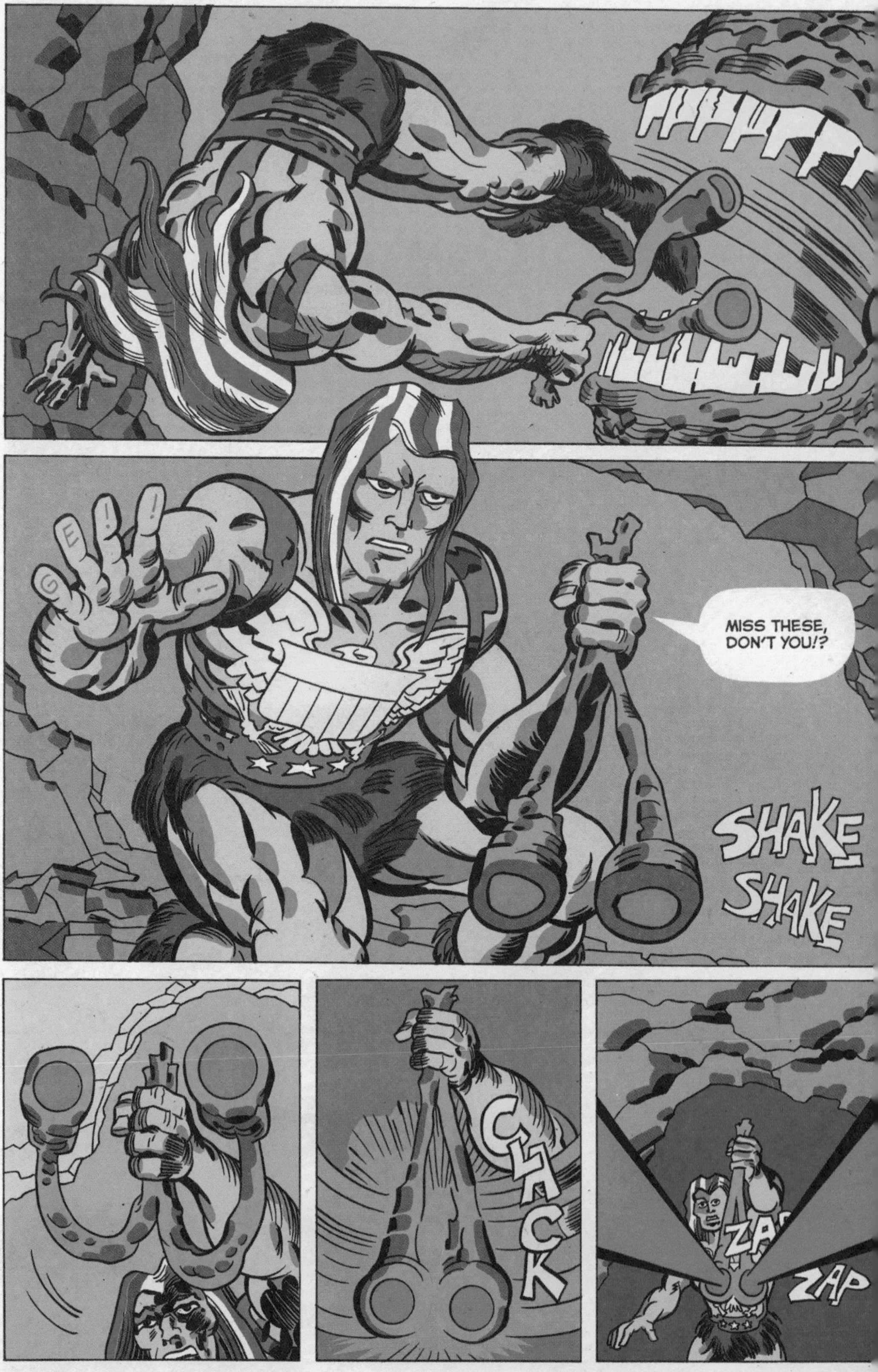
MISS THESE, DON'T YOU!?
SHAKE
SHAKE
CLACK
ZAP

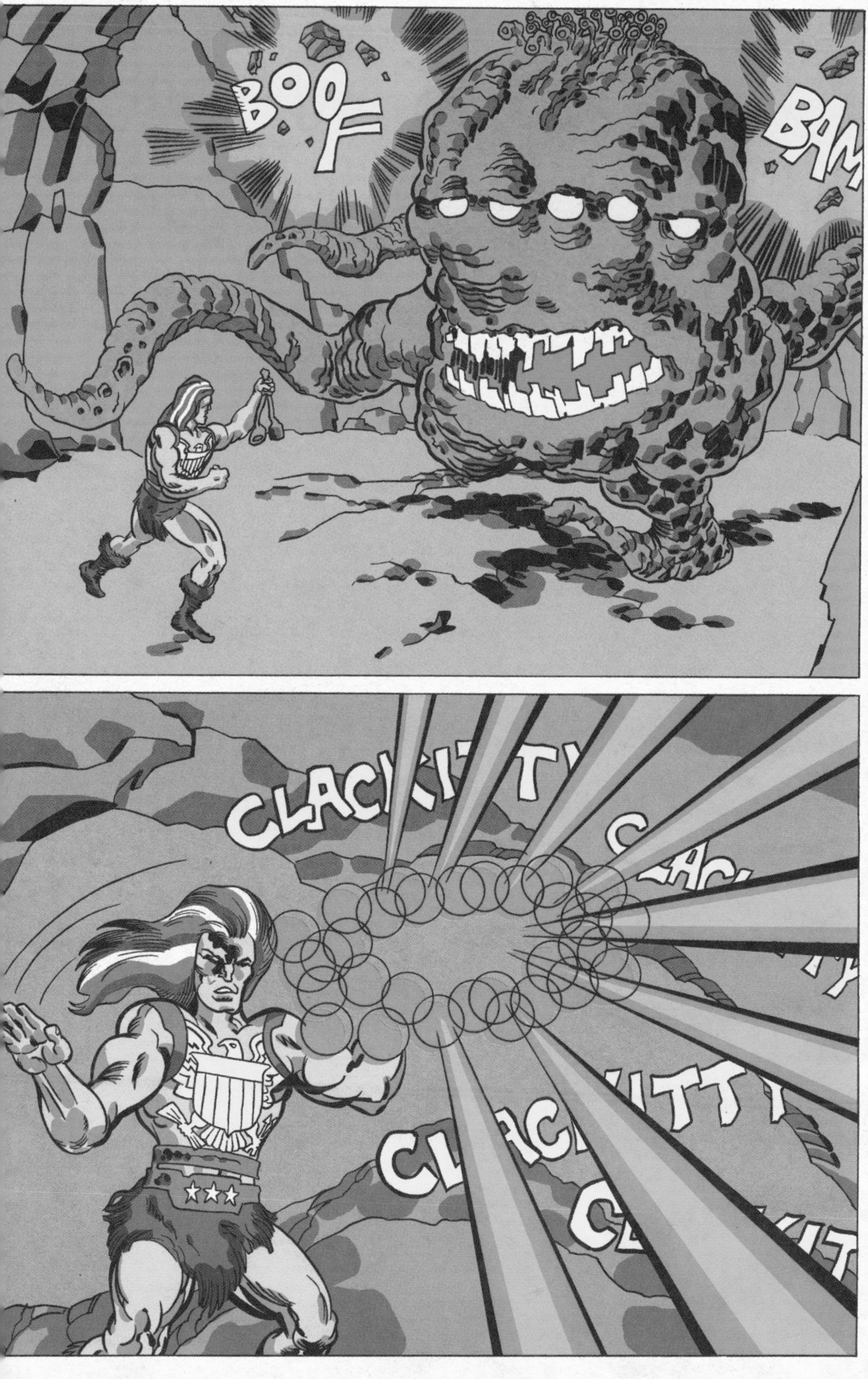
BOOF
BAM
CLACKITTY

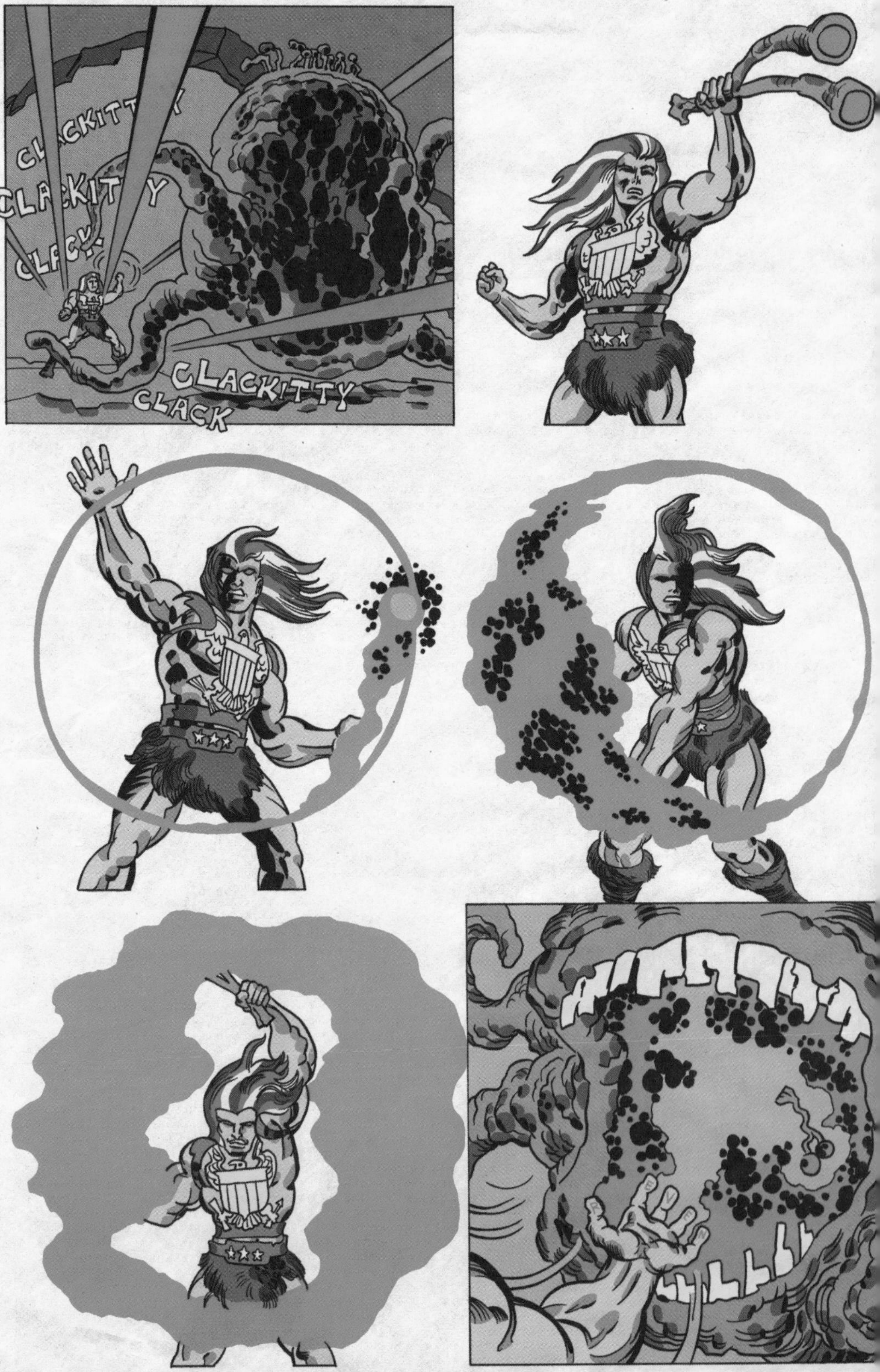
CLACKITTY
CLACKITTY
CLACK
CLACKITTY
CLACK

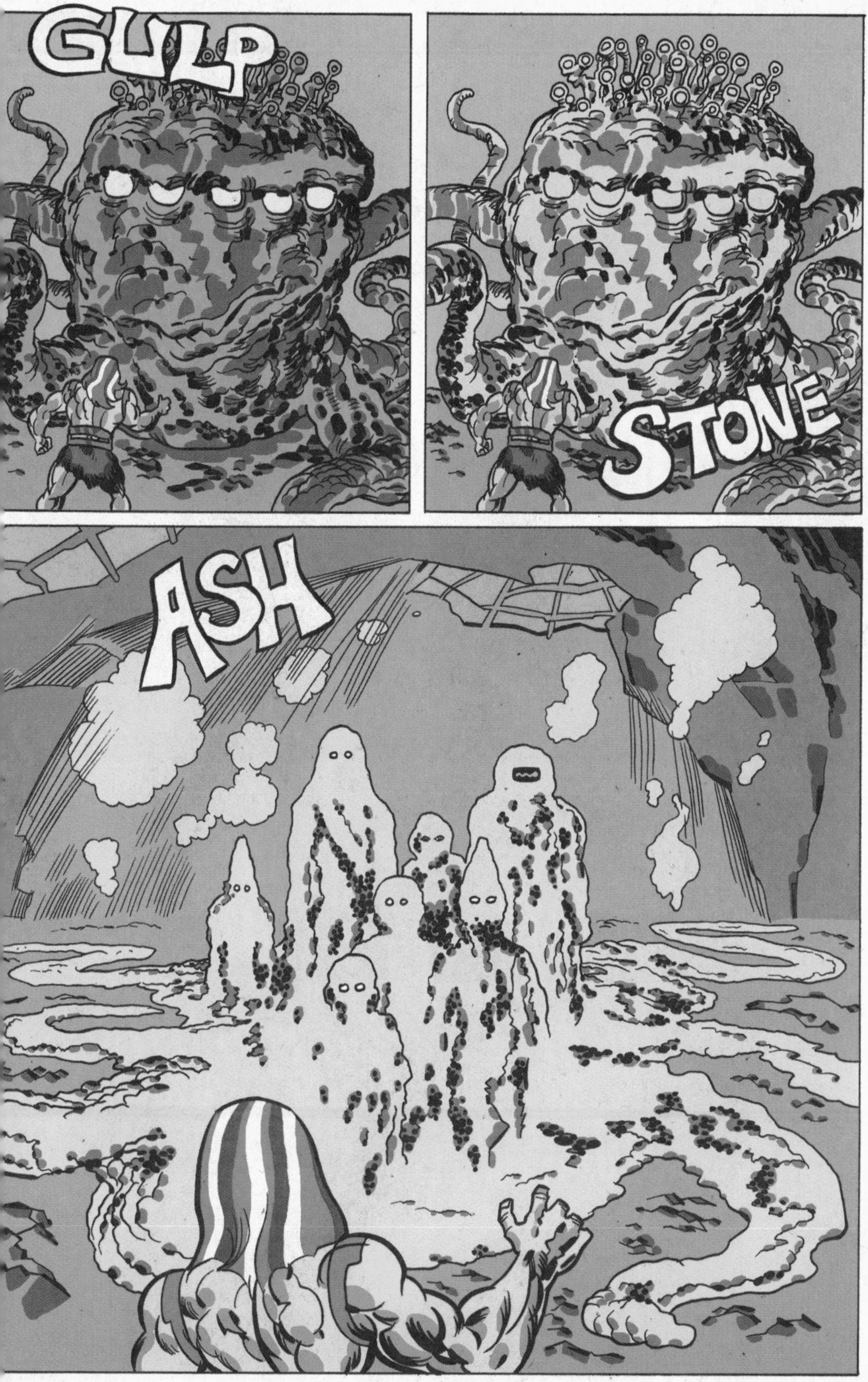
GULP
STONE
ASH

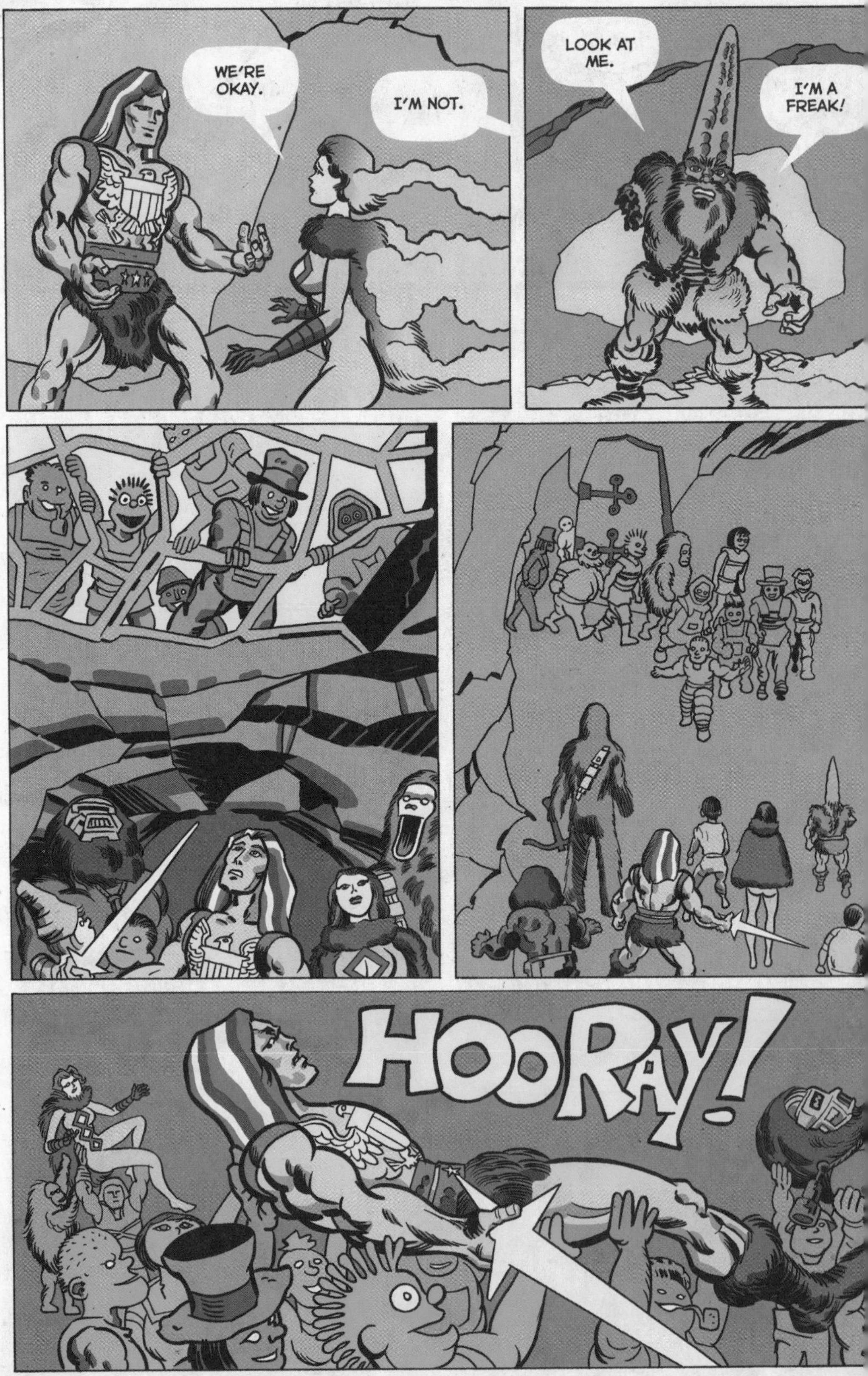
WE'RE OKAY.
I'M NOT.
LOOK AT ME.
I'M A FREAK!
HOORAY!

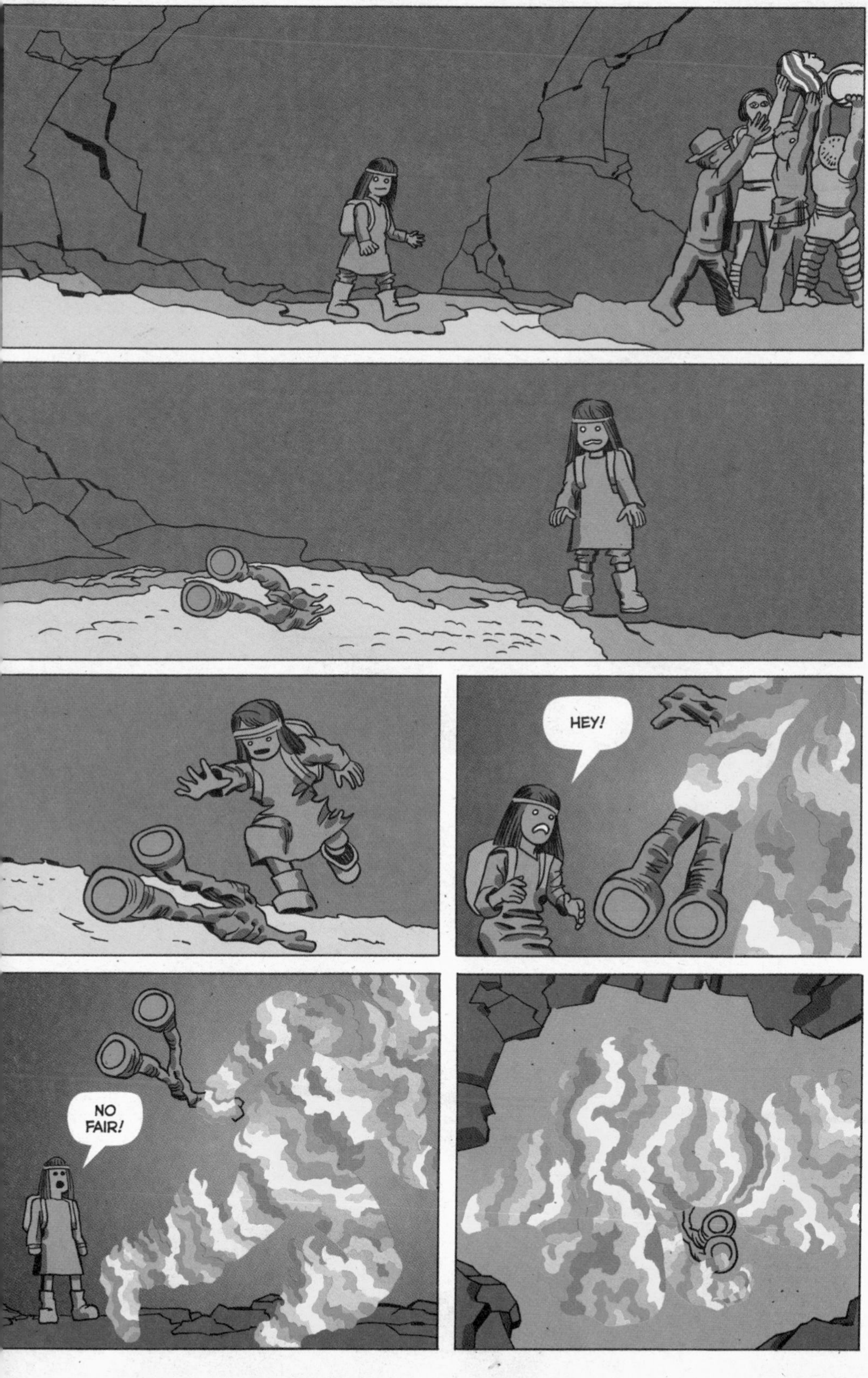
HEY!
NO FAIR!

THANKS FOR THE PRIZE!
LISTEN UP, EVERYBODY!
I'M HEADING OUT TO KICK SOME MORE ASS, BUT I NEED AN ARMY.
ANYBODY WANT TO COME WITH ME?

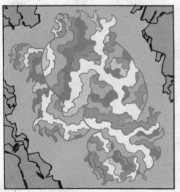

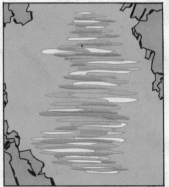

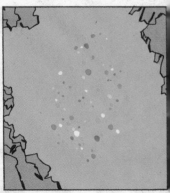

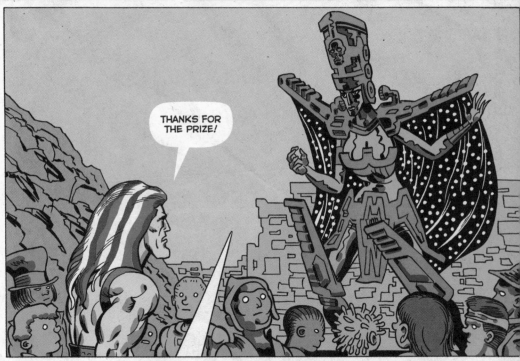

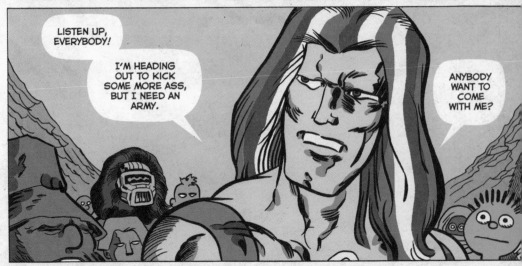

AMERICAN BARBARIAN

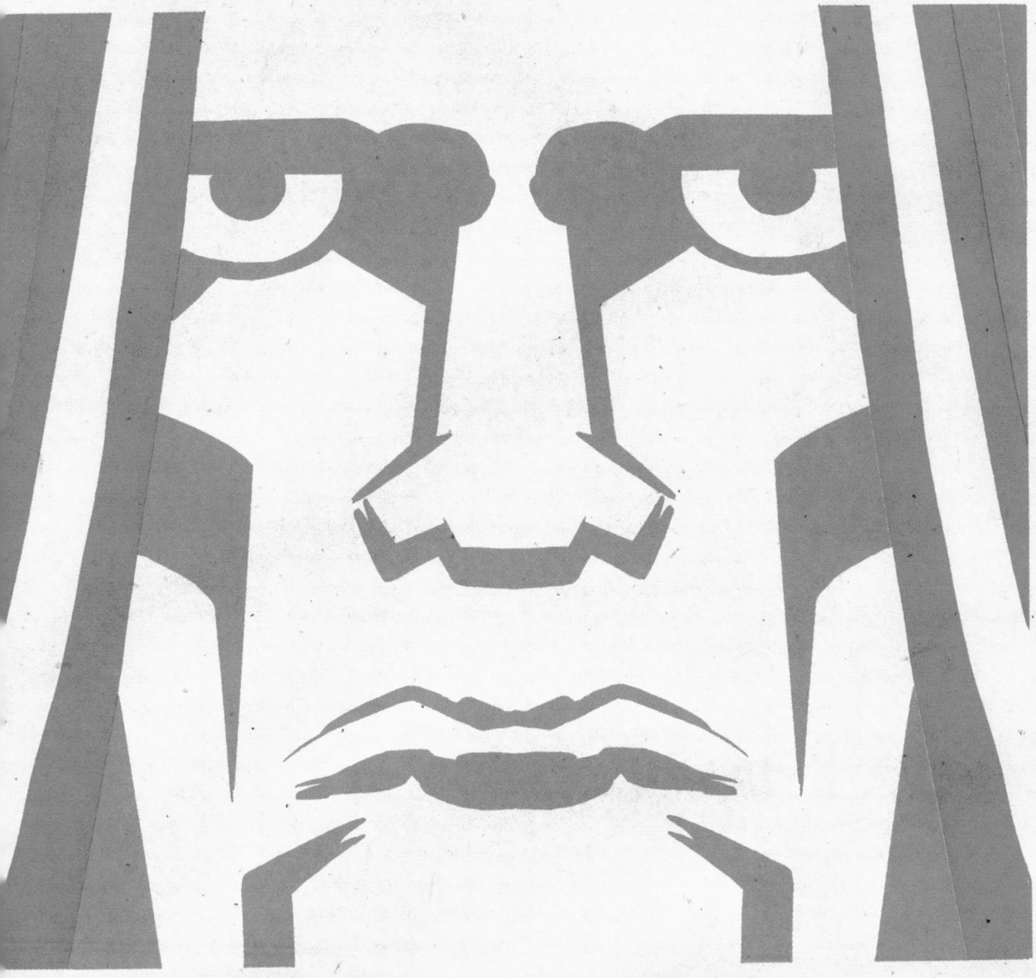

HAS A POSSE

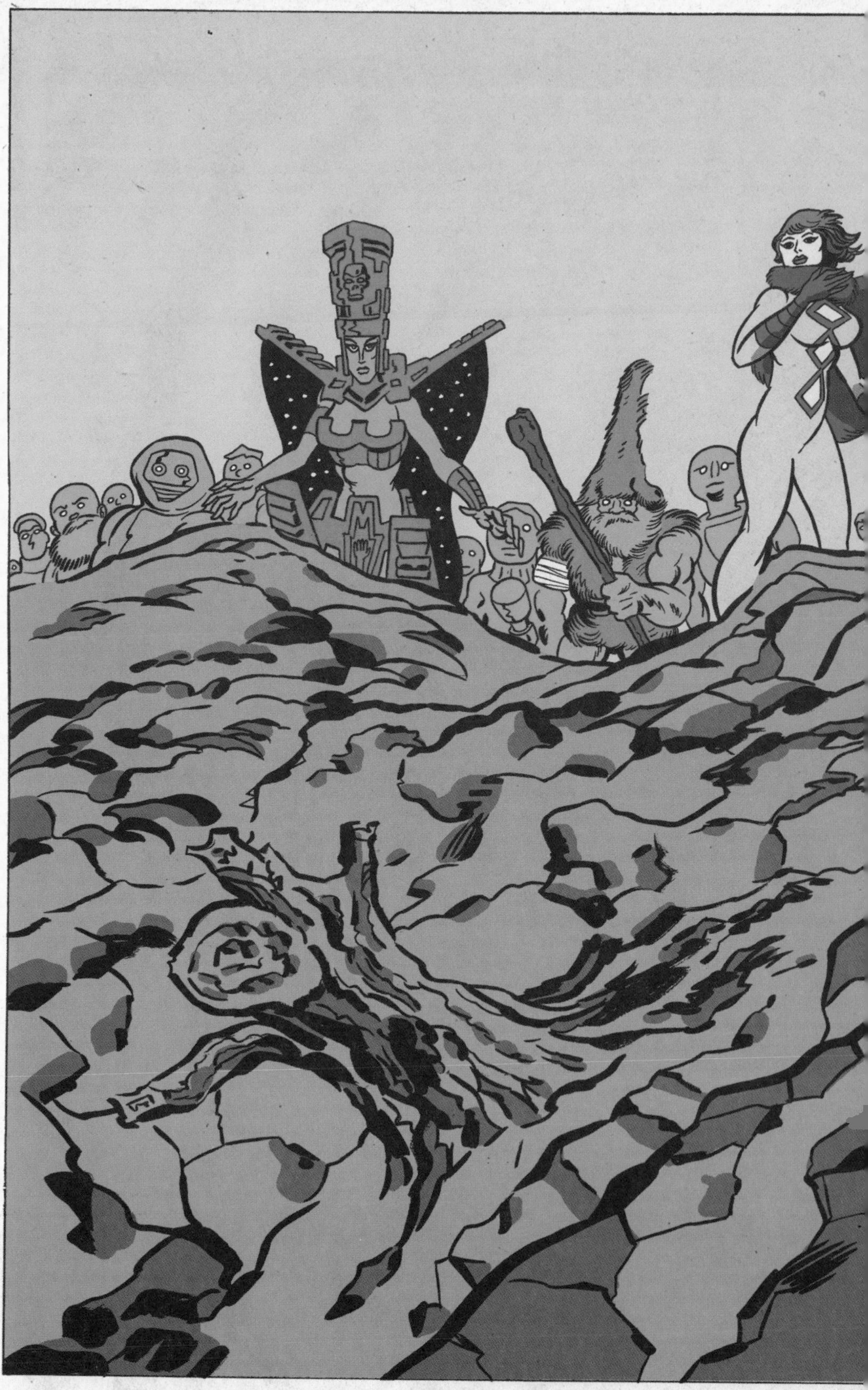

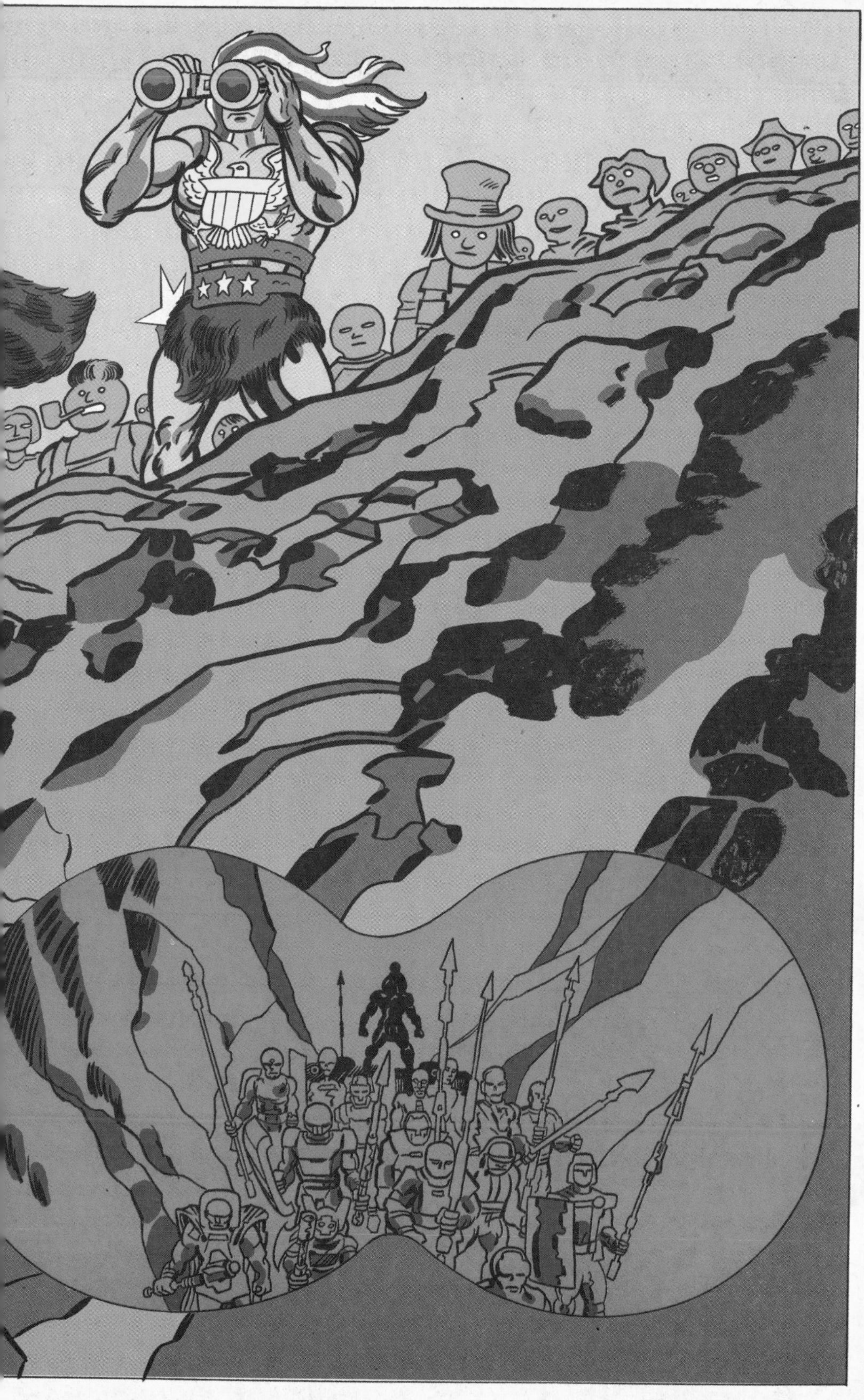

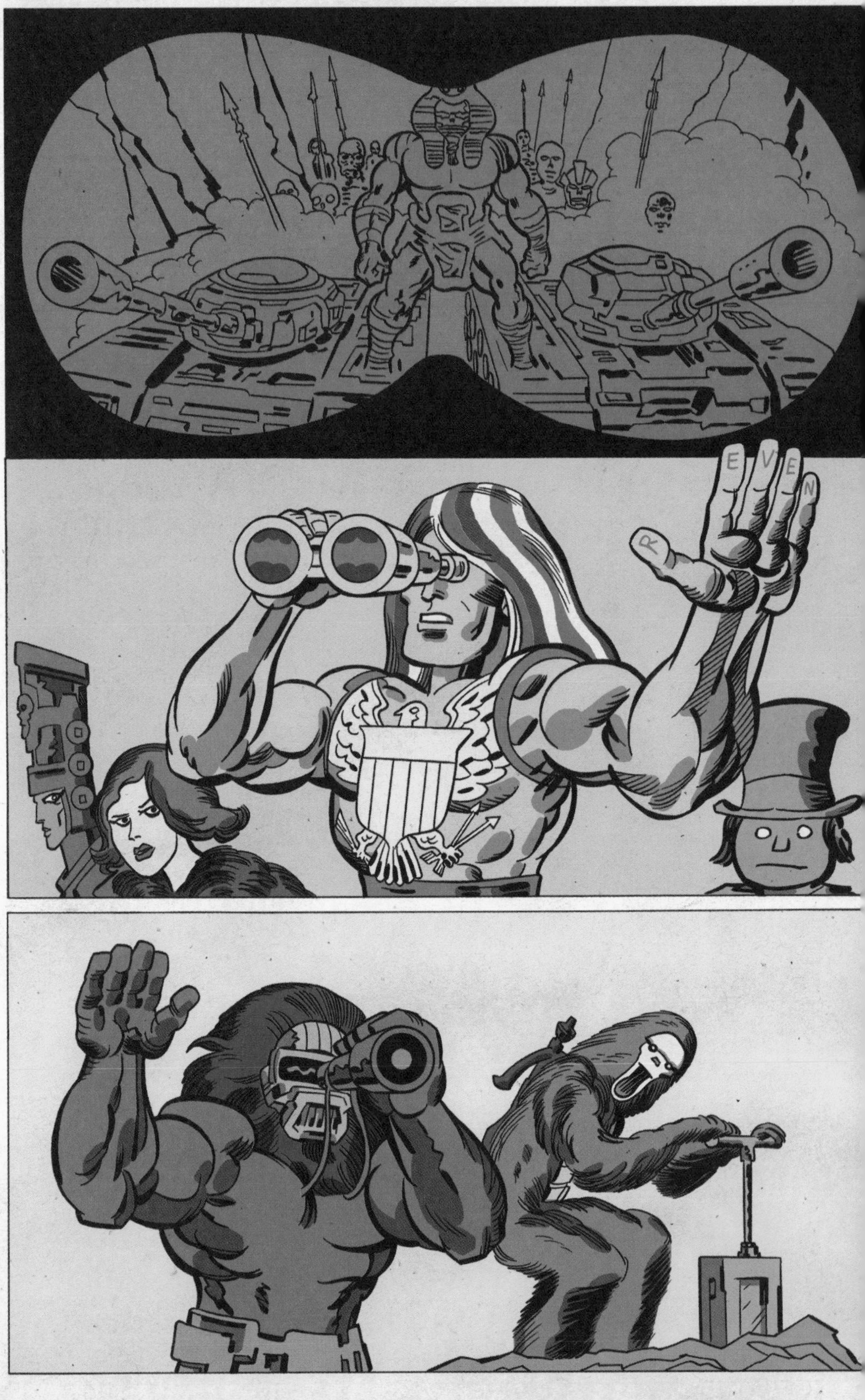
E V E N
R

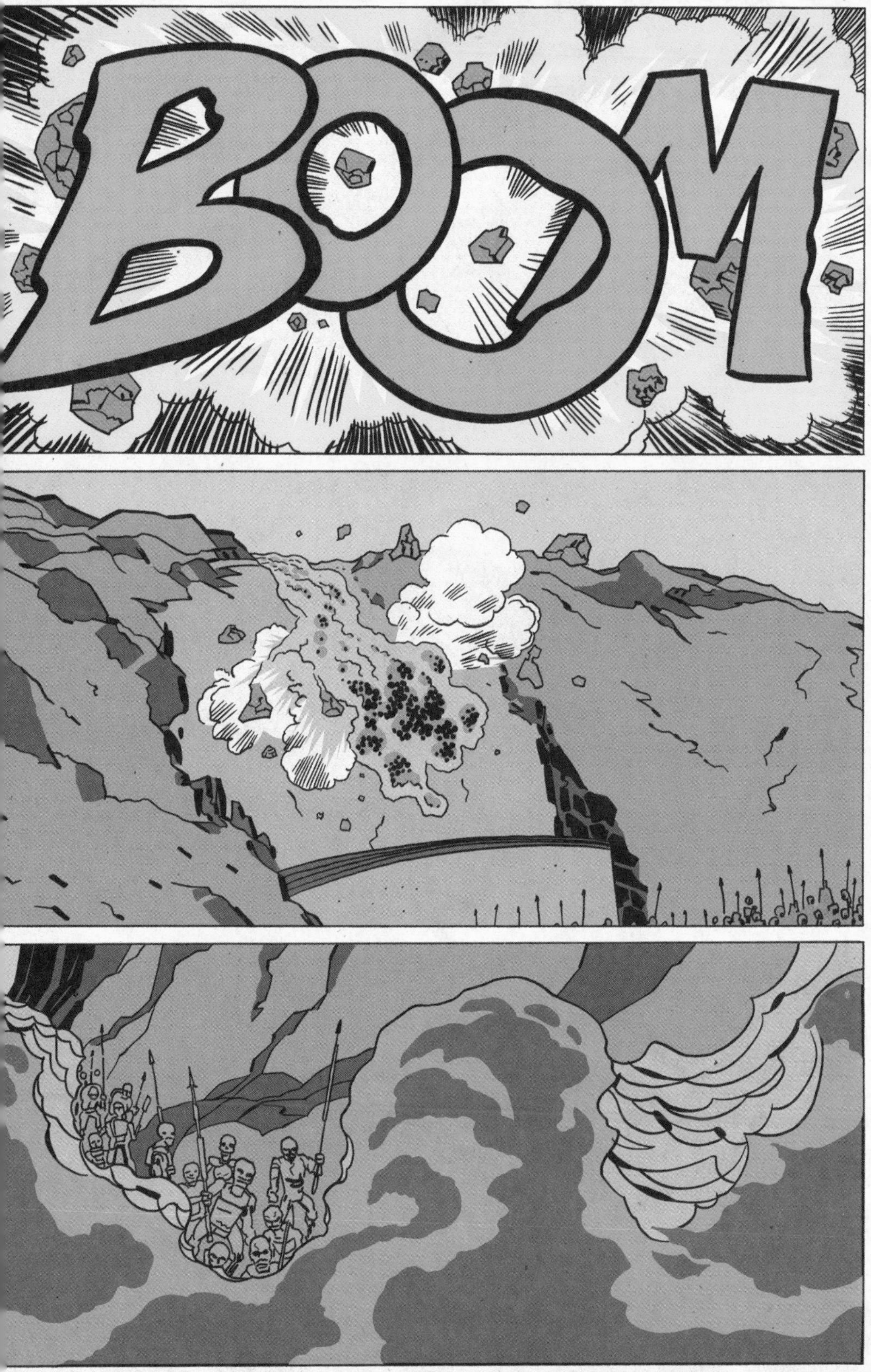
BOOM

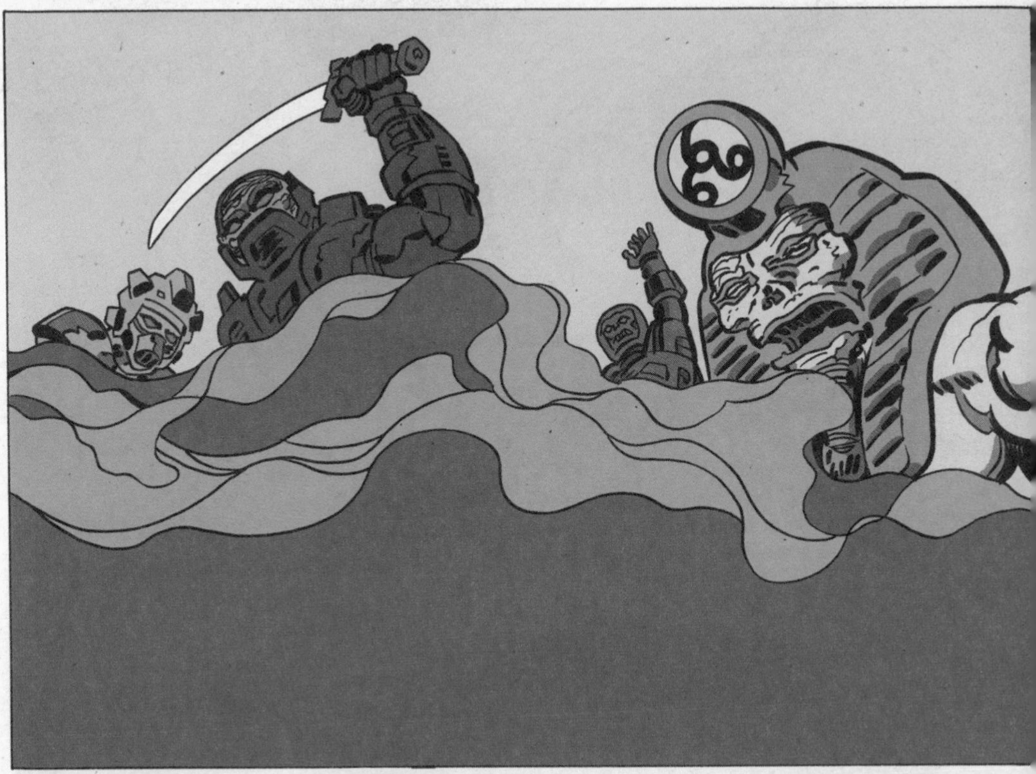

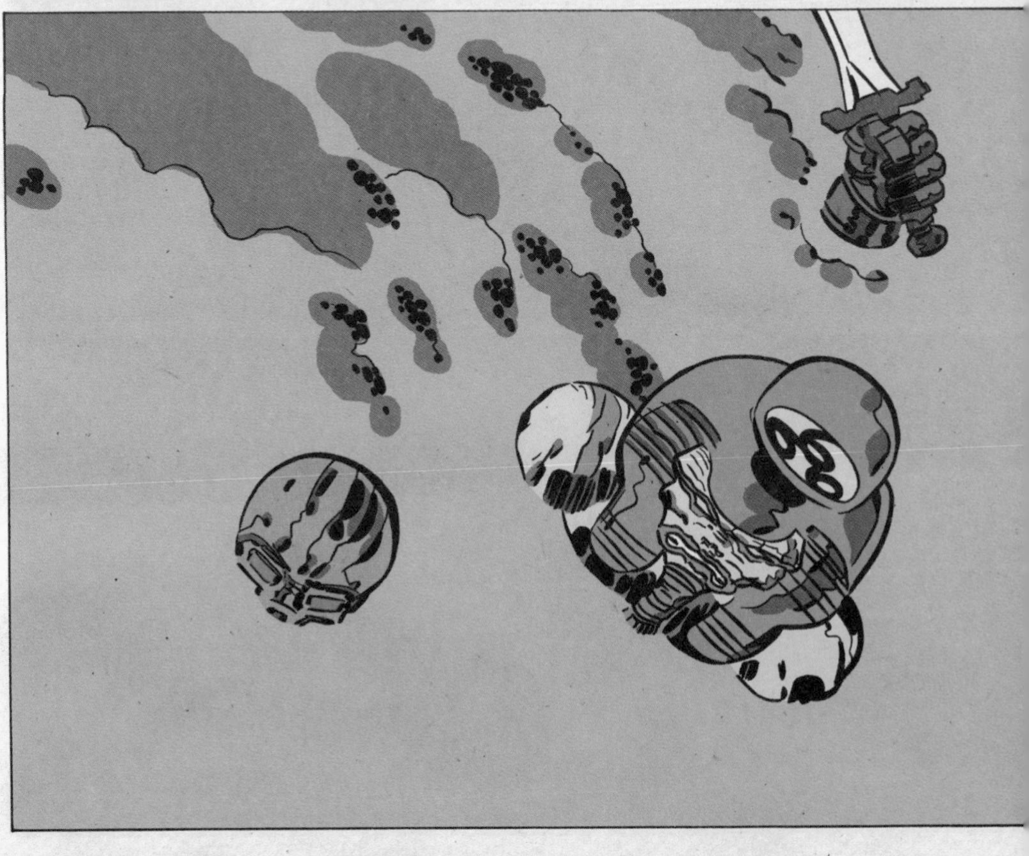

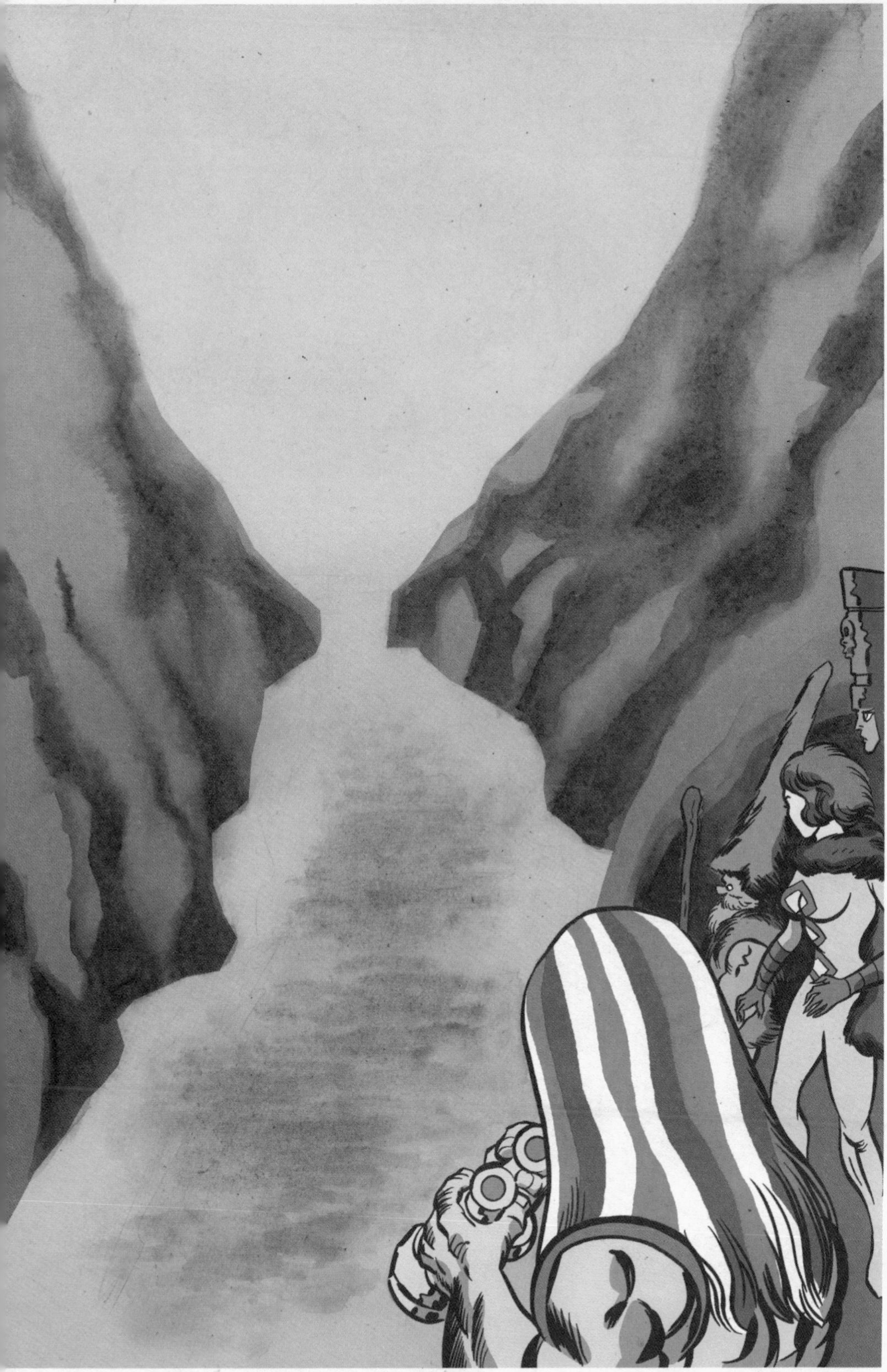

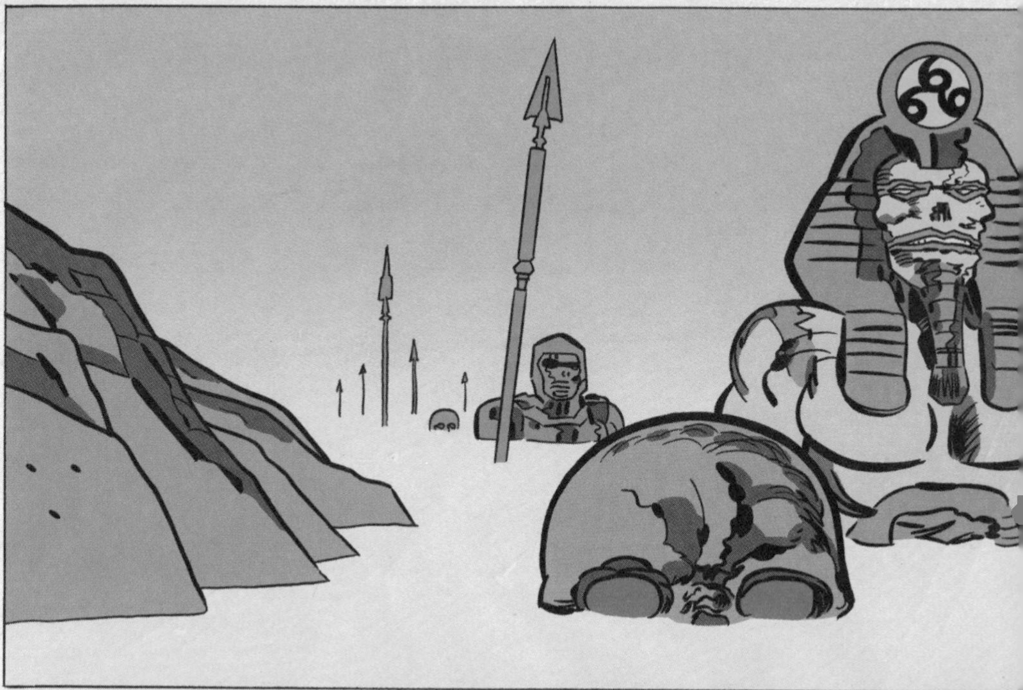

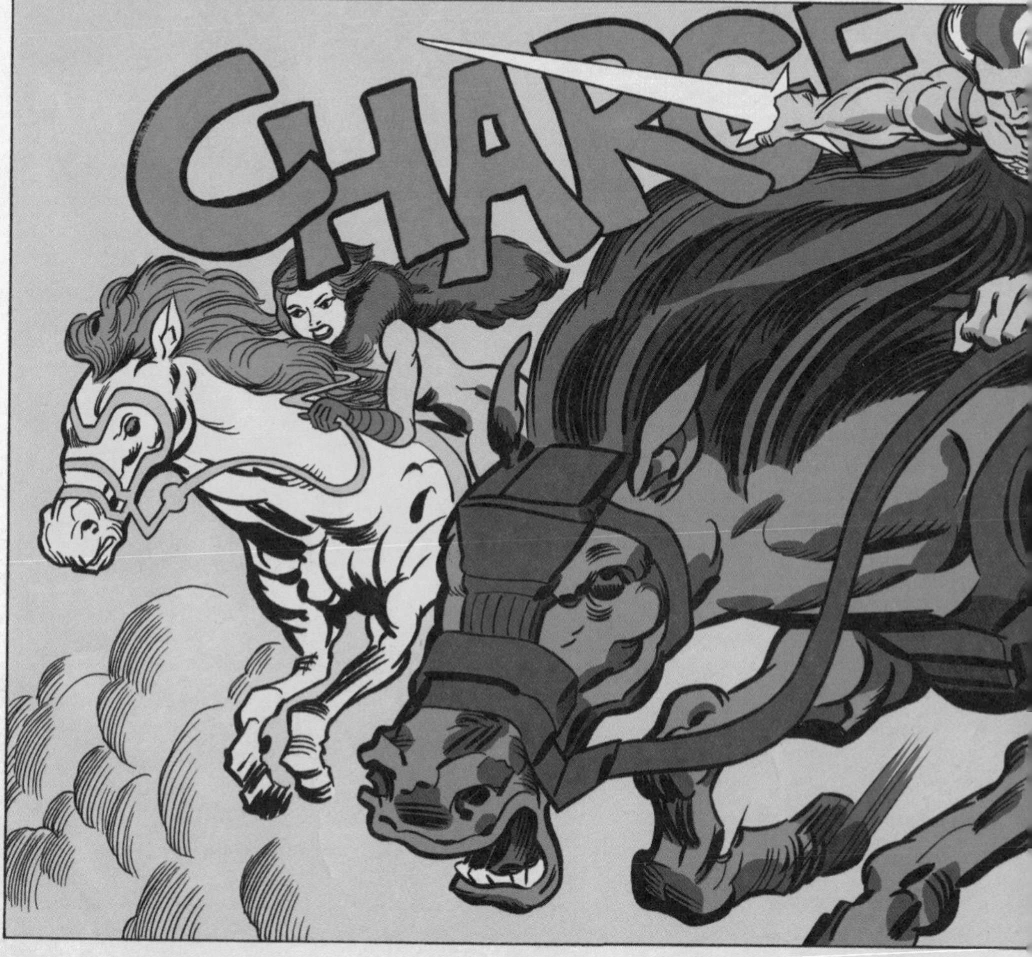
CHARGE

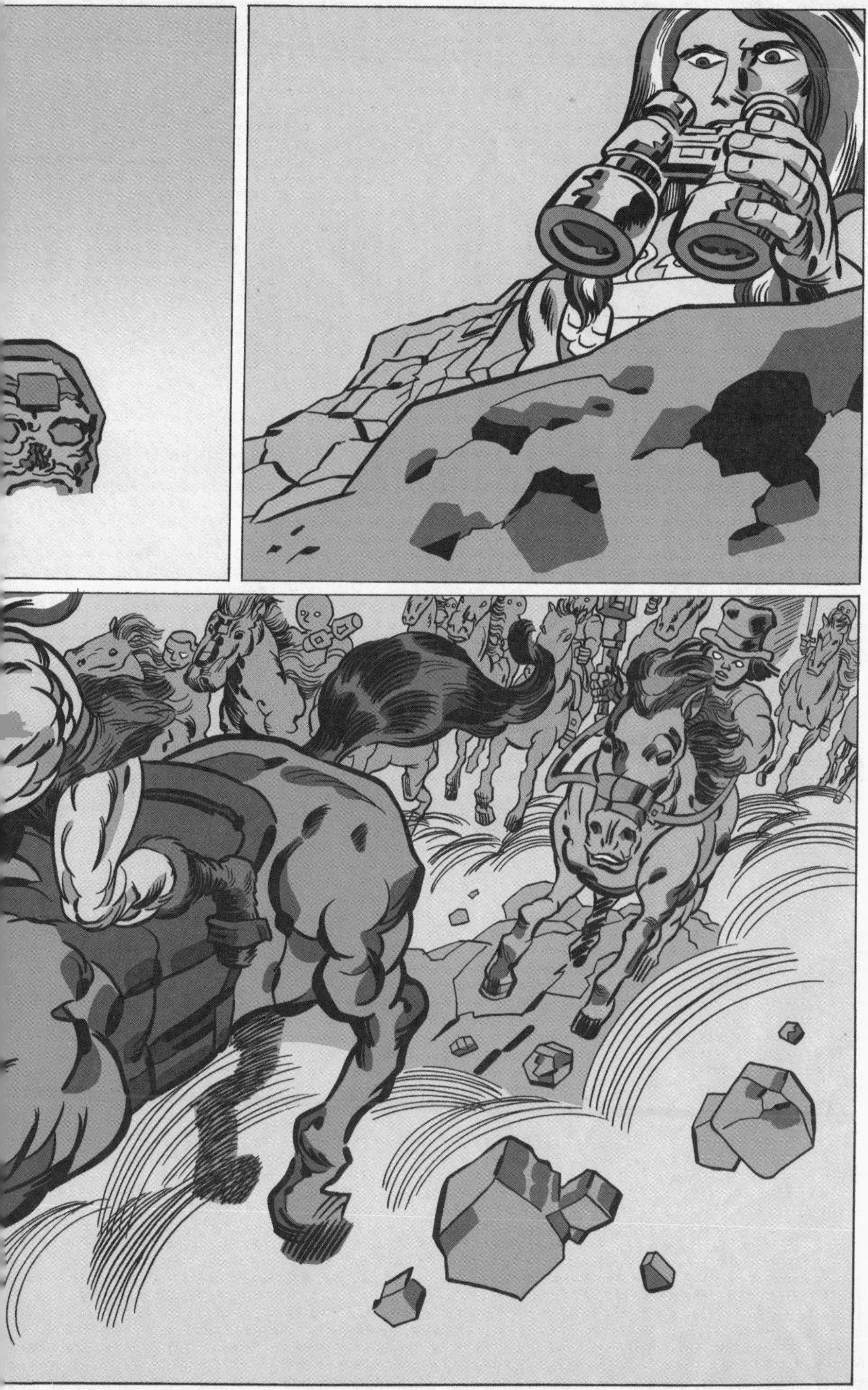

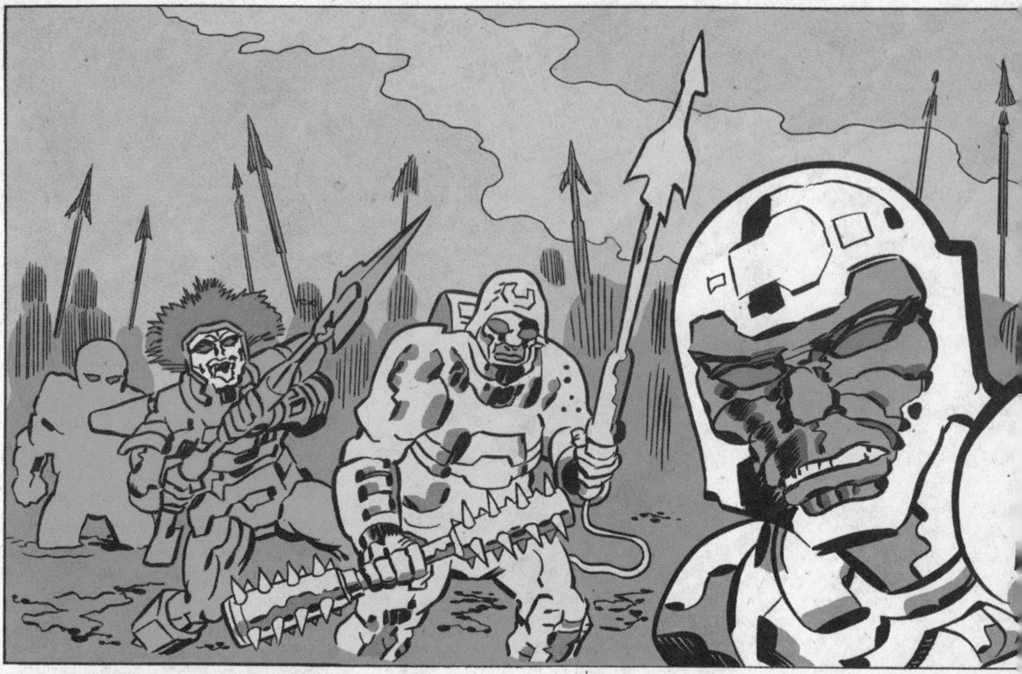

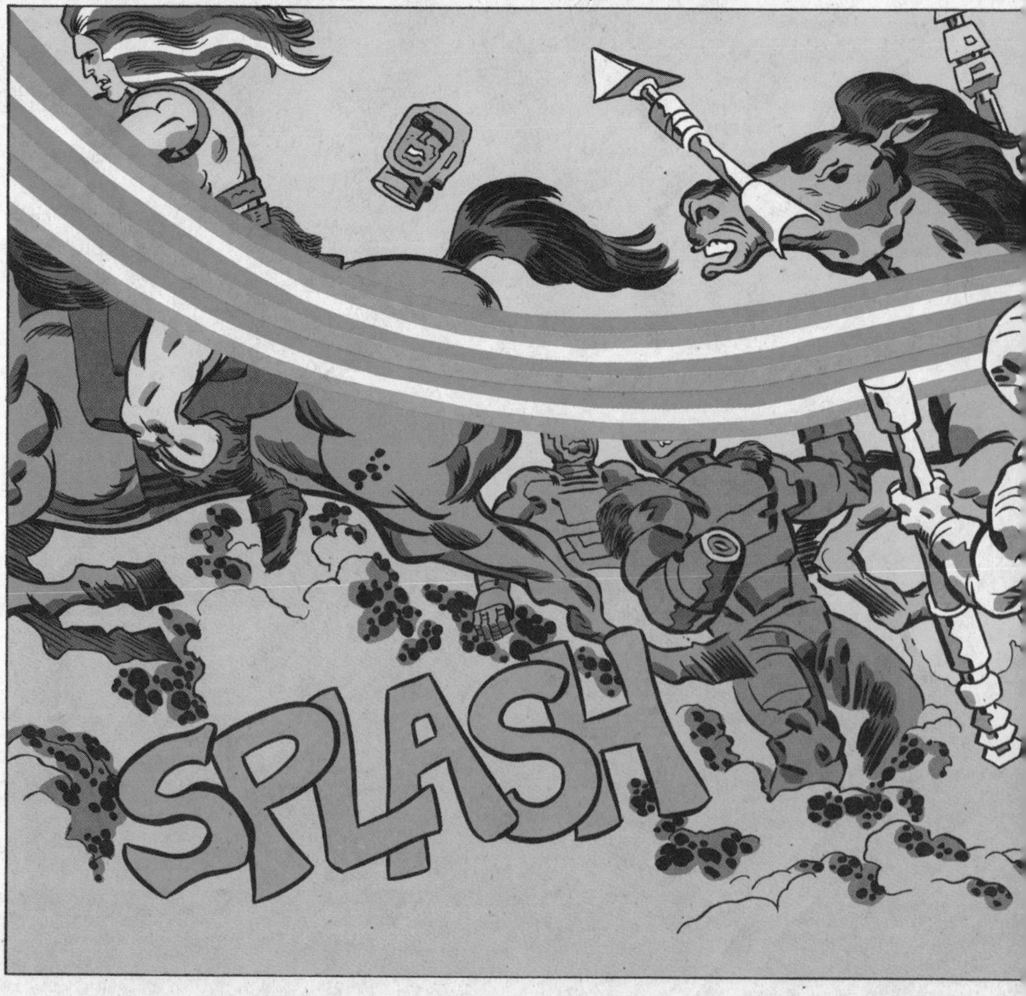
SPLASH

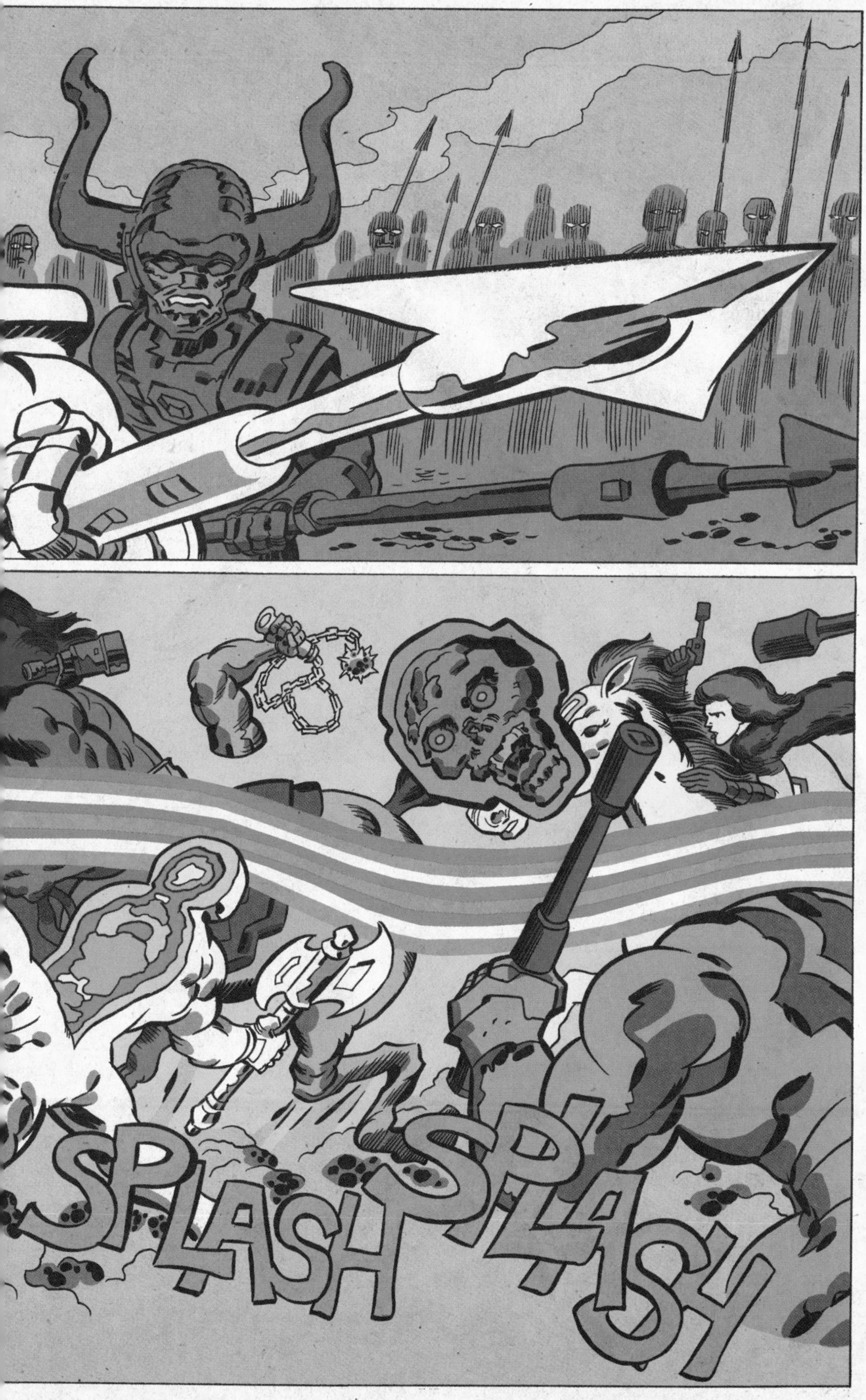
SPLASH
SPLASH

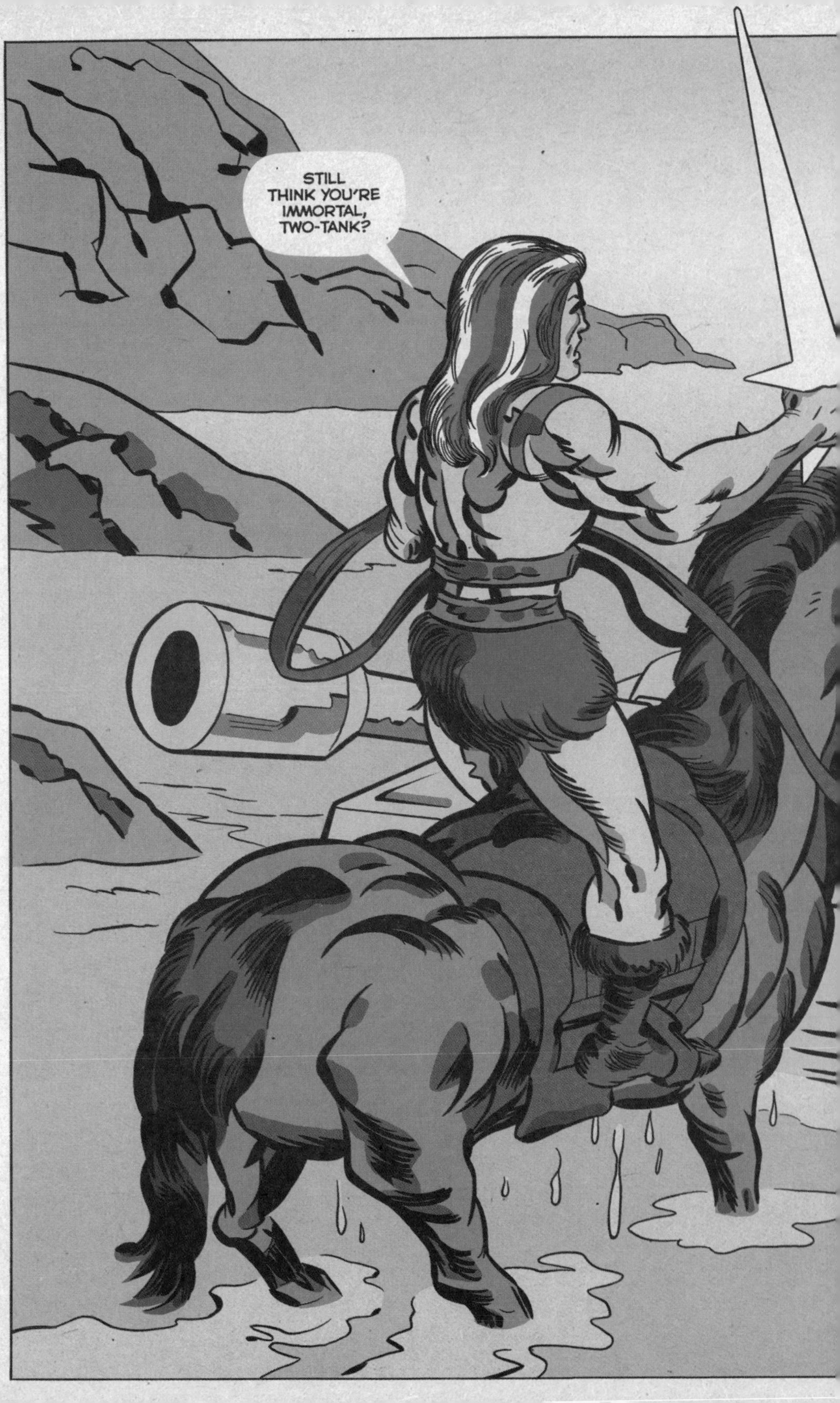
STILL THINK YOU'RE IMMORTAL, TWO-TANK?

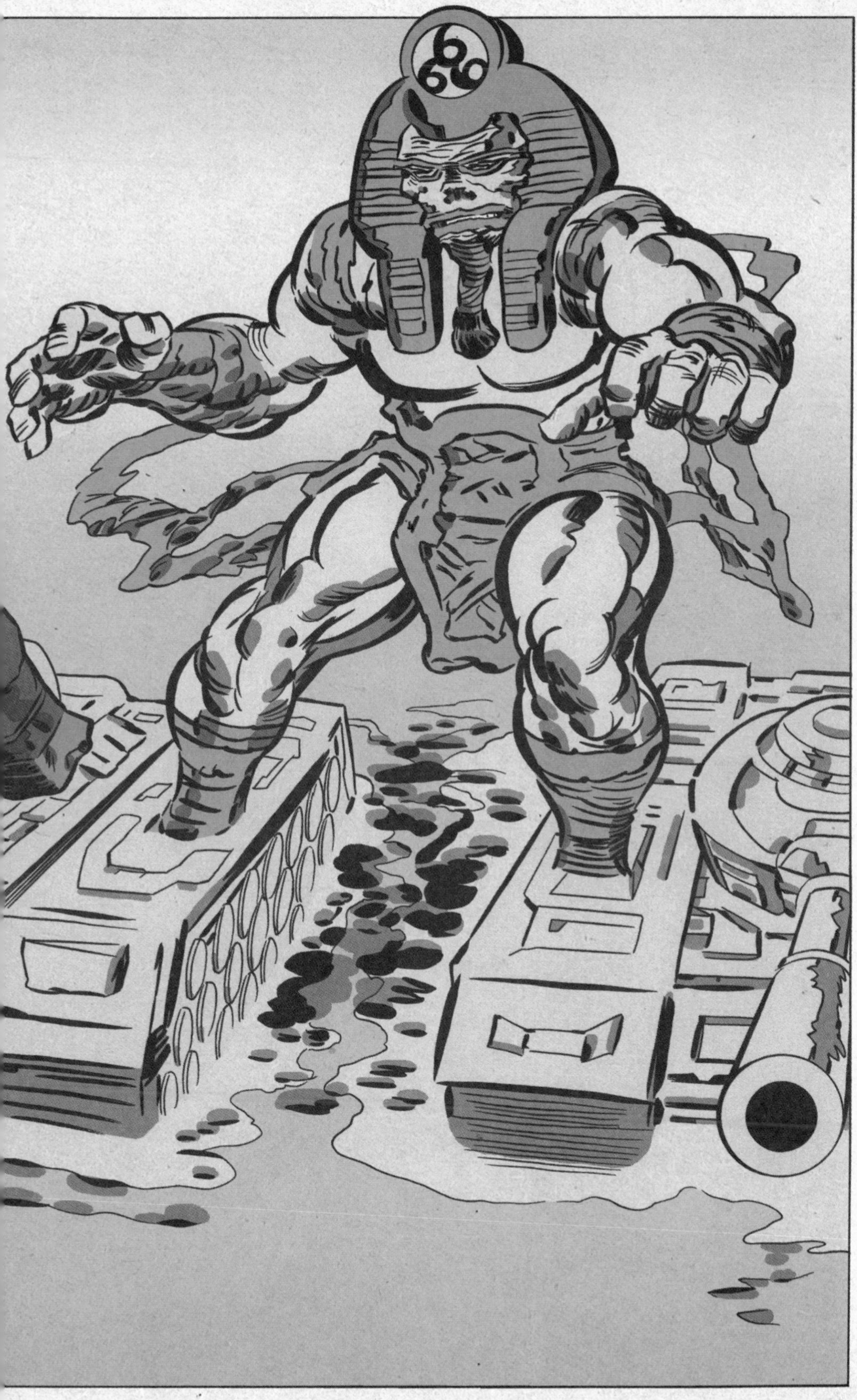

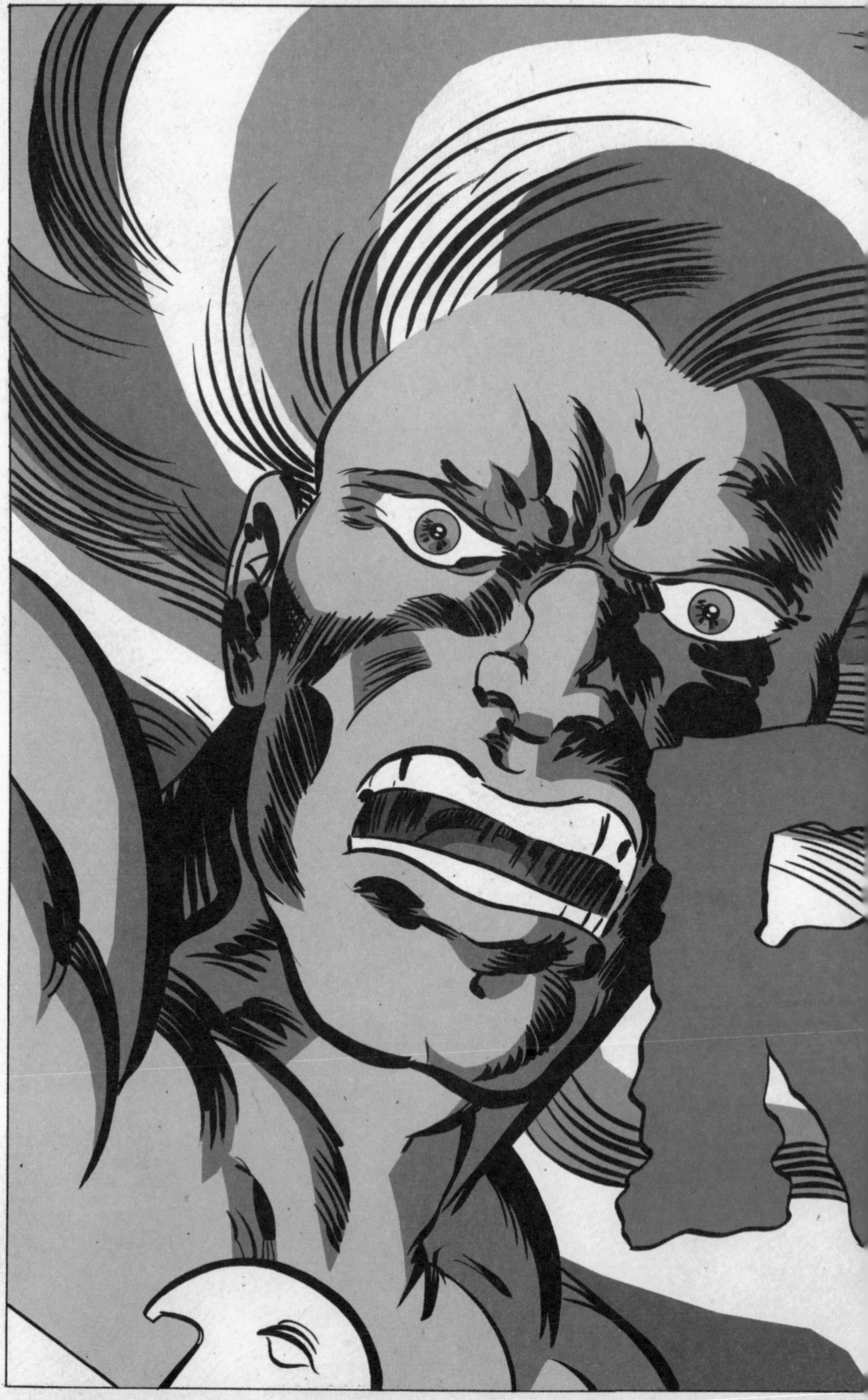

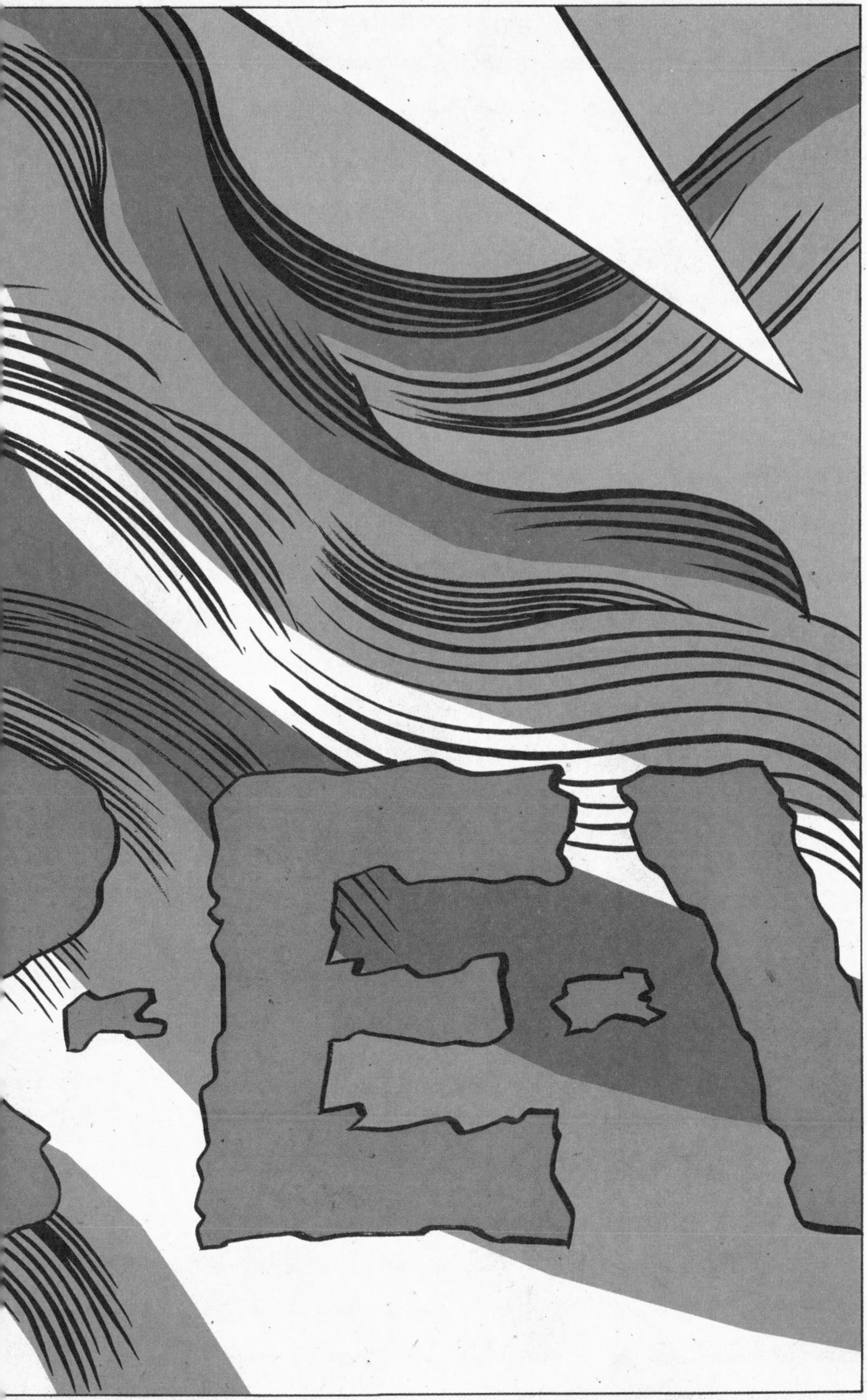

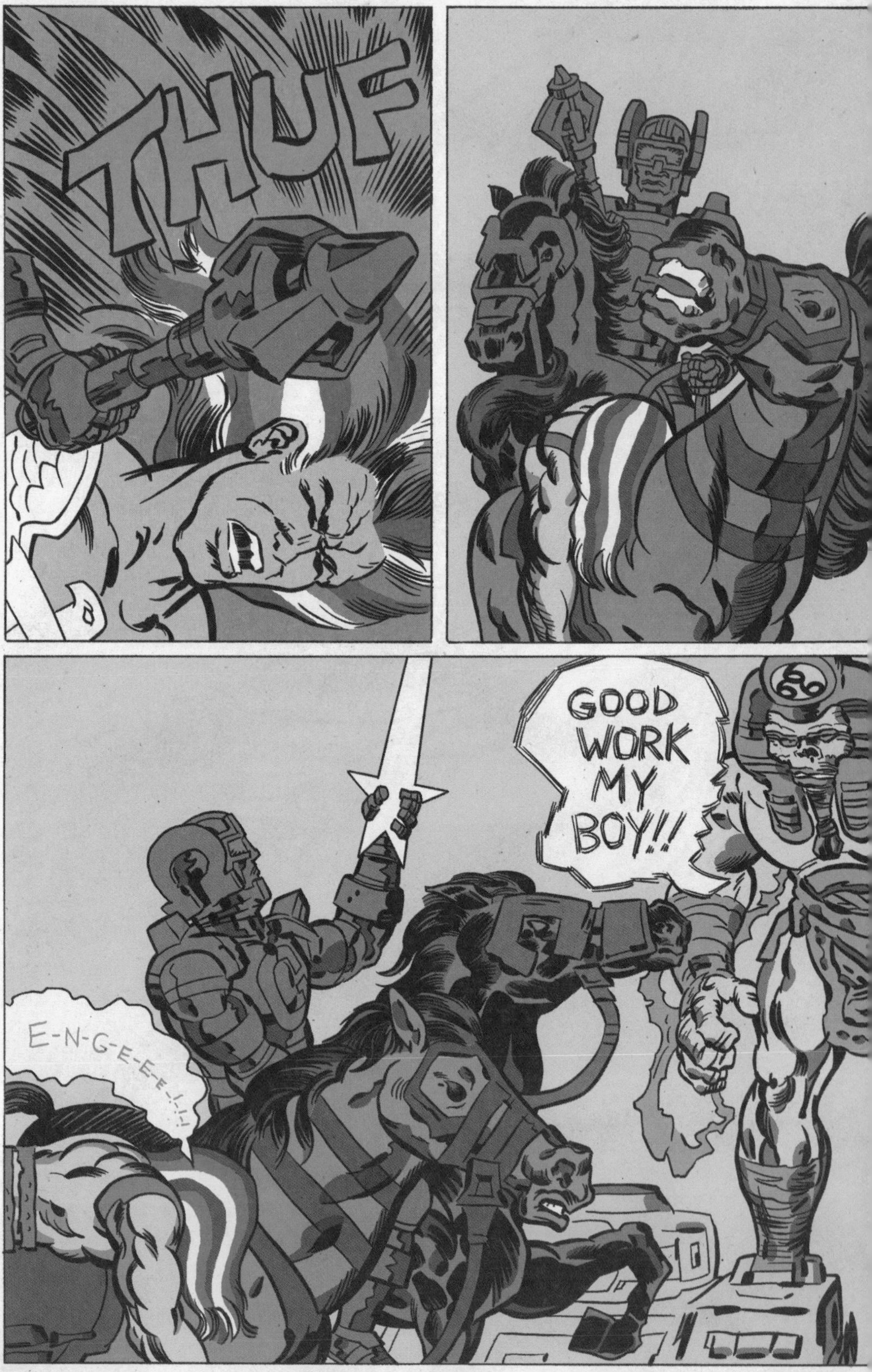
THUF
GOOD WORK MY BOY!!
E-N-G-E-E-E-E-!-!-!

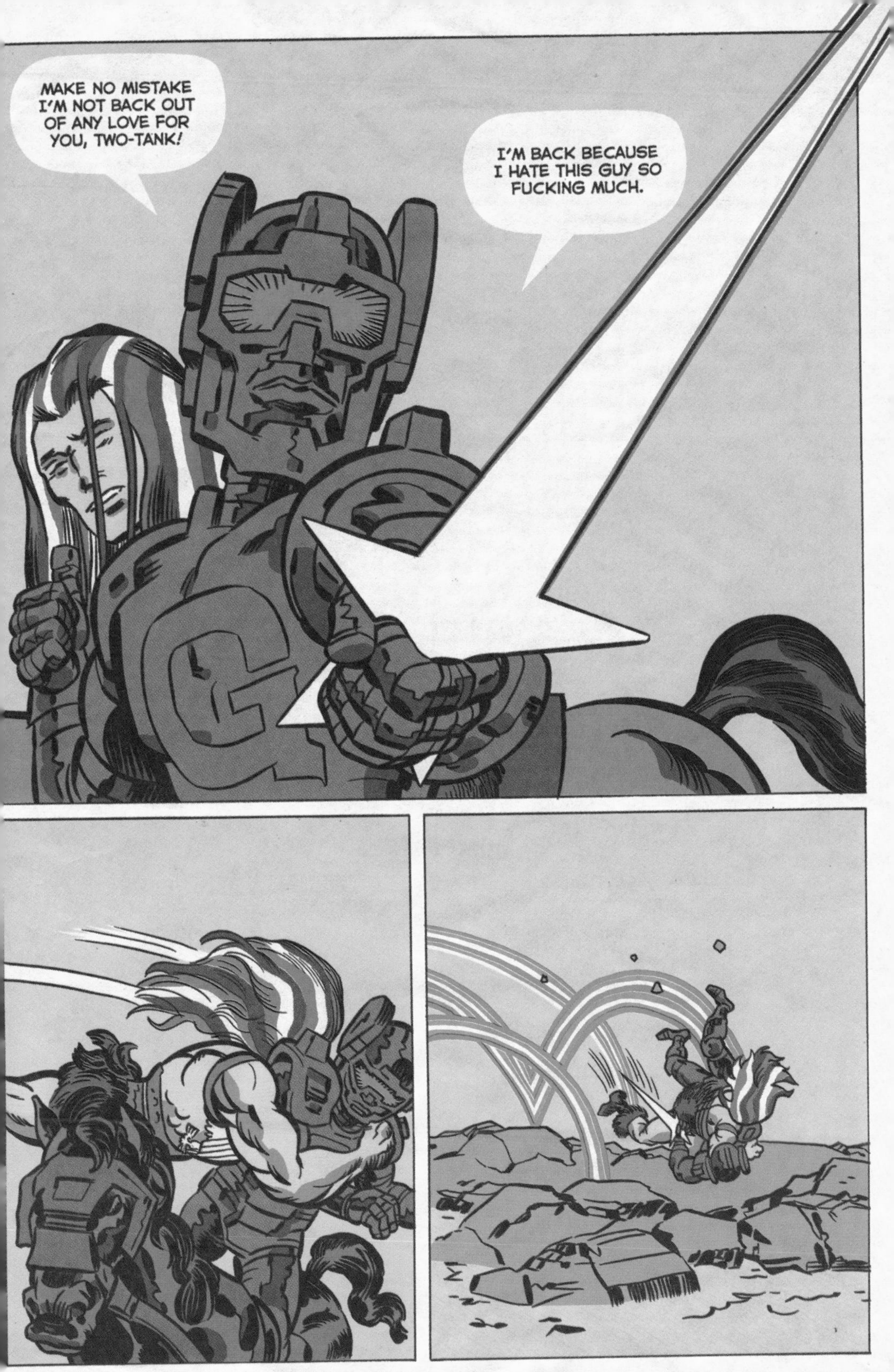
MAKE NO MISTAKE I'M NOT BACK OUT OF ANY LOVE FOR YOU, TWO-TANK!
I'M BACK BECAUSE I HATE THIS GUY SO FUCKING MUCH.

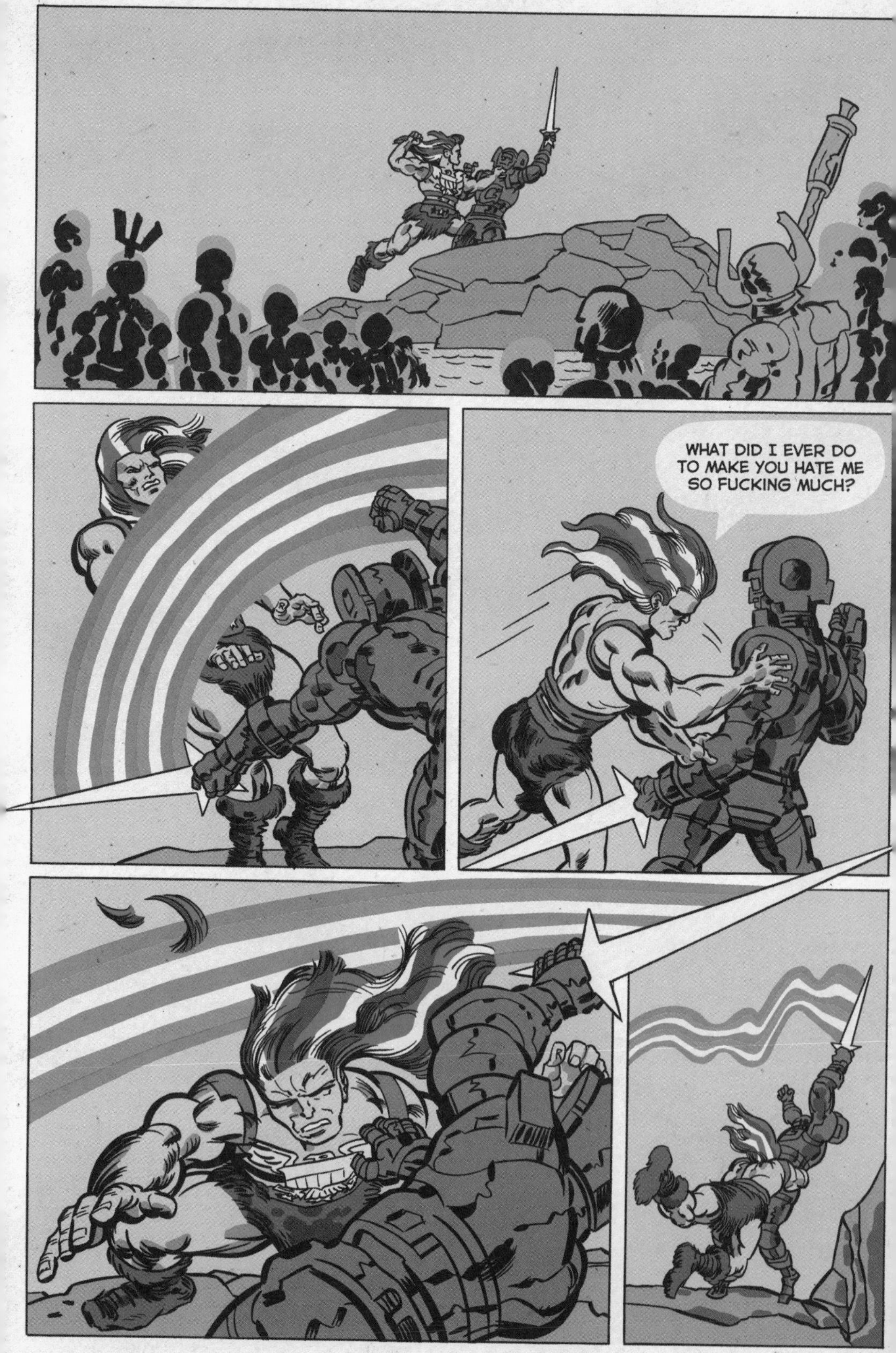
WHAT DID I EVER DO TO MAKE YOU HATE ME SO FUCKING MUCH?

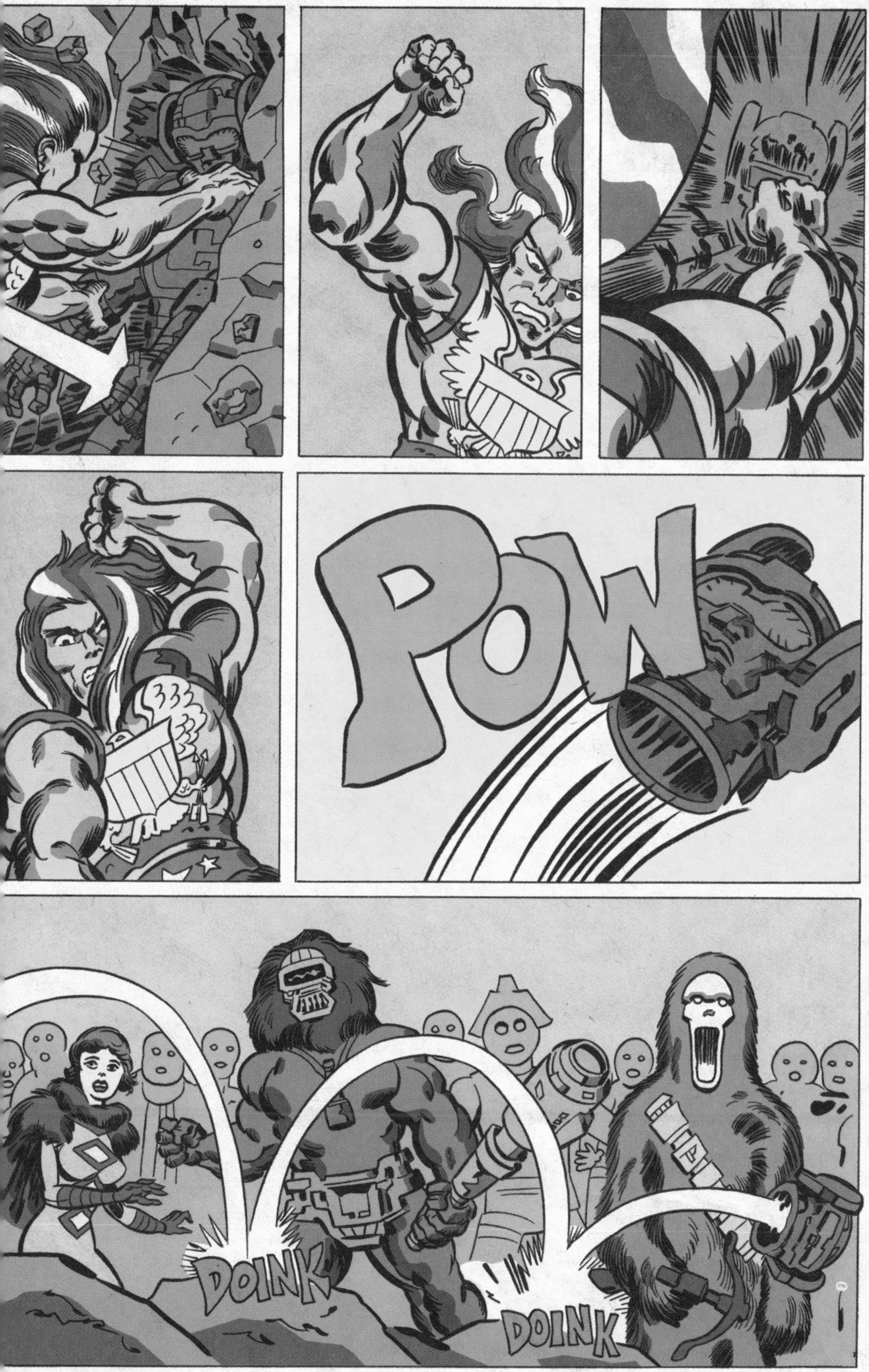
POW
DOINK
DOINK

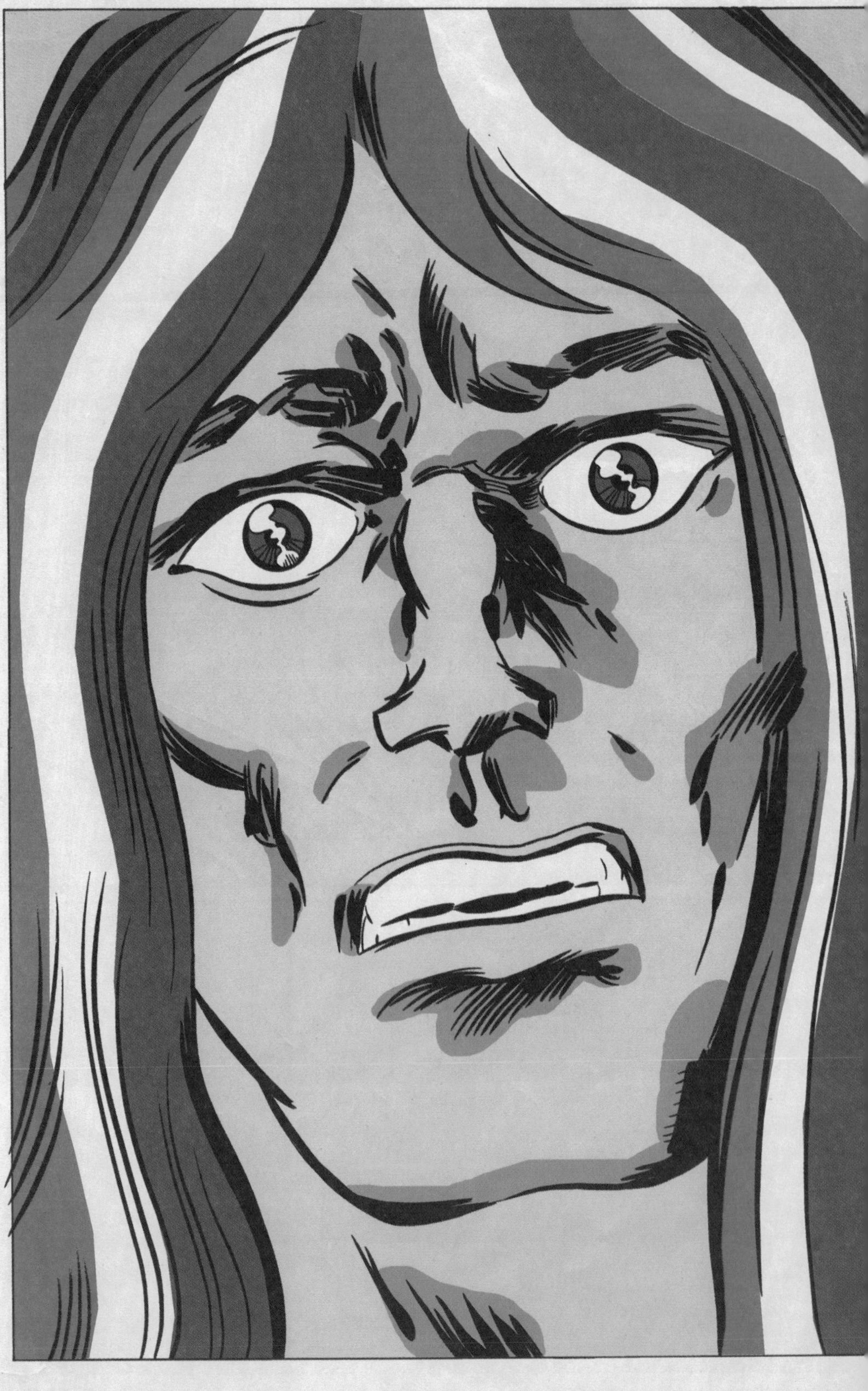

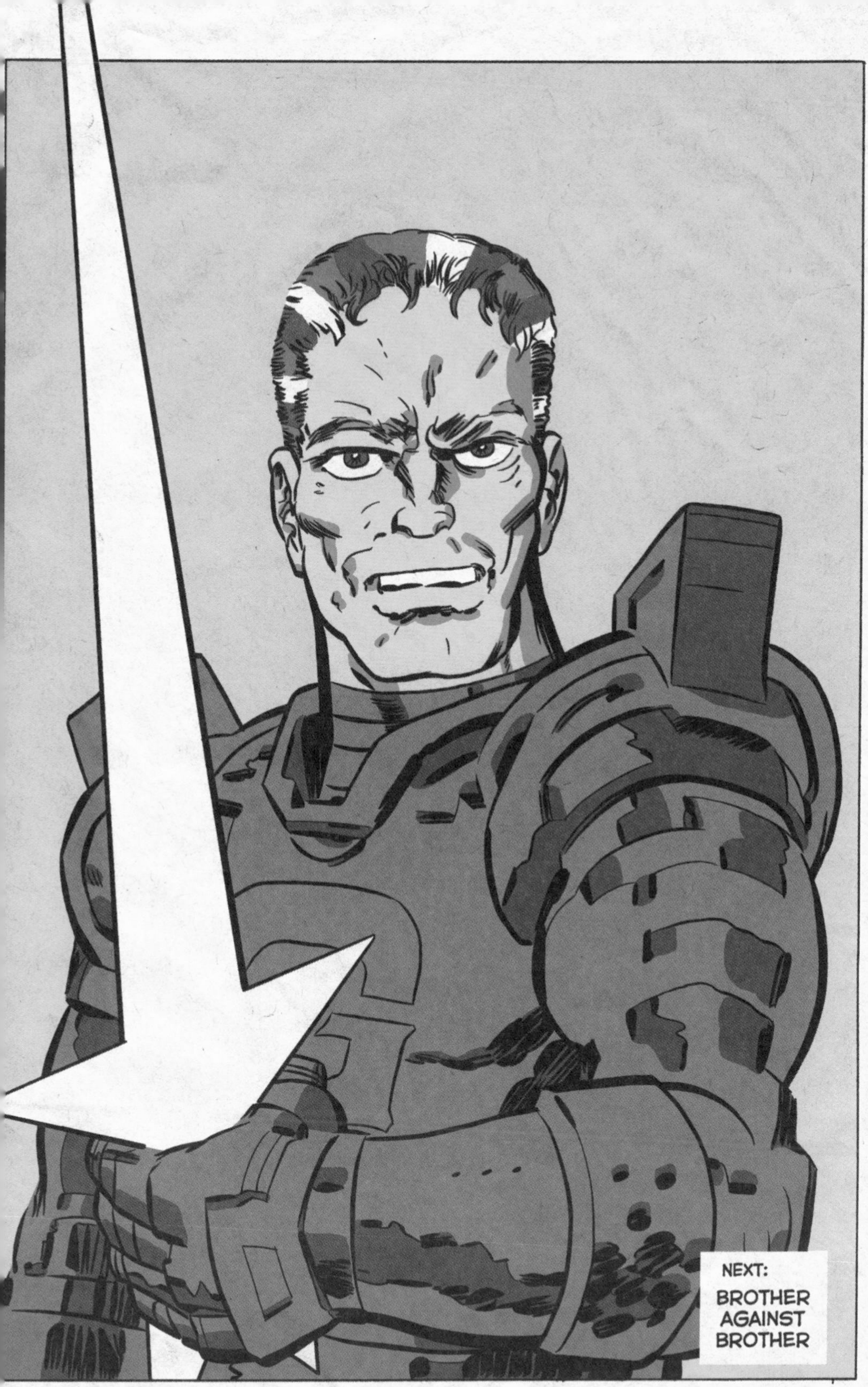
NEXT:
BROTHER AGAINST BROTHER

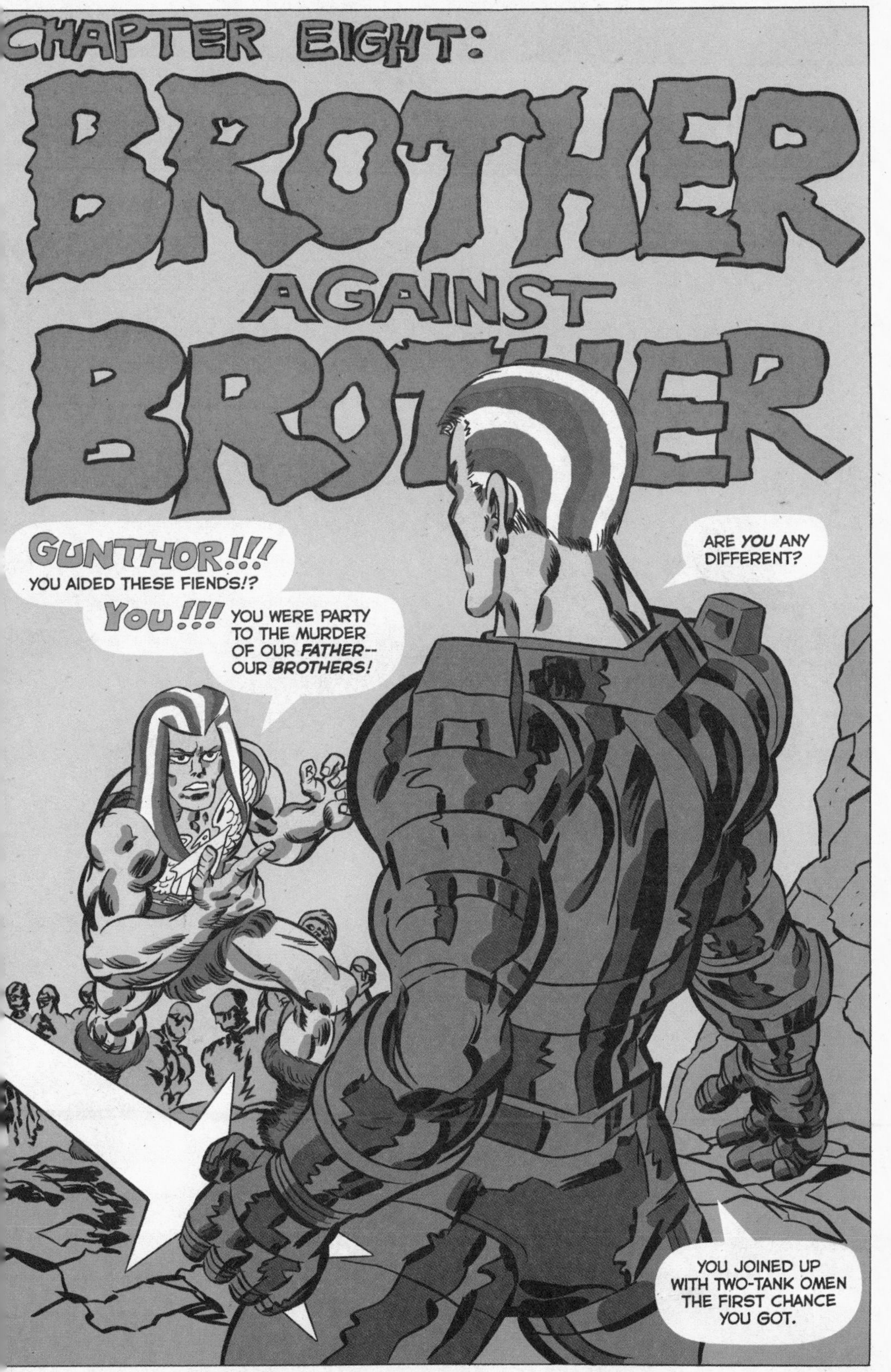
CHAPTER EIGHT:
BROTHER AGAINST BROTHER
GUNTHOR!!! YOU AIDED THESE FIENDS!?
YOU!!! YOU WERE PARTY TO THE MURDER OF OUR FATHER-- OUR BROTHERS!
ARE YOU ANY DIFFERENT?
YOU JOINED UP WITH TWO-TANK OMEN THE FIRST CHANCE YOU GOT.

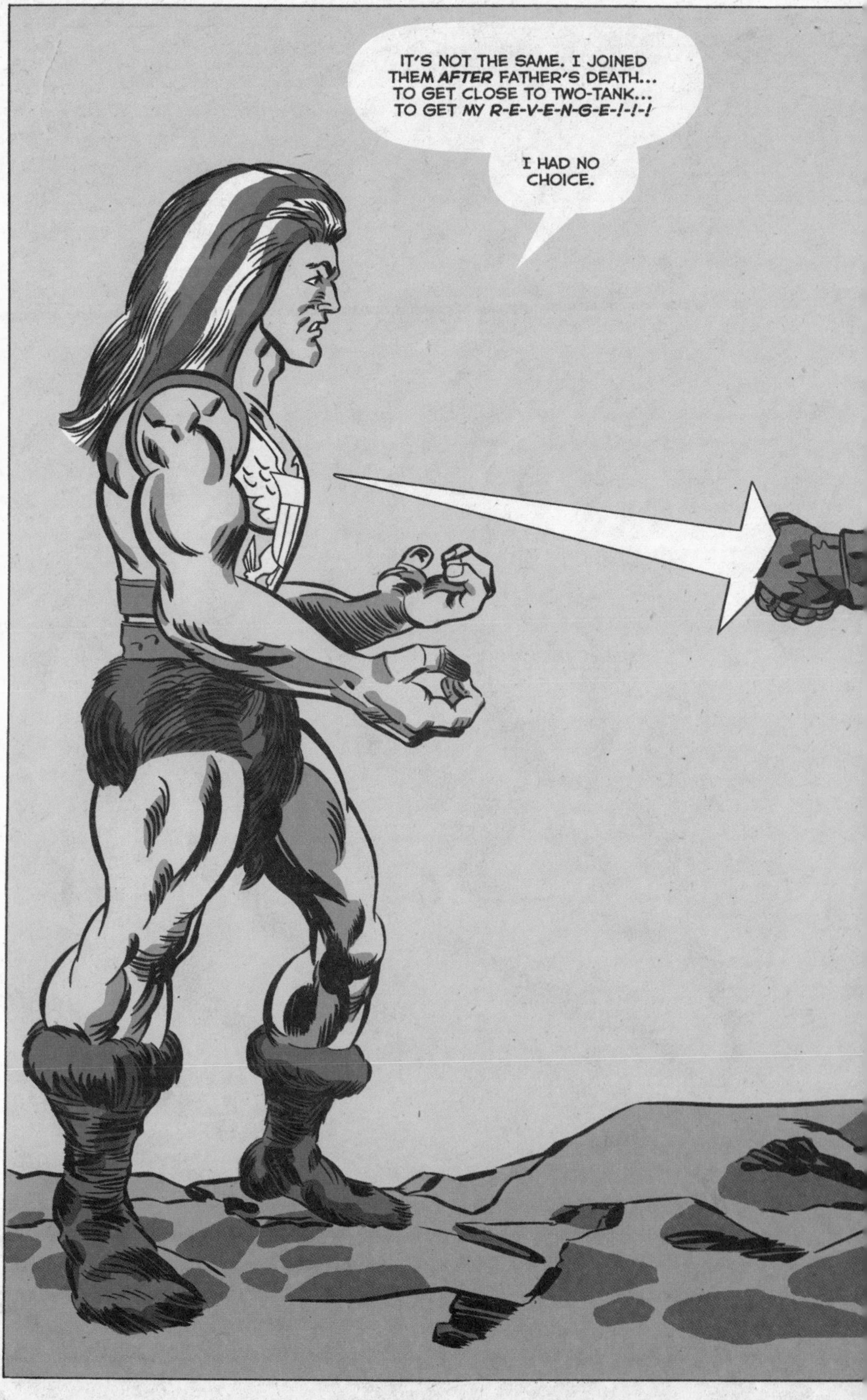
IT'S NOT THE SAME. I JOINED THEM *AFTER* FATHER'S DEATH... TO GET CLOSE TO TWO-TANK... TO GET MY *R-E-V-E-N-G-E-!-!-!*
I HAD NO CHOICE.

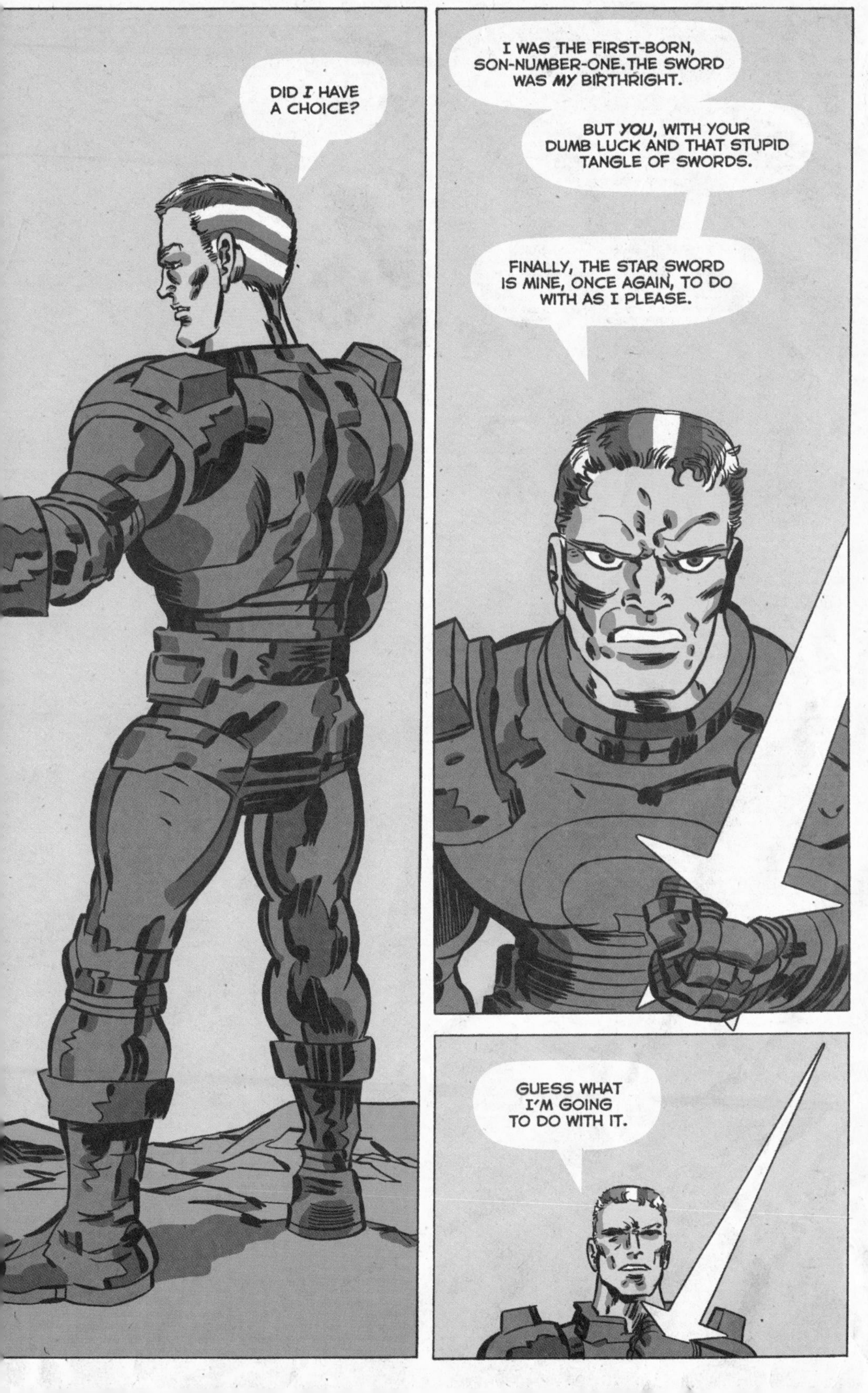
DID I HAVE A CHOICE?
I WAS THE FIRST-BORN, SON-NUMBER-ONE. THE SWORD WAS MY BIRTHRIGHT.
BUT YOU, WITH YOUR DUMB LUCK AND THAT STUPID TANGLE OF SWORDS.
FINALLY, THE STAR SWORD IS MINE, ONCE AGAIN, TO DO WITH AS I PLEASE.
GUESS WHAT I'M GOING TO DO WITH IT.

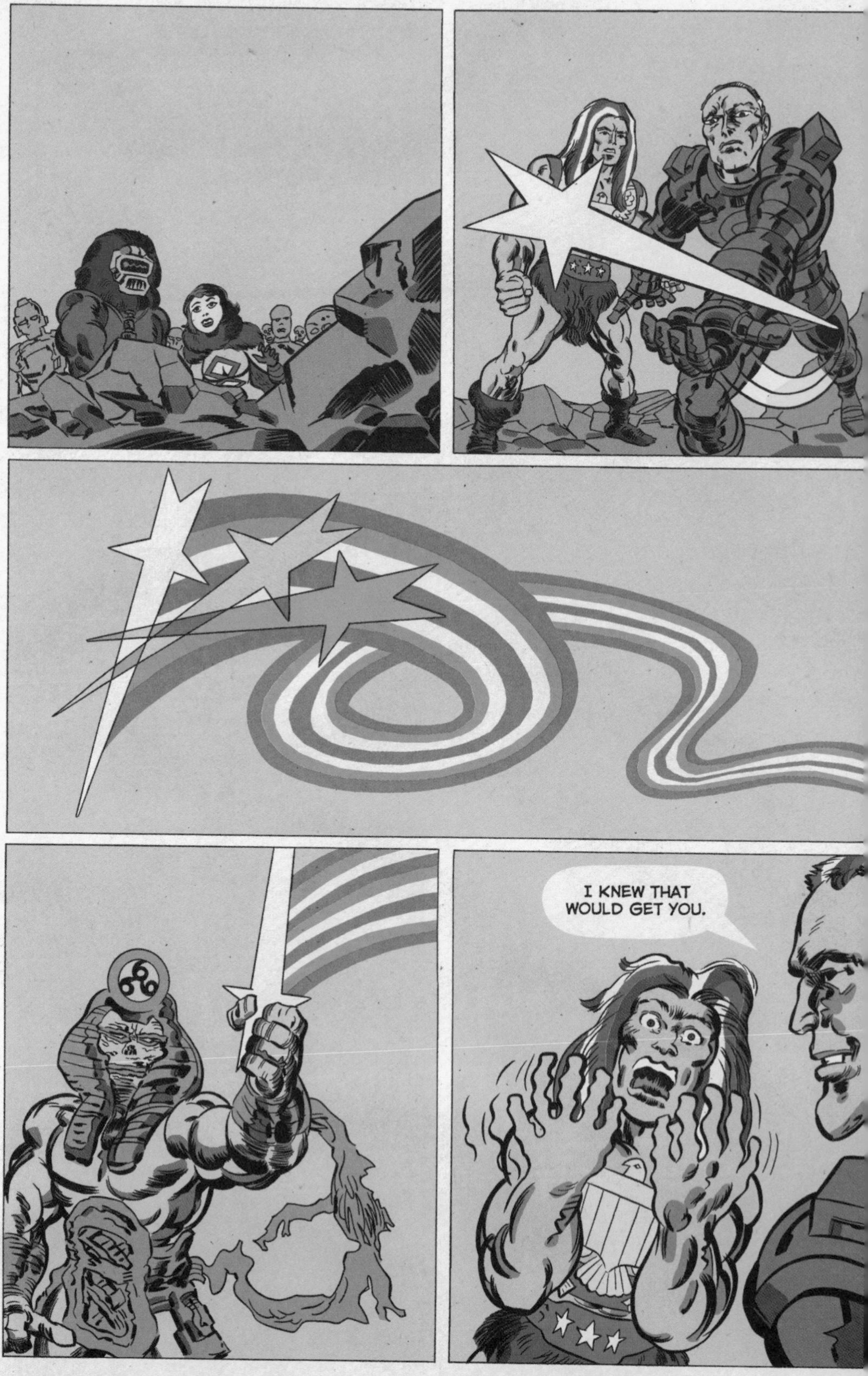
I KNEW THAT WOULD GET YOU.

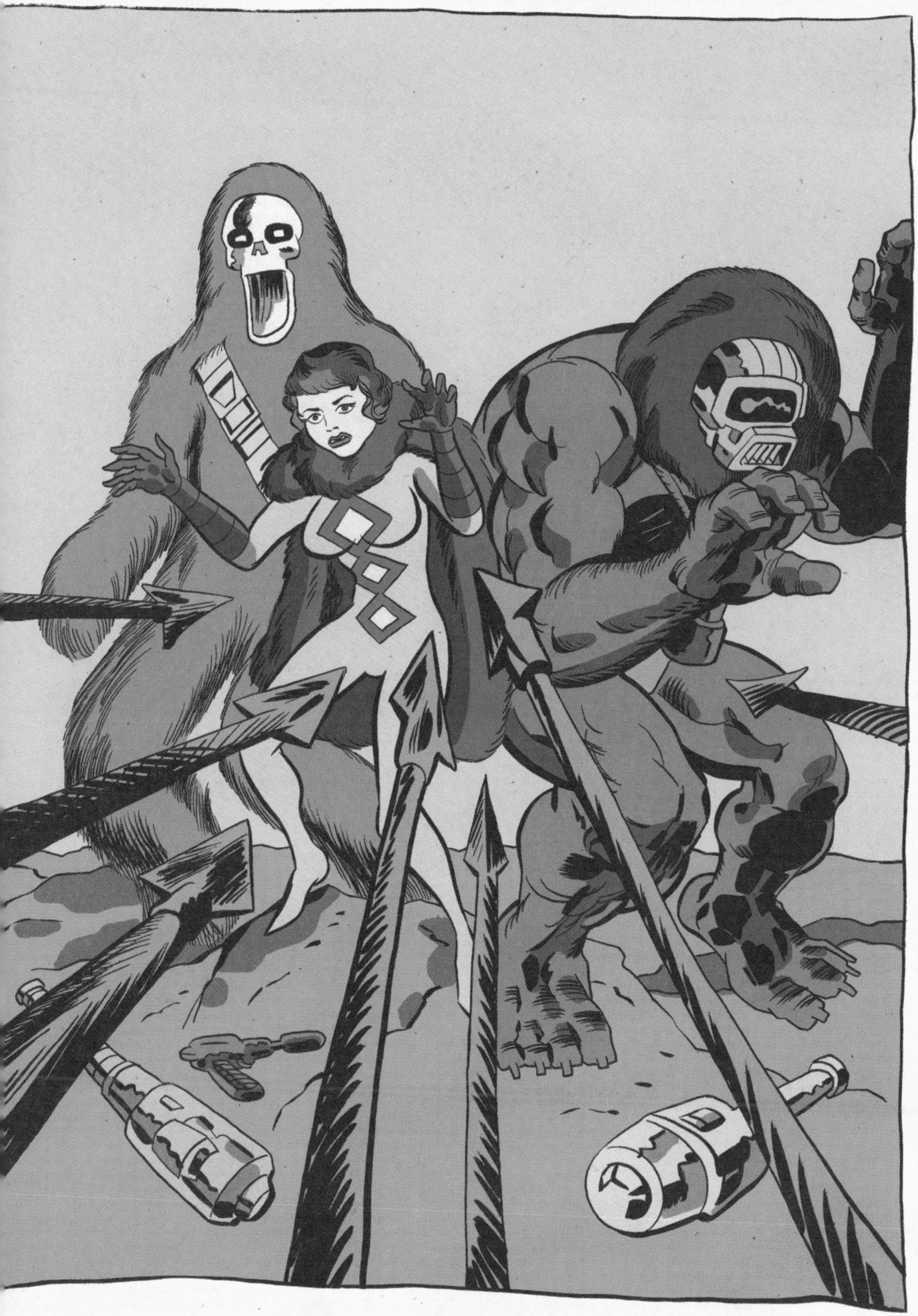

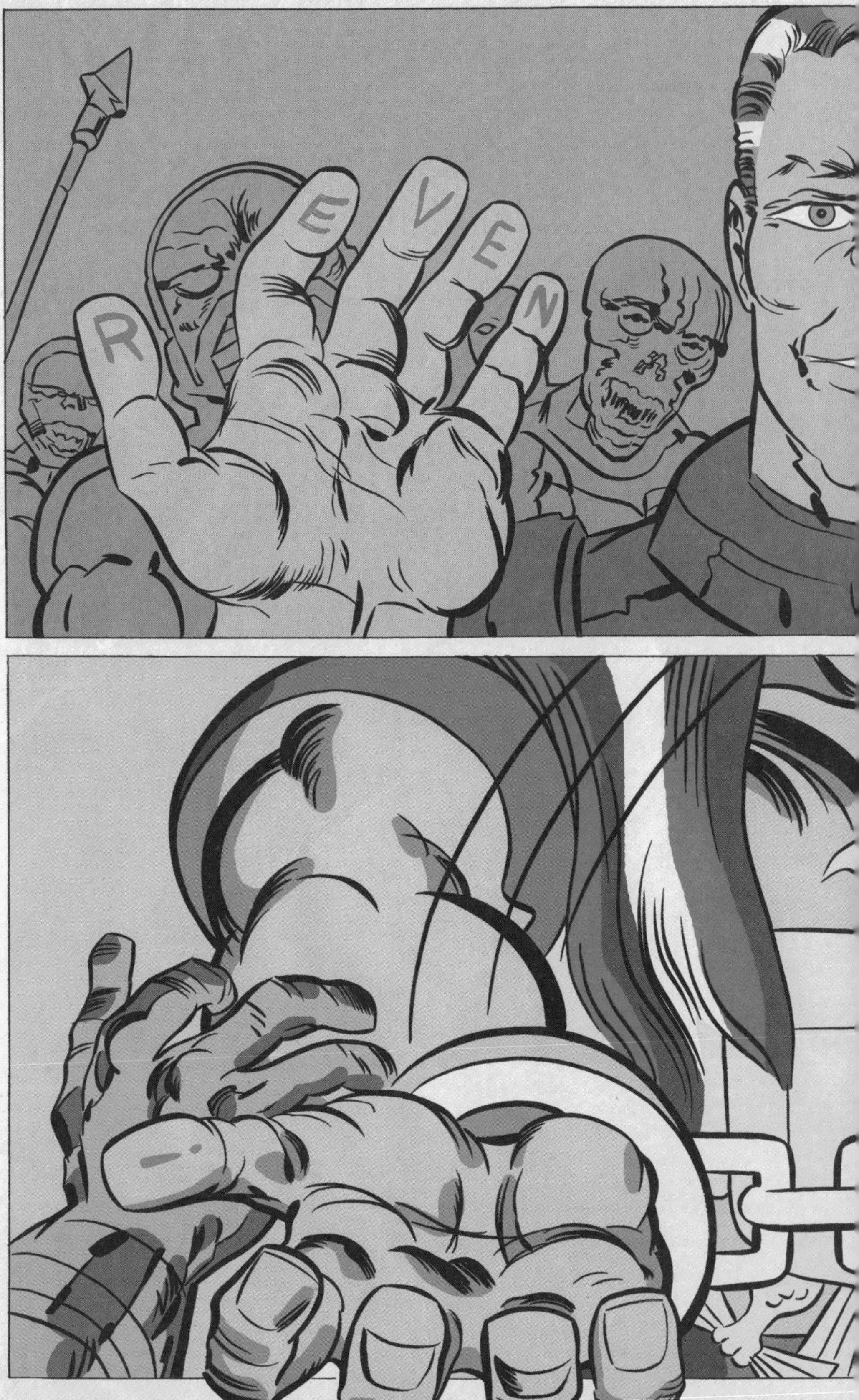
R E V E N

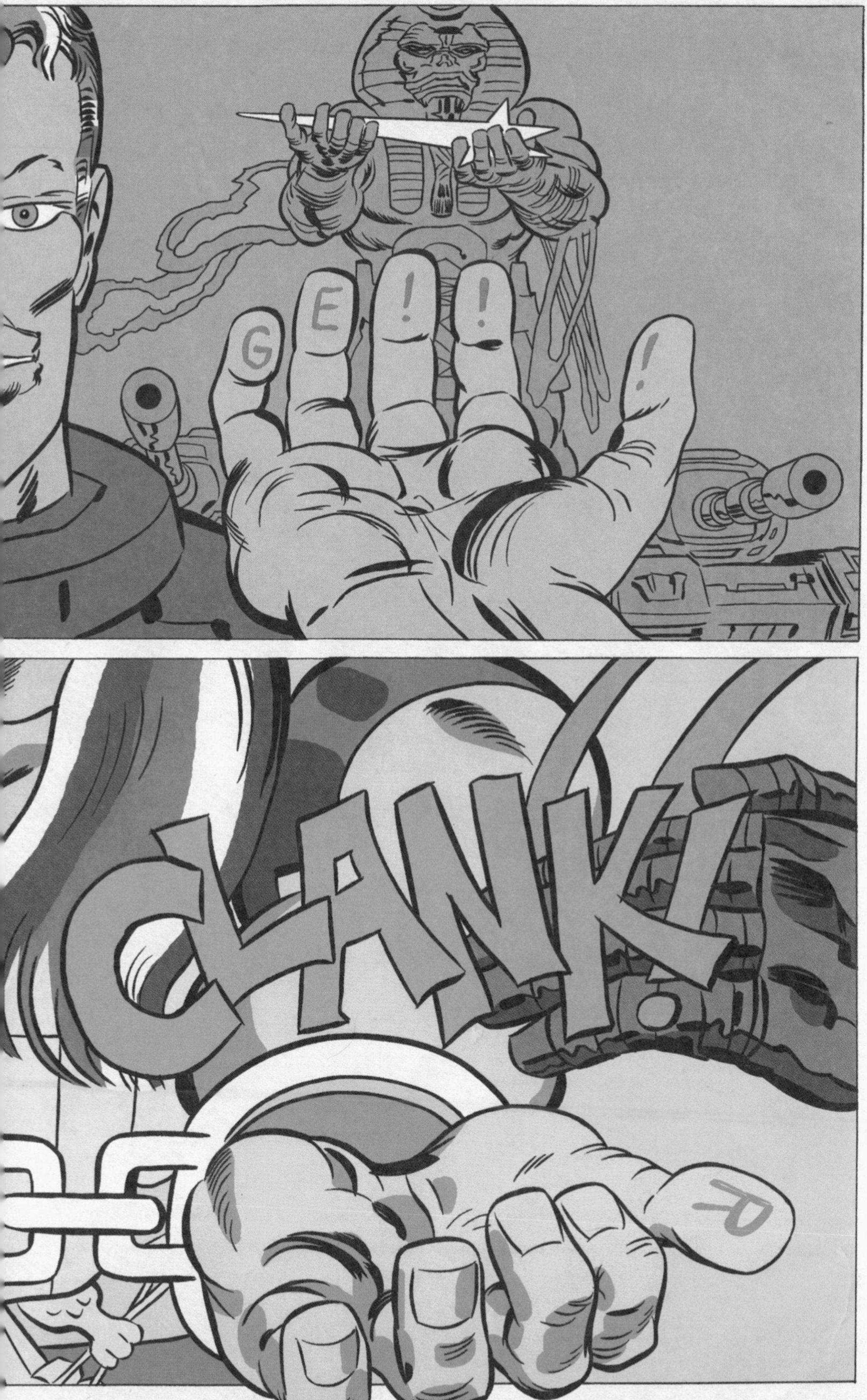
CLANK!

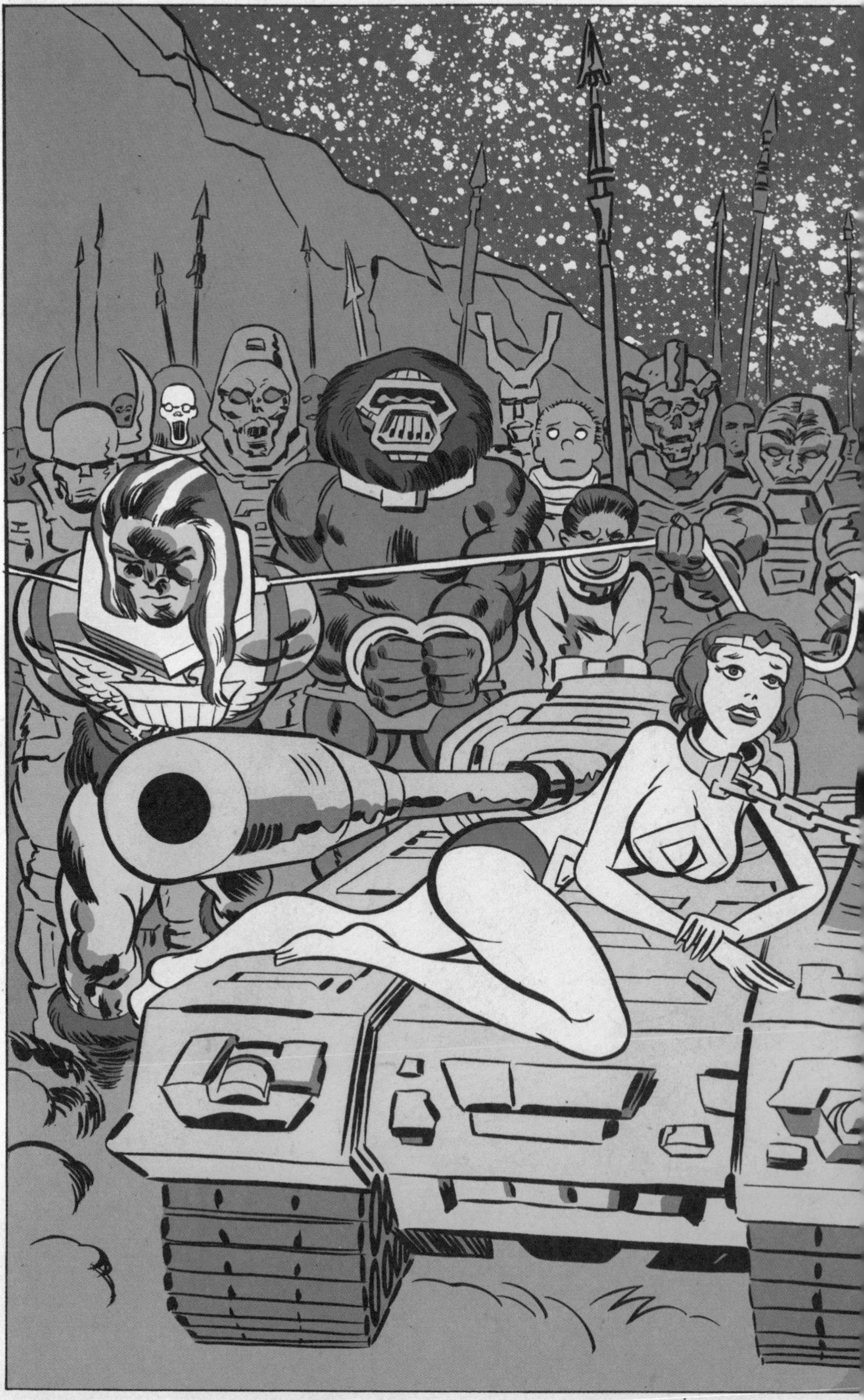

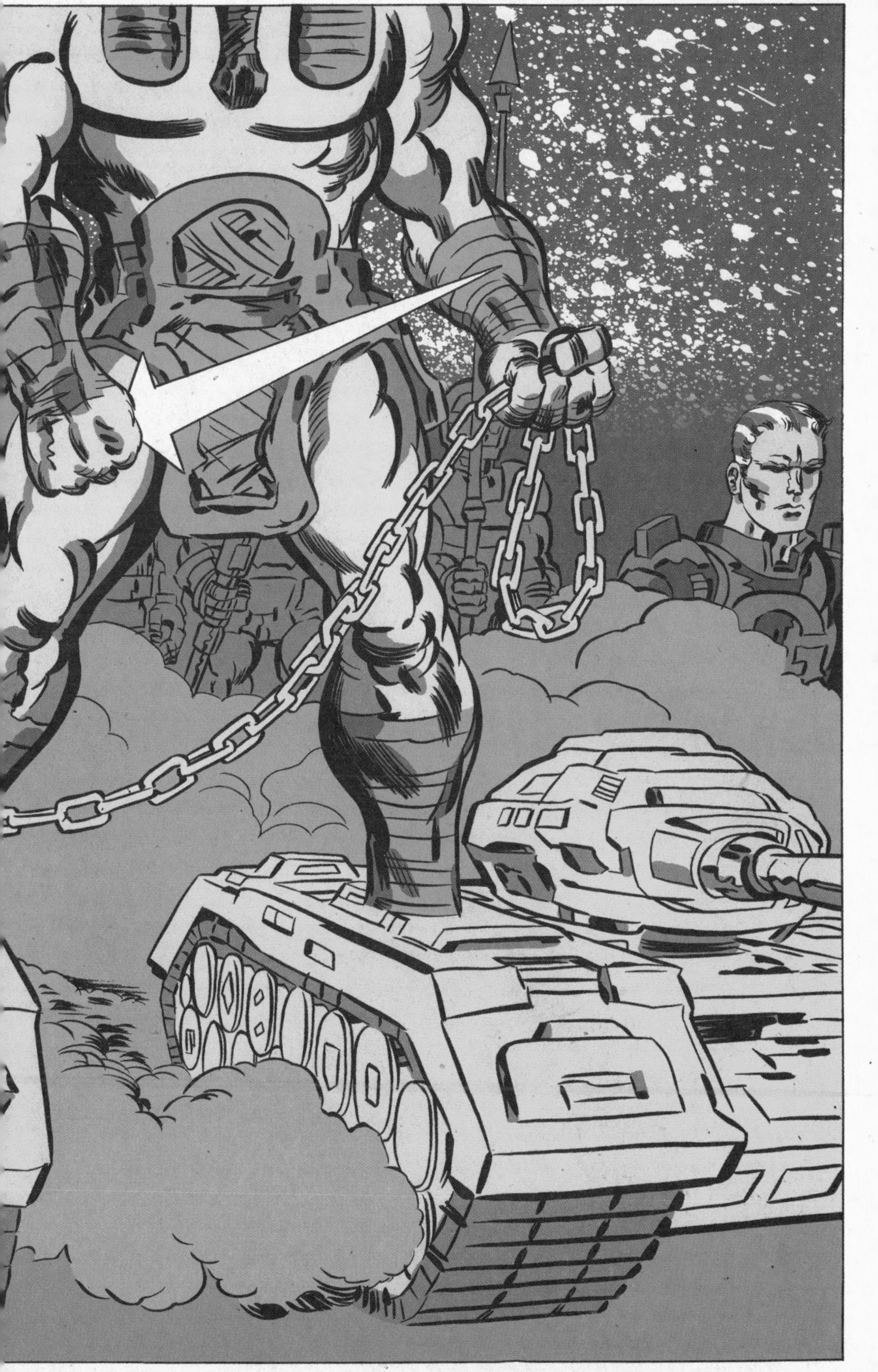

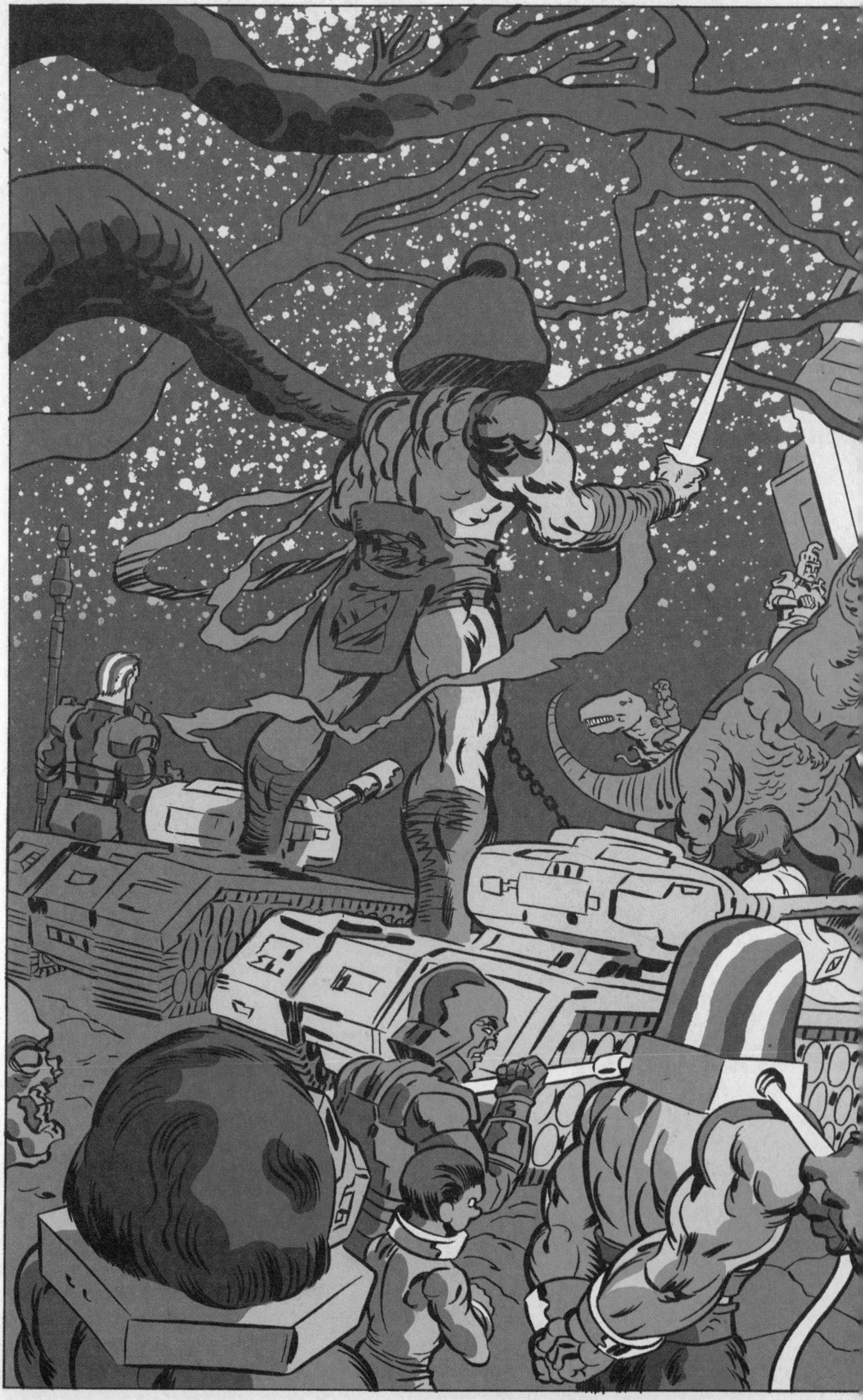

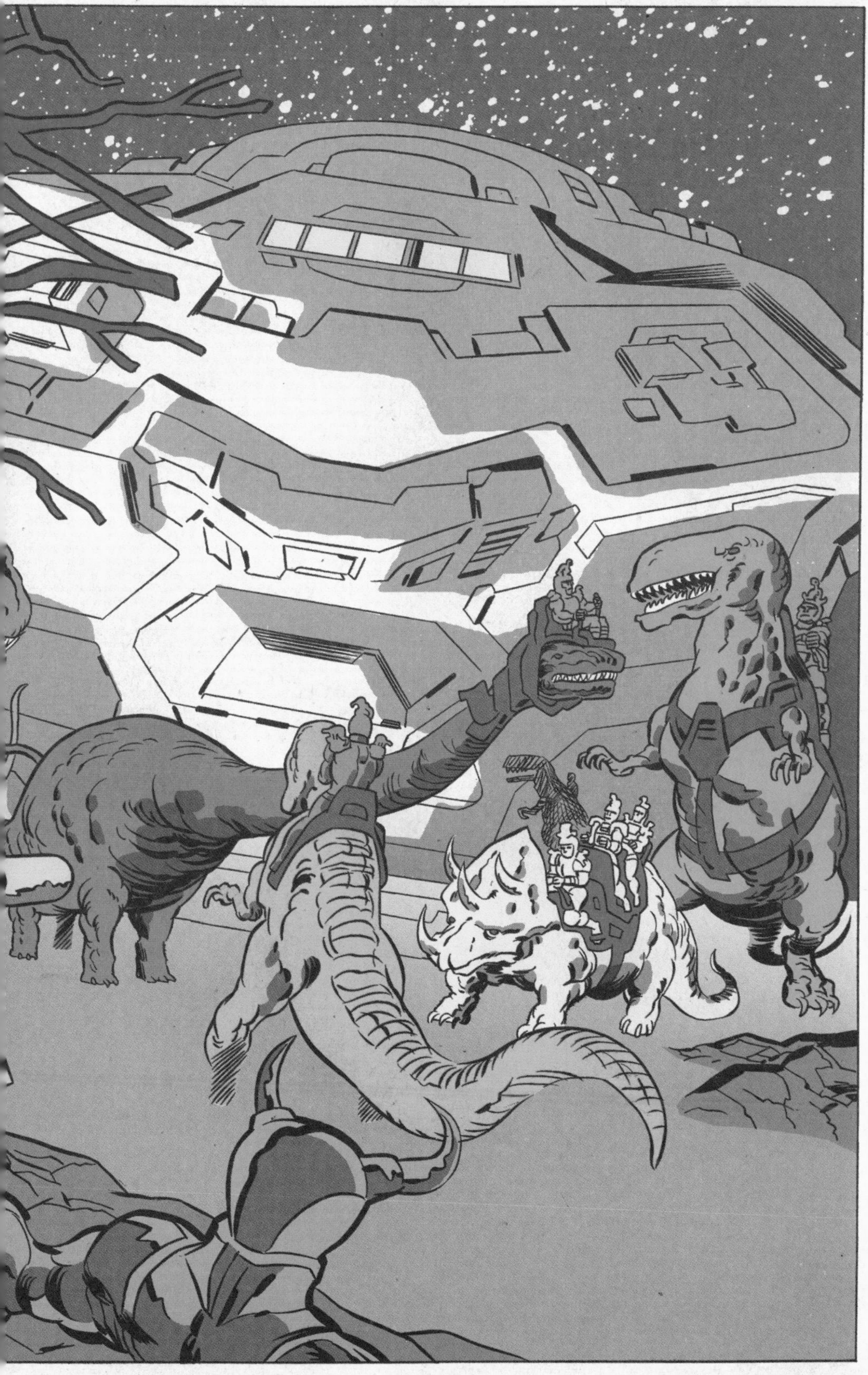

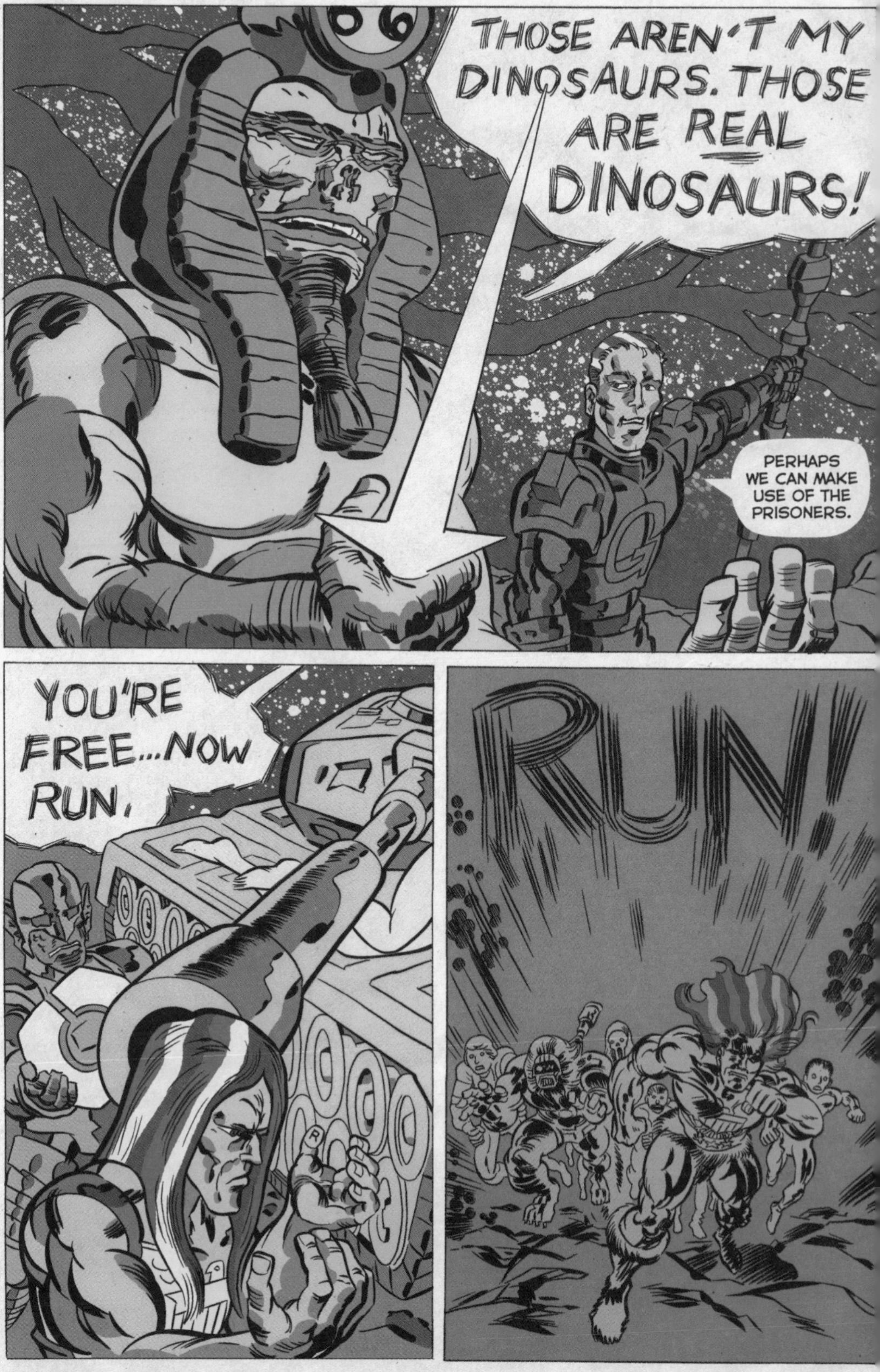
THOSE AREN'T MY DINOSAURS. THOSE ARE REAL DINOSAURS!
PERHAPS WE CAN MAKE USE OF THE PRISONERS.
YOU'RE FREE...NOW RUN.
RUN!

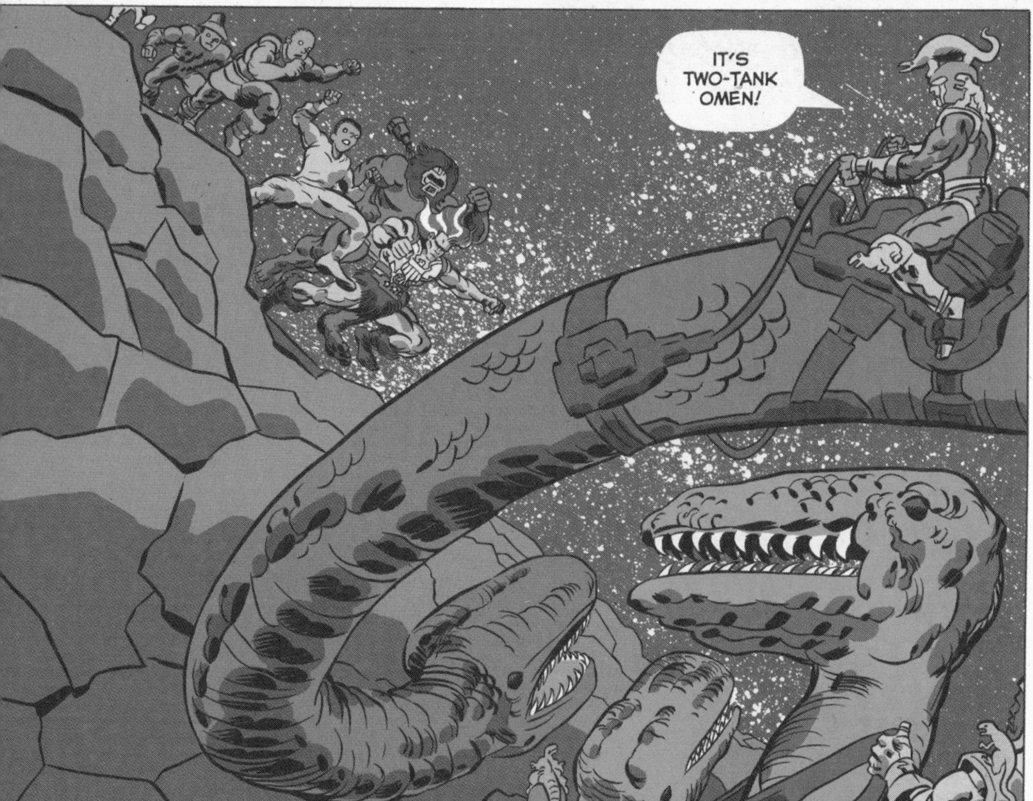
IT'S TWO-TANK OMEN!

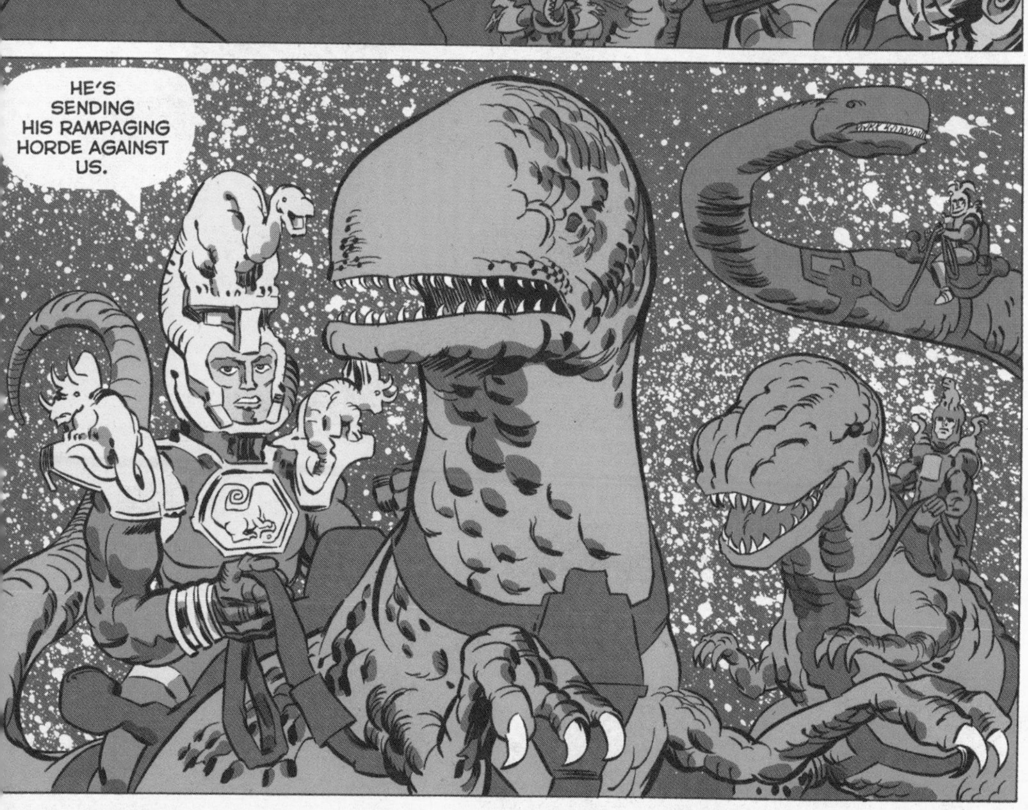
HE'S SENDING HIS RAMPAGING HORDE AGAINST US.

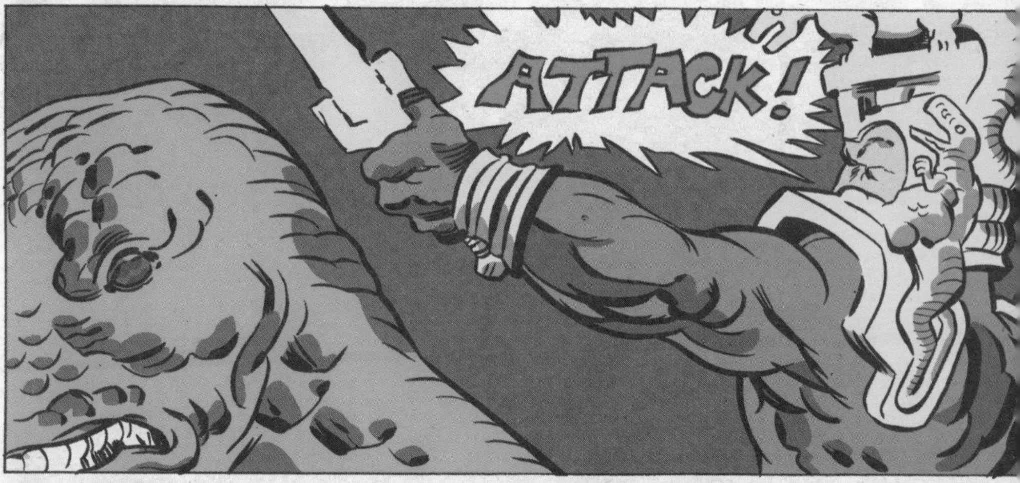
ATTACK!

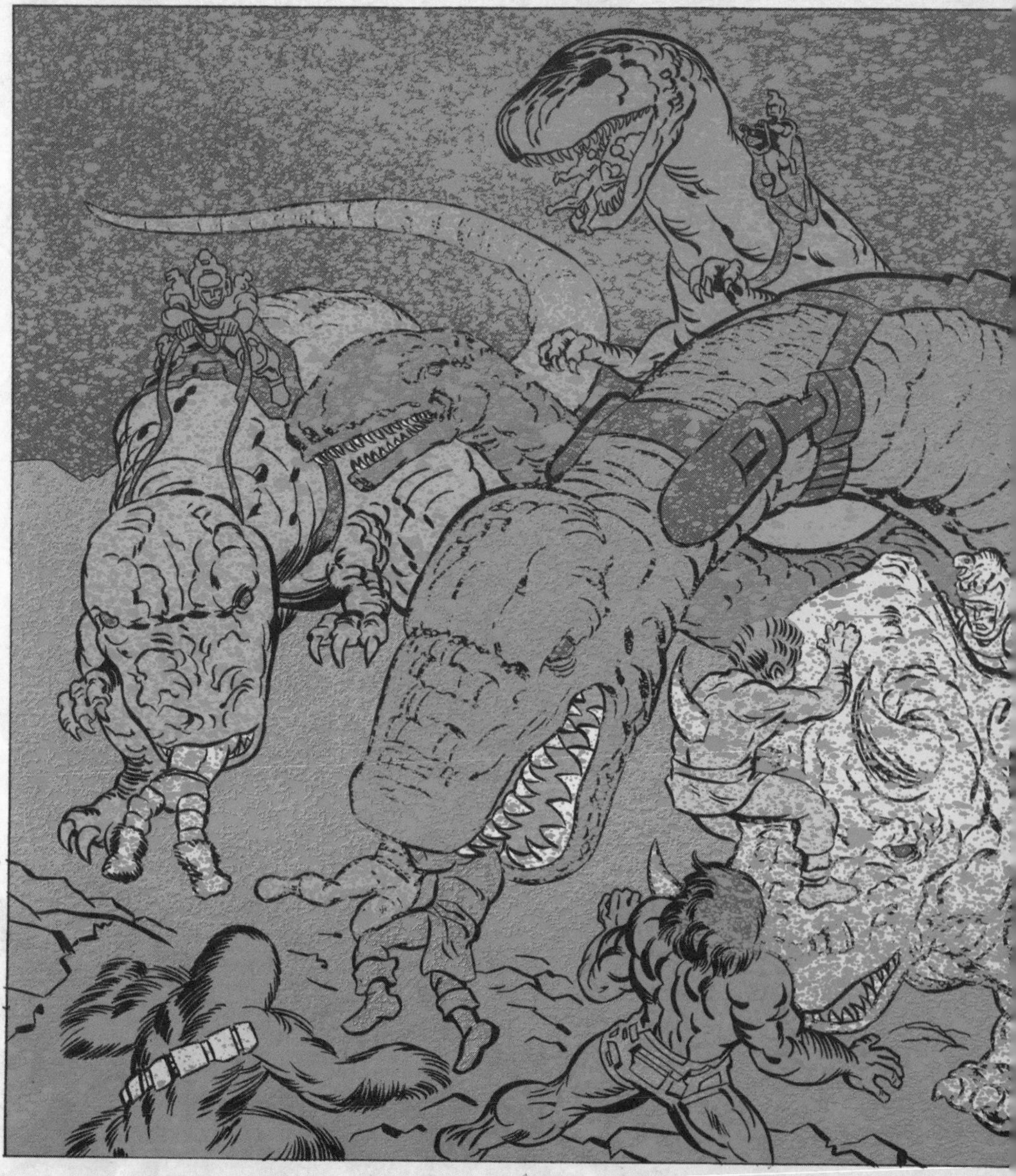

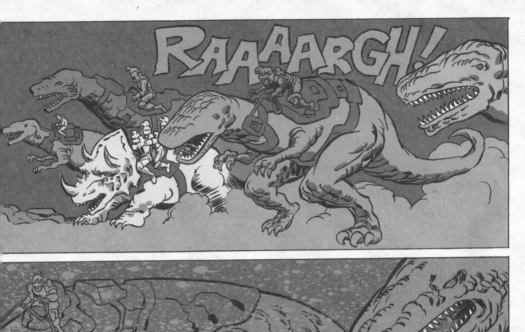

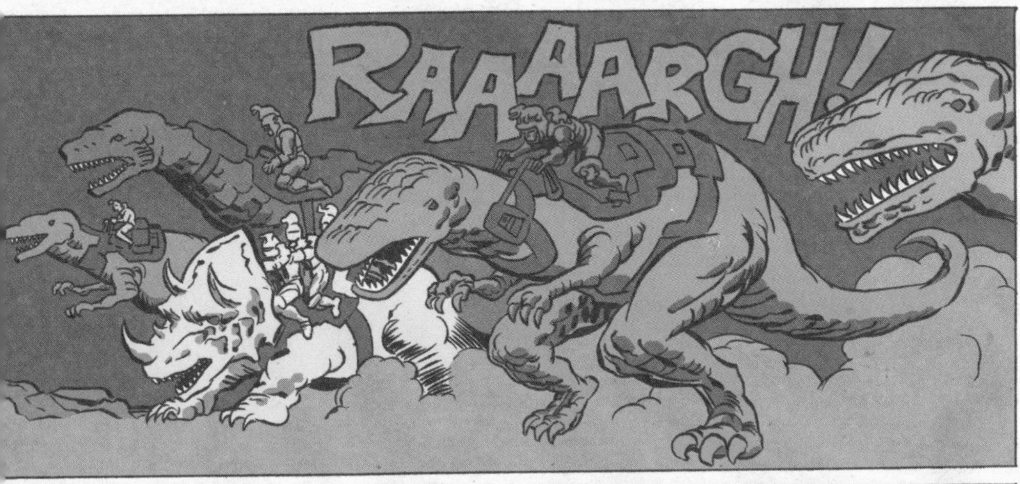
RAAAARGH!

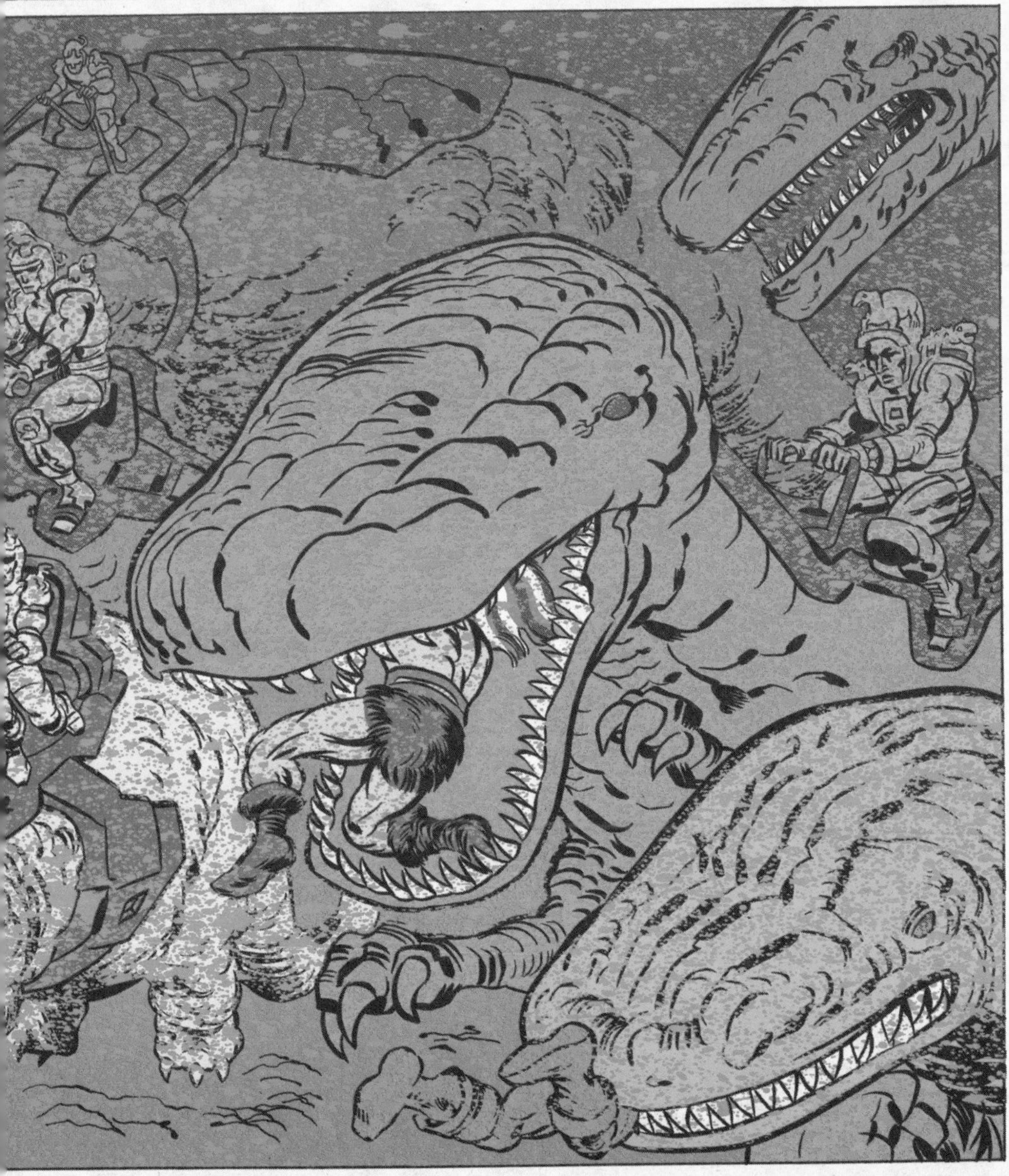

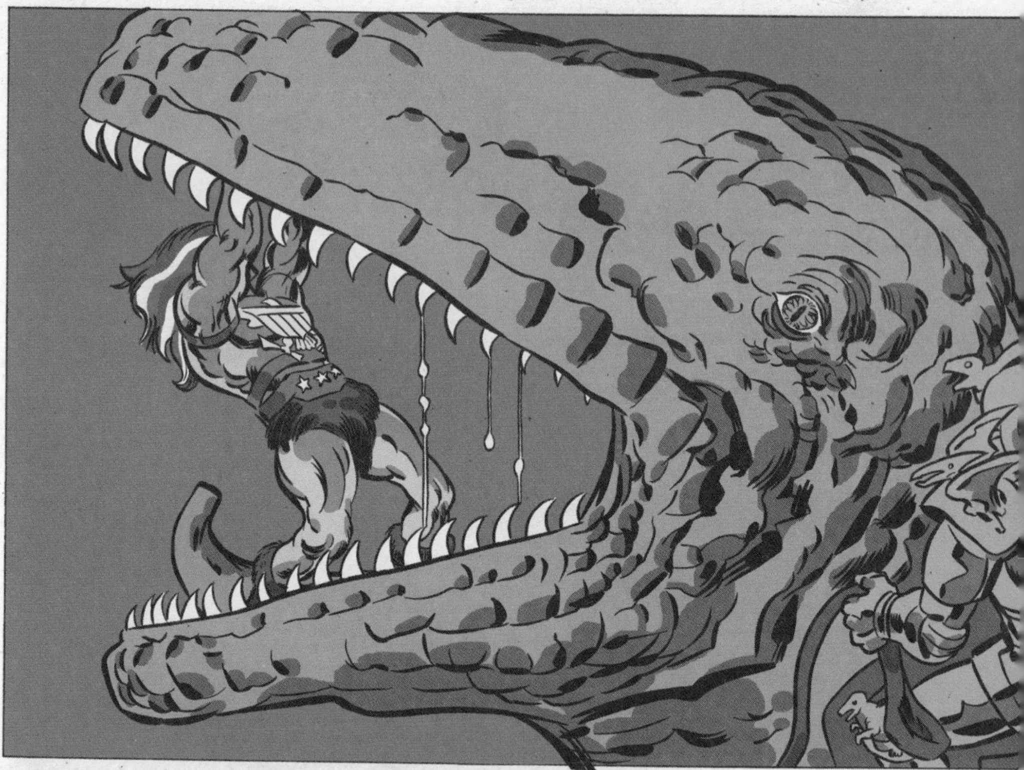

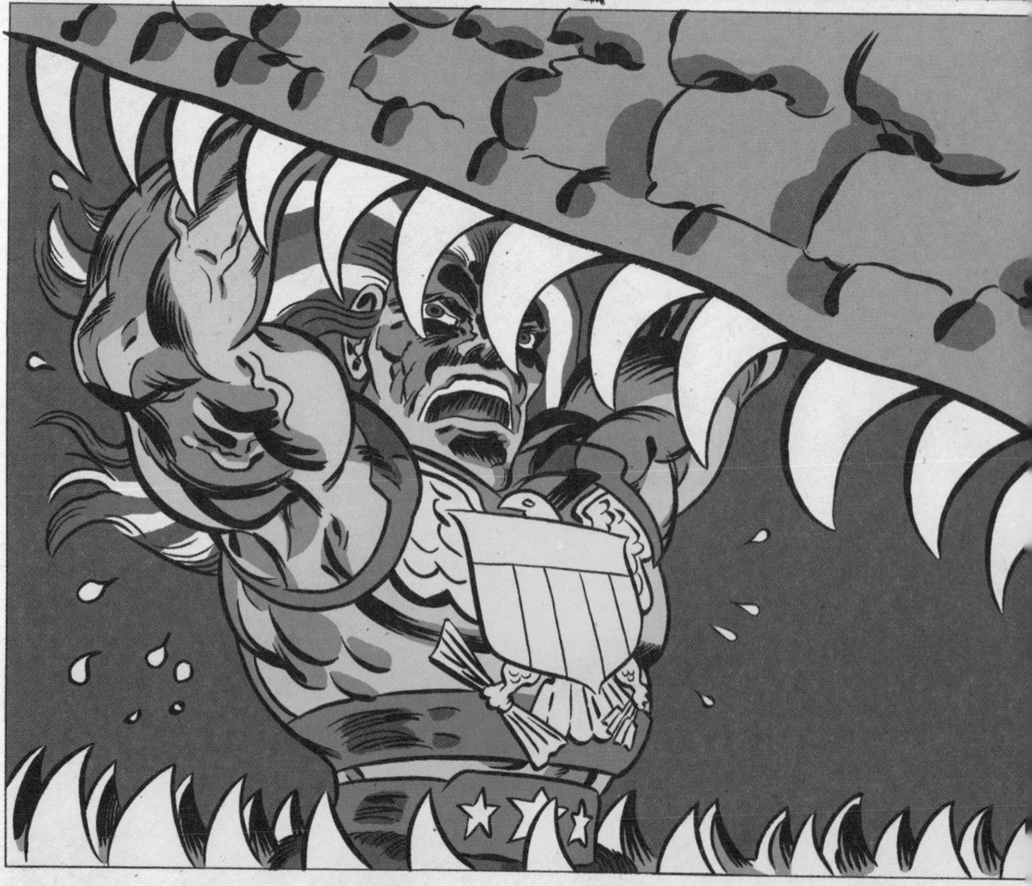

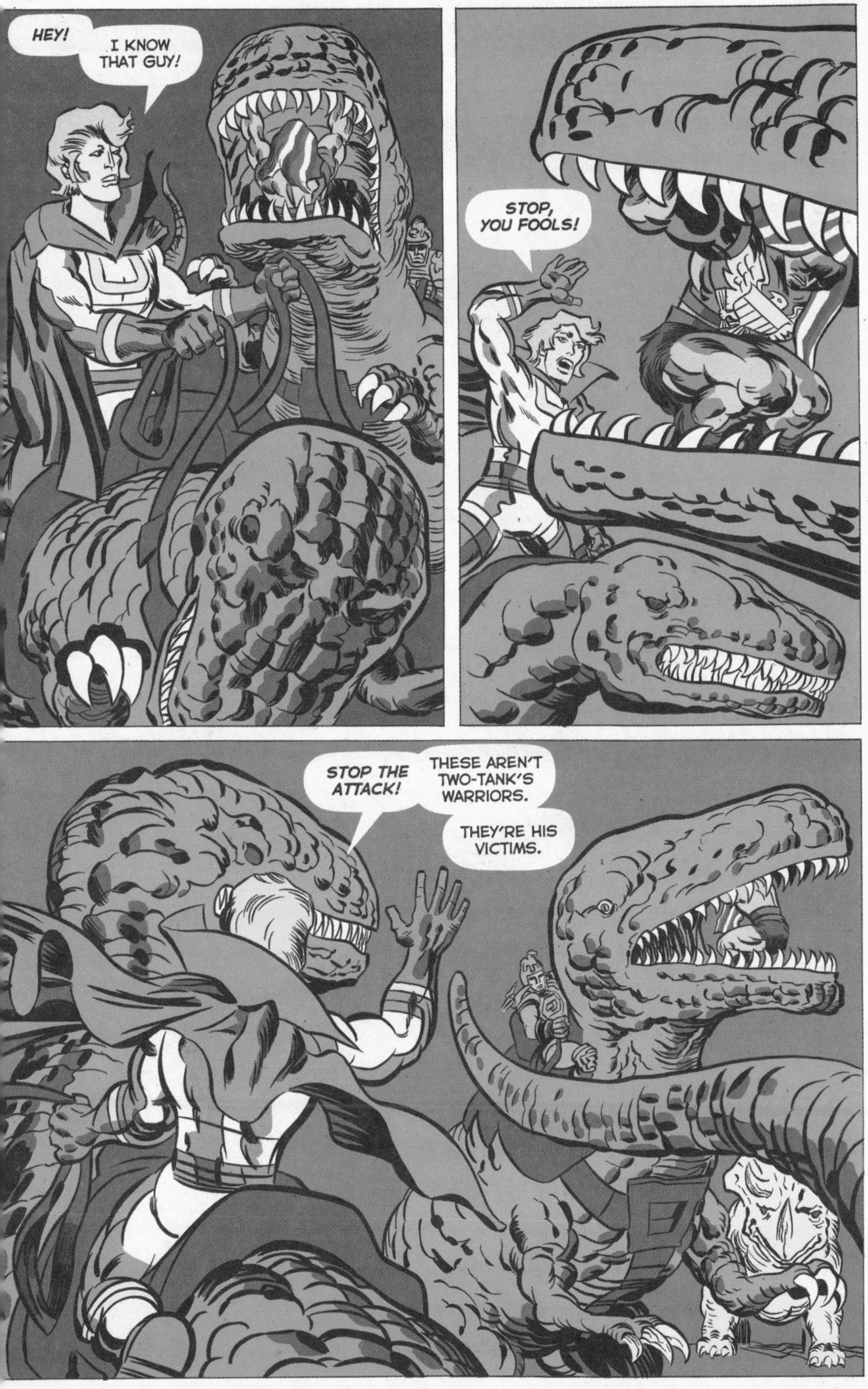
HEY!
I KNOW THAT GUY!
STOP, YOU FOOLS!
STOP THE ATTACK!
THESE AREN'T TWO-TANK'S WARRIORS.
THEY'RE HIS VICTIMS.

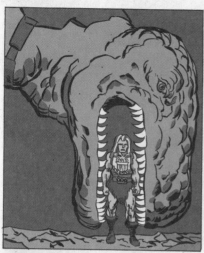

THINK NEXT TIME!

WHERE'S MY SISTER?

TWO-TANK'S GOT HER.

SMICK

I DESERVED THAT, BUT FIGHTING EACH OTHER WON'T GET US ANYTHING.

TWO-TANK IS OUT THERE.

THIS IS WAR.

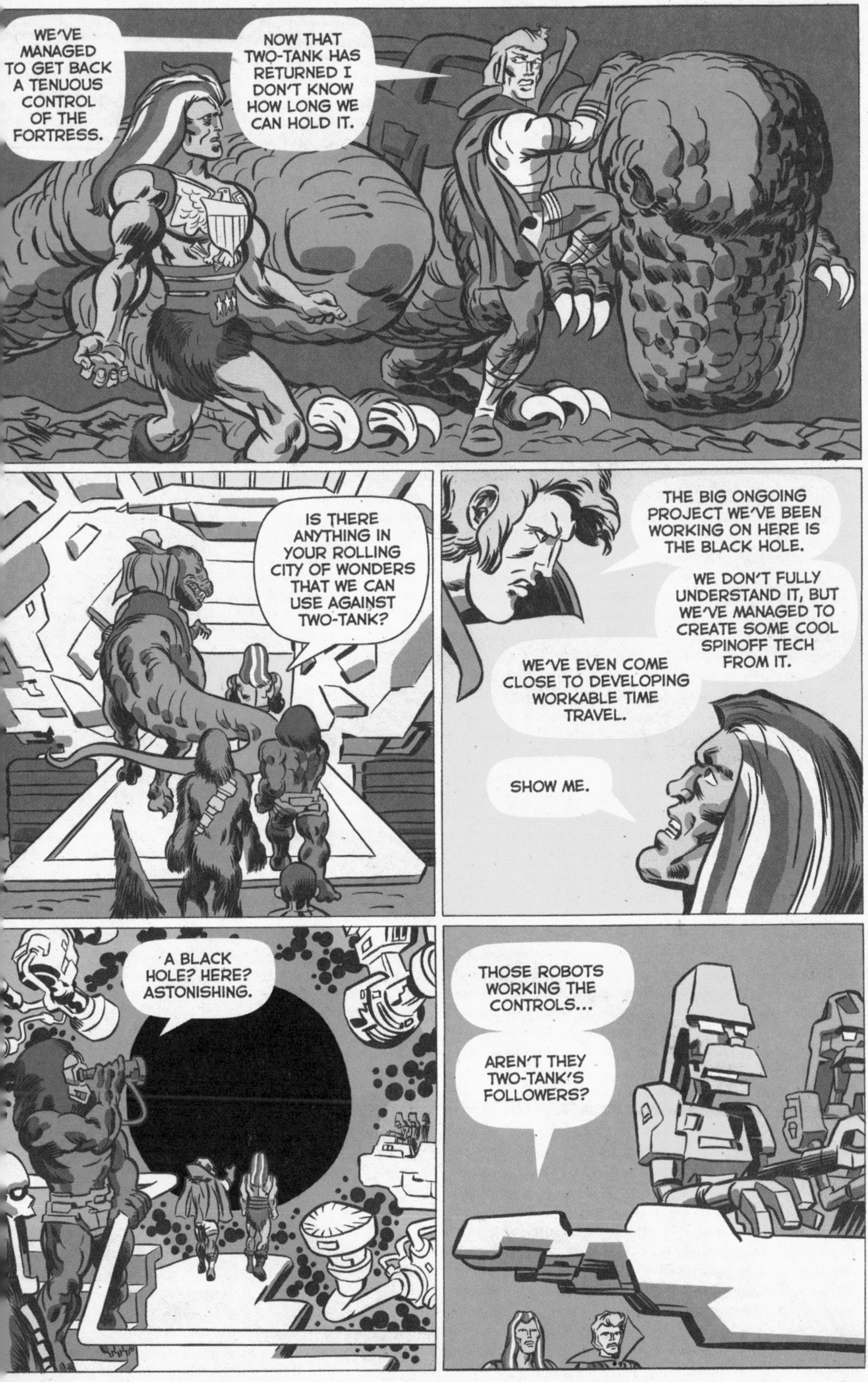
WE'VE MANAGED TO GET BACK A TENUOUS CONTROL OF THE FORTRESS.
NOW THAT TWO-TANK HAS RETURNED I DON'T KNOW HOW LONG WE CAN HOLD IT.
IS THERE ANYTHING IN YOUR ROLLING CITY OF WONDERS THAT WE CAN USE AGAINST TWO-TANK?
THE BIG ONGOING PROJECT WE'VE BEEN WORKING ON HERE IS THE BLACK HOLE.
WE DON'T FULLY UNDERSTAND IT, BUT WE'VE MANAGED TO CREATE SOME COOL SPINOFF TECH FROM IT.
WE'VE EVEN COME CLOSE TO DEVELOPING WORKABLE TIME TRAVEL.
SHOW ME.
A BLACK HOLE? HERE? ASTONISHING.
THOSE ROBOTS WORKING THE CONTROLS...
AREN'T THEY TWO-TANK'S FOLLOWERS?

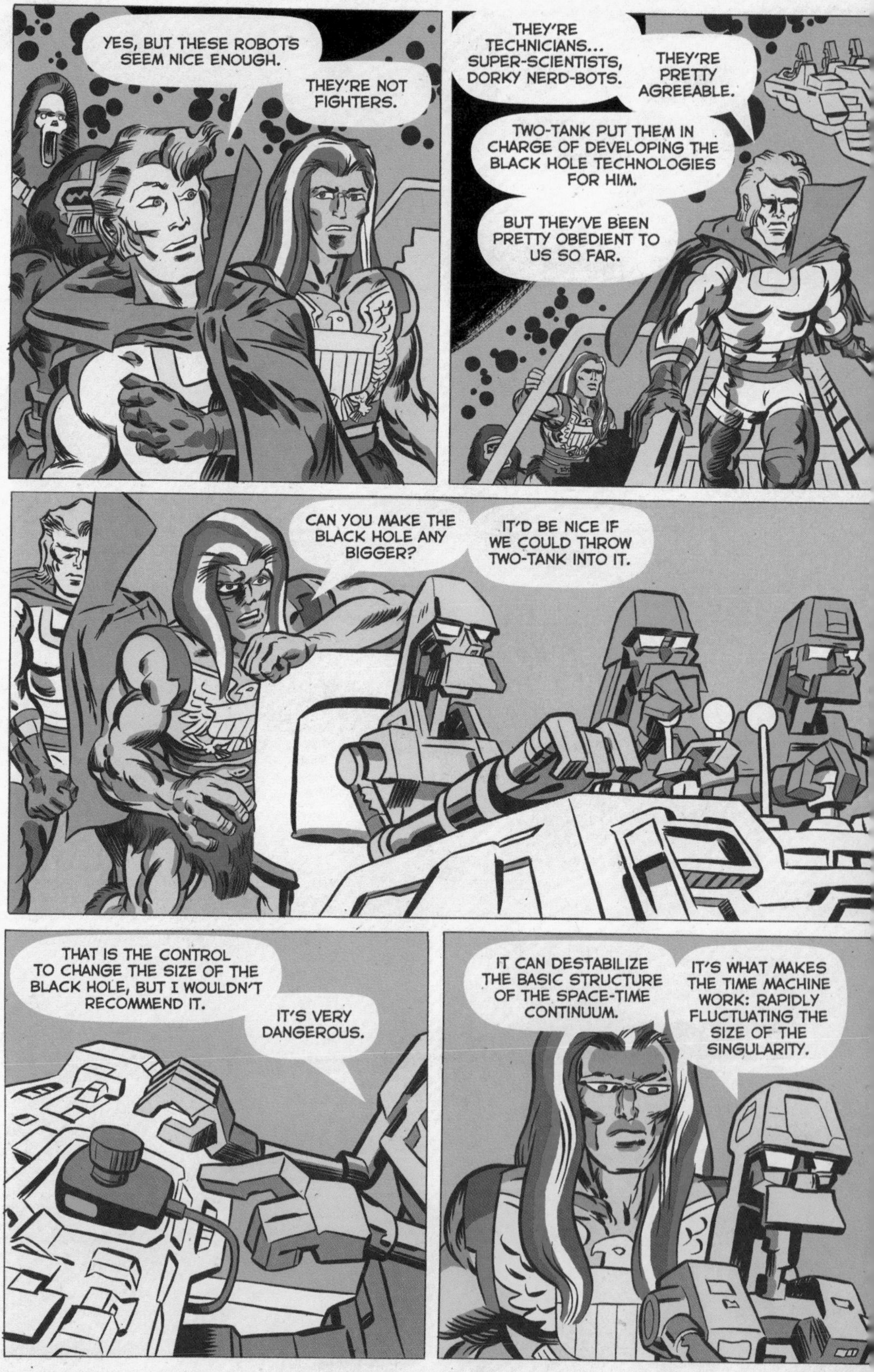

YES, BUT THESE ROBOTS SEEM NICE ENOUGH.
THEY'RE NOT FIGHTERS.
THEY'RE TECHNICIANS... SUPER-SCIENTISTS, DORKY NERD-BOTS.
THEY'RE PRETTY AGREEABLE.
TWO-TANK PUT THEM IN CHARGE OF DEVELOPING THE BLACK HOLE TECHNOLOGIES FOR HIM.
BUT THEY'VE BEEN PRETTY OBEDIENT TO US SO FAR.
CAN YOU MAKE THE BLACK HOLE ANY BIGGER?
IT'D BE NICE IF WE COULD THROW TWO-TANK INTO IT.
THAT IS THE CONTROL TO CHANGE THE SIZE OF THE BLACK HOLE, BUT I WOULDN'T RECOMMEND IT.
IT'S VERY DANGEROUS.
IT CAN DESTABILIZE THE BASIC STRUCTURE OF THE SPACE-TIME CONTINUUM.
IT'S WHAT MAKES THE TIME MACHINE WORK: RAPIDLY FLUCTUATING THE SIZE OF THE SINGULARITY.

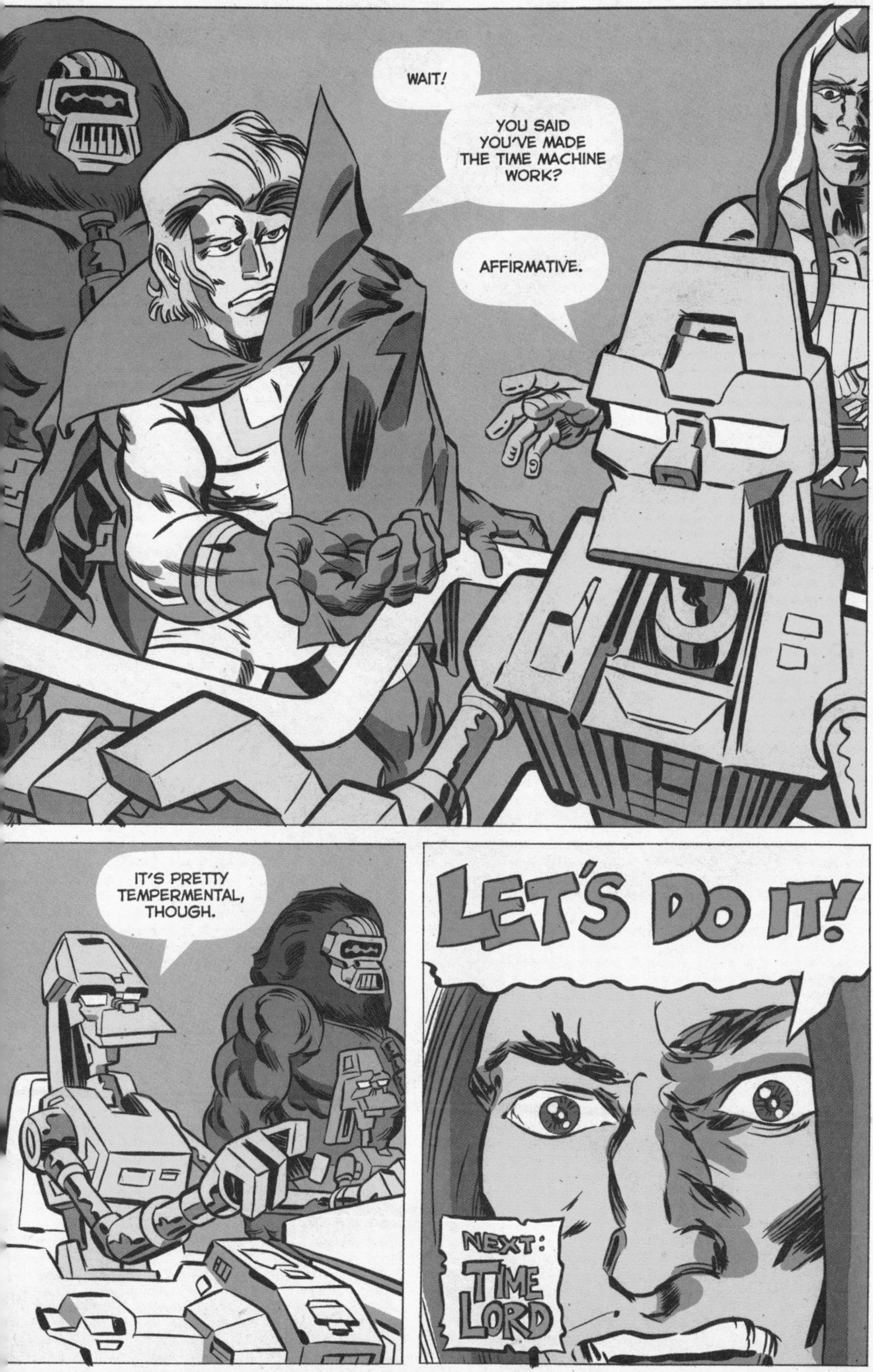

WAIT!
YOU SAID YOU'VE MADE THE TIME MACHINE WORK?
AFFIRMATIVE.
IT'S PRETTY TEMPERMENTAL, THOUGH.
LET'S DO IT!
NEXT: TIME LORD

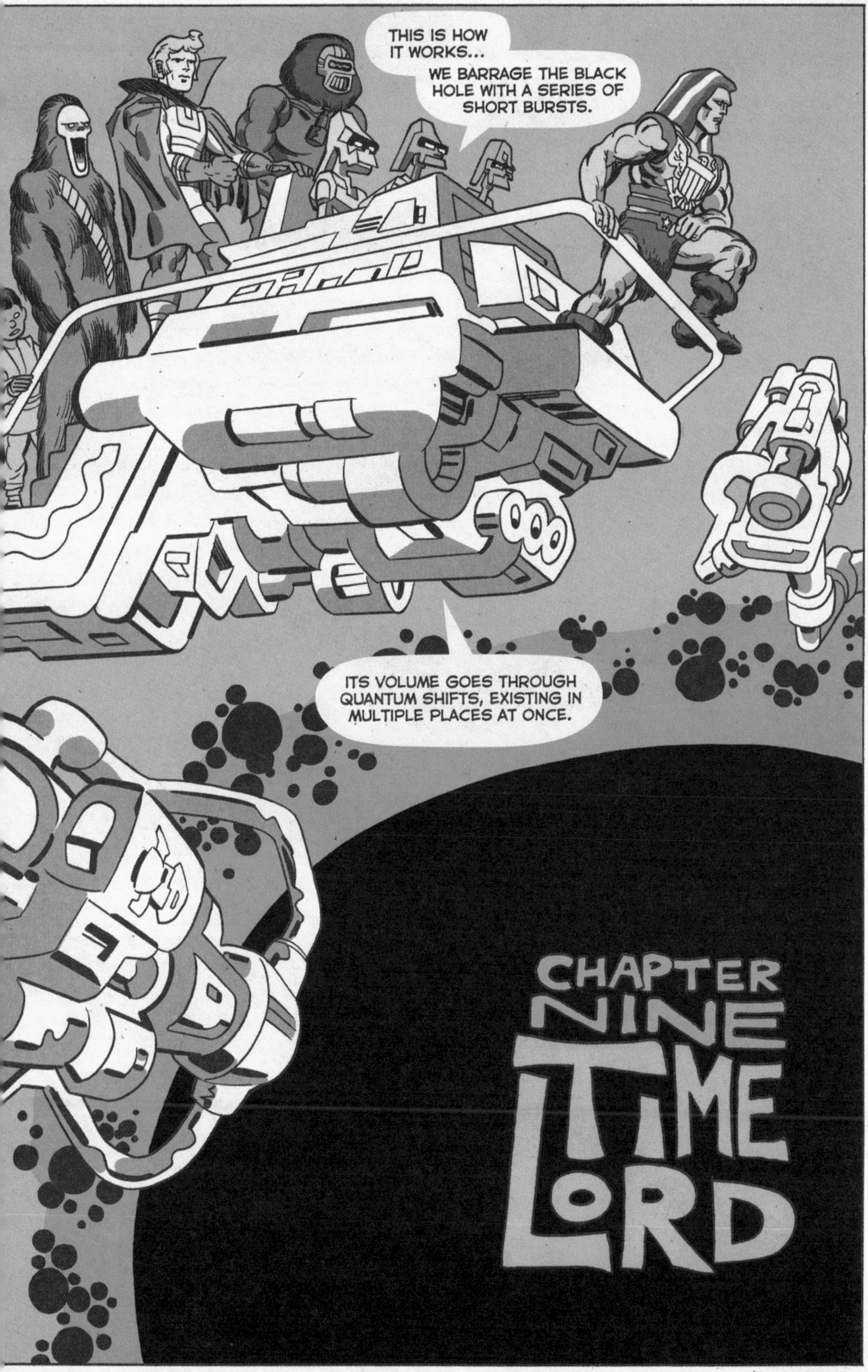
THIS IS HOW IT WORKS...
WE BARRAGE THE BLACK HOLE WITH A SERIES OF SHORT BURSTS.
ITS VOLUME GOES THROUGH QUANTUM SHIFTS, EXISTING IN MULTIPLE PLACES AT ONCE.
CHAPTER NINE
TIME LORD

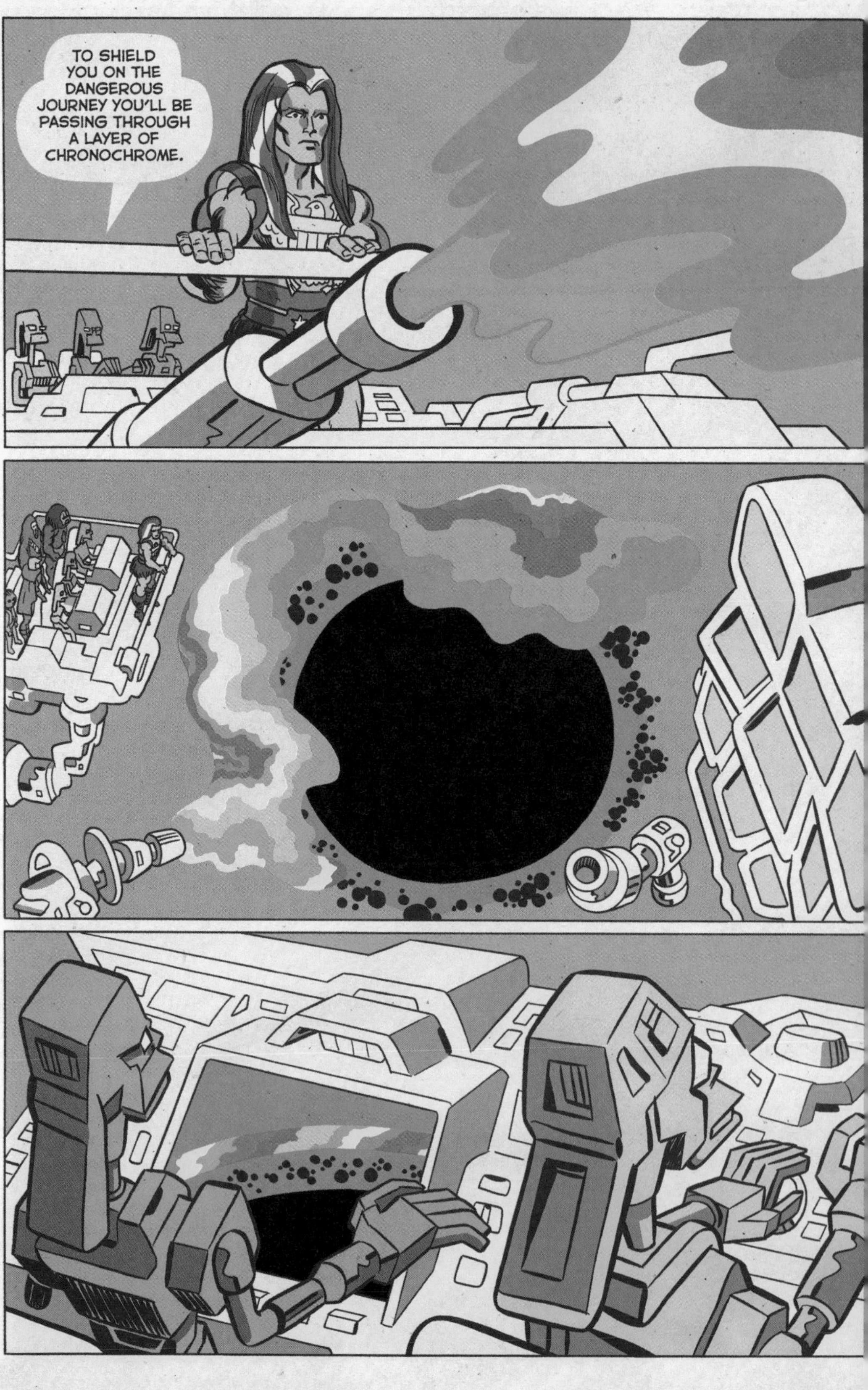
TO SHIELD YOU ON THE DANGEROUS JOURNEY YOU'LL BE PASSING THROUGH A LAYER OF CHRONOCHROME.

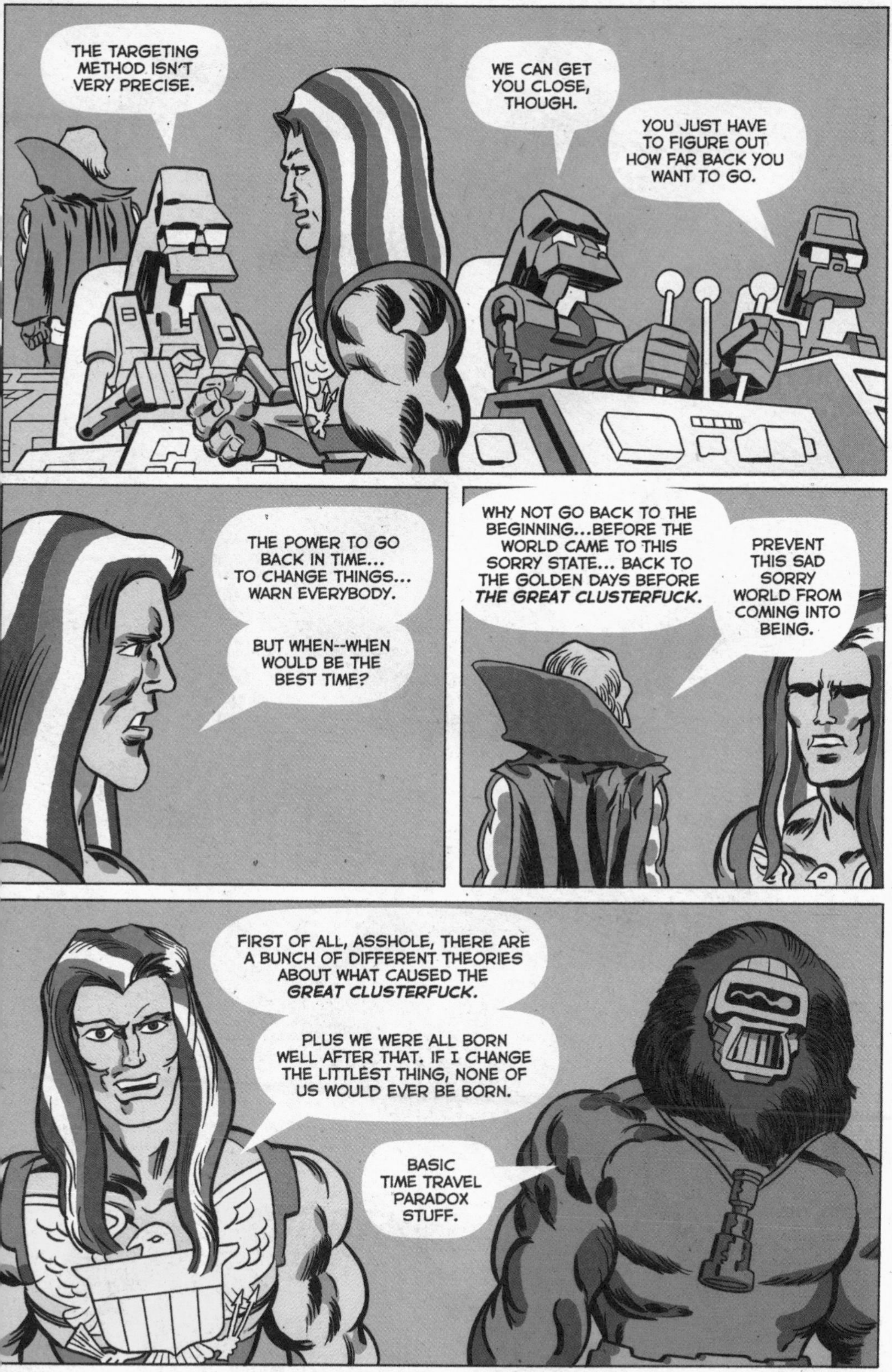
THE TARGETING METHOD ISN'T VERY PRECISE.
WE CAN GET YOU CLOSE, THOUGH.
YOU JUST HAVE TO FIGURE OUT HOW FAR BACK YOU WANT TO GO.
THE POWER TO GO BACK IN TIME... TO CHANGE THINGS... WARN EVERYBODY.
BUT WHEN--WHEN WOULD BE THE BEST TIME?
WHY NOT GO BACK TO THE BEGINNING...BEFORE THE WORLD CAME TO THIS SORRY STATE... BACK TO THE GOLDEN DAYS BEFORE *THE GREAT CLUSTERFUCK.*
PREVENT THIS SAD SORRY WORLD FROM COMING INTO BEING.
FIRST OF ALL, ASSHOLE, THERE ARE A BUNCH OF DIFFERENT THEORIES ABOUT WHAT CAUSED THE *GREAT CLUSTERFUCK.*
PLUS WE WERE ALL BORN WELL AFTER THAT. IF I CHANGE THE LITTLEST THING, NONE OF US WOULD EVER BE BORN.
BASIC TIME TRAVEL PARADOX STUFF.

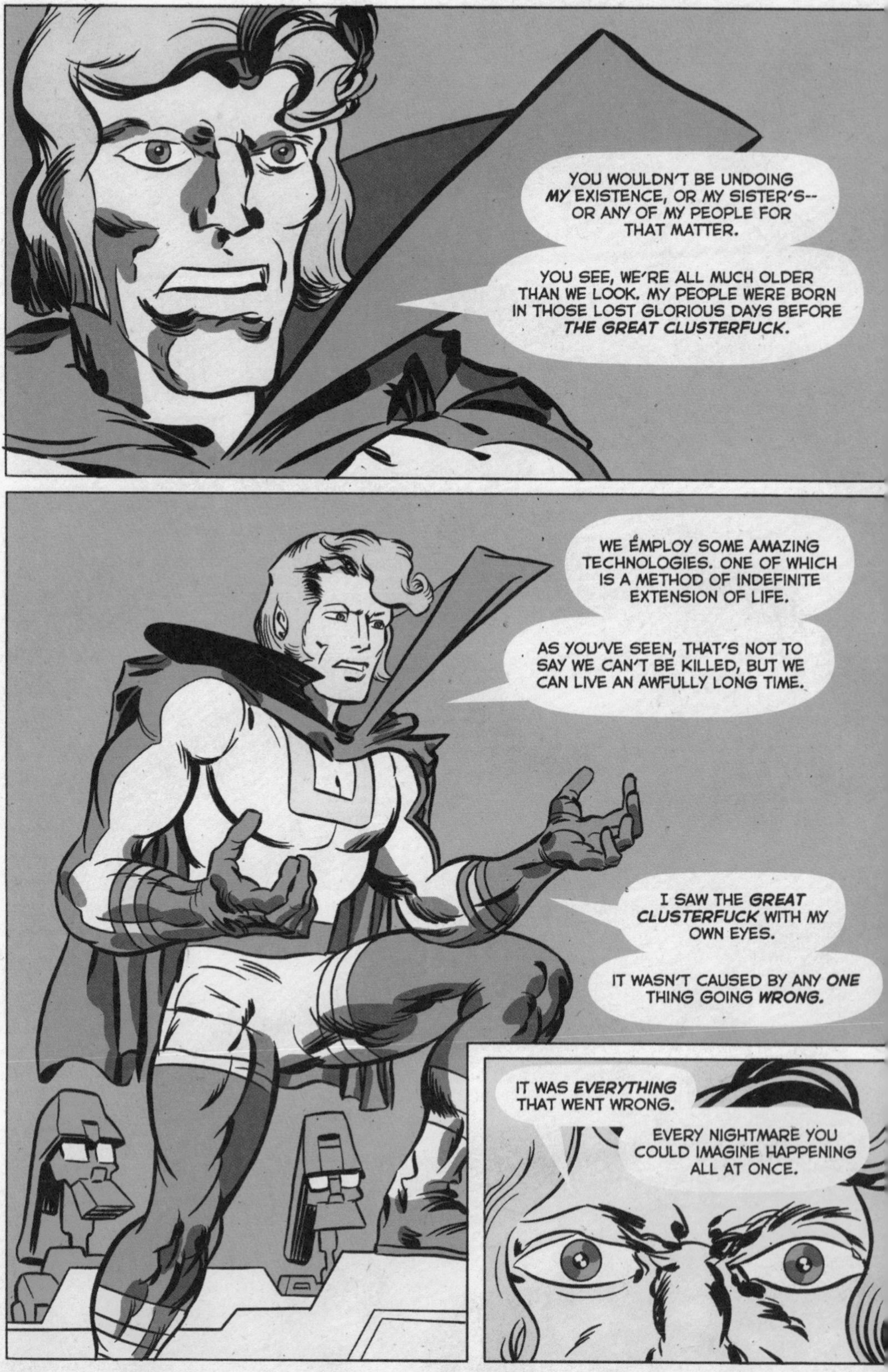
YOU WOULDN'T BE UNDOING MY EXISTENCE, OR MY SISTER'S-- OR ANY OF MY PEOPLE FOR THAT MATTER.
YOU SEE, WE'RE ALL MUCH OLDER THAN WE LOOK. MY PEOPLE WERE BORN IN THOSE LOST GLORIOUS DAYS BEFORE THE GREAT CLUSTERFUCK.
WE EMPLOY SOME AMAZING TECHNOLOGIES. ONE OF WHICH IS A METHOD OF INDEFINITE EXTENSION OF LIFE.
AS YOU'VE SEEN, THAT'S NOT TO SAY WE CAN'T BE KILLED, BUT WE CAN LIVE AN AWFULLY LONG TIME.
I SAW THE GREAT CLUSTERFUCK WITH MY OWN EYES.
IT WASN'T CAUSED BY ANY ONE THING GOING WRONG.
IT WAS EVERYTHING THAT WENT WRONG.
EVERY NIGHTMARE YOU COULD IMAGINE HAPPENING ALL AT ONCE.

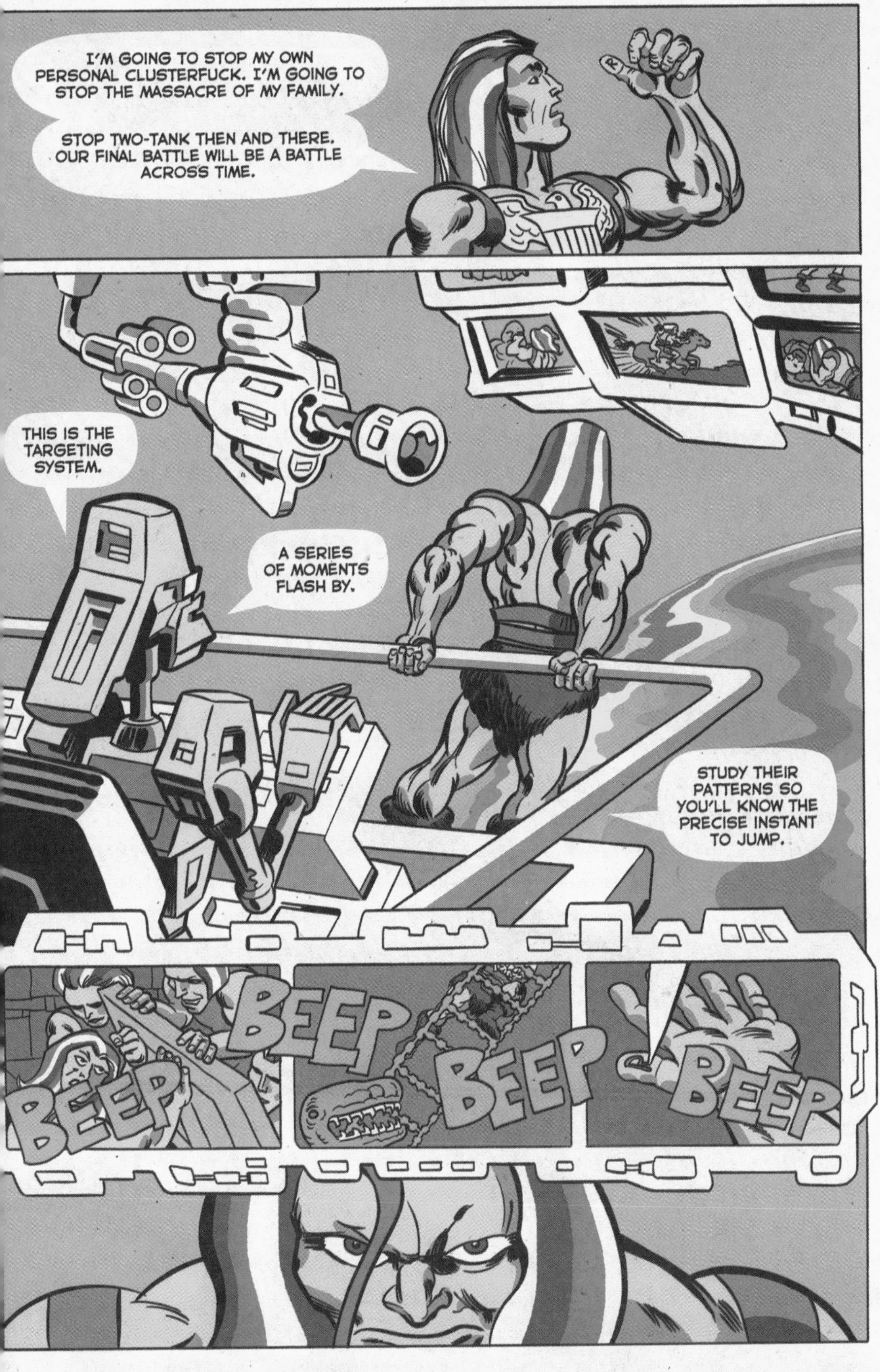
I'M GOING TO STOP MY OWN PERSONAL CLUSTERFUCK. I'M GOING TO STOP THE MASSACRE OF MY FAMILY.
STOP TWO-TANK THEN AND THERE. OUR FINAL BATTLE WILL BE A BATTLE ACROSS TIME.
THIS IS THE TARGETING SYSTEM.
A SERIES OF MOMENTS FLASH BY.
STUDY THEIR PATTERNS SO YOU'LL KNOW THE PRECISE INSTANT TO JUMP.
BEEP
BEEP
BEEP
BEEP

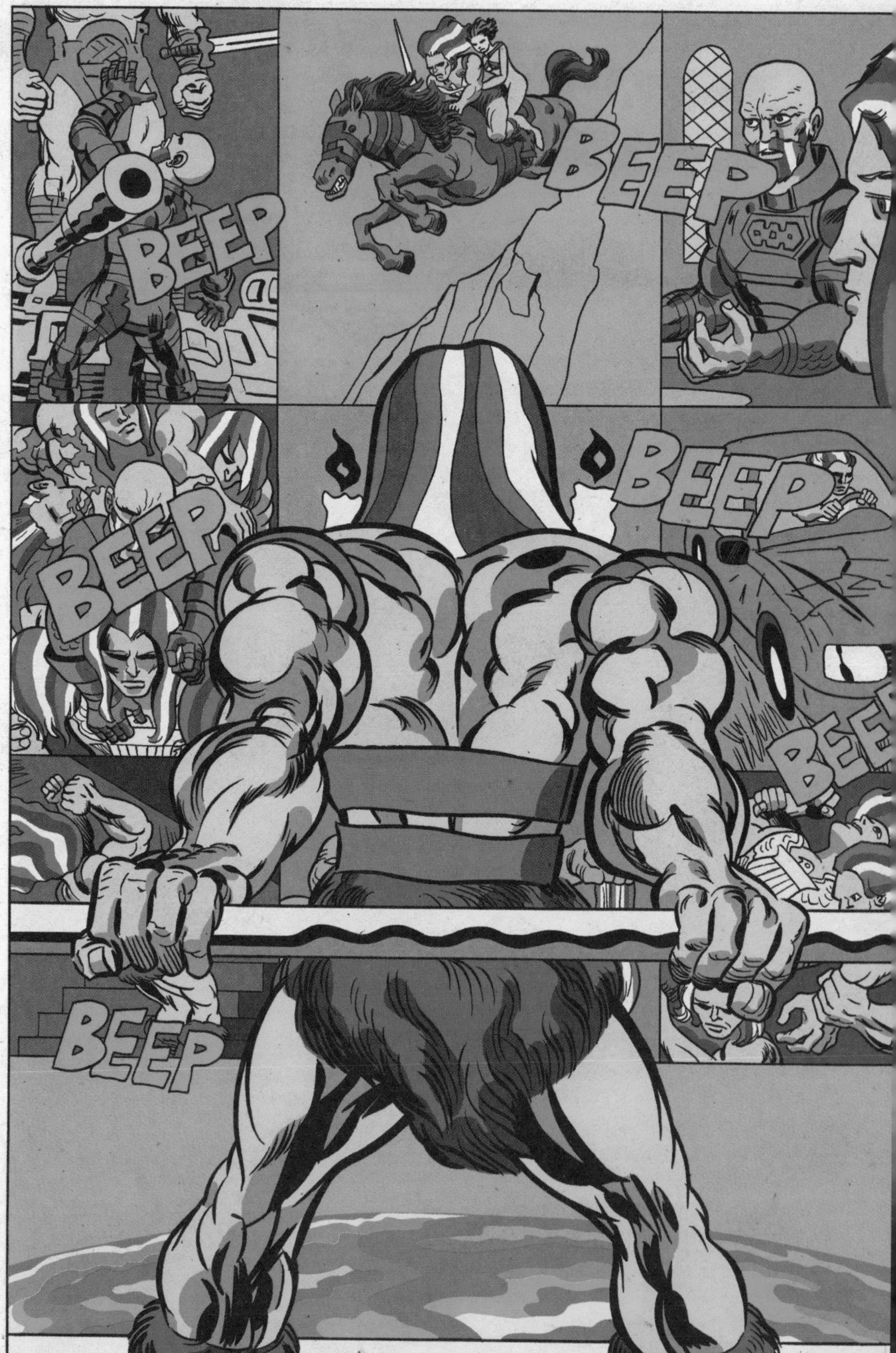
BEEP
BEEP
BEEP
BEEP
BEEP
BEEP

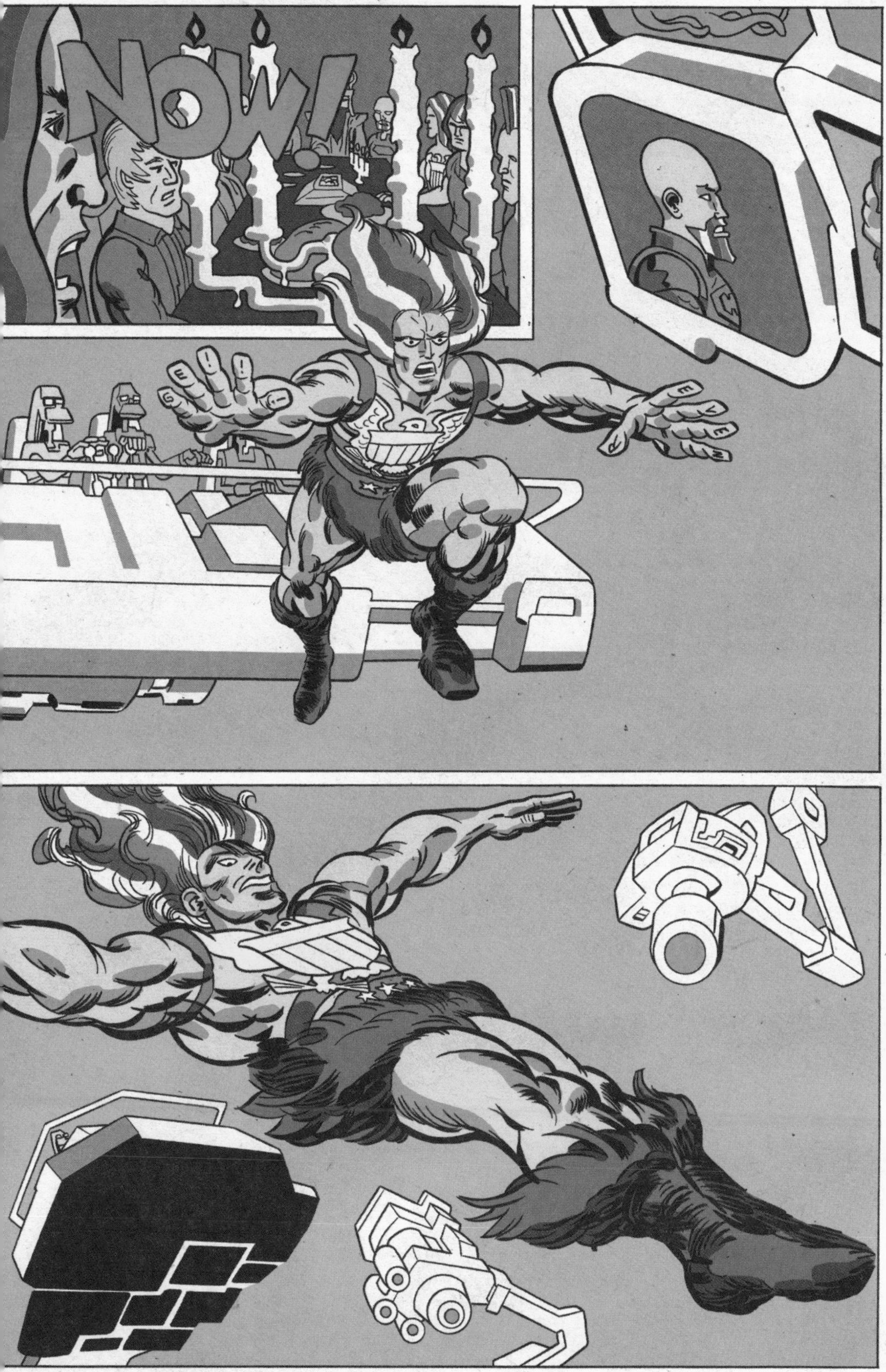
NOW!

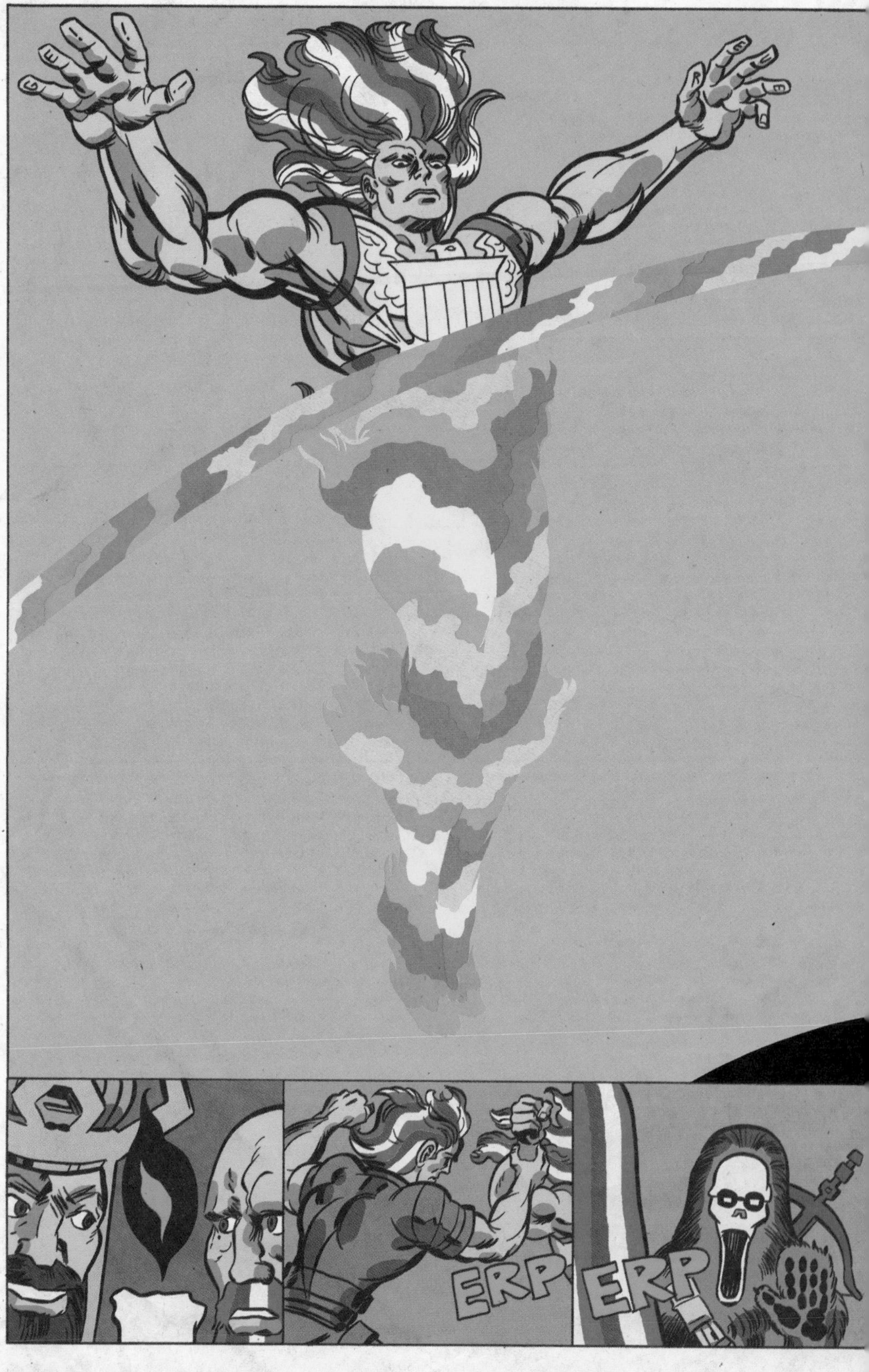
ERP
ERP

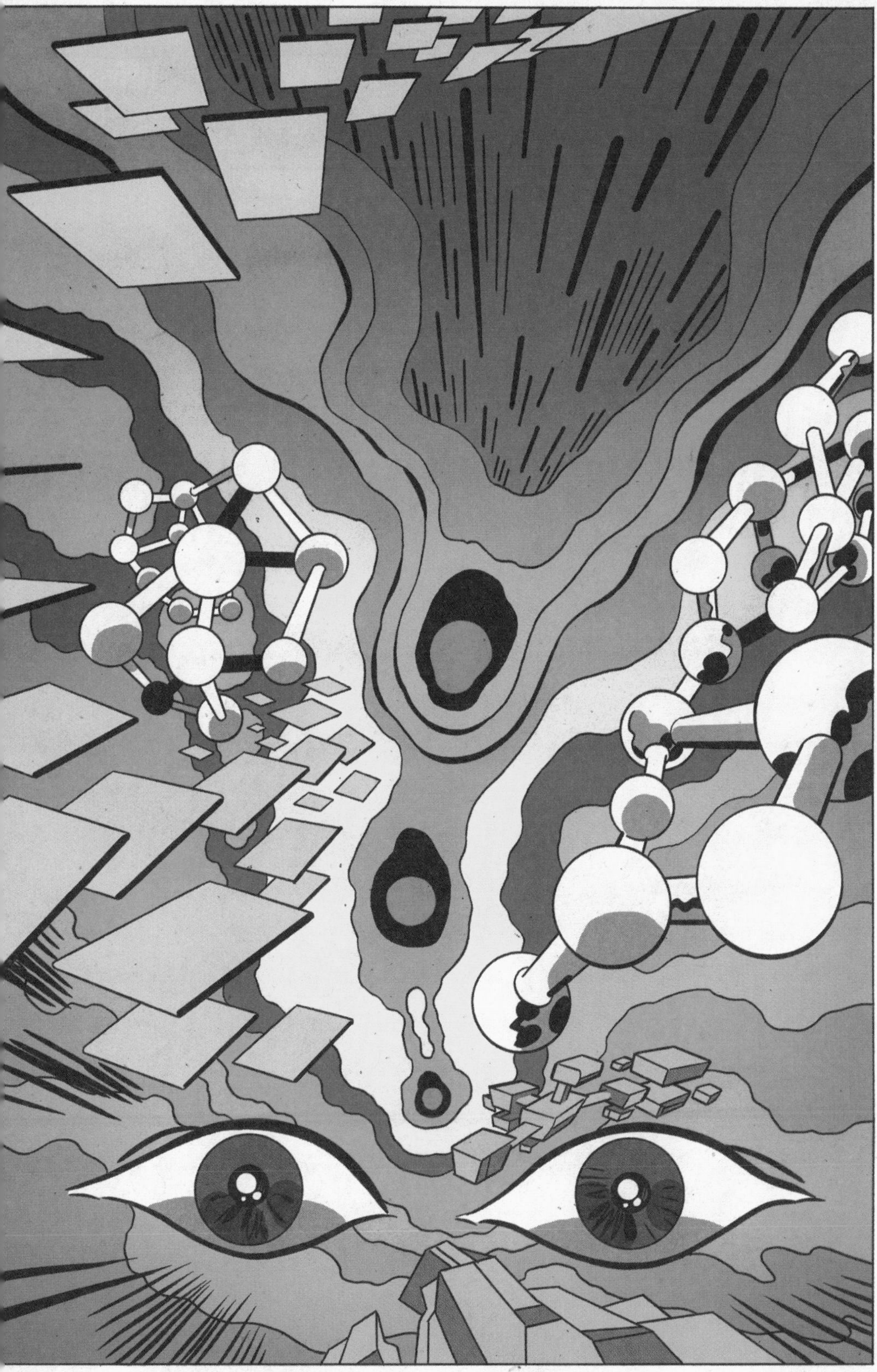

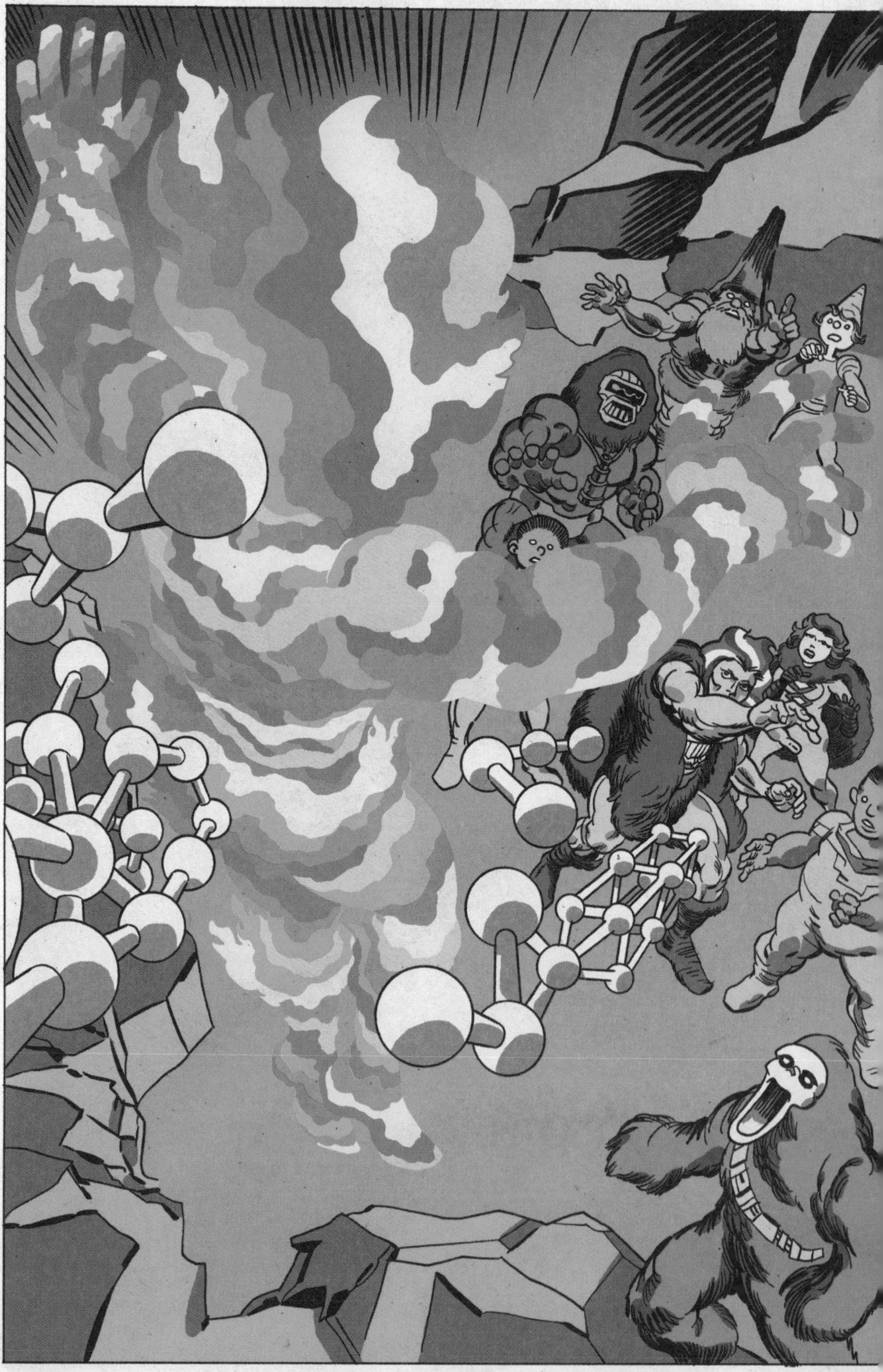

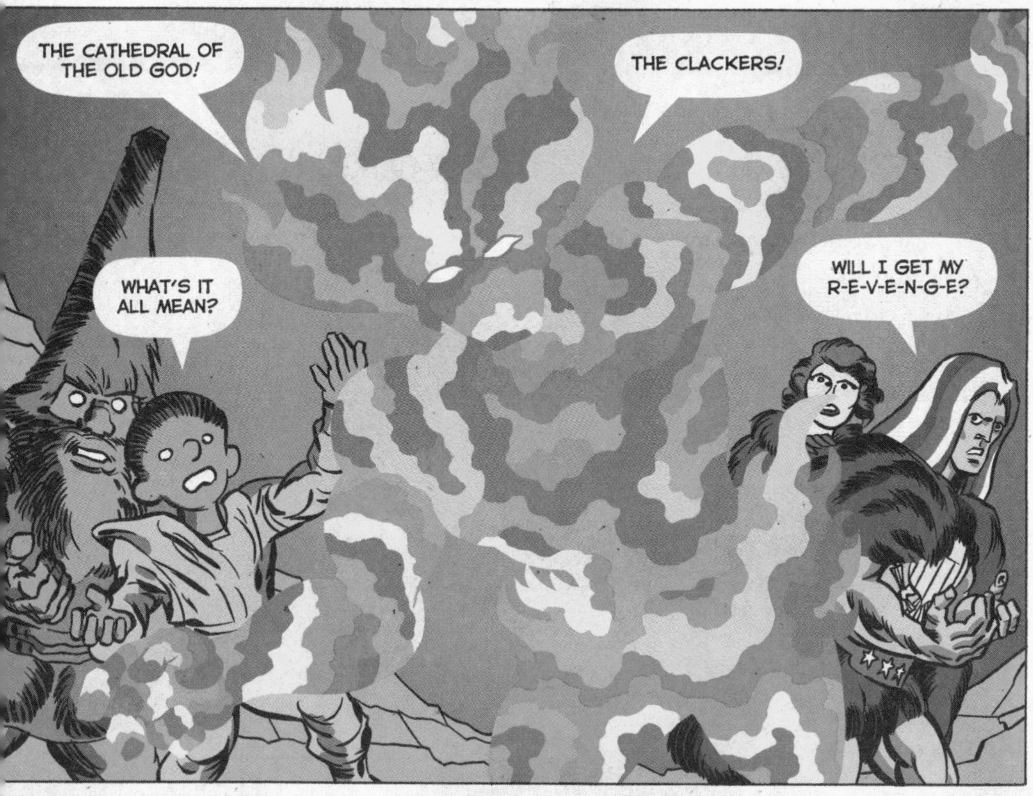
THE CATHEDRAL OF THE OLD GOD!
THE CLACKERS!
WHAT'S IT ALL MEAN?
WILL I GET MY R-E-V-E-N-G-E?

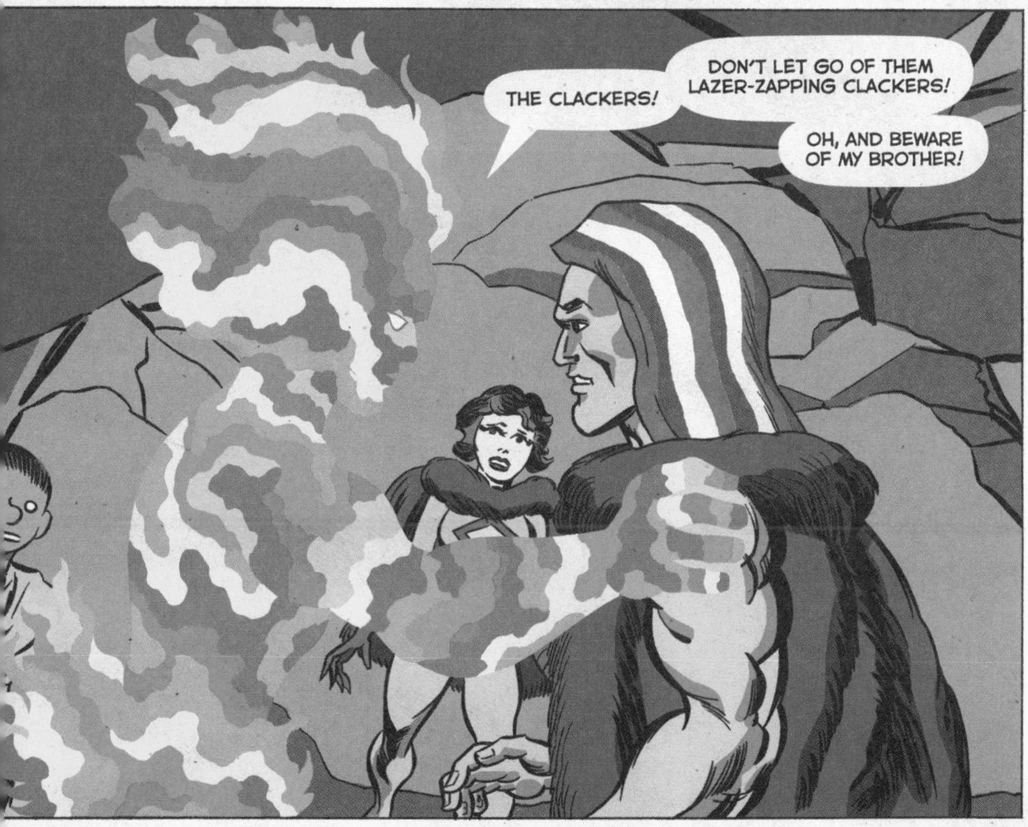
THE CLACKERS!
DON'T LET GO OF THEM LAZER-ZAPPING CLACKERS!
OH, AND BEWARE OF MY BROTHER!

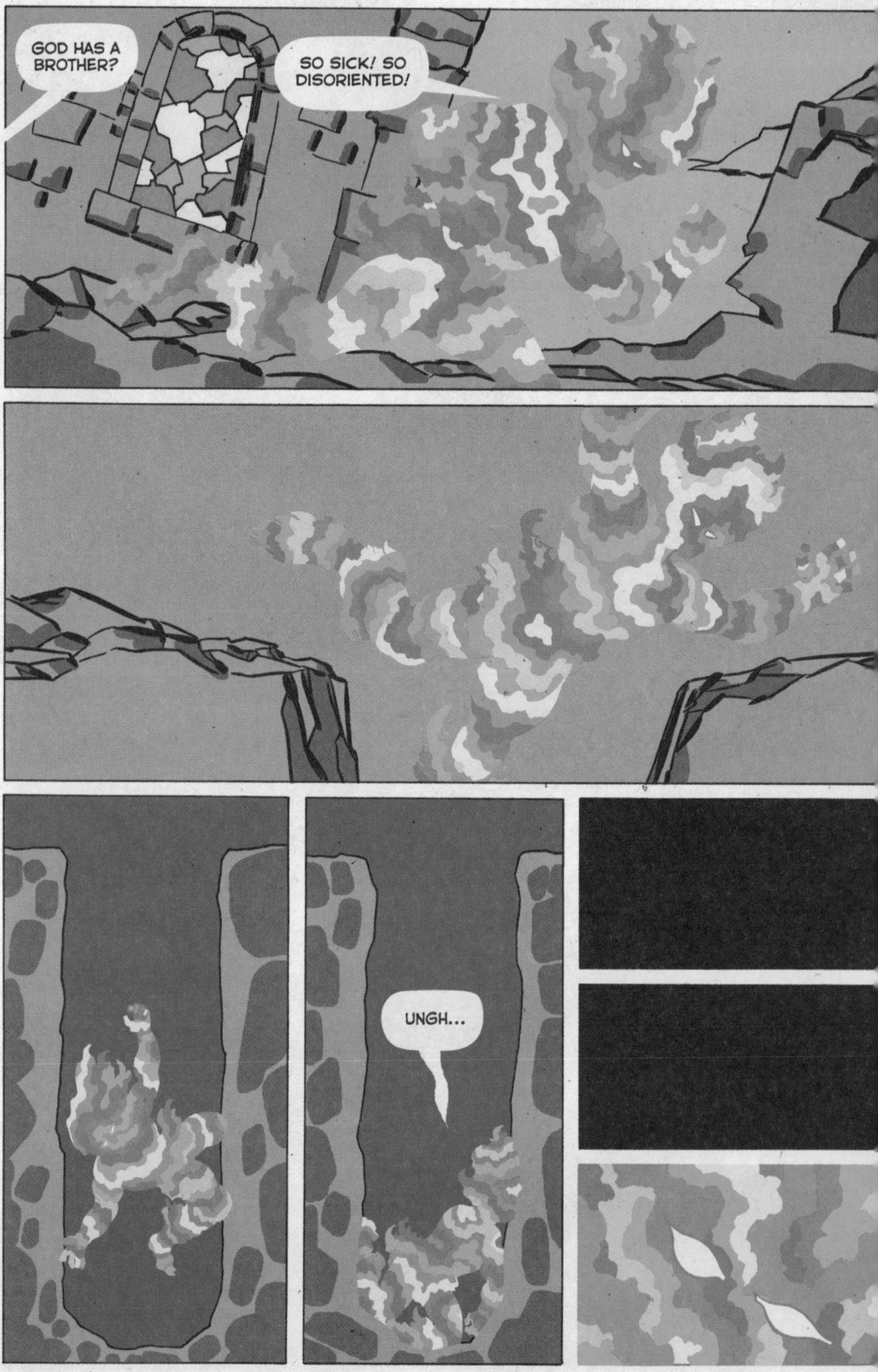
GOD HAS A BROTHER?
SO SICK! SO DISORIENTED!
UNGH...

HOORAY

THE CLACKERS!

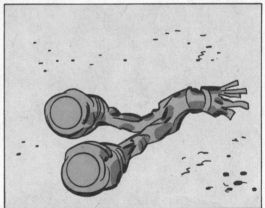

HEY!

NO FAIR!

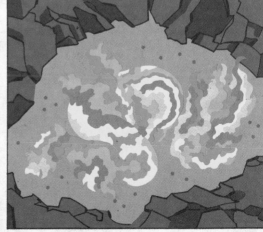

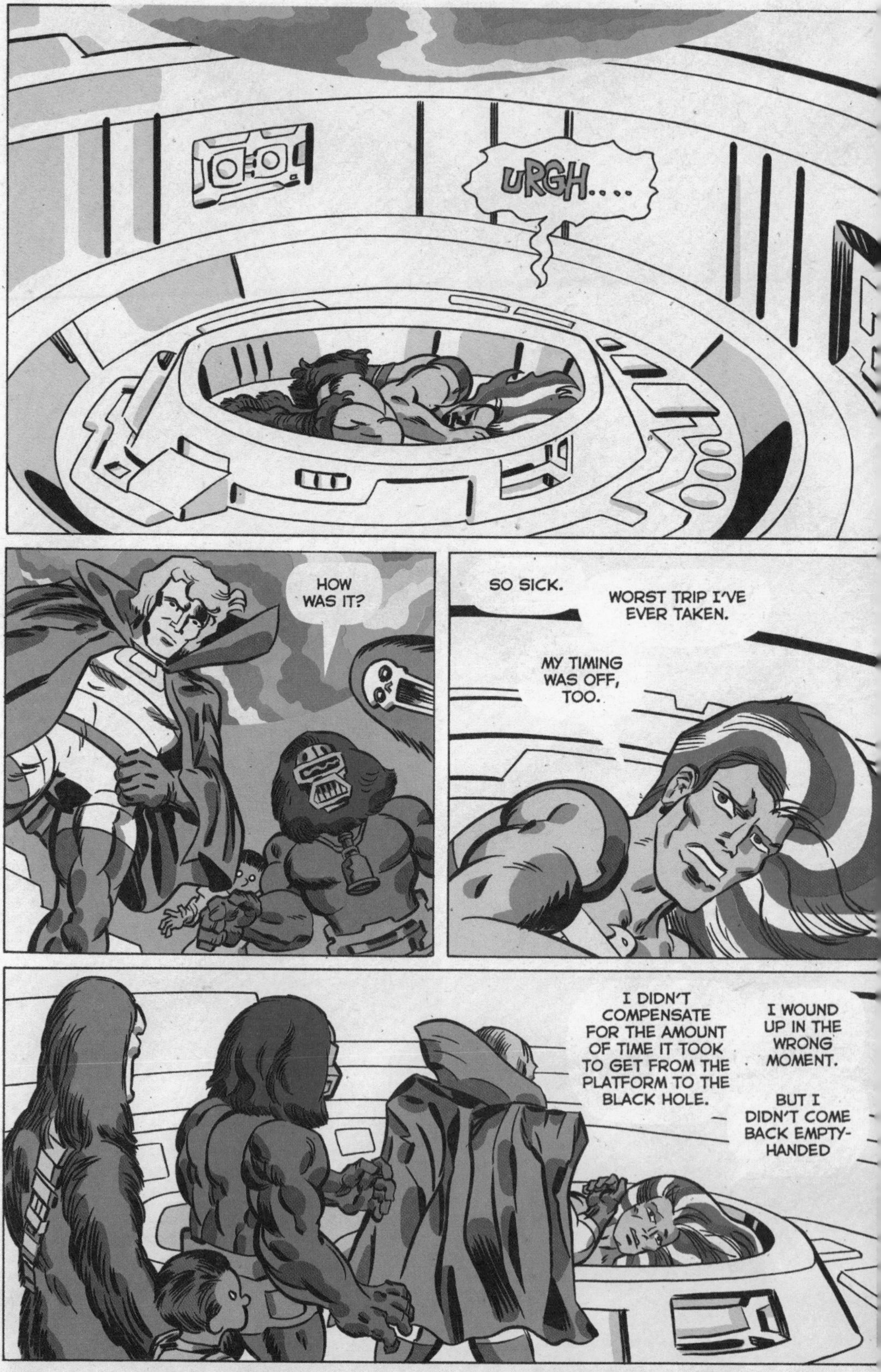
URGH.....
HOW WAS IT?
SO SICK.
WORST TRIP I'VE EVER TAKEN.
MY TIMING WAS OFF, TOO.
I DIDN'T COMPENSATE FOR THE AMOUNT OF TIME IT TOOK TO GET FROM THE PLATFORM TO THE BLACK HOLE.
I WOUND UP IN THE WRONG MOMENT.
BUT I DIDN'T COME BACK EMPTY-HANDED

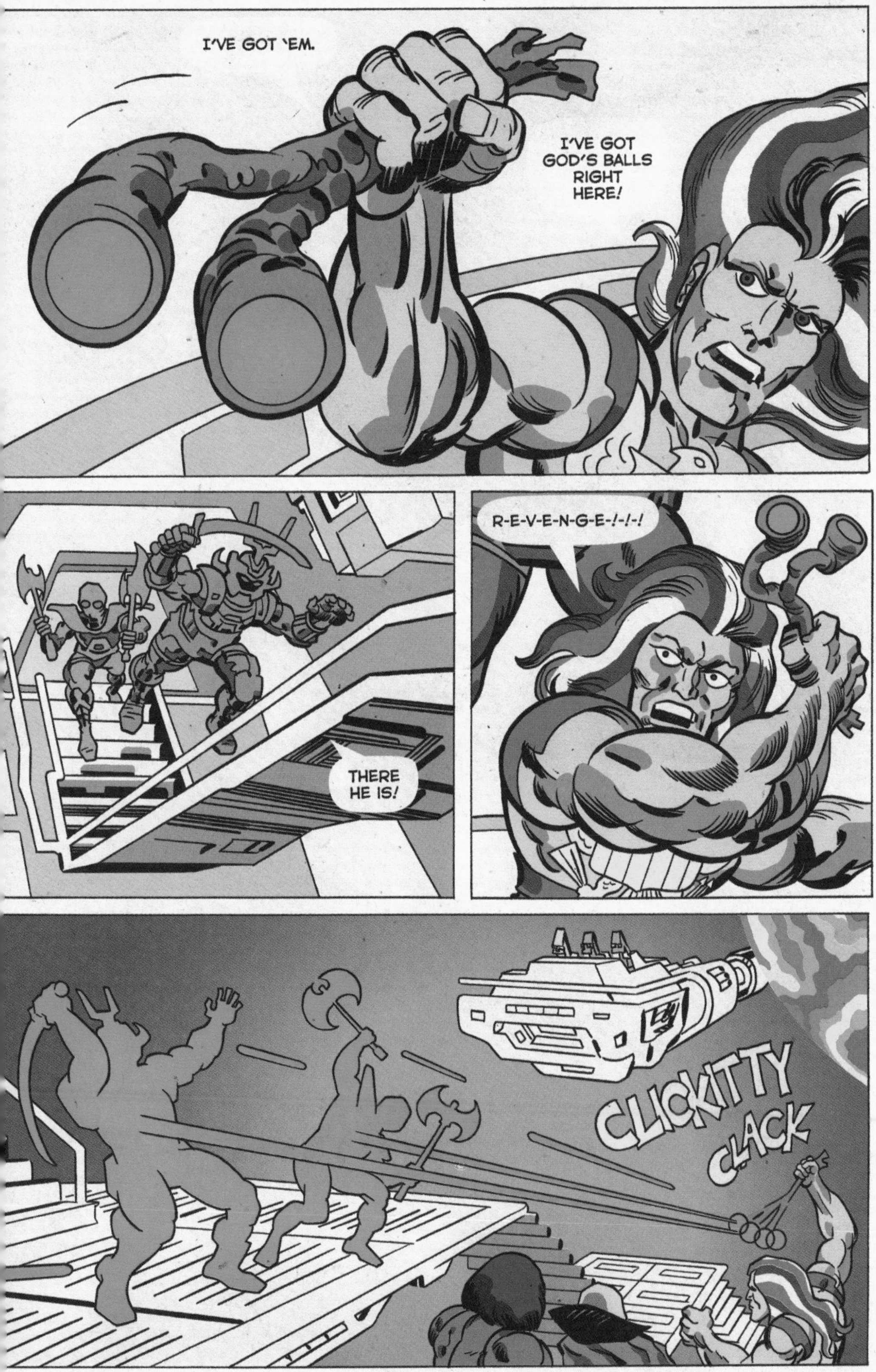
I'VE GOT 'EM.
I'VE GOT GOD'S BALLS RIGHT HERE!
THERE HE IS!
R-E-V-E-N-G-E-!-!-!
CLICKITTY CLACK

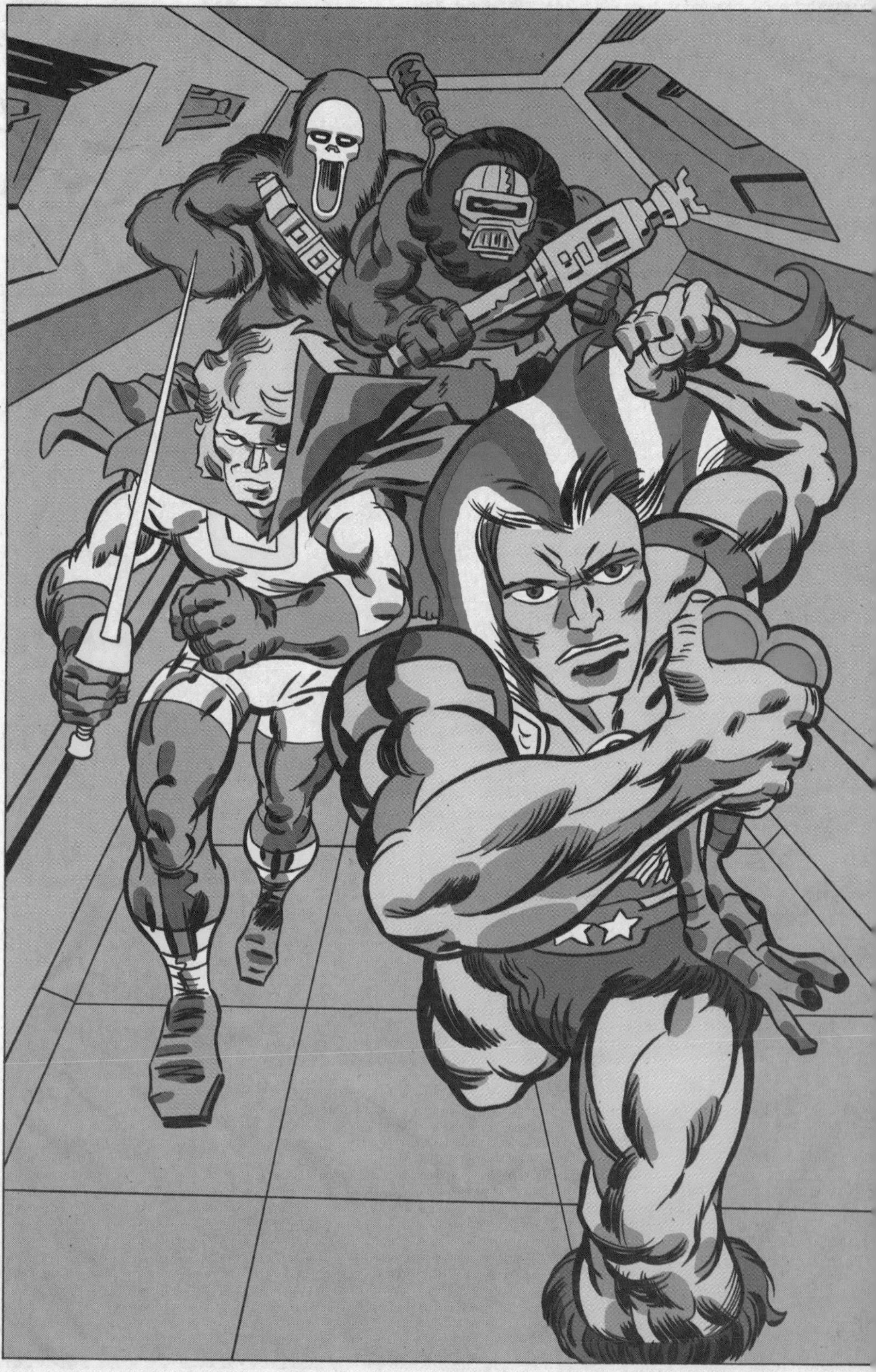

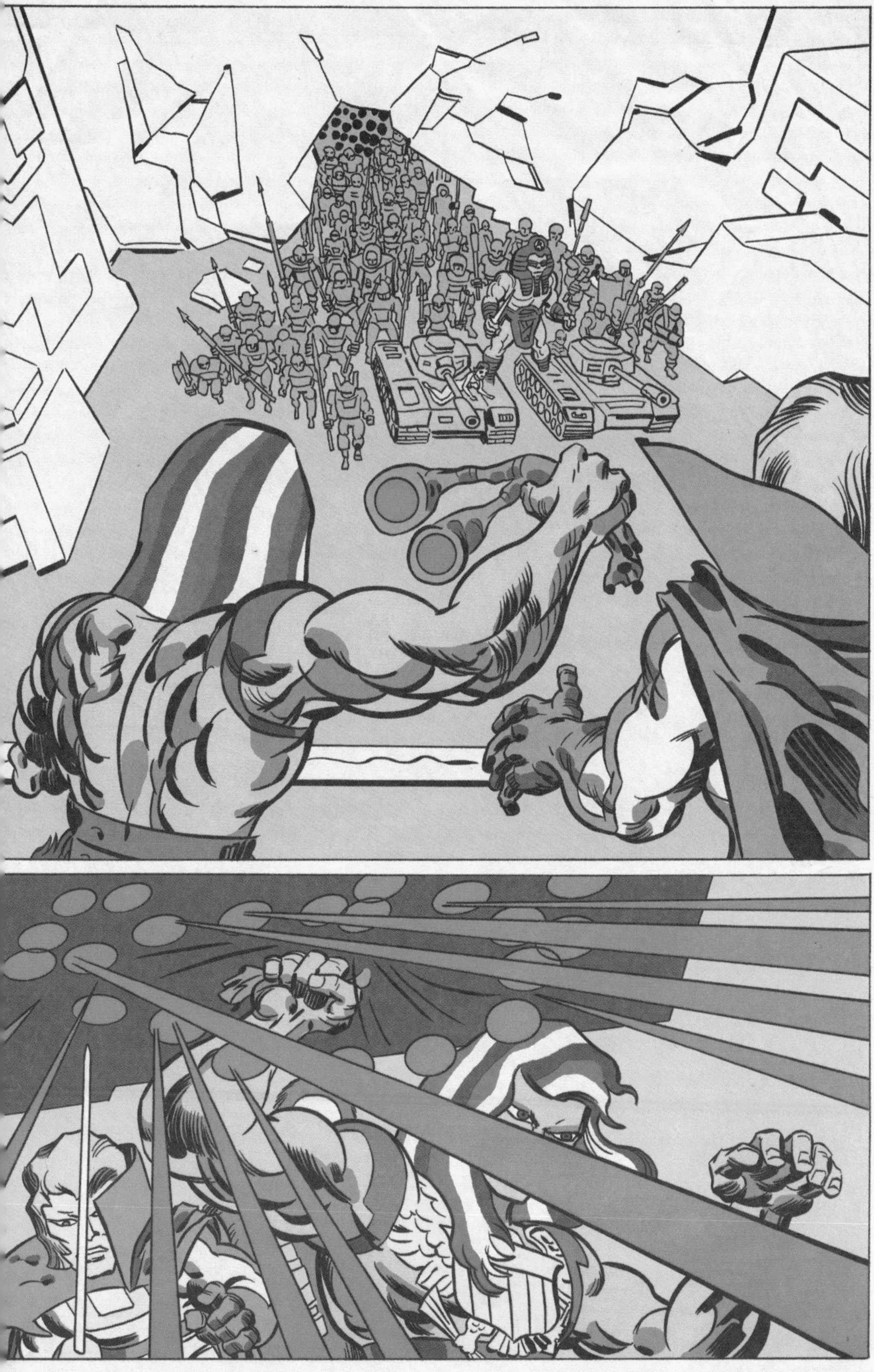

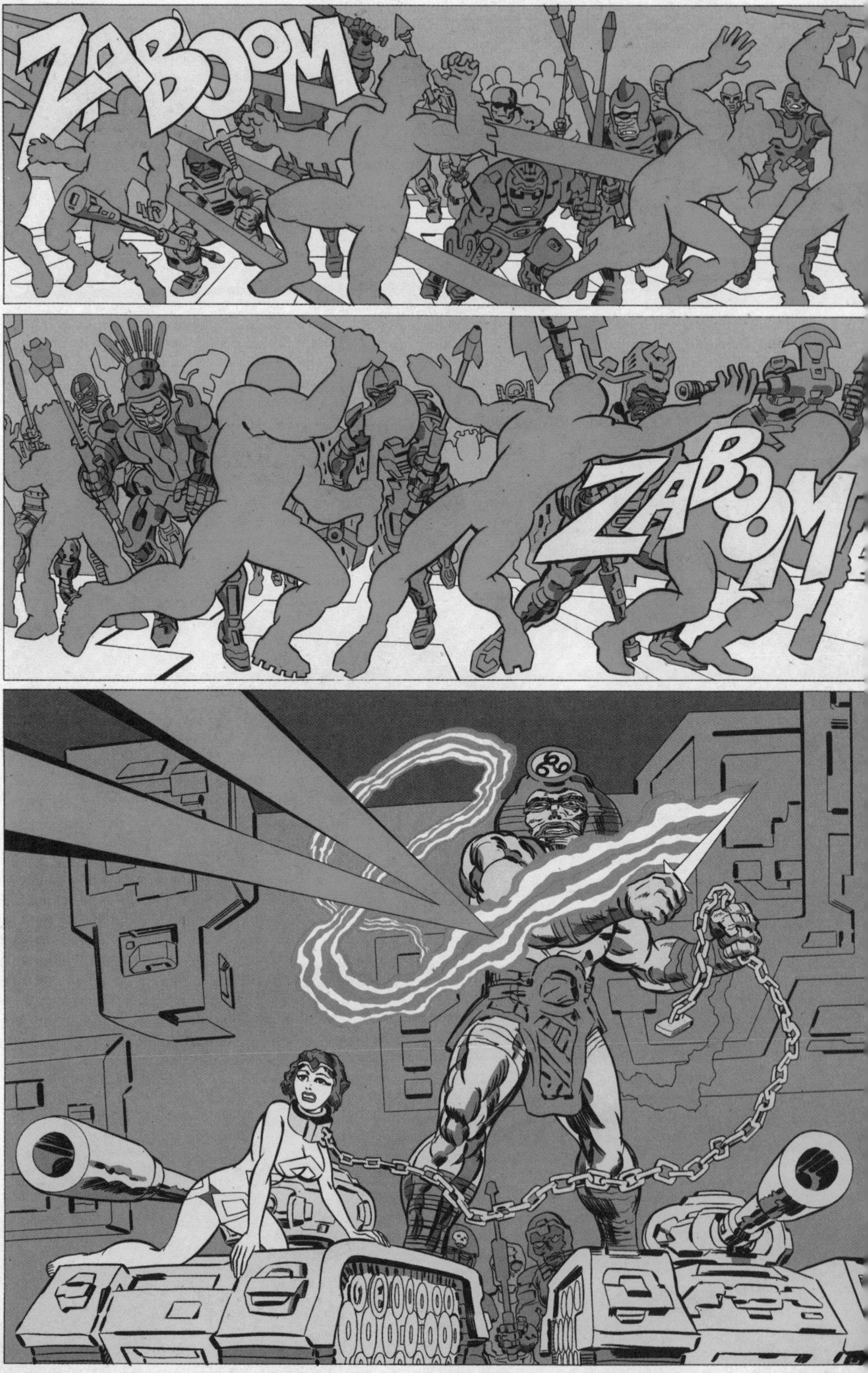
ZABOOM
ZABOOM

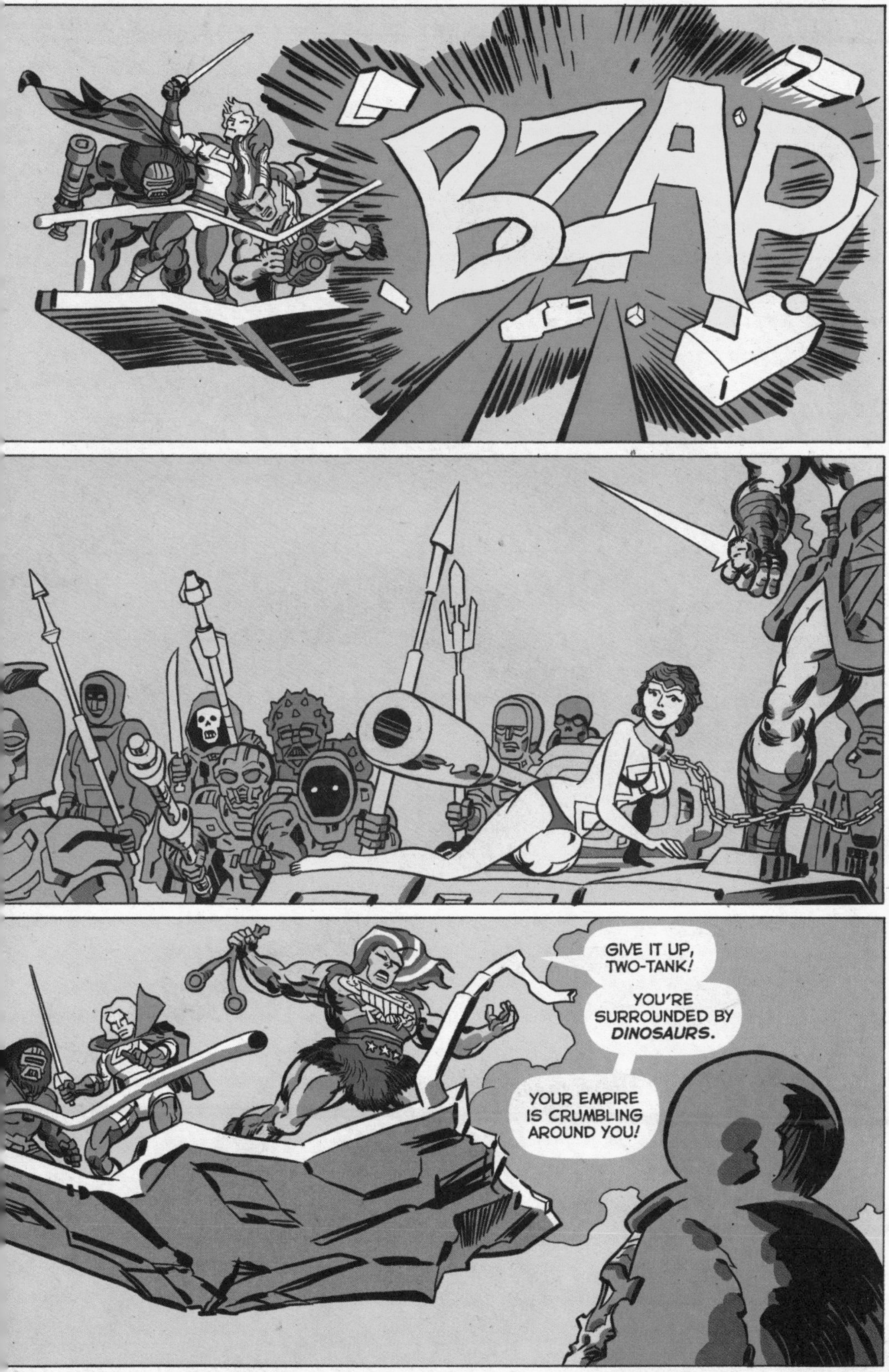
BZAP!
GIVE IT UP, TWO-TANK!
YOU'RE SURROUNDED BY *DINOSAURS*.
YOUR EMPIRE IS CRUMBLING AROUND YOU!

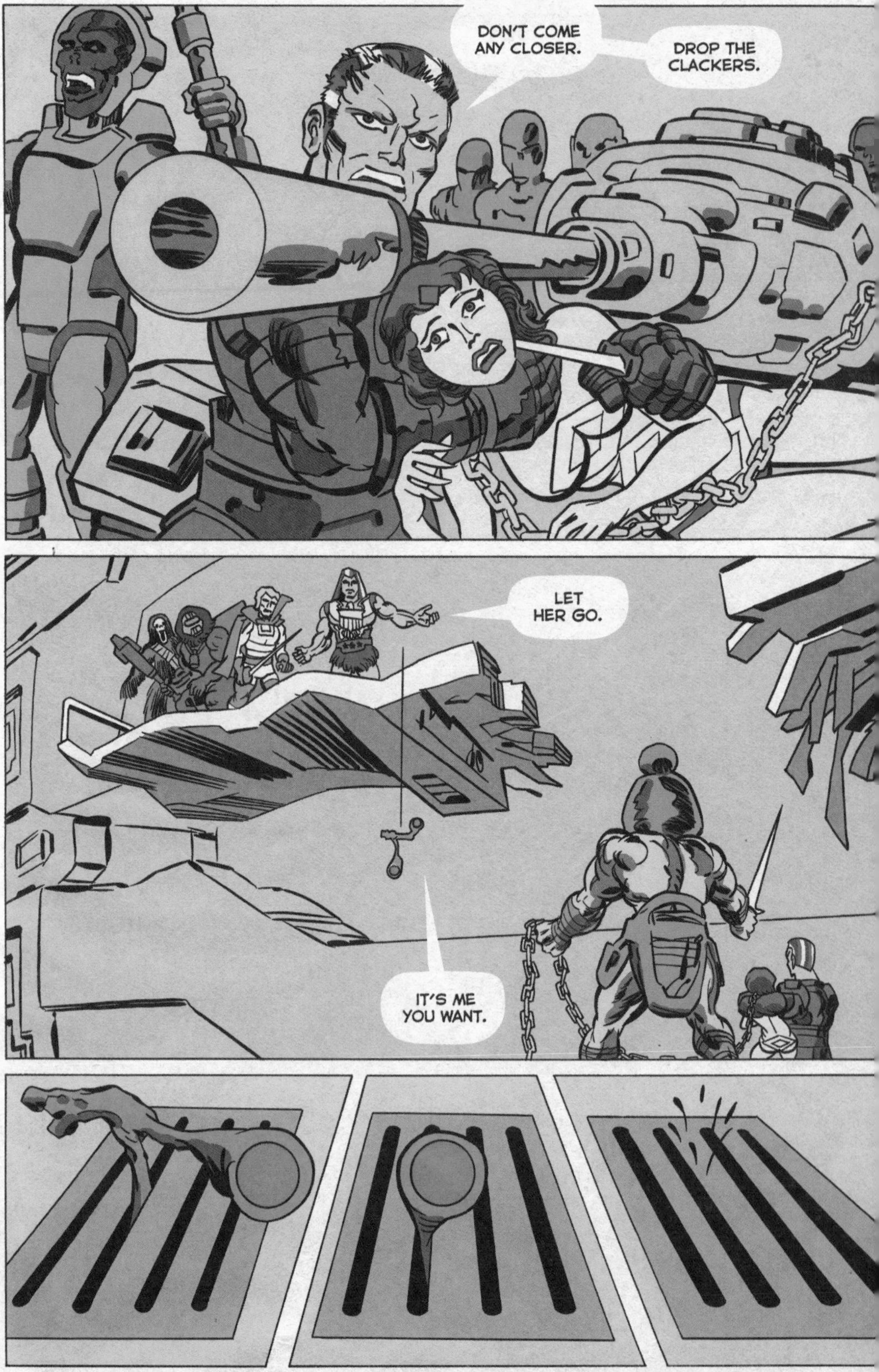
DON'T COME ANY CLOSER.
DROP THE CLACKERS.
LET HER GO.
IT'S ME YOU WANT.

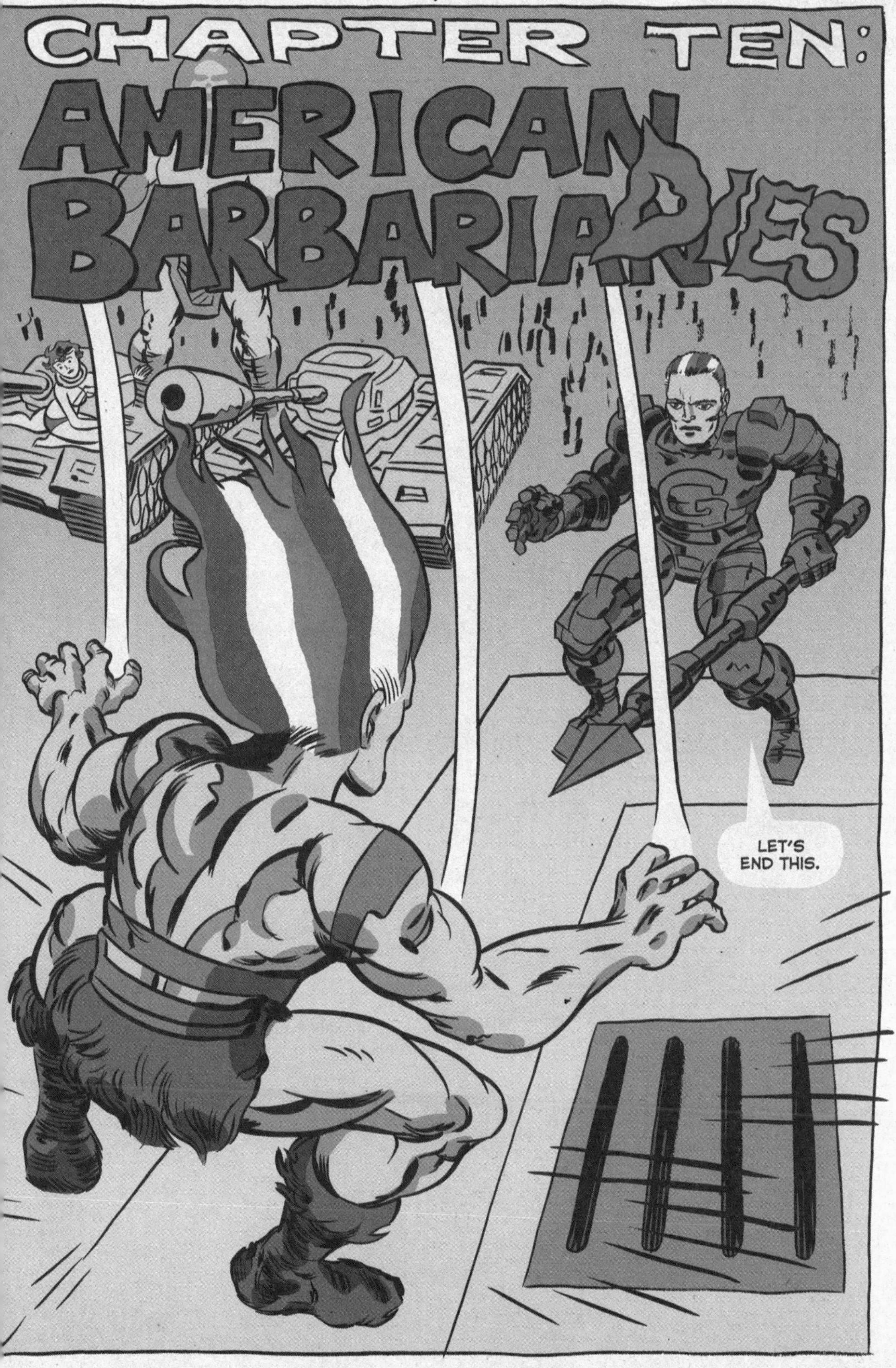
CHAPTER TEN:
AMERICAN BARBARIAN DIES
LET'S END THIS.

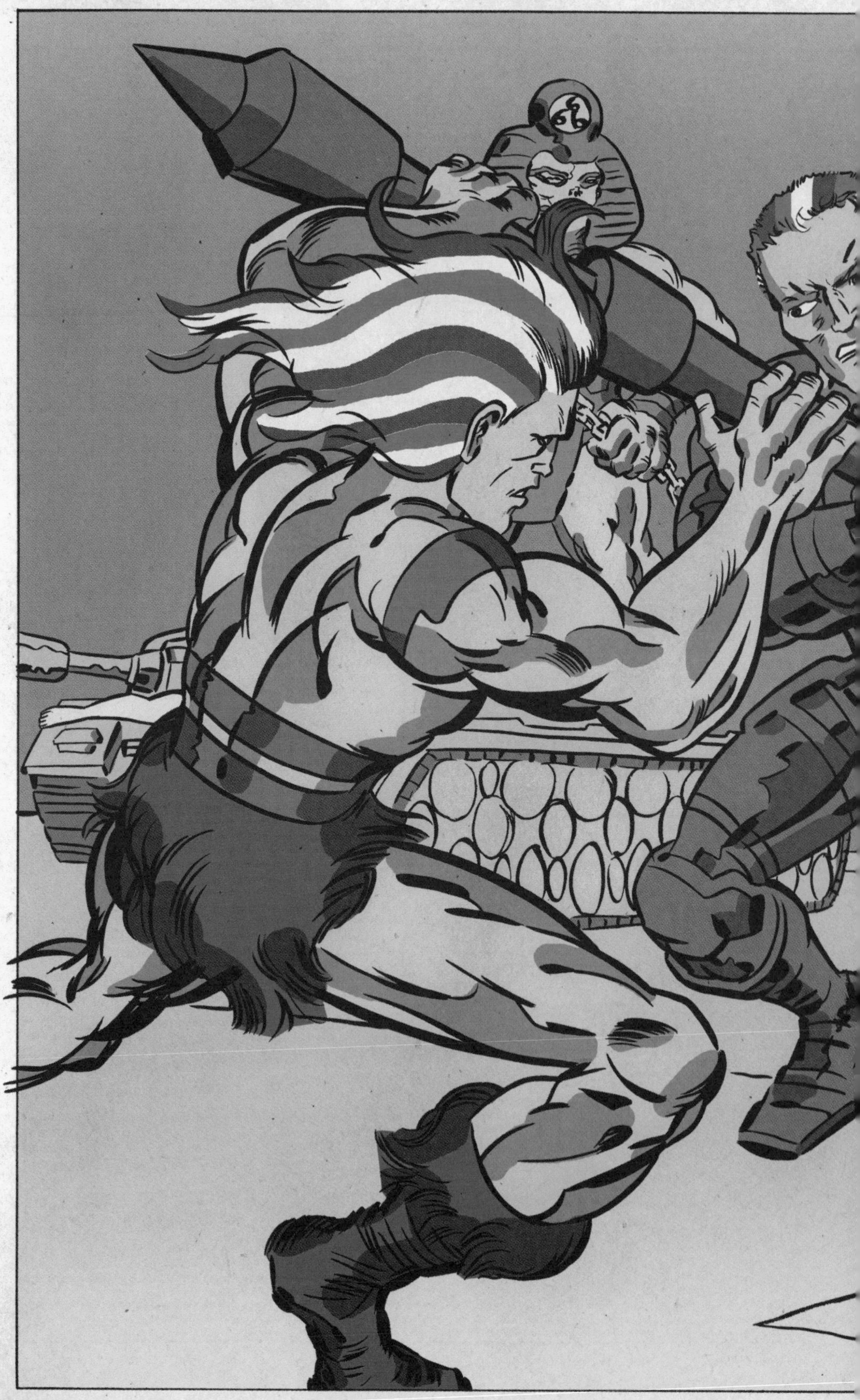

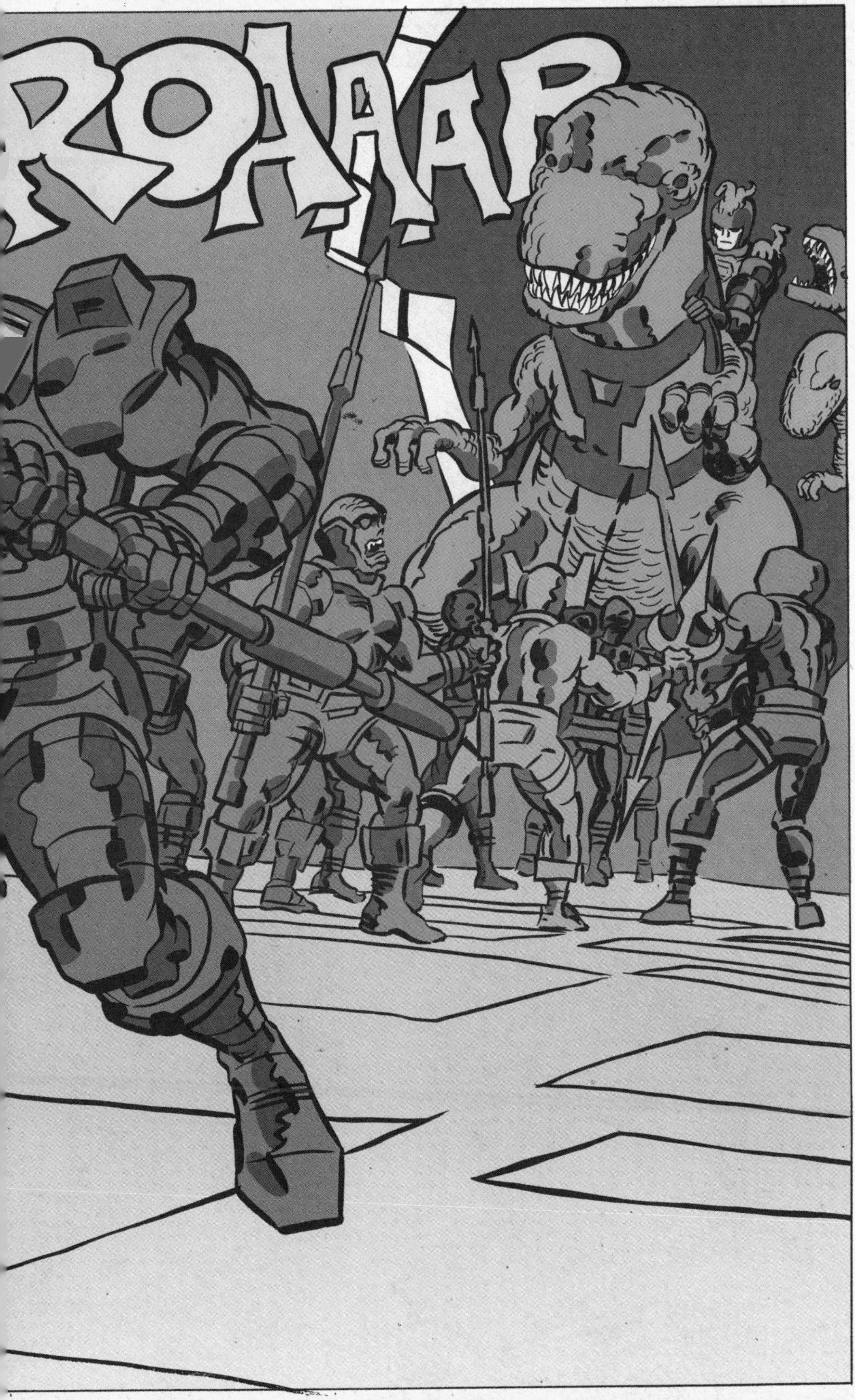
ROAAAR

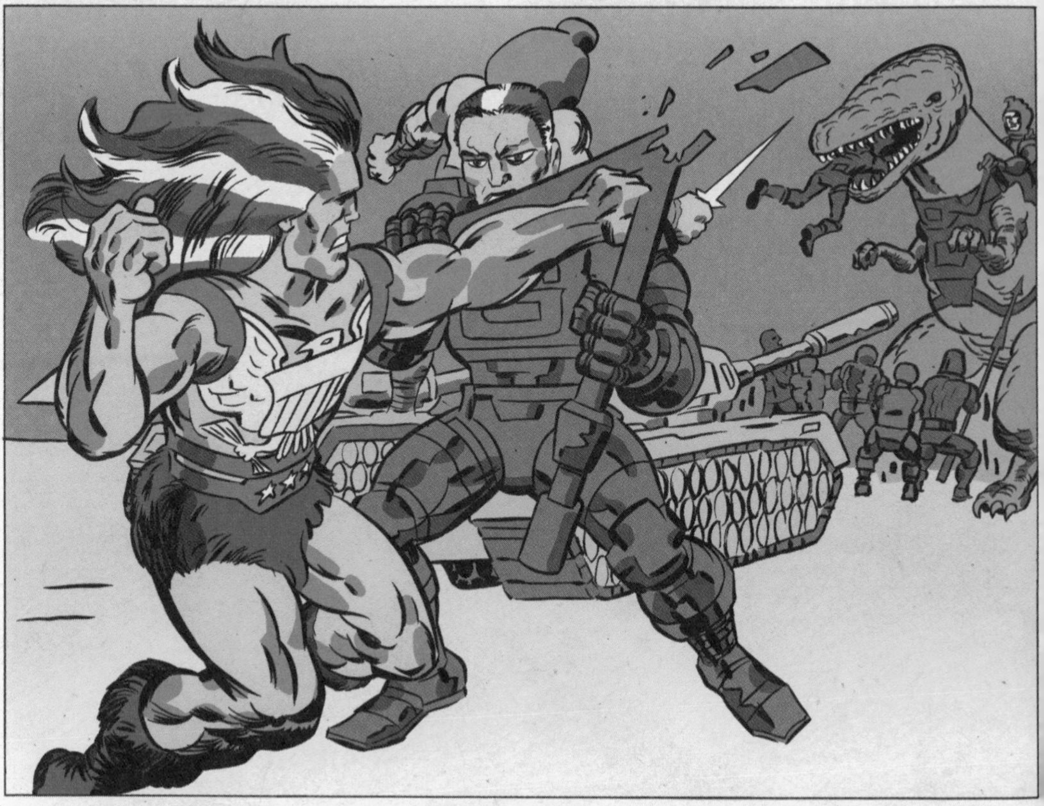

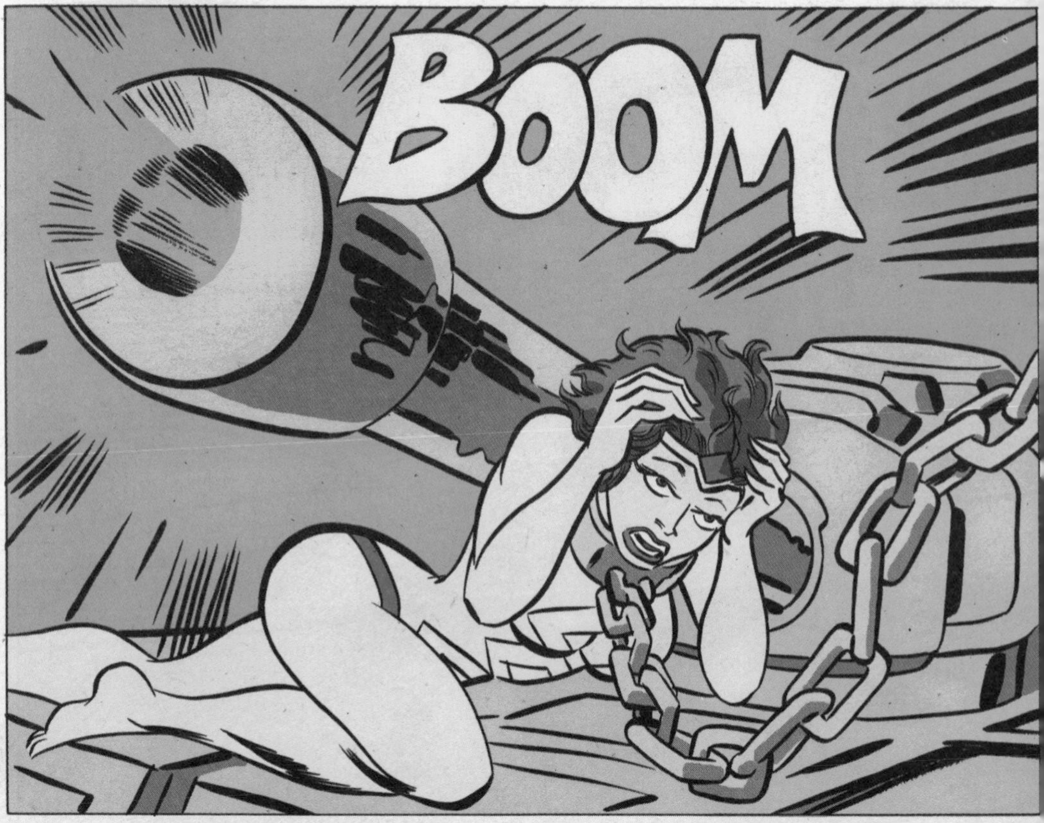
BOOM

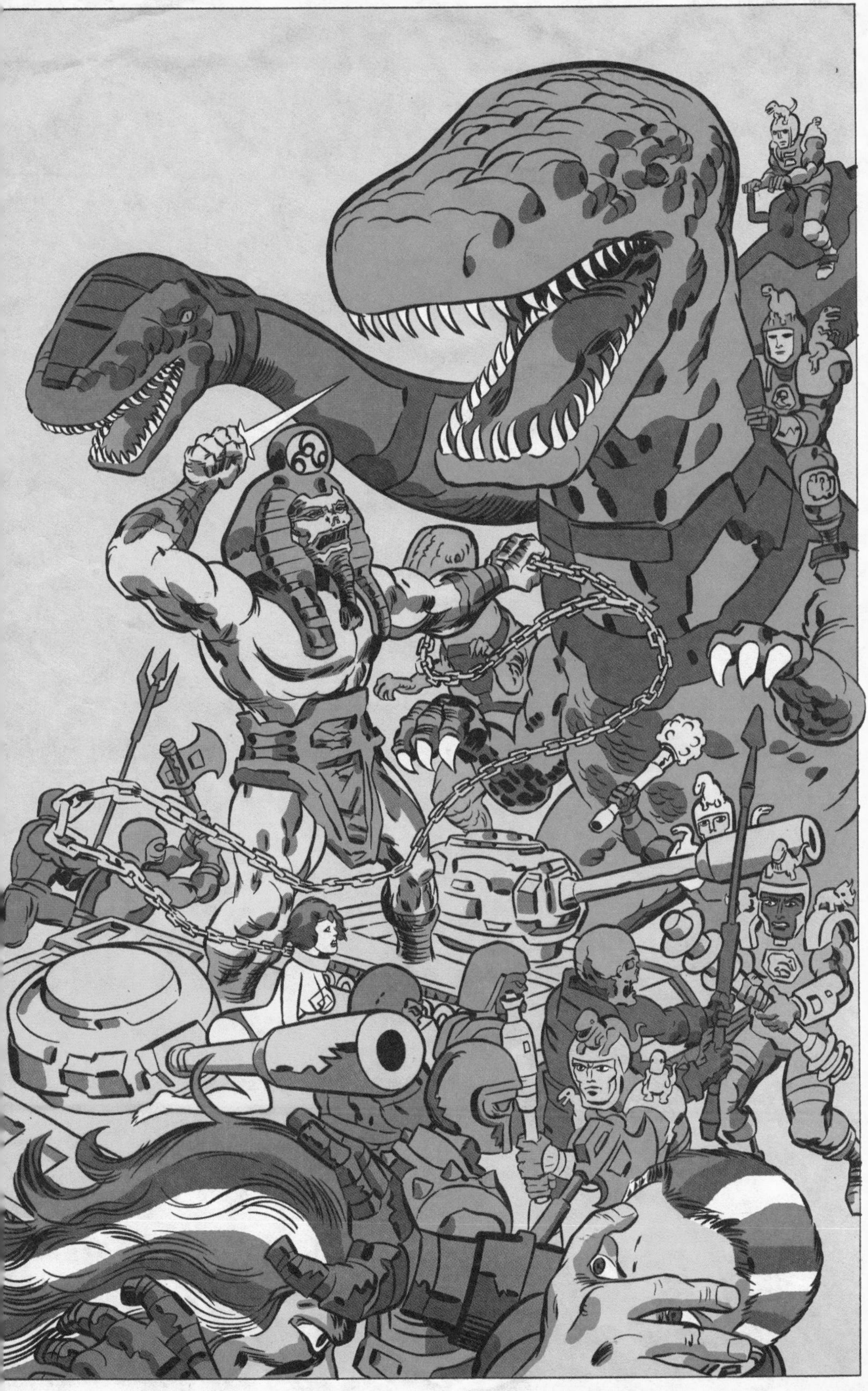

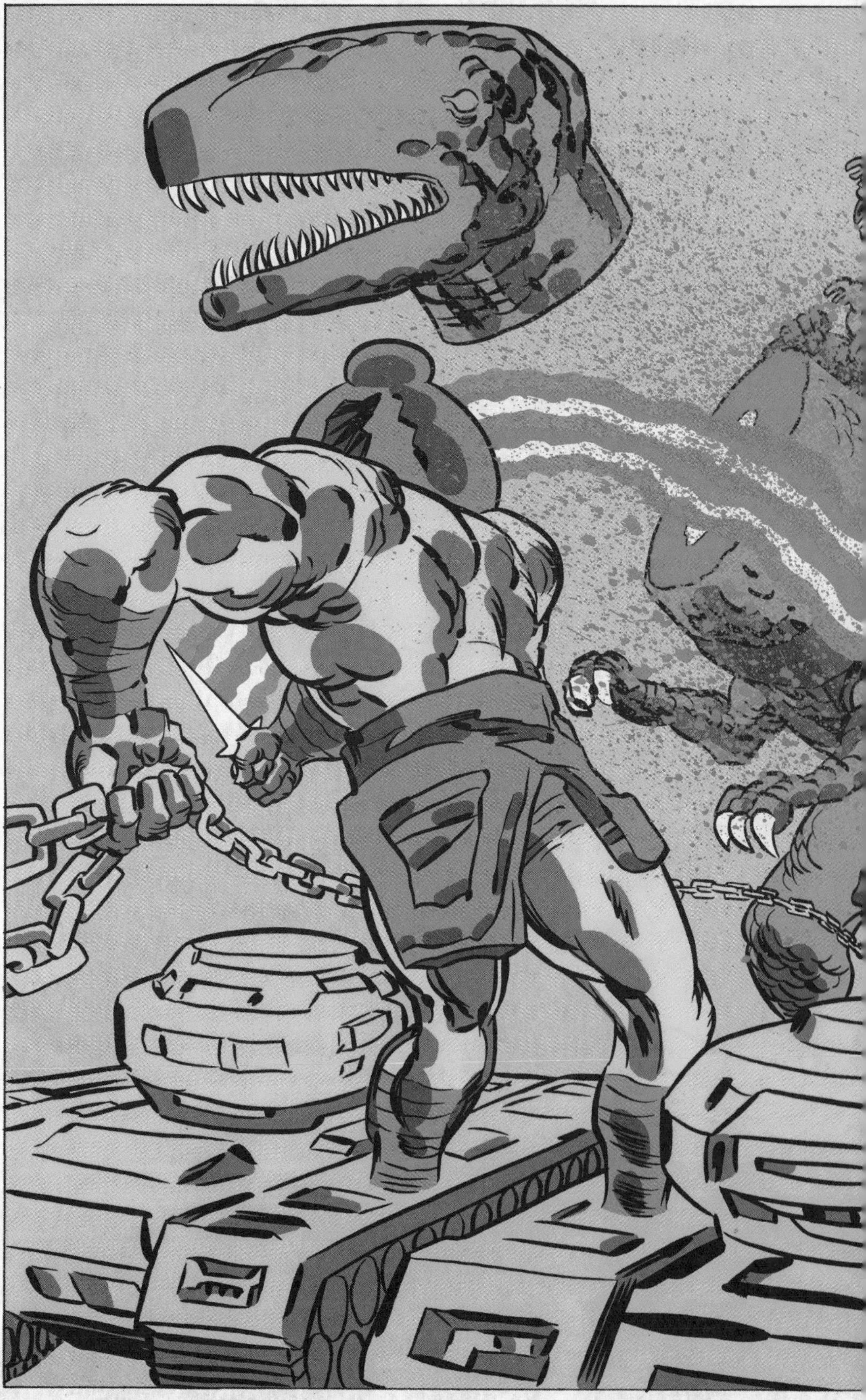

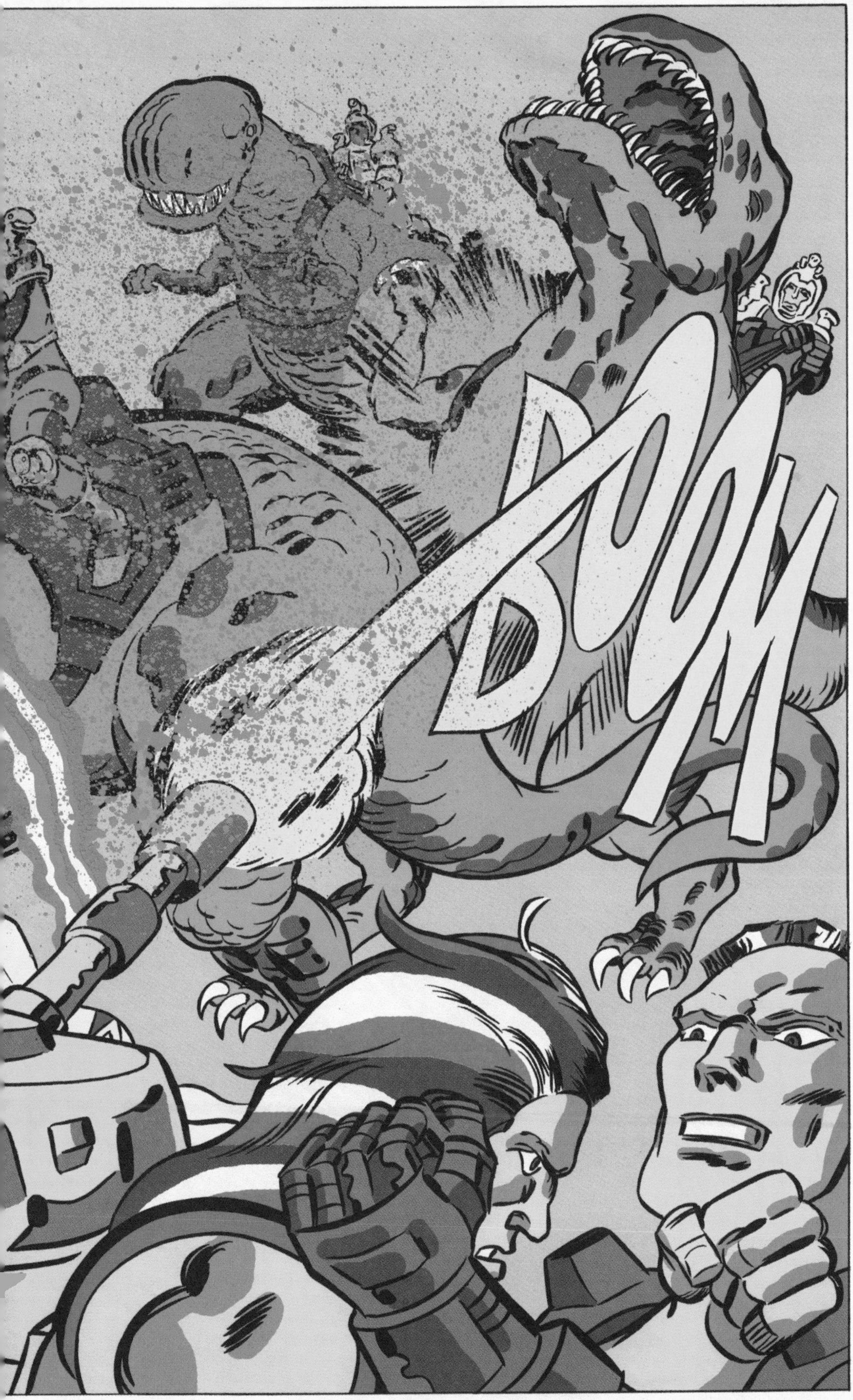
BOOM

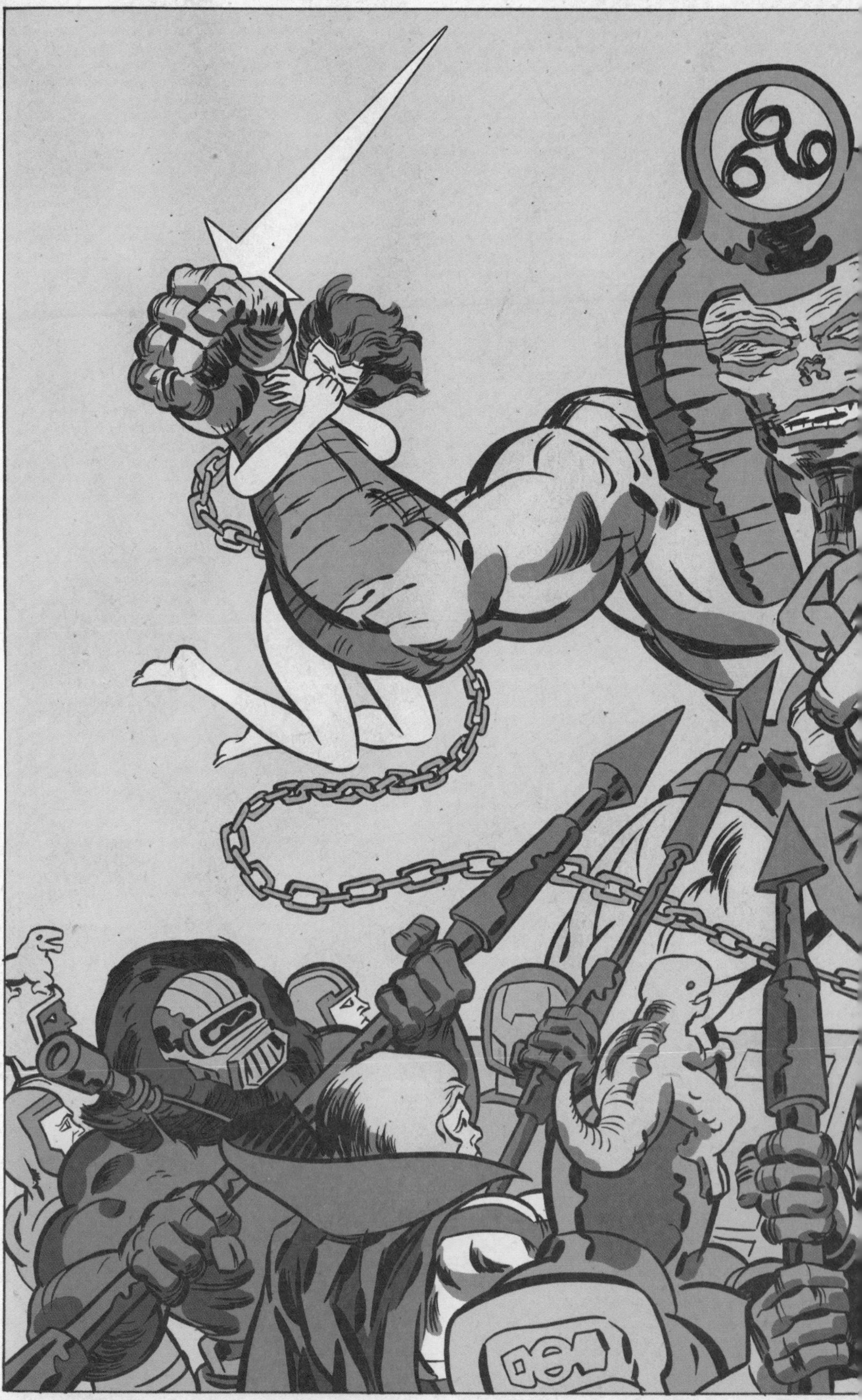

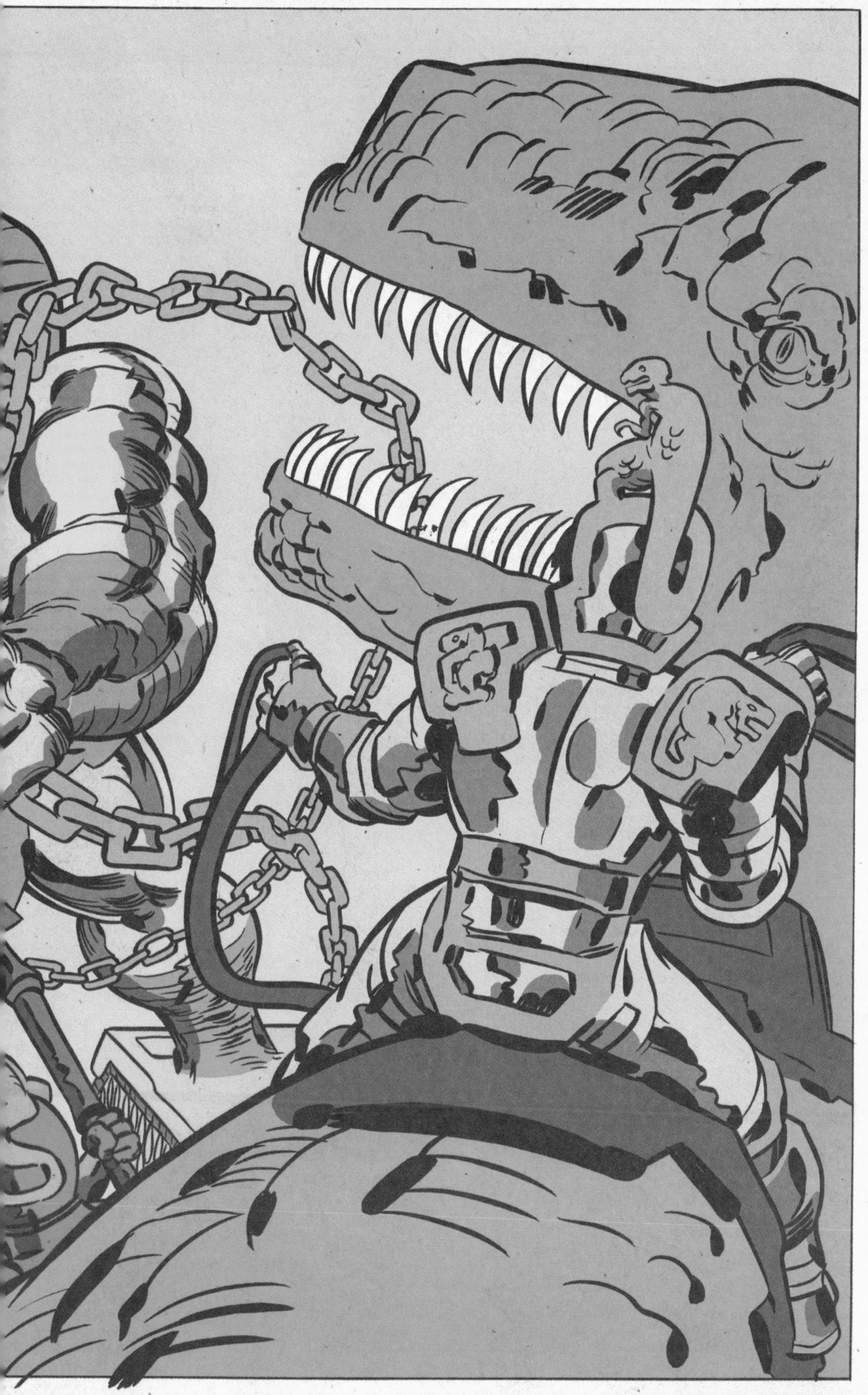

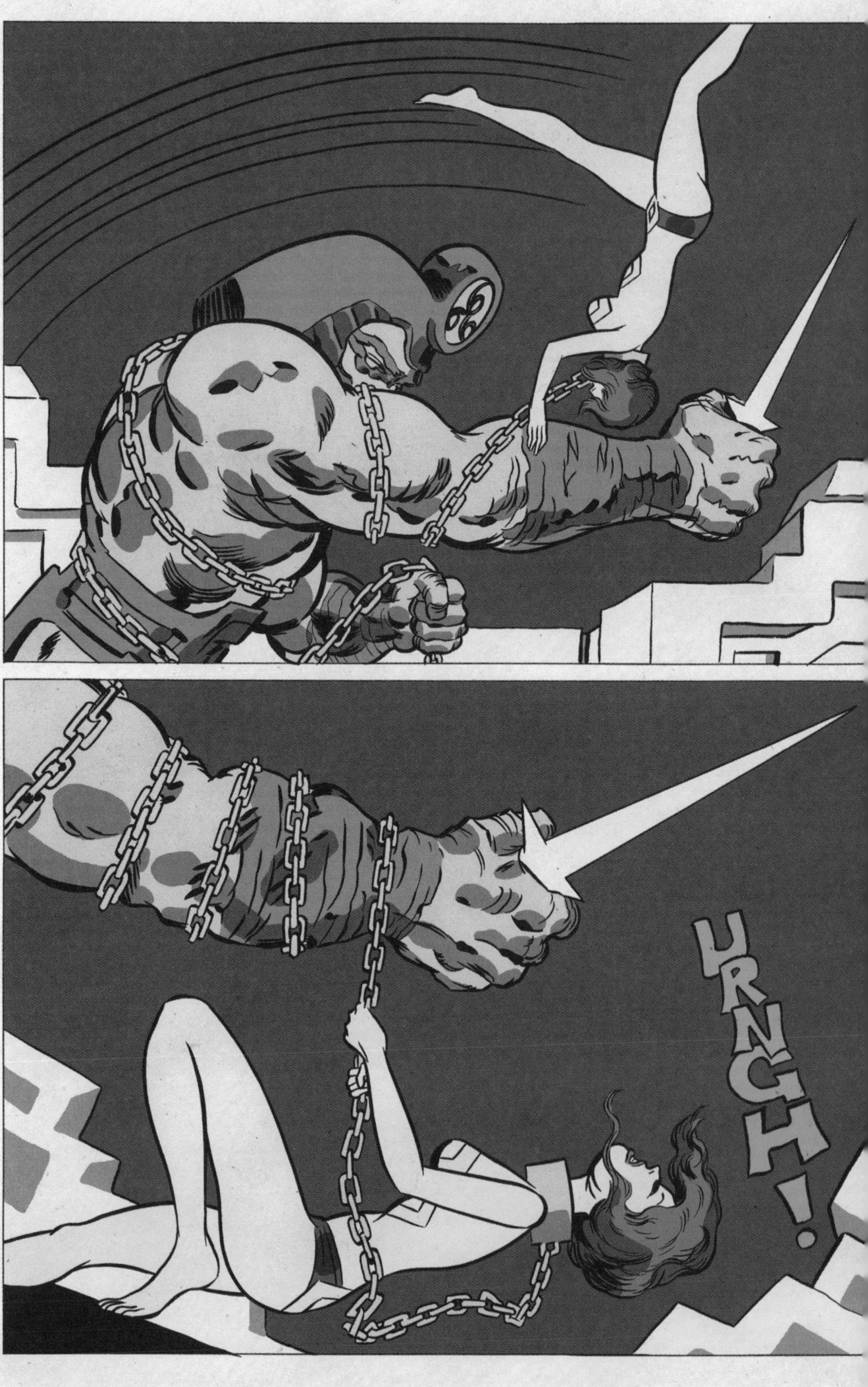
URNGH!

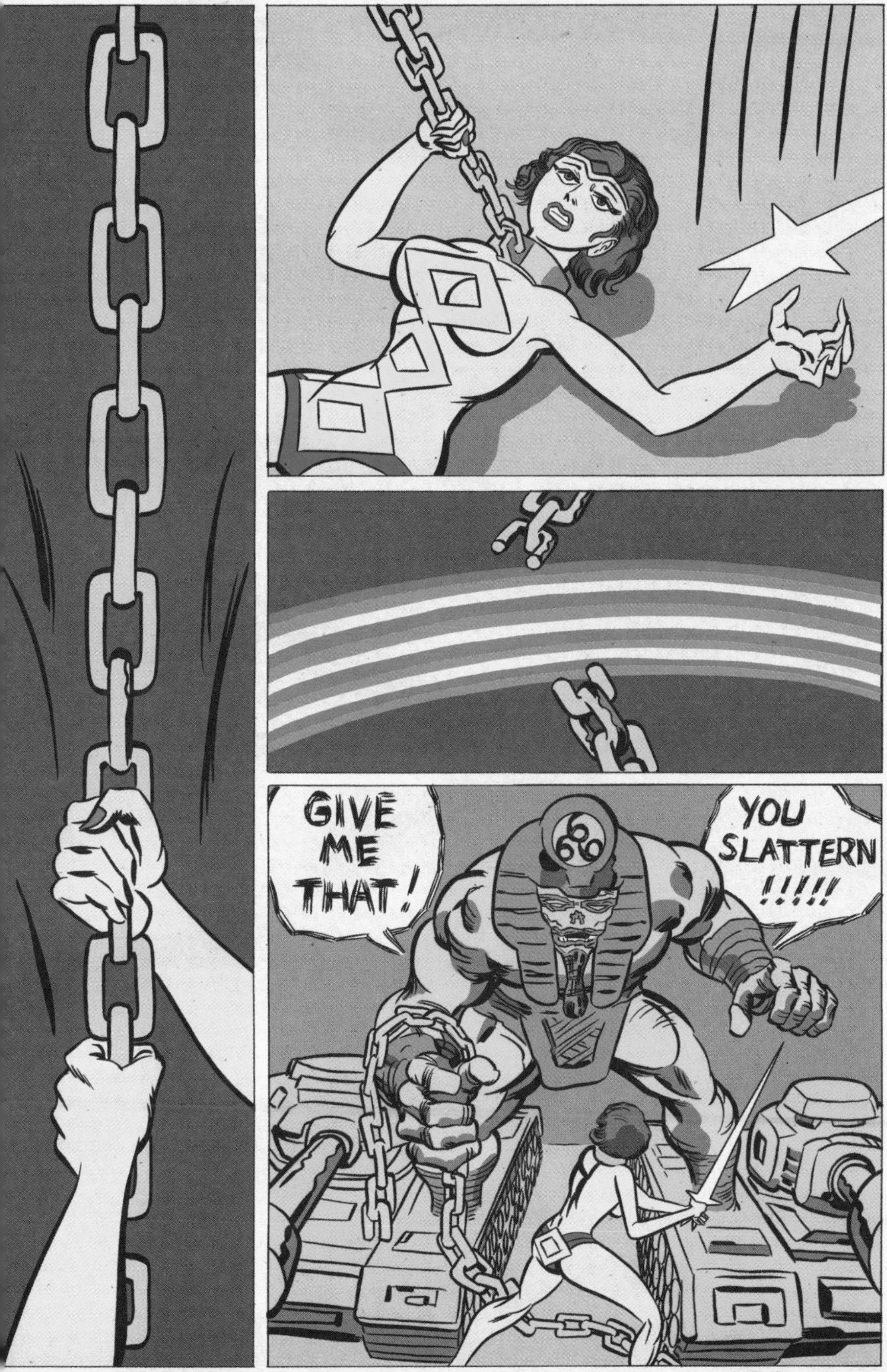
GIVE ME THAT!
YOU SLATTERN !!!!!!

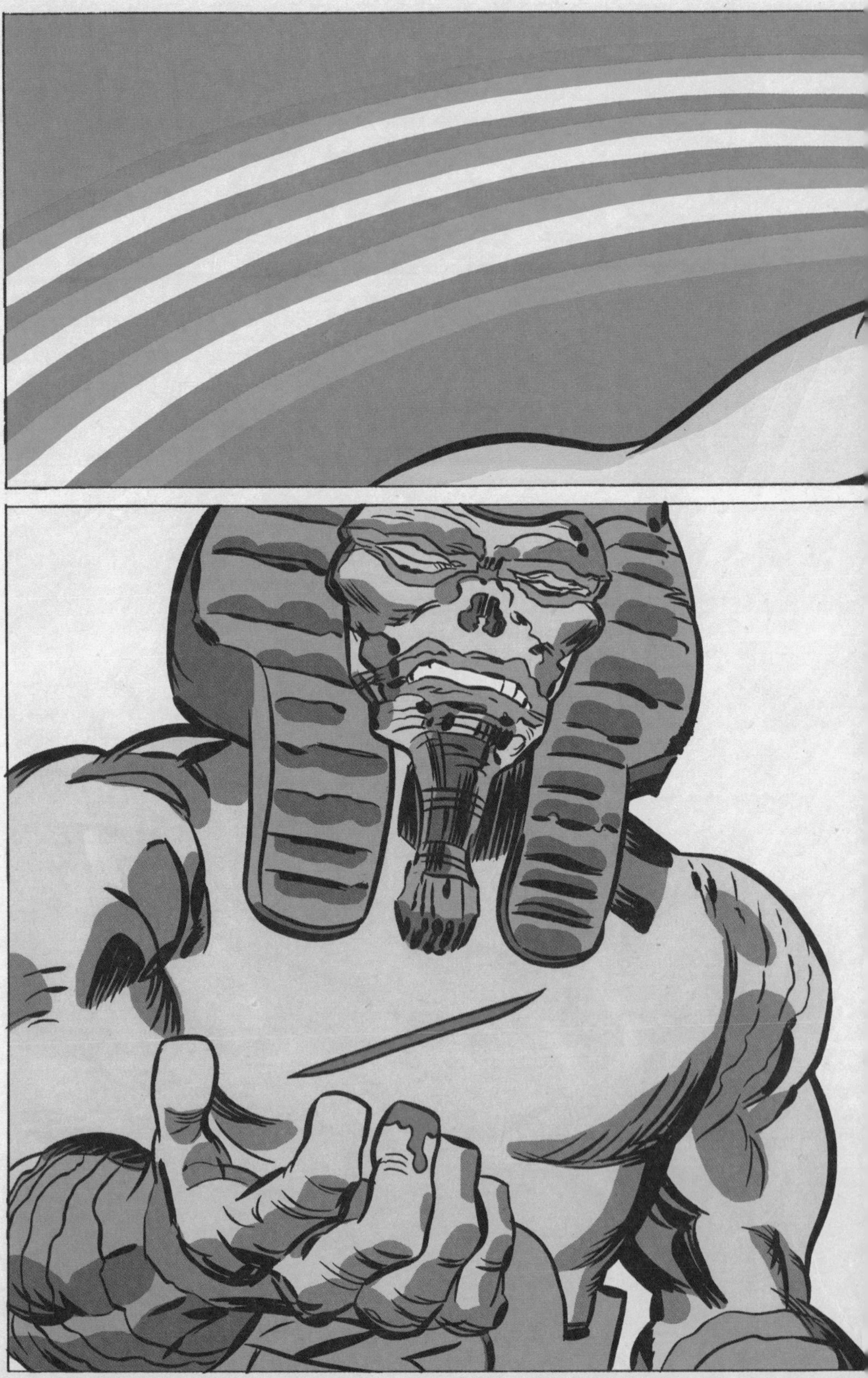

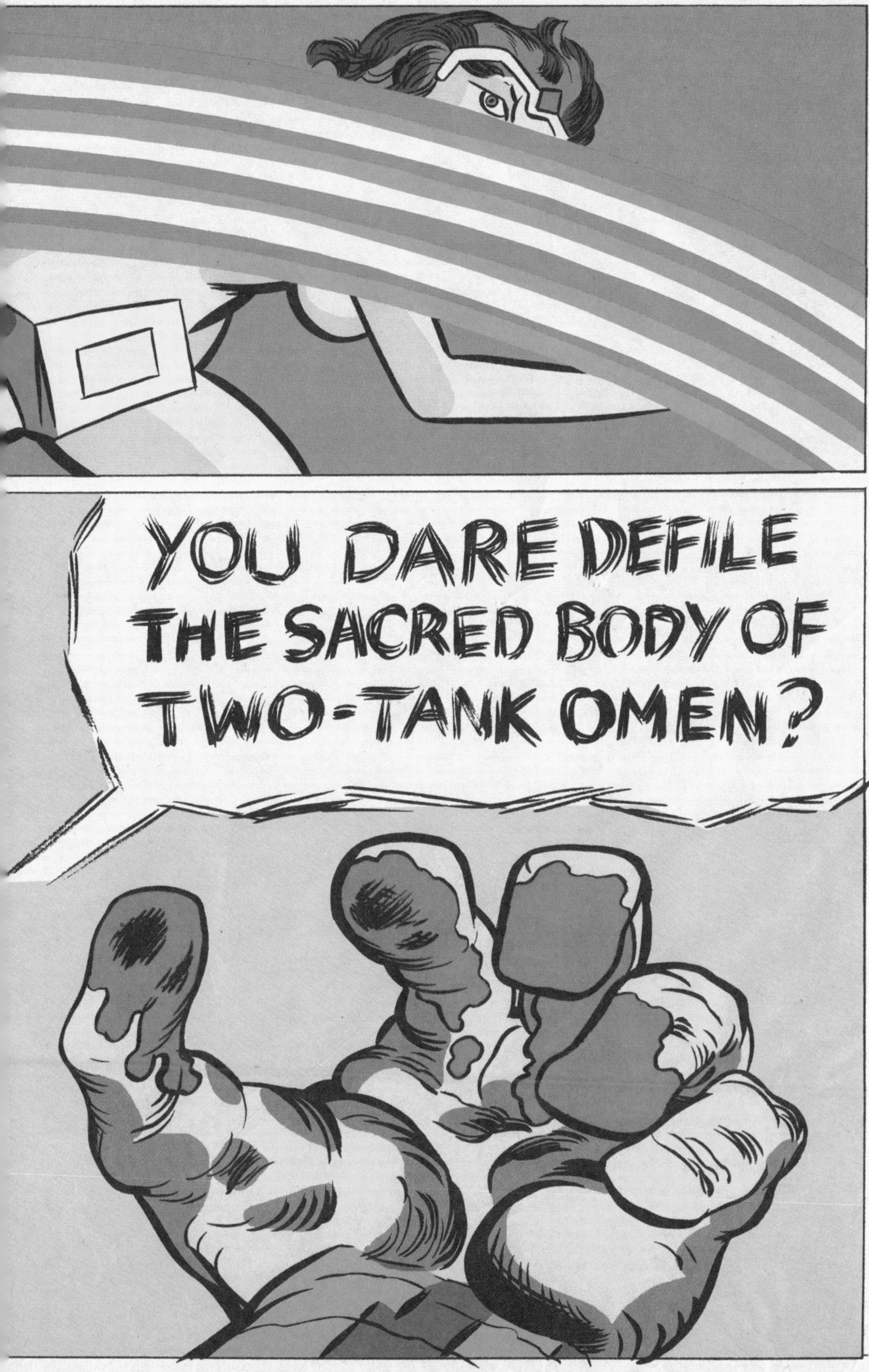
YOU DARE DEFILE THE SACRED BODY OF TWO-TANK OMEN?

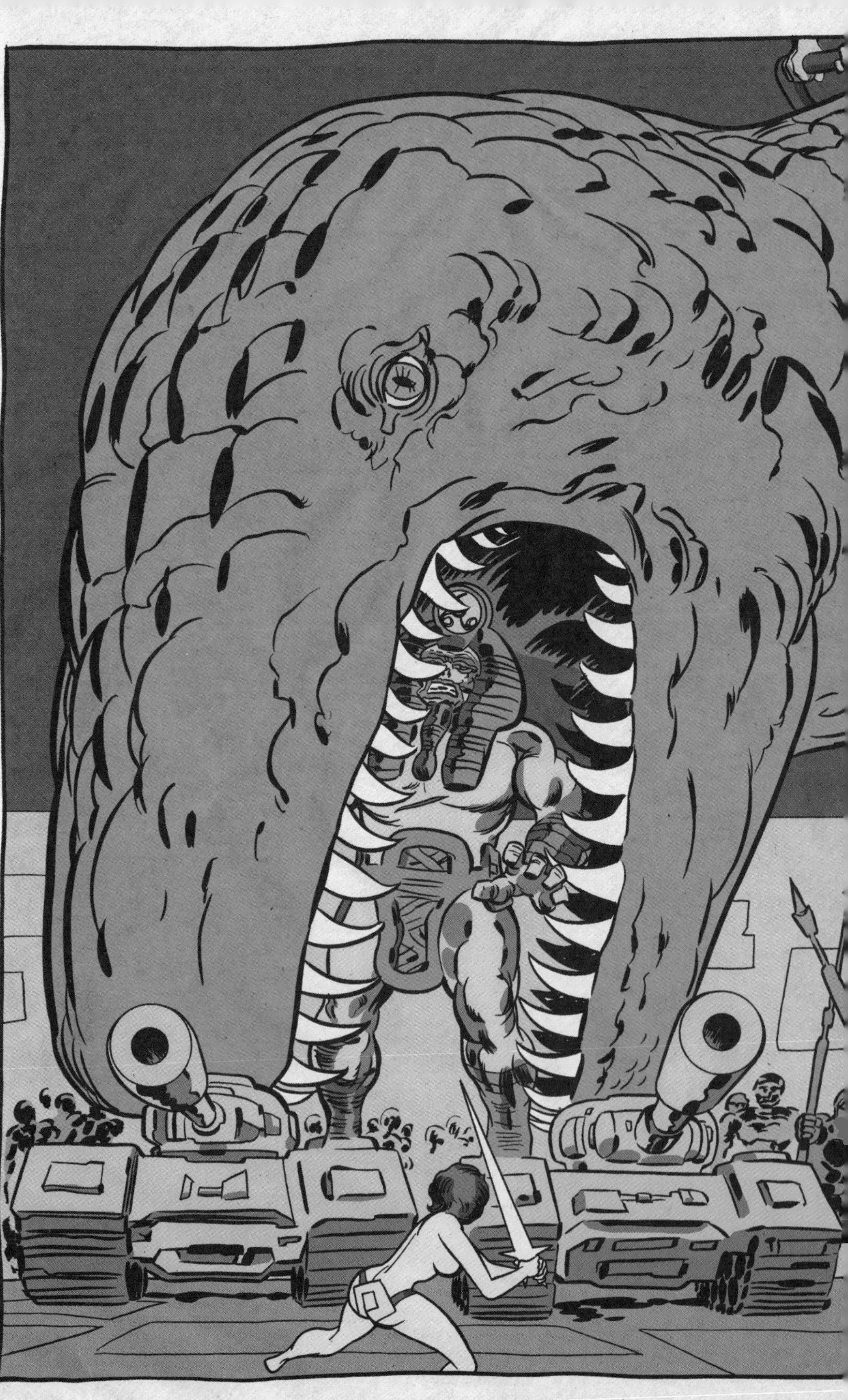

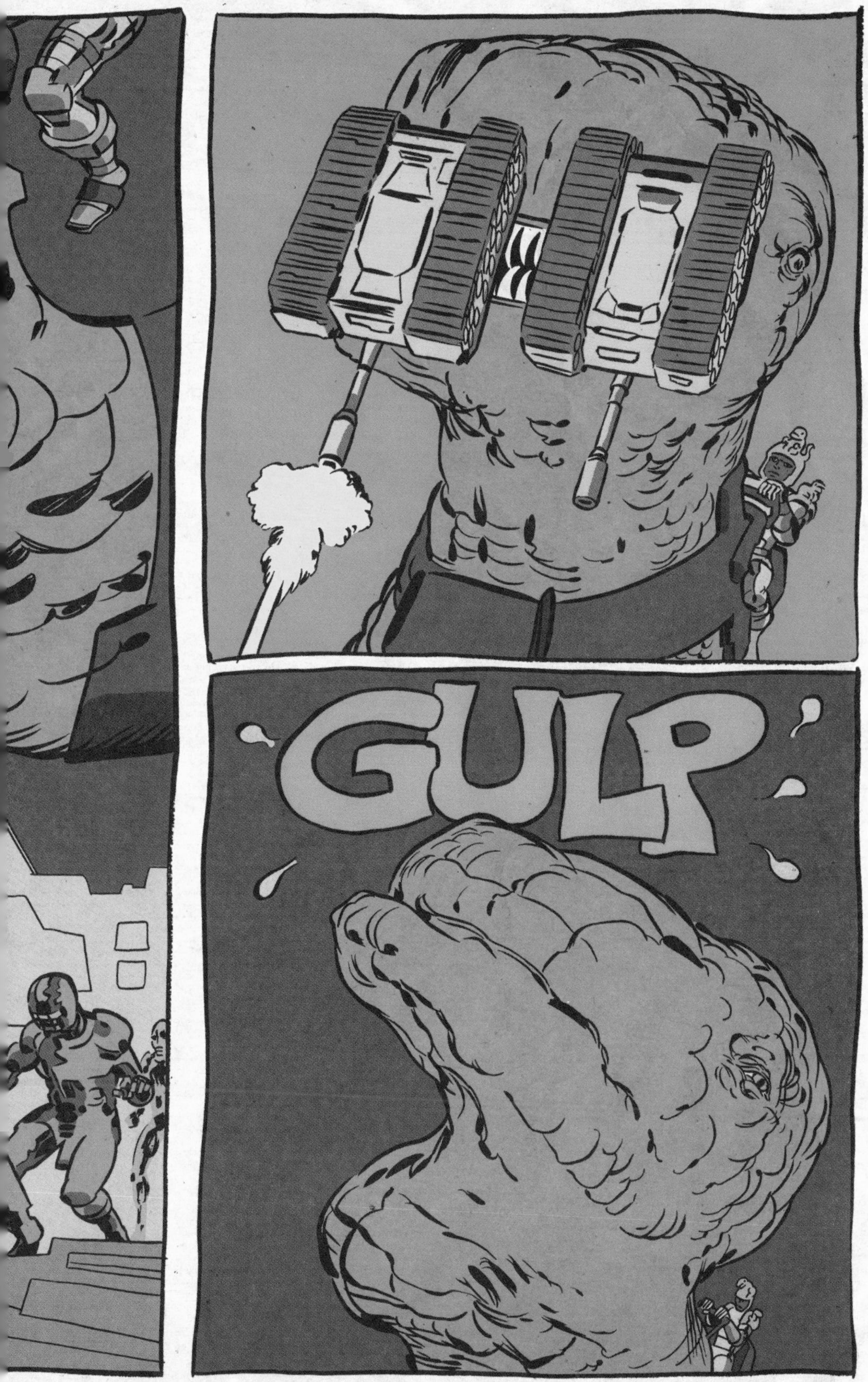
GULP

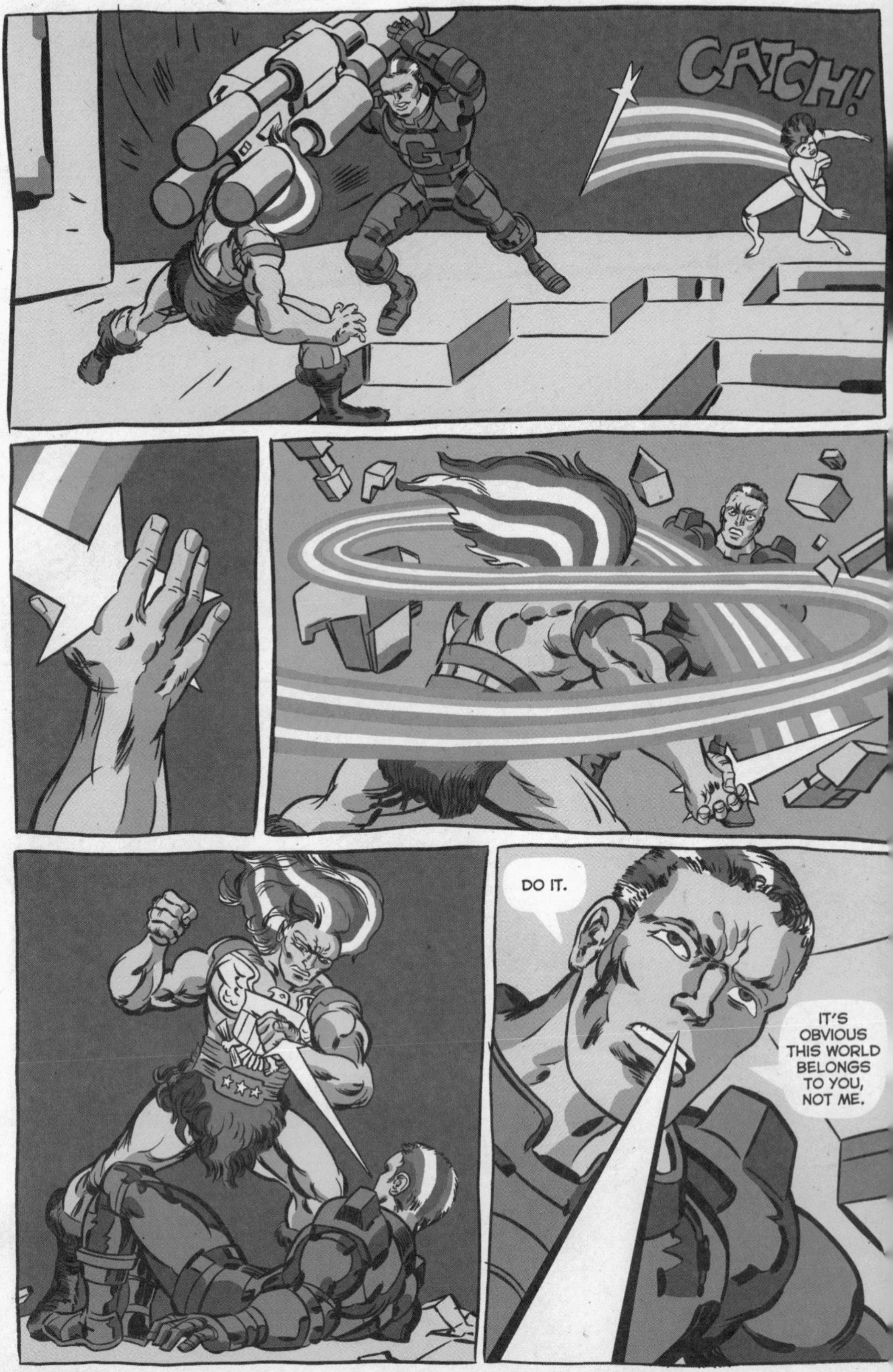
CATCH!
DO IT.
IT'S OBVIOUS THIS WORLD BELONGS TO YOU, NOT ME.

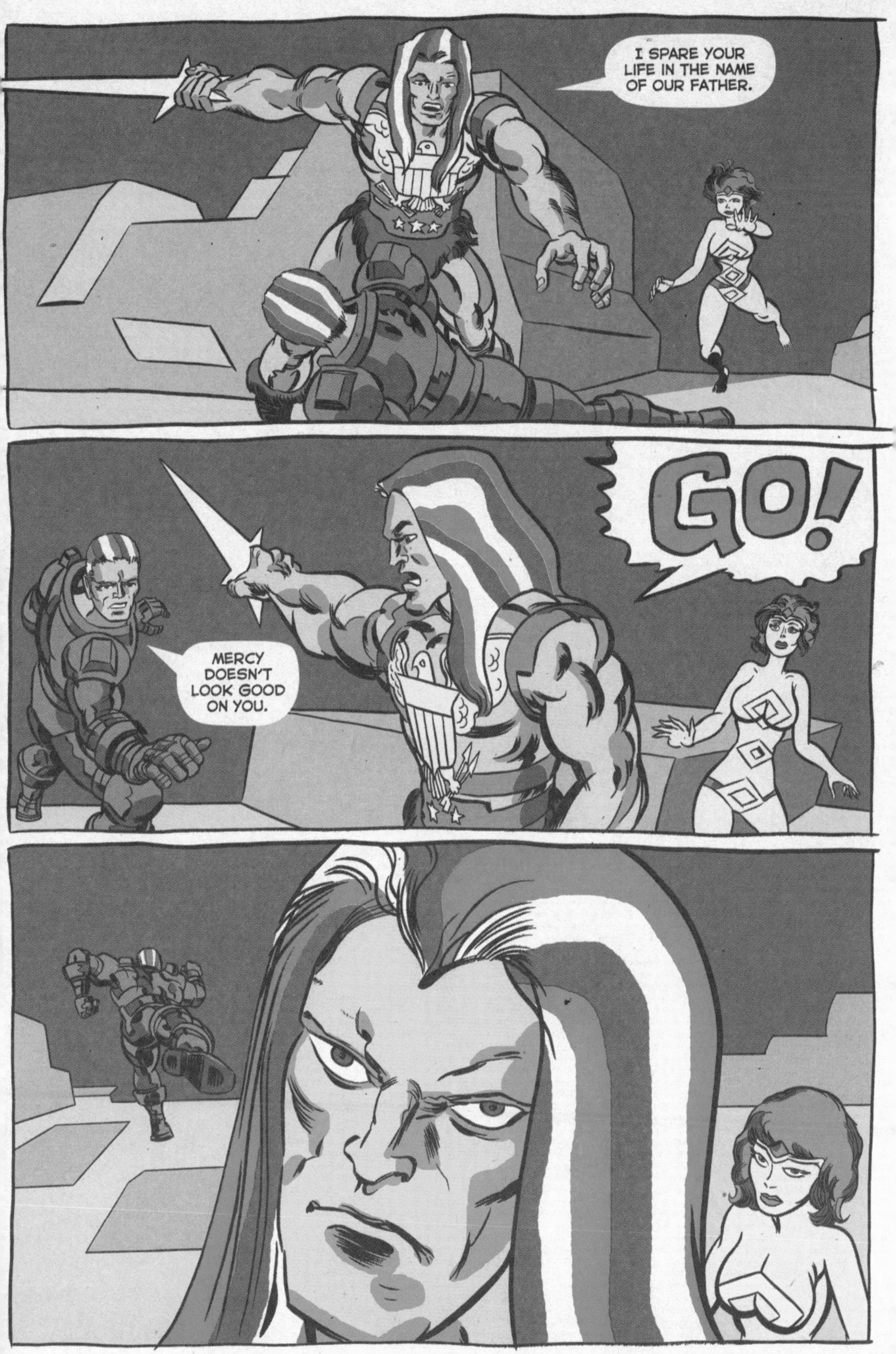
I SPARE YOUR LIFE IN THE NAME OF OUR FATHER.
GO!
MERCY DOESN'T LOOK GOOD ON YOU.

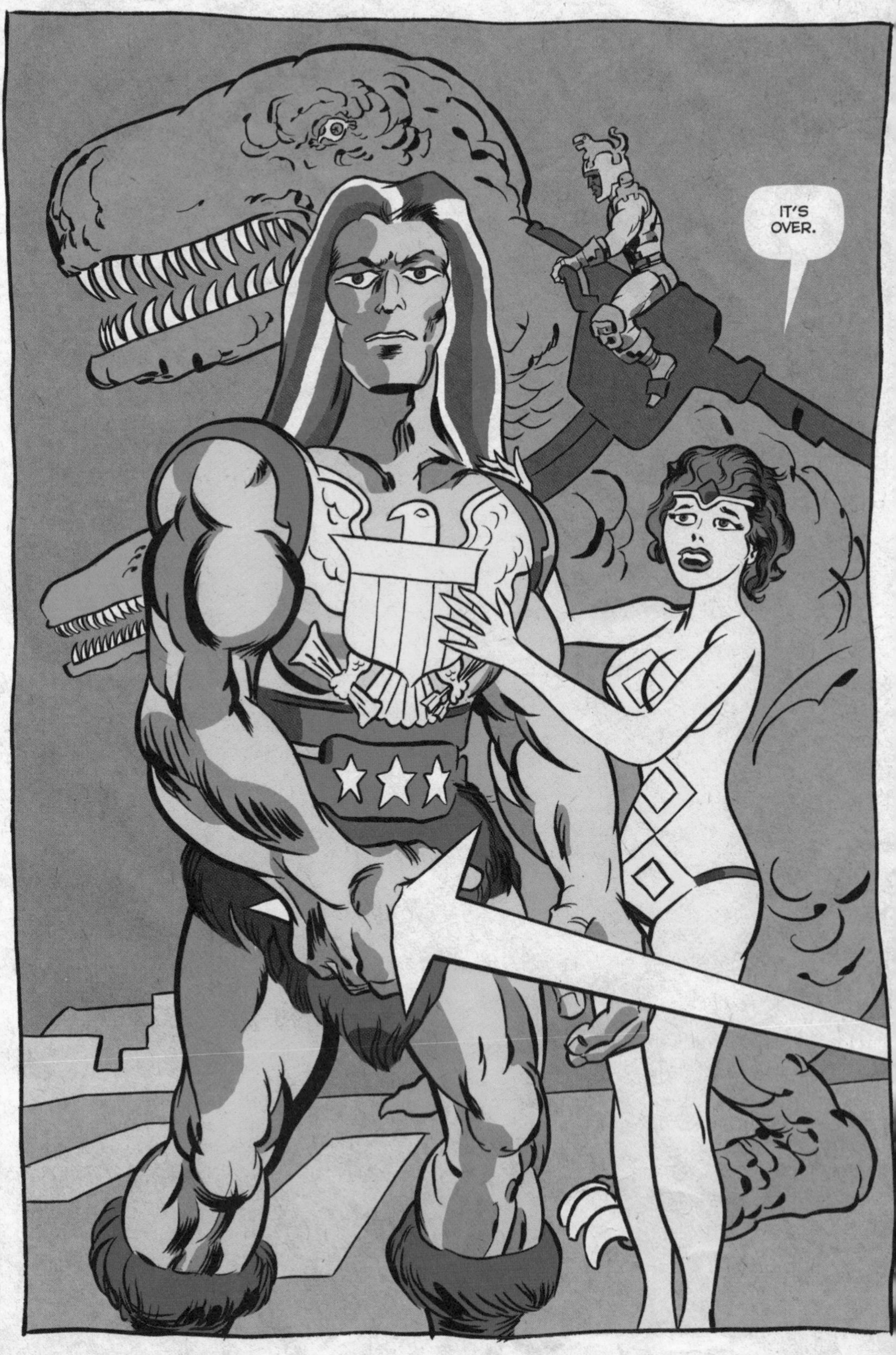
IT'S OVER.

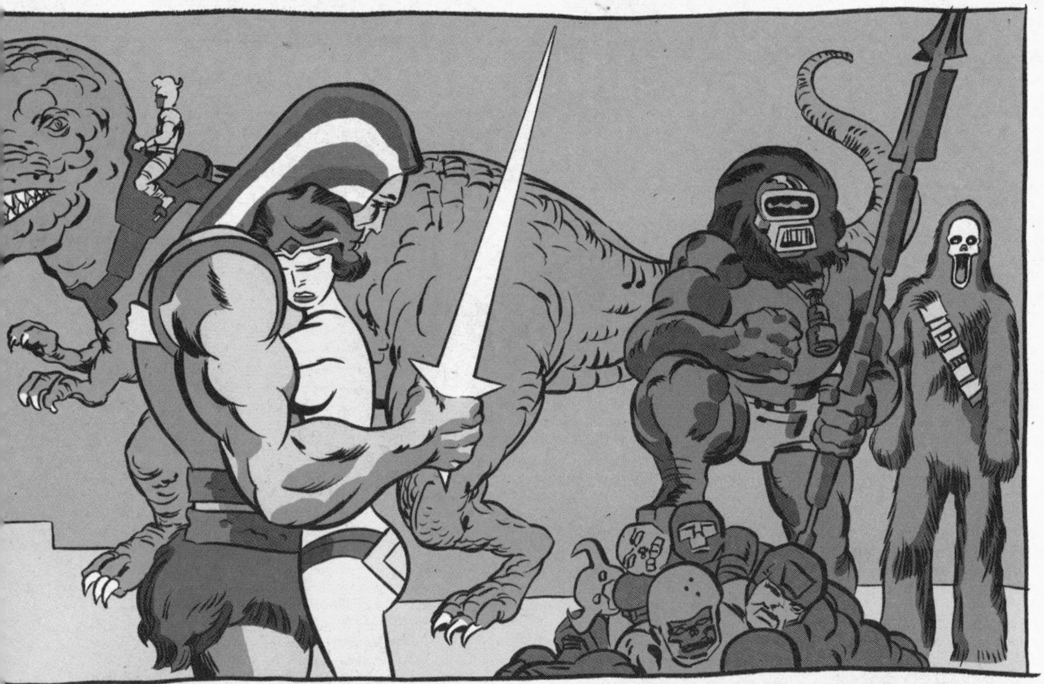
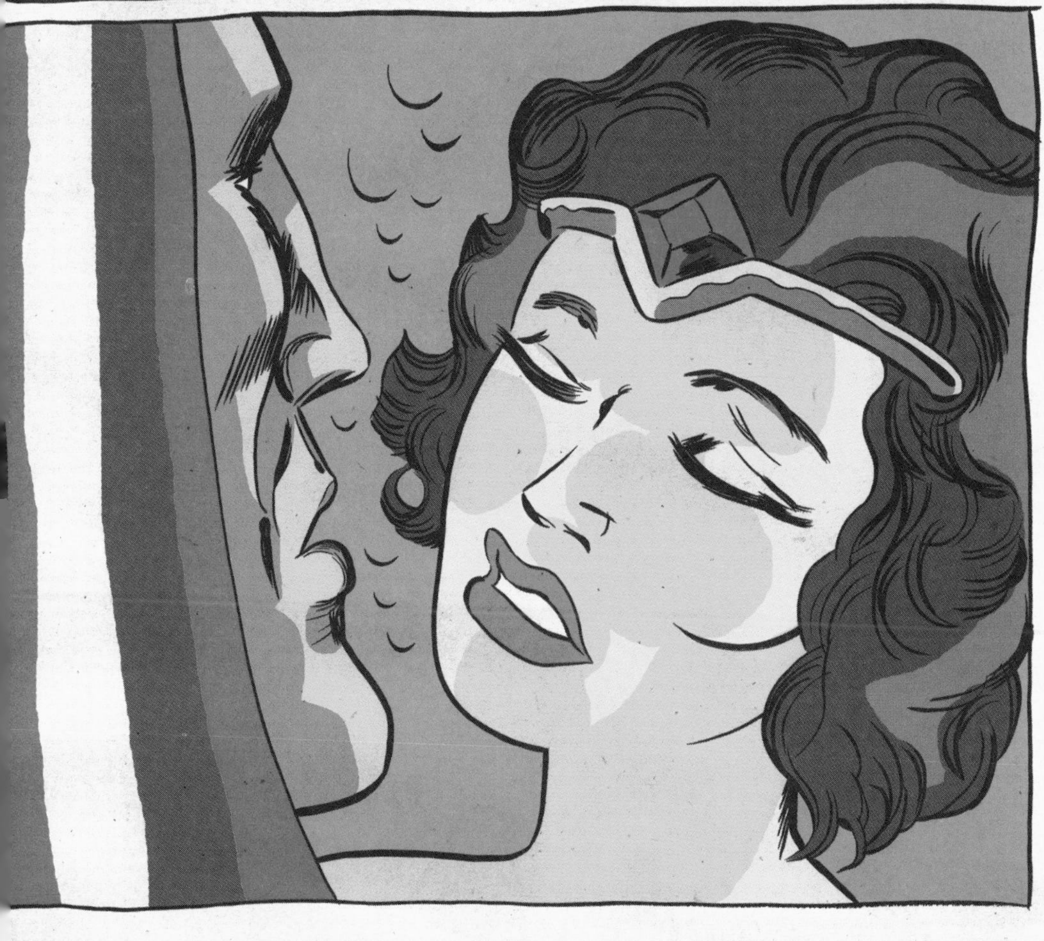

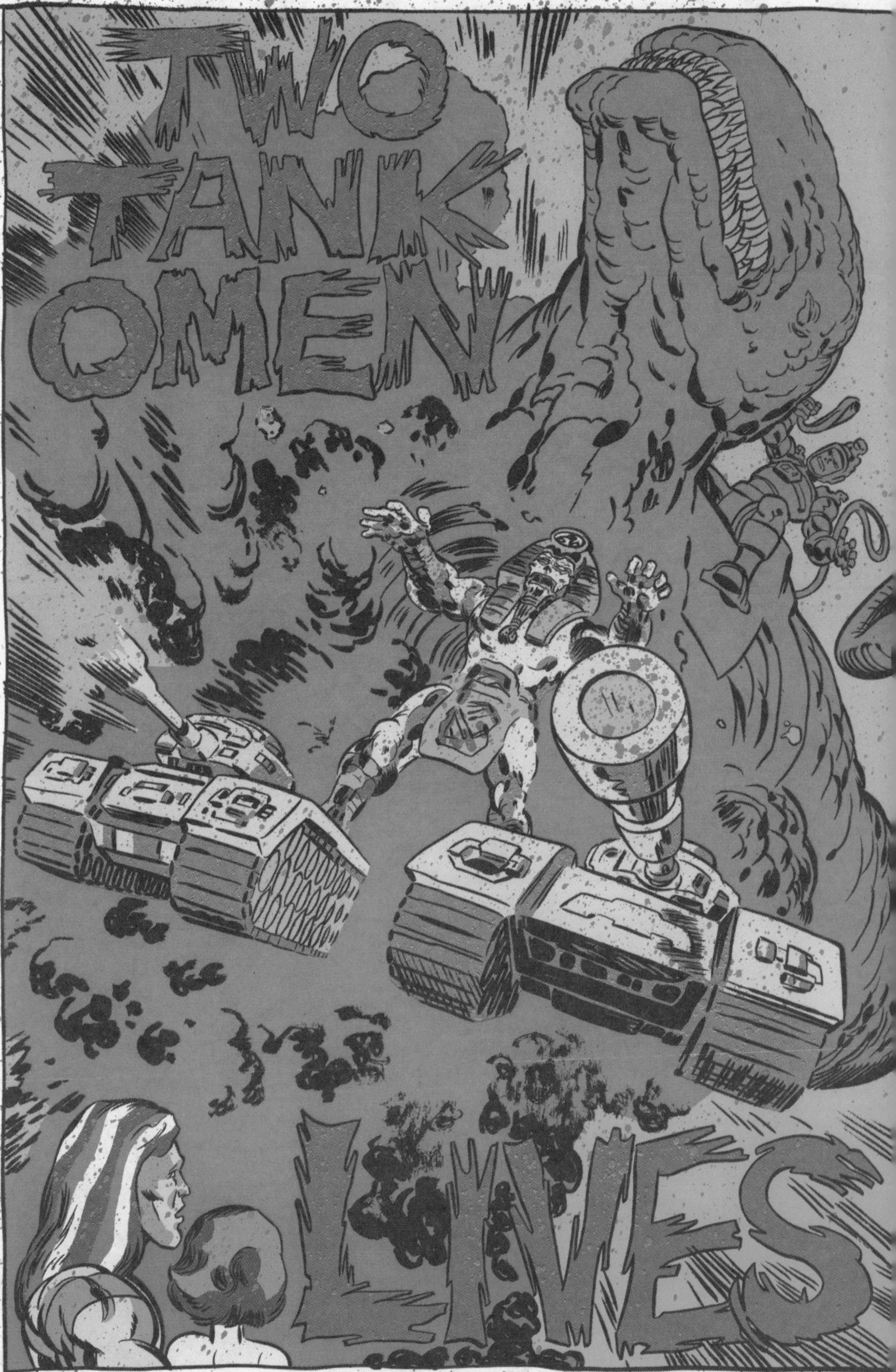
TWO TANK OMEN
LIVES

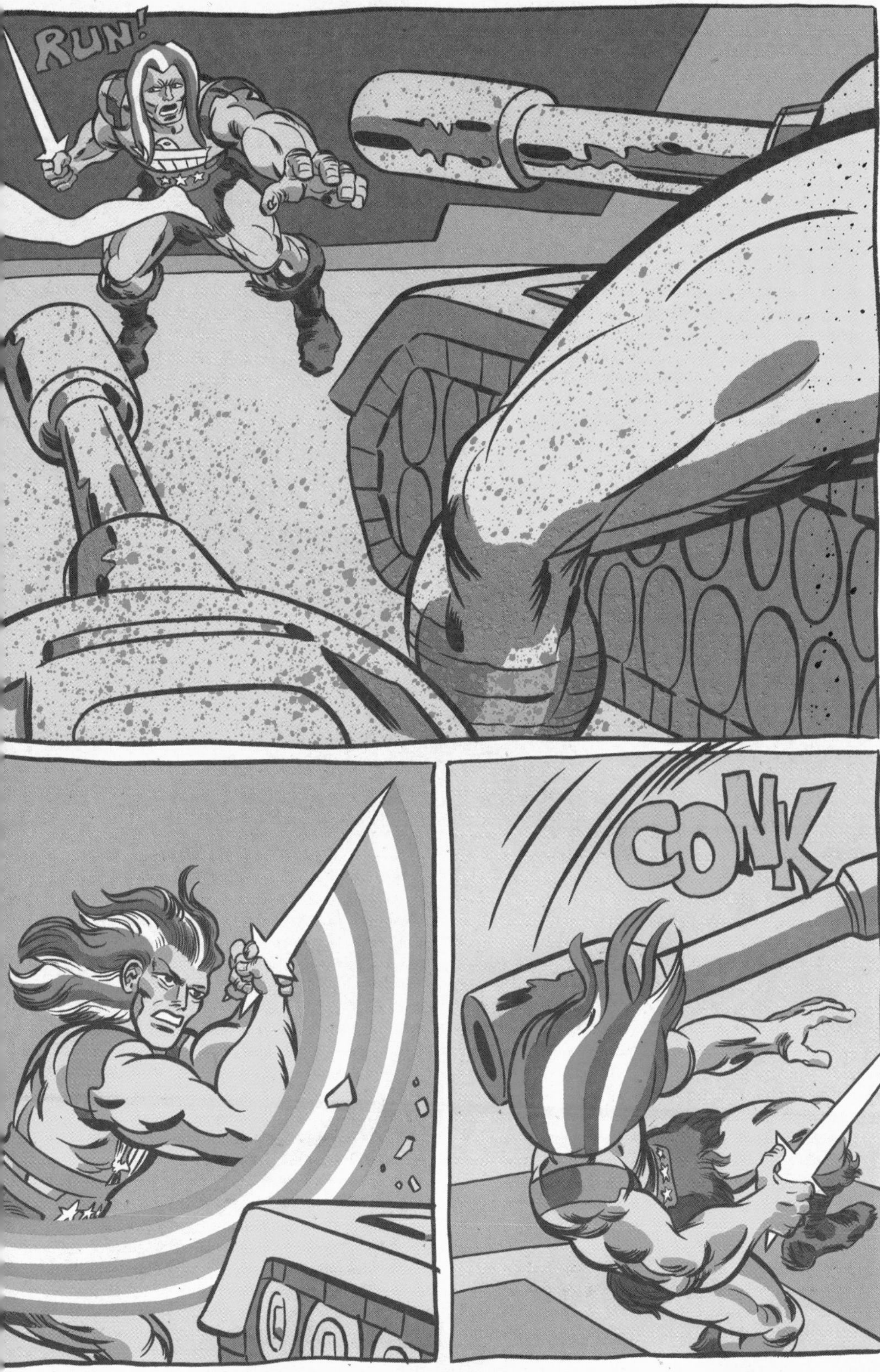
RUN!
CONK

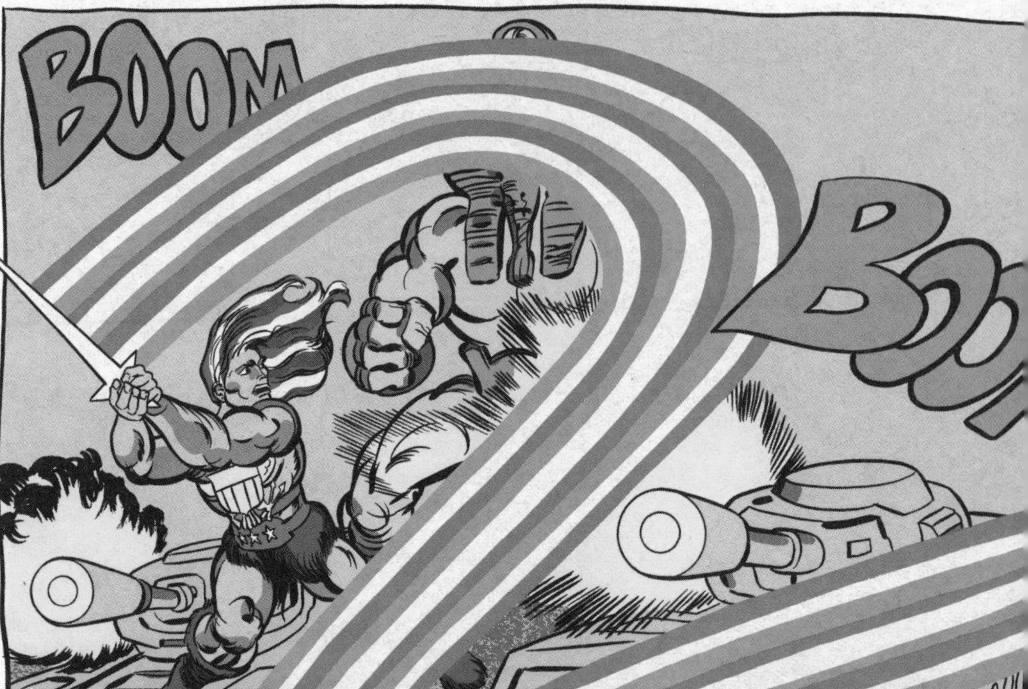
BOOM
BOOM

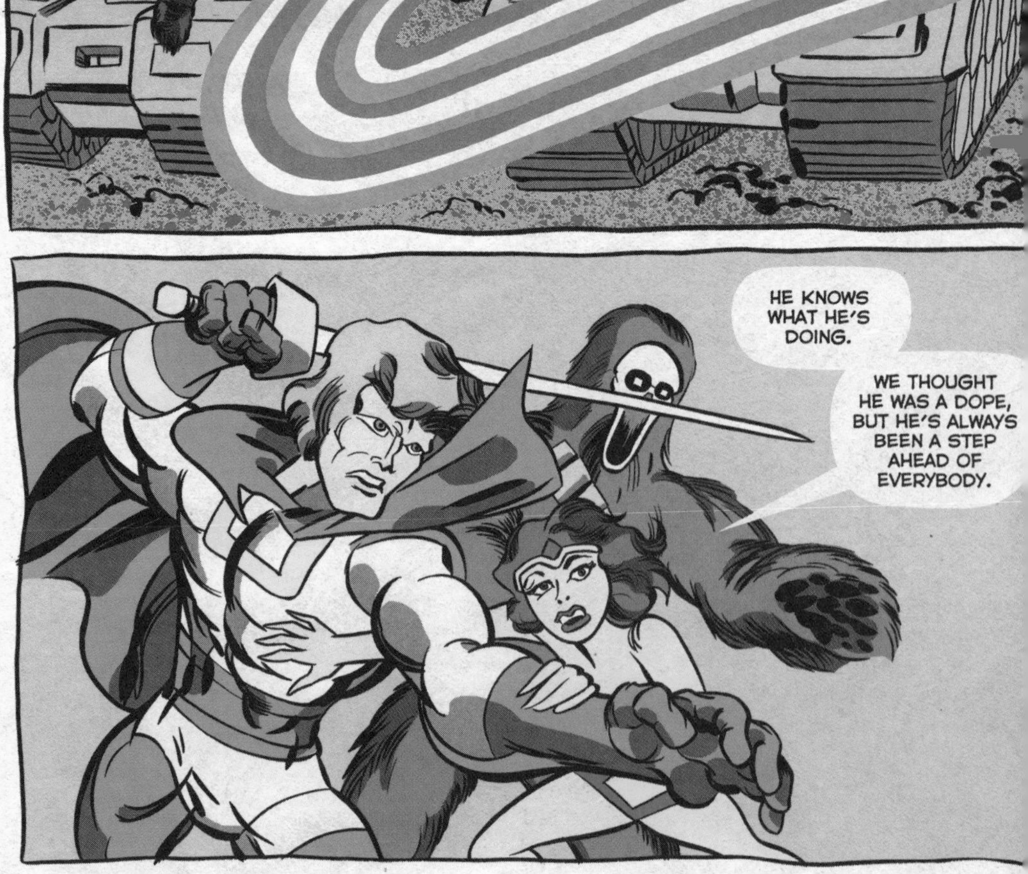
HE KNOWS WHAT HE'S DOING.
WE THOUGHT HE WAS A DOPE, BUT HE'S ALWAYS BEEN A STEP AHEAD OF EVERYBODY.

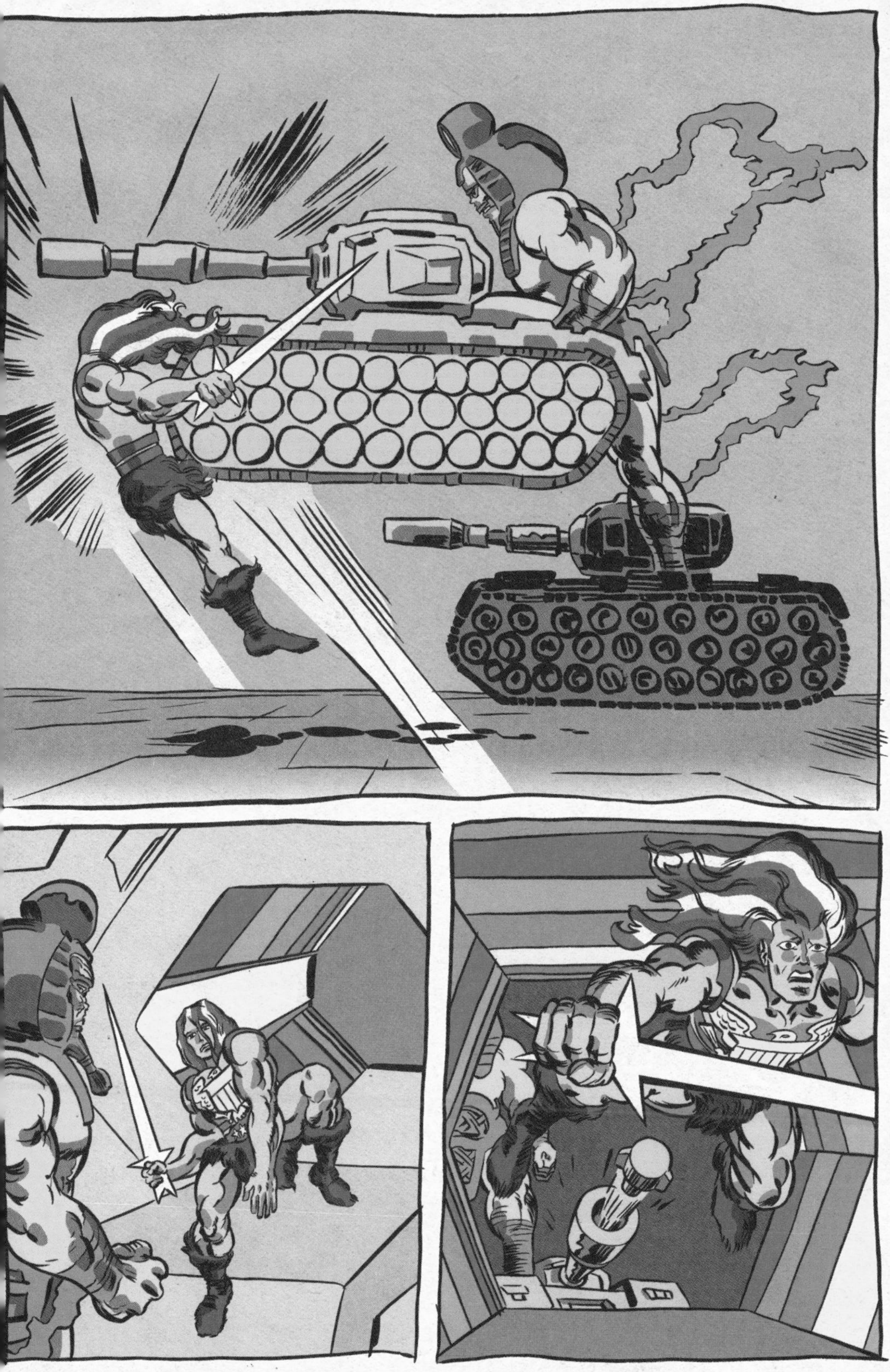

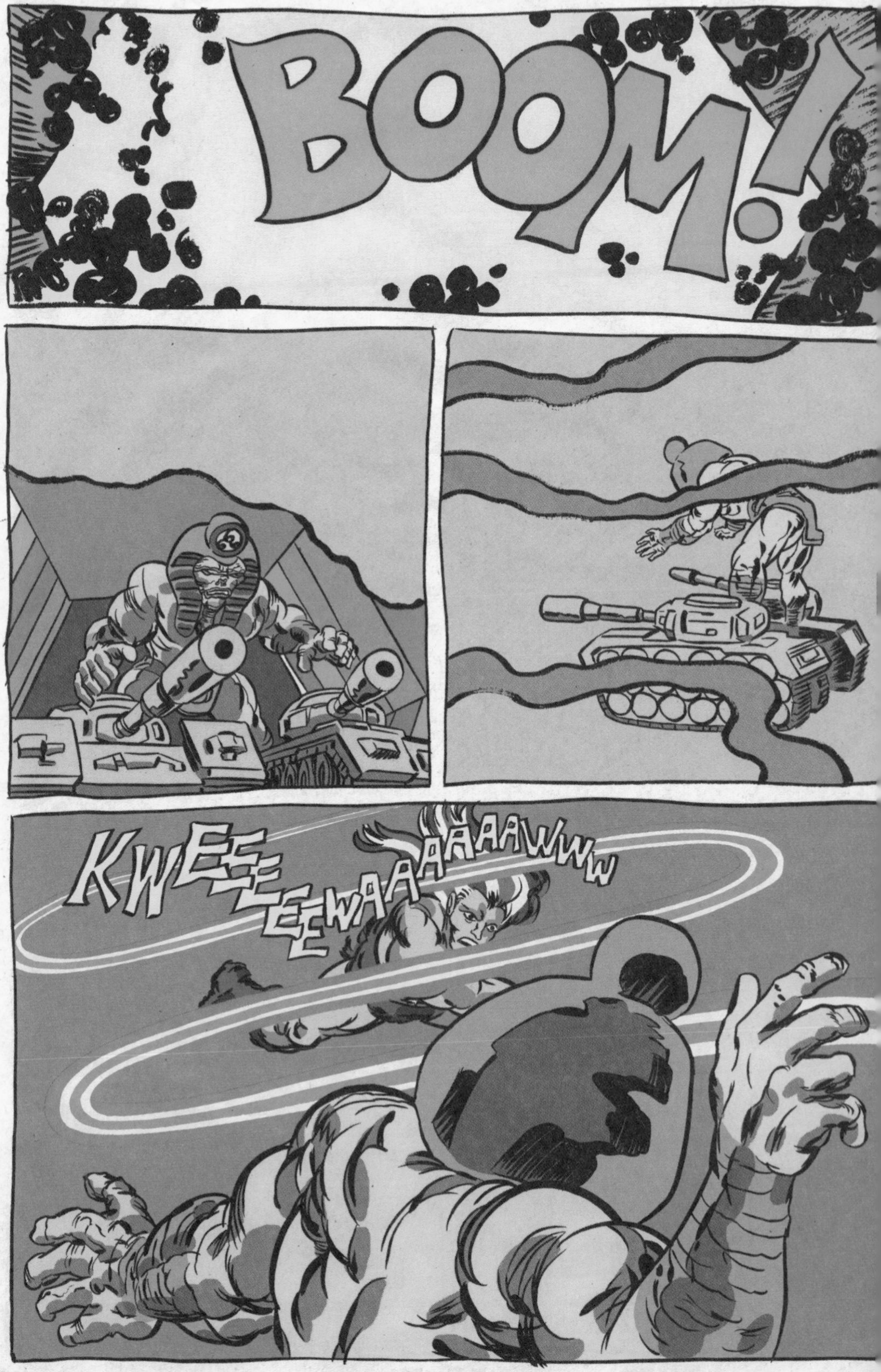
BOOM!
KWEEEEEEWAAAAAAAAWWWW

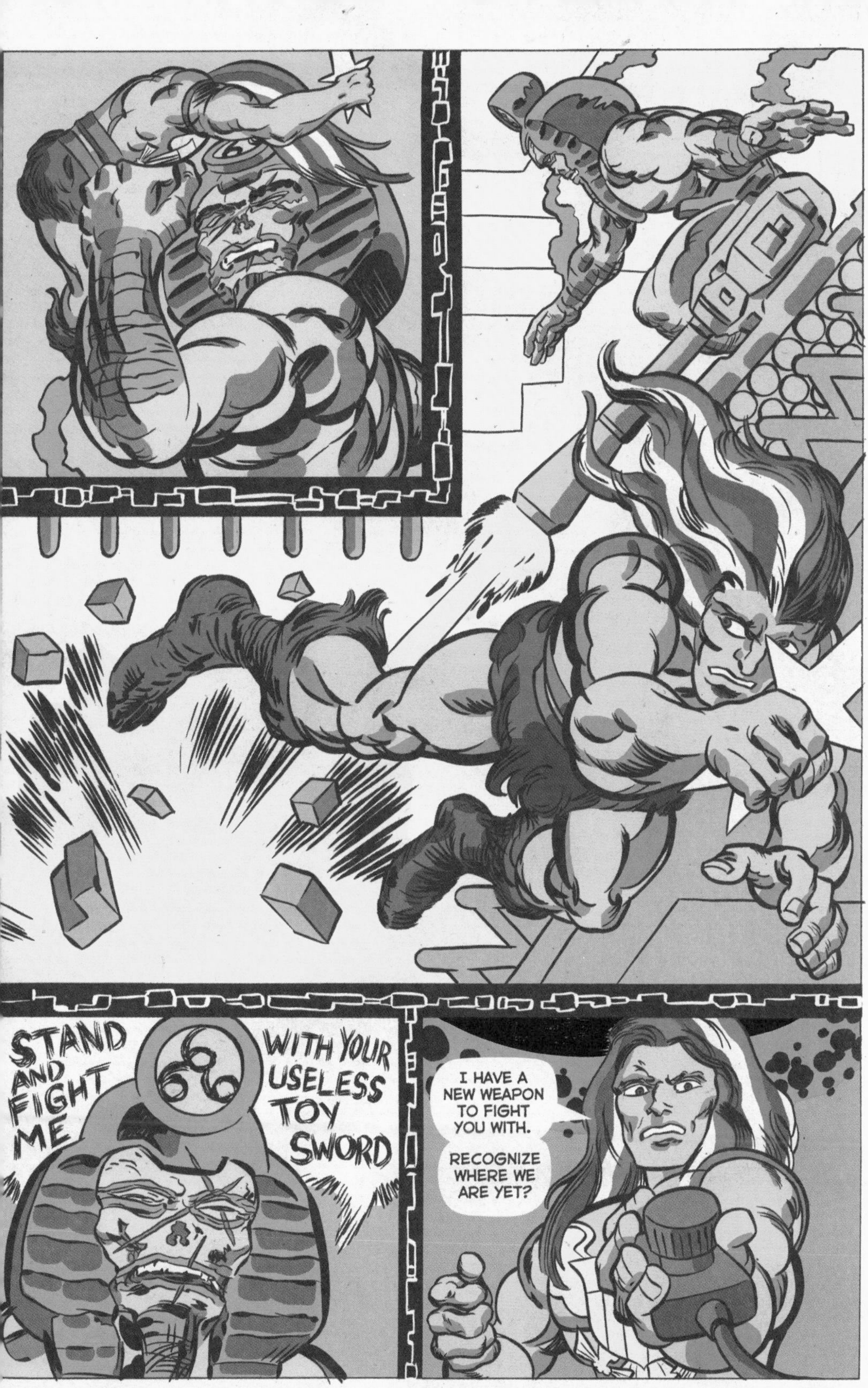
STAND AND FIGHT ME
WITH YOUR USELESS TOY SWORD
I HAVE A NEW WEAPON TO FIGHT YOU WITH.
RECOGNIZE WHERE WE ARE YET?

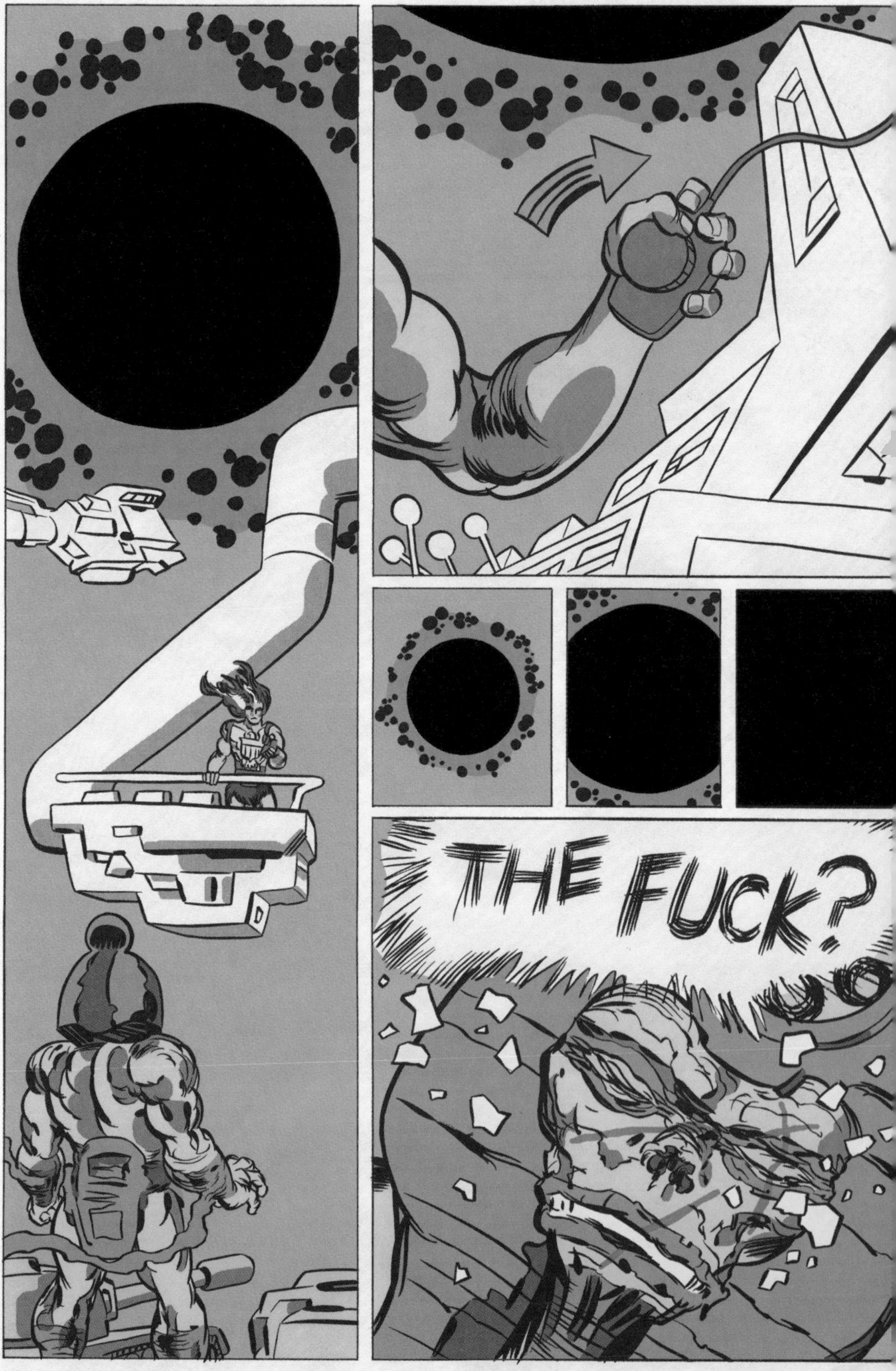
THE FUCK?

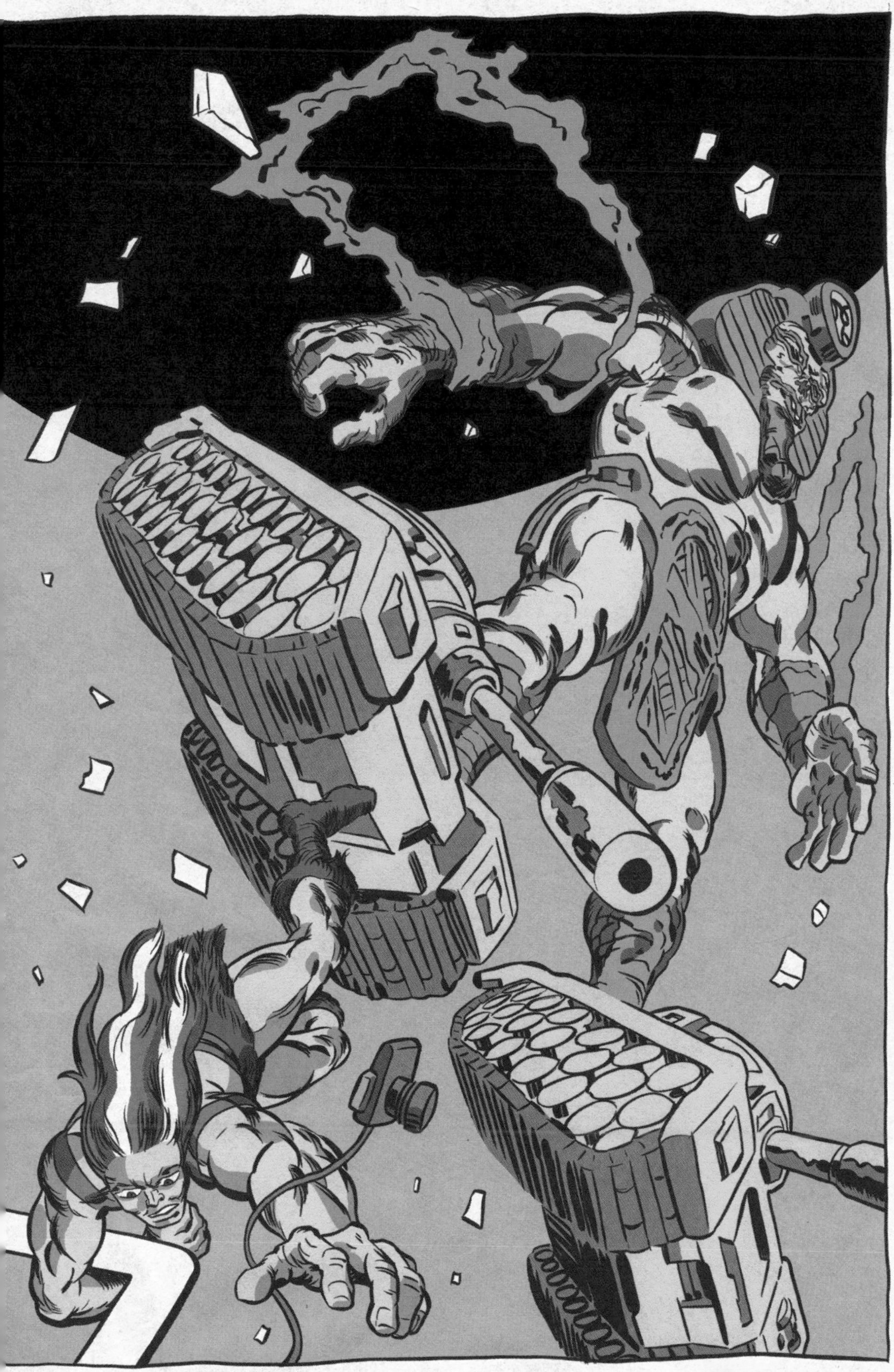

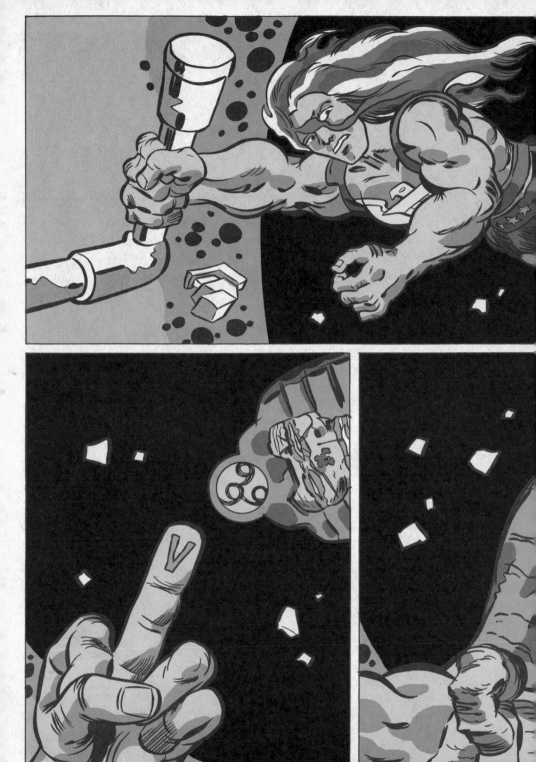

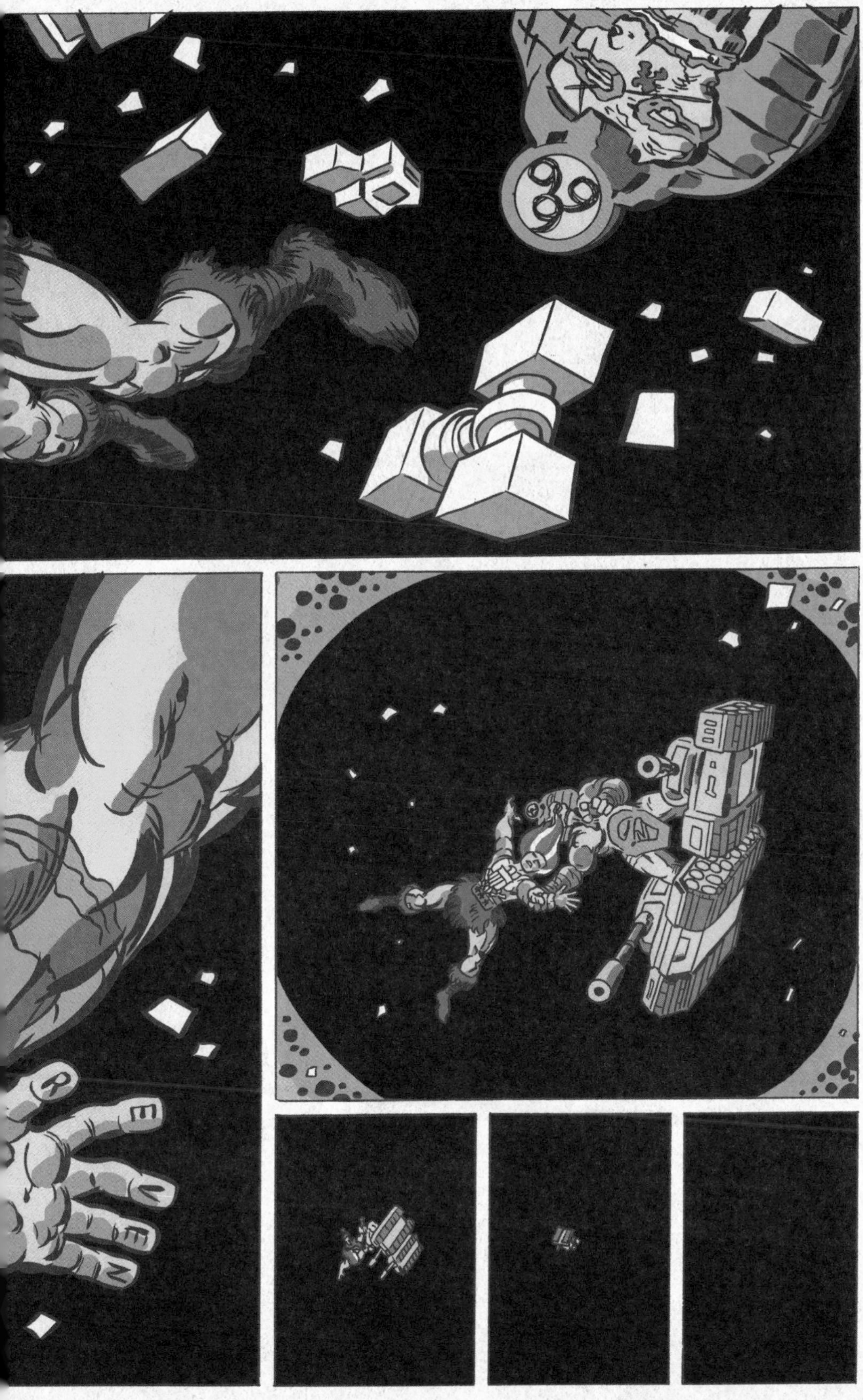

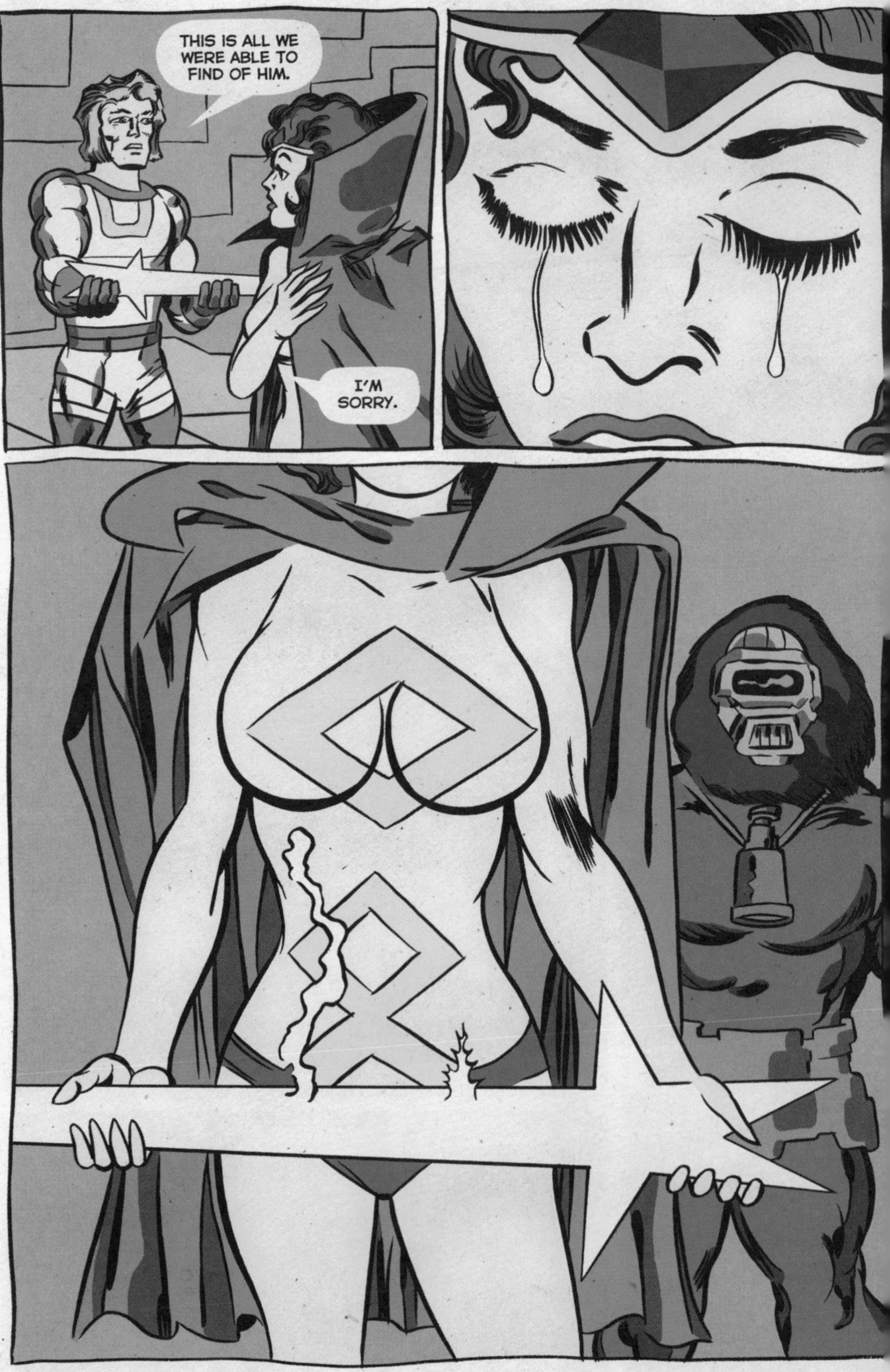
THIS IS ALL WE WERE ABLE TO FIND OF HIM.
I'M SORRY.

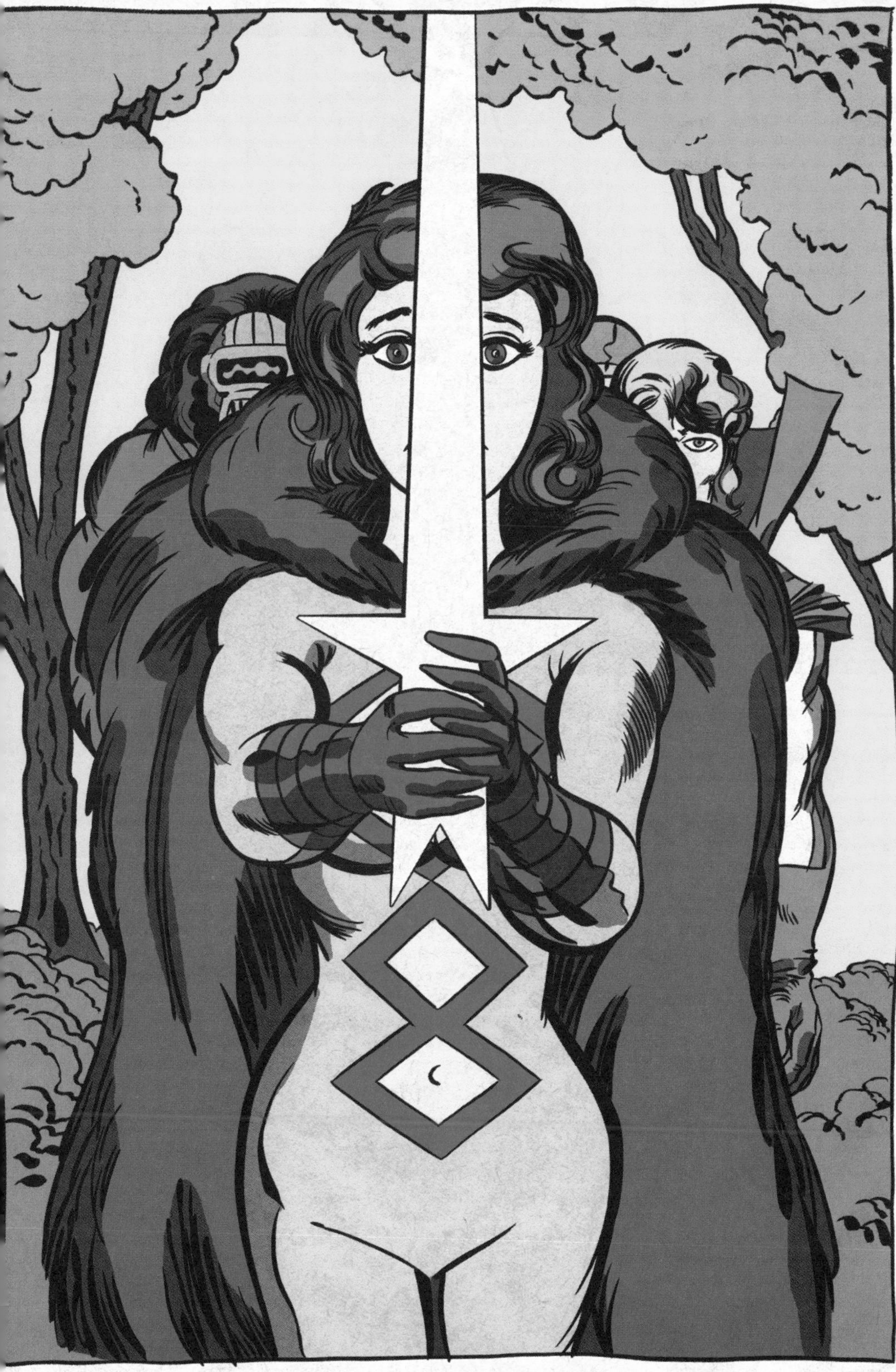

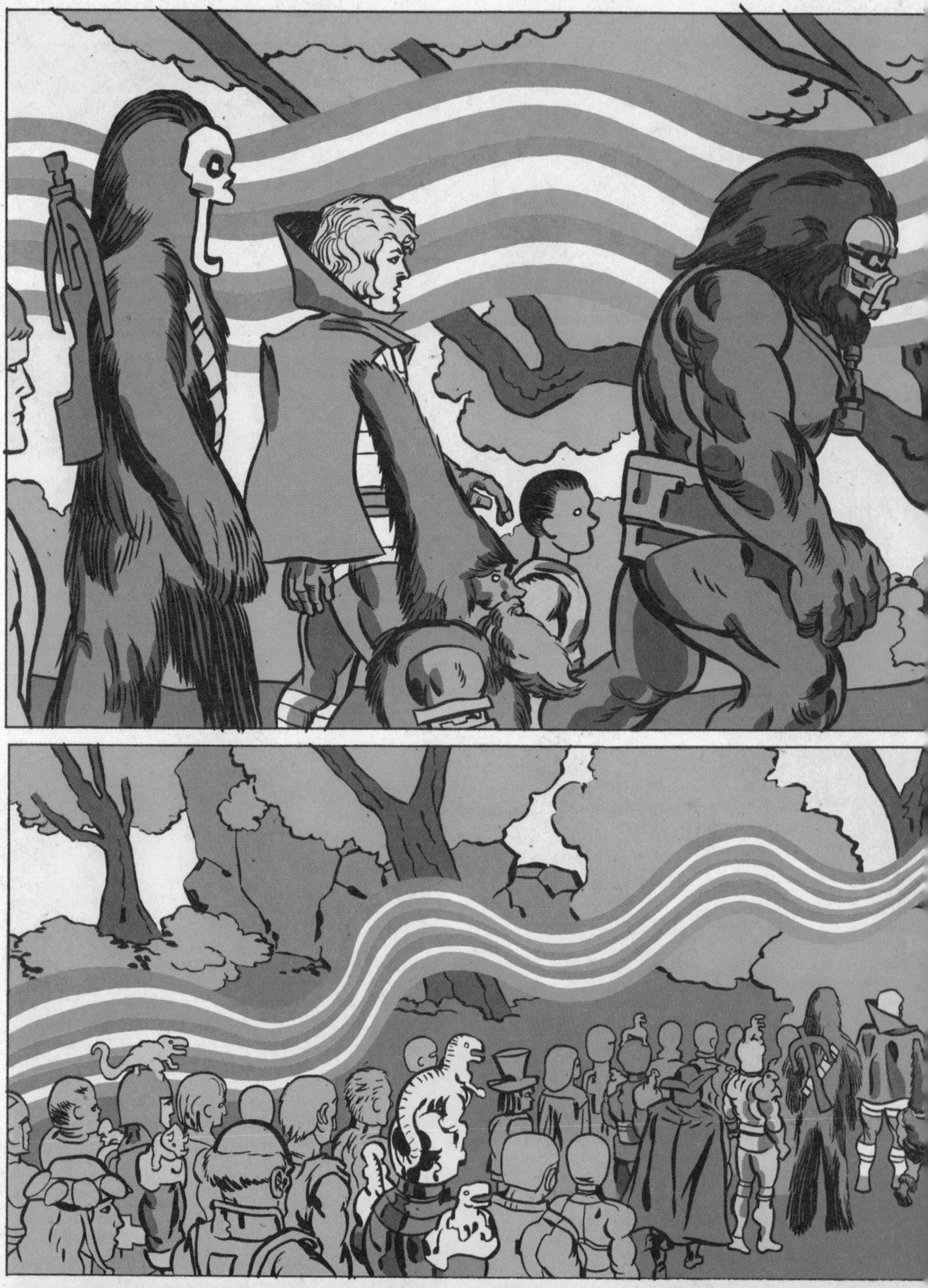

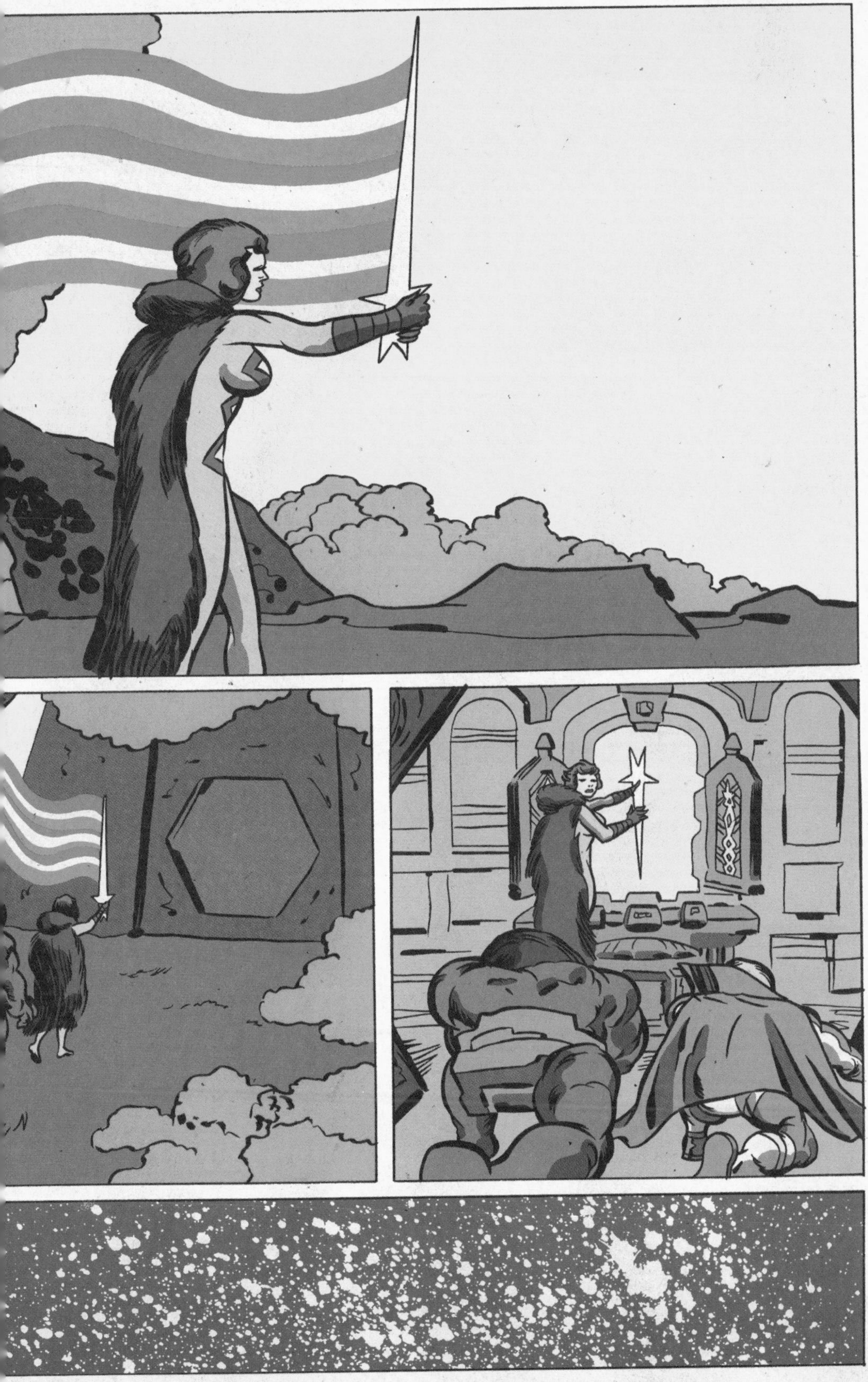

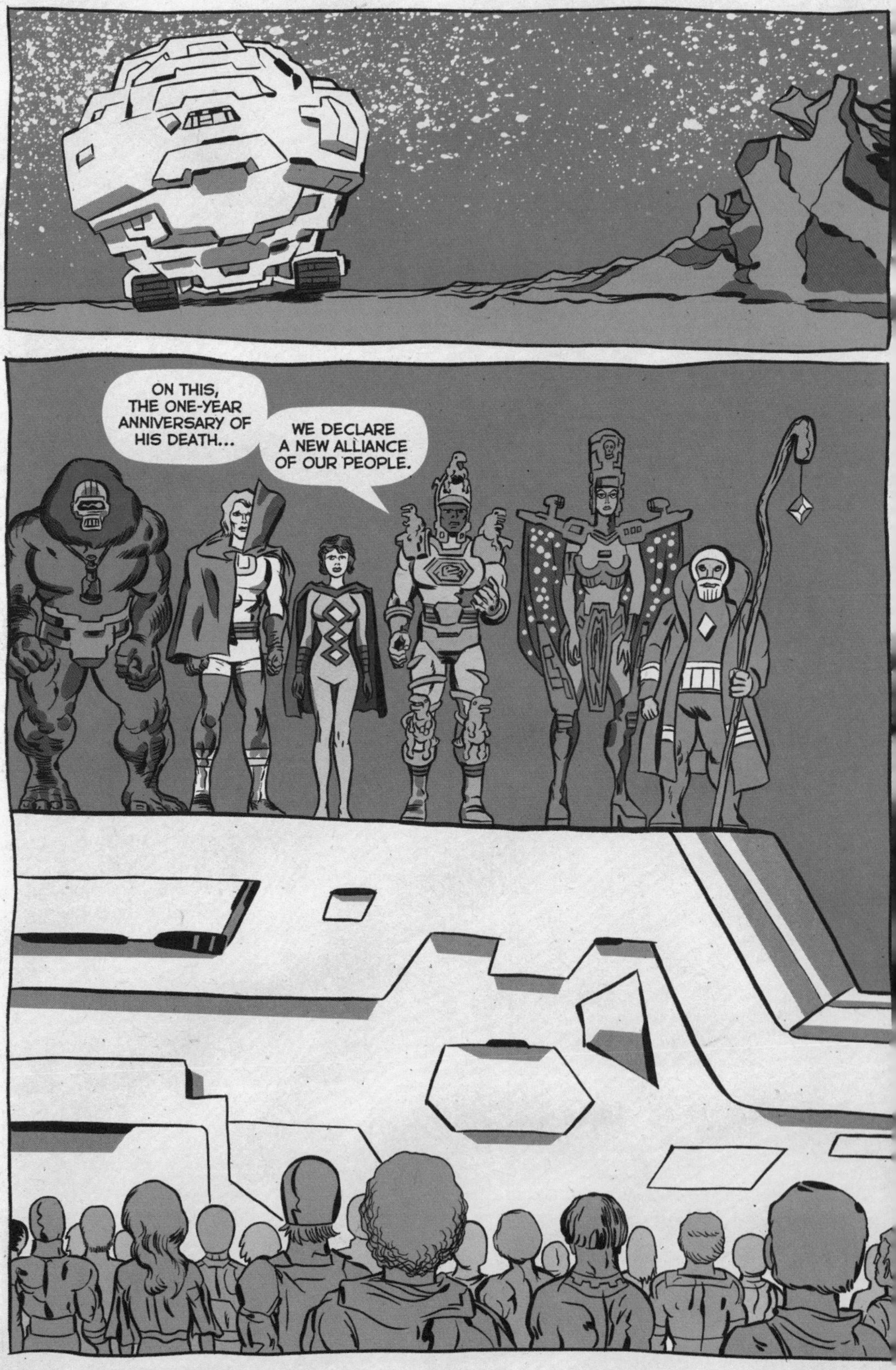
ON THIS, THE ONE-YEAR ANNIVERSARY OF HIS DEATH...
WE DECLARE A NEW ALLIANCE OF OUR PEOPLE.

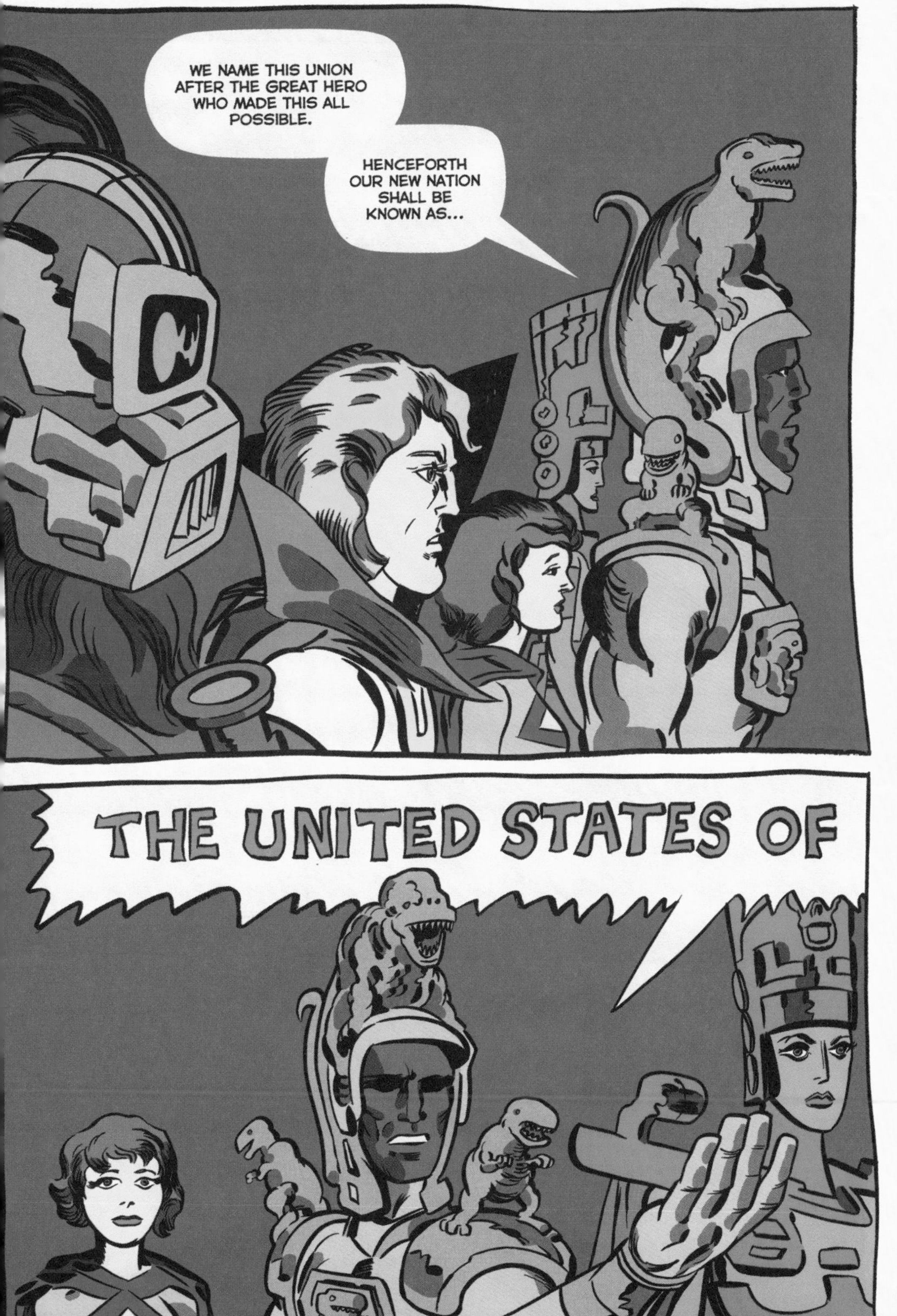
WE NAME THIS UNION AFTER THE GREAT HERO WHO MADE THIS ALL POSSIBLE.
HENCEFORTH OUR NEW NATION SHALL BE KNOWN AS...
THE UNITED STATES OF

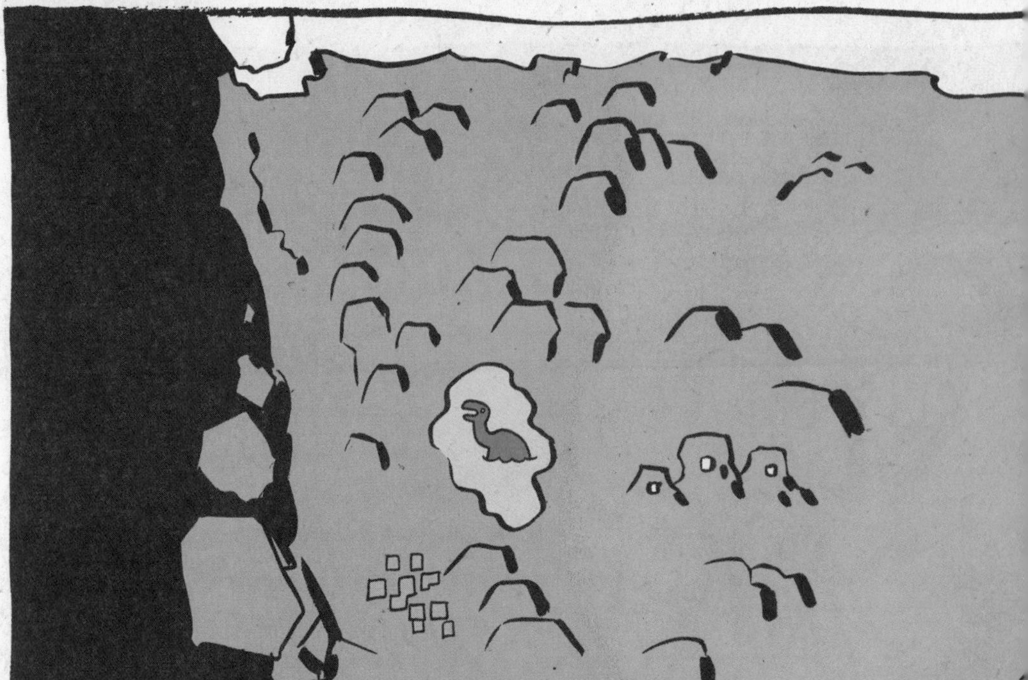
BARBARIA

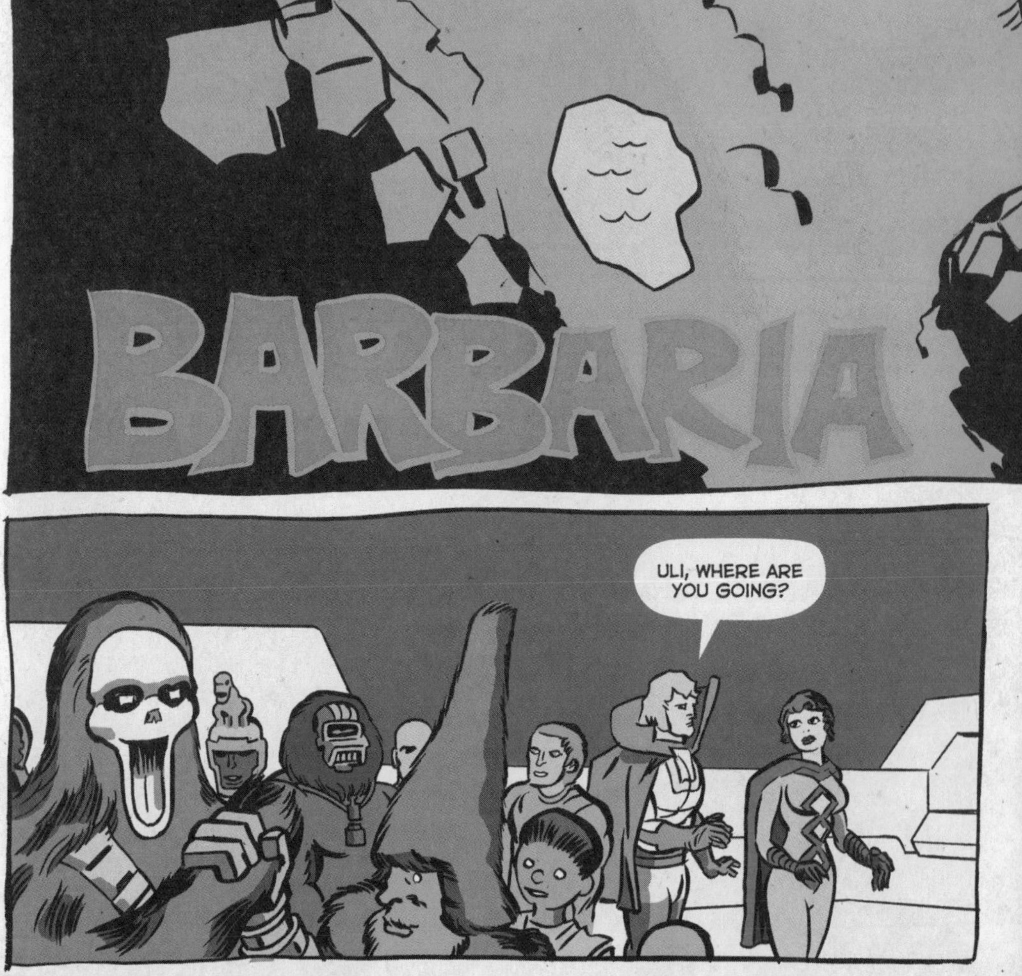
ULI, WHERE ARE YOU GOING?

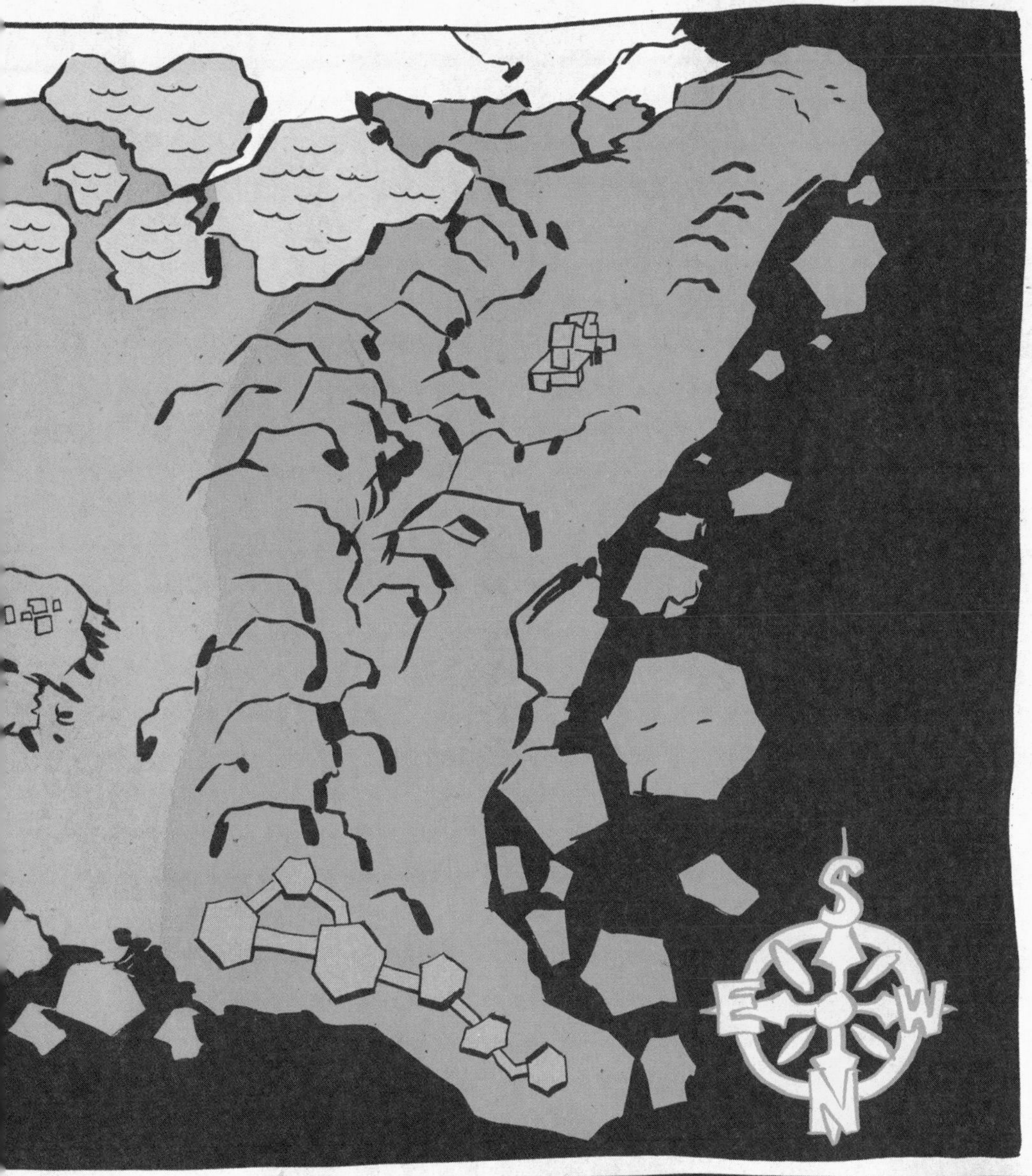
S
E
W
N

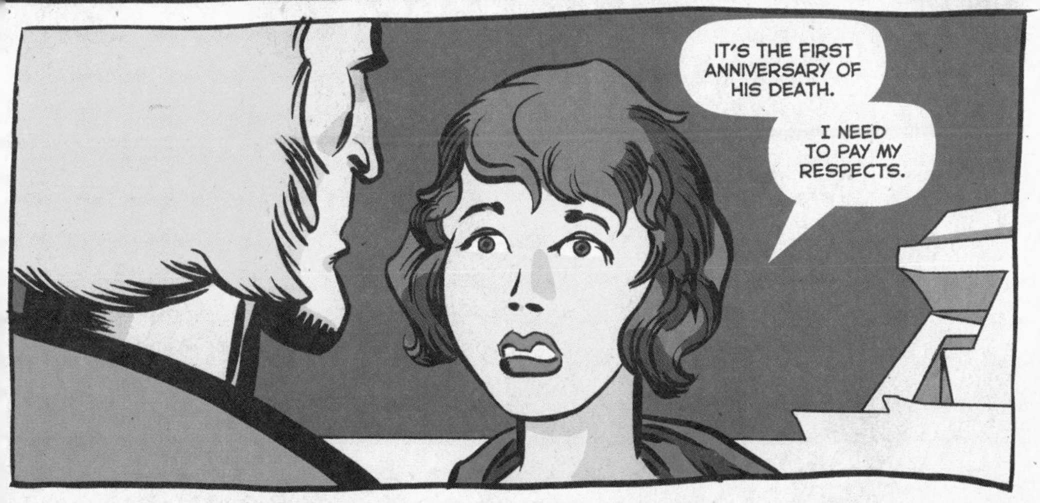
IT'S THE FIRST ANNIVERSARY OF HIS DEATH.
I NEED TO PAY MY RESPECTS.

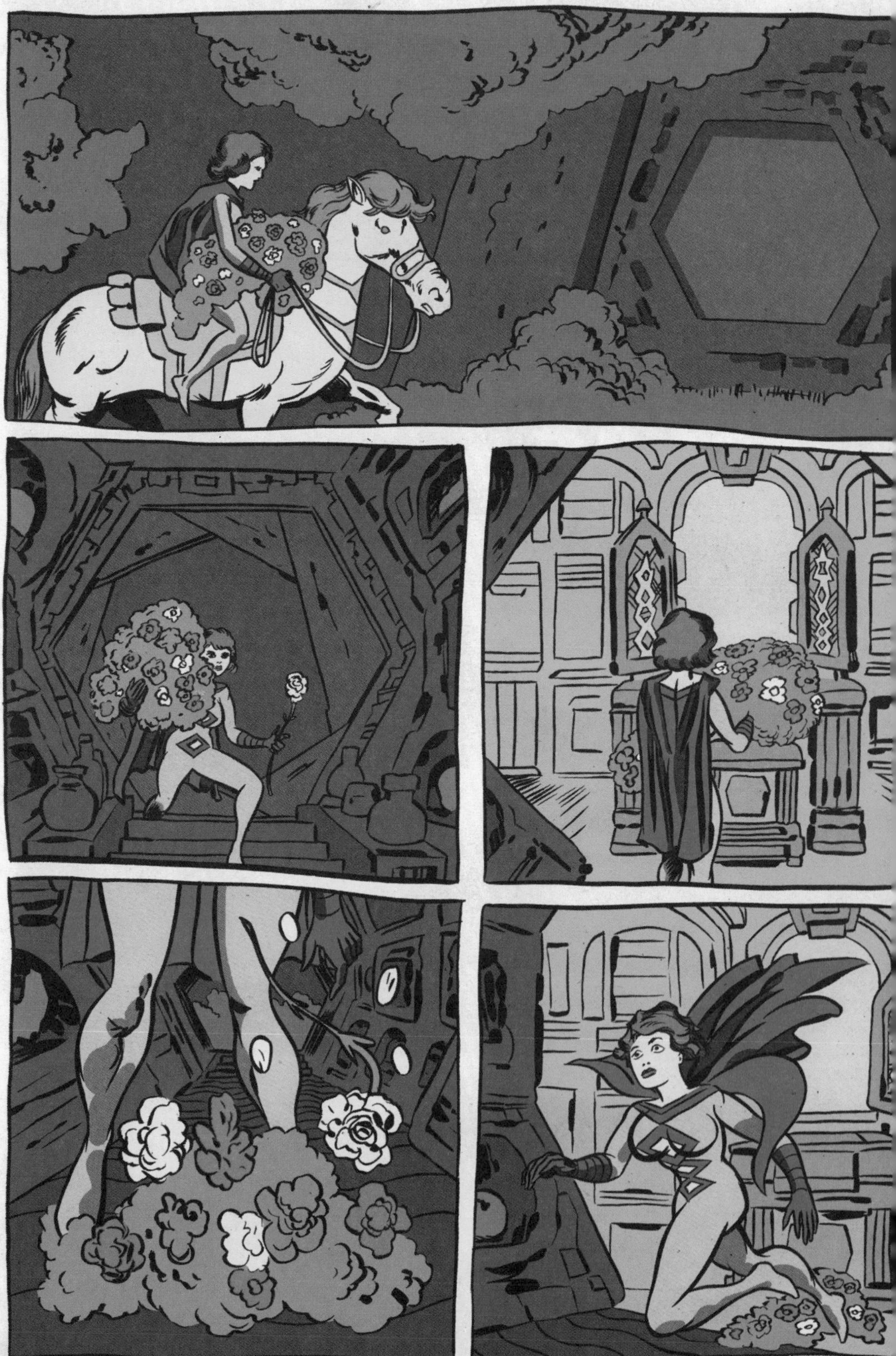

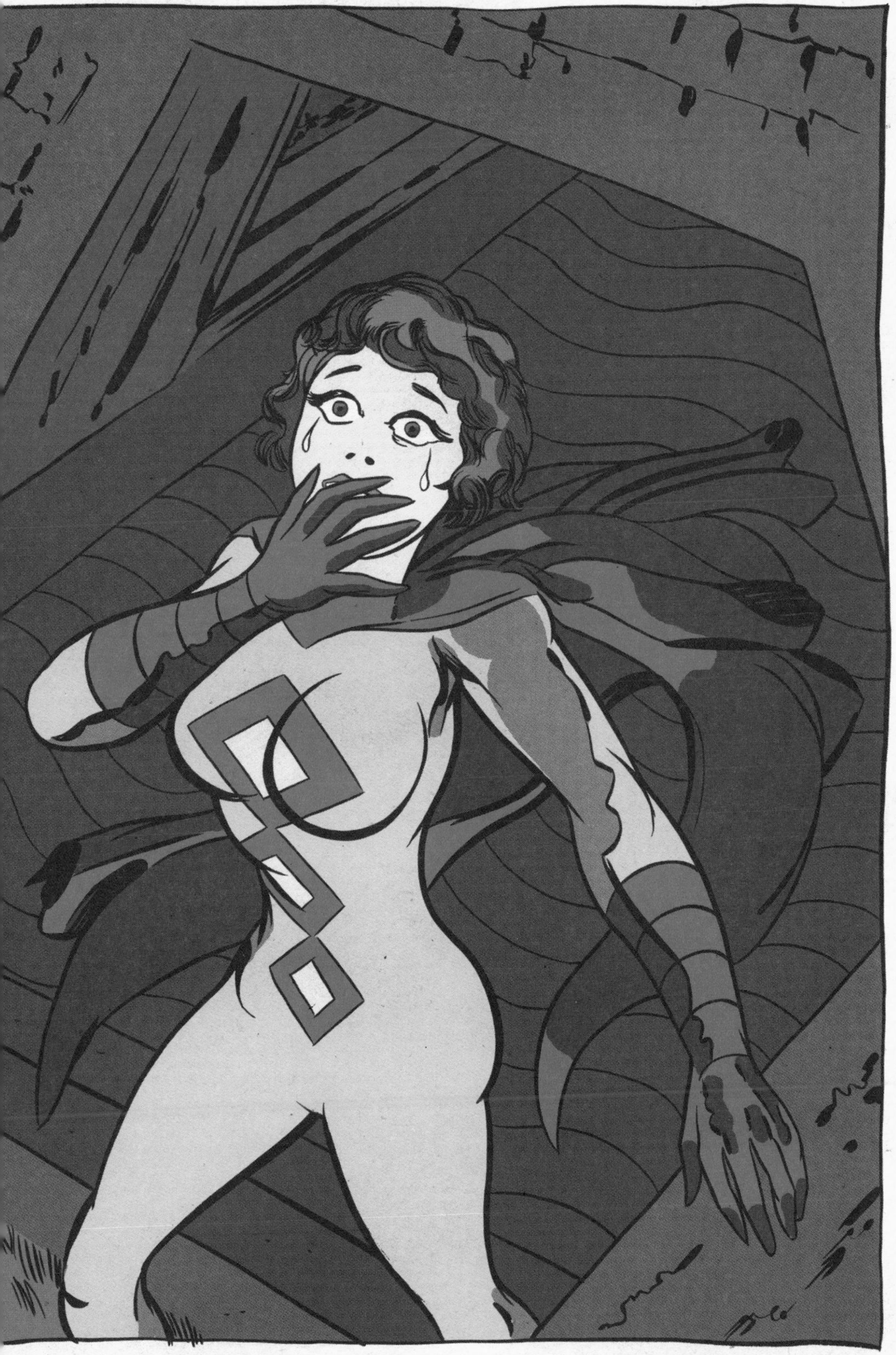

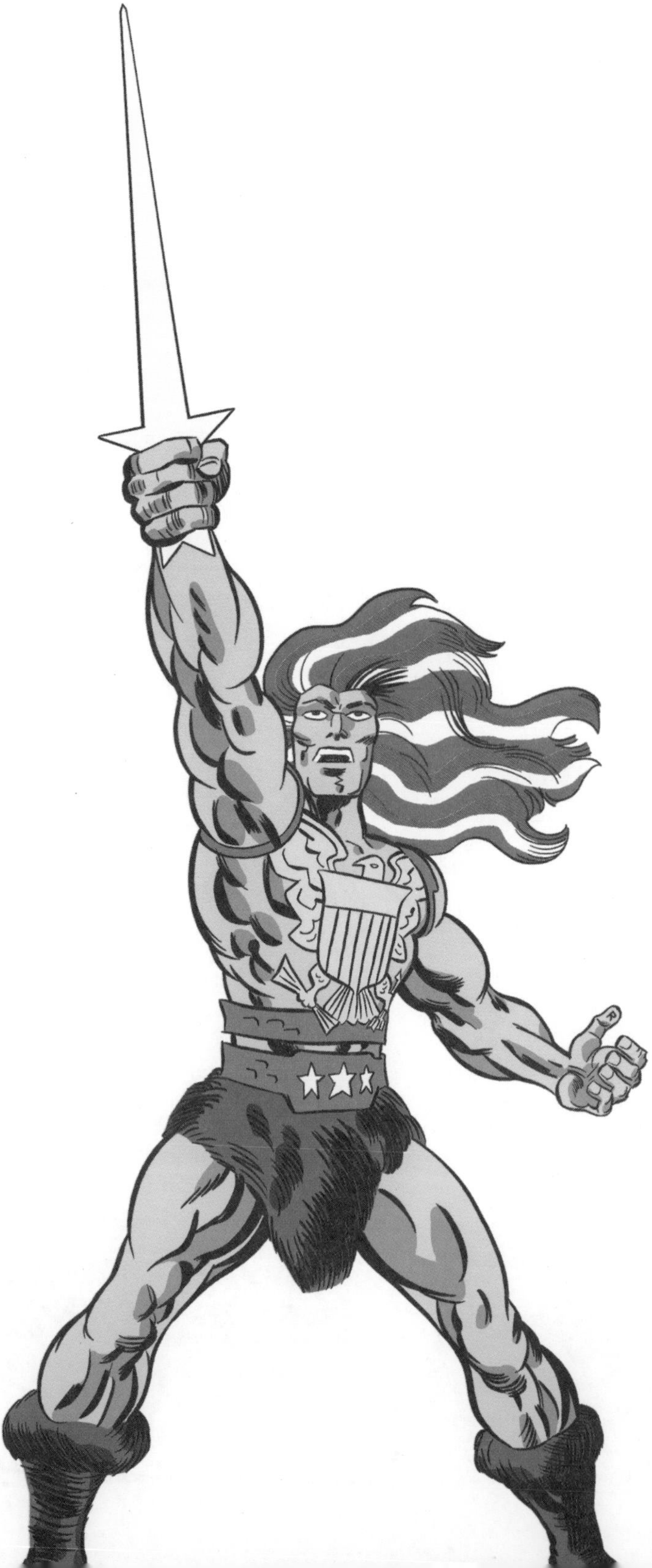

THE END

Tom Scioli lives in Pittsburgh. He's been making comics for years, including the Xeric-winning UnMortals: The Myth of 8-Opus and the Eisner-nominated Godland. With American Barbarian he's moved into the realm of webcomics and is currently serializing his next major work, Final Frontier.

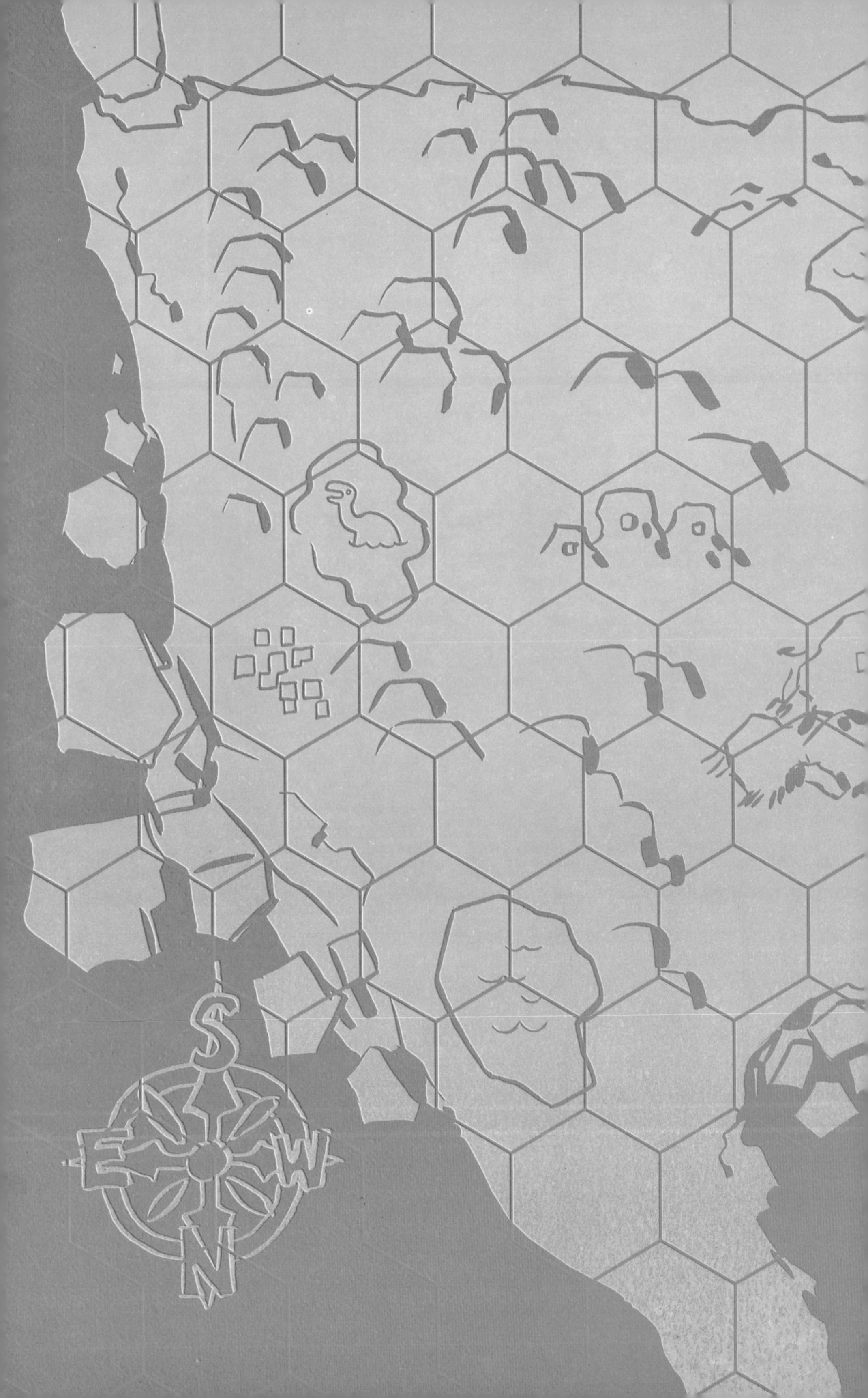
S
E
W
N